INFLUENCES ON HUMAN
DEVELOPMENT

INFLUENCES ON HUMAN DEVELOPMENT
SECOND EDITION

Edited by

Urie Bronfenbrenner
Cornell University

Maureen A. Mahoney
Cornell University

The Dryden Press
Hinsdale, Illinois

CONTENTS

INTRODUCTION

This collection of readings reflects a new theoretical perspective in the study of human development and behavior. The change has not yet, and may never, become the norm, but it has significantly altered and enriched our understanding of the forces that shape the development of the human being.

The nature of the change is reflected in a superficial sign. Ten years ago, it would have been difficult to find research literature with a rigorous study that was not couched in terms of S and E. S was of course the subject, and E the experimenter. The latter, and often the former, had or needed no further identity—no name, no age, no sex, no role in life other than to participate in an experiment that ended on the same day, or even in the same hour, in which it began. In fact, in most experiments, the only participant besides S was a graduate student, whose prior relationship with the child was nonexistent, or, if existent, trivial in character. Indeed, it can be said that *much of American developmental psychology, even today, is the science of the behavior of children with adult strangers.*

More correctly, we should say it is a study of the behavior of a child with *one* strange adult. Existing theoretical models in human development typically assume a two-person system only. This assumption continues to be true even when the other person is a familiar figure—such as a parent, teacher, or therapist. Even if more than one is included in the research, e.g. mother and father, they are still treated separately. Three-person models are found in theory (e.g. Parsons & Bales) but rarely in practice. The S-and-E model also reflects the fact that, with a few exceptions, the process taking place is viewed as unidirectional. One is concerned, for example, with the effect of the experimenter's behavior—or that of the parent, teacher, or therapist—on the child, not the reverse.

Inevitably in a two-person model, and typically in the rare N-person (multi-person) system attention is limited to direct effects, i.e. the influence of A on B. There is neither interest in nor, often, the possibility of examining how the interaction of A and B (mother with child) might be affected by a third party C—say the father, or a second child, a grandparent, or teacher. One might call this the *second-order effect.* Only one substantial body of research in our field focuses on second-order effects; again, the other participant is a stranger. We refer to the growing literature on the effect of a stranger on the interaction of a child with his mother.

Finally, and most important of all, in much of our research the two-person system exists, or is treated as if it existed, in isolation from any other social context that could impinge on or encompass it.

These features so common in our research are hardly characteristic of the situations in which children actually live and develop. Thus in the family, the day care center, preschool, play group, school classroom, or neighborhood:

1. There are usually more than two people.
2. The child invariably influences those who influence him.

3. The other participants are not strangers but persons who have enduring roles and relationships vis-à-vis the child.
4. Finally, the behavior of all these persons is profoundly affected by other social systems in which these same persons participate in significant roles and relationships, both toward the child and each other.

The contrast between the conditions that have traditionally prevailed in our experiments and those that exist in the child's everyday life situation points up the fact that much of our research has been *ecologically invalid.* By removing the child from the environment in which he ordinarily finds himself and placing him in another setting which is typically unfamiliar, short-lived, and devoid of the persons, objects, and experiences that have been central in his life, we are getting only a partial picture both of the child and his environment. As a result, the potentialities of each to influence the other may be substantially greater than we have thus far seen.

Furthermore, existing theoretical models in human development typically focus attention on processes occurring within a single setting (e.g. family, day-care center, classroom, peer group). An ecological orientation points to the additional importance of relations *between systems* as critical to the child's development (e.g. the interaction between home and school, family and peer group).

Present theoretical orientations also tend to be limited to those ecological systems that actually contain the child himself (e.g. family, preschool, classroom, peer group); they seldom include the adjacent or encompassing system which may in fact determine what can or cannot occur in the more immediate context. Such encompassing systems include the nature and requirements of the parents' work, characteristics of the neighborhood, transportation facilities, the relation between school and community, and the role of television (not only in its direct effect on the child but in its indirect influence on patterns of family and community life). These, along with a host of other ecological circumstances and changes determine with whom and how the child spends his time: for example, the separation of residential and business areas, the disappearance of neighborhoods, zoning ordinances, geographic and social mobility, child labor laws, moonlighting, super markets, welfare policies, age segregation, the growth of single parent families, the abolition of the apprentice system, consolidated schools, commuting, the working mother, the delegation of child care to specialists and others outside the home, urban renewal, or the existence and character of an explicit national policy on children and families.

The emphasis, then, in this new theoretical perspective, is on the enduring environment of the child. This enduring environment, which we shall refer to as the *child's ecology,* consists of two concentric layers, the first superimposed upon the second.

A. The upper layer and the most visible is the immediate setting actually containing the child—home, school, street, playground, camp, etc. Every setting, in turn, is viewed along three dimensions:
   1. Design of physical space and materials.

2. People, in differing roles and relationships toward the child.
3. Activities in which the people are engaging—both with each other and with the child—including the *social meaning* of these activities.

B. The supporting and surrounding layer, in which the immediate setting is embedded, limits and shapes what can and does occur within the immediate setting:
1. Geographic and physical, for example, a housing project in which people live.
2. Institutions—the social systems which affect what can occur in the immediate setting—not just social class—but much more explicit systems such as health services and homemaker services.

But perhaps even more important are systems not directly or primarily focused on the child—shopping facilities, public transportation, parental working hours, traffic regulations, and a variety of other arrangements and customs that determine where children can be, and what activities they engage in with what kinds of people. In some countries, but not in our own, such arrangements grow in part out of an explicit national policy on children and family life.

The readings which follow reflect our concern with the scientific investigation of the child in his enduring environment and are examples of the new direction of research in human development. By and large, the participants in the experiments and investigations cited have lost their anonymity. They are not merely passive strangers, but active and familiar agents who play significant roles in each other's lives as family members, friends, pupils, teachers, and fellow workers. They come from particular segments of society and share common experiences. Indeed, the experiments in which they participate, whether made by man or nature, often continue over a period of days, weeks, or months—or, on occasion, even a lifetime. And these experiments are conducted not only in the laboratory, but also in the setting in which the activities under investigation normally occur, such as the home, play group, school, or community. In short, the new approach combines rigorous scientific method with the study of the developing person in the contexts in which he lives.

Our broad perspective on human development is reflected in the range of sources of material. The investigations here are drawn not only from psychological research, but also from biology, human genetics, sociology, and anthropology. The principal concern is the interplay of biological factors, human interaction, social structures, and cultural forces in shaping the individual. Thus we have selected articles which document specific influences—biological and social—on the process of development. Special emphasis is given to the implications of science for social policy, and in turn, to the manner in which social policy shapes, and sometimes stifles, scientific endeavor.

Some of the readings, like the articles of Spitz, and Skodak and Skeels, have stood the test of a quarter of a century of discussion; others are as yet untried, having been published only in the past year or specially written for this volume. But we commend them all to our readers as invitations to a new—ecological—perspective on the understanding of the process of human development.

The editors wish to express appreciation to Lorraine Sharpe, who typed, telephoned, and generally kept track of the proceedings. Nancy Burston also deserves special acknowledgment for her patience and judgment in preparing the index. Above all, our thanks go to the authors represented in these pages for making the real contribution—first in research and now in teaching.

Ithaca, New York
January, 1975

Urie Bronfenbrenner
Maureen Mahoney

INFLUENCES ON HUMAN
DEVELOPMENT

part one
SCIENTIFIC METHOD IN THE STUDY OF HUMAN BEHAVIOR

Whatever the subject matter, the aims and methods of science are fundamentally the same: to formulate and verify general principles through the joint application of logic and objective, controlled observation. Science begins with a question and proceeds to a tentative answer. This tentative answer is referred to as a hypothesis. A hypothesis is usually derived from observation, theory, or a combination of both.

But, while there are no restrictions on the source of a hypothesis, there are rather rigorous technical requirements on the form that a hypothesis must take and on the conditions that must be met if the hypothesis is to be considered as verified or, more properly, as not rejected. Unfortunately, these technical matters are typically presented in abstract terms, without reference to concrete research problems. This is particularly true in discussions of the structure of hypotheses, the logic of verification, and the problems of measurement in the study of human behavior. For this reason, a special chapter has been written to deal with these topics.

1.1

The Structure and Verification of Hypotheses

Urie Bronfenbrenner
Maureen A. Mahoney

I. THE STRUCTURE OF HYPOTHESES

What Is a Hypothesis?

The scientific process begins with the asking of a question about the nature of objective reality. The scientist then tries to obtain an answer to his question through observing, classifying, and relating what he sees. He tries to arrive at tentative answers. Such tentative answers are called *hypotheses.*

Actually, in science, the term *hypothesis* is used with several different meanings. If we seek a general definition, one that encompasses all uses of the term, we can say that *a hypothesis is any supposition about a fact.*

Let us examine what forms such suppositions may take.

Forms of Hypotheses

Some years ago, Dr. Louis DiCarlo, then the director of a speech clinic in Syracuse, New York, was surprised by the unexpectedly high proportion of cases of cleft palate coming from certain sparsely populated counties in upstate New York. He was so struck by the phenomenon that he reported it to the district office of the U.S. Public Health Service directed by Dr. John Gentry. Gentry responded by doing what public health physicians have done for decades; he started putting up pins on a map, in this instance a map of New York State, one pin for each case, not only of cleft palate, but of all reported congenital malformations (which are deformities present at birth). When all the pins were in place, they made a pattern that Gentry found familiar. Where had he seen it before? After some effort, he remembered. It was in a geology course, on a map of igneous rock formations in New York State. Igneous rocks are those that were originally extracted from within the earth's surface. They are found in mountainous areas and glacial deposits. What is more, some of these rocks emit natural radiation, and, as Gentry knew, radiation had been suspected as a possible source of cleft palate and other deformities present at birth.

In short, Gentry had arrived at a hypothesis about DiCarlo's original observation. He had a "supposition about a fact." Indeed, he had several. In his published paper, Gentry (1959) investigated a series of hypotheses. Let us examine three of them:

1. Igneous rocks are radioactive.
2. Rates of congenital malformation are higher among residents of mountain areas than of plains and valleys.

3. An increase in the amount of natural radiation increases the rate of congenital malformation in the population living in the area.

Each of these three statements is a supposition about a fact, but the propositions differ in kind. To begin with, note how the first statement can be distinguished from the other two. The latter both postulate a relation between variation in one factor and variation in another, whereas the former involves no variation at all; it merely claims the presence of a particular characteristic in a class of objects, in this case of radioactivity in igneous rocks. A supposition that simply postulates the presence of a phenomenon we shall refer to as an *attributive* hypothesis. It merely asserts that a particular entity or event exists and can be observed. Witness the following examples:

1. In 1869, Mendelyev (1869), using his periodic table as a basis, predicted the existence of three then-unknown elements and specified their properties. The elements were subsequently discovered and found to have precisely the properties Mendelyev had attributed to them.
2. In 1929, the German psychiatrist, Hans Berger (1930), found evidence for the hypothesis that the human brain exhibited constant electrical activity, even during sleep.
3. In 1956, the Swedish biologists, Tjio and Levan (1956), using a new method for handling cells, obtained photographic evidence that the normal number of chromosomes in man was not 48, as had been thought previously, but 46. This hypothesis was subsequently confirmed by numerous investigators.
4. For over a quarter of a century, the American psychologist, J. B. Rhine (1964), has claimed validity for the hypothesis of *extrasensory perception*—the ability to receive information without benefit of the known physical senses (for example, thought transference, clairvoyance, etc.). Although much evidence has been adduced in support of the phenomena, most psychologists remain unconvinced, because of flaws in the methods used (for a critical review, see Gerden, 1962).

If we now turn our attention to hypotheses involving two variables, we observe a difference in the two examples given from Gentry's research. Strictly speaking, the first simply posits a statistical relationship between two variables, rate of congenital malformation on the one hand, geographical environment on the other. In contrast, the last proposition explicitly goes beyond a merely statistical association in claiming a cause and effect relationship: natural radiation is presumed to contribute to the development of congenital malformations.

To distinguish one kind of statement from the other, we shall designate the first as an *associative hypothesis,* and the second as a *causal hypothesis.* In other words, an *associative* hypothesis is one that stipulates a statistical relationship between two variables without explicitly asserting that one of these variables influences the other. A *causal* hypothesis does add this additional specification; it asserts that variation in one factor produces variation in the other.

It is true that many associative hypotheses, when proved correct, add weight to an existing causal hypothesis, or suggest a new explanatory principle. We have an instance of the latter when confirmation of the purely geographical hypothesis proposed by DiCarlo led Gentry (1959) to identify natural radiation as a possible cause of congenital malformation.

But the associative hypothesis may not imply or suggest any explanations at all; it may merely call attention to a phenomenon to be explained. Consider, for example, the hypothesis proposed by Bronfenbrenner (1958) that over recent decades child rearing practices in the United States have become more permissive. Certainly one cannot conclude that the sheer passage of time makes successive generations more lenient in bringing up their children. We are left with the question as to what factors lead parents to treat their own children differently from the way in which they themselves were treated. In reply to this question Bronfenbrenner suggests that one explanation is to be found in the changing pattern of advice given to parents in successive editions of such widely read publications as the Children's Bureau bulletin on Infant Care (1951) and Benjamin Spock's pocketbook on the same subject (1957).

The foregoing example illustrates the nature and uses of the associative hypothesis. What this type of hypothesis does is to raise the question of a possible pattern among the variables observed. If the presence of the pattern is confirmed, this fact in time may serve one of three purposes: call attention to a new research problem, suggest a new causal hypothesis for investigation, or provide evidence in support or rejection of an already existing one.

The Causal Hypothesis Analyzed

We have said that a causal hypothesis differs from a purely associative one in stipulating a cause-and-effect relationship. What do we mean by this term?

The answer to this question turns out to be rather complex. We may begin with a formal definition. A cause-and-effect relationship exists when *a change in one variable is a necessary or sufficient condition to produce a given effect on another variable.*

Independent and Dependent Variables

Let us now look at the definition in greater detail. Notice first of all that the hypothesis postulates a relation between two factors, one which produces the change, the other the one in which the change is produced. The first, the one that produces the change, is called the *independent* or *antecedent* variable. The other, the one that is changed, is called the *dependent* or *consequent* variable, because it hangs (depends) on the independent variable and follows from it. Thus in Gentry's causal hypothesis the amount of natural radiation is the independent variable, the rate of congenital malformation the dependent variable.

Usually, the causal hypothesis is a one-way street. It works in only one direction. For example, changing the amount of natural radiation increases congenital malformation, but a change in the malformation rate, say by medical intervention, cannot have the slightest effect on the radioactivity of the rocks. But there can be causal relationships which operate in both directions. Contemporary theories of interpersonal relations (Homans, 1950; Heider, 1958; Newcomb, 1953) contain many hypotheses of this character. For example: the more similar two people are, the more likely they are to have positive feelings toward one another. But the process also operates in the reverse direction: the more two people like each other, the more they take on each other's characteristics. In other words, in this particular instance, independent and dependent variables are interchangeable. For this and other reasons, statements of causal hypotheses can be deceptive and may require careful analysis to ascertain which variable is which.

A helpful device in this connection is to conduct a hypothetical experiment in your mind—what the German psychologists call a Gedanken Experiment, a "thought experiment." Try changing each of the variables, and see what happens to the other one. If a change in A leads to a change in B, then A is an independent variable and B dependent. Conversely, if A varies with the change in B, it is A which is the dependent variable. If both change, we have what may be called a *reciprocal* causal relationship.

This does not mean, however, that a directional relationship, in which a change in one variable is followed by a change in the other, necessarily implies cause and effect. A case in point is provided by Bronfenbrenner's hypothesis, already cited, that over the past 25 years American child rearing practices have become more permissive. Clearly, it is the practices that have changed with time, rather than the reverse. In other words, the passage of time is the independent variable, parental behavior the dependent. But one cannot regard time as the factor which makes successive generations more lenient.

Necessary and Sufficient Conditions

This brings us to the main feature which distinguishes the causal hypothesis from its purely associative counterpart: the former always stipulates that one variable actually *influences* the other. This requirement may take two different forms, specified in the definition by the terms "necessary" or "sufficient." What does each of these terms mean?

Necessary means that *the effect cannot occur except under the* specified condition. For example, the disease process known as tuberculosis cannot occur in animal or man in the absence of a creature known as *Microbacterium tuberculosis,* the bacterium which we say "causes" the illness. It is a *necessary* condition.

Although the tubercular bacillus is necessary for the development of the disease, it is quite possible for a person to be a carrier of this baccillus and yet be perfectly healthy, because the human organism develops antibodies which keep the bacillus under control. In other words, the bacillus is a necessary condition, but not a *sufficient* one. A sufficient condition is one that produces a given effect: for example, stick a healthy baby with a pin, and it cries. Of course inflicting pain is not the only condition that will make a baby cry. He will also cry if deprived of food. But sticking him with a pin will do the job. It is a *sufficient* condition.

An example of a less obvious sufficient condition is provided by a study conducted by Rheingold, Gewirtz, and Ross (1959) at the National Institute of Health. These investigators were interested in what it takes to make a baby vocalize more —that is, make more sounds. They showed that the rate of vocalizing among three-month-old infants could be increased markedly by such simple actions on the part of the adult as touching the baby's abdomen with the finger every time the infant made a sound, smiling at it, and clucking at it ("tsk, tsk, tsk") in return. When the adult experimenter reacted in this way, the baby's vocalization rate just about doubled. None of these things was *necessary* to make the baby vocalize more, but they were *sufficient.*

Notice that in actual practice, a sufficient condition may not produce the given effect in every case. A baby will not vocalize every time an adult touches, smiles, or makes noises at it. It may be tired, fearful, or simply distracted by some other event. Nor will an infant cry every time it is stuck with a pin; it may have a bad case of laryngitis, the pin may not hit a pain spot, or the baby may be crying already. In other words, something can interfere.

To put it in another way, a given phenomenon can occur only under certain *boundary conditions.* These boundary conditions are of two kinds. First, all *necessary* conditions to make possible variation in the dependent variable must be satisfied. Thus a baby cannot cry without a functioning voice box (larynx); it cannot smile if the facial nerve is injured; it can do neither if it is seriously ill or exhausted. In other words, a sufficient condition cannot be effective until all necessary conditions are met. But even if all necessary conditions for producing the effect are satisfied, the infant may not be able to perceive the stimulus, and hence not make the response. He may not hear the "tsk, tsk," see the smiling face, or feel the touch or the pin because the stimulus doesn't hit a functioning touch receptor. These are conditions that must be met—not for the effect to occur in the dependent variable (a blind, deaf, or tactilely insensitive baby may be perfectly able to smile and cry) but for the independent variable to be functional in producing the effect. In other words, we are dealing here with a class of variables which limits not the dependent variables but the *relation* between the independent and dependent variables. To distinguish such requirements from what we have called necessary conditions—those that apply to the dependent variable itself—we shall refer to them as *contingent* conditions. Given an independent variable x and a dependent variable y, a contingent condition is one that is not necessary to produce a given effect in y but is required *for x* to produce the given effect in y. Boundary conditions, then, include all necessary and contingent conditions.

We are now in a position to offer a definition of a sufficient condition: *within a given set of boundary conditions, x is a sufficient condition if a change in x produces a change in y.*

Interrelation of the Three Types of Hypotheses

A causal hypothesis, then, is one that stipulates one variable as a necessary or sufficient condition for another. Note also that the causal hypothesis always implies an associative hypothesis as well, since a necessary or sufficient condition inevitably produces a statistical relationship between independent and dependent variables. Finally, an associative hypothesis assumes that each of its components is an observable phenomenon; in other words, it implies two attributive hypotheses. In short, the three types of hypotheses fall into a nested arrangement, like a set of Russian dolls, with the causal hypothesis containing the associative hypothesis, and the associative containing two attributive hypotheses.

If one asks whether there exists still a higher order construct encompassing more than one causal hypothesis, the answer is of course found in the concept of a *theory.* Although this term has no rigorous definition or use, it usually refers to a body of interrelated hypotheses such as Freudian theory, learning theory, dissonance theory, or role theory, all of which have been employed in the attempt to understand the development of human behavior.

As we shall see, the hierarchical structure of the causal hypothesis dictates the steps to be followed in proving a cause-and-effect relationship. The investigator begins by specifying a procedure for observing each of the separate variables in the investigation. By demonstrating that such observations can be made, he in effect confirms the attributive hypothesis for each factor. He then proceeds to demonstrate a statistical association between two of the variables under circumstances which require such an association to be the product of a cause-and-effect relationship.

We turn next to an examination of the principles and procedures involved in the process of hypothesis testing.

II. THE LOGIC OF VERIFICATION

In our discussion we shall focus attention on the causal hypothesis since, as we have seen, this incorporates all other types as well.

Given our definition of a cause-and-effect relationship, the task of verification becomes that of demonstrating that a given condition is necessary or sufficient. As we shall see, the proof begins somewhat differently for the two cases, but ends with a similar exacting requirement.

The Logic of Demonstrating a Cause-and-Effect Relationship

Let us begin with the case of a necessary condition. Since necessary means that the dependent variable (B) cannot occur without the independent variable (A), one must show first of all that all possible instances of (B) are preceded or accompanied by (A). The situation with a sufficient condition involves a different requirement. Here variation in one factor must produce a given effect on the other. In other words, a change in A must be followed by the specified effect in B.

Now let us suppose that one or the other of the above requirements is fulfilled. Does this mean that a necessary condition has in fact been demonstrated in the one case, and a sufficient condition in the other? Unfortunately not. If that were all there was to it, the work of the scientist would be much easier than it is, and much less interesting.

The inadequacy of either of the above demonstrations is brought home by the tale of a man who obviously understood exactly what he was doing. This chap discovered that every time he drank a highball of scotch and ginger ale, he became drunk. The next time he tried gin and ginger ale and got the same effect. Then he experimented with rye and ginger ale and you know what happened. What to do? "Aha,' " he said, "I know what does it." And the next time he eliminated the ginger ale.

This example shows that, to demonstrate a necessary or sufficient condition, it is not enough to show the required kind of relationship between the independent variable A and the dependent variable B. One must also establish that no other factor X is functioning as an independent variable. For if it is, then the results are *confounded;* that is, one cannot separate the effect of A from the effect of X. And if X is actually responsible for the effect, then A is neither necessary nor sufficient.

Demonstrating that a given effect is produced by A, and not by some other factor, can turn out to be a fairly complicated task, especially if people in general—and scientists in particular—are sure they already know what the necessary or sufficient condition is.

The Goldberger Story

To show how complicated it can be, let us look at the case history of a hypothesis that is all inclusive, since it postulates a condition which is both necessary and sufficient at the same time. The case history begins back in the early 1900's.[1] At that time they were having trouble down in the South—Virginia, South Carolina, Mississippi, and Georgia. It was a different kind of trouble. But they did what they so often do when there is trouble in the South; they sent a man from Washington. This man's name was Joseph Goldberger.

In the period 1900 to 1914, 100,000 people died every year in the American South from a disease called *pellagra.* In Italian, pellagra means "rough skin," one of the symptoms of the disease. Other symptoms, which come on gradually, include running sores, foul odor, vomiting, diarrhea, terrible pain, nervous and mental disturbances, and finally that ultimate symptom—death.

In 1912, just before Goldberger was sent down from Washington, a top medical commission had surveyed all the available evidence and had concluded that pellagra was "a specific infectious disease communicable from person to person by means at present unknown." Goldberger got off the train at Spartanberg, South Carolina, where there was a pellagra hospital. As an investigator he saw his first task as one of observing. Pellagra cases were everywhere; not only in the hospital but all round the countryside. Goldberger saw emaciated bodies, sallow sunken faces, cases of insanity.

But he noticed other things too. It was cotton country. In the mill towns and villages everyone was trying to live by cotton, and not succeeding. Families were attempting to survive on fifteen dollars a week, and they looked it. If they paid the rent and bought the barest necessities in clothes, there wasn't half enough left for food. And it was the same in Georgia, in Florida, Alabama, and Virginia. In fact, you can still see it—not the pellagra, but the poverty. And it still takes a toll, both physically and psychologically.

But back to Goldberger. As he visited hospitals and institutions, he noticed a strange thing: none of the nurses, attendants or other employees, who were in daily contact with the pellagra cases, had ever developed the disease. He also observed that in an orphanage he visited, there were virtually no pellagra cases below the age of six or above the age of twelve, but in the middle group, practically all the children had pellagra. Goldberger knew that he had run onto a critical natural experiment. He was hot on the trail of a hypothesis. In the institutional setting, it didn't take him very long to find what he was looking for. It had to do with food.

1. The middle group ate only the regular institutional diet.
2. The little ones got a regular milk supplement.
3. The older group supplemented their diet by foraging on their own.

And what did the regular institutional menu consist of? Traditional Southern dishes—but low cost ones—biscuits, hominy grits, corn mush, syrup, molasses, gravy, sowbelly. Plenty to eat, but no milk, no eggs, no butter, no meat—in short, no animal proteins.

It would seem he had found the answer. All that remained was to publish it to the world. But Goldberger didn't. Instead, he went to another institution with lots of pellagra cases, instituted dietary changes, and the pellagra went away. Just like that.

Then Goldberger published. And what was the reaction? Leaders of the medical profession were unconvinced. Goldberger had not found the agent of contagion, and "as is well known, pellagra is a contagious disease."

So Goldberger decided to do an experiment that would be convincing. He would show that he could produce pellagra in healthy human beings. But he needed volunteers. So he went to the Governor of Mississippi with a request. Would the Governor grant pardons to 12 convicts with long-term sentences in state prison if they volunteered to stay in Goldberger's experiment for six months. The risk: pellagra, the gain: freedom.

The Governor of Mississippi was an understanding man, Goldberger got his volunteers—twelve enterprising fellows—embezzlers, highwaymen, murderers—and in the best of health.

When the experiment started, the volunteers were sure they had a good thing going. Instead of the regular prison fare, they were being given special meals—and what meals! The food was well cooked, tasted fine, and every man got all he wanted. For breakfast there was: biscuits, fried mush, syrup. For dinner: corn bread, cabbage, sweet potatoes, grits. For supper: rice, gravy, fried mush, coffee with sugar.

Eighty additional convicts, who were designated as a control group, lived under the same conditions as the volunteers—except for diet. After a few weeks, the volunteers began to doubt that they had made such a fine bargain. They began to feel queer—headache, stomach ache, dizziness. By the fifth month, the skin began to scale, and all the classical symptoms of pellagra were present.

The convicts were pardoned, released, and offered a cure, but they were too frightened to take it. Goldberger hastened to report his findings at a meeting of public health experts in Washington. At the meeting, the Chairman had some remarks to make. He said he wished "to enunciate certain beliefs concerning pellagra, these beliefs being backed by research done by good American citizens such as Siler, Garrison, and MacNeal." The Chairman then went on to state that pellagra was "a specific infectious disease, communicable from person to person by unknown means."

In short, Goldberger's argument was unconvincing in the light of prevailing views. How did Goldberger react? With another experiment. He recognized that he had not yet proved his point. He still had a requirement to fulfill. He had built a case for his own independent variable—diet, but he had not shown that another independent variable, X, had not influenced the results. Specifically, he had not dealt with the accepted explanation for pellagra, and for virtually all the other diseases known at that time—contagion. He hadn't really answered the principal argument of his opponents.

Goldberger set out to eliminate the contagion hypothesis once and for all. This is how he did it.

He drew an ounce of blood from a pellagra patient suffering an acute attack. A colleague then injected five cubic centimeters of the patient's blood into Goldberger's shoulder. In addition, secretions from the patient's nose and throat were swabbed into Goldberger's nose and throat. Finally, he selected two patients—one with scaling sores and the other with diarrhea. He scraped the scales from the sores, mixed the scales with four cubic centimeters of urine from the same patients, added an equal amount of liquid feces, and rolled the mixture into little dough balls by the addition of a few pinches of flour. The pills were then taken voluntarily by him, by his assistants and by his wife. Publication of the experiment was withheld for five months to make sure that there were no delayed effects. The report mentioned no names. It simply spoke of 15 men and a housewife.

The experiment made its point. Finally, the "infectionists" were silenced. Years after Goldberger's death the substance contained in animal protein necessary to prevent pellagra was named Vitamin G. But the name didn't stick. Personal tribute had to give way to scientific progress. In 1936, the critical substance was identified more specifically as nicotinic acid.

Proof as a Psychological Problem

As Goldberger's experience demonstrates, the process of proof may demand more than satisfying logical requirements. It may also necessitate overcoming psychological barriers. Verification does not take place in a vacuum; it occurs in the minds of men. The human mind is not always capable of seeing objectively, let alone thinking objectively. Both perception and thought can be distorted by conviction and desire. Nor are scientists any more immune to such distortions than other men. The medical scientists who heard and read Goldberger's reports were neither stupid nor evil. They simply *knew* that pellagra was a contagious disease, and—what is more important —they knew this was the opinion of the "best authorities."

Since one does not have to be a social scientist to regard himself or be regarded by others as an authority on problems of human behavior, the researcher in this sphere frequently finds himself confronted with a task of psychological as well as logical persuasion.

Some Principles of Verification

Nevertheless, it is logic that lies at the heart of the matter. To make explicit the principles involved, let us analyze the steps in the argument as exemplified in Goldberger's work.

What was Goldberger's line of reasoning? Where did he begin?

First he established that every case of pellagra he observed ate a certain diet; persons not eating the diet never contracted pellagra.

In other words, Goldberger showed that two variables were related statistically. He confirmed what we have called an associative hypothesis.

What does this demonstration accomplish?

Does it prove a necessary condition? He had shown that every case of pellagra had eaten the same kind of diet.

Could some other factor have accounted for the same results?

Yes, contagion—through infected food; through sewage.

Does his demonstration prove a sufficient condition? He had shown that a difference in diet was related to pellagra, but could some other factor have accounted for the same results? Again the answer is yes. The food could have been infected. This brings us to our first principle.

Principle I

A causal hypothesis is not proved so long as an alternative hypothesis can be offered to explain the same findings.

In other words, no causal hypothesis can be regarded as confirmed until all plausible alternative hypotheses have been eliminated. This requirement points up a critical limitation of any purely associative hypothesis, such as the one we have just been considering. The demonstration that a particular kind of association exists of course does not eliminate the possibility that this association is the product of some third factor. This is one of the reasons why—

Principle II

The demonstration that a particular kind of association between two variables exists cannot, by itself, prove that one of these variables is a necessary or sufficient condition for the other.

So what did Goldberger's first step accomplish? Could he draw any inferences from it at all?

What was his associative hypothesis? Was it simply that diet and pellagra tend to occur together?

Suppose Goldberger had found the following:

	PERCENT PELLAGRA CASES
Eating diet	85%
Not eating diet	5%

Do we have an association? Yes.

Do we have a necessary condition? No.

Putting the matter more generally—in establishing a necessary condition, *all* positive instances of the dependent variable must be associated with *presence* of the independent variable. There can be no exceptions.

And Goldberger didn't find any. The actual percentage among those not eating the diet was zero.

So the results for an associative hypothesis can be useful after all. They can be used to *disprove* a hypothesis about a necessary condition. We may put this as a general principle.

Principle III

Results for a hypothesis of association can disprove a hypothesis of necessity so long as there is even a single case in which the dependent variable occurs without the independent variable.

Can results for a hypothesis of association disprove a hypothesis of sufficient condition as well?

The answer to this question turns out to be somewhat more complicated. To demonstrate the point, we must take a different example. Suppose that instead of working with pellagra, Goldberger had been working with a still unsolved mystery, the common cold, and was investigating the hypothesis that exposure to damp weather increases susceptibility. In studying case records of visits to general practitioners by persons complaining of colds, he finds the following:

	% OF ALL PATIENTS WITH COLDS
Persons working mainly indoors (businessmen, secretaries, etc.)	50%
Persons working mainly outdoors (laborers, policemen, etc.)	50%

In other words, no association. Does this mean that exposure to dampness does not increase susceptibility to colds? No.

Persons working outdoors may be healthier.

Persons working indoors may take their complaints to a doctor more often.

Principle IV

A negative result for a hypothesis of association cannot, by itself, disprove a hypothesis of sufficiency, since it does not eliminate the possibility that an association in fact exists but is counteracted by some third factor.

Since results for a purely associative hypothesis can neither prove nor disprove that a variable is a sufficient condition, do they have any utility at all in investigating hypotheses of sufficiency?

Did it make any difference to Gentry that the association between congenital malformation and rock formations came out as it did?

Of course; the association suggested that he was on the right track.

Since an association between two variables can imply a possible causal relation—

Principle V

A positive result for an associative hypothesis increases the probability that the implied causal hypothesis can be sustained; a negative result decreases that probability, eliminating it completely in the case of a hypothesis of necessity.

In view of the above principle, tests of associative hypotheses are very useful in the early stages of research, not only to narrow down the independent variables that are to become the foci of further investigation, but also tentatively to identify or eliminate other factors that may have to be controlled in order to establish the hypothesis in question.

We had just identified one such factor in relation to the first step in Goldberger's investigation; namely, we pointed out that the observed association between diet and pellagra did not rule out the possibility of contagion.

Let us now eliminate that possibility and see where we stand then. Suppose Goldberger had done both the first step and the last; that is, he

1. Showed an association between diet and pellagra, with all cases of pellagra eating a deficient diet,
2. Showed by his experiment that pellagra was not contagious.

Would he have proved his hypothesis?

Remember: a hypothesis is not proved until no alternative hypothesis can be given to explain the observed findings.

Can an alternative explanation be offered?

...till single out the lower socioeconomic ...h separately are being the group where child abuse occurs the most?

Psychol. implications for child - for mother - etc...

Who were the people who ate the deficient diet? Poor cotton workers. What about the following possibilities:

1. Contact with some poison associated with processing cotton.
2. Excessive exposure to sunlight.
3. Exposure to natural radiation.
4. Exposure to extremes of temperatures.

Notice that in the groups that Goldberger studied these are factors that were associated with eating a deficient diet—that is, with the independent variable of the hypothesis.

Does this mean that you have to rule out any factor that happens to be associated with the independent variable of the hypothesis?

What about the evil eye? Some people think you can get sick from being given the evil eye. And poor people are more likely to have such beliefs than the well-to-do and well educated.

Is it necessary to rule out the evil eye as a possible influence?

No. Because there is no scientific basis for believing that an evil eye could have such an effect.

So what alternative hypotheses do you have to rule out? Any and all? When must a variable be considered as a potentially confounding factor?

Principle VI

In testing a hypothesis, a variable must be considered as a potentially confounding factor when it is associated with the independent variable of the hypothesis, and scientific ground exists for believing that the variable in question could influence the dependent variable.

Poison encountered either in the course of cotton processing or—more important—simply in the diet eaten by poor families, would satisfy both of the above conditions. And in Goldberger's time, perhaps so could exposure to dampness, sunlight, or extremes of temperature.

How would one rule out the possibility that such factors could explain the observed results?

Would one have to disprove each of them the way Goldberger did with contagion?

That would have been an awful lot of work. Did Goldberger do all that?

No, he didn't.

Then Goldberger didn't prove his case after all? We have all been taken in—and so have all the scientists—then and today.

What did Goldberger do that eliminated all of these alternative hypotheses—and some others as well—at one fell swoop?

He supplemented the diet of pellagra cases with animal proteins and the pellagra disappeared.

Notice that this procedure immediately eliminates the possibility that poison, climate, sleep, etc. could influence the results. Since the same individuals are involved throughout, and they remain in the same environment, all of the above variables—and a host of others—are held constant. Only one factor is allowed to vary —the independent variable of the hypothesis—change in diet. If, under the circumstances, the dependent variable then also changes, the change can be attributable only to the independent variable.

We have just illustrated the fundamental principle for verifying causal hypotheses.

Principle VII

To establish a cause-and-effect relationship, one demonstrates that variable x has an effect on variable y by allowing x to vary, holding constant other sources of variation for y, and then showing that y varies in a specified fashion as a function of the variation in x.

There are a number of different methods for varying x while holding constant other sources of variation for y; these are discussed in textbooks on experimental design. One more step remains to complete our examination of principles of verification as illustrated by Goldberger's classic investigation.

Suppose Goldberger had carried out only the second and the last steps of his research. That is, he had shown that

> Step 2. Supplementing the diet of pellagra cases with animal proteins made the pellagra disappear.

> Step 4. Pellagra could not be contracted through contagion.

Are these two steps enough to prove that deficient diet is a necessary condition for pellagra?

To prove a hypothesis of necessity you have to show two things:

> 1. that without the independent variable (diet), the effect cannot take place,

Has this been shown? Yes.

> 2. and that no other independent variable can explain the obtained results.

Does any alternative explanation remain? Note that contagion was eliminated by the experiment in Step 4. Such things as amount of sleep, exposure to sunlight, natural radiation, etc. are held constant by having the same individuals be sick and well in the same environment.

In other words, the combination of Step 2 and Step 4 has established the hypothesis of necessity. What about the hypothesis of sufficiency. Do Steps 2 and 4 confirm that as well?

To prove a hypothesis of sufficiency, one has to demonstrate that a change in the independent variable A produces a given effect B, and that no other independent variable can explain the obtained results. Thus far we have shown only that diet A is a necessary condition for producing pellagra and that a normal diet is sufficient to cure pellagra. What we still have to do is prove that diet A is sufficient to produce pellagra. How to do it?—by means of Goldberg's experiment producing pellagra in convict volunteers. Other variables were controlled by feeding a comparable group in the same institution on a normal diet. Here change in A produces the effect in question. And no alternative hypothesis remains.

Quod erat demonstrandum!

Taken together, the results of Goldberger's three experiments "prove" his hypothesis. By producing pellagra through the removal of animal protein from the diet, by curing pellagra through adding this same ingredient to the diet, and by showing that pellagra was not transmitted through contagion, Goldberger established that the necessary and sufficient condition for pellagra is absence of animal proteins in the diet. The cause of the disease—what medical scientists call its etiology—was now fully known.

The Problem of Levels of Analysis

But was it really? Perhaps a medical scientist would be satisfied, but what about a chemist? After all, subsequent investigation showed that pellagra was actually caused not by protein deficiency in general but by the absence in the diet of a specific chemical substance known as nicotinic acid. And if biological hypotheses have to be reduced to chemical ones, what about psychological explanations, or sociological ones—must each be reduced ultimately to the level of charged particles?

Clearly not. The scientist is free to choose the level of analysis at which he wishes to work. His independent and dependent variables may be at the same or at different levels. The only restriction upon him is that he may not claim conclusions beyond the levels at which he has worked, although his results may suggest new problems and hypotheses at these other levels.

Thus we shall find students of human behavior working at different levels of analysis. Some attempt to relate the behavior of the individual to its physiological and even chemical substrata. Others seek to explain the actions and attitudes of one person as a function of the behavior of others acting individually or in concert as groups, communities, and societies.

But at whatever the level the causal hypothesis is couched, the logic of proof remains the same. We may summarize this logic by offering a paradox: *the process of proof is actually one of disproof.* The scientist never really demonstrates that a hypothesis is true; what he does is to eliminate all other possible explanations. In sum, scientific truth is established by default.

III. THE MEASUREMENT OF VARIABLES

We have examined the *logic* of science—the principles involved in formulating and testing hypotheses. What about the method? How does one translate the logic into actual research operations?

Operational Definition

Since variables constitute the building blocks of every hypothesis, the first step calls for expressing these variables in some concrete form, in terms of some operation which enables the investigator to determine a change, or lack of change, in the variable in question. Thus, Goldberger had to have some way of knowing when the subjects in his experiments developed pellagra and when they were cured of this affliction. For this purpose, he used as an index the symptoms of the disease, primarily the appearance of the characteristic rash for which the condition was named. In other words, the measure of the dependent variable in his hypothesis was simply the diagnosis made by a physician as to whether pellagra was present or absent. Similarly, Goldberger's independent variable was defined by presence or absence of animal proteins in the diet fed to his research subjects.

Of course, we are often interested in intermediate points between complete absence and full development of a variable. For example, as his measure of the relative degree of congenital malformation in a given area, Gentry used the rate of such cases per thousand births as determined from entries in the infants' birth and death certificates of abnormalities observed by the attending physician.

In science, the procedure one employs to determine the degree to which a particular variable is present is called *operational definition*. It is also referred to as *indexing* or just plain *measuring*.

Scales of Measurement

As the foregoing examples illustrate, measuring always involves specification of the category into which a particular observation falls. Categories may differ from each other in one of two ways, in quality or in quantity. Examples of the former are classifications of disease, nationality, occupation, or sex. When a system of classification is based on qualitative distinctions without any implication of order among the categories, we refer to such a system as a *nominal scale*. In a nominal scale, the classes differ by name and not by number; that is, they do not fall into any fixed sequence.

Where the categories do fall into a regular order, but the interval between steps is not fixed in terms of a constant unit of measurement, we speak of an *ordinal scale*. The most simple example of an ordinal scale is a ranking. Ranks, however, have the disadvantage that their significance depends on the number of persons ranked. Thus the student ranking 10th in a class of 10 is clearly not comparable to one who ranks 10th in a class of 100. For this reason, distributions of ordinal position are often broken up into divisions with an equal number of cases in each division. Thus one speaks of a measurement in the top *quartile* (upper fourth of all the cases), *decile* (tenth) or *percentile* (hundredth). All of these are examples of ordinal scales.

The chief limitation of ordinal measurements is that the distance between successive ordinal positions may not be equal (e.g., the difference between the tallest and the second tallest may not be the same as that between the second tallest and third tallest). It is of course much more convenient when the units of measurement are stable. When this condition is satisfied we have what is called an *interval scale,* illustrated by the common thermometer. Notice that the location of the zero point on such a scale is usually quite arbitrary; on an ordinary thermometer, zero does not mean the absence of any temperature at all. It is for this reason that one cannot say that a temperature of 40° C is twice as hot as 20° C. To be able to make such proportional statements, it is necessary to have an absolute zero point, as in measurements of weight, time, and distance. When an interval scale has this property it is referred to as a *ratio scale.* The scale of cardinal numbers—the one we use to count a series of objects—is of course a ratio scale.

Except for their use in counting people or frequencies of an event, ratio scales are a rarity in the behavioral sciences, since it is difficult to establish an absolute zero point for psychological characteristics. It is usually possible, however, to construct interval scales for most aspects of human behavior. This is fortunate, since the interval scale has many advantages for scientific work. In particular, because of its equally spaced intervals, it permits the calculation of stable indices which summarize the characteristics of a whole series of measurements.

But before considering how and for what purpose measurements themselves can be manipulated and summarized, we must confront a prior problem regarding their basic soundness.

The Problem of Validity

Whenever one undertakes to translate theoretical variables into concrete indices, one must take into account an omnipresent danger—the danger of mistranslation. The index may not be *measuring what it is supposed to measure.* In scientific terminology, it may not be *valid.* For example, in measuring brain waves, the meter may be plugged into the wrong circuit, with the result that what is being recorded is not the perturbations of electric current in the brain but in the overhead light fixture.

The foregoing example may not be so outlandish as it may seem. In the age of computers, the possibility that one set of data has been substituted for another is hardly negligible. Take the experience of one of the writers. A dozen years ago, in a Presidential address (Bronfenbrenner, 1958), I reported some fascinating findings on the effects of different types of parental treatment on the behavior of the child. The results were rather complex, some seemingly contradictory, but I managed to show how they all really fitted together into a single theory. It was rather impressive.

Unfortunately, at the next convention of the American Psychological Association a year later I had to present the same material again to much the same audience (Bronfenbrenner, 1959). I was able to assure my listeners, however, that no one would be bored. You see, through a misunderstanding at the computing center, the signs on all the computations had been reversed, so every relationship that I had reported a year before was in fact exactly backwards. In my second address, I had to set everything right side up. And of course, I came up with a new theory that fitted the "new" results, but somehow it was not so impressive any more. ·

Here, then, was an instance in which the measurements, as they were being used, were completely *invalid*. The more typical case, however, is that of partial validity—the index reflects the variable in question plus other factors as well, which may account for much if not most of the variation. For example, years ago, before the French psychologists Binet and Simon (1905) invented an "objective method" for testing functional intelligence, the evaluation of a child's mental ability was made simply by asking some adult who knew him—usually the teacher—to make a judgment. We know now that although teachers' judgments show a positive relation to more objective measures of the child's intellectual performance, they are also influenced by other factors such as the child's social class level, how he behaves in school, or—perhaps most importantly—the degree to which the teacher likes him. To the extent that these other factors affect the teacher's judgment, her evaluation of the child's mental ability is an invalid index.

Of course, so-called objective measures—such as paper-and-pencil tests with predetermined scoring schemes—also present problems of validity. For example, group tests that purport to measure intelligence, or achievement in a particular subject like history, biology, or even mathematics, may actually be measuring little more than speed of reading. Another source of confounding arises with paper-and-pencil tests of personality, for here the respondent often gives not the real answer but what he thinks he ought to say—the socially desirable response.

There are various ways for getting around such difficulties more or less satisfactorily, but these are technical problems which need not concern us at the moment. The point we wish to make here is that the investigator must always consider the issue of validity with respect to each of the variables included in his investigation and provide some evidence that the procedures he is using—his operational definitions—do in fact measure what they are supposed to measure.

Validation Against an Outside Criterion

How does one establish that his methods of measurement are valid? When the senior author was himself a student, this question was simply answered. To show that your technique was valid, you simply tested it against some *external criterion* presumed to measure the same variable. This outside criterion usually took the form of a judgment by a person or persons deemed to be experts on the phenomenon in question. For example, the Stanford-Binet, the best and most widely used individual test of intelligence,[2] was originally validated against teachers' judgments. In other words, to see whether the test was measuring what it was supposed to, Lewis M. Terman, the famous Stanford psychologist, examined the degree of correspondence between the results of the test and the ratings of each child's intelligence made by his classroom teacher. There was a positive relationship between the two sets of measures, but there were also some exceptions. Some pupils whom the teachers rated high in intelligence turned out low on the test and *vice versa*. Which measure was right? We know now that the Stanford-Binet is usually a more valid measure of intellectual performance than a teacher's rating, but this could not be determined simply from the degree of association between two measures where the validity of each was in question.

The foregoing consideration points to the principal limitation of the *outside criterion* method for evaluating validity; namely, the method is limited by the *validity* of the outside criterion. This approach, therefore, is most applicable in those situations where a valid criterion already exists. But then why develop a new method? Actually, there may be very good reason to do so. The existing valid method may be excellent but expensive of time and resources. The Stanford-Binet is a case in point. It can only be given to one child at a time, requires a trained examiner, and takes anywhere from thirty minutes to an hour and a half to administer. In contrast, group tests of intelligence can be given to an entire classroom within a specified period of time by persons without a high degree of specialized training. Such group tests are invariably validated against the Stanford-Binet as an external criterion.

But what if the outside criterion is itself of inadequate validity, or at least of poorer validity than is desired of the new instrument? Does testing against the outside criterion then have any utility at all? Clearly, yes, provided this criterion is believed to have *some* validity, for, then, as in the case of teachers' ratings, it provides some reassurance that the investigator is on the right track. But equally clearly, additional evidence of validity is required, especially in those instances where no external criterion is available, as would occur when the variable was being measured for the first time. How can one establish the validity of a measuring technique without relying on some external index of the variable in question?

Construct Validity

The answer to the foregoing question is suggested by the following fact. The ability of the Stanford-Binet to predict school grades was also offered as evidence for its validity. The argument ran as follows: since intelligence is necessary for academic achievement, there should be a positive relation between measures of intelligence and measures of achievement. Since scores on the Stanford-Binet show such a positive association, this fact is *consistent with* the position that the Stanford-Binet does in fact measure intellectual capacity. Notice that, taken by itself, the existence of the expected relationship does not *prove* the validity of the measure of intelligence, it is merely *consistent* with the presence of such validity. But if one could identify a variety of such expected relationships, and if all of these expectations were in fact fulfilled, this would obviously increase the probability that the index was actually measuring what it was presumed to measure.

Here we have the guiding principle of the process known as *construct validation.* It may be stated somewhat more formally in the following terms: *a measure has construct validity if it shows a pattern of relationships with other variables that is to be expected from a theoretical analysis of the phenomenon.*

To make clear what is implied by this definition let us take an example of construct validation carried out by Richard Christie and his associates (Christie, 1964; Geis, Christie, and Nelson, 1963; Geis, 1964; Geis and Christie, 1965; Christie and

Geis, 1968; Christie and Geis, 1970) at Columbia University. These investigators posit the wide prevalence in contemporary American society of a personality trait which they call Machiavellianism. The origin and nature of this characteristic are described in the following excerpt.

> Since the publication of *The Prince* in 1532, the name of its author has come to designate the use of guile, deceit, and opportunism in interpersonal relations. These behaviors are usually conceived as accompanied by congruent perceptual and attitudinal personality dispositions, characteristically including a dispassionate readiness to expect and detect human weaknesses, failings, and foibles, and the willingness to exploit them. More generally, a Machiavellian is one who views and evaluates others impersonally and amorally in terms of their usefulness for his own purposes. The Machiavellian would thus appear to correspond to the ideal type— or stereotype—of the "operator" or "manipulator."
>
> Whatever the labels applied, the syndrome of impersonal, manipulative attitudes and behavior is socially significant. As society becomes more and more organized, increasing proportions of interpersonal contacts become impersonal and means-oriented. As major activity in all areas of society is increasingly conducted by organizations, the ability to influence, direct, and use others effectively becomes increasingly valuable. (Geis, *et al.,* 1963)

To measure the Machiavellian syndrome, Christie and his colleagues have developed a questionnaire of 20 items, of which the following are examples.

> *Never tell anyone the real reason you did something unless it is useful to do so.
> *The biggest difference between most criminals and other people is that the criminals are stupid enough to get caught.
> *Most men forget more easily the death of their father than the loss of their property.
> One should take action only when sure it is morally right. It is safest to assume that all people have a vicious streak and it will come out when they are given a chance.
> Barnum was wrong when he said that there's a sucker born every minute.

The respondent indicates his degree of agreement with each item on a seven point scale ranging from "strongly disagree" to "strongly agree." Starred items are scored in the opposite direction. The measure of Machiavellianism is the sum of the person's score across all 20 items.

How is the validity of such a scale to be established? Clearly an external criterion is hard to come by. This is particularly true of what might be thought of as the ideal validating index—obtaining Machiavelli's own response to the items (although some would not deny the ultimate availability of this criterion to the originators of the scale!). The authors themselves have sought to demonstrate validity by testing and confirming a variety of hypotheses about differences between high and low scores. Here are some of them:

1. When given an opportunity to deceive others in an experimental situation, high scorers were much more active than low scorers in thinking up and carrying out activities which confused, annoyed, and frustrated the other person.
2. In a sample of Washington lobbyists, high scorers spent more time contacting and entertaining Congressmen than low scorers. The high scorers also had more clients.
3. In group discussions, high scorers were more persuasive than low scorers.
4. In a sample of Hungarian immigrants, high scorers adapted to the American way of life more quickly than low scorers.
5. In an experimental game requiring convincing a partner to join in a coalition at a loss to the partner, high scorers generally won, low scorers lost.
6. In a sample of medical students, high scorers were more likely to choose psychiatry over surgery as a specialty.
7. The more ambiguous the rules in an experimental game, the more likely high scorers were to win it.
8. Mach (short for Machiavelli) score tended to be unrelated to amount of education, socioeconomic status, or level of intelligence.
9. When high and low scorers played strategy games over a period of time, the high scorers tended to win in the early stages, but low scorers won in the final stages. The investigators interpreted these results as supporting the hypothesis that "honesty is the best policy—in the long run."
10. When shown slides of past contestants in the Miss Rheingold contest, high scorers were more successful in selecting the winners for each year than were low scorers.
11. Persons reaching 21 years of age after 1942 had higher Mach scores than those attaining their maturity before that date. In other words, the tendency toward Machiavellianism has increased since World War II.
12. High scores on the Mach scale were associated with a history of disrupted relationships in childhood (parents separated or divorced, many moves from one location to another.)
13. "Graduate students in social psychology are more in tune with Machiavelli than any other aggregate of subjects yet tested." (Christie 1964, p. 14)

Note the following characteristics of this set of findings.

A. The variables with which the Mach score shows positive (Hypotheses 1–8. 10–12), negative (Hypothesis 9), and no relationships (Hypothesis 8) are those for which such relationships would be expected, given a valid measure of Machiavellianism as theoretically defined.

B. The hypotheses involve Machiavellianism both as an independent (Hypotheses 1–8, 9–10), and as a dependent variable (Hypotheses 8, 11, 12).

C. Since the presence of a statistical association can serve as corroborative but not as conclusive evidence for verifying a hypothesis (see preceding section), the data submitted include not only evidence of appropriate statistical relations (Hypotheses 2, 4, 6, 7, 8, 10–13), but also relevant results of controlled experiments (Hypotheses 1, 3, 5, 7, 9).

D. Since a laboratory situation necessarily leaves out aspects of the "real world" in which behavior occurs, validating hypotheses involve events outside the laboratory (Hypotheses 2, 4, 6, 8, 10–13) as well as controlled experiments.

As we see from the foregoing analysis, construct validation involves demonstrating that the antecedents, consequents, and correlates of the variable under consideration are consistent with the presumed nature of that variable. In a sentence, *construct validation involves testing the theory associated with the construct*—the body of interrelated hypotheses involving the variable in question. Confirmation of this set of hypotheses constitutes evidence that the operational definition of the variable does represent what it is supposed to represent, that the variable in question does exist and can be measured. In short, construct validation is a method for confirming what we have called a single variable hypothesis.

Notice that the confirmation is accomplished by taking advantage of the hierarchical, nested structure of a theory and its component causal hypotheses. Specifically, where a set of causal hypotheses have in common a particular variable, either as an independent or dependent factor, then confirmation of these hypotheses is also a validation of their component elements, including the single hypothesis about the existence of the focal variable.

Does this mean that every operational definition must be validated in this comprehensive fashion? If so, this would mean that no measurement could be considered valid until a whole body of hypotheses involving that variable have been confirmed. Actually, this is necessary only in those instances where the operational definition is only remotely or indirectly related to the theoretical variable. Such a state of affairs is likely to occur in two kinds of situations. The first, illustrated by Christie's concept of Machiavellianism as a personality trait, involves a characteristic which is not accessible to direct observation but is inferred as a *hypothetical construct.* Hence the term "construct validity."

A second circumstance in which construct validation is indicated occurs when a theoretical variable could be measured directly, but for reasons of economy the investigator makes use of some indirect index relatively removed from the original phenomenon but more quickly and cheaply obtained. A case in point is provided by Gentry's research (1959). Here the independent variable, natural radiation, could have been measured directly, through the use of portable Geiger counters, but the cost of carrying out a radiological survey for the entire state would have been prohibitive. In its place, Gentry ingeniously employed the far cheaper alternative of utilizing already available geological survey maps of rock formations. But since his index is indirect, he is under obligation to establish its validity. This he does by demonstrating a chain of relationships as follows:

1. He cites laboratory studies showing that igneous rocks exhibit higher radioactivity than sedimentary rocks.
2. For the few sections of the state where direct field studies of rate of natural radiation had been made, he shows that areas with higher rates are those containing greater concentration of igneous rocks (eg., the Adirondacks).
3. Finally, he shows that the rate of congenital malformation is highest among persons who live in areas with the greatest concentration of igneous rocks and whose way of life involves close contact with rocky soil (e.g., obtaining drinking water from wells and springs).

Notice that where an outside criterion exists, (as in this instance) construct validation includes testing the index against the outside criterion (i.e., laboratory measurement of radioactivity of rock specimens). But, as before, evidence is presented for the validity of the measure outside the laboratory as well. Finally, the ultimate validation of the construct is supplied by confirmation of the causal relationships involving that construct.

The Dangers of Face Validity

But what if the existence of the theoretical variable is not in doubt and its operational definition is fairly direct rather than inferential? For example, suppose the independent variable in our hypothesis is the sex of the child and the dependent variable "crying." Obviously, one does not need to confirm a complete theory of genetics to be sure that one child is a boy or another a girl. Nor does one need to demonstrate the causes or consequences of crying to be assured that Mary or Johnny is shedding tears. Under such circumstances, a variable is said to have *face validity;* that is, the validity of the operational definition is regarded as self-evident.

But even though the validity seems self-evident, it is good practice not to take it for granted but to consider possible sources of confounding. Suppose, for example, that in testing for a sex difference in susceptibility to crying among nursery school children, the dependent variable is measured by the amount of time per hour that each child is observed to be in tears. The problem with such an index becomes readily apparent when we examine the kinds of activities engaged in by boys and girls in the nursery playroom or out of doors: the boys are at greater risk to physical injury with the result that they may actually cry more than the girls busily playing in the doll corner. In other words, for the measure of crying to be valid, one must control for the degree of instigation in the environment.

The foregoing example illustrates how the problem of validity becomes part of the more general problem of experimental design—that is, controlling for the influence of confounding variables. Such sources of confounding variables are readily overlooked when the face validity of an index is taken for granted. The index may indeed reflect the theoretical variable in question, but one or more extraneous variables as well.

Systematic and Variable Errors

To the extent that a measurement is only partially valid, it is said to be in error. There are two kinds of errors, *systematic* and *random.* A systematic error is one that deviates in one direction more than in another. For example, in a special validating study of the measure of his dependent variable, Gentry found that entries of congenital malformation in birth certificates actually underestimates the true rate of such defects in the population. This fact was established by visiting the family of every n*th* child born in a given region and obtaining more direct information about the presence or absence of congenital defect. The rate of congenital malformation compiled on this basis turned out to be three times as high as that obtained from looking at birth and death certificates. In other words, the information on certificates was often incomplete, producing a systematic underestimate.

The second type of error is illustrated by the following example. The following are estimates of John Jones' height by five of his classmates who observe him as he stands at the front of the class:

5'6", 5'8", 5'4", 4'11", 5'8"—Jones' height actually is 5'4½". This is very close to the average of the above estimates, which equals 5'5". The estimates are obviously in error, but not in any systematic way. The chance of an error in one direction is just about as great as in the other. Errors of this type are known as *variable* or *random* errors and they reflect the degree of precision of the measuring instrument.

It would be easy to increase this precision by using a measuring tape in place of the naked eye, but even so, some degree of variability in successive measurements of the same thing would remain.

Reliability

The extent to which a measuring procedure is free of such random variability, *the degree to which it yields stable or consistent results in measuring the same thing, is referred to as the reliability of the measure.* Reliability, then, is a special form of validity reflecting the extent to which a measuring technique is free of random variation or uncontrolled wobble. Notice that if an index is completely valid, it must also be completely reliable, since a totally valid measure must be completely free of error, random as well as systematic. A reliable measure, however, is not necessarily valid. For example, at one time it was thought that head size was directly related to mental ability; the larger the head, the more intelligent the person. It is, of course, possible to obtain highly reliable measures of the circumference of the skull, precise to the fraction of a centimeter, but as indices of mental capacity, such exact measurements have virtually no validity.

Reliability is obviously a relative matter, one measuring procedure being more precise than another. For this reason, it is useful to have an index of the degree of reliability of a given measuring procedure. The most direct index would be some indication of the size of the random variations obtained when the same thing is measured several times. For example, in the case of the five estimates of John Jones' height, one could index the extent to which these estimates vary around their average or mean value of 5'5". For this purpose we need a measure of *dispersion or spread.* The most commonly used index of this type is called the *standard deviation,* designated by the Greek letter σ (sigma).

When applied to a distribution of errors in measurement, as is the case in assessing reliability, the index is referred to as a *standard error,* abbreviated as S. E. The standard deviation of a distribution, when extended on either side of the mean, will include about two-thirds of all the observations.

A standard deviation is always expressed in the same units as were employed in making the original measurement. Thus, the standard error in estimating heights would be expressed in inches, that of an intelligence test in I.Q. points, of an achievement test in grade levels, etc. Obviously, it would be desirable to be able to compare the relative reliability of different measuring instruments irrespective of what they were measuring, to be able to determine, for example, whether an intelligence scale is more or less reliable than a personality test being used in the same research. Such comparability becomes possible through the use of a statistic called a *correlation coefficient,* designated by the letter r, which measures the degree of association between two sets of measurements; for example, height and weight. The correlation coefficient varies in magnitude from −1.00 to + 1.00. A value of + 1.00 indicates a perfect and direct association between two variables. The higher the one, the higher the other, with perfect prediction between. A correlation of −1.00 also implies perfect predictability, but in an inverse relationship; as one variable gets bigger, the other gets smaller. A correlation of zero means no association predictability between the two variables. Most observed correlations range somewhere between these two extremes. For example, the correlation between height and weight is about .40.[3]

The correlation coefficient can also be used to measure the extent of correspondence between two sets of measures of the same variable; for example, two versions, or forms, of a test. When used for this purpose, the correlation coefficient is referred to as a *reliability coefficient,* for it measures the consistency of a given measuring instrument when applied more than once to the same set of phenomena. For example, the reliability of a test may be assessed by giving it twice to the same group. This is called "test-retest" reliability. Such a procedure of course, has the disadvantage that the person's responses the second time may be influenced by memory, thus producing an artificial consistency between the results of the two administrations. To avoid this artifact, the same test may be divided into two parts (for example, odd-numbered items vs. even numbered) and observing the correspondence between them; this is called "split-half reliability." Individually administered measuring instruments, such as the Stanford-Binet, often have reliability coefficients in the .90's. Group administered techniques typically have lower reliabilities, ranging from .40 to .60.

The measurement of variables is a necessary step in the testing of a hypothesis, but not a sufficient one. The process of proof, which, as we have already seen, is actually a process of disproof, requires the use of an appropriate strategy of analysis, involving statistical methods and research design. These matters are discussed in the next section.

IV. RESEARCH DESIGN

Suppose we have a hypothesis we wish to verify. What do we do next?

Several years ago, the senior author and his colleagues conducted an experiment in a large introductory course, testing a series of hypotheses. We wanted to determine the effects on academic performance of three kinds of grading procedures—letter grades, pass-fail, and guaranteed pass. We were also interested in whether the students' participation in a discussion section influenced their learning. Finally, we wanted to see if attending lectures delivered "live" by the professor produced a different result from seeing the same lectures on videotape in a smaller classroom setting. Effects were examined in terms of performance on examinations (all students took the same tests regardless of grading condition), in academic and career choices, and in attitudes toward the subject matter and the lecturer.

Let us take one of the above variations to demonstrate how research methods are applied to verify a hypothesis, specifically, the hypothesis that students do better in courses in which they see the lecturer "live" rather than on a television screen.

Sampling

The first problem that arises is how to pick our sample. One possibility might be to ask for volunteers. At the first meeting of the class, we might ask who would be willing to view the lecturer on television, and let the remaining students stay in the lecture hall and watch the course "live." What would be wrong with this plan?

The difficulty, of course, is that the groups would probably not be comparable. Those who volunteered for television might be the students more eager to please the lecturer, or less willing to risk being called on. A similar problem occurs in many other research situations, for example in trying to measure the effect of group preschool programs, like Head Start. Many investigators have compared Head Start children with non-Head Start children from the same neighborhood without regard to the possibility that the parents of the Head Start children might have been more motivated to enroll their children in the program, whereas parents in the control group were less interested or able to make the necessary arrangements. How can we get around this kind of problem? How would we make the two groups comparable?

One strategy is to ask for volunteers willing to participate in the program, and then assign them at random to either the experimental or control group. "Assigning at random" means forming the two groups in such a way that every individual has an equal chance of being chosen for one or the other. This can be accomplished by pulling names out of a hat, or, more effectively, by using a computer which can pull names out of a hat far faster than a human can. The names are fed into the computer, a distinctive number is assigned to each name, and then the computer is asked to select numbers at random either for one or the other experimental condition.

Suppose we had followed this procedure in our course experiment; that is, asked for volunteers from among the students in the class and then assigned these volunteers at random to the TV or non-TV treatments. Would this have been a good way to select our sample?

The answer to this question depends on the population to which we wish to generalize our findings. The nature of the problem is exemplified by a famous error in scientific method that occurred in the 1932 presidential election in which the candidates were Franklin D. Roosevelt and Herbert Hoover. Polls had just come into fashion, and a leading weekly magazine of the period, the *Literary Digest,* conducted a survey to predict the outcome. On the basis of its national polls, the magazine announced that Hoover would win by a substantial margin. On Election Day Roosevelt won by a landslide. As a result, the *Literary Digest* lost subscribers and eventually disappeared. What had gone wrong? The problem was in the selection of the people to be interviewed. All were subscribers to the magazine, and all were contacted by telephone. In retrospect, it became clear that most of the subscribers, especially those who in 1932 owned a telephone, were Republicans. In other words, the sample was biased. The error made by the *Literary Digest* pollsters highlights a fundamental requirement in any research design: *the sample must be representative of the population to which the researcher wishes to generalize.*

How does this requirement relate to our own example? What are the likely biases in asking for volunteers in an introductory course in child development? First, only those most interested in the subject are likely to volunteer. Also, past research has shown that firstborns and females are more likely to volunteer than those born later and males.

How do we solve this problem? How do we obtain a cross-section of university students? Ideally, we could take a random sample from the student directory. But how would we get all the students so selected to take the course, since it is not a university-wide requirement? What we did was to announce in the student daily that only those willing to be in the experiment could enroll in the course, and each participant would have to agree in advance to accept the experimental condition to which he would be assigned at random. The result was the highest enrollment ever experienced in the history of the course, with representation from all college years and undergraduate divisions.

But even so, to what population can we generalize these results? American college students? Students at a particular university? In a particular course? With a particular professor? There are problems in generalizing even to the latter, because this was the first, and probably the only time that students enrolled in the class were also all volunteers for an experiment. So do we restrict our findings to "student volunteers in this course with this professor in this university"?

If so, and if the goal of science is to establish universal laws, on what grounds was the experiment worth doing at all? Let us consider the answer to this question in terms of one of our major research findings: students in the letter grade condition averaged 30 points higher on exams than students in the guaranteed pass condition, and 9 points more than students in the pass-fail condition. We certainly cannot generalize the results to all students in all courses. But the finding does increase the probability that the implied causal hypotheses will be sustained in similar situations. A skeptic is obligated to come up with a plausible counter-hypothesis explaining why the same relation would not obtain elsewhere. If no reasonable alternative hypothesis can be offered, it is only reasonable to assume that a similar result would be obtained with other students in other courses at other universities.

This means that, with one important qualification, the researcher does not have to test his hypothesis with every group in every kind of situation that he believes the hypothesis covers. It is a scientific contribution to demonstrate that the hypothesis is confirmed in one such group in one such situation, *provided there is nothing about the group or situation which would make the observed relation peculiar to that group or setting*—as occurred in the case of the *Literary Digest* poll.

Incidentally, how could the *Literary Digest* have avoided its fatal error? How does one obtain a representative sample of American voters? A random sample—in which every voter in the United States had an equal chance of being selected—would be too complicated and time-consuming to obtain. Instead, a random sample of census tracts—or other units—is more efficient. This type of sample is not completely satisfactory since some important element, for example, a large city, may be overlooked. To avoid this danger, the researcher can specify the proportions within his sample of known components of the universe to which he wishes to generalize. For example, he may determine ratios in the population by sex, age, race, urban-rural residence, city size, and then select randomly *within* these strata. Thus, one would draw random census tracts within a city, and select households and family members within them, adhering to desired sex, age, and race distributions. This strategy of selection is called *stratified cluster sampling.*

Making use of known characteristics of the sample increases the accuracy of estimation. For example, a stratified sample of 1200 voters can predict election results within one or two percentage points. In addition, one can get information about a critical component group of the stratified sample—for example, the black vote.

Most psychologists however, do not employ stratified random sampling or any other technique for assuming broad representativeness. Typically, the investigator uses what is called an "accidental" sample, composed of the people and situations at hand. He then tries to demonstrate that his hypothesis does obtain for these people and this situation, and leaves it to someone else to show that the relation does or does not hold true for other people somewhere else. As we have already indicated, such a limited research can be altogether legitimate and scientifically valuable provided there are no grounds for regarding the observed finding as a special or restricted case.

To return to the results of our experiment: can our finding that students receiving letter grades performed better on exams than students in other grading conditions be interpreted as a special case? For example, the students in our sample were taking all their other courses for a letter grade; perhaps those with a guaranteed pass in this course simply devoted more time and energy to earning better marks in the other courses they were taking.

Although we did not test this alternative hypothesis in our experiment, a professor at another university did so. In his research, students in the experimental group, took *all* their courses during one semester on a pass-fail basis (Gold, 1971). Their grades were not only lower during that term but also in the next one, when all courses were again marked on a letter-grade basis.[4] This example demonstrated another important fact about the process of research: science is the product of *a community of scholars.* Different people make different and often complementary contributions to the investigation of the same general problem. One researcher's design need not and cannot cover all the possibilities.

Usually the first question to be answered is not whether some relation is true for everyone everywhere but whether it is true at all. For example, in our research, only after we show that TV instruction is superior or inferior in one course, does the question arise whether the same result will obtain in other courses.

Methods of Control

In addition to sampling, a second major problem of experimental design is to devise valid measures for the independent and dependent variables. In our case, this was a fairly easy task. We assigned students at random to the "live" vs. TV condition and assessed course performance through six examinations, three of the essay and three of the multiple choice type.

But now we come to the third and crucial feature of the experimental design. We must be able to examine variation in the dependent variable under different degrees (or conditions) of the independent variable, *in such a way that the possible influence of other factors can be ruled out.* One way of achieving this objective is to employ two groups or treatments; the group in which the independent variable is present or maximal is called the *experimental* group. The group in which the independent variable is absent is called the *control* group. The methodology of experimental design can be extremely complex and ingenious. Consider, for example, some of the problems we encounter in our course experiment. If we are interested in the effect of TV on course performance, and, say, half of the students are in the TV condition and half not, for what variables would it be important to control? For one thing, it has been repeatedly demonstrated that, from the primary grades through college, women get better grades than men. This means that we need to make sure that the sex of the student is not the confounding variable. One way of accomplishing this is to place an equal number of males and females in each group, or in our case, in each discussion section. This technique is called a *balanced design.*

Actually, the number of women and men in each section need not be equal; it is necessary only that the proportion in each group be the same. Indeed, nowadays even the condition of proportionality can be dispensed with, since computers make it possible to correct for unequal numbers in the design and even for missing cases. Bear in mind, however, that if a design is not balanced or proportional, the researcher must make the appropriate corrections. Otherwise, his results will be confounded.

Sex of subject is only one of the many possible sources of confounding that are encountered in research with human beings. For example, in our experiment one might wish to control for such factors as the socioeconomic status of the student's family, his year in college, field of major study, previous courses in the same area, or the student's age, race, and ordinal position in the family. It would clearly be impossible to assign students to sections that were balanced or proportional with respect to all of these possible confounding variables. How are we to meet this practical problem? Fortunately, there is a method that simultaneously controls not only for all these variables but *all others* that might be a source of confounding, even those which might not have occurred to the investigator. This powerful strategy is one we have already discussed—random assignment. Such a procedure avoids systematic bias on any and all variables in the allocation of subjects to experimental or control groups.

Effective as it is, however, random assignment possesses two limitations. First, it is applicable only to experiments done by man—not those done by nature—for it requires that the experimenter be able to determine who goes into which group. For example, in studying the effects of upbringing in a kibbutz versus a conventional family, the researcher cannot assign families at random to one or another setting. He must take them as they come.

The methods of control applicable in this kind of situation are the same as those employed to deal with a second limitation of random assignment. Even when subjects are assigned to different conditions on a chance basis, the possibility of some bias is not eliminated. In our experiment, for example, one might by accident end up having more psychology majors in the "television" treatment than in the "live" condition. Because of this possibility of bias, it is essential not to leave control of the most important confounding variables purely to chance. Instead, we can resort to the already familiar procedure of classifying subjects in terms of these variables and controlling for them by means of a balanced proportional or other type of statistical design. If this is done, there are two critical conditions that must be met. First, *the same independent and control variables must appear in both the experimental and control groups, and in the same combinations.* For example, if we have boys and girls in the TV condition, we must also have boys and girls in the "live" condition. The same requirement applies for the various combinations of sex and grading systems. For example, if there were girls receiving a letter grade in the "live" condition but not in TV, this could produce a spurious result for the experiment as a whole.

The second requirement is that *there be at least two cases in each "cell" of the design—that is, at least two cases representing every combination.* This requirement is necessary in order to be able to carry out certain crucial statistical analyses to be described in the next section.

When these two conditions are met, it is possible to analyze the independent effect of each independent variable controlling for all other variables. This very powerful type of experimental design is called *analysis of variance.* Variance is the variation of scores about the average. In analysis of variance, the total variation is divided into components, and each component is evaluated for its independent contribution. For example, in our experiment, TV vs. live, grading condition, and sex were each evaluated for their effect on course performance—independent of the others. Moreover, in this technique we can examine not just the independent effects of each variable, but the variables in combination. For example, we can ask whether the effect of TV was the same for boys and girls. If not—if, say, the boys did better with TV whereas the girls scored higher in the live lecture—we would have what is called an *interaction effect,* a joint effect of two or more variables which differs from that of any of the variables taken separately.

What happens when the available data do not meet the strict requirements of an analysis of variance design? For example, it may be impossible, or just too complicated, to find cases at every level and combination of several independent and control variables. Under these circumstances, the correct strategy is often simply a reduction in scale. For instance, instead of working with both sexes at each of three socioeconomic levels, the investigator limits himself to one sex and one socioeconomic level only (e.g. just middle class girls). If this is done, the researcher must bear in mind that his findings are limited and may obtain only for the restricted population he has sampled.

The procedure of controlling for a variable by having it appear at only one level represents one form of a more general technique for equaling experimental and control groups, called *matching.* Matching can be applied not only with qualitative categories, like sex or ethnicity, but also with variables that can fall along a continuous scale, such as age or intelligence quotient. For example, age or intelligence can be controlled by insuring that both experimental and control groups show the same averages on each of these variables. Such a procedure is known as *group matching.*

Matching can also be done at the level of individual cases. For example, each member of the experimental group is compared to a partner from the control group who is of the same sex, age, social class, IQ, etc. This procedure, called *pair matching,* allows for precise control on several variables, but it has a number of disadvantages. First, in pair matching, the several control variables are confounded so that it is impossible to assess their independent effects and interactions. Second, it may become very difficult to find pairs that match on several variables at once, so that most of the cases remain unused. Finally, the matched sample one ends up with may be so restricted that it is no longer representative of the population to which one wishes to generalize.

Finally, there are some situations to which analysis of variance cannot be applied without distorting or eliminating valuable information. For instance, in all the situations we have considered thus far, the independent variable, and most of the control variables, have been measured in terms of mutually exclusive, qualitative categories (boys vs. girls, letter grade vs. pass-fail, etc.), whereas the dependent variable (e.g. scores on exams) has been quantitative and continuous (i.e., the scores go from low to high). Suppose that the independent and control variables are also quantitative and continuous: for instance, we wish to know whether attendance in the course is related to course grade, or weight at birth is related to a child's psychological development.

A second powerful method can handle this situation. It is one we have already encountered in the form of the correlation coefficient (r) which measures the degree of association between two continuous variables. If two variables are correlated, it means that a researcher can predict one from the other as a linear relation ($y = bx + c$). For example, we can predict the weight of the baby from the mother's food intake. We can also look at the effect of two variables on a third—for example, the mother's weight and food intake as both affect the baby's weight. This method is called *multiple correlation.* Finally, we can look at the relation between two variables controlling for the third—for example, the effect of food intake on baby's weight controlling for the mother's weight. This is called *partial correlation.* This general method is known as correlational analysis, and also as regression analysis.

There is one final situation we need to consider. What does one do when the independent and control variables are mixed and include *both* continuous and discontinuous components; for example, we may wish to examine the effect both of television and of attendance controlling for sex and for age. Under such circumstances one can resort to a procedure called *analysis of covariance,* which combines the strategies of correlation and analysis of variance within the same design.

There are many other statistical designs for achieving control of variables, and they can become rather complex. In fact, there is an increasing danger that methods can become so complex that they depart too far from reality—especially with the availability of computers. Another unfortunate consequence of sophisticated methodology is that researchers can often overlook more effective and direct designs in favor of the complicated ones. It is for this reason that, in our brief description of different strategies in research design, we have emphasized the underlying logic and not the statistical procedures involved. For information on the latter score, the reader can consult readily available textbooks on statistical methods. It is important to bear in mind that the choice of design should depend primarily not on statistical but logical considerations—the nature of the questions being asked, of possibly confounding variables, and of the subjects and situations to which the investigator wishes to generalize.

Testing the Null Hypothesis

One final task remains. Most alternative hypotheses are specific to a particular problem. But there is one alternative hypothesis that applies to every research design, and must be eliminated before the major hypothesis can be accepted.

To take a simple example: suppose we are interested in whether there is any difference in the heights of men and women in a given class. We pick a random sample from the class of one male and one female and measure the difference in heights. The problem is obvious: when the sample is small, the obtained result may differ by chance, to an appreciable degree, from the situation that obtains in the parent population as a whole, in this case the entire class. In such circumstances the observed difference between the small experimental and control samples may be larger or smaller than it really is; it may show no difference when one actually exists; or it can even reverse the direction of the true difference.

Note, however, that as we add more cases to our sample, we get a more stable, more reliable estimate of the average height of boys and girls in the class. If we were to look at the variation of height *within* sexes (from one girl to the next) and that between sexes (boys vs. girls) we would find that the latter was greater than the former and the ratio of the two will be greater than one. In contrast, if there is *no* real difference in height between males and females, the variation between sexes would equal the variation within sexes, and the ratio between the two would on the average, approach unity—sometimes a little less than one, sometimes more as a function of chance fluctuation.

Statisticians have calculated the probability of obtaining a ratio greater than one by chance for samples of different sizes. If this probability is less than 5 percent (or sometimes 1 percent), the researcher concludes that there *is* a difference between the means.

Analysis of variance uses this principle. The experimenter calculates the variance within an experimental group and then the variance among experimental groups. The ratio of the latter to the former is called an F ratio, for Sir Ronald Fisher, an English statistician who developed the method. If we get a ratio of, say, 3.5, we can consult a table of probabilities of F (available in most statistics texts) to see whether such a ratio could have occurred by chance. If not, we have what is called a *statistically significant difference,* one that is not very likely to have occurred simply by chance.

Now we can answer the question as to why analysis of variance requires more than one observation within each cell. Such repeated observations are needed to provide an estimate of *within* group variation against which to test the variation among groups in order to determine whether the latter is significantly larger.

An F test can be applied to any number of means—for example, three grading conditions. If only two groups are involved, it is possible to test the observed difference in means without computing their variance. Such a procedure is known as a *t* test. The logic underlying the *t* and F tests is exactly the same. In fact, in the case of two groups, $F = t^2$. A test of statistical significance can be applied to any measure of association between two variables, such as the correlation coefficient (r).

Another example arises in assessing differences between proportions, when the variable of interest is measured in mutually exclusive categories. For example, we may wish to know whether the incidence of congenital malformation is greater among boys than girls. Under these circumstances we use a technique called *chi square* (symbolized by the Greek letter X^2), which tells us whether the observed difference between two proportions is greater than what could have occurred by chance.

We can now state the universal alternative hypothesis that must always be tested. We must be able to show that the obtained differences are not due simply to chance. The alternative hypothesis is called the *null hypothesis:* it stipulates that *no* true difference exists, that such variation as we see can be attributed to chance fluctuation. The null hypothesis applies to all hypotheses —not only causal, but also associative and even attributive. We must always consider the possibility that observed differences are a function of random variation.

To illustrate the application of the null hypothesis to a hypothesis of association, we may consider an observation by Pasamanick (1958) that a larger proportion of mentally retarded children in Ohio institutions were born in January and February than in other months of the year. He rejected the null hypothesis in his research—the relationship was not due merely to chance. Rather, he showed that it was related to mean temperature during the summer, when the mother was in the third month of pregnancy.

This example illustrates the point that in science there are few purely associative hypotheses. A causal hypothesis, or at least a search for a causal hypothesis, is usually implied. Variable X, or some variable X_1 associated with variable X, is presumed to be a necessary or sufficient condition for variable Y. In other words, there is almost always an implicit independent variable and the associative hypothesis is a test of a potential causal hypothesis. If the association is not explainable as a chance phenomenon—i.e., if the null hypothesis is rejected, then the original hypothesis is supported, *provided* of course that no other plausible alternative hypothesis remains.

Note that the demonstration of statistical significance always implies some degree of reliability. If men are significantly taller than women, this implies that the difference cannot be due to chance; hence measurements must contain more than error.

In summary:

1. Every causal hypothesis implies one or more associative hypotheses. For example, Madigan's thesis (1957) that women are biologically hardier than men, led him to the associative hypothesis that they would outlive men under constant environments.
2. Every associative hypothesis is challenged by a null hypothesis. Thus Madigan had to reject the possibility that the observed

differential mortality rates between the two sexes could be due to chance.

3. If the null hypothesis is rejected, then the original causal hypothesis is supported, *provided there exists no plausible alternative explanation for the observed relation.* For example, Madigan's finding that nuns outlive monks living under virtually identical conditions of monastic life leaves little room for other explanations besides biological sex differences.

One final caution: failure to demonstrate a statistically significant relation does not necessarily mean that no difference exists—that is, that the means are equal. Suppose when we chose class members, to determine if men are taller than women, we happened to pick persons of each sex who, on the average, were of similar height. The difference would not be statistically significant, even though, in the general population, a difference in fact exists. In other words, failure to reject the null hypothesis does not mean the absence of association; it means only that we have not been able to show a significant effect, perhaps because the N (number of people in the sample) was too small. If, under these circumstances, we had concluded there was no difference in heights, we would have made an error. There are, then, two types of error inherent in experimental designs. A so-called *Type I error* is the result of asserting a difference when none exists. A *Type II error* occurs in claiming no difference when a difference does in fact exist. In the case of our sampling of sex differences in height, we made a Type II error.

For some reason, researchers on human behavior have been much more concerned about Type I than Type II errors. They are more worried about being caught wrong than about failing to state the right. Scientists, for the most part, are conservatives, at least those who have engaged in the study of human behavior. This trend is reflected in the studies which follow, although there are some in which even the possibility of a Type I error has been overlooked. The reader is therefore well advised to be on his guard, or, still better, to do his own thinking, which is the essence of scientific inquiry.

NOTES

[1]The account which follows is condensed from R. P. Parsons, Joseph Goldberger and Pellagra, in *Trail to Light* (New York: Bobbs-Merrill, 1943).

[2]In recent years, serious questions have been raised about the validity of this instrument when applied to persons from a different social and cultural background from that of the predominantly white, middle class samples for whom the test was originally developed.

[3]The correlation coefficient should not be interpreted as a percent. It is simply a number varying between − 1.00 and + 1.00.

[4]Still, one might argue that taking courses of pass-fail grades within a university which otherwise assigns grades for courses may be quite different from taking all courses for pass-fail when all other students are evaluated in the same way. This particular case, so far as the authors know, has not been investigated.

REFERENCES

Bechtold, H. P. Construct validity: A critique. *American Psychologist,* 1959, *5,* (14), 619–629.

Berger, H. Ueber das Elektroenkephalogramm des Menschens, *Archiv fur Psychologie and Neurologie,* 1930, 40, 160–179.

Binet, A., & Simon, T. Methodes nouvelles pour le diagnostic du niveau intellectuel des anormaux. *Annee Pschologique,* 1905, 191–244.

Bronfenbrenner, U. Family structure and development. Presidential Address to the Division of Development Psychology, September, 1958.

Bronfenbrenner, U. Socialization and social class through time and space. In E. E. Maccoby: T. M. Newcomb, and E. L. Hartley (Eds.) *Readings in social psychology.* New York: Henry Holt and Co., 1958. Pp. 400–425.

Bronfenbrenner, U. Parental behavior and adolescent responsibility: a reorientation. Paper presented at the annual meeting of the American Psychological Association, September, 1959.

Christie, R. The prevalence of Machiavellian orientations. Paper presented at the annual meeting of the American Psychological Association, September 7, 1964.

Christie, R., Geis, F. Some consequences of taking Machiavelli seriously. In Borgatta, E. F. and W. W. Lambert, (Eds.), *Handbook of Personality Theory and Research.* Chicago: Rand McNally, 1968, 959–973.

Christie, R., & Geis, F. *Studies in Machiavellianism.* New York: Academic Press, 1970.

Cronbach, L. J. and Meehl, P. E. Construct validity in psychological tests. *Psychological Bulletin,* 1965, 52, 281–302.

Geis, F. Machiavellianism and the manipulation of one's fellow man. Paper presented at the annual meeting of the American Psychological Association, Los Angeles, 1964.

Geis, F., Christie, R. Machiavellianism and the tactics of manipulation. Paper presented at the annual meeting of the American Psychological Association, Chicago, 1965.

Geis, F., Christie, R., & Nelson, C. Some Machiavellian manipulations. Unpublished paper, Department of Psychology, Columbia University, 1963.

Gentry, J. P. An epidemiological study of congenital malformations in New York State. *American Journal of Public Health,* 1959, *49,* (4), 1–22.

Gerden, E. A review of psychokinesis. *Psychol. Bull.,* 1962, *59,* 353–388.

Gold, R. C., Reilly, A., Silberman, R., & Lehr, R. Academic achievement declines under pass-fail grading. *The Journal of Experimental Education,* 1971, 17–21.

Grollman, A. *Functional pathology of disease.* (2nd ed.) New York: McGraw-Hill, 1963, 172–176.
This is an account of present day knowledge about pellagra and the chemistry of its effects.

Heider, F. *The psychology of interpersonal relations.* New York: John Wiley, 1958.

Homans, G. C. *The human group.* New York: Harcourt, Brace, 1950.

Knoblach, H., & Pasamanick, B. Seasonal variation in the births of the mentally deficient. *American Journal of Public Health,* 1958, *48,* 1201–1208.

Madigan, Francis C. Are sex mortality differentials biologically caused? *Milbank Memorial Fund Quarterly,* 1957 (April), 35, *2,* 202–223.

Mendelyev, D. I. *The principles of chemistry.* Translated from the Russian (5th ed.) by George Kamensky. New York: Longmans, Green, 1891.

Newcomb, F. An approach to the study of communicative acts. *Psychological Review,* 1953, *60,* 393–404.

Parsons, R. P. Joseph Goldberger and Pellagra. In *Trail to light.* New York: Bobbs-Merrill, 1943. Also reprinted in Rapport, S., and H. Wright, *Great adventures in medicine.* New York: Dial Press, 1952, 586–604.

Rheingold, H. L., Gewirtz, J. L., & Ross, Helen W. Social conditioning of vocalizations in the infant. *J. Comp. Physiol. Psychol.,* 1959, *52,* 68–73.

Rhine, J. B. *Extrasensory perception.* Boston: Humphries, 1964.

Spock, B. *Baby and child care.* New York: Pocket Books, 1957.

Terris, Milton. *Goldberger on pellagra.* Baton Rouge: Louisiana State Press, 1964. This is the most recent and complete account of Goldberger's pursuit on pellagra including original reports by him and his critics.

Tjio, J. H., & Levan. The chromosome number of man. *Hereditas,* 1956, *42,* 1–6.

United States Children's Bureau. Infant care. (Rev. ed.) Washington: United States Government Printing Office, 1951.

part two
NATURE WITH NURTURE

The articles in this section all speak to the same vital principle: namely, heredity and environment never operate in isolation from each other. With respect to human development, neither factor can exert an influence without the other. This point is beautifully illustrated in the initial presentation by Freedman of a series of researches growing out of a study undertaken when he was still a student. What originally appeared as an elegant demonstration of the impact of different training methods on the development of "conscience" in puppies turned out to be mediated critically by genetic predispositions. The fact that analogous effects have been reported for man and attributed primarily to differential patterns of child rearing serves as a reminder that, for human young as well, patterns of indulgence vs. discipline work on a genetic base.

Along the same line, at a time when observed psychological differences between the sexes are being criticized as products of discriminatory child rearing practices, Madigan's ingenious demonstration of the persistence of sex differences in men and women exposed to highly similar ways of life raises the possibility of innate foundations for psychological differences between the sexes.

Finally, the intricate question of the interplay between genetic and social factors in the development of human ability is examined in three articles. It is in this area that the critical relation between science and social policy is most clearly apparent. Skodak and Skeels' pioneering study of the impact of true vs. foster mothers on the development of children adopted in the first six months of life presents a classic example of the difficulties of gaining acceptance for a new idea before its time. One of the first studies to demonstrate how an enriched environment can enhance intellectual capacity, this research ironically continues to be cited in support of the opposite conclusion.

A similarly unwarranted genetic bias, with even more serious social consequences, is analyzed and demolished by Scarr-Salapatek in her critique of the thesis of innate race differences in intelligence—a thesis promulgated in recent years by Jensen, Herrnstein, Eysenck, and others.

Finally, Bronfenbrenner takes on the major thesis of Jensen and others that intelligence is primarily determined by genetic factors; from a review of the evidence, he concludes that the argument for an 80 percent genetic effect is contradicted by the data, which in fact testify to the power of the environment in enabling the developing child to realize his genetic potential.

2.1

The Origins of Social Behavior

Daniel G. Freedman

The studies that form the basis of this article had their origin on the campus of Brandeis University, near Boston, Massachusetts, in 1953. In the winter of that year the campus mascot, a motley bitch with what looked like a beagle and dachshund background, gave birth to a litter of four. We were not sure who the father was. As graduate students in the newly formed graduate school Norbett Mintz and I had sufficient time to 'play around' and we had the happy notion that puppies might prove enjoyable experimental subjects—as indeed they did.

In considering what we might do with the puppies we had two previous studies in mind. The first was that of J. P. Scott and M. Marston at Bar Harbor who, in 1950, had suggested that three to eight weeks of age was a critical period in the social development of puppies. Although this was little more than an impression then, it had subsequently turned out to be largely correct within the breeds studied. Secondly, John Whiting, a psychoanalytically orientated anthropologist, had been working with adult dogs and had developed a test to measure their 'conscience'. This was assessed by the extent to which they remained obedient in the absence of the handler. The test was attractively simple and merely involved a person punishing a dog for eating food that had been forbidden him. The person then left the room and, watching through a one way glass, recorded the amount of time the animal stayed away from the forbidden food. In this way the extent to which punishment was 'incorporated' received a quantitative score.

Our chore became one of using this information in a meaningful study of development, and when the idea finally came to us it seemed the most natural study possible. As clinical psychologists, Mintz and I were aware of the work of the child psychiatrist, David Levy. As a result of his extensive experience with behaviour disorders in children, Levy had hypothesized that extreme permissiveness on the part of parents could lead to a psychiatric condition called psychopathy. This is characterized by an abnormal inability to inhibit one's impulses. These people are asocial in that their own desires and wishes always take precedence over those of others. Levy found that in many families which produced such individuals the parents allowed themselves to become complete slaves to the tyrannical wilfullness of the child.

With Levy's work in mind we carried out the following study. Two puppies were to act as 'control'. One was given to a family which we decided was typically 'middle class'—in other words, a home in which the puppy would receive plenty of affection, but would also be restricted to certain areas, prevented from biting, be housebroken and so on. A second puppy was raised separately in a room by itself, save for the few minutes each day it took to put food in and take the old bowls out. As for the 'psychopathic' puppies, Mintz and I decided to enlist the aid of the boys in the

Reprinted from *Science Journal*, 1967, *3* 69–73, by permission.

dormitories of which we were proctors. The puppies were to have complete freedom in the dormitory. Urine and faeces were to be cleaned up after them. If they wished to climb on someone's bed or lap, they were to be helped up. If they wished to get off, they were helped off. If they wished to sleep in someone's bed, they were allowed that. (If they nipped an ear in bed, one was allowed to duck under the covers.) They were not to be punished for any offense. Since the study was to last only six weeks (from three to nine weeks of age), all the students agreed to cooperate.

At nine weeks we had two distinctly different groups of dogs, and this was nicely shown by the 'incorporation of punishment' test. Beginning at the ninth week of age and continuing for eight consecutive days we administered the test devised by Whiting. We placed each pup, which had not been fed for at least four hours, in a room with a bowl of meat at its centre. When the pup attempted to eat, the experimenter hit it on the rump with a newspaper and shouted, "No". After the experimenter left the room, the time to eat was recorded. In this early version of the test the experimenter rushed back in and punished the pup each time it ate.

We found that whereas the home reared dog averaged 37.5 minutes and the isolate 9.5 minutes between each transgression, the permissively reared pups averaged a lightning 2.2 minutes. By the eighth day of testing, in fact, the permissively reared pups managed to eat all the meat before the tester had a chance to leave the room. He would smack the pup only to have it immediately circle back through his legs for another bite. This happened so fast that we could not measure the time between transgressions accurately and consequently we overestimated the time between transgressions in the seventh and eighth test sessions.

The subsequent history of these two pups was not a happy one. Although people were initially taken with them because of their uninhibited friskiness, they were passed from home to home as each owner found something else to complain about. They seemed to have become untrainable.

The isolate's behaviour was typical of pups raised in this fashion. She was hyperexcitable and initiated contacts only to run off when a hand was reached out or when another pup tried to play with her. After the fourth session of testing, however, she calmed down somewhat and was able to learn what was demanded of her. We are happy to report that she subsequently became a beloved and loving pet, and we could not help but reflect that a dog with no experiences with people may be preferable to one with the wrong experiences.

Having become completely captured by the study, we decided to try another experiment. David Levy had postulated that a second class of psychopaths are formed by extreme cruelty or great emotional deprivation in childhood. With this second hypothesis in mind, we raised a beagle from four to nine weeks of age under conditions in which all his contacts with people were negative. Each time he tried to make contact he was either ignored or pushed aside, and it is not surprising that he developed a rather depressed, fearful personality. True to Levy's hypothesis, his performance on the test was like that of the overindulged puppies, although the average time between transgressions was higher: 8.14 minutes. Again the controls were a home reared littermate and a littermate kept in isolation. Both quickly learned to stay away from the food and averaged one transgression each 31.13 minutes. Thus once again Levy's hypothesis, developed from studies of problem children, appeared to hold when applied to puppies.

It was clearly time to do these studies on a larger scale and in a systematic and repeatable fashion, and I proposed such a project for my PhD thesis. After interesting Paul Scott, Chairman of the Division of Behaviour Studies at the Jackson Laboratories, Bar Harbor, Maine, it was arranged that the work be done there.

In the Bar Harbor study, eight litters of four pups each were used. They included two litters each of Shetland sheepdogs, basenjis, wire-haired fox terriers, and beagles. Following weaning at three weeks of age, each litter of four was divided into two pairs which were equated as closely as possible on the basis of sex, weight, activity, vocalizations, maturation of eyes and ears, and reactivity to a startling stimulus. Thereafter, each member of one pair was indulged and each member of the second pair was disciplined. However, because of the numbers involved, this treatment could be given only during two daily 15 minute periods, again from the third to the eighth week of age.

Indulgence consisted of encouraging a pup in any activity it initiated, such as play, aggression and climbing on the supine handler. As before, these pups were never punished. By contrast, the disciplined pups were at first restrained in the experimenter's lap and were later taught to sit, to stay, and to come upon command. When still older they were trained to follow on the leash. I handled all the pups and tested them individually; they lived with the identically treated littermate in isolation boxes the remainder of the time.

A revised punishment test was initiated at eight weeks of age. As before, when the pup ate meat from a bowl he was punished with a swat on the rump and a shout of, "No!" After three minutes the experimenter left the room and, observing through a one way glass, recorded the time that elapsed before the pup again ate. This time the experimenter did not return to the room until the allotted ten minutes were up.

The first breed that went through this experimental rearing and testing was a basenji litter. By the fourth day of testing all basenjis tended to eat soon after the experimenter left the room, the method of rearing having little effect. This was most discouraging, since we had failed to duplicate the results of the pilot experiment, but we decided to carry on.

The second group was a Shetland sheepdog litter and they were equally disappointing, except this time all tended to refuse the food. At least one thing was clear at this point: the breed of dog was a major factor to consider. Second litters of basenjis and of Shetland sheepdogs from our inbred stocks bore this out, for they performed much like the first litters.

The next breed which became available was a beagle litter. We found that their behaviour depended upon the way they were reared but, paradoxically, in a direction opposite to our pilot studies. A second beagle litter, from the same mating, performed exactly the same way and so did the two litters of wire-haired fox terriers.

The conditions of rearing were continued over a second period, when the pups were 11 to 15 weeks of age, and all tests were readministered with essentially the same results. At this point we were so fascinated by breed differences that we postponed thinking about the contradictions to our pilot work. Our question now was how could the breed characteristics explain the differences in performance?

It was clear that, during training, beagles and wire-haired terriers were strongly orientated to the experimenter and sought contact with him continuously. Basenjis, by contrast, were interested in all phases of the environment and often ignored the experimenter in favour of inanimate objects. Shetland sheep dogs showed yet another pattern; all became fearful of physical contact with the experimenter and tended to maintain distance from him. Thus the two breeds that were highly attracted to the experimenter showed behavioural differences as a result of the mode of rearing, whereas the breeds that exhibited aloofness (basenjis) and excessive timidity (Shetland sheep dogs) did not. Apparently it was the strong constitutional attraction combined with indulgent treatment that enhanced the effectiveness of later punishment.

It should be noted that basenjis and Shetland sheep dogs were not entirely unaffected by the differential treatment. The scores of all indulged animals were significantly different from those of their disciplined counterparts on five of ten tests administered. In general, these tests indicated that the indulged pups were more active, more vocal, less timid (although more easily inhibited with punishment), and more attracted to people than the disciplined pups.

We now had to reconcile the findings of the pilot studies of Brandeis and the major study at the Bar Harbor. In the first we found that overindulged rearing in the dormitories led to 'psychopathic' performance, but in the Bar Harbor work the disciplined animals of all breeds tended to be more disobedient, although this was true of the Shetland sheep dogs and basenjis over only the first three days of testing.

To recapitulate the pilot studies, a regimen of affection and freedom and no discipline produced hyperactive, disobedient pups. A regimen of discipline and no affection likewise produced a disobedient pup, albeit within a depressed and fearful personality. Actually, none of the Bar Harbor findings contradict these 'rules'.

In the Bar Harbor studies the permissive group was given free reign to express affection, to investigate and to bite, but each time they were returned to their boxes they were under enforced control; as their cries to get out attested. On thinking it over, it became clear that they were treated much like normal home reared dogs in that restrictions were regularly imposed on their freedom. We therefore changed their official title from 'over indulged,' to 'indulged', although this was still not a complete description.

The disciplined group, on the other hand, received considerably less affection than do home reared dogs and, in addition, few dogs at home have so much demanded of them at so early an age. When we had initially planned the study we called this group 'normal', but very early we changed to the word 'disciplined'. It was clear that in terms of affection and play they were a *deprived* group and that 'disciplined' was only partially descriptive of the treatment they received.

It was in this way that we attempted to resolve the contradiction between the Bar Harbor results and the Brandeis pilot studies and, setting aside any genetic factors for the moment, the general hypothesis still appeared viable: dogs who did not 'incorporate' punishment were those reared under conditions of excessive freedom *vis-à-vis* humans or, conversely, under conditions in which human contacts were largely negative. It is of interest that some of the great trainers of field trail champions, such as Tetzloff and Spandet of the Danish Kennel Club, stress the importance of basing discipline on deeply affectionate relationships between trainer and dog . . .

REFERENCES

Freedman, D. G. An ethological approach to the genetical study of human behaviour. *In Methods and Goals in Human Behaviour Genetics.* New York: Academic Press, 1965.

Freedman, D. G., King, J. A., & Elliott, O. Critical period in the social development of dogs. *Science. 331,* 1016–1017. 1961.

Levy, D. M. The deprived and the indulged forms of psychopathic behaviour. *American Journal of Orothopsychiatry, 21,* 250–254, 1951.

Melzack, R. The genesis of emotional behavior: an experimental study of the dog. *Journal of Comparative Physiology and Psychology, 47* 166–168.

Scott, J. P., & Marston, Mary. Critical periods affecting the development of normal and maladjusted social behaviour of puppies. *Journal of Genetic Psychology, 77,* 26–60, 1950.

Juel-Nielsen N. Individual and environment. *Acta Psychiatrica Scandinavica, Supplementum 183,* Copenhagen, 1965.

Newman, H. H., Freeman, F. N., & Holzinger, K. J., *Twins: study of heredity and environment.* Chicago: University of Chicago Press, 1937.

Shields, J. Monozygotic twins brought up apart and together. London: Oxford University Press, 1962.

2.2

Are Sex Mortality Differentials Biologically Caused?

Francis C. Madigan, S.J.

Several previous studies by demographers have drawn attention to the continuous divergence of male and female expectations of life in this country since 1900. Wiehl in 1938 pointed out the widening gap between the sexes, suggested the need for research into the causes, and called for medical specialization in care for men just as gynecologists have specialized in care of women.[1] Yerushalmy in a sex and age investigation of our population composition showed the striking increases which had occurred in the percentage of women among the older people of our country during the period from the census of 1920 to that of 1940.[2] More recently, Bowerman has produced new data which prove that the gap has continued to widen rather than to narrow.[3]

In 1900, the white women of this country enjoyed but a 2.85 year advantage over comparable males in expectation of life at birth. By 1950, this female advantage had doubled to 5.8 years, and the national abridged tables for 1954 show a difference of 6.2 years.

Why have men not profited from the better conditions of this century to the same extent as women? What are the chances that their days of life can be prolonged to equal those of the female sex?

Such questions raise further ones. Are these differentials in rates of dying chiefly reflections of the greater sociocultural pressures and strains which our culture lays upon male shoulders? Or are the differentials rather to be associated mainly with biological factors related to sex? If the former is the case, then probably little can be done to enable men to enjoy a life as long as women's. Short of a profound cultural revolution in our society, it appears that men must continue to experience greater stresses. However, if sex-linked biological factors principally underlie the differentials, the prognosis is more hopeful. It seems likely in this case that medical research can isolate the factors responsible for greater female viability, and use this knowledge to advantage in the treatment of middle-aged and old men, assuming of course that this can be done without disturbing psychological balance or causing observable physical reactions.

A quickening of interest in the problem of the diverging death trends of our men and women has occurred during the past few years and has resulted in a rather large amount of journal literature upon the question. However, most of this has been descriptive and speculative rather than analytic and research-oriented. The present article reports upon the results of a study which has attempted to shed some light upon the problem through the tools of demographic research.

Reprinted from the *Millbank Memorial Fund Quarterly*, 1957 (April), *35*, No. 2, 202–223, by permission of the Millbank Memorial Fund.

RESEARCH DESIGN

There seems to be no question that the differentials between the sexes in perinatal and infant mortality are due to biological rather than to sociocultural factors.[4] Accordingly, this study is concerned only with that part of the life from age 15 onwards.

The design chosen was that of the "ex post facto experiment." Thus the problem was one of finding a male group and a female group in which cultural stresses and strains had been so standardized between sexes that one could observe the operation of biological factors in comparative isolation.

The subjects chosen for study were teachers and personnel of administrative staffs of Roman Catholic religious Brotherhoods and Sisterhoods engaged in educational work. Communities of these which operated hospitals were eliminated from the universe, and in communities actually studied the life records of Brothers and Sisters devoting their energies to household and manual duties were discarded as were those of infirmarians and nurses (who are in charge not of extern patients but of sick members).

Also eliminated from consideration were the records of those who had served in foreign missions, those who had been married before entrance into religious life, the foreign-born, the nonwhite, and those who had entered into the religious community on or after their 27th birthday. The reason for all these eliminations was the imposition of controls that would yield as homogeneous a group of subjects as possible.

While in the general public single men are more given to dissipation than single women, a life of dissipation is equally out of the question for both sexes in religious communities. Moreover, Brothers are not subject to military service after their entrance into religious life. Further, the daily regime of Brothers and Sisters is extremely similar as regards time for sleep, work, study, and recreation, and with respect to diet, housing, and medical care. (However, the life of the young Sisters seems to be slightly more stressful.)

It must be admitted that the Brothers are more likely to smoke and take an occasional drink. Only recently have Sisters been permitted to smoke and only in a limited number of communities. An important factor that is not controlled because of the absence of relevent data is the relative incidence of obesity or of overeating within each sex group. However, it may be observed that Sisters do not have the same motives for slimness found among their sex in the general public.

Such control of sociocultural factors, it was assumed, would permit the desired operation of biological factors working in comparative isolation. Five highly significant sources of differential stress between the sexes had been eliminated: (1) male service in armed forces; (2) greater male liberty to dissipate; (3) the dissimilar roles of husband and wife; (4) male employment in hazardous and life-shortening occupations; and (5) the employment of men and women in diverse occupations. Other sources of differential sociocultural stress also appear to have been eliminated or greatly curtailed. Maternal mortality, of course, had also been excluded by the very nature of the female group under observation.[5]

Health requirements suitable for the teaching occupation were demanded of candidates for entrance into the religious life by both Brothers and Sisters during the entire period of observation. Such screening was based upon personal knowledge of the candidate's past health, his or her condition at time of entrance, and the person's health record during the one or more years of trial before the first vows are pronounced. It appears that Sisters required a medical examination by a physician earlier and more widely than the Brothers. This requirement seems to have become the common practice by about 1930.

Since stable death rates were desired, a large number of years of exposure to risk to dying was needed. Because the number of religious persons, especially of Brothers, was limited, the person-year of life was chosen as the unit of study, and the period of observation was extended from January 1, 1900 to December 31, 1954.

Sampling lists of all teaching communities of Brothers and Sisters in the United States were prepared from various editions of THE OFFICIAL CATHOLIC DIRECTORY.[6] A sample of 22 Brothers' communities and of 53 Sisters' communities was drawn by probability sampling from these lists. In terms of members living in 1927, which we treated as the mid-year of the study, the sample of Brothers comprised 100 percent of the Brothers' universe, while that of the Sisters included 59.3 percent of the Sisters' universe. The response from these communities was good with 20 communities of Brothers cooperating, representing more than 98 percent of the Brothers' membership as measured in terms of 1927, and with 41 communities of Sisters cooperating, representing 83.9 percent of the membership in the Sisters' sample as measured, again, in terms of 1927.

In each of these communities life records were collected for the full membership of Brothers and Sisters since January 1, 1900, with the exception of persons who had not persevered for some part of three calendar years in the community. (The person-years in religious life of these latter were estimated on a sample basis.) All deaths were recorded, even if such death had occurred within the calendar year of entrance. When eliminations had been made according to the "experimental" controls described above, this left 9,813 life records of Brothers and 32,041 for Sisters.

In studying the literature, it had appeared to us that the greater weight of expert opinion lay on the side favoring biological factors as the principal causes for the sex differentials in the death rates. Accordingly, the research hypotheses were framed from this point of view and were expressed as follows:

1. Given two groups of American adults, one all male, the other all female, both drawn from the universe of healthy, native white persons in the United States who have reached age 15: if both groups are subjected to closely similar sociocultural stresses and strains over a long period of time, the female group will continue to show significantly more favorable death rates than the males.

2. The mortality differentials between the two experimental groups will not differ significantly from the patterns exhibited by the

national population, or else will show increased female superiority.

While these hypotheses assume for testing purposes that biological factors linked with sex chiefly underlie women's pervasive advantage in length of life, and that the differing amounts of sociocultural stress borne by men and women have little relation to this female advantage, neither hypothesis should be misinterpreted to mean that social strains and pressures are believed to be unimportant in the chain of events which leads to an individual's death. In fact, evidence is strong that social strains may play a leading role in the deaths of both sexes. Rather, proper interpretation of these hypotheses understands them to mean that, other things being equal, the same objective stresses and strains upon equal numbers of men and women will lead to the deaths of more men than women during a given period of time.

METHODOLOGY

From the life records of these Sisters and Brothers age-specific death rates by ten year age groups were worked out for each decade, 1900–1950, and for the five years, 1950–1954, as well as for the entire period, 1900–1954. Ratios were formed by dividing the death rates of Brothers by those of American native white males, and the rates of Sisters by the corresponding females.

THEORETICAL MODEL

On the assumption that the Brothers and Sisters studied constitute a group in which sociocultural stresses have been very greatly standardized between sexes, what results would indicate that such sociocultural factors are chiefly responsible for the differentials in mortality trends of American men and women? On the other hand, what results would point to biological factors as being the chief agents?

If the death rates of the Brothers should prove to have been lower than those of males of the general public, while Sisters exhibited death rates approximately equivalent to those of Brothers, the sociocultural hypothesis would be confirmed. For this would show that the variation in death rates of each sex is closely associated with variations in the amount of sociocultural stresses undergone.

On the other hand, this null hypothesis would be rejected and the biological hypothesis strengthened if the differences between the death rates of Brothers and Sisters should remain rather similar to the differentials found between death rates of men and women of the general public.

However, two points need emphasis here. The first concerns the Brothers. No matter which hypothesis is actually closer to the truth, Brothers should have experienced death rates somewhat lower than those of white males of the general public, at least at ages under forty-five. First of all, they presumably suffer accident rates—especially motor vehicle accident rates—far below those of white males of the same age. Secondly, they would not have been exposed to the disabilities often resulting from military service (except Brothers who had been in service before entrance, none of whom would have been admitted to religious life if they had shown serious disability). Thirdly, their occupation, teaching, seems to be less stressful and dangerous than that of the average white male outside religious life. Finally, they have not carried on their shoulders the worries of a husband or a father about the security of his family.

The second point relates to the Sisters. Young Sisters at least (those up to about age 40) lead a life which appears more stressful than that of the average female in the general public. They teach long hours, and work on college and graduate degrees during their spare time. Most of them do not have a summer vacation but rather attend classes, teach catechism, take parish censuses, or participate in other activities.

Accordingly, even if sociocultural factors should be only of slight importance in relation to the observed sex mortality differentials of the general public, one would still not anticipate finding that young Sisters, at least, had experienced greater gains over females of the general public in mortality rates than Brothers had made over the corresponding males. Thus if Sisters have experienced significantly lower death rates than Brothers, and if at the same time the gains they made over females of the general public were not much smaller than those made by Brothers over the males, this would constitute strong evidence for rejecting the second null hypothesis. This hypothesis states that although biological factors may prove more important than sociocultural stresses, nevertheless sociocultural stresses still will be found to play an important part in the total effect of differential sex mortality.

FINDINGS

Results confirm both research hypotheses and indicate (1) that biological factors are *more* important than sociocultural pressures and strains in relation to the differential sex death rates; and (2) that the greater sociocultural stresses associated with the male role in our society play only a small and unimportant part in producing the differentials between male and female death rates.

ANALYSIS OF RESULTS BY EXPECTATION OF LIFE

In general, life expectations of Brothers at all ages but the oldest (where the frequencies were very small) proved to be considerably greater than those of white males of the general public.[7] Such a result was to have been anticipated under either biological or sociocultural hypotheses.

The important point, however, is that Sisters' expectations of life did not in general recede from the favored position of white females. Rather, they too usually made gains over these females. In thirty-eight cases Sisters had greater expectations of life than these white females, whereas the latter had greater expectations in only four cases.

Moreover, in these culturally standardized groups, Sisters' and Brothers' expectations of life did not tend to vary about the same means, but Sisters consistently exhibited greater expectations of life, and Brothers shorter expectations. Only seven times in the abridged life tables did Brothers enjoy longer expectations of life, while Sisters were favored in this manner thirty-three times. It is noteworthy that most of the Brothers' advantage came at ages 15–34 when they would be favored by accident rates, and in the years 1900–1919 when young Sisters appear to have had extremely high rates of tuberculosis.[8]

FIGURE 1. EXPECTATIONS OF LIFE IN YEARS AT AGE 15, BROTHERS AND SISTERS, 1900–1954

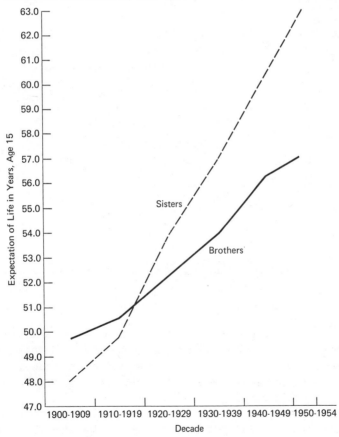

Comprehension of these results is aided by studying expectation of life at age 15, which summarizes results for the entire period of religious life from entrance until death; and expectation of life at age 45, which summarizes the experience for middle and old age only. This latter expectation is particularly important, in fact is crucial in this research design, because if social pressures were the main reason for the differentials in death rates of men and women in our general public, then at ages 45 and above in these standardized groups Brothers' and Sisters' death rates should show great convergence. For in the general public it is during the years from 45 to 65 that men seem to undergo greatest social strains and pressures. Accordingly, one would expect such pressures to exert an ever greater cumulative weight and to exact an increasing toll in the years following age 45. Therefore, on the hypothesis of sociocultural causation, standardization of such pressures ought to result in Brothers' and Sisters' death rates which vary about the same averages for each age group.

FIGURE 2. EXPECTATIONS OF LIFE IN YEARS AT AGE 45,
BROTHERS AND SISTERS, 1900–1954

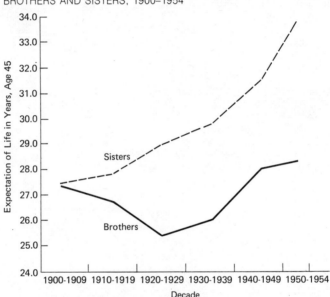

Figures 1 and 2 make it abundantly clear that such convergence has not occurred at the middle and older ages, and they also show that even at age 15 the expectations have favored Sisters without exception from the third decade onwards. A comparison of the two figures also makes it evident that the Brothers' chief period of advantage was between ages 15 and 44.

The trends over time are important, too, for the consistency of the trend lines at age 15 minimizes the probability that Sisters' advantages after 1919 are due to chance factors, while the consistent upward secular trend of Sisters at age 45 and the fluctuation of Brothers' expectations around a mean of about 27.5 years of remaining life, appears even more cogent.

Are these differences between Brothers' and Sisters' expectations of life statistically significant? If so, the null hypothesis that sociocultural factors are the chief reasons for the differentials between male and female death rates may be rejected.

In order to make this test, the data for the entire period of observation were pooled.

Such pooling gave more stable death rates; they were based on totals of 788 deaths and 130,863 person-years of life for Brothers, and 6,144 deaths and 718,435 person-years of life for Sisters.

When expectations of life at age 15 and age 45 were tested, the advantages of Sisters in both cases proved significant at beyond the .001 level. Thus the first research hypothesis, that biological factors mainly underlie the differential death rates, was supported. It is interesting to note in this connection that the ratios showing Sisters' advantages became larger at each successive age interval—exactly the opposite of what would be expected under the sociocultural hypothesis. A somewhat similar trend appears in the ratios for the national population.

ANALYSIS OF RESULTS BY AGE-SPECIFIC DEATH RATES[9]

We now turn our attention to the second research hypothesis, that not only are sociocultural pressures less important than biological factors in relation to the mortality differentials of the sexes, but they are of comparatively small importance in this respect. This hypothesis was examined by means of age-specific death rates.

A point of interest in these death rates, is the spatial location of rates which favor Brothers over Sisters. Seventy-seven per cent of all rates unfavorable to Sisters are found within early ages during the period 1900–1939. On the other hand, Sisters showed a clear advantage from age 45 upwards in all decades, and at all ages after 1939.

This finding supports the conclusion already reached in studying expectations of life that sociocultural pressures are not the main factors underlying sex differences in death rates, because it shows that Sisters enjoyed more favorable rates than Brothers at the crucial middle and older ages. It also indicates that Sisters' death rates at ages under 45 in the period 1900–1939 were anomalous. Analysis of the table for these ages and years makes it clear that Sisters' rates therein were at times exceptionally high. Since social pressures and degenerative diseases would hardly cause such high death rates between ages 15 and 24, and between ages 25 and 34, the conclusion seems warranted that some infectious or contagious disease or diseases plagued young Sisters in the early part of this century with unusually lethal effects.

A number of reasons suggest that this disease was tuberculosis. First, there was the greater difficulty of detecting incipient cases during the first quarter of the century in the medical examination required of candidates for admission, due to the less frequent use of X-ray pictures. Even in 1936, according to Dr. Frost, a large proportion of tubercular cases in the general public were not discovered until they had reached an advanced stage.[10] We may be fairly sure that the same would be true among

Sisters in regard to those incipient cases of tuberculosis which had escaped detection at time of entrance. Secondly, the dangers of infection would be multiplied by the close life of the Sisters among themselves in the Convent, and the lack of general understanding then prevalent of prophylactic methods to prevent the spread of the germ. "Age and prior exposure bring no such immunity against tuberculosis as they establish against many of the acute infections."[11]

Again, the highest tuberculosis mortality of cohorts of birth appears to occur between ages 20-29.[12] Moreover, it has been a fairly common observation that females between ages 10 and about 29 show higher susceptibility to tuberculosis than males of these ages, so much so, indeed, that in 1929 Sydenstricker called such women "relatively neglected groups" and found their death rates from tuberculosis were 59 per cent higher than the male rate at 10–14 years of age, 106 per cent higher at 15–29 years, and 43 per cent higher at 20–24 years.[13]

Finally, Fecher's work[14] as well as the British experience of 1930–1932[15] makes it evident that Catholic Sisters and nuns aged 15 to 34 years during the period 1900–1932 had rates of tuberculosis which were unusually high and which were far above the rates for single women. Single women at these ages generally showed rates higher than those of married women or of males. Dr. Taylor found similar results among Sisters in three American communities she studied from their foundation in the last century up through 1953.[16]

Ratios were formed by dividing Brothers' death rates by those of native white males, and Sisters' death rates by those of native white females. In order not to bias the comparison, each ratio was weighted by the number of person-years out of the total that Brothers or Sisters had lived in the particular decade-age-group, and thus average weighted ratios were formed for ages 15–44, ages 15 and above, and ages 45 and above.

These average ratios show whether Brothers made greater gains over native white males than Sisters made over native white females and vice versa. Thus they permit comparison of the differences of patterns between sexes in death rates for the "experimental" groups and for the national population. Where the ratios are equal, this shows that the patterns between sexes of the national groups are perfectly reflected in the differential rates of Brothers and Sisters. However, where male ratios are lower, this indicates that Brothers have made greater gains, and that there has been convergence between death rates of Brothers and Sisters, when these are measured from the positions of male and female of the national population. On the other hand, where female ratios are lower, it indicates Sisters have made greater gains, and that there has been divergence.

We may again ask, what results would lead to the non-rejection of the second null hypothesis, that sociocultural factors are of more than small importance in effecting the sex differences in mortality rates? Taking into account the lower accident rates of younger Brothers, and the less hazardous and stressful occupation in which they are engaged in comparison with that of the average native white male, as well as the fact that young Sisters are probably under greater stresses than the average native white female, non-rejection of the null hypothesis would call for large divergences from the patterns of the general public which would (a) be particularly manifested during the crucial middle and old-age periods of life, and (b) which would be in the direction of convergence between Brothers and Sisters' death rates, rather than in the direction of greater divergence.

TABLE 1. AVERAGE WEIGHTED RATIOS OF BROTHERS' DEATH RATES TO DEATH RATES OF UNITED STATES' NATIVE WHITE MALES, AND OF SISTERS' DEATH RATES TO DEATH RATES OF UNITED STATES' NATIVE WHITE FEMALES, FOR AGES 15– 44, 15 AND ALL AGES OVER, AND 45 AND ALL AGES OVER, 1900–1954[1]

GROUP	1900–09	1910–19	1920–29	1930–39	1940–49	1950–54	1900–54	AGES
Brothers[2]	.94	.84	.73	.36	.44	.36	.61	15–44
Sisters	1.26	1.18	.97	.80	.55	.44	.96	
Brothers	.97	.85	.77	.45	.50	.44	.66	15 and
Sisters	1.18	1.09	.93	.83	.66	.56	.92	Over
Brothers	1.13	.87	.96	1.00	.83	.84	.92	45 and
Sisters	.85	.86	.82	.90	.85	.71	.84	Over

[1]The United States rates for 1950–1954 used were for the white rather than the native white population.
[2]"Brothers" was used here as a shorthand expression for the death rates of Brothers divided by the death rates of United States native white males and weighted according to the number of person years of exposure; similarly "Sisters."
Source: The Differential Mortality of the Sexes, pp. 169–171, and p. 173.

The results shown in Table 1 do not present a picture of convergence of Sisters' death rates towards Brothers nor divergence from the general public pattern of superior female death rates at the middle and the old ages. An examination of this table reveals that Sisters exhibited as much superiority over Brothers at these ages as females over males of the general public. Almost all comparative gains of Brothers occurred at ages 15–44, a period in which it is difficult to believe that the underlying causation could have been influenced much by social stress and strain. Rather the difference, particularly in the last 15 years of observation, appears due to gains of Brothers over native white males in lower deaths rates from motor vehicle and other types of accidents, on the one hand, and on the other to high death rates from infectious disease such as tuberculosis among Sisters in the first quarter of this century.

Tests of significance were made by weighted analyses of variance upon each of the values shown in Table 1.[17] Brothers' ratios proved significantly lower than Sisters' at ages 15–44 in the 1900, 1910, and 1950 decades, and for the period 1900–1954 (at .05 for each period, except 1910–1919 when the difference was significant at .001). In the decades 1920, 1930, and 1940 the differences were not significant.

At all ages, 15 and above, Brothers' ratios proved significantly lower in the 1910, and the 1930 decades, as well as in the period 1900–1954. (The level of significance was .01 except for 1930 when it stood at .05.)

At ages 45 and above, no differences were significant within decades, but the Sisters' lower ratio for the entire period 1900–1954 was significant at the .01 level.

Since there were no large departures among Brothers and Sisters at the middle and older ages from the patterns of female superiority observed in the general public and since, in fact, at these ages Sisters' ratios were generally somewhat lower, the null hypothesis was rejected and the research hypothesis, that sociocultural pressures made only small contributions to the differential mortality rates of the sexes, was supported. Because of the nature of the tests, it was not possible to set any precise level of probability for this rejection of the null hypothesis.

EVALUATION OF RESULTS

The-finding that biological factors played by far the chief part in differentiating the death rates of members of the universe studied is very important. Since these members were native white Americans of sufficient health to be admitted into religious communities engaged in the active occupation of teaching, the results point to the operation of similar biological factors as the chief agents in the differential death rates of the two sexes of the American general public.

An interesting lead for further research is the notable, even spectacular improvement of young Sisters under observation from the early to the late years of the study. From showing the poorest records of the four populations compared in the period 1900–1909, they improved rapidly to exhibit by far the best mortality records for the years after 1939. This suggests the hypothesis that *under conditions of equal stress* women may be no more resistant to the *infectious and contagious* diseases than men —perhaps even less so—and that the gains which women have been making over men in this century may be chiefly bound up with a greater constitutional resistance to the *degenerative* diseases. This would account for the remarkable improvement of young Sisters vis-à-vis the other three populations, because of the spectacular advances made during this century in controlling the ravages of the infectious and contagious diseases. If this hypothesis is born out by further research, one might then say that the growing advantage of American women over men is a function of the transition from conditions when infectious and contagious diseases were the main causes of death to conditions wherein the degenerative diseases play this role.

Of course, an alternative hypothesis is possible. There may have been some hidden selection of Sisters in the earlier quarter of the century which operated at a much reduced degree in the second quarter. What this selection would be is obscure. None of the convents took in girls to "let them die in the religious life." Nor was the ascetical life of the Sisters apparently more rigorous than that of the Brothers, although both regimes were more severe at the start of the century than they are now. Further, the physical examination of candidates for admission seems to have been more careful than that of the Brothers rather than less painstaking.[18]

The continuing phase of this study should allow some test of these hypotheses, as well as the hypothesis that the chief reason for the poor showing of young Sisters during the first quarter century was tuberculosis. However, it is hoped that the results of the present study will stimulate further research by other interested parties, including both replications of the present study among other matched groups of men and women, and medical research, first, into causes of death which carry off more men than women when social stress differentials have been minimized, and secondly, into specific biological factors which may be associated with the longer life of women. Such studies may advance the date when our men can enjoy an average lifetime as long as that of women.

NOTES

[1] Dorothy G. Wiehl, Sex Differences in Mortality in the United States. Milbank Memorial Fund *Quarterly* (April, 1938), XVI, pp. 145–55.

[2] Jacob Yerushalmy, The Age-Sex Composition of the Population Resulting from Natality and Mortality Conditions. Milbank Memorial Fund *Quarterly* (January, 1943), XXI, 37–63.

[3] Walter G. Bowerman, Annuity Mortality. *Actuarial Society of America: Transactions* (1950), II, 76–102.

[4] The most pertinent and forceful of the many studies showing the existence of these differentials is that of Sam Shapiro, the influence of Weight, Sex, and Plurality on Neonatal Loss in the United States, *American Journal of Public Health and the Nation's Health* (1954), XLIV, 1142–1153.

[5] A detailed discussion of the research design will be found in a previous article by Rupert B. Vance and Francis C. Madigan, S.J., Differential Mortality and the "Style of Life" of Men and Women: Research Design. *Trends and Differentials in Mortality.* 1955 Annual Conference of Milbank Memorial Fund, New York, Milbank Memorial Fund, 1956, pp. 150–163. A later and more comprehensive treatment is also available in the writer's unpublished doctoral dissertation available in the University of North Carolina Library: The Differential Mortality of the Sexes, 1900–1954: Cultural and Biological Factors in the Diverging Life Chances of American Men and Women (Chapel Hill: University of North Carolina, 1956).

[6] *The Official Catholic Directory.* (Milwaukee: Wiltzius and Company, 1900–1911; New York, Kenedy and Son, 1912–1955).

[7] When comparing Brothers' expectations with those of males of the general public, one must bear in mind that a small part of the Brothers' advantage is a statistical artifact. In the first four decades, for the age group 85 years and above, the central death rate used for the life tables of both Brothers and Sisters was the United States native white rate as common to both sexes. This device was employed because of the paucity of Brothers at these ages, and because of the desire to hold constant death rates of Brothers and Sisters at previous ages, while still finishing off the tables. A similar procedure was used in the first two decades for ages 75–84. Stable Brothers' rates—if they had been obtainable—would probably have been nearer those of native white males than the rates for both sexes taken together. On the other hand, Sisters' expectations were somewhat deflated, since in general at these ages the actual rates of Sisters were more favorable than the native white rates not specific for sex.

[8] See Footnotes [10–15].

[9] The fractions upon which these rates were based will be found in the writer's dissertation. *The Differential Mortality,* 225–253.

[10] Wade Hampton Frost, How Much Control of Tuberculsis, in *Papers of Wade Hampton Frost,* M.D. Ed., Kenneth F. Maxcy, M.D. (New York: Commonwealth Fund, 1941), p. 607.

[11] Wade Hampton Frost: The Age Selection of Mortality from Tuberculosis in Successive Decades, *In Papers of Wade Hampton Frost,* 594.

[12] *Ibid., American Journal of Hygiene* (1939), XXX, Sec. A. p. 91, footnote (in letter of Dr. Frost to Dr. Sydenstricker, quoted).

[13] Edgar Sydenstricker, Tuberculosis Among Relatively Neglected Groups, *Transactions of the National Tuberculosis Association* (1929), XXV, p. 268.

[14] Constantine J. Fecher, *The Longevity of Members of Catholic Religious Sisterhoods* (Washington: Catholic University of America, 1927), pp. 42–44. Fecher is at present bringing his interesting study up to date.

[15]Registrar General's Office, *The Registrar General's Decennial Supplement, England and Wales,* 1931. Part IIa. Occupational Mortality (London: His Majesty's Stationery Office, 1938), Table 4c, 303.

[16]It is the writer's understanding that Dr. Ruth Taylor and Mr. Ben Carroll of the National Institutes of Health expect to publish these results in the near future.

[17]The Method of Fitting Constants was used to obtain adjusted sums of squares for sex and for age. Cf. George W. Snedecor: *Statistical Methods* (Ames, Iowa: Collegiate Press, 1946), 296–299.

[18]The writer learned these facts from a questionnaire which he circulated among the communities in his sample after the results had become available.

2.3

A Final Follow-Up Study of One Hundred Adopted Children

Marie Skodak
Harold M. Skeels

A. HISTORICAL BACKGROUND

... This report constitutes a final chapter in a long-range study in which the same group of adopted children have had intelligence tests on four occasions. ...

The foster homes into which the children described in this study were placed became available through a number of sources. The child-placing programs of the State Board of Control and the Iowa Children's Home Society were well known throughout the state since the majority of agency placements were made through them. Both organizations had travelling workers, assigned to certain areas whose duties included: (*a*) The supervision of children placed in wage, free, and adoptive homes to insure proper care, protection, education, and home relationships. (*b*) The evaluation of homes and foster families for children in terms of financial resources, physical set-up, attitudes toward children, future demands on children. (*c*) The development of community interest in child care, adoption, and placement.

Parents interested in adoption would write directly to the state office, the institution, agency, or one of the field workers. The application blanks contained only the minimum information regarding the type of child desired, the family's financial and vocational status, and the names of at least three references. The field worker would then visit the home, interview the applicants, evaluate the physical and emotional

Excerpted, adapted and reprinted from *The Journal of Genetic Psychology,* 1949, 75, 85–125, by permission of the authors and The Journal Press.

resources and the possible future demands with regard to education and vocation. References were contacted by mail, phone, or visit. The degree of investigation varied. Families who were well known or who were manifestly capable were accepted with less scrutiny than families in more modest circumstances or where there were questions regarding the present or future adequacy of the home. It is not known what proportion of applicants was rejected, but in many cases families were dissuaded from completing an application if it seemed unlikely that a child would be placed with them.

On the whole, the foster families were above the average of their communities in economic security and educational and cultural status. They were highly regarded by the town's business, professional, and religious leaders and usually had demonstrated a long-time interest in children through church or community activities.

The placement procedure in both organizations was essentially similar. In the state agency after the application was accepted the family was placed on the waiting list and their name was considered at the monthly staff meetings when assignments were made. At these case conferences, attended by the head of the Children's Division, the superintendent of the institution, the psychologists, and head nurse, the available babies and available homes were discussed. Factors in the assignment included religion, sex, age, color or complexion, physique, medical history, and report of the family background. Pre-placement psychological examinations were not available for the children in this study. In many instances the information about the child's family background was so meager that it was of little or no value. The primary factors in matching were the stipulations of the foster parents regarding religion, sex, and hair color in that order.

This method of placement of children from relatively inferior socioeconomic backgrounds into substantial homes thus provided the setting for the study. Perusal of the child's social history as recorded in the institution and comparison with the field's agent's pre-placement evaluation of the adopting home was disheartening. It did not seem possible that children with such meager possibilities, as projected from the intellectual, academic, and occupational attainments of their parents, could measure up to the demands of cultured, educated parents. Yet careful examination of one child after another showed none of the retardation or misplacement which might have been anticipated. Following a preliminary survey of results (24) it was decided that a follow-up study was imperative, and the cooperation of the foster parents was solicited and received.

B. DESCRIPTION OF THE SAMPLE

In general there are three levels of society from which children for adoptive placements originate. It is believed that children from culturally, socially, and educationally superior homes tend to be placed among relatives or in adoptive homes through various private sources. Because of the extreme difficulty of identifying and locating such placements, no studies have been made of the subsequent development or adjustment of these children nor is the exact number of these children known to official agencies. At what may be described as the second socioeconomic level, the children tend to become the charges of private or semiprivate child caring or placing agencies. Many of these children's aid and protective societies exercise considerable control over their intake. Policies may, for instance, preclude the acceptance of children of mentally defective parents, or of other children who may be judged "unplaceable" or in need of care which that particular organization does not feel equipped to offer. These organizations tend to draw from the various middle economic classes but also have a fair number of children from extremely ineffective homes as the study by Roe and Burks indicates (21). The third group of children from the lowest socioeconomic levels are usually known to various public welfare agencies. The public agencies, in contrast to the private ones, are usually obligated to accept all children committed to their care and naturally receive children no other agency feels able to accept. There is no doubt that the general social, vocational, and adjustment level of the parents of children committed to public agency care is substantially below that of children who become wards of private agencies or who are adopted through private channels.

It is necessary to differentiate between observations regarding the natural families of infants committed for care and the natural families of preschool or older children. All studies which have published reports on the education of the true parents of children placed in foster homes agree that the true parents of the older children are more apt to be inadequate, unstable, retarded, unemployed, in other words, less competent by any criterion of measurement which has been used. The social factors behind this difference are not difficult to identify. The youngest children, the infants, are primarily illegitimate children. In the first place, their parents are relatively younger. While parents-out-of-wedlock show various signs of emotional instability, the psychoses, alcoholism, and cumulating effects of maladjustment characterizing the parents of older dependent children have not yet indelibly affixed themselves. With the rest of their generation, the younger parents enjoy higher educational opportunities together with the dubious benefits of being "lifted" from grade to grade on the basis of the physical size rather than academic accomplishment. Vocationally it is understandable that an 18-year-old youth is a farm hand or truck driver's helper, while an adult of 40 on the same job is prima facie scored well down on the scale of occupational success. The young illegitimate parents have not had the accumulating frustration of economic deprivation, children in unwanted numbers, and the growing weight of community disapproval of their inefficient way of living. For many it is the first, and often the only, social transgression and after this experience many, perhaps even the majority of illegitimate parents, go on to establish secure, socially acceptable homes and families. A study of what happens to illegitimate parents who decide to establish a family together, as compared to those who release their child, may shed some interesting light on the factors which operate to produce the poorer histories among the older children as compared to the younger. There is a significant socioeconomic difference between the parents of the younger and older groups of children who become dependent. It does not necessarily follow, however, that this difference is genetically determined.

1. Subjects of this Study

The criteria for inclusion in this study were as follows: (a) The child was placed in an adoptive home under the age of six months. (b) The child had been given an intelligence test prior to November, 1936, and after one year's residence in the adoptive home. (c) Some information, though of variable amount and reliability, existed concerning the natural and adoptive parents. (d) The child was white, of North European background (it so happened that no children of South European, Latin, or other social backgrounds met the other criteria either).

In this study all of the children were received for care as infants. The Iowa Soldiers' Orphan's Home, identified as the public agency, was the placing agency in 76 percent of the cases and the Iowa Children's Home Society, a state-wide, private, nonsectarian organization placed 21 percent. The remaining three children were privately placed and were included because they were available and met the criteria set up for the other children.

It was earlier pointed out (26) that 96.6 percent of the 319 children committed to the two agencies under the age of six months between 1933–1937, were placed in adoptive homes. In only four cases was the child withheld from adoptive placement because of poor family history. The remaining seven had serious health problems. Since the majority of the children originally in the study had been placed during this period, and the remainder had been placed earlier during a time when the policies regarding family background had been even more lenient, it was concluded that the children in the study were representative of all those placed by these organizations.

During 1934–1936, when the mental testing program was coördinated for the two agencies, and 1933–1937 for the public agency alone, it was found that 90 percent of the children placed under six months of age had been given at least one intelligence test. The mean IQ of this group was 119, slightly above the mean IQ of 116 achieved by the members of the follow-up group on the first examination during the same calendar years.

It was evident that the group of children who constituted the first sample were representative of the available children since there was no systematic withholding of numbers of children because of poor histories, nor was there a group with lower initial intelligence test scores who were excluded from the study.

In the first follow-up report (25), out of a total of 180 children who met the criteria of age at placement, race and date of examination, it was possible to retest 152 children during 1937–1938. On the third examination 139 children were seen during 1940–41 (26) and the fourth and final visit in 1946 resulted in the present sample of 100. The major factor in the reduction of the size of the sample has been time and expense. The families, all originally in Iowa, are now scattered over many states and Canada. To locate and visit the 100 children in the 10 weeks available for the study, it was necessary to drive over 12,000 miles even though accurate addresses were available and careful preliminary arrangements had been made with planned appointments acceptable for the parents and the child. . . .

Comparisons were made between the continuous group of 100 and those who dropped out at the various retest points. Systematic selection which would influence the character of the final group of 100 is not evident from the comparisons between the mean IQ's of the group at the various reexamination periods. The standard deviations for all means are large, ranging from 11.9 to 17.2, and none of the differences is statistically significant.

It may be concluded that this group of 100 children is probably representative of the total group placed by these agencies at comparable ages, and that conclusions based on the pattern of mental development of these children are probably applicable to others with similar experience and social backgrounds and placed under similar circumstances into comparable homes.

2. Test Techniques

The purpose throughout the study was to secure the most reliable and valid measure of the child's intellectual ability at the time of examination. On first examination the children ranged from 11 months to six years in age with 78 percent of the children between one and three years. Four children had been placed at a few days of age and were tested shortly before the expiration of the one-year observation period. The 1916 Stanford-Binet was suitable for use with the 19 percent over three years of age and was occasionally used with younger children who were obviously accelerated in mental development. The Kuhlman Binet was routinely used with all children under three years, and occasionally as a clinical supplement with some children over three.

The reexaminations were begun in 1936 when the Revised Stanford-Binet was not generally available and the 1916 revision was consequently used. In this series of tests, although 17 percent of the children were under 3–0 years of age, they were all over 2–6 and sufficiently accelerated to make the 1916 Stanford-Binet a usable test. Therefore, all test scores reported for the second examination were based on the 1916 revision.

When the third examination was scheduled in 1939–1940, the question of "best test" was raised. From the standpoint of fatigue and future rapport, it seemed advisable to limit the number of tests given and the 1916 revision was again selected. Survey of the literature (7, 14, 18) showed that between 5 and 11 years, the ages of these children at the third examination, the results of the 1916 and 1937 scales were most nearly identical. Not only had the 1916 test been used in the earlier examinations, but it also had been used in examinations of the mothers and a few of the fathers of the children. Direct comparisons of test scores were thus made possible without getting into the knotty problems of comparability of standardization of the different revisions. The problems of such a long-time research underscore the need for an intelligence test which results in comparable scores at all ages.

When the fourth and last examination was scheduled in 1946, the children were between 11 and 17 years of age. In view of the problems surrounding the 1916 revision at these ages, it was decided to impose on the good nature of the subjects and give both the 1916 revision and Form L of the 1937 revision. This set up a program involving approximately two hours, often a great deal more, if there was marked scatter on either or both tests. Since there are a number of overlapping items, these were given and scored simultaneously. The 1916 revision was completed first and the 1937, Form L, second. Whatever advantage of practice effect there might have been, was judged to be cancelled by fatigue. Every effort was made to keep the interest and effort of the examinees at an optimum level. No subject refused to take the tests after an appointment was made and only two were openly antagonistic in typical adolescent behavior. Even these were persuaded to cooperate and no greater compliment to the intrinsic interests of the tests can be made than to say that in spite of themselves even these reluctant subjects became interested and made scores consistent with their earlier test results and their current school placements.

All of the third and fourth tests, and all but five or six of the first two tests were given in the foster homes. This made it possible to observe the relationships between child and parents, the fluctuation in family economic and cultural status of the 13-year period, and to sample the child's behavior in the home situation. A cordial relationship developed between the parents and the examiners as a result of these repeated visits. The first examination was usually a highly emotional experience for the parents, who understood that the psychologist's word was final in approving or disapproving the completion of adoption. In a sense this was even more crucial than the court action since as one parent stated "we were taking an examination in parenthood. Our success was shown by the results in our child." The majority of the families, located in areas where clinics and psychologists were not available but who were familiar with these resources through reading and the radio, availed themselves of the opportunity to discuss various child rearing problems. As would be anticipated, the character of the problems changed with age, and on the fourth visit dealt with problems of adolescence, vocational choices, educational plans, emancipation from the home, etc. There seemed to be no problem which was unique to this group of children as compared to any other group of similar age. The problem of information concerning their own adoption had been well solved by nearly all the families. Surprisingly enough two families had still not "told," but other evidence indicated that these children probably guessed. In two or three instances there had been community problems in which, despite the efforts of the foster parents, the children had had a very difficult adjustment to the adoptive status.

All parents were aware of the research nature of the re-tests and were, on the whole, proud of the distinction. Through their contribution they felt they could facilitate early placement of children in adoptive homes and provide reassurance to families uncertain about adoption.

Relationships between the children and the examiners were more casual. Some of the children recalled the examiner's visits from one occasion to the next, and when they did, it was in terms of the fun of playing games with an unusually agreeable person. An explanation was made to all participants during the fourth examination following the general pattern that:

When you were a younger boy, you were a member of a group of boys and girls all over the state who were given tests like this. We wanted to find out how well children could do different sorts of things, how well they could remember, figure things out and so on. Now that they are older, we would like to see how much they have changed and in what way. The tests are a little like a quiz program on the radio and most people find them rather fun.

In a few instances the question was raised as to whether children who were not adopted were also tested and the subjects were assured that children in many places also took similar tests. Two of the participants, one, the oldest subject, who had completed one year in college, and one a superior high school senior with decided research interests, were familiar with the published reports of the study and cooperated delightfully.

C. MENTAL DEVELOPMENT OF THE CHILDREN

All of the children had been seen on four occasions and a few for various reasons had been given additional tests. In these cases the test given at an age nearest the mean age for the group was selected for use in the major comparisons. The mean age at first examination was *2 years 2 months,* at second examination *4 years 3 months,* at third examination *7 years 0 months* and at fourth examination *13 years 6 months.*

The group included 60 girls and 40 boys. The range, median, and mean ages for both sexes were essentially the same.

TABLE 1.

TEST	AGE	MEAN IQ	SD	RANGE	MEDIAN
I	2 yrs. 2 mo.	117	13.6	80–154	118
II	4 yrs. 3 mo.	112	13.8	85–149	111
III	7 yrs. 0 mo.	115	13.2	80–149	114
IV (1916)	13 yrs. 6 mo.	107	14.4	65–144	107
IV (1937)	13 yrs. 6 mo.	117	15.5	70–154	117

Ages and results may be summarized for the 100 children as given in Table 1 —the mean IQ of this group of children has remained above the average for the general population throughout early childhood, school age, and into adolescence. It would be generally accepted that if major changes in intellectual functioning occur after this age, they probably result from psychiatric and emotional problems rather than from developmental abnormalities. . . .

Repeated cross-section analysis of the general trend of IQ's where tests are distributed by age shows that the group has consistently achieved a higher average mental age than would be found in a representative sampling of the total child population of the same age. Detailed statistical analysis of this material is not possible since every test for each child is presented, including some which are not used in the major comparisons. While fluctuations do occur, accentuated by the small numbers of cases at single age levels, the findings are essentially the same as in the earlier reports. The mean IQ of this group has remained consistently above the average of the population as a whole at each age level.

Rather wide fluctuations in IQ between tests were found throughout the entire period. The general trend is toward losses when the first test is taken as the basis of comparison, as the mean IQ on succeeding tests would indicate. Since the total number of cases is 100, the percentages may be computed automatically and only the actual number of cases is given in the table.

These results, together with the correlations reported later, are consistent with findings from other studies (3, 4, 13, 23), which show that IQ fluctuations of considerable magnitude are found among children who live with their own parents. The greater the time span between tests the greater the probability of wide difference between successive test scores. . . .

D. RELATIONSHIPS BETWEEN MENTAL DEVELOPMENT OF ADOPTED CHILDREN AND CHARACTERISTICS OF THEIR FOSTER PARENTS

1. Occupational Level

In the selection of foster homes all agencies give preference to families who not only have sufficient financial resources to assure adequate care for the child, but who show signs of culture, refinement, and intellectual and emotional understanding of the needs of children and the special problems of adoption.

TABLE 2.   DISTRIBUTIONS OF TRUE AND FOSTER FATHER OCCUPATIONS

OCCUPATIONAL CLASSIFICATION	GENERAL U.S. POPULATION EMPLOYED MALES, 1930 PERCENT	TRUE FATHERS NUMBER	TRUE FATHERS PERCENT	FOSTER FATHERS NUMBER	FOSTER FATHERS PERCENT
I. Professional	3.1	2	2.7	14	14.0
II. Semiprofessional and managerial	5.2	3	4.1	17	17.0
III. Skilled trades	15.0	9	12.3	27	27.0
IV. Farmers	15.3	5	6.8	29	29.0
V. Semiskilled	30.6	10	13.7	8	8.0
VI. Slightly skilled	11.3	9	12.3	5	5.0
VII. Day laborers	19.5	35	48.0		
Number	100.0	73		100	
Mean	4.8	6.47		2.85	
Median	5	6		3	
Standard deviation	1.5	1.77		1.33	

The occupational level of foster families reflects this initial selection and has remained consistently well above the average for the general population. Table 2 shows the foster father and the true father occupations compared with the occupational distribution of the population as a whole, based on the 1930 census and classified according to Goodenough's seven-point scale (9). Figures for the 1940 census are not directly comparable because of differences in classification method, particularly in the clerical, sales, skilled, and slightly skilled occupations.

In 1940 in the U.S. as a whole, 4.4 percent of the employed males were in professional occupations. In Iowa they constituted 3.7 percent of the employed population while 14 percent of the foster fathers were so employed. Although only 14 percent of employed U.S. males are farm proprietors or managers, 29.5 percent of Iowa men and 29 percent of the foster fathers are so employed, thus farmers were adequately represented. In the U.S. approximately 17 percent of men and in Iowa 19 percent are unskilled laborers. None of the foster fathers, but 48 percent of the natural fathers are so classified.

Further comparison between the figures for the foster parents, the general population, and the data for 73 true fathers for whom occupational information was available shows that the foster fathers are not only above the average of the population with a mean scale score of 2.85 as against 4.8 for the U.S. as a whole, but are conspicuously above the mean for the true fathers. The latter are, in addition, well below the mean for the total population with an average scale score of 6.47, equivalent to the status of an unskilled or very slightly skilled workman. The children whose natural parents, as a group, come from one extreme of the population were placed in foster homes representing the opposite extreme in occupational status.

Observation of the homes over the 13-year period showed that, although they were above the average in culture, resources, and financial security at the time the child was placed, they were, on the whole, even more prosperous at the end of the study. Only two fathers had been in military service, one as a professional man and one as a noncommissioned draftee. While some had benefited from high war wages, others on fixed incomes had been at a slight disadvantage. The general economic prosperity of 1945–1947 was evident in most cases. . . .

Relationships between the child's IQ and foster father's occupation are obscured because the personal qualities, the cultural opportunities, and intellectual stimulation of the homes are not directly reflected by the occupational classification of the families. The opportunities of many of the farm (Class IV) and skilled trades (Class III) homes exceeded some of the teachers', physicians', and managerial homes (Classes I and II). The results, however, show persistent slight differences in favor of homes in the upper three categories. Comparisons for all years except the first two are based on the 1916 Stanford-Binet. Since all available test scores were utilized and the number of cases at any year is small, detailed analysis is not attempted.

It can be concluded that, on the whole, children in homes in the higher occupational categories tend to have somewhat higher mean IQ's at all ages. However, all the children, including those in homes of lesser occupational levels, are above the mean for the total population at all age levels where the number of cases is sufficient to warrant consideration.

2. Education

The distribution of educational attainment of the natural and foster parents is shown in Table 3. The average school attainment of the foster parents as recorded on the application record and verified in 1946 showed that mean and median attainment for the foster parents was high school graduation, with 15 percent having completed college. According to the 1940 census figures the median education for native Iowans in a comparable age group (35–44 years of age in 1940) was 8.8 for males and 9.3 for females. In general, urban populations have an average of one more year of education than rural populations.

TABLE 3. DISTRIBUTION OF TRUE AND FOSTER PARENT EDUCATION

SCHOOL ATTAINMENT	TRUE FATHERS NO.	TRUE MOTHERS NO.	FOSTER FATHERS NO.	FOSTER MOTHERS NO.
Number	59	92	100	100
Mean	10.05	9.80	12.09	12.31
Median	10.57	9.78	12.13	12.56
SD	2.73	2.31	3.54	2.89

The educational status of the true parents is significantly below that of the foster parents and is below the average of a comparable age group for the state. The 1940 census showed that native Iowans 25–34 years of age had a mean education of 10.2 for the males and 11.0 for the females. While the information on the education of foster parents is reasonably accurate, there is evidence that the education of the natural mother has been overstated by an average of one year (12, 26).

These data again show that while the education of the foster parents is superior to the average for their age and region, the natural parents' education is below the average for their age and region.

TABLE 4.

	FOSTER MOTHER EDUCATION	FOSTER FATHER EDUCATION
Child's Test I	−.03 ± .07	.05 ± .07
Child's Test II	+.04 ± .07	.03 ± .07
Child's Test III	.10 ± .07	.03 ± .07
Child's Test IV (1916)	.04 ± .07	.06 ± .07
Child's Test IV (1937)	.02 ± .07	.00 ± .07

Correlations between foster parent education and child IQ on successive tests are summarized in Table 4.

Earlier reports on somewhat larger numbers of children showed a slight positive correlation between foster child IQ and foster parent education (24, 25, 26). In this array of correlations there is no discernible trend except a consistent lack of statistical relationship. Inspection of the original scatter diagram confirms the lack of relationship. However, it should be pointed out that both the IQ's and the educations represented here are confined to the upper segment of the total possible range. As long as the parents are highly selected, and the children as a group also have a limited range of IQ's and are in the upper half of the total population, it is not likely that repetition of similar studies will produce any more significant correlations. Increasing the number of cases may extend the range and sharpen the focus on what little differences exists. These figures are lower than correlations generally reported in the literature for both foster child-foster parent and own-child-parent correlations. However, in other cases, the range for both distributions has been wider.

The only conclusions which may be drawn from these data are that the foster parents are above the average of their age and regional group in education and that the children in these homes are above the average in mental development. The differences between these adoptive parents in amount of formal education completed are not reflected in differences in intelligence between the children.

E. RELATIONSHIPS BETWEEN MENTAL DEVELOPMENT OF ADOPTED CHILDREN AND CHARACTERISTICS OF THEIR TRUE PARENTS

1. Intelligence

Intelligence test results were available for 63 of the true mothers. All were based on the 1916 Stanford-Binet except one Terman Group Test, two Otis, and one Wechsler-Bellevue. Since the scores on these tests were consistent with other evidence on the mental adequacy of the mothers, the scores were included. The tests were given by trained examiners, under ordinary testing conditions, usually after the mother had decided to release the baby for adoption. The release was not contingent on the mother's test score and examinations were not made when the mother was ill or obviously upset emotionally.

TABLE 5.   COMPARISON BETWEEN DISTRIBUTION OF IQ'S (1916 STANFORD-BINET) OF TRUE MOTHERS AND THEIR CHILDREN

IQ	MOTHERS	CHILDREN
Number	63	63
Mean	85.7	106
Median	86.3	107
Standard deviation	15.75	15.10

Table 5 shows the distribution of the true-mother IQ's and child IQ's at a mean age of 13.6 based on the 1916 Stanford-Binet. This test was selected since it offered the maximum available degree of comparability for parent and child intelligence test scores. The mean IQ of these children on the 1937 revision is 10 points higher than on the 1916 revision. If a correction were to be made for the IQ's of the mothers, as some investigators have suggested, the 1937 test scores of the children would be used, with the same relative difference between the two arrays of scores.

A difference of 20 points between the means of mothers and children is not only a statistically reliable difference (CR 9.2) but is also of considerable social consequence.

Previous analysis (26) showed that there was no difference between the mean IQ's of children whose mothers had been examined and those whose mothers' IQ's were unknown. This was confirmed by examination of the present data.

Relationships between mother-child pairs, with regard to IQ, expressed in terms of correlation coefficients on 63 cases, are summarized in Table 6.

TABLE 6.

Test I	.00 ± .09
Test II	.28 ± .08*
Test III	.35 ± .07**
Test IV (1916)	.38 ± .07**
Test IV (1937)	.44 ± .07**

*Reliable at the 5 percent level of confidence (17, p. 212).
**Reliable at the 1 percent level of confidence (Ibid.).

It is apparent that the above tabulation contains more questions than it answers and can be the source of considerable controversy. Certain conclusions can be drawn, however. Among these are the following: test scores of children secured during the first two years of life bear no statistical relationship to the scores of their mothers, nor, it should be noted, do they show a very high relationship to their own later scores ($r = .35$). By seven years of age a substantial correlation with true mother's IQ is reached which remains of the same magnitude in adolescence provided the 1916 Stanford-Binet test is used with both children and mothers. The correlation is still further increased if the 1937 revision of the Binet is used.

Many reasons can and have been advanced for the low correlation between infant tests and later measures which will not be reviewed here. There is considerable evidence for the position that as a group these children received maximal stimulation in infancy with optimum security and affection following placement at an average of three months of age. The quality and amount of this stimulation during early childhood seemed to have little relation to the foster family's educational and cultural status.

The available data which can be statistically used—occupational classification and formal education—are not sufficiently sensitive to be useful in measuring these less tangible differences in child rearing practices. This point is important for the interpretation of the correlations between the child's IQ and his mother's IQ because it is possible to throw the weight of interpretation in the direction of either genetic or environmental determinants. If the former point of view is accepted, then the mother's mental level at the time of her examination is considered to reflect her fundamental genetic constitution, and ignores the effects of whatever environmental deprivations or advantages may have influenced her own mental development. Thus it would be assumed that the children of brighter mothers would in turn be brighter than the children of less capable mothers regardless of the type of foster home in which they were placed. The increasing correlation might be interpreted to support this point of view, since the occupational differences between foster parents are not large. It is, however, inconsistent with the evidence that the children's IQ's substantially exceed those of their mothers and that none of them are mentally defective even though a number of the mothers were institution residents. The role of the unknown father adds to the complication although the evidence indicates that the fathers resembled their unwed partners in mental level and education (1).

If the so-called environmental point of view is accepted, then the question is raised whether the increasing correlation between child and true mother IQ possibly reflects the tendency to place the children of brighter mothers in the more outstanding foster homes, and the influence of these homes becomes increasingly prominent as the child grows older.

The question regarding selective placement can be approached in at least two ways. The first is an inspection of the relationships between such characteristics of the true and foster families as education and occupation. Using these crude measures, correlations of .24 between true mother IQ and foster parent education and .27 between true mother and foster parent education were found in this sample. Comparisons between true mother characteristics and foster father occupation for the present sampling are summarized in Table 7.

TABLE 7.

	FOSTER FATHER OCCUPATION					
	I	II	III	IV	V	VI
Number of foster fathers	14	17	27	29	2	5
Mean *IQ* of mothers of children in these homes	86	89	87	83	77	90
Number of cases	9	13	20	15	4	2
Mean education of mothers of children in these homes	10	10	10	8	8	8
Number of cases	12	16	28	25	9	2

It is apparent from both types of analyses that while a trend existed, selective placement, as evaluated by these measures was not consistently practiced.

Another approach to this problem of relationship is to examine the data for two contrasting groups of children. Selected for this purpose were: (*a*) Those children whose mothers were known to be mentally defective, with other evidence supporting the known IQ of under 70 (N = 11). (*b*) Those children whose mothers were above average in intelligence as measured by tests. Since there were only three cases above 110 IQ, the next five, in the 105–109 IQ range, were also included (N = 8).

TABLE 8.   COMPARISONS BETWEEN CHILDREN OF MOTHERS OF INFERIOR AND OF ABOVE AVERAGE INTELLIGENCE

	TRUE MOTHER'S IQ	TRUE MOTHER'S EDUC.	FOSTER MID-PAR. EDUC.	FOSTER FATHER OCCUP.	CHILD'S IQ TEST I	TEST II	TEST III	TEST IV	TEST IV '37
			GROUP A (N = 11)						
Mean	63	7	12	3.2	113	109	105	96	104
Median	64	8	12	III	114	111	96	96	106
			GROUP B (N = 8)						
Mean	111	12	12.5	3.3	116	117	125	118	129
Median	109	12.5	11.5	III	117	112.5	125	117	130

Comparisons between the two groups are shown in Table 8. It is evident from the table that there is a marked difference between the intelligence and education of the true mothers of children in Groups (*a*) and (*b*). On the basis of education and occupation the foster parents of both groups are essentially similar, with perhaps a slight advantage for Group (*b*). On the first examination both groups of children were above average. By seven years of age a marked difference in mental level between the two groups is observable which persists into adolescence and is reflected by both the 1916 and 1937 Stanford-Binet tests. While children in Group (*a*) show average mental development as a group, the children in (*b*) show superior mental development. A difference of 25 points in IQ has significance socially, educationally, and vocationally.

If reliance were to be placed on these data alone, the inference would be fairly clear. However, comparison of the actual situation in the homes leads to a different conclusion. As a group, the homes of Group (*b*) are superior to the homes of Group (*a*) on every count on which homes can be evaluated. The average income of Group (*b*) is easily double the average income of Group (*a*) families. Five of the eight had sent their children to private schools, nursery schools, or camps for more than one year, reflecting an intelligent interest in superior opportunities, financial stability, and social status. None of the families in Group (*a*) had been either interested or able to afford similar opportunities. All the children in Group (*b*) had had music, dancing, or art lessons, while only 5 of the 11 in Group (*a*) had such training. In the number of books, the extent of participation in church, civic, social, recreational, and cultural organizations, participation in Child Study and PTA groups, familiarity with and application of approved child rearing practices and attitudes, the number of toys, school equipment, typewriters, personal radios, the degree of freedom in spending allowances, deciding recreation, hours to be kept and other factors now believed to be essential for optimum social and emotional adjustment, the homes in Group (*b*) were definitely superior to the homes in Group (*a*). The one exception was 72G. This was the home in which the foster mother had been hospitalized for mental illness. The foster father, well educated in a foreign country, is a railroad section supervisor. Finances are limited, intellectual interests are nonexistent. For several years this girl has competently managed a household. It is possible to speculate that under more favorable circumstances she too, might have attained higher test scores.

The general conclusions which may be drawn indicate that while in this study an increasing correlation between child IQ and true mother IQ is observed with increasing age, it cannot be attributed to genetic determinants alone. A more sensitive measure of foster parental competence in child development is necessary before small sample techniques of comparisons and analyses of differences can be fruitful. The present measures of education and occupation do not evaluate the crucial differences between outstanding, average, or less effective homes. The fact remains that the children are considerably superior to their mothers in mental development. There is a socially important difference between a group of people whose average IQ is 107–117, depending on the test selected, and another group whose IQ is 87. Since the mean for the children is above the average for the population as a whole, it cannot be attributed to the phenomenon of regression alone.

2. Education

In addition to the intelligence test scores there was information on the education of 92 of the true mothers. Recognizing that it was an unreliable and questionably valid measure of ability, nevertheless, correlations between true mothers' education and child *IQ* were computed. Table 9 summarizes the results.

TABLE 9.

Test I	.04 ± .09
Test II	.31 ± .07*
Test III	.37 ± .06*
Test IV (1916)	.31 ± .06*
Test IV (1937)	.32 ± .06*

*Reliable at the 1 per cent level of confidence (17, p. 212).

Here, too, there was an increase in correlations between the first and second tests, but the relationships then became stationary instead of showing a further increase with subsequent tests. Recalling the still lower correlations between child *IQ* and foster parent education, here again it is advisable to guard against an inclination to over value the significance of correlations of this size.

3. Occupation

Since both the true mothers and true fathers of the children originated primarily from the two lowest occupational classifications, attempts to identify a relationship between the mental development of the children and the occupational ranking of the parents were fruitless. The occupational status of the true fathers was occasionally considered in placement plans, but usually the information was not felt to be sufficiently reliable to influence the decision.

Goodenough (8), Terman (29) and others have found that children living with their own parents in the two lower occupational categories have mean *IQ*'s of approximately 95. In contrast, children living with their own parents in the professional and managerial occupations have a mean *IQ* of approximately 115. It is apparent that foster children in adoptive homes of all the occupational levels represented here compare favorably with own children in homes of the upper socio-economic level, rather than following the pattern found in the families from which they originated.

F. CONCLUSIONS

Perhaps the most important contribution this study can make to the planning of future research is to point out the inadequacies of easily available data, and the necessity of formulating more clearly the various criteria used in the selection and assessment of the foster homes and the children. It is clear that the objective data used here, education and occupation, do not represent the real basis for selection and are not closely related to the child's mental development. Judging from the trend of correlations between mother's and child's IQ's, one might conclude that a relationship exists which became increasingly apparent with age. This is complicated by the evidence of selective placement, yet without a parallel relationship between foster parent education and child IQ. This one set of figures must not be permitted to overshadow the more significant finding that the children are consistently and unmistakably superior to their natural parents and in fact, follow and improve upon the pattern of mental development found among own children in families like the foster families. What may be the salient features in the foster homes which have produced this development of the children, is only suggested in this study. It is inferred that maximum security, an environment rich in intellectual stimulation, a well-balanced emotional relationship, intellectual agility on the part of the foster parents—all these and other factors contributed to the growth of the child. Unfortunately, there is still no scale for the measurement of these dynamic aspects of the foster home situation. The futility of arguments based on correlations involving measures of education and occupation applies to both sides of the discussion.

The conclusions which may be drawn from the material presented here suggest that:

1. The above average mental development of the children adopted in infancy has been maintained into early adolescence. There has been no large scale decline

in IQ either for the group or for large segments of it, although certain children have shown either wide fluctuation or a steady decline or rise as compared with the first test results.

2. The educational or occupational data available for foster or natural parents in the typical social history record are not sufficient to predict the course of mental development of the children. Other factors, primarily emotional and personal, and probably located in the foster home, appear to have more significant influence in determining the mental growth of the children in this group.

3. The intellectual level of the children has remained consistently higher than would have been predicted from the intellectual, educational, or socioeconomic level of the true parents, and is equal to or surpasses the mental level of own children in environments similar to those which have been provided by the foster parents.

The implications for placing agencies justify a policy of early placement in adoptive homes offering emotional warmth and security in an above average educational and social setting.

REFERENCES

1. Anderson, C. L., & Skeels, H. M. A follow-up study on a small sampling of the putative fathers in Skodak's study. Unpublished study. Iowa Child Welfare Research Station. State University of Iowa, December, 1941.

2. Bradway, K. P. IQ constancy on the revised Stanford-Binet from the pre-school to the Junior High School level. *J. Genet. Psychol.*, 1944, *65*, 197–217.

3. Bradway, K. P. An experimental study of factors associated with Stanford-Binet IQ changes from the preschool to the Junior High School. *J. Genet. Psychol.*, 1945, *66*, 107–128.

4. Cunningham, B. V. Infant IQ ratings evaluated after an interval of seven years. *J. Exper. Educ.*, 1934, *3*, 84–87.

5. Dexter, E. S. The relation between occupation of parent and intelligence of children. *Sch & Soc.*, 1923, *17*, 612–614.

6. Driscoll, G. P. The developmental status of the preschool child as a prognosis of future development. Teach. Coll., Columbia Univ., *Child Devel. Monog.*, 1933, No. 13, 111.

7. Ebert, E. H. A comparison of the original and revised Stanford-Binet scales. *J. of Psychol.*, 1941, *11*, 47–61.

8. Goodenough, F. The relation of the intelligence of preschool children to the occupation of their fathers. *Amer J. Psychol.*, 1928, *40*, 284–302.

9. Goodenough, F. L., & Anderson, J. E. Experimental child Study. New York: Century, 1931. Pp xii+546.

10. Hallowell, D. K. Stability of mental test ratings for preschool children. *J. Genet. Psychol.*, 1932, *40*, 406–421.

11. Hallowell, D. K., Validity of mental tests for young children. *J. Genet. Psychol.*, 1941, *58*, 265–288.

12. Harms, I. E., & Skeels, H. M. Reported education and verified education of mothers of infants committed to the Iowa Soldiers' Orphans' Home during 1940. Unpublished study. Iowa Child Welfare Research Station, State University of Iowa, September, 1941.

13. Hirt, Z. I. Another study of retests with the 1916 Stanford-Binet Scale. *J. Genet. Psychol.*, 1945, *66*, 83–105.

14. Hoakley, Z. P. A comparison of the results of the Stanford and Terman-Merrill revisions of the Binet. *J. Appl. Psychol.*, 1940, *24*, 75–81.

15. Layman, J. W. IQ changes in older-age children placed for foster-home care. *J. Genet. Psychol.*, 1942, *60*, 61–70.

16. Leahy, A. M. A study of certain selective factors influencing prediction of the mental status of adopted children in nature-nurture research. *J. Genet. Psychol.*, 1932, *41*, 294–329.

17. Lindquist, E. F. Statistical Analysis in Educational Research. New York: Houghton Mifflin, 1940. Pp. xii+266.

18. Merrill, M. A. The significance of IQ's on the Revised Stanford-Binet Scales. *J. Educ. Psychol.*, 1938, 641–651.

19. National Society for the Study of Education: The Twenty-Seventh Yearbook of the National Society for the Study of Education. Nature and Nurture. Part I. Their Influence Upon Intelligence. Part II. Their Influence Upon Achievement. Bloomington, Ill.: Public School Publishing, 1928. Pp. ix+465, xv+397.

20. National Society for the Study of Education: The Thirty-Ninth Yearbook of the National Society for the Study of Education. Intelligence: Its Nature and Nurture. Part I. Comparative and Critical Exposition. Part II. Original Studies and Experiments. Bloomington, Ill.: Public School Publishing, 1940. Pp. xviii+471, xviii+409.

21. Roe, A., Burks, B., & Mittelmann, B. Adult adjustment of foster children of alcoholic and psychotic parentage and the influence of the foster home. *Quart. J. Stud. Alcohol,* 1945, No. 3, p. 164.

22. Satzman, S. The influence of social and economic background on Stanford-Binet performance. *J. Soc. Psychol.*, 1940, *12*, 71–81.

23. Schmidt, B. G. Changes in personal, social, and intellectual behavior of children originally classified as feebleminded. *Psychol. Monog.*, 1946, *60*, No. 5.

24. Skeels, H. M. Mental development of children in foster homes. *J. Consult* Psychol., 1938, *2*, 33–43.

25. Skodak, M. Children in Foster Homes. *Univ. Iowa Stud. Child Welf.,* 1939, *16*, No. 1, p. 165.

26. Skodak, M., & Skeels, H. A follow-up study of children in adoptive homes. *J. Genet. Psychol.*, 1945, *66*, 21–58.

27. Snygg, D. The relation between the intelligence of mothers and of their children living in foster homes. *J. Genet. Psychol.*, 1938, *52*, 401–406.

28. Speer, G. S. The intelligence of foster children. *J. Genet. Psychol.*, 1940, *57*, 49–55.

29. Terman, L. M., & Merrill, M. A. Measuring Intelligence: A guide to the administration of the new revised Stanford-Binet tests of intelligence. Boston, Mass.: Houghton-Mifflin, 1937. Pp. xiv+461.

30. Theis, S. Van S. How foster children turn out. New York: New York State Charities Aid Assoc., 1924. P. 239.

31. Woodworth, R. S. Heredity and Environment. New York: Social Science Research Council Bulletin 47, 1941.

2.4

Unknowns in the IQ Equation: A Review of Three Monographs

Sandra Scarr-Salapatek

Environment, Heredity, and Intelligence. Compiled from the *Harvard Educational Review*. Reprint Series No. 2. Harvard Educational Review, Cambridge, Mass. 969.iv, 248 pp., illus. Paper, $4.95.

The IQ Argument. Race, Intelligence and Education. H. J. Eysenck. Library Press, New York, 1971.iv, 156 pp., illus. $5.95.

IQ. Richard Herrnstein, in the *Atlantic,* Vol. 228, No. 3, Sept. 1971, pp. 44–64.

IQ scores have been repeatedly estimated to have a large heritable component in United States and Northern European white populations.[1] Individual differences in IQ, many authors have concluded, arise far more from genetic than from environmental differences among people in these populations, at the present time, and under present environmental conditions. It has also been known for many years that white lower class and black groups have lower IQ's, on the average, than white middle class

Reprinted from *Science,* 17 Dec. 1971, *174,* 1223–1228, by permission of the author and the American Association for the Advancement of Science. Copyright 1971 by the American Association for the Advancement of Science.

groups. Most behavioral scientists comfortably "explained" these group differences by appealing to obvious environmental differences between the groups in standards of living, educational opportunities, and the like. But recently an explosive controversy has developed over the heritability of between-group differences in IQ, the question at issue being: If individual differences within the white population as a whole can be attributed largely to heredity, is it not plausible that the average differences between social class groups and between racial groups also reflect significant genetic differences? Can the former data be used to explain the latter?

To propose genetically based racial and social-class differences is anathema to most behavioral scientists, who fear any scientific confirmation of the pernicious racial and ethnic prejudices that abound in our society. But now that the issue has been openly raised, and has been projected into the public context of social and educational policies, a hard scientific look must be taken at what is known and at what inferences can be drawn from that knowledge.

The public controversy began when A. R. Jensen, in a long paper in the *Harvard Educational Review,* persuasively juxtaposed data on the heritability of IQ and the observed differences between groups. Jensen suggested that current large-scale educational attempts to raise the IQ's of lower class children, white and black, were failing because of the high heritability of IQ. In a series of papers and rebuttals to criticism, in the same journal and elsewhere,[2] Jensen put forth the hypothesis that social class and racial differences in mean IQ were due largely to differences in the gene distributions of these populations. At least, he said, the genetic-differences hypothesis was no less likely, and probably more likely, than a simple environmental hypothesis to explain the mean difference of 15 IQ points between blacks and whites[3] and the even larger average IQ differences between professionals and manual laborers within the white population.

Jensen's articles have been directed primarily at an academic audience. Herrnstein's article in the *Atlantic* and Eysenck's book (first published in England) have brought the argument to the attention of the wider lay audience. Both Herrnstein and Eysenck agree with Jensen's genetic-differences hypothesis as it pertains to individual differences and to social class groups but Eysenck centers his attention on the genetic explanation of racial group differences, which Herrnstein only touches on. Needless to say, many other scientists will take issue with them.

EYSENCK'S RACIAL THESIS

Eysenck has written a popular account of the race, social class, and IQ controversy in a generally inflammatory book. The provocative title and the disturbing cover picture of a forlorn black boy are clearly designed to tempt the lay reader into a pseudo-battle between Truth and Ignorance. In this case Truth is genetic-environmental interactionism[4] and Ignorance is naive environmentalism. For the careful reader, the battle fades out inconclusively as Eysenck admits that scientific evidence to date does not permit a clear choice of the genetic-differences interpretation of black inferiority on intelligence tests. A quick reading of the book, however, is sure to leave the reader believing that scientific evidence today strongly supports the conclusion that U.S. blacks are genetically inferior to whites in IQ.

The basic theses of the book are as follows:

1. IQ is a highly heritable characteristic in the U.S. white population and probably equally heritable in the U.S. black population.
2. On the average, blacks score considerably lower than whites on IQ tests.
3. U.S. blacks are probably a nonrandom, lower IQ, sample of native African populations.
4. The average IQ difference between blacks and whites probably represents important genetic differences between the races.
5. Drastic environmental changes will have to be made to improve the poor phenotypes that U.S. blacks now achieve.

The evidence and nonevidence that Eysenck cites to support his genetic hypothesis of racial differences make a curious assortment. Audrey Shuey's review[5] of hundreds of studies showing mean phenotypic differences between black and white IQ's leads Eysenck to conclude:

> All the evidence to date suggests the strong and indeed overwhelming importance of genetic factors in producing the great variety of intellectual differences which we observe in our culture, and much of the difference observed between certain racial groups. This evidence cannot be argued away by niggling and very minor criticisms of details which do not really throw doubts on the major points made in this book (p. 126).

To "explain" the genetic origins of these mean IQ differences he offers these suppositions:

> White slavers wanted dull beasts of burden, ready to work themselves to death in the plantations, and under those conditions intelligence would have been counter-selective. Thus there is every reason to expect that the particular sub-sample of the Negro race which is constituted of American Negroes is not an unselected sample of Negroes, but has been selected throughout history according to criteria which would put the highly intelligent at a disadvantage. The inevitable outcome of such selection would of course be a gene pool lacking some of the genes making for higher intelligence (p. 42).

Other ethnic minorities in the U.S. are also, in his view, genetically inferior, again because of the selective migration of lower IQ genotypes:

It is known (*sic*) that many other groups came to the U.S.A. due to pressures which made them very poor samples of the original populations. Italians, Spaniards, and Portuguese, as well as Greeks, are examples where the less able, less intelligent were forced through circumstances to emigrate, and where their American progeny showed significantly lower IQ's than would have been shown by a random sample of the original population (p. 43).

Although Eysenck is careful to say that these are not established facts (because no IQ tests were given to the immigrants or nonimmigrants in question?), the tone of his writing leaves no doubt about his judgment. There is something in this book to insult almost everyone except WASP's and Jews.

Despite his conviction that U.S. blacks are genetically inferior in IQ to whites, Eysenck is optimistic about the potential effects of radical environmental changes on the present array of Negro IQ phenotypes. He points to the very large IQ gains produced by intensive one-to-one tutoring of black urban children with low IQ mothers, contrasting large environmental changes and large IQ gains in intensive programs of this sort with insignificant environmental improvements and small IQ changes obtained by Headstart and related programs. He correctly observes that, whatever the heritability of IQ (or, it should be added, of any characteristic), large phenotypic changes may be produced by creating appropriate, radically different environments never before encountered by those genotypes. On this basis, Eysenck calls for further research to determine the requisites of such environments.

Since Eysenck comes to this relatively benign position regarding potential improvement in IQ's, why, one may ask, is he at such pains to "prove" the genetic inferiority of blacks? Surprisingly, he expects that new environments, such as that provided by intensive educational tutoring, will not affect the black-white IQ differential, because black children and white will probably profit equally from such treatment. Since many middle class white children already have learning environments similar to that provided by tutors for the urban black children, we must suppose that Eysenck expects great IQ gains from relatively small changes in white, middle class environments.

This book is an uncritical popularization of Jensen's ideas without the nuances and qualifiers that make much of Jensen's writing credible or at least responsible. Both authors rely on Shuey's review (note 5), but Eysenck's way of doing it is to devote some 25 pages to quotes and paraphrases of her chapter summaries. For readers to whom the original Jensen article is accessible, Eysenck's book is a poor substitute; although he defends Jensen and Shuey, he does neither a service.

It is a maddeningly inconsistent book filled with contradictory caution and incaution; with hypotheses stated both as hypotheses and as conclusions; with both accurate and inaccurate statements on matters of fact. For example, Eysenck thinks evoked potentials offer a better measure of "innate" intelligence than IQ tests. But on what basis? Recently F. B. Davis[6] has failed to find any relationship whatsoever between evoked potentials and either IQ scores or scholastic achievement, to which intelligence is supposed to be related. Another example is Eysenck's curious use of data to support a peculiar line of reasoning about the evolutionary inferiority of blacks: First, he reports that African and U.S. Negro babies have been shown to have precocious sensorimotor development by white norms (the difference, by several accounts, appears only in gross motor skills and even there is slight). Second, he notes that by three years of age U.S. white exceed U.S. black children in mean IQ scores. Finally he cites a (very slight) negative correlation, found in an early study, between sensorimotor intelligence in the first year of life and later IQ. From exaggerated statements of these various data, he concludes:

> These findings are important because of a very general view in biology according to which the more prolonged the infancy the greater in general are the cognitive or intellectual abilities of the species. This law appears to work even within a given species (p. 79).

Eysenck would apparently have us believe that Africans and their relatives in the U.S. are less highly evolved than Caucasians, whose longer infancy is related to later higher intelligence. I am aware of no evidence whatsoever to support a within-species relationship between longer infancy and higher adult capacities. . . .

HERRNSTEIN'S SOCIAL THESIS

Thanks to Jensen's provocative article, many academic psychologists who thought IQ tests belonged in the closet with the Rorschach inkblots have now explored the psychometric literature and found it to be a trove of scientific treasure. One of these is Richard Herrnstein, who from a Skinnerian background has become an admirer of intelligence tests—a considerable leap from shaping the behavior of pigeons and rats. In contrast to Eysenck's book, Herrnstein's popular account in the *Atlantic* of IQ testing and its values is generally responsible, if overly enthusiastic in parts.

Herrnstein unabashedly espouses IQ testing as "psychology's most telling accomplishment to date," despite the current controversy over the fairness of testing poor and minority group children with IQ items devised by middle class whites. His historical review of IQ test development, including tests of general intelligence and multiple abilities, is interesting and accurate. His account of the validity and usefulness of the tests centers on the fairly accurate prediction that can be made from IQ scores to academic and occupational achievement and income level. He clarifies the pattern of relationship between IQ and these criterion variables: High IQ is a necessary but not sufficient condition for high achievement, while low IQ virtually assures failure at high academic and occupational levels. About the usefulness of the tests, he concludes:

> An IQ test can be given in an hour or two to a child, and from this infinitesimally small sample of his output, deeply important predictions follow—about schoolwork, occupation, income, satisfaction

with life, and even life expectancy. The predictions are not perfect, for other factors always enter in, but no other single factor matters as much in as many spheres of life (p. 53).

One must assume that Herrnstein's enthusiasm for intelligence tests rests on population statistics, not on predictions for a particular child, because many children studied longitudinally have been shown to change IQ scores by 20 points or more from childhood to adulthood. It is likely that extremes of giftedness and retardation can be sorted out relatively early by IQ tests, but what about the 95 percent of the population in between? Their IQ scores may vary from dull to bright normal for many years. Important variations in IQ can occur up to late adolescence.[7] On a population basis Herrnstein is correct; the best early predictors of later achievement are ability measures taken from age five on. Predictions are based on correlations, however, which are not sensitive to absolute changes in value, only to rank orders. This is an important point to be discussed later.

After reviewing the evidence for average IQ differences by social class and race, Herrnstein poses the nature-nurture problem of "which is primary" in determining phenotypic differences in IQ. For racial groups, he explains, the origins of mean IQ differences are indeterminate at the present time because we have no information from heritability studies in the black population or from other, unspecified, lines of research which could favor primarily genetic or primarily environmental hypotheses. He is thoroughly convinced, however, that individual differences and social class differences in IQ are highly heritable at the present time, and are destined, by environmental improvements, to become even more so:

> If we make the relevant environment much more uniform (by making it as good as we can for everyone), then an even larger proportion of the variation in IQ will be attributable to the genes. The average person would be smarter, but intelligence would run in families even more obviously and with less regression toward the mean than we see today (p. 58).

For Herrnstein, society is, and will be even more strongly, a meritocracy based largely on inherited differences in IQ. He presents a "syllogism" (p. 58) to make his message clear.

1. If differences in mental abilities are inherited, and
2. If success requires those abilities, and
3. If earnings and prestige depend on success,
4. Then social standing (which reflects earnings and prestige) will be based to some extent on inherited differences among people.

Five "corollaries" for the future predict that the heritability of IQ will rise; that social mobility will become more strongly related to inherited IQ differences; that most bright people will be gathered in the top of the social structure, with the IQ dregs at the bottom; that many at the bottom will not have the intelligence needed for new jobs; and that the meritocracy will be built not just on inherited intelligence but on all inherited traits affecting success, which will presumably become correlated characters. Thus from the successful realization of our most precious egalitarian, political and social goals, there will arise a much more rigidly stratified society, a "virtual caste system" based on inborn ability.

To ameliorate this effect, society may have to move toward the socialist dictum, "From each according to his abilities, to each according to his needs," but Herrnstein sees complete equality of earnings and prestige as impossible because high-grade intelligence is scarce and must be recruited into those critical jobs that require it, by the promise of high earnings and high prestige. Although garbage collecting is critical to the health of the society, almost anyone can do it; to waste high IQ persons on such jobs is to misallocate scarce resources at society's peril.

Herrnstein points to an ironic contrast between the effects of caste and class systems. Castes, which established artificial hereditary limits on social mobility, guarantee the inequality of opportunity that preserves IQ heterogeneity at all levels of the system. Many bright people are arbitrarily kept down and many unintelligent people are artificially maintained at the top. When arbitrary bounds on mobility are removed, as in our class system, most of the bright rise to the top and most of the dull fall to the bottom of the social system, and IQ differences between top and bottom become increasingly hereditary. The greater the environmental equality, the greater the hereditary differences between levels in the social structure. The thesis of egalitarianism surely leads to its antithesis in a way that Karl Marx never anticipated.

Herrnstein proposes that our best strategy, in the face of increasing biological stratification, is publicly to recognize genetic human differences but to reallocate wealth to a considerable extent. The IQ have-nots need not be poor. Herrnstein does not delve into the psychological consequences of being publicly marked as genetically inferior.

Does the evidence support Herrnstein's view of hereditary social classes, now or in some future Utopia? Given his assumptions about the high heritability of IQ, the importance of IQ to social mobility, and the increasing environmental equality of rearing and opportunity, hereditary social classes are to some extent inevitable. But one can question the limits of genetic homogeneity in social class groups and the evidence for his syllogism at present.

Is IQ as highly heritable throughout the social structure as Herrnstein assumes? Probably not. In a recent study of IQ heritability in various racial and social class groups,[8] I found much lower proportions of genetic variance that would account for aptitude differences among lower class than among middle class children, in both black and white groups. Social disadvantage in prenatal and postnatal development can substantially lower phenotypic IQ and reduce the genotype-phenotype correlation. Thus, average phenotypic IQ differences between the social classes may be considerably larger than the genotypic differences.

Are social classes largely based on hereditary IQ differences now? Probably not as much as Herrnstein believes. Since opportunities for social mobility act at the phenotypic level, there still may be considerable genetic diversity for IQ at the bottom of the social structure. In earlier days arbitrary social barriers maintained genetic variability throughout the social structure. At present, individuals with high phenotypic IQ's are often upwardly mobile; but inherited wealth acts to maintain genetic diversity at the top, and nongenetic biological and social barriers to phenotypic development act to maintain a considerable genetic diversity of intelligence in the lower classes.

As P. E. Vernon has pointed out,[9] we are inclined to forget that the majority of gifted children in recent generations have come from working class, not middle class, families. A larger percentage of middle class children are gifted, but the working and lower classes produce gifted children in larger numbers. How many more disadvantaged children would have been bright if they had had the middle class gestation and rearing conditions?

I am inclined to think that intergenerational class mobility will always be with us, for three reasons. First, since normal IQ is a polygenic characteristic, various recombinations of parental genotypes will always produce more variable genotypes in the offspring than in the parents of all social class groups, especially the extremes. Even if both parents, instead of primarily the male, achieved social class status based on their IQ's, recombinations of their genes would always produce a range of offspring, who would be upwardly or downwardly mobile relative to their families of origin.

Second, since, as Herrnstein acknowledges, factors other than IQ—motivational, personality, and undetermined—also contribute to success or the lack of it, high IQ's will always be found among lower class adults, in combination with schizophrenia, alcoholism, drug addiction, psychopathy, and other limiting factors. When recombined in offspring, high IQ can readily segregate with facilitating motivational and personality characteristics, thereby leading to upward mobility for many offspring. Similarly, middle class parents will always produce some offspring with debilitating personal characteristics which lead to downward mobility.

Third, for all children to develop phenotypes that represent their best genotypic outcome (in current environments) would require enormous changes in the present social system. To improve and equalize all rearing environments would involve such massive intervention as to make Herrnstein's view of the future more problematic than he seems to believe.

RACE AS CASTE

Races are castes between which there is very little mobility. Unlike the social class system, where mobility based on IQ is sanctioned, the racial caste system, like the hereditary aristocracy of medieval Europe and the caste system of India, preserves within each group its full range of genetic diversity of intelligence. The Indian caste system was, according to Dobzhansky,[10] a colossal genetic failure—or success, according to egalitarian values. After the abolition of castes at independence, Brahmins and untouchables were found to be equally educable despite—or because of—their many generations of segregated reproduction.

While we may tentatively conclude that there are some genetic IQ differences between social class groups, we can make only wild speculations about racial groups. Average phenotypic IQ differences between races are not evidence for genetic differences (any more than they are evidence for environmental differences). Even if the heritabilities of IQ are extremely high in all races, there is still no warrant for equating within-group and between-group heritabilities.[11] There are examples in agricultural experiments of within-group differences that are highly heritable but between-group differences that are entirely environmental. Draw two random samples of seeds from the same genetically heterogeneous population. Plant one sample in uniformly good conditions, the other in uniformly poor conditions. The average height difference between the populations of plants will be entirely environmental, although the individual differences in height within each sample will be entirely genetic. With known genotypes for seeds and known environments, genetic and environmental variances between groups can be studied. But racial groups are not random samples from the same population, nor are members reared in uniform conditions within each race. Racial groups are of unknown genetic equivalence for polygenic characteristics like IQ, and the differences in environments within and between the races may have as yet unquantified effects.

There is little to be gained from approaching the nature-nurture problem of race differences in IQ directly.[12] Direct comparisons of estimated within-group heritabilities and the calculation of between-group heritabilities require assumptions that few investigators are willing to make, such as that all environmental differences are quantifiable, that differences in the environments of blacks and whites can be assumed to affect IQ in the same way in the two groups, and that differences in environments between groups can be "statistically controlled." A direct assault on race differences in IQ is vulnerable to many criticisms.

Indirect approaches may be less vulnerable. These include predictions of parent-child regression effects and admixture studies. Regression effects can be predicted to differ for blacks and whites if the two races indeed have genetically different population means. If the population mean for blacks is 15 IQ points lower than that of whites, then the offspring of high IQ black parents should show greater regression (toward a lower population mean) than the offspring of whites of equally high IQ. Similarly, the offspring of low IQ black parents should show less regression than those of white parents of equally low IQ. This hypothesis assumes that assortative mating for IQ is equal in the two races, which could be empirically determined but has not been studied as yet. Interpretable results from a parent-child regression study would also depend upon careful attention to intergenerational environmental changes, which could be greater in one race than the other.

Studies based on correlations between degree of white admixture and IQ scores *within* the black group would avoid many of the pitfalls of between-group comparisons. If serological genotypes can be used to identify persons with more and less white admixture, and if estimates of admixture based on blood groups are relatively independent of visible characteristics like skin color, then any positive correlation between degree of admixture and IQ would suggest genetic racial differences in IQ. Since blood groups have not been used directly as the basis of racial discrimination, positive findings would be relatively immune from environmentalist criticisms. The trick is to estimate individual admixture reliably. Several loci which have fairly different distributions of alleles in contemporary African and white populations have been proposed.[13] No one has yet attempted a study of this sort.

h² AND PHENOTYPE

Suppose that the heritabilities of IQ differences within all racial and social class groups were .80, as Jensen estimates, and suppose that the children in all groups were reared under an equal range of conditions. Now, suppose that racial and social class differences in mean IQ still remained. We would probably infer some degree of genetic difference between the groups. So what? The question now turns from a strictly scientific one to one of science and social policy.

As Eysenck, Jensen, and others (note 13) have noted, eugenic and euthenic strategies are both possible interventions to reduce the number of low IQ individuals in all populations. Eugenic policies could be advanced to encourage or require reproductive abstinence by people who fall below a certain level of intelligence. The Reeds[14] have determined that one-fifth of the mental retardation among whites of the next generation could be prevented if no mentally retarded persons of this generation reproduced. There is no question that a eugenic program applied at the phenotypic level of parents' IQ would substantially reduce the number of low IQ children in the future white population. I am aware of no studies in the black population to support a similar program, but some proportion of future retardation could surely be eliminated. It would be extremely important, however, to sort out genetic and environmental sources of low IQ both in racial and in social class groups before advancing a eugenic program. The request or demand that some persons refrain from any reproduction should be a last resort, based on sure knowledge that their retardation is caused primarily by genetic factors and is not easily remedied by environmental intervention. Studies of the IQ levels of adopted children with mentally retarded natural parents would be most instructive, since some of the retardation observed among children of retarded parents may stem from the rearing environments provided by the parents.

In a pioneering study of adopted children and their adoptive and natural parents, Skodak[15] reported greater *correlations* of children's IQ's with their natural than with their adoptive parents' IQ's. This statement has been often misunderstood to mean that the children's *levels* of intelligence more closely resembled their natural parents' which is completely false. Although the rank order of the children's IQ's resembled that of their mothers' IQ's, the children's IQ's were higher, being distributed, like those of the adoptive parents, around a mean above 100, whereas their natural mothers' IQ's averaged only 85. The children, in fact, averaged 21 IQ points higher than their natural mothers. If the (unstudied) natural fathers' IQ's averaged around the population mean of 100, the mean of the children's would be expected to be 94, or 12 points lower than the mean obtained. The unexpected boost in IQ was presumably due to the better social environments provided by the adoptive families. Does this mean that phenotypic IQ can be substantially changed?

Even under existing conditions of child rearing, phenotypes of children reared by low IQ parents could be markedly changed by giving them the same rearing environment as the top IQ group provide for their children. According to DeFries,[16] if children whose parents average 20 IQ points below the population mean were reared in environments such as usually are provided only by parents in the top .01 percent of the population, these same children would average 5 points *above* the population mean instead of 15 points below, as they do when reared by their own families.

Euthenic policies depend upon the demonstration that different rearing conditions can change phenotypic IQ sufficiently to enable most people in a social class or racial group to function in future society. I think there is great promise in this line of research and practice, although its efficacy will depend ultimately on the cost and feasibility of implementing radical intervention programs. Regardless of the present heritability of IQ in any population, phenotypes can be changed by the introduction of new and different environments. (One merit of Eysenck's book is the attention he gives to this point.) Furthermore, it is impossible to predict phenotypic outcomes under very different conditions. For example, in the Milwaukee Project,[17] in which the subjects are ghetto children whose mothers' IQ's are less than 70, intervention began soon after the children were born. Over a four-year period Heber has intensively tutored the children for several hours every day and has produced an enormous IQ difference between the experimental group (mean IQ 127) and a control group (mean IQ 90). If the tutored children continue to advance in environments which are radically different from their homes with retarded mothers, we shall have some measure of the present phenotypic range of reaction[18] of children whose average IQ's might have been in the 80 to 90 range. These data support Crow's comment on h^2 in his contribution to the *Harvard Educational Review* discussion (p. 158):

> It does not directly tell us how much improvement in IQ to expect from a given change in environment. In particular, it offers no guidance as to the consequences of a new kind of environmental influence. For example, conventional heritability measures for height show a value of nearly 1. Yet, because of unidentified environmental influences, the mean height in the United States and in Japan has risen by a spectacular amount. Another kind of illustration is provided by the discovery of a cure for a hereditary disease. In such cases, any information on prior heritability may become irrelevant. Furthermore, heritability predictions are less dependable at the tails of the distribution.

To illustrate the phenotypic changes that can be produced by radically different environments for children with clear genetic anomalies, Rynders[19] has provided daily intensive tutoring for Down's syndrome infants. At the age of two, these children have average IQ's of 85 while control group children, who are enrolled in a variety of other programs, average 68. Untreated children have even lower average IQ scores.

The efficacy of intervention programs for children whose expected IQ's are too low to permit full participation in society depends on their long-term effects on intelligence. Early childhood programs may be necessary but insufficient to produce functioning adults. There are critical research questions yet to be answered about euthenic programs, including what kinds, how much, how long, how soon, and toward what goals?

DOES h^2 MATTER?

There is growing disillusionment with the concept of heritability, as it is understood and misunderstood. Some who understand it very well would like to eliminate h^2 from human studies for at least two reasons. First, the usefulness of h^2 estimates in animal and plant genetics pertains to decisions about the efficacy of selective breeding to produce more desirable phenotypes. Selective breeding does not apply to the human case, at least so far. Second, if important phenotypic changes can be produced by radically different environments, then, it is asked, who cares about the heritability of IQ? Morton[20] has expressed these sentiments well:

> Considerable popular interest attaches to such questions as "is one class or ethnic group innately superior to another on a particular test?" The reasons are entirely emotional, since such a difference, if established, would serve as no better guide to provision of educational or other facilities than an unpretentious assessment of phenotypic differences.

I disagree. The simple assessment of phenotypic performance does not suggest any particular intervention strategy. Heritability estimates can have merit as indicators of the effects to be expected from various types of intervention programs. If, for example, IQ tests, which predict well to achievements in the larger society, show low heritabilities in a population, then it is probable that simply providing better environments which now exist will improve average performance in that population. If h^2 is high but environments sampled in that population are largely unfavorable, then (again) simple environmental improvement will probably change the mean phenotypic level. If h^2 is high and the environments sampled are largely favorable, then novel environmental manipulations are probably required to change phenotypes, and eugenic programs may be advocated.

The most common misunderstanding of the concept "heritability" relates to the myth of fixed intelligence: if h^2 is high, this reasoning goes, then intelligence is genetically fixed and unchangeable at the phenotypic level. This misconception ignores the fact that h^2 is a population statistic, bound to a given set of environmental conditions at a given point in time. Neither intelligence nor h^2 estimates are fixed.

It is absurd to deny that the frequencies of genes for behavior may vary between populations. For individual differences within populations, and for social-class differences, a genetic hypothesis is almost a necessity to explain some of the variance in IQ, especially among adults in contemporary white populations living in average or better environments. But what Jensen, Shuey, and Eysenck (and others) propose is that genetic racial differences are necessary to account for the current phenotypic differences in mean IQ between populations. That may be so, but it would be extremely difficult, given current methodological limitations, to gather evidence that would dislodge an environmental hypothesis to account for the same data. And to assert, despite the absence of evidence, and in the present social climate, that a particular race is genetically disfavored in intelligence is to scream "FIRE! . . . I think" in a crowded theater. Given that so little is known, further scientific study seems far more justifiable than public speculations.

NOTES

[1]For a review of studies, see L. Erlenmeyer-Kimling and L. F. Jarvik, *Science* 142, 1477 (1963). Heritability is the ratio of genetic variance to total phenotypic variance. For human studies, heritability is used in its broad sense of total genetic variance/total phenotypic variance.

[2]The *Harvard Educational Review* compilation includes Jensen's paper, How much can we boost IQ and scholastic achievement? comments on it by J. S. Kagan, J. McV. Hunt, J. F. Crow, C. Bereiter, D. Elkind, L. J. Cronbach and W. F. Brazziel, and a rejoinder by Jensen. See also A. R. Jensen, in J. Hellmuth, *Disadvantaged Child.* vol. 3 (Seattle, Wash.: Special Child Publ., 1970).

[3]P. L. Nichols, thesis, University of Minnesota (1970). Nichols reports that in two large samples of black and white children, seven-year WISC IQ scores showed the same means and distributions for the two racial groups, once social class variables were equated. These results are unlike those of several other studies, which found that matching socioeconomic status did not create equal means in the two racial groups [A. Shuey (5); A. B. Wilson, *Racial Isolation in the Public Schools,* vol. 2 (Washington, D.C.: Government Printing Office, 1967)]. In Nichols's samples, prenatal and postnatal medical care was equally available to blacks and whites which may have contributed to the relatively high IQ scores of the blacks in these samples.

[4]By interaction, Eysenck means simply $P = G + E$, or "heredity and environment acting together to produce the observed phenotype" (p. 111). He does not mean what most geneticists and behavior geneticists mean by interaction; that is, the *differential* phenotypic effects produced by various combinations of genotypes and environments, as in the interaction term of analysis-of-variance statistics. Few thinking people are not interactionists in Eysenck's sense of the term, because that's the only way to get the organism and the environment into the same equation to account for variance in any phenotypic trait. How much of the phenotypic variance is accounted for by each of the terms in the equation is the real issue.

[5]A. Shuey, *The Testing of Negro Intelligence* (New York: Social Science Press, 1966), pp. 499–519.

[6]F. B. Davis, *The Measurement of Mental Capacity through Evoked-Potential Recordings* (Greenwich, Conn.: Educational Records Bureau, 1971). "As it turned out, no evidence was found that the latency periods obtained . . . displayed serviceable utility for predicting school performance or level of mental ability among pupils in preschool through grade 8" (p. v).

[7]J. Kagan and H. A. Moss, *Birth to Maturity* (New York: Wiley, 1962).

[8]S. Scarr-Salapatek, *Science,* in press.

[9]P. E. Vernon, *Intelligence and Cultural Environment* (London: Methuen, 1969).

[10]T. Dobzhansky, *Mankind Evolving* (New Haven: Yale Univ. Press, 1962), pp. 234–238.

[11]J. Thoday, *J. Biosocial Science* 1, suppl. 3, 4 (1969).

[12]L. L. Cavalli-Sforza and W. F. Bodmer, *The Genetics of Human Populations* (San Francisco: Freeman, 1971), pp. 753–804. They propose that the study of racial differences is useless and not scientifically supportable at the present time.

[13]T. E. Reed, *Science* 165, 762 (1969); *Am. J. Hum. Genet.* 21, 1 (1969); C. MacLean and P. L. Workman, paper at a meeting of the American Society of Human Genetics (1970, Indianapolis).

[14]E. W. Reed and S. C. Reed, *Mental Retardation: A Family Study* (Philadelphia: Saunders, 1965); *Social Biol.* 18, suppl., 42 (1971).

[15]M. Skodak and H. M. Skeels, *J. Genet. Psychol.* 75, 85 (1949).

[16]J. C. DeFries, paper for the C.O.B.R.E. Research Workshop on Genetic Endowment and Environment in the Determination of Behavior (3–8 Oct. 1971, Rye, N.Y.).

[17]R. Heber, *Rehabilitation of Families at Risk for Mental Retardation* (Regional Rehabilitation Center, Univ. of Wisconsin, 1969). S. P. Strickland, *Am. Ed.* 7, 3 (1971).

[18]I. I. Gottesman, in *Social Class, Race, and Psychological Development,* M. Deutsch, I. Katz, and A. R. Jensen, Eds. (New York: Holt, Rinehart, and Winston, 1968), pp. 11–51.

[19]J. Rynders, personal communication, November 1971.

[20]N. E. Morton, paper for the C.O.B.R.E. Research Workshop on Genetic Endowment and Environment in the Determination of Behavior (3–8 Oct. 1971, Rye, N.Y.).

2.5

Is 80% of Intelligence Genetically Determined?[1]

Urie Bronfenbrenner

Although Jensen's (1969a, 1969b) argument claiming genetically based race differences in intelligence has been repeatedly and forcefully attacked (e.g., Scarr-Salapatek, 1971a; Gage, 1972; Lewontin, 1970), his thesis that 80 percent of the variation in intelligence is determined by heredity has been cited as an unassailable fact by his supporters (e.g., Eysenck, 1971; Herrnstein, 1971; Shockley, 1972) and, by and large, has been left unchallenged by his critics (e.g., Lewontin, 1970; Scarr-Salapatek, 1971b). To quote but one representative statement from each quarter, Herrnstein, a leading protagonist of Jensen's views, asserts, "Jensen concluded (as have most other experts in the field) that the genetic factor is worth about 80 percent and that only 20 percent is left to everything else" (1971, p. 56). Lewontin, in his forceful critique and rejection of Jensen's argument for genetically based race differences, takes no issue with the latter's 80 percent figure for the contribution of heredity: "I shall accept Jensen's rather high estimate without serious argument." (1970, p. 6).

Since Jensen takes his thesis of 80 percent genetic effect as the foundation both for his argument for innate differences in ability between the races, and for his contention that intervention programs with disadvantaged groups have little hope of success, it becomes important, both from the point of view of science and of social policy, to examine the evidence and line of reasoning that underlie his initial thesis. Jensen's argument rests on inferences drawn primarily from three sets of data:

1. Studies of resemblance between identical twins reared apart.
2. Studies of resemblance within families having own children vs. adopted children.
3. Studies of resemblance between identical vs. fraternal twins reared in the same home.

1. IDENTICAL TWINS REARED APART

Jensen's conclusion from these studies (Burt, 1966; Newman, Freeman, and Holzinger, 1937; Juel-Nielsen, 1964; Shields, 1962) that at least 75 percent of variance in intelligence is due to heredity is based on two critical assumptions. First, the environments of separated twins must be uncorrelated; in other words, there must be no tendency to place the twins in similar foster homes. Second, the range of environments into which twins are separated must be as great as that for unrelated children. There is evidence to indicate that neither of these assumptions is met. For example, in the Newman, Freeman, and Holzinger study (1937), rated differences between the social or educational environments of each pair were usually small, and there was a correlation of .55 between separated twins in the number of years of schooling that each received. In addition, although separated, the twins were often brought up by related persons, such as a mother and an aunt. This was true in all four of the published studies. An examination of the 128 pairs of separated twins described in these investigations revealed that 42, or a third of all the cases, were brought up by relatives. In the three researches in which such information was made available, almost half (44 percent) were found to have been brought up in the same town, and 31 percent attended the same school, usually in the same classroom.

Such findings illustrate the more general phenomenon of *selective placement,* which has been shown to operate whenever children are separated from their true parents and placed in foster homes or other settings (e.g., Skodak and Skeels, 1949). The effects of this process are manifested in correlations between the characteristics of the home into which the child was born and those of the foster home. The selection operates with respect to a variety of variables relevant to psychological development including social status, religion, ethnicity, family structure, and, in particular, values and practices of child rearing. The operation of selective placement with respect to one or more such variables cannot be ruled out in any of the studies, and the resulting correlation between the environments means that estimates of 75 percent for genetic influence are confounded by environmental variance. Further evidence for the presence and effect of correlated environments is presented below.

The evidence also calls into question the assumption that the range of environments into which twins are separated is unrestricted. Findings from adoption studies indicate "a surprising uniformity among adoptive parents" (Pringle, 1966) both in their social and psychological characteristics.

The importance of degree of environmental variation in influencing the correlation between identical twins reared apart, and hence the estimate of heritability based on this statistic, is revealed by the following examples:

1.   Among 35 pairs of separated twins for whom information was available about the community in which they lived, the correlation in Binet IQ for those raised in the same town was .83; for those brought up in different towns, the figure was .67.

2.   In another sample of 38 separated twins, tested with a combination of verbal and nonverbal intelligence scales, the correlation for those attending the same school in the same town was .87; for those attending schools in different towns, the coefficient was .66. In the same sample, separated twins raised by relatives showed a correlation of .82; for those brought up by unrelated persons, the coefficient was .63.

3.   When the communities in the preceding sample were classified as similar vs. dissimilar on the basis of size and economic base (e.g. mining vs. agricultural), the correlation for separated twins living in similar communities was .86; for those residing in dissimilar localities the coefficient was .26.

4.   In the Newman, Holzinger, and Freeman study, ratings are reported of the degree of similarity between the environments into which the twins were separated. When these ratings were divided at the median, the twins reared in the more similar environments showed a correlation of .91 between their IQ's; for those brought up in less similar environments, the coefficient was .42.

The foregoing examples by no means exhaust the environmental variables in terms of which selection can occur in the placement of separated twins. As a result, the possible contribution of environment to differences between separated twins is considerably less than it would be in a population of unrelated children.

In view of these facts, the correlation of .75 or higher between IQ's of identical twins reared apart cannot be interpreted as reflecting the proportion of variance attributable solely to heredity. There is no question that genetic factors play a significant role in the determination of intelligence. Witness the fact that the correlation in IQ between identical twins reared apart is greater than that for fraternal twins raised in the same home. But, for the reasons given, the conclusion that 70 to 80 percent of the variance in mental ability is due to heredity represents an inflated estimate.[2]

2. CHILDREN FROM ADOPTED FAMILIES

Jensen concludes that since the correlation between unrelated children brought up in the same home is only .24, the remaining fraction of .76 is due to heredity (1969a, pp. 50–51). This argument requires the rather extraordinary assumption that all differences between children raised in the same home are due only and entirely to genetic differences between them. The possible role of environment (in terms of such factors as differential treatment by parents, or varying experiences in school, peer group, or other settings) is ruled out of consideration. Clearly such an assumption is untenable.

Jensen also relies heavily on studies reporting higher similarity among own vs. adopted children, in particular the finding cited by Honzik (1957) that the correlation between IQ of adopted childern was .40 with the IQ of their true mothers but unrelated to the educational level of the foster mothers. In point of fact, in the original study from which these data were taken, Skodak and Skeels (1949) had shown that the correlations for the mothers were significantly confounded by the selective placement of children of more intelligent and better educated mothers in better foster homes. Moreover, the mean IQ of the foster children at age twelve was 106, whereas that of their true mothers was only 86. In an attempt to account for this marked difference, Skodak and Skeels analyzed the characteristics of the home environments among both true and foster families and concluded that the critical factor was the "maternal stimulation . . . and optimum security" provided in the foster homes as a group and especially in those in which the children had shown a marked gain in IQ over a ten-year period. None of these facts bearing on the substantial impact of the environment are reflected in Honzik's conclusions or Jensen's interpretation.

In sum, as in the case of identical twins reared apart, the data from studies of own vs. adopted children likewise fail to support Jensen's claim that 80 percent of the variance in intelligence is genetically determined.

3. IDENTICAL VS. FRATERNAL TWINS REARED TOGETHER

The most widely employed method for estimating the proportion of variance attributable to genetic factors is based on the comparison of within-pair differences for identical vs. same sex fraternal twins, both groups reared in their own homes. Without getting into technicalities, the basic argument runs as follows. Differences between identical twins can be attributable only to environment since their genetic endowments are the same. Differences between fraternal twins, however, reflect both environmental and genetic effects, and are larger for that reason. Accordingly, if one subtracts the former variance from the latter, the resulting difference is the amount of variance attributable to heredity. By expressing this variance as a fraction of total variance among individuals, one obtains an estimate of the proportion of total variation attributable to genetic factors in fraternal twins. Since such twins have half their genes in common, the contribution of heredity to variation among unrelated children would be about twice as large. The resulting ratio is referred to as the *heritability coefficient,* and is usually designated as h^2, after Holzinger (1929), who first developed such an index.

Drawing on the results from 25 studies of identical and fraternal twins reared together, as well as other kinship correlations, Jensen obtained a heritability coefficient of .80, which constitutes the primary basis of his claim.

The interpretation of the heritability coefficient as measuring the proportion of variance due to heredity rests on two critical assumptions. First, the environments of identical twins must be no more alike than those for fraternal twins. In the past, investigators have acknowledged that identical twins do grow up in more similar environments but have regarded the difference as a negligible one. An analysis of data published in the last decade reveals that the difference is in fact substantial and contributes significantly to the observed resemblance between identical twins. The analysis draws on three types of evidence. First, systematic studies of the environments of identical vs. fraternal twins indicate that the former are more often placed in similar situations (Husen, 1959; Jones, 1946; Koch, 1966; Shields, 1954) and are consistently treated more similarly by their parents (Scarr, 1968).

Second, if their more similar environments have significant impact, then identical twins should resemble each other most in those characteristics which are the product of common experience in the family. For example, they should be more similar in verbal than in non verbal tests of intelligence and in personality traits which relate to interpersonal relations (e.g., extraversion-introversion, dominance-submissiveness) than in intrapsychic qualities (e.g., anxiety, flexibility). Moreover, since parents do not treat boys and girls in the same way, male and female twins should differ in the abilities and traits in which they are most alike, with boys showing greater similarity, and therefore show higher heritability coefficients, in mathematical ability or dominance, and girls in languages or sociability. The results of a series of independent studies (Husen, 1959; Gottesman, 1966; Nichols, 1965a. 1965b; Scarr-Salapatek, 1969, 1971b) are in accord with these expectations.

Third, if their more similar environments affect their development, identical twins should be most alike in those social contexts in which parent-child interaction is most intensive, sustained, and focused on the development of the child. For example, the similarity of identical twins should vary directly with social class and, given present inequities in American society, should be greater among white than black families. In line with these expectations Scarr-Salapatek (1971b) reports greater similarity, and hence higher heritability coefficients, for twins from advantaged than from disadvantaged socioeconomic groups and in white as against black families. These findings indicate that for genetic potential to be realized requires an appropriately complex, sustained, and stimulating environment. In accord with this principle, twins from lower class black groups, who in our society live in suppressive environments, exhibit lower levels of ability and reduced genetic variability as reflected in lower heritability coefficients.

Independent confirmation for this conclusion comes from recent studies of intellectual development in children of mixed black-white marriages (Willerman *et al.,*

1970). From the point of view of genetic theory, which parent is of which race should make no difference for the child's mental capacity. Yet the data showed a differential effect. Specifically, if the mother was black, then the child's IQ was closer to the average IQ for blacks than if the father was black. Since it is the mother who is the primary agent of child rearing, this result is consistent with the conclusion that the suppressive environments in which blacks grow up in our society disrupts the process of socialization, with the result that the child of the impoverished environment fails to realize his genetic potential.

The foregoing findings indicate that, contrary to Jensen's assumptions, the greater similarity of environments for identical twins contributes substantially to their greater psychological resemblance. As a result, the heritability coefficient again reflects substantial environmental as well as genetic variance.

Finally, Jensen's argument suffers from an even more serious restrictive condition. To the extent that it is a valid measure, the heritability coefficient reflects the relative contribution of genetic and environmental variance *within* but not *between* families. Yet, it is precisely *between families* that most of the differences in ability occur. It may be true that individual differences among children *within the same family* are more influenced by genetic than by environmental factors, but such a finding implies nothing about variation among children from *different* families. Evidence for the effect of such environmental restriction on the magnitude of heritability coefficients based only on samples of twins can be obtained from data cited by Jensen himself. For example, twins are necessarily of the same age, a circumstance which obviously reduces differences in their environmental experience. Utilizing data provided by Jensen (1969a), one can compute a heritability coefficient from a comparison of siblings with unrelated children raised in the same family. Siblings, of course, are no more alike than fraternal twins. Just as identical twins have about twice as many genes in common as fraternal twins, so do the latter have about twice as many genes in common as children who are completely unrelated. Accordingly, from this point of view, the genetic contribution to differences in intelligence, as measured by the heritability coefficient, should be approximately the same in both cases. Of course, the critical element is the fact that we are now dealing with children who, though raised in the same family, are of different ages. Although just as similar genetically as fraternal twins, they do not look as alike *at the same point in time.* Hence they are more likely to be treated differently than fraternal twins are, so that the environmental variation is greater. This fact is reflected in the heritability coefficient computed by Jensen's formula from the data cited in his article on siblings vs. unrelated children raised together. The obtained estimate of genetic effect was 68 percent, clearly lower than the 80 percent derived by Jensen from the data on twins. Which value is correct? Obviously, the answer depends on the range of variation present in the environment.

But the contribution of the environment to differences among children raised in the same family is of course less than would obtain for children raised in different households. As Newman, Freeman, and Holzinger pointed out in their pioneering study (1937, p. 347), an unbiased estimate of the relative contribution of heredity and environment to differences between children raised in *different* families could be obtained from a heritability coefficient based on separated identical and separated fraternal twins. They further speculated that, under these circumstances, the percentage of genetic effect, "instead of being about .75 as for twins reared together, might be of the order of .50 or even smaller. . . . The relative role of heredity and environment is thus a function of the type of environment." (p. 347).

It is surprising that no one has followed up on this suggestion. Nor do any published data exist on the degree of similarity between fraternal twins reared apart. Fehr (1969), however, has carried out an alternate analysis comparing separated identical twins with siblings reared apart. As Fehr acknowledges (p. 576), such a comparison is biased toward heredity since identical twins are probably more likely to come from and be placed in correlated environments and, unlike siblings, are always of the same age and sex. As a result, a heritability coefficient based on a comparison of identical twins reared apart with separated siblings would be higher than one in which the contrast group was separated, same-sex fraternal twins. Even so, the estimate of heritability obtained by Fehr was .53, a value substantially below Jensen's figure of .80. Fehr's result also lends support to Newman, Freeman, and Holzinger's prediction of a coefficient of ".50 or even smaller" for separated twins of both types.

But even this estimate can not be generalized to the population at large, in view of the restricted range of environments into which foster children are placed.

We have now concluded our reexamination of evidence and assumptions underlying the thesis of Jensen and others that 80 percent of the variation in human intelligence is genetically determined. The results of our analysis lead to rejection of this thesis both on theoretical and empirical grounds. But what of the fundamental question to which Jensen was so ready to supply an answer? What can be said about the relative contributions of heredity and environment to psychological development? On the basis of the analysis we have undertaken, several conclusions appear to be in order:

1. There can be no question that genetic factors play a substantial role in producing individual differences in mental ability. Many research findings testify to the validity of this statement. Perhaps the most impressive is the fact that the similarity of identical twins reared apart is clearly greater than that of fraternal twins reared together.

2. It is impossible to establish a single fixed figure representing the proportion of variation in intelligence, or any other human trait, independently attributable to heredity vs. environment. Even if one assumes the absolute degree of genetic variation to be a constant, the fact that the relative contribution of each factor depends on the degree of variability present in given environment and its capacity to evoke innate potential means that the influence of genetic factors will vary from one environmental context to another. *Specifically, whereas the impact of hereditary endowment is considerable in accounting for individual differences among children raised in the same family, the relative importance of the environment becomes much greater in accounting for differences among children raised in different families. This fact is of*

special importance since the greatest variation in human abilities occurs across families rather than within them.

3. Any attempt to identify the independent contribution of heredity and environment to human development confronts the fact of a substantial correlation between these two factors. Moreover, the relation is not unidirectional. It is true, as Jensen points out (1969a, p. 38), that parents of better genetic endowment are likely to create better environments for their children, and that the child, as a function of his genetic characteristics, in fact partially determines the environment that he experiences. The genetically instigated greater environmental similarity of identical vs. fraternal twins is a case in point. But Scarr-Salapatek's (1971b) research on this same phenomenon provides dramatic evidence that the environment can also determine the extent to which genetic potential is realized. This reverse relationship calls into question the legitimacy of including covariance between heredity and environment in the proportion of variance due solely to genetic factors, as Jensen does (1969a p.39). The impossibility of assigning this covariance unequivocally to one or the other source is further ground for the conclusion that a fixed, single figure representing the proportion of variance attributable to genetic factors cannot be established.

4. For genetic potential to find expression in terms of level and diversity, requires an appropriately complex and stimulating environment. This fact leads to a new and somewhat ironic interpretation of measures of heritability. Since heritability coefficients are lowest in environments that are most inpoverished and suppressive, and highest in those that are most stimulating and enriched, *the heritability coefficient should be viewed not solely as a measure of the genetic loading underlying a particular ability or trait, but also as an index of the capacity of a given environment to evoke and nurture the development of that ability or trait.*

5. Even when the heritability coefficient for a trait in a particular environment is very high, this in no way restricts what might occur in some new environment that might come about or be deliberately constructed. Specifically, contrary to Jensen's contention, *a high heritability coefficient for a particular ability or trait cannot be taken as evidence that the ability or trait in question cannot be substantially enhanced through environmental intervention.* An instructive example is cited by Gage (1972) in a reply to Shockley and Jensen. Gage calls attention to the striking gain in stature exhibited by adults in Western countries over the past 200 years as a function of improved conditions of health and nutrition. He notes further that the heritability of height as determined from twin studies is about .90—higher than that for IQ. "If this high heritability index had been derived in the year 1800, would it then have been safe to conclude that height cannot be increased through environmental influences? If that conclusion had been drawn, it would have been wrong." (Gage, 1972, p. 422).

6. If the heritability coefficient for a given ability or trait in a particular environment is low in comparison with other social contexts, this means that the environment is inadequate for the development of that capacity. Specifically, the low heritability

coefficients and depressed levels of measured intelligence, observed in disadvantaged populations, especially Blacks, indicate that the environments in which these persons live do not permit the realization of their genetic potential.

7. In terms of implications for social policy, the foregoing conclusions argue against reliance on methods of selective mating and population control and in favor of measure aimed at improving existing environments, and even creating new ones better suited to evoke and nurture the expression of genetic potential.

Thus, our analysis has brought us to a paradoxical conclusion. An inquiry into the heritability of inborn capacities has shed new light on the power and potential of the environment to bring about the fuller realization of genetic possibilities.

NOTES

[1]A more detailed and technical analysis of evidence and argument bearing on the issues raised in this article is contained in Bronfenbrenner (1974).
[2]Similar considerations apply to the interpretation of data on adopted vs. own children. The fact that intrafamilial correlations in IQ tend to be higher for families with own than with adopted children is in part a function of the greater homogeneity of adoptive parents as a group both in terms of social background characteristics and values. Hence the greater similarity among blood related vs. adoptive family members cannot be attributed solely or even primarily to genetic factors.

REFERENCES

Bronfenbrenner, U. Nature with nurture: A reinterpretation of the evidence. In A. Montaju (Ed.) *Race and IQ,* New York: Oxford University Press. In Press, 1974.

Burt C. The genetic determination of differences in intelligence: A study of monozygotic twins reared together and apart. *British Journal of Psychology,* 1966, *57,* 137–153.

Eysenck, H. J. *The IQ argument.* New York: Library Press, 1971.

Fehr, F. S. Critique of hereditarian accounts. *Harvard Educational Review,* 1969, 39, 571–580.

Gage, N. L. I.Q. heritability, race differences, and educational research. *Phi Delta Kappan,* January, 1972, 297–307.

Gottesman, I. I. Genetic variance and adaptive personaiity traits. *Journal of Child Psychology and Psychiatry,* 1966, *7,* 199–208.

Herrnstein, R. IQ. *Atlantic Monthly,* September, 1971, 43–64.

Holzinger, J. The relative effect of nature and nurture influences on twin differences. *Journal of Educational Psychology,* 1929, *20,* 241–248.

Honzik, M. P. Developmental studies of parent-child resemblance in intelligence. *Child Development*, 1957, *28*, 215–228.

Husen, T. *Psychological twin research*. Stockholm: Almqvist & Wiksell, 1959.

Jensen, A. R. Estimation of the limits of heritability of traits by comparison of monozygotic and dizygotic twins. *Proceedings of the National Academy of Sciences*, 1967, *58*, 149–157.

Jensen, A. R. How much can we boost I.Q. and scholastic achievement? *Harvard Educational Review*, Winter, 1969, 1–123. (a)

Jensen, A. R. Reducing the heredity-environment uncertainty: A reply. *Harvard Educational Review*, 1969, *39*, 449–483. (b)

Jones, A. G. Environmental influences on mental development. In Earl Carmichael (Ed.), *Manual of child psychology*. New York: Wiley & Sons, 1946, 582–632.

Juel-Nielsen, N. *Individual and environment*. Copenhagen: Munksgaard, 1965.

Koch, H. L. *Twins and twin relations*. Chicago: University of Chicago Press, 1966.

Lewontin, R. C. Race and intelligence. *Bulletin of the Atomic Scientists*, March, 1970, *26*, 2–8.

Newman, H. H., Freeman, F. N., & Holzinger, K. J. *Twins: A study of heredity and environment*, Chicago: University of Chicago Press, 1937.

Nichols, R. C. The inheritance of general and specific abilities. *National Merit Scholarship Corporation Research Reports*, 1965, *1*, 1–13. (a)

Nichols, R. C. The National Merit twin study. In G. Vandenberg (Ed.), *Methods and goals in human behavior genetics*. New York: Academic Press, 1965, 231–245. (b)

Pringle, M. L. K. *Adoption—facts and fallacies*. London, England: Longmans, Green, 1966.

Scarr, S. Environmental bias in twin studies. *Eugenics Quarterly*, 1968, *15*, 34–40.

Scarr, S. Social introversion-extraversion. *Child Development*, 1969, *40*, 823–833.

Scarr-Salapatek, S. Unknowns in the IQ equation. *Science*, 1971, *174*, 1223–1228. (a)

Scarr-Salapatek, S. Race, social class and IQ. *Science*, 1971, *174*, 1285–1295. (b)

Shields, J. Personality differences and neurotic traits in normal twin school children. *Eugenics Review*, 1954, *45*, 213–247.

Shields, J. *Monozygotic twins brought up apart and brought up together*. London: Oxford University Press, 1962. Shockley, W. A. debate challenge: Geneticity is 80% for white identical twins I.Q.'s. *Phi Delta Kappan*, March, 1972, 415–419.

Skodak, M., & Skeels, H. M. A final follow-up study of one hundred adopted children. *Journal of genetic psychology*, 1949, *75*, 85–125.

Willerman, L., Naylor, A. F. & Myrianthopoulos, N. C. Intellectual development of children from interracial matings. *Science*, 1970, *170*, 1329–1331.

part three
INFANCY

In the history of human development, the past decade may well come to be known as the period in which science discovered the human infant, his powers, and his vulnerabilities. From a scientific point of view, infancy was long regarded as a rather dull affair in which a largely passive organism was maturing primarily as a function of inexorable, internally mediated neurological development. The studies included in this section document the demise of this traditional view. The infant emerges not only as vulnerable to external influences, even while still in the womb, but also as an active agent, who, given minimum support from his environment, can recoup and even shape his own destiny.

This double theme is first demonstrated by Willerman in his discussion of the interaction between biological and social influences on human development. The power of both the infant and his environment to shape the course of development in the early weeks of life is then illustrated in a series of studies of mother-infant interaction. Both Korner and Grobstein, working with neonates, and Moss, observing infants at three weeks and three months, call attention to the critical part played by the infant in the formation of a system of mother-infant interaction which then develops its own momentum. Caudill and Frost, as if in complement, demonstrate the impact of cultural factors on the infant's behavior.

The possibility that the mother-child system differs for male and female infants is explored by Goldberg and Lewis, who demonstrate marked sex differences in the first year of life. Tulkin and Kagan then take us back to a consideration of the child's larger environment and show how social class affects the mother's treatment of her child and his corresponding reactions.

The nature of the mother-infant bond, and the consequences of its disruption, are reflected in the final group of papers. Spitz offers a classical study of the effects of maternal separation, whereas Gil provides a view of the reality of violence in the lives of many of the nation's children. Finally, the reversibility of retardation associated with maternal separation is demonstrated by Skeels in his pioneer study of the adult status of institutionalized children.

3.1

Biosocial Influences on Human Development

Lee Willerman

The confluence of heredity and environment begins from the moment of conception. At every instant these forces provide interacting challenges and responses that mostly go undetected by the outer world. For example, it is almost impossible to assess directly the health of a fetus. Except for heart sounds and fetal position, almost all information about its status is inferred from the mother's condition. That a pregnant woman, appearing only mildly ill, can be carrying a desperately sick fetus is seen in the tragic consequences of rubella, and the frequency of apparently healthy mothers carrying abnormal fetuses is unknown. In those rare instances when family histories suggest genetic or chromosomal aberrations, aminocentesis can perhaps be utilized, but these occasions are still too few and far between. There is no good substitute for direct measurement of the fetus, and it is likely that any substantial progress in the future will require new techniques for such measurement.

The present report begins with the observation that racial and socioeconomic differences in the incidence of maternal complications during pregnancy parallel the findings of mean differences in IQ between races and socioeconomic groups.(19) In both instances, those worse off are in the lowest socioeconomic categories for their race and, even when attempts are made to control "statistically" for social class differences, Negroes fare worse than whites.

The present effort attempts to amplify on that parallel and deals with social and biological influences on prenatal and postnatal functioning. It presents recently developed data on (1) socioeconomic and race correlates of the sex ratio; (2) birthweight as a perinatal correlate of IQ; and (3) some efforts to accelerate intellectual functioning through biological and environmental influences.

The Collaborative Study from which the present data are drawn is sponsored by the National Institute of Neurological Diseases and Stroke. The Study, still in progress, has included pregnant women who registered for prenatal care and delivered approximately 56,000 infants at twelve collaborating hospitals throughout the country. The children are now being followed until eight years of age with batteries of neurological, speech, language, hearing, and psychological tests.

The socioeconomic index (SEI) employed throughout this paper for Collaborative Study data is a modification of the Bureau of the Census Socioeconomic Index. (17) It is based on the average of a set of ratings on head of household education, occupation, and family income. Though the SEI does not include other variables that would probably add validity to a measure of socioeconomic status, such as housing

Reprinted from Willerman, Lee. Biosocial influences on human development. *American Journal of Orthopsychiatry*, 1972, *42*, 452–462. Copyright ©, The American Orthopsychiatric Association, Inc. Reproduced by permission.

quality and density, family nutrition, and intellectual stimulation around the home,(2) it has the advantage of being available for almost the entire Collaborative Study population and is similar to other measures in wide use.

SEX RATIO, RACE, AND SOCIAL CLASS

Predicated on the assumption that male fetuses are more suscepti- ble to adverse prenatal conditions than are female fetuses, it was hypothesized that with increasingly adverse prenatal conditions, there should be a decrease in the proportion of male births relative to female births. This then might serve as an indirect means of estimating adverse prenatal environ- mental influences. The conventional way of designating this sex proportion is by the secondary sex ratio, which is equal to the number of male births divided by the number of female births multiplied by 100. A value of 100 then means that equal numbers of males and females were born, a value greater than 100 means that more males than females were born, and a value less than 100 means that less males than females were born.

It has long been established that the sex ratio for whites exceeds that for Negroes, but it has been impossible to determine whether this difference is primarily genetic or environmental in origin. Conceivably, poorer prenatal environments are associated more strongly with being black, and given the greater vulnerability of the male fetus, the sex ratio depression among Negroes might be the result of dispropor- tionate numbers of male fetuses aborting.

FIGURE 1. SEX RATIO BY RACE AND SOCIOECONOMIC INDEX

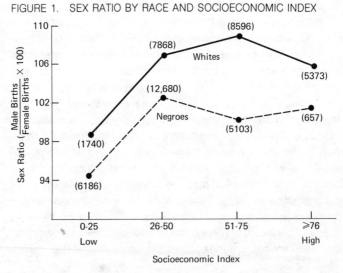

Ns given in parentheses.

To investigate this possibility, data from the Collaborative Study on the sex ratio at birth for Negroes and whites are displayed in Figure 1. The idea is that with lower

SEI, there should be an increase in adverse prenatal conditions, and consequently a decrease in the sex ratio.

These sex ratio data show roughly the same pattern as a function of socioeconomic status and race as that for maternal pregnancy complications and IQ. The lowest sex ratios are in the lowest socioeconomic group and, even when statistical controls for socioeconomic status are provided, the Negro population still tends to have lower sex ratios.

The curves for both races indicate a depression in the sex ratio for the lowest SEI groups ($X^2 = 15.3$, $p < .01$, $df = 3$) with the sex ratio for whites always exceeding that for the Negroes within the same SEI category. Though this latter finding is not novel and has been reported before, (5) it is interesting to note that even among the highest SEI category the sex ratio for whites exceeds that for Negroes. The fact that the sex ratio among the higher SEI Negro group is also depressed relative to most of the white population is difficult to explain. It may be that large numbers of these Negro women during their formative years were in the lower social strata and have retained some legacy of poverty from that time.

Within a race, the sex ratios for the three higher SEI categories do not differ significantly from one another and they lend support to the notion that there may be a threshold above which excess males begin to abort. The most striking illustration of this sex ratio depression for the lowest SEI category is found in the sex ratio distribution for the hospital with the lowest average socioeconomic status in the Collaborative Study. This southern hospital has only Negro patients, and all mothers receive free prenatal care from the time of first registration at the clinic. The sex ratio for births in the 0–25 SEI category for this Negro population is 82 (n = 1039), with no evidence of a sex ratio depression among the higher SEI groups there.

The factors responsible for the reduced sex ratios for the lowest SEI are unknown. Neither higher mean maternal ages nor higher birth orders, which have been shown by others to be related to depression in the sex ratio,(15) were found in this low SEI category. Relevant variables may involve SEI correlates of poor antenatal care such as poorer maternal nutrition or increased infection rates among the poor.

Caution must be exercised, however, before assuming that the observed sex ratio depresssion is solely environmental in origin and due to excessive numbers of males being killed off *in utero*. Ciocco, (5) using population statistics gathered from seven states over a ten-year period beginning in 1925, was unable to demonstrate that a depression in the sex ratio for live births was related to an increase in the stillbirth sex ratio in that population, as might be predicted from such a theory. Information on sex ratios for early abortions, which account for the great majority of fetal deaths, was lacking in that study, so the results are not themselves conclusive.

BIRTHWEIGHT AS A PERINATAL CORRELATE OF IQ

Do prenatal influences have effects on postnatal behavioral functioning among the liveborn in the absence of pregnancy complications and prematurity? One question of concern to large numbers of researchers is that of performance of Negroes on IQ tests. Controversy continues over whether the lower mean IQ's of Negroes are due largely to genetic or to environmental differences between the races. If there are more adverse prenatal influences on the poor, however, and a greater proportion of Negroes than whites are poor, it could be that adverse prenatal influences account for part of the reduction in mean Negro IQ.(15) Pasamanick and Knobloch(20) suggested from retrospective data, that prenatal complications are associated with an increased incidence of mental retardation and behavior disorder. The study now to be reported focuses on high IQ Negroes and asks whether birth weight distinguishes them from their lower IQ counterparts.

In one institution, each of the four-year-old Negro children with Stanford-Binet IQs of 120 or greater (n = 40) was matched to six others by age, race, sex, and SEI.(30) One case in each of the IQ categories ≤69, 70–79, 80–89, 90–99, 100–109, and 110–119 was matched to the 120 IQ subject. In some instances, always among the two lowest IQ groups, it was impossible to find a suitable match so that all frequencies were not always equal to 40. The birth weights of these children as a function of their IQ categories were subjected to a one-way analysis of variance, first with all children, regardless of their gestational ages, and then excluding all cases premature by gestational age (≤37 weeks as determined from the mother's report of her last menstrual period).

FIGURE 2. MEAN BIRTH WEIGHT BY IQ CATEGORY FOR NEGRO FOUR-YEAR-OLD CHILDREN

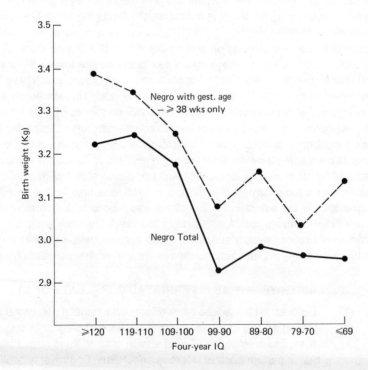

Figure 2 shows mean birth weights both with and without the premature children. Looking first at the means for all the children it can be seen that those with the higher IQ's tend to have the highest birth weights (F = 11.2, $p < .001$ on 1 and 276 degrees of freedom). The slope of the curve tends to be much the same when the prematures by gestational age are excluded (F = 8.0, $p < .005$ on 1 and 207 degrees of freedom). The higher IQ children have greater birth weights than do the lower IQ children, though some inversions in the curve occur. Whereas the 120 IQ group had the highest mean birth weight, the ≤ 69 IQ group did not have the lowest birth weight. The fact that the results are still significant when those premature by gestational age are excluded suggests that it is the low birth weight and not the short gestational age that is associated with the low IQ. Parallel data on Collaborative Study whites tended to confirm the results for Negroes. Among the whites there was an IQ-birth weight relationship of borderline significance at the .10 level for the total group. However, excluding the prematures by gestational age strengthened this relationship slightly, with the results being significant at the .05 level.

These results suggest that higher birth weight antedates high IQ performance and that excluding gestationally premature children does not substantially alter the IQ-birth weight relationship.

One problem in the interpretation of these data is the possibility that a good prenatal environment varies with a good postnatal environment and that mothers who provide good prenatal care to their fetuses are also better able to provide good postnatal environments. If true, higher birth weights then may be a nonessential manifestation of this relationship. Matching the high IQ children with lower IQ children on SEI should tend to minimize this possibility, but, as indicated above, the SEI is only a crude measure of family life. The mechanism behind this relationship is unknown; but it may be that the higher birth weight infant is less susceptible to adverse postnatal environmental influence.

In the Collaborative Study, SEI has been found to correlate positively with four-year Stanford-Binet IQ within the Negro population as within the white group. Those in the Negro group seem to average about 8–13 points lower at all socioeconomic levels than their white counterparts of the same SEI.(30)

That the lower IQ's among Negroes is not simply a function of such gross indexes of social class as parental occupation, education, and income, seems clear from Collaborative Study data. When one obtains mean IQ scores for the children of Negroes who have good jobs, adequate incomes, and a minimum of some college education, lower mean scores compared to whites still exist. The implication of such results is that higher parental socioeconomic status among Negroes does not confer upon the child that degree of advantage conferred upon whites of high socioeconomic status.

Evidence on this point comes from those highest SEI Negroes whose indexes were greater than 8.0. This value is obtained by only 1 percent of Negroes and 10 percent of whites in the Collaborative Study. The Negro children whose parents met this criterion were compared to the entire white population. Mean four-year Stanford-Binet IQ for this subgroup of high-SEI Negroes (n = 131) was 102.1, whereas the mean IQ for the entire Collaborative Study white population on the Stanford-Binet was 104.2 (n = 10,104). There is little reason to believe these results to be atypical and not representative of the findings in the general population, since Myrianthopoulos and French(17) have shown, using data from the Bureau of the Census, that with regard to the distribution of socioeconomic status, Negroes in the Collaborative Study are quite similar to the entire Negro population in the United States.

In view of the often reported finding of increased risk associated with prematurity, it's important to note that there is evidence that the mean gestational age of Negro children is somewhat shorter than that of white children, even when efforts are made at controlling for SEI. Those Negroes from the highest quartile of SEI (n = 299) in one northern institution were identified, and the gestational ages of these infants were calculated from mother's reports of their last menstrual period. These Negro mothers were in the highest quartile of social class for the 3000 plus whites there also. The high-SEI Negro children averaged three days shorter gestational age than all the whites in that institution (t = 4.12, p < .001).

An interpretation that there is a genetically determined difference between the races in gestational age, should be treated with skepticism at this point since there are data suggesting that nutrition of the prospective mother during her own formative years may affect her ability optimally to carry her child and thus increase the likelihood of prematurity.(7) Such a factor could well relate to SEI and points out the need for intergenerational studies of prenatal influences.

There are, in addition, factors occurring more frequently among the poor, such as close spacing of children, which may operate adversely on the latter born child via a suboptimal prenatal environment. Holley et al. (14) showed that children conceived within three months after the birth of an older sib have lower birth weights, eight-month Bayley Mental and Motor scores, and Stanford-Binet IQ's than do children matched for race, sex, SEI, and institution of birth, and who were conceived at least two years after the birth of an older sib. That this effect on the closely spaced child operated via some biological mechanism is suggested by the lowered birth weights in these children. It also suggests that increased spacing between births may be biologically advantageous and that a positive consequence of family planning programs may be to increase the likelihood of healthy children being born.

BIOLOGICAL CORRELATES OF HIGH ACHIEVEMENT

We have more questions than answers regarding the nature of intelligence and how it may be influenced. From the biological side, a little known bit of information, if confirmed, may provide a most exciting clue to the understanding of this question. Retinoblastoma, a rare tumor of childhood (approximately 1 in 25,000 live births) often results in bilateral blindness. The familial form of this tumor is believed to be transmitted as an autosomal dominant with incomplete penetrance. Thurrell and Josephson(25) were the first to document strikingly high intelligence among retinoblastoma subjects (median IQ = 128, n = 14). In a larger controlled study, Williams (32) reported that 50 English school children bilaterally blinded from retinoblastoma averaged 119.7 IQ, whereas children blinded from other causes averaged 102.8 IQ, and sighted controls obtained a mean of 102.7 IQ. Besides the elevated IQ in the retinoblastoma group only one child with retinoblastoma had an IQ below 100, though the expected number of children with IQ's below 100 was approximately 20–25 in this population. These results strongly suggest a unique association between the tumor itself and high intelligence. Thus far, only bilaterally blind children have been tested and it remains to be demonstrated that sighted retinoblastoma children also have superior performance. But the fascinating aspect of this finding is the possibility that either a single major gene or some specific metabolite secreted by the tumor is associated with high intelligence. The current view is that the gifted are at the extreme end on a polygenic continuum and it would be important to demonstrate that some giftedness may not be polygenic, but rather due to a single gene. Investigations into the biochemical correlates of retinoblastoma have already begun, but as yet only suggestive evidence has been developed. One report (3) suggested, by a nonsignificant trend, that there may be elevated amounts of norepinephrine metabolites associated with these tumors.

Another disease perhaps associated with high IQ is asthma. In a survey of asthmatic children in Aberdeen, Dawson et al.(6) found that asthmatic children at seven years had higher IQ's than did controls, after controlling for social class. That this disease may have a significant inherited component has been long suggested.(26)

Other sources of evidence may provide additional clues to the search for correlates of high performance. There have been a number of reports suggesting a positive relationship between serum uric acid levels and high achievement. Extremely high levels of uric acid are found in gout, long believed to be a "rich man's" disease and associated in anecdotal reports with high achievement. These studies, (16) however, have not shown any meaningfully significant relationships between intelligence and urate levels. Also, these reports of elevated uric acid levels have not shown it to be a true ontogenetic variable since no studies have been done on elevated uric acid levels and achievement in children. These relationships nevertheless merit full exploration because high achievement motivation can often substitute for what is lacking in intelligence.

In view of some reports of significant correlations between birth weight and intelligence, it is of interest to note that Churchill et al.(4) showed a correlation between maternal amino acid blood levels and birth weights of the children in a population of Negro mothers living in poverty. However, maternal protein intake by a dietician's estimates bore no significant relationship to either the blood amino acid levels or the birth weights of the children. Protein intake was estimated from the pregnant woman's recall of what she had eaten during the previous 24 hours. The unreliability of that method of determining protein intake was clear to the authors, and such results need to be replicated with finer techniques before they can be accepted.

Direct manipulation of the biochemistry of the organism has brought to light some significant insights and dangers of accelerating behavioral development through this mode. On the positive side, Harrell et al., (11) in a double blind study, have shown that the mothers given vitamin supplementation during pregnancy and lactation had children with higher preschool IQ's compared to the children of mothers given placebo. This study is extremely important and needs to be replicated.

On the other hand, Schapiro's (24) results suggest that a cautious approach be taken toward biochemical behavioral acceleration. He administered thyroxine to neonatal rats and found that during infancy these animals behaved similarly to more mature rats on a variety of biochemical, anatomical, and behavioral measures. Interestingly enough, these animals, although accelerated learners during infancy, were slower learners than were controls at a later age (between 35 and 45 days). Schapiro suggested that the thyroxine "appears to have advanced the brain prematurely through those critical ontogenetic stages associated with plasticity and the gradual acquisition of an expanding behavioral repertoire" (p. 225). Holden *et al.* (12) have reported results suggesting similar superior neurological and behavioral status in human infants whose mothers were treated during pregnancy with desiccated thyroid extract because of subclinical thyroid gland deficiency. It will be worthwhile to test these children later to see if this advanced status is maintained. Because prolonged infantilization seems to be a characteristic of humans, acceleration of infant development via some biochemical treatment may not be unequivocally desirable if Schapiro's findings are correct.

Exposing the organism to "positive" environmental experiences may be a different story, however. Some studies in both rats and humans have suggested that environmental enrichment, besides producing superior behavioral achievement, results in prolonged infantilization. Altman *et al.* (1) have shown that rats handled early in infancy have brains that weigh less than the brains of unhandled control infant rats. Also these handled rats have a higher "rate in the acquisition of late forming, short-axoned neurons." These authors hypothesize that delayed maturation "extends the time available for the exertion of environmental modulatory influences on the organization of the brain."

White (28) has reported some data that are nicely consistent with the Altman *et al.* (1) finding of delayed maturation among supposedly "enriched" animals. White found a delay in onset of sustained hand regard in infants exposed to environmental enrichment (though these same infants were advanced in visual attention). White suggested that the delay in hand regard was "partly a function of the availability of interesting objects" that helped to distract the infants from focusing on their hands. Without knowing the experiential histories of these infants, the delay might have been viewed more negatively.

Somewhat at variance to the Altman *et al.* data are the findings of the research team at Berkeley.(23) In rats, a cognitively enriched environment was associated with heavier brains, particularly cortex.

INTERACTIONS BETWEEN BIOLOGICAL AND SOCIAL STATUS

Turning now to social influences on intellectual functioning, the evidence seems very convincing that high social class among whites can compensate for impairments in biological status. Drillien(8) found that social class differences in developmental quotient were approximately of the same magnitude at four years of age as they had been at six months of age among full-term infants; among very premature infants, differences in developmental quotient between the higher and lower class children were far greater at four years than they had been at six months. Similarly, Werner *et al.* (27) assessed severity of complications around delivery for a large number of neonates. Using the Cattell Intelligence Scale at 20 months, it was found that social class was associated with only small differences in IQ among deliveries that had been uncomplicated, but that social class was strongly related to IQ among deliveries with severe complications.

Willerman *et al.* (29) demonstrated that in whites the incidence of four-year IQ's less than 80 for infants originally in the lowest quartiles of mental and motor development at eight months were strongly related to the social class of their parents. Retarded eight-month-old infants from the lowest social class were seven times more likely to have four-year IQ's below 80 than were similarly retarded eight-month-old infants from the highest social class when they were again tested at four years of age. The converse finding was that infants in the highest quartiles in mental and motor development at eight months did not differ in the incidence of IQ's below 80 at four years of age. The implication of such results is that biological impairments in infancy do not have univocal outcomes with respect to IQs measured later, and that there is often cause for optimism with respect to the intellectual fate of some impaired infants, if given a stimulating environment.

COMMENT

Other factors besides sex ratios, maternal pregnancy complications, and IQ vary roughly in the same manner with race and social class. Birth weight increases with increasing social class but Negro infants weigh less than whites at all social class levels.(30) Father absence also follows the same pattern, with the rates for Negroes much higher than those for whites.(2)

It seems likely that these similarities in pattern have multiple origins, but often it appears that the source of the differences between Negroes and whites is in the inadequate assessment of social class. As Pettigrew says,

> Indeed, the economic floor for Negroes . . . is so distinctly below the floor of whites that not even comparison of lower class Negroes with lower class whites is generally an adequate test of racial factors. (p. 70)

Because there is considerable evidence of plasticity in the developing nervous system, early diagnosis of defect may therefore provide the opportunity for environmental compensation. It would appear that a good place to look for effective methods of remediation is in the child rearing practices of the higher social classes. These classes only rarely have children with intellectual impairments, even when there is definite central nervous damage. For example, Holden and Willerman(13) found that only 5 percent of neurologically abnormal one-year-old infants (excluding children with Down's syndrome) were retarded at age four, whereas 35 percent of similarly damaged infants from lower class homes were retarded at four. None of the higher social class and only 14 percent of the lower social class matched controls were retarded at age four. Though there were no data on whether neurological diagnoses themselves had changed during that interval, the fact that so few damaged children from the higher class were retarded is cause for optimism.

There are other indications that it is the maternal child rearing practices that are crucial in determining the intellectual fate of children. Reed and Reed (22) showed that in matings where the tested intelligence of the mother fell in the retarded range and the father in the average range, the children were two and one-half times more likely to be retarded than if the mother was of average intelligence and the father retarded.

In a different context, the maternal effect hypothesis was investigated by looking at the intelligence test performance of four-year-old offspring of interracial matings.(31) The supposition was that if intelligence test data were available, the Negro members would have tested lower than the white members. The results indicated that the children of white mothers (and Negro fathers) had higher Stanford-Binet IQ's than the children of Negro mothers (and white fathers). The interpretation was that the mother, as the primary agent of socialization during the early years, was more closely associated with the children's performance.

Even casual observation of child rearing shows that the maternal input dwarfs, by comparison, any other sources of socialization, and that compensatory or enrichment programs will need to be much more intensive if they are to compete successfully with the influence of the mothers of their target children.

On the biological side, the possibility that there may be a biochemical product from a single gene associated with high intelligence, as in retinoblastoma, increases the likelihood that such a product will be found from among the enormous array of biochemical products, most of whose genetic modes of transmission are unknown. The fact that retinoblastoma is almost exclusively a disease of early childhood (89 percent are diagnosed by age three) when the brain is still developing means that the brain is susceptible to biochemical manipulation in a positive sense, and that there may be multiple paths towards the rectification of intellectual inadequacies or in the fashioning of the talented.

REFERENCES

1. Altman, J., Das, G., & Anderson, W. Effects of infantile handling on morphological development in the rat brain: An exploratory study. *Develpm. Psychobiol.* 1968 *1*, 10–20.

2. Bloom, R., Whiteman, M. and Deutsch, M. Race and social class as separate factors related to environment. *In* M. Deutsch (Ed.). *The disadvantaged child,* New York: Basic Books, 1967.

3. Brown, D. The urinary secretion of vanilmandelic acid (VMA) and homovanilic acid (HVA) in children with retinoblastoma. *Amer. J. Ophthamol.,* 1966, *62*; 238–243.

4. Churchill, J. *et al.* Relationships of maternal amino acid blood levels to fetal development. *Obstet. Gynecol.,* 1969, *33,* 492–495.

5. Ciocco, A. Variation in the sex ratio at birth in the United States. *Human Biol.,* 1938, *10,* 36–64.

6. Dawson, B. *et al.* A survey of childhood asthma in Aberdeen. *Lancet,* 1969, *1* (7599), 827–830.

7. Drillien, C. The social and economic factors affecting the incidence of premature birth. *J. Obstet. Gynecol. of the British Empire,* 1957, *LXIV,* 161–184.

8. Drillien, C. *The growth and development of the prematurely born infant.* Baltimore: Williams & Wilkins, 1964.

9. Eastman, N., Hellman, L. *Williams obstetrics.* New York: Appleton-Century-Crofts, 1966.

10. Ganong, W. *Review of medical physiology.* Los Altos, California, 1967.

11. Harrell, R., Woodyard, E., & Gates, A. *The effects of mother's diets on the intelligence of offspring: A study of the influence of vitamin supplementation in the diets of pregnant and lactating women on the intelligence of their children.* New York: Columbia University Press, 1955.

12. Holden, R., Man, E., & Jones, W. Hypothyroxinemia in pregnancy and deviant development in the first year of life. Paper presented at the 1969 Biennial Meetings of the Society for Research in Child Development, Santa Monica, Calif., 1969.

13. Holden, R., and Willerman, L. Neurological abnormality in infancy, preschool intelligence, and social class. In Trapp, P., & Himmelstein, P. (Eds.), New York: Appleton-Century-Crofts, in press.

14. Holley, W., Rosenbaum, A., & Churchill, J. Effects of rapid succession of pregnancy. In *Perinatal factors affecting human development.* Washington D.C.: Paho Science Publications, 1969.

15. Montagu, A. *Prenatal influences.* Springfield, Ill.: Charles C. Thomas, 1962.

16. Mueller, E., *et al.* 1970. Psychosocial correlates of serum urate levels. *Psychol. Bull.,* 1970, *73,* 238–257.

17. Myrianthopoulos, N., French, K. An application of the United States Bureau of the Census Socioeconomic Index to a large diversified patient population. *Soc. Sci. and Med,* 1968, *2,* 283–299.

18. Naylor, A., & Myrianthopoulos, N. The relation of ethnic and selected socio-economic factors to human birthweight. *Annals Human Genet.,* 1967. *31,* 71–83.

19. Pasamanick, B., Knobloch, H., & Lilienfeld, A. Socioeconomic status and some precursors of neuropsychiatric disorder. *Amer. J. Orthopsychiat.,* 1956, *26,* 594–601.

20. Pasamanick, B., & Knobloch, H. Brain damage and reproductive casualty. *Amer. J. Orthopsychiat.*, 1960, *30*, 298–305.

21. Pettigrew, T. *A profile of the negro american.* Princeton, N.J.: Van Nostrand Company, 1964.

22. Reed, E., Reed, S. *Mental retardation: A family study.* Philadelphia: W. B. Saunders, 1965.

23. Rosenzweig, M. Environmental complexity, cerebral change, and behavior. *Am. Psychol.*, 1966, *21*, 321–332.

24. Schápiro, S. Some physiological, biochemical, and behavioral consequences of neonatal hormone administration: cortisol and thyroxine. *Gen. Compar. Endocrinol.*, 1968, *10*, 214–228.

25. Thurrell, R., & Josephson, T. Retinoblastoma and intelligence. Psychosomatics, 1966, *1*, 368–372.

26. Tuft, L., & Mueller, H. *Allergy in man.* Philadelphia: W. B. Saunders, 1970.

27. Werner, E. *et al.* Cumulative effect of perinatal complications and deprived environment on physical, intellectual and social development of preschool children. *Pediatrics,* 1967, *39*, 490–505.

28. White, B. An experimental approach to the effects of experience on early human behavior. *In* Hill, J. (Ed.), Minnesota Symposia on Child Psychology. Minneapolis: University of Minnesota Press, 1968.

29. Willerman, L., Broman, S., & Fiedler, M. Infant development, preschool IQ and social class. *Child Developm., 41,* 69–77.

30. Willerman, L., & Churchill, J. Birthweight as a perinatal correlate of superior IQ. Manuscript in preparation, 1969.

31. Willerman, L., Naylor, A., & Myrianthopoulos, N. 1970. Intellectual development of children from interracial matings. *Science,* 1970, *170,* 1329–1331.

32. Williams, M. Superior intelligence of children blinded from retinoblastoma. *Arch. Dis. Childhood,* 1968, *43,* 204–210.

3.2

Visual Alertness as Related to Soothing in Neonates: Implications for Maternal Stimulation and Early Deprivation

Anneliese F. Korner
Rose Grobstein

Observations incidental to a study of behavior genetics in neonates (Korner, 1964) suggest that when babies cry and are picked up to the shoulder, they not only stop crying, but they frequently become visually alert, and they scan the environment. We were struck by several implications of this observation: if generally true, this type of soothing would induce a state which is otherwise quite rare in the neonate and which is considered by some to be the optimal state for the infant's earliest learning. According to P. H. Wolff's (1965) observations, this state of alertness occurs spontaneously but from 8 to 16 percent of the time in the first postnatal week, and it only very gradually increases over subsequent weeks. The infant thus spends only a very minor part of his day in alertness. Yet, in terms of his locomotor helplessness, visual apprehension is one of the few avenues at his disposal to make contact and to get acquainted with the environment. If regular soothing of this type induces a state of alertness, it follows that a baby picked up for crying will have earlier and many more opportunities to scan the environment than an infant left crying in his crib.

In a recent symposium entitled "The Crucial Early Influence: Mother Love or Environmental Stimulation" Fantz (1966), referring to his findings that infants discriminate from birth among visual stimuli, concluded that perceptual experiences play a crucial role in early development. In fact, he could distinguish babies reared at home from institutional infants through their visual responses by the second month of life. While Fantz stressed the importance of perceptual experiences through environmental stimulation, he also stated that the effects of early stimulation would be better understood "if one could pin down the specific kinds of sensory stimulation and perceptual experience often provided optimally by a loving mother." Our observation that babies, when picked up for crying, frequently become visually alert may thus capture one important pathway by which maternal ministrations may inadvertently provide visual experiences.

In this study we set out to investigate how frequently soothing of the type described elicited visual alertness. With the design used to study this problem, it was possible to explore an additional hypothesis. Bell (1963) suggested that infants born to primiparous mothers may, for a number of reasons, respond differently to tactile

Reprinted from *Child Development,* 1966 *37,* No. 4, 867–876, by permission of author and The Society for Research in Child Development, Inc. Copyright © 1966 by The Society for Research in Child Development, Inc.

stimulation than infants of multiparous mothers. We explored the relation between parity and visual alertness in response to soothing by including both types of infants.

SAMPLE

The sample consisted of 12 newborn, breastfed baby girls; six were born to primiparous mothers and six to multiparae. Boys were excluded because it was quite apparent that the comfort derived from being picked up and put to the shoulder was offset by the discomfort of being held close within hours of a circumcision. The babies ranged from 45–79 hours in age; the average was 55 hours old. All were Caucasian. Their birth weights ranged from 6 pounds 8 ounces to 8 pounds 13 ounces. They all had normal vaginal deliveries, received Apgar scores of 8 and above at birth, and they were found to be healthy newborn infants on physical examination.

METHOD

The infants were tested in a treatment room adjoining the nursery. Temperature and illumination approximated conditions in the nursery. The infants were tested individually after being brought to the treatment room in their own bassinets. They were dressed in shirts and diapers. To facilitate pickups, the infants were placed on the mattress underneath the plastic bassinet usually used for diapering and dressing infants. Since we were interested in soothing crying babies, they were all tested within 1½ hours before a feeding. Occasionally, we had to rouse a sleepy baby by moving her or by flicking her foot. The tests described below were initiated only when the baby was crying. Minimum time between experiments was 1 minute. Since we were interested in comparing each infant with her own tendencies in the various experimental positions, it was of little consequence whether some infants cried harder than others at any given trial. Also, enough trials were given to each infant to randomize the degree of agitation over all the trials.

Diapers were changed before the experiments were started irrespective of need. All infants were tested in four positions:

1. Six trials on the left shoulder.
2. Six trials on the right shoulder.
3. Six trials sitting up.
4. Six control trials in which the baby lay on her back without intervention by the observers.

The "situp" experiments were introduced because it was noted that handling and the upright position alone frequently induced alertness. It was noted, for example, that many babies are alert when they are carried out to their mothers for feeding. In addition to the handling and the upright position, the experience of being put to the shoulder involves warmth, containment, the sense of smell, and the opportunity to establish mouth contact with the shoulder. Differential effects of the two positions could thus be studied.

To insure comparability of handling, the same person did all the interventions. When picked up, the baby's head was supported, and her hands were kept out of reach of her mouth. The same was done in sitting up a baby. Trials in the various positions were done at random.

For 30 seconds following an intervention, alert and scanning behavior was recorded. During the control experiments, the same was done for 30 seconds without an intervention. When the infant opened her eyes during the 30-second experimental period, the trial was scored a "yes." In each instance, the same was done for scanning behavior. Babies varied a great deal in the degree of alertness. Some drowsily opened their eyes; others actively looked around, lifting the head and exploring the experimenter. Some had brief, others had sustained, periods of alertness. Since visual pursuit can be elicited even in drowsy babies (see Wolff, in press), and since it is difficult to equate several brief periods of alertness with one sustained period, the degree and the duration of alertness were not considered in the ratings. "Yes" was scored when the infant opened her eyes and when she scanned the environment at any one time during the 30 seconds of observations. In addition to these observations, the number of spontaneous alert and scanning episodes between experiments was noted for 10 of the 12 subjects.

OBSERVER RELIABILITIES

Reliabilities between two observers were calculated on the basis of dividing the number of agreements by the combined number of agreements and disagreements. Percentages of agreement were as follows:

1.   Opening eyes during "situps" and during controls: 96 percent.
2.   Opening eyes between experiments: 98 percent.
3.   Scanning during "situps" and during controls: 97 percent.
4.   Scanning episodes between experiments: 95 percent.

Reliability ratings for opening of eyes and scanning during "pickups" would have required a third observer. Since there was very little disagreement between what constituted alerting and scanning behavior during "situps" and controls and between experiments (the percentages of agreement ranging from 95 to 98), it was felt to be unnecessary to introduce a third observer to rate alert and scanning behavior during "pickups."

RESULTS

Incidence of Alerting in Response to Soothing

Our data confirmed the observation that, when crying infants were put to the shoulder, they not only stopped crying, but each of them also opened her eyes and alerted in the large majority of trials.

An analysis of variance was performed. The difference between "primips"[1] and "multips" was not found to be significant. By contrast, the difference of reactions to the various positions was found to be significant at the 1 percent level.

The results suggest that handling and the upright position alone did not result in the infant's opening her eyes significantly more often than when no intervention was made.

Incidence of Scanning in Response to Soothing

Since the degree of alertness varied when an infant opened her eyes, active scanning probably was a better measure for testing the effect of soothing on visual alertness. Even with this more stringent criterion for alertness, each baby in this sample alerted and scanned when put to the shoulder, and most did in the majority of the trials.

An analysis of variance was performed. Even though, in absolute terms, the "primips" scanned more, the difference was not statistically significant. By contrast, the difference of reactions to the various positions was again significant at the 1 percent level.

Spontaneous Alerting and Scanning Between Experiments

Spontaneous alerting and scanning between experiments were recorded only in 10 out of 12 cases. The incidence among babies of these episodes varied greatly. The average number of times the "primips" opened their eyes between experiments was 7.8; for "multips," the average was only 3.2. The "primips" scanned on the average of 6.5 times, the "multips" only 3 times. These differences between "primips" and "multips" did not reach significance, probably because of the small number of observations. It is of interest, however, that there is a consistent trend among the three types of observations: In each instance, the "primips" alerted and scanned more frequently than the "multips." This suggests that differences may exist in arousal levels between "primips" and "multips." Our data on crying, not reported here, which shows highly significant differences between "multips" and "primips," would support this hypothesis.

Individual Differences

There were marked differences among babies in their tendency to alert and scan. For example, P4, P5, and M5, tended to alert and scan readily in all positions. By contrast,

M3 and P6 had difficulty with both, even when put to the shoulder. There also were marked differences in the capacity to sustain alertness. In some babies these episodes were fleeting; in others they were maintained for long periods of time.

There were particularly marked differences among the infants in their proneness to alert and to scan between experiments. Some babies never did alert and scan, others did very rarely, and a few did quite frequently (range from 0–15 instances, with a mean of 5.5). Infants M3 and P6, who had difficulty alerting when put to the shoulder, also showed very few instances of alerting and scanning between experiments (3 and 0 instances, respectively). By contrast, those infants who alerted and scanned most between experiments were not necessarily the same babies who had the highest frequency of these behaviors when picked up. Very probably, the amount of handling during the entire experimental session affected babies differently, arousing some, not affecting others. One may infer from this that there may be individual differences among babies in the case with which the state of arousal is changed through manipulation.

DISCUSSION

Visual alertness in the neonate has become the concern of many studies (e.g., Fantz, 1958, 1966; Ling, 1942; White, 1963; Wolff, 1965, 1966; Wolff & White, 1965). This concern on the part of some investigators stems from the observation that visual alertness is not as reflex as most neonatal behavior and, to a large extent, qualitatively resembles the later capacity of attentiveness. In terms of psychoanalytic theory, visual alertness is probably the clearest example of a primary autonomous ego function observable in the newborn. In view of the neonate's locomotor helplessness, visual prehension is one of the infant's few avenues for learning and for getting acquainted with the environment.

Our experiments show that this state of visual alertness, so important for learning, can readily be induced by picking up a crying newborn and putting him to the shoulder. It was possible to do this without difficulty even at a time when, according to Wolff's (1965) findings, the newborn is least likely to be alert, namely, when he is hungry. Wolff's observations demonstrated that during the first week of life his subjects spent, on the average, only 11 percent of the time in the state of alert inactivity and that 86.4 percent of this 11 percent occurred within the first hour after a feeding.

One can only speculate about the causes of the association between this kind of soothing and visual alertness. Neurophysiologically, what may occur is that the soothing action of this intervention lowers the infant's state of arousal, with the result that the infant goes from crying into the next lower state on the continuum of states and arousal.[2] Waking activity, the next lower state on this continuum, was prevented by the motor restraint imposed by being held to the shoulder. This restraint may have lowered the infant's state of arousal one step further, resulting in the state of alert inactivity. In fact, by preventing the distracting effects on the infant's motor activity, the physical restraint may have enhanced the likelihood of alert behavior. Wolff and

White (1965) found this relation to hold. They increased the infant's capacity for attentive behavior by inhibiting motor activity through the use of a pacifier.

In psychological terms, the association of soothing and visual alertness may involve the prototype of a reaction which may hold true throughout life. By reducing the intensity of internal needs, the organism can turn outward and attend the external world. Descriptively, this corresponds well with the sequence of events as we observed them.

Our data did not suggest that handling or the upright position alone induced a state of alertness. This was true because, in most cases, handling alone did not lower the infant's state of arousal sufficiently to reduce crying to the point of alertness. The observation that many infants are quietly alert when brought to a feeding suggests that handling and the upright position are more successful in inducing alertness in noncrying or sleepy infants. In those states of arousal, the stimulation of touch, motion, and positional change are rousing rather than soothing. In an intense form, labor and birth which entail extreme stimulation of this type may have arousing effects with similar results. Brazelton (1961) observed that, for a few hours after delivery and before going into a relative state of disorganization, all of his subjects were alert and responsive. They fixed and followed a red ring visually for several minutes at a time. They also attended and often visually followed auditory stimuli. Brazelton's observations of the alertness of the newly delivered baby are easily confirmed by casual observation. All one has to do is to watch babies as they are admitted to the newborn nursery from the delivery room: most of them have their eyes wide open and are highly alert.

Of relevance to the alertness-producing effects of both soothing and handling are the numerous studies dealing with the effects of handling and early stimulation on both animals and infants. For the most part, these studies show the importance of early stimulation for the growth and development of the young organism. The specific factors which account for the more favorable development of the "handled" group are usually not spelled out. Levine (1962), noting profound psychophysiological effects of infantile stimulation in the rat, concluded that the sensory routes and mechanisms underlying these effects are not known. He suspects that proprioceptive and kinesthetic stimulation may indicate the sensory routs of effective stimulation. Casler (1961) and Yarrow (1961), in reviews of maternal deprivation studies, concluded that early tactile stimulation appears necessary for normal human development. Our own observations suggest that tactile stimulation may activate visual behavior. Activation of the visual modality through tactile stimulation may thus be one of the pathways through which early stimulation takes effect. We find support of this hypothesis in White and Castle's (1964) study which demonstrated that institution-reared infants given small amounts of extra handling during their first weeks of life later showed significantly more visual interest in their environment than nonhandled controls.

In the earliest days of life, infant care, for the most part, invites soothing rather than rousing interventions. It is the handling involved in soothing rather than rousing which may make the difference in the neonates' earliest opportunities for visual experiences. Infants in institutions, while usually given adequate physical care, generally are not picked up and soothed when they cry. This may be partly responsible for their earliest deficit.

Mothers of home-reared infants differ, of course, in their readiness to soothe their crying newborn. Our observations suggest that picked-up infants will have many more opportunities to get acquainted with the environment than babies left crying in their cribs. In particular, they will have many more occasions to explore their mothers. Their visual explorations will occur when comforted. This may lower their stimulus barrier under conditions which minimize the danger of being overwhelmed.

Fantz's (1966) findings suggest that visual and perceptual experiences during the neonatal period have lasting developmental effects. With this in mind, our observations raise a host of developmental questions. For example, do babies who are carried around a great deal learn to rely more heavily on the visual modality in their exploration of the environment than babies who do not have this experience as much? How does the development of the infant of another culture who is constantly carried around by his mother differ in this respect? With the added opportunities of exploring the mother, are there differences in time and depth in the infant-mother bond formation and in the development of differentiating self from nonself? Also, are there differences in the onset and strength of stranger and separation anxiety? As Benjamin (1959) has shown, babies who rely heavily on the visual modality will experience stranger and separation anxiety earlier and more severely.

Our observations have not only experiential implications. We also found organismic differences among the infants. Babies differed greatly in their capacity for alert behavior. This finding is confirmed by our larger study (Korner, 1964) involving a bigger sample of neonates and much longer observations. It is reasonable to believe that varying opportunities for visual experiences will affect babies differently depending on their own disposition. Thus an infant with high sensory thresholds may demonstrate the effects of maternal neglect or sensory deprivation more acutely than the infant more capable of providing visual experiences for himself.

NOTES

[1]The terms "primips" and "multips" will be used for convenience henceforth to refer to the offspring of primiparous and multiparous mothers, respectively.
[2]For a definition of states of arousal, see Wolff (1959).

REFERENCES

Bell, R. Q. Some factors to be controlled in studies of the behavior of newborns. *Biol. Neonat.,* 1963,*5,* 200–214.

Benjamin, J. D. Prediction and psychopathological theory. In Lucie Jessner & Eleanor Pavenstedt (Eds.), *Dynamic psychopathology in childhood,* New York: Grune & Stratton, 1959, 6–77.

Brazelton, T. B. Psychophysiologic reactions in the neonate: II. Effect of maternal medication on the neonate and his behavior. *J. Pediat.,* 1961, *58,* No. 4, 513–518.

Casler, L. Maternal deprivation: a critical review of the literature. *Monogr. Soc. Res. Child Develpm.,* 1961, *26,* No. 2 (Serial No. 80).

Fantz, R. L. Pattern vision in young infants. *Psychol. Rec.,* 1958, 8, 43–47.

Fantz, R. L. The crucial early influence: mother love or environmental stimulation? *Amer. J. Orthopsychiat.,* 1966,*36,* No. 2, 330–331. (Abstract)

Korner, Anneliese F. Some hypotheses regarding the significance of individual differences at birth for later development. *The psychoanalytic study of the child.* Vol. 19. New York: International Universities Pr., 1964, 58–72.

Levine, S. Psychophysiological effects of infantile stimulation. In E. Bliss (Ed.), *Roots of behavior.* New York: Paul Hoeber, 1962, 246–253.

Ling, Bing-Chung. A genetic study of sustained visual fixation and associated behavior in the human infant from birth to six months: I. *J. genet. Psychol.,* 1942, 227–277.

White, B. L. The development of perception during the first six months of life. Paper read at Amer. Ass. of Advancement of Science, December 30, 1963.

White, B. L., & Castle, P. W. Visual exploratory behavior following postnatal handling of human infants. *Percept. mot. Skills,* 1964, *18,* 497–502.

Wolff, P. H. Observations of newborn infants. *Psychosom. Med.,* 1959, *21,* 110–118.

Wolff, P. H. The development of attention in young infants. Ann. N. Y. *Acad. Sci.,* 1965, *118,* 815–830.

Wolff, P. H. The causes, controls and organization of behavior in the newborn. *Psychological issues.* New York: International Universities Pr., 1966.

Wolff, P. H, & White, B. L. Visual pursuit and attention in young infants. J. *Amer. Acad. Child Psychiat.,* 1965, *4,* No. 3, 473–484.

Yarrow, L. J. Maternal deprivation: toward an empirical and conceptual re-evaluation. *Psychol. Bull.,* 1961, *58,* 459–590.

3.3

Sex, Age, and State as Determinants of Mother-Infant Interaction

Howard A. Moss

A major reason for conducting research on human infants is derived from the popular assumption that adult behavior, to a considerable degree, is influenced by early experience. A corollary of this assumption is that if we can precisely conceptualize and measure significant aspects of infant experience and behavior we will be able to predict more sensitively and better understand adult functioning. The basis for this conviction concerning the enduring effects of early experience varies considerably according to the developmental model that is employed. Yet there remains considerable consensus as to the long-term and pervasive influence of the infant's experience.

Bloom (1964) contends that characteristics become increasingly resistant to change as the mature status of the characteristic is achieved and that environmental effects are most influential during periods of most rapid growth. This is essentially a refinement of the critical period hypothesis which argues in favor of the enduring and irreversible effects of many infant experiences. Certainly the studies on imprinting and the effects of controlled sensory input are impressive in this respect (Hess, 1959; White and Held, 1963). Learning theory also lends itself to support the potency of early experience. Since the occurrence of variable interval and variable ratio reinforcement schedules are highly probable in infancy (as they are in many other situations), the learnings associated with these schedules will be highly resistant to extinction. Also, the preverbal learning that characterizes infancy should be more difficult to extinguish since these responses are less available to linguistic control which later serves to mediate and regulate many important stimulus-response and reinforcement relationships. Psychoanalytic theory and behavioristic psychology probably have been the most influential forces in emphasizing the long-range consequences of infant experience. These theories, as well as others, stress the importance of the mother-infant relationship. In light of the widespread acceptance of the importance of early development, it is paradoxical that there is such a dearth of direct observational data concerning the functioning of infants in their natural environment, and in relation to their primary caretakers.

Observational studies of the infant are necessary in order to test existing theoretical propositions and to generate new propositions based on empirical evidence. In addition, the infant is an ideally suitable subject for investigating many aspects of behavior because of the early stage in life. Such phenomena as temperament, reac-

Reprinted from the *Merrill-Palmer Quarterly*, 1967, *13*, No. 1, 19–36, by permission of the author and the Merrill-Palmer Institute.

tions to stimulation, efficacy of different learning contingencies, perceptual functioning, and social attachment can be investigated while they are still in rudimentary form
and not yet entwined in the immensely complex behavioral configurations that
progressively emerge.

The research to be reported in this paper involves descriptive-normative data of
maternal and infant behaviors in the naturalistic setting of the home. These data are
viewed in terms of how the infant's experience structures potential learning patterns.
Although the learning process itself is of primary eventual importance, it is necessary
initially to identify the organizational factors, in situ, that structure learning opportunities and shape response systems.

A sample of 30 firstborn children and their mothers were studied by means of
direct observations over the first 3 months of life. Two periods were studied during
this 3-month interval. Period one included a cluster of three observations made at
weekly intervals during the first month of life in order to evaluate the initial adaptation
of mother and infant to one another. Period two consisted of another cluster of three
observations, made around 3 months of age when relatively stable patterns of behavior were likely to have been established. Each cluster included two 3-hour observations and one 8-hour observation. The 3-hour observations were made with the use
of a keyboard that operates in conjunction with a 20-channel Esterline-Angus Event
Recorder. Each of 30 keys represents a maternal or infant behavior, and when a key
is depressed it activates one or a combination of pens on the recorder, leaving a trace
that shows the total duration of the observed behavior. This technique allows for a
continuous record showing the total time and the sequence of behavior. For the
8-hour observation the same behaviors were studied but with the use of a modified
time-sampling technique. The time-sampled units were one minute in length and the
observer, using a stenciled form, placed a number opposite the appropriate behaviors
to indicate their respective order of occurrence. Since each variable can be coded
only once for each observational unit, a score of 480 is the maximum that can be
received. The data to be presented in this paper are limited to the two 8-hour observations. The data obtained with the use of the keyboard will be dealt with elsewhere in
terms of the sequencing of events.

The mothers who participated in these observations were told that this was a
normative study of infant functioning under natural living conditions. It was stressed
that they proceed with their normal routines and care of the infant as they would if
the observer were not present. This structure was presented to the mothers during
a brief introductory visit prior to the first observation. In addition, in order to reduce
the mother's self-consciousness and facilitate her behaving in relatively typical fashion, the observer emphasized that it was the infant who was being studied and that
her actions would be noted only in relation to what was happening to the infant. This
approach seemed to be effective, since a number of mothers commented after the
observations were completed that they were relieved that they were not the ones
being studied. The extensiveness of the observations and the frequent use of informal
conversation between the observer and mother seemed to contribute further to the
naturalness of her behavior.

TABLE 1. MEAN FREQUENCY OF MATERNAL AND INFANT BEHAVIOR AT 3 WEEKS AND 3 MONTHS

	3-WEEK OBSERVATION		3-MONTH OBSERVATION[a]	
BEHAVIOR	MALES[b] (N = 14)	FEMALES (N = 15)	MALES[b] (N = 13)	FEMALES (N = 12)
MATERNAL VARIABLES				
Holds infant close	121.4	99.2	77.4	58.6
Holds infant distant	32.2	18.3	26.7	27.2
Total holds	131.3	105.5	86.9	73.4
Attends infant	61.7	44.2	93.0	81.8
Maternal contact (holds and attends)	171.1	134.5	158.8	133.8
Feeds infant	60.8	60.7	46.6	41.4
Stimulates feeding	10.1	14.0	1.6	3.6
Burps infant	39.0	25.9	20.9	15.3
Affectionate contact	19.9	15.9	32.8	22.7
Rocks infant	35.1	20.7	20.0	23.9
Stresses musculature	11.7	3.3	25.8	16.6
Stimulates/arouses infant	23.1	10.6	38.9	26.1
Imitates infant	1.9	2.9	5.3	7.6
Looks at infant	182.8	148.1	179.5	161.9
Talks to infant	104.1	82.2	117.5	116.1
Smiles at infant	23.2	18.6	45.9	46.4
INFANT VARIABLES				
Cry	43.6	30.2	28.5	16.9
Fuss	65.7	44.0	59.0	36.0
Irritable (cry and fuss)	78.7	56.8	67.3	42.9
Awake active	79.6	55.1	115.8	85.6
Awake passive	190.0	138.6	257.8	241.1
Drowsy	74.3	74.7	27.8	11.1
Sleep	261.7	322.1	194.3	235.6
Supine	133.7	59.3	152.7	134.8
Eyes on mother	72.3	49.0	91.0	90.6
Vocalizes	152.3	179.3	207.2	207.4
Infant smiles	11.1	11.7	32.1	35.3
Mouths	36.8	30.6	61.2	116.2

[a]Four of the subjects were unable to participate in the 3-month observation. Two moved out of the area, one mother became seriously ill, and another mother chose not to participate in all the observations.
[b]One subject who had had an extremely difficult delivery was omitted from the descriptive data but is included in the findings concerning mother-infant interaction.

The observational variables, mean scores and sample sizes are presented in Table 1. These data are presented separately for the 3-week and the 3-month observations. The inter-rater reliabilities for these variables range from .74 to 1.00 with a median reliability of .97. Much of the data in this paper are presented for males and females separately, since by describing and comparing these two groups we are able to work from an established context that helps to clarify the theoretical meaning of the results. Also, the importance of sex differences is heavily emphasized in contemporary developmental theory and it is felt that infant data concerning these differences would provide a worthwhile addition to the literature that already exists on this matter for older subjects.

The variables selected for study are those which would seem to influence or reflect aspects of maternal contact. An additional, but related consideration in the selection of variables was that they have an apparent bearing on the organization of the infant's experience. Peter Wolff (1959), Janet Brown (1964), and Sibylle Escalona (1962) have described qualitative variations in infant state or activity level and others have shown that the response patterns of the infant are highly influenced by the state he is in (Bridger, 1965). Moreover, Levy (1958) has demonstrated that maternal behavior varies as a function of the state or activity level of the infant. Consequently, we have given particular attention to the variables concerning state (cry, fuss, awake active, awake passive, and sleep) because of the extent to which these behaviors seem to shape the infant's experience. Most of the variables listed in Table 1 are quite descriptive of what was observed. Those which might not be as clear are as follows: *attends infant*—denotes standing close or leaning over infant, usually while in the process of caretaking activities; *stimulates feeding*—stroking the infant's cheek and manipulating the nipple so as to induce sucking responses; *affectionate contact*— kissing and caressing infant; *stresses musculature*—holding the infant in either a sitting or standing position so that he is required to support his own weight; *stimulates/ arouses infant*—mother provides tactile and visual stimulation for the infant or attempts to arouse him to a higher activity level; and *imitates infant*—mother repeats a behavior, usually a vocalization, immediately after it is observed in the infant.

The sex differences and shifts in behavior from 3 weeks to 3 months are in many instances pronounced. For example, at 3 weeks of age mothers held male infants about 27 minutes more per 8 hours than they held females, and at 3 months males were held 14 minutes longer. By the time they were 3 months of age there was a decrease of over 30 percent for both sexes in the total time they were held by their mothers. Sleep time also showed marked sex differences and changes over time. For the earlier observations females slept about an hour longer than males, and this difference tended to be maintained by 3 months with the female infants sleeping about 41 minutes longer. Again, there was a substantial reduction with age in this behavior for both sexes; a decrease of 67 and 86 minutes in sleep time for males and females, respectively. What is particularly striking is the variability for these infant and maternal variables. The range for sleep time is 137–391 minutes at 3 weeks and 120–344 minutes at 3 months, and the range for mother holding is 38–218 minutes at 3 weeks and 26–168 minutes for the 3-month observation. The extent of the individual differences reflected by these ranges seem to have important implications. For instance, if an infant spends more time at a higher level of consciousness this should increase his experience and contact with the mother, and through greater learning opportunities, facilitate the perceptual discriminations he makes, and affect the quality of his cognitive organization. The finding that some of the infants in our sample slept a little over 2 hours, or about 25 percent of the observation time and others around 6 hours or 75 percent of the time, is a fact that has implications for important developmental processes. The sum crying and fussing, what we term irritability level of the infant, is another potentially important variable. The range of scores for this behavior was from 5–136 minutes at 3 weeks and 7–98 at 3 months. The fact that infants are capable through their behavior of shaping maternal treatment is a point that has gained increasing recognition. The cry is a signal for the mother to respond and variation among infants in this behavior could lead to differential experiences with the mother.

TABLE 2. CHANGES IN BEHAVIOR BETWEEN 3 WEEKS AND 3 MONTHS (N = 26)

MATERNAL VARIABLES	t-VALUES	INFANT VARIABLES	t-VALUES
HIGHER AT 3 WEEKS:		**HIGHER AT 3 WEEKS:**	
Holds infant close	4.43****	Cry	2.84***
Holds infant distant	.56	Fuss	1.33
Total holds	4.00****	Irritable (cry and fuss)	1.73*
Maternal contact		Drowsy	9.02****
(holds and attends)	.74	Sleep	4.51****
Feeds infant	3.49***		
Stimulates feeding	3.42***		
Burps infant	3.28***		
Rocks infant	1.08		
HIGHER AT 3 MONTHS:		**HIGHER AT 3 MONTHS:**	
Attends infant	5.15****	Awake active	2.47**
Affectionate contact	2.50**	Awake passive	5.22****
Stresses musculature	3.42***	Supine	1.75*
Stimulates/arouses infant	2.63**	Eyes on mother	3.21***
Imitates infant	4.26****	Vocalizes	3.56***
Looks at infant	.38	Infant smiles	6.84****
Talks to infant	2.67**	Mouths	3.69***
Smiles at infant	4.79****		

* $p < .10$
** $p < .05$
***$< .01$
**** $p < .001$

Table 2 presents *t* values showing changes in the maternal and infant behaviors from the 3-week to the 3-month observation. In this case, the data for the males and females are combined since the trends, in most instances, are the same for both sexes. It is not surprising that there are a number of marked shifts in behavior from 3 weeks to 3 months, since the early months of life are characterized by enormous growth and change. The maternal variables that show the greatest decrement are those involving feeding behaviors and close physical contact. It is of interest that the decrease in close contact is paralleled by an equally pronounced increase in attending behavior, so that the net amount of maternal contact remains similar for the 3-week and 3-month observations. The main difference was that the mothers, for the later observation, tended to hold their infants less but spent considerably more time near them, in what usually was a vis-à-vis posture, while interacting and ministering to their needs. Along with this shift, the mothers showed a marked increase in affectionate behavior toward the older infant, positioned him more so that he was required to make active use of his muscles, presented him with a greater amount of stimulation and finally, she exhibited more social behavior (imitated, smiled, and talked) toward the older child.

The changes in maternal behavior from 3 weeks to 3 months probably are largely a function of the maturation of various characteristics of the infant. However, the increased confidence of the mother, her greater familiarity with her infant, and her developing attachment toward him will also account for some of the changes that occurred over this period of time.

By 3 months of age the infant is crying less and awake more. Moreover he is becoming an interesting and responsive person. There are substantial increases in the total time spent by him in smiling, vocalizing, and looking at the mother's face, so that the greater amount of social-type behavior he manifested at three months parallels the increments shown in the mother's social responsiveness toward him over this same period. The increase with age in the time the infant is kept in a supine position also should facilitate his participation in vis-à-vis interactions with the mother as well as provide him with greater opportunity for varied visual experiences.

TABLE 3. CORRELATIONS BETWEEN OBSERVATIONS AT 3 WEEKS AND AT 3 MONTHS (N = 26)

MATERNAL VARIABLES	$r =$	INFANT VARIABLES	$r =$
Holds infant close	.23	Cry	.28
Holds infant distant	.04	Fuss	.42**
Total holds	.18	Irritable (cry and fuss)	.37*
Attends infant	.36*	Awake active	.25
Maternal contact		Awake passive	.26
(holds and attends)	.25	Drowsy	.44**
Feeds infant	.21	Sleep	.24
Stimulates feeding	.37*	Supine	.29
Burps infant	.20	Eyes on mother	-.12
Affectionate contact	.64****	Vocalizes	.41**
Rocks infant	.29	Infant smiles	.32
Stresses musculature	.06	Mouths	-.17
Stimulates/arouses infant	.23		
Imitates infant	.45**		
Looks at infant	.37*		
Talks to infant	.58***		
Smiles at infant	.66****		

* $p < .10$
** $p < .05$
*** $< .01$
**** $p < .001$

Table 3 presents the correlations between the 3-week and the 3-month observations for the maternal and infant behaviors we studied. These findings further reflect the relative instability of the mother- infant system over the first few months of life. Moderate correlation coefficients were obtained only for the class of maternal variables concerning affectionate-social responses. It thus may be that these behaviors are more sensitive indicators of enduring maternal attitudes than the absolute amount of time the mother devoted to such activities as feeding and physical contact. The few infant variables that show some stability are, with the exception of vocalizing, those concerning the state of the organism. Even though some of the behaviors are moderately stable from 3 weeks to 3 months, the overall magnitude of the correlations reported in Table 3 seem quite low considering that they represent repeated measures of the same individual over a relatively short period.

TABLE 4. SEX DIFFERENCES IN FREQUENCY OF MATERNAL AND INFANT BEHAVIORS AT 3 WEEKS AND 3 MONTHS

MATERNAL VARIABLES	t-VALUES		INFANT VARIABLES	t-VALUES	
	3 WEEKS	3 MONTHS		3 WEEKS	3 MONTHS
MALE HIGHER:			MALE HIGHER:		
Holds infant close	1.42	1.52	Cry	1.68	1.11
Holds infant distant	2.64**		Fuss	2.48**	3.47***
Total holds	1.65	1.12	Irritable (cry		
Attends infant	2.66**	1.10	and fuss)	2.23**	2.68**
Maternal contact			Awake active	1.66	.57
(holds and attends)	2.09**	1.57	Awake passive	2.94***	1.77*
Feeds infant	.06	.27	Drowsy		.41
Burps infant	1.67	.69	Supine	2.30**	1.07
Affectionate contact	.90	1.00	Eyes on mother	1.99*	.75
Rocks infant	1.21		Mouths	.64	
Stresses musculature	2.48**	1.67			
Stimulates/arouses					
infant	2.20**	1.53			
Looks at infant	1.97*	1.36			
Talks to infant	1.02	.79			
Smiles at infant	.57				
FEMALE HIGHER:			FEMALE HIGHER:		
Holds infant distant		.05	Drowsy	.03	
Stimulates feeding	.62	1.47	Sleep	3.15***	2.87***
Rocks infant		.82	Vocalizes	1.34	.23
Imitates infant	.80	1.76*	Infant smiles	.02	.08
Smiles at infant		.44	Mouths		2.57**

* $p < .10$
** $p < .05$
*** $p < .01$

Table 4 presents t-values based on comparisons between the sexes for the 3-week and 3-month observations. A number of statistically significant differences were obtained with, in most instances, the boys having higher mean scores than the girls. The sex differences are most pronounced at 3 weeks for both maternal and infant variables. By 3 months the boys and girls are no longer as clearly differentiated on the maternal variables although the trend persists for the males to tend to have higher mean scores. On the other hand, the findings for the infant variables concerning state remain relatively similar at 3 weeks and 3 months. Thus, the sex differences are relatively stable for the two observations even though the stability coefficients for the total sample are low (in terms of our variables).

TABLE 5. SEX DIFFERENCES AFTER CONTROLLING FOR IRRITABILITY AND SLEEP TIME THROUGH ANALYSIS OF COVARIANCE[a]

MATERNAL OR INFANT BEHAVIORS	SLEEP TIME CONTROLLED FOR		SEX WITH HIGHER MEAN SCORE	IRRITABILITY CONTROLLED FOR		SEX WITH HIGHER MEAN SCORE
	3 WEEKS	3 MONTHS		3 WEEKS	3 MONTHS	
VARIABLES	t	t		t	t	
Holds infant close	.30	1.22		.64	1.70	
Holds infant distant	.59	-.20		.92	-.20	
Total holds	.43	.88		.86	1.08	
Attends infant	1.12	1.36		1.91*	.94	Males
Maternal contact (holds and attends)	.62	1.04		1.20	1.12	
Stimulates feeding	.55	-1.12		-.09	-1.06	
Affectionate contact	-.46	.91		.56	1.27	
Rocks	.35	-.70		.44	-1.44	
Stresses musculature	1.84*	.71	Males	1.97*	1.40	
Stimulates/arouses infant	2.09**	1.82*	Males	2.43**	2.31**	Males
Imitates infant	-.91	-2.73**	Females	-.63	-2.14**	Females
Looks at infant	.58	1.35		1.17	1.02	
Talks to infant	-.48	.24		.70	.59	
Infant supine	.82	-.03		1.36	.69	
Eyes on mother	.37	.58		1.76*	-.37	Males

* $p < .10$
** $p < .05$
[a]A positive t-value indicates that males had the higher mean score, a negative t-value indicates a higher mean score for females.

In general these results indicate that much more was happening with the male infants than with the female infants. Males slept less and cried more during both observations and these behaviors probably contributed to the more extensive and stimulating interaction the boys experienced with the mother, particularly for the 3-week observation. In order to determine the effect of state we selected the 15 variables, excluding those dealing with state, where the sex differences were most marked and did an analysis of covariance with these variables, controlling for irritability and another analysis of covariance controlling for sleep. These results are presented in Table 5. When the state of the infant was controlled for, most of the sex differences were no longer statistically significant. The exceptions were that the t-values were greater, after controlling for state, for the variables "mother stimulates-

/arouses infant" and "mother imitates infant." The higher score for "stimulates-/arouses" was obtained for the males and the higher score for "imitates" by the females. The variable "imitates" involves repeating vocalizations made by the child, and it is interesting that mothers exhibited more of this behavior with the girls. This response could be viewed as the reinforcement of verbal behavior, and the evidence presented here suggests that the mothers differentially reinforce this behavior on the basis of the sex of the child.

In order to further clarify the relation between infant state and maternal treatment, product-moment correlations were computed relating the infant irritability score with the degree of maternal contact. The maternal contact variable is based on the sum of the holding and attending scores with the time devoted to feeding behaviors subtracted out. These correlations were computed for the 3-week and 3-month observations for the male and female samples combined and separate. At 3 weeks a correlation of .52 ($p < .01$) was obtained between irritability and maternal contact for the total sample. However, for the female subsample this correlation was .68 ($p < .02$) and for males only .20 (non. sig.). Furthermore, a somewhat similar pattern occurred for the correlations between maternal contact and infant irritability for the 3-month observation. At this age the correlation is .37 ($p < .10$ level) for the combined sample and .54 ($p < .05$ level) for females and $-.47$ ($p < .10$ level) for males. A statistically significant difference was obtained ($t = 2.40$, $p < .05$ level) in a test comparing the difference between the female and male correlations for the 3-month observation. In other words maternal contact and irritability positively covaried for females at both ages; whereas for males, there was no relationship at 3 weeks, and by 3 months the mothers tended to spend less time with the more irritable male babies. It should be emphasized that these correlations reflect within-group patterns, and that when we combine the female and male samples positive correlations still emerge for both ages. Since the males had substantially higher scores for irritability and maternal contact than the females, the correlation for the male subjects does not strongly attenuate the correlations derived for the total sample, even when the males within group covariation seems random or negative. That is, in terms of the total sample, the patterning of the male scores is still consistent with a positive relationship between irritability and maternal contact.

From these findings it is difficult to posit a causal relationship. However, it seems most plausible that it is the infant's cry that is determining the maternal behavior. Mothers describe the cry as a signal that the infant needs attention and they often report their nurturant actions in response to the cry. Furthermore, the cry is a noxious and often painful stimulus that probably has biological utility for the infant, propelling the mother into action for her own comfort as well as out of concern for the infant. Ethological reports confirm the proposition that the cry functions as a "releaser" of maternal behavior (Bowlby, 1958; Hinde, *et al.,* 1964; Hoffman, *et al.,* 1966). Bowlby (1958) states:

> It is my belief that both of them (crying and smiling), act as social releasers of instinctual responses in mothers. As regards crying, there is plentiful evidence from the animal world that this is so:

probably in all cases the mother responds promptly and unfailingly to her infant's bleat, call or cry. It seems to me clear that similar impulses are also evoked in the human mother. . . .

Thus, we are adopting the hypothesis that the correlations we have obtained reflect a causal sequence whereby the cry acts to instigate maternal intervention. Certainly there are other important determinants of maternal contact, and it is evident that mothers exhibit considerable variability concerning how responsive they are to the stimulus signal of the cry. Yet it seems that the effect of the cry is sufficient to account at least partially for the structure of the mother-infant relationship. We further maintain the thesis that the infant's cry shapes maternal behavior even for the instance where the negative correlation was noted at 3 months for the males. The effect is still present, but in this case the more irritable infants were responded to *less* by the mothers. Our speculation for explaining this relationship and the fact that, conversely, a positive correlation was obtained for the female infants is that the mothers probably were negatively reinforced for responding to a number of the boys but tended to be positively reinforced for their responses toward the girls. That is, mothers of the more irritable boys may have learned that they could not be successful in quieting boys whereas the girls were more uniformly responsive (quieted by) to maternal handling. There is not much present in our data to bear out this contention, with the exception that the males were significantly more irritable than the girls for both observations. However, evidence that suggests males are more subject to inconsolable states comes from studies (Serr and Ismajovich, 1963; McDonald, Gynther, and Christakos, 1963; Stechler, 1964) which indicate that males have less well-organized physiological reactions and are more vulnerable to adverse conditions than females. The relatively more efficient functioning of the female organism should thus contribute to their responding more favorably to maternal intervention.

In summary, we propose that maternal behavior initially tends to be under the control of the stimulus and reinforcing conditions provided by the young infant. As the infant gets older, the mother, if she behaved contingently toward his signals, gradually acquires reinforcement value which in turn increases her efficacy in regulating infant behaviors. Concurrently, the earlier control asserted by the infant becomes less functional and diminishes. In a sense, the point where the infant's control over the mother declines and the mother's reinforcement value emerges could be regarded as the first manifestation of socialization, or at least represents the initial conditions favoring social learning. Thus, at first the mother is shaped by the infant and this later facilitates her shaping the behavior of the infant. We would therefore say that the infant, through his own temperament or signal system, contributes to establishing the stimulus and reinforcement value eventually associated with the mother. According to this reasoning, the more irritable infants (who can be soothed) whose mothers respond in a contingent manner to their signals should become most amenable to the effects of social reinforcement and manifest a higher degree of attachment behavior. The fact that the mothers responded more contingently toward the female infants should maximize the ease with which females learn social responses.

This statement is consistent with data on older children which indicate that girls learn social responses earlier and with greater facility than boys. (Becker, 1964). Previously we argued that the mothers learned to be more contingent toward the girls because they probably were more responsive to maternal intervention. An alternative explanation is that mothers respond contingently to the girls and not to the boys as a form of differential reinforcement, whereby, in keeping with cultural expectations, the mother is initiating a pattern that contributes to males being more aggressive or assertive, and less responsive to socialization. Indeed, these two explanations are not inconsistent with one another since the mother who is unable to soothe an upset male infant may eventually come to classify this intractable irritability as an expression of "maleness."

There are certain environmental settings where noncontingent caretaking is more likely and these situations should impede social learning and result in weaker attachment responses. Lennenberg (1965) found that deaf parents tended not to respond to the infant's cry. One would have to assume that it was more than the inability to hear the infant that influenced their behavior, since even when they observed their crying infants these parents tended not to make any effort to quiet them. The function of the cry as a noxious stimulus or "releaser" of maternal behaviour did not pertain under these unusual circumstances. Infants in institutions also are more likely to be cared for in terms of some arbitrary schedule with little opportunity for them to shape caretakers in accordance with their own behavioral vicissitudes.

Although we have shown that there is a covariation between maternal contact and infant irritability and have attempted to develop some theoretical implications concerning this relationship, considerable variability remains as to how responsive different mothers are to their infants' crying behavior. This variability probably reflects differences in maternal attitudes. Women who express positive feelings about babies and who consider the well-being of the infant to be of essential importance should tend to be more responsive to signals of distress from the infant than women who exhibit negative maternal attitudes. In order to test this assumption, we first derived a score for measuring maternal responsiveness. This score was obtained through a regression analysis where we determined the amount of maternal contact that would be expected for each mother by controlling for her infant's irritability score. The expected maternal contact score was then subtracted from the mother's actual contact score and this difference was used as the measure of maternal responsivity. The maternal responsivity scores were obtained separately for the 3-week and the 3-month observations. The parents of 23 of the infants in our sample were interviewed for a project investigating marital careers, approximately 2 years prior to the birth of their child, and these interviews provided us with the unusual opportunity of having antecedent data relevant to prospective parental functioning. A number of variables from this material were rated and two of them, "acceptance of nurturant role," and the "degree that the baby is seen in a positive sense" were correlated with the scores on the maternal responsivity measure.[1] Annotated definitions of these interview variables are as follows:

"Acceptance of nurturant role" concerns the degree to which the subject is invested in caring for others and in acquiring domestic and homemaking skills such as cooking, sewing, and cleaning house. Evidence for a high rating would be describing the care of infants and children with much pleasure and satisfaction even when this involves subordinating her own needs.

The interview variable concerning the "degree that the baby is seen in a positive sense" assesses the extent to which the subject views a baby as gratifying, pleasant and nonburdensome. In discussing what she imagines infants to be like she stresses the warmer, more personal, and rewarding aspects of the baby and anticipates these qualities as primary.

Correlations of .40 ($p < .10$ level) and .48 ($p < .05$ level) were obtained between the ratings on "acceptance of nurturant role" and the maternal responsivity scores for the 3-week and 3-month observations, respectively. The "degree that the baby is seen in a positive sense" correlated 38 ($p < .10$ level) and .44 ($p < .05$ level) with maternal responsivity for the two ages. However, the two interview variables were so highly intercorrelated ($r = .93$) that they clearly involve the same dimension. Thus, the psychological status of the mother, assessed substantially before the birth of her infant, as well as the infant's state, are predictive of her maternal behavior. Schaffer and Emerson (1964) found that maternal responsiveness to the cry was associated with the attachment behavior of infants. Extrapolating from our findings, we now have some basis for assuming that the early attitudes of the mother represent antecedent conditions for facilitating the attachment behavior observed by Schaffer and Emerson.

The discussion to this point has focused on some of the conditions that seemingly affect the structure of the mother-infant relationship and influence the reinforcement and stimulus values associated with the mother. Next we would like to consider, in a more speculative vein, one particular class of maternal behaviors that has important reinforcing properties for the infant. This discussion will be more general and depart from a direct consideration of the data. There has been mounting evidence in the psychological literature that the organism has a "need for stimulation" and that variations in the quantity and quality of stimulation received can have a significant effect on many aspects of development (Moss, 1965; Murphy, et al., 1962; White and Held, 1963). Additional reports indicate that, not only does the infant require stimulation, but that excessive or chaotic dosages of stimulation can be highly disruptive of normal functioning (Murphy, et al., 1962). Furthermore, there appear to be substantial individual differences in the stimulation that is needed or in the extremes that can be tolerated. As the infant gets older he becomes somewhat capable of regulating the stimulation that is assimilated. However, the very young infant is completely dependent on the caretaking environment to provide and modulate the stimulation he experiences. It is in this regard that the mother has a vital role.

The main points emphasized in the literature are that stimulation serves to modulate the state or arousal level of the infant, organize and direct attentional processes, and facilitate normal growth and development. Bridger (1965) has shown that stimulation tends to have either an arousing or quieting effect, depending on the existing state of the infant. Infants who are quiet tend to be aroused, whereas aroused infants tend to be quieted by moderate stimulation. Moreover, according to data collected by Birns (1965), these effects occur for several stimulus modalities and with stable individual differences in responsivity. (We found that mothers made greater use of techniques involving stimulation—"stresses musculature" and "stimulates/arouses"—with the males who as a group were more irritable than the females.)

The capacity for stimulus configurations to direct attention, once the infant is in an optimally receptive state also has been demonstrated by a number of studies. Young infants have been observed to orient toward many stimuli (Razran, 1961;Fantz, 1963), and certain stimuli are so compelling that they tend to "capture" the infant in a fixed orientation (Stechler, 1965). Other studies have demonstrated that infants show clear preferences for gazing at more complex visual patterns (Fantz, 1963). Thus, stimulation can influence the set of the infant to respond by modifying the state of the organism as well as structure learning possibilities through directing the infant's attention. White (1959) has systematically described how stimulation contributes to the learning process in infants. He points out that the infant is provided with the opportunity to activate behavioral potentials in attempting to cope with control stimulation. Motor and perceptual skills eventually become refined and sharpened in the process of responding to stimulus configurations and it is this pattern of learning which White calls "effectance behavior."

Not all levels of stimulation are equally effective in producing a condition whereby the infant is optimally alert and attentive. Excessive stimulation has a disruptive effect and according to drive reduction theorists the organism behaves in ways aimed at reducing stimulation that exceeds certain limits. Leuba (1955), in an attempt to establish rapprochement between the drive reduction view and the research evidence that shows that there is a need for stimulation, states that there is an optimal level of stimulation that is required, and that the organism acts either to reduce or to increase stimulation so as to stay within this optimal range.

The mother is necessarily highly instrumental in mediating much of the stimulation that is experienced by the infant. Her very presence in moving about and caring for the infant provides a constant source of visual, auditory, tactile, kinesthetic and proprioceptive stimulation. In addition to the incidental stimulation she provides, the mother deliberately uses stimulation to regulate the arousal level or state of the infant and to evoke specific responses from him. However, once the infant learns, through conditioning, that the mother is a source of stimulation he can in turn employ existing responses that are instrumental in eliciting stimulation from her. Certain infant behaviors, such as the cry, are so compelling that they readily evoke many forms of stimulation from the mother. It is common knowledge that mothers in attempting to quiet upset infants, often resort to such tactics as using rocking motion, waving bright objects or rattles, or holding the infant close and thus provide warmth and physical contact. The specific function of stimulation in placating the crying infant can be somewhat obscured because of the possibility of confounding conditions. In our discussion so far we have indicated that stimulation inherently has a quieting effect irrespective of learning but that crying also can become a learned instrumental behavior which terminates once the reinforcement of stimulation is presented. However, it is often difficult to distinguish the unlearned from the learned patterns of functioning, since the infant behavior (crying) and the outcome (quieting) are highly similar in both instances. Perhaps the best means for determining whether learning has occurred would be if we could demonstrate that the infant makes anticipatory responses, such as the reduction in crying behavior to cues, prior to the actual occurrence of stimulation. In addition to the cry, the smile and the vocalization of the infant can become highly effective, and consequently well-learned conditioned responses for evoking stimulation from adult caretakers. Rheingold (1956) has shown that when institutional children are given more caretaking by an adult they show an increase in their smiling rate to that caretaker as well as to other adults. Moreover, for a few weeks after the intensive caretaking stopped there were further substantial increments in the smiling rate, which suggests that the infant after experiencing relative deprivation worked harder in attempting to restitute the stimulation level experienced earlier.

It seems plausible that much of the early social behavior seen in infants and children consists of attempts to elicit responses from others. We mentioned earlier that it has been stressed in recent psychological literature that individuals have a basic need for stimulation. Since the mother, and eventually others, are highly instrumental in providing and monitoring the stimulation that is experienced by the infant, it seems likely that the child acquires expectancies for having this need satisfied through social interactions and that stimulation comes to serve as a basis for relating to others. Indeed, Schaffer and Emerson (1964) have shown that the amount of stimulation provided by adults is one of the major determinants of infants' attachment behavior. Strange as well as familiar adults who have been temporarily separated from an infant often attempt to gain rapport with the infant through acts of stimulation. It is quite common for the father, upon returning home from work, to initiate actions aimed at stimulating the child, and these actions are usually responded to with clear pleasure. Because of the expectancies that are built up some of the provocative behaviors seen in children, particularly when confronted with a nonresponsive adult, could be interpreted as attempts to elicit socially mediated stimulation.

The learning we have discussed is largely social since the infant is dependent on others, particularly the mother, for reinforcements. This dependency on others is what constitutes attachment behavior, and the specific makeup of the attachment is determined by the class of reinforcements that are involved. The strength of these learned attachment behaviors is maximized through stimulation, since the mother is often the embodiment of this reinforcement as well as the agent for delivering it. The social aspect of this learning is further enhanced because of the reciprocal dependence of the mother on the infant for reinforcement. That is, the mother learns certain conditioned responses, often involving acts of stimulation, that are aimed at evoking desired states or responses from the infant.

In conclusion, what we did was study and analyze some of the factors which structure the mother-infant relationship. A central point is that the state of the infant affects the quantity and quality of maternal behavior, and this in turn would seem to influence the course of future social learning. Furthermore, through controlling for the state of the infant, we were able to demonstrate the effects of pre-parental attitudes on one aspect of maternal behavior, namely, the mother's responsiveness toward her infant. Many investigators, in conducting controlled laboratory studies, have stressed that the state of the infant is crucial in determining the nature of his responses to different stimuli. This concern is certainly highly relevant to our data, collected under naturalistic conditions.

NOTES

[1]Dr. Kenneth Robson collaborated in developing these variables, and made the ratings.

REFERENCES

Becker, W. C. Consequences of different kinds of parental discipline. In M. L. Hoffman & Lois W. Hoffman (Eds.), *Review of child development research: I.* New York: Russell Sage Found., 1964, 169–208.

Birns, B. Individual differences in human neonates' responses to stimulation. *Child Develpm.,* 1965, *36,* 249–256.

Bloom, B. S. *Stability and change in human characteristics.* New York: Wiley, 1964.

Bowlby, J. The nature of a child's tie to his mother. *Internat. J. Psychoanal.,* 1958, *39,* 350–373.

Bridger, W. H. Psychophysiological measurement of the roles of state in the human neonate. Paper presented at Soc. Res. Child Develpm., Minneapolis, April, 1965.

Brown, Janet L. States in newborn infants. *Merrill-Palmer Quart.,* 1964, *10,* 313–327.

Escalona, Sibylle K. The study of individual differences and the problem of state. *J. Child Psychiat.,* 1962, *1,* 11–37.

Fantz, R. Pattern vision in newborn infants. *Science,* 1963, *140,* 296–297.

Hess, E. H. Imprinting. *Science,* 1959, *130,* 133–141.

Hinde, R. A., Rowell, T. E., & Spencer-Booth, Y. Behavior of living rhesus monkeys in their first six months. *Proc. Zool. Soc., London,* 1964, *143,* 609–649.

Hoffman, H., *et al.* Enhanced distress vocalization through selective reinforcement. *Science,* 1966, *151,* 354–356.

Lennenberg, E. H., Rebelsky, Freda., & Nichols, I. A. The vocalizations of infants born to deaf and to hearing parents. *Vita Humana,* 1965, *8,* 23–37.

Leuba, C. Toward some integration of learning theories: The concept of optimal stimulation. *Psychol. Rep.,* 1955, *1,* 27–33.

Levy, D. M. *Behavioral analysis.* Springfield, Ill.: Charles C Thomas, 1958.

McDonald, R. L., Gynther, M. D., & Christakos, A. C. Relations between maternal anxiety and obstetric complications. *Psychosom. Med.,* 1963, *25,* 357–362.

Moss, H. A. Coping behavior, the need for stimulation, and normal development. *Merrill-Palmer Quart.,* 1965, *11,* 171–179.

Murphy, Lois B., *et al. The widening world of childhood.* New York: Basic Books, 1962.

Noirot, Eliane. Changes in responsiveness to young in the adult mouse: the effect of external stimuli. *J. comp. physiol. Psychol.,* 1964, *57,* 97–99.

Razran, G. The observable unconscious and the inferable conscious in current Soviet psychophysiology: Interoceptive conditioning, semantic conditioning, and the orienting reflex. *Psychol. Rev.,* 1961, *68,* 81–146.

Rheingold, Harriet L. The modification of social responsiveness in institutional babies. *Monogr. Soc. Res. Child Develpm.,* 1956, *21,* No. 2 (Serial No. 23).

Schaffer, H. R., & Emerson, Peggy E. The development of social attachments in infancy. *Monogr. Soc. Res. Child Develpm.,* 1964, *29,* (Serial No. 94).

Serr, D. M., & Ismajovich, B. Determination of the primary sex ratio from human abortions. *Amer J. Obstet. Gyncol.,* 1963, *87,* 63–65.

Stechler, G. A longitudinal follow-up of neonatal apnea. *Child Develpm.,* 1964, *35,* 333–348.

White, B. L. & Held, R. Plasticity in perceptual development during the first six months of life. Paper presented at Amer. Ass. Advncmnt. Sci., Cleveland, Ohio, December, 1963.

White, R. W. Motivation reconsidered: the concept of competence. *Psychol. Rev.,* 1959, *66,* 297–323.

Wolff, P. H. Observations on newborn infants. *Psychosom. Med.,* 1959, *21,* 110–118.

3.4

A Comparison of Maternal Care and Infant Behavior in Japanese-American, American, and Japanese Families

William Caudill
Lois Frost

Earlier reports from this ongoing research project have dealt with a comparison of the everyday behavior of mothers and 3 to 4 month old infants in middle class homes in Japan and America (Caudill and Weinstein, 1969; Caudill, 1971). These earlier analyses show that the American mothers do more lively chatting to their babies, and that as a result the American babies have a generally higher level of vocalization and particularly they respond with greater amounts of happy vocalization and gross motor activity. The Japanese mothers, on the other hand, do more vocal lulling, carrying, and rocking of their babies, and as a result the Japanese babies are more physically passive; in addition, the Japanese babies have a greater amount of unhappy vocalization as their mothers take longer to respond to such signals for attention. Thus, because of the different styles of caretaking in the two cultures it appears that by 3 to 4 months of age the infants have already learned (or have been conditioned) to behave in culturally distinctive ways and that this has happened out of awareness and well before the development of language. If true, these findings have major thoretical implications for the understanding of personality development in relation to the transmission and persistence of cultural patterns of emotion, cognition, and behavior in human groups.

Two somewhat opposed arguments might be directed against the interpretation just given to the earlier findings. The first argument is that the behavioral differences between the Japanese and American infants might be due more to group genetic factors than to cultural learning or conditioning (see, for example, Freedman and Freedman, 1969). The second argument is that as social change takes place in a human group, succeeding generations of mothers will care for their babies in a different fashion and that this will result in significant shifts in the behavior of the babies (see, for example, Bronfenbrenner, 1958).

Comparable data obtained from Japanese-American mothers and infants can provide information to help settle both of these arguments, and this is the task set for this paper. Japanese-Americans tend to marry within their own group, and hence the children of these intragroup marriages are genetically Japanese. If the first argument is the more true, then group genetic factors should remain as an important influence on the behavior of Japanese-American infants and they should be closer to Japanese than to American infants in their degree of physical passivity, lesser total vocalization, and greater unhappy vocalization.[1] In support of the second argument, the vast majority of Japanese immigrants came to the mainland of the United States between 1890–1924, and Japanese-American mothers are now having the third generation of babies to be born in this country. Since, as indicated more fully below, Japanese-Americans have so successfully adapted to American middle class life, the present generation of mothers ought to be rearing their babies in American style and the babies should be responding accordingly; that is, the Japanese-American infants should be closer to American than to Japanese infants in their degree of high physical activity, greater total vocalization, and particularly greater happy vocalization.

BACKGROUND OF THE JAPANESE-AMERICANS

The Japanese-Americans are an extraordinarily interesting group of people to study (see Caudill, 1952; Caudill and DeVos, 1956; Kitano, 1969). At the end of the nineteenth, and during the beginning of the twentieth century, fairly large groups of Japanese immigrated either directly to the mainland of the United States, or to Hawaii. These people called themselves Issei—meaning first generation. They came largely from farming families in the southern part of the Japanese islands, and for a short while they worked as laborers in the United States, but on the mainland they soon shifted to being independent truck and garden farmers and small businessmen in and around the major cities of California, Washington, and Oregon. At first the immigrant Issei were largely men, but as they found that they were not going to return to Japan, they arranged for marriages in their home prefectures and the brides came to join them in the United States.

At the beginning of World War II the Japanese-Americans on the Pacific Coast numbered about 130,000 persons (with an additional 160,000 persons in Hawaii). By this time the citizen children of the Issei, known as Nisei—meaning second generation —had achieved a very high educational level and were in their early to mid-twenties when war broke out. During the war, the Japanese-Americans were first placed in relocation camps, and later allowed to migrate to middle western and eastern cities, but could not return to the Pacific Coast until after the war. The Nisei made an outstanding record in the armed services of the United States.

Both during and after World War II, the Nisei moved quickly into predominantly white collar and professional occupations and established themselves as solidly middle class. They were able to do this, despite highly visible racial differences, because of the high degree of compatibility between Japanese and American middle class values—both cultures emphasizing at that time educational attainment, hard work, and long-range goals (see Caudill and DeVos, 1956). The phrase "compatibility of values" is important because although the values of the Nisei and those of middle class Americans were similar, they were far from being the same. Americans looking at the Nisei thought that they were just like themselves when, in considerable part, the Nisei were operating on a Japanese set of values that worked very well in the middle class American world.

By 1970 the Nisei were well into middle age, and their children, known as Sansei —meaning third generation—also had achieved a very high educational level, and were beginning to establish their own families. The children in these families are known as Yonsei—meaning fourth generation—and this article is concerned with the behavior of Sansei mothers and their Yonsei babies.

At the present time many of the Sansei are critical of their Nisei parents for being so establishment-minded and so successful in the white American middle class world; and some of the Sansei, at least on university campuses, are beginning to try to form themselves into a radical group. As a group, however, the Sansei have come rather late to radicalism and are rather mild in their demonstration of it compared with their black, Spanish-American, and white counterparts. Most of those Sansei who have graduated from high school and college, established families, and are working in white collar and professional jobs, give every evidence of being law-abiding, middle class American citizens.

Given the foregoing historical background, the Sansei should in the area of family life and child rearing look very much like middle class Americans. At the same time, and in light of the compatibility rather than identity of values discussed earlier, it could be expected that a good many Japanese ideas on how to care for and rear children will have been passed down, largely out of awareness, from Issei to Nisei to Sansei mothers. In research terms then, the expectation is that the behavior both of Sansei mothers and their Yonsei babies will, for the most part, be closer to that of the American sample, but in some regards there will still be evidence of a Japanese cultural heritage.[2]

SAMPLE POPULATIONS AND METHOD

The Japanese and American samples have been fully described in Caudill and Weinstein (1969). In general, naturalistic observations were made on two consecutive days during 1961–1964 in the homes of 30 Japanese and 30 white American firstborn, 3 to 4 month old infants equally divided by sex, and living in intact middle class urban families. Data on the ordinary daily life of the infant were obtained by time-sampling, one observation being made every 15th second over a 10-minute period in terms of a predetermined set of categories concerning the behavior of the mother (or other caretaker) and the behavior of the infant, resulting in a sheet containing 40 equally spaced observations. There was a 5-minute break between observation periods, and 10 observation sheets were completed on each of the 2 days, giving a total of 800 observations for each case. In the analysis already published, these data were analyzed by multivariate analysis of variance using three independent variables: culture (Japanese, American), father's occupation (salaried, independent), and sex of infant (male, female). The effects of each of these independent variables were examined while controlling on the other two variables, and culture proved overwhelmingly to be the most important variable. Interactions between the independent variables revealed nothing of importance. Essentially the same methods of data analysis are used in arriving at the results reported in this article, except that, for reasons given below, only culture and sex of infant are used as independent variables.

TABLE 1.   OBSERVER RELIABILITY AND WEIGHTS USED FOR STANDARDIZATION OF FREQUENCIES OF OBSERVATIONS ACROSS CULTURES

DEPENDENT VARIABLES	AVERAGE PERCENT AGREEMENT PER CASE*			WEIGHT USED FOR STANDARDIZATION†		
	JAPANESE (7 CASES)	AMERICAN (3 CASES)	JAPANESE AMERICAN (4 CASES)	JAPANESE (7 CASES)	AMERICAN (3 CASES)	JAPANESE AMERICAN (4 CASES)
INFANT BEHAVIOR						
Awake	98	100	100	. . .	. . .	. . .
Breast or bottle	99	100	97	. . .	. . .	. . .
All food	99	99	98	. . .	.98	. . .
Finger or pacifier	92	84	85	. . .	.94	1.02
Total vocal	91	80	73	1.04	.86	. . .
Unhappy	89	88	73	1.05	1.07	.97
Happy	70	70	72	1.10	.64	1.04
Active	69	74	77	.91	.75	.90
Baby plays	85	93	75	.96	1.07	1.28
CARETAKER BEHAVIOR						
Presence of	99	100	100	. . .	. . .	. . .
Feeds	99	100	99	. . .	. . .	. . .
Diapers	95	96	94	.98	.93	1.09
Dresses	84	99	85	1.06	1.03	1.17
Positions	49	77	56	1.75	.71	.62
Pats or touches	78	87	59	.82	.84	.69
Other care	85	85	72	.97	.86	.80
Plays with	67	86	85	1.34	1.16	.93
Looks at	94	90	99	. . .	1.06	. . .
Talks to	90	83	88	. . .	.83	.94
Chats	90	83	89	. . .	.83	.96
Lulls	94	100	78	. . .	. . .	. . .
In arms	100	99	97	. . .	. . .	. . .
Rocks	90	88	91	.95	. . .	1.02

*Agreement between two observers as to the presence (Yes) or absence (No) of a behavior is classified within four cells: (a) Yes/Yes, (b) Yes/No, (c) No/Yes, (d) No/No. Percent agreement is computed as the ratio of (2a) to (2a + b + c), thus avoiding the use of the somewhat spurious agreement on absence of behavior.
Weight used to standardize frequencies across cultures is computed as the ratio of (Sum of Caudill's Presence Scores) to (Sum of Other Observer's Presence Scores).

The Japanese-American sample was gathered by the junior author, Lois Frost, after she had read the article by Caudill and Weinstein (1969). Using the same methods, she carried out observations during 1969–1970 in Sacramento, California, in the homes of 21 Sansei mothers having a 3 to 4 month old Yonsei baby (in general, see Frost 1970). All of the Sansei families are middle class as measured by the occupation and education of the father, and the education of the mother. By occupation, 11 of the fathers have professional and managerial positions, 7 are white collar and clerical workers, and 3 are in skilled trades; by education, 10 of the fathers are college graduates, 4 have some college training, and 7 are high school graduates. By education, 8 of the mothers are college graduates, 11 have some college training, and 2 are high school graduates. All of the fathers work as salaried employees in large businesses, and for this reason the classification by father's occupation into salaried and independent families is omitted as a variable in the analyses in this article.[3]

Among the 21 Yonsei infants, 7 are male and 14 are female, and 11 are firstborn and 10 are later born. Because the sex distribution is more equal and all infants are firstborn in the Japanese and American samples, we did a complete internal analysis of the Japanese-American data using sex and birth order as independent variables. The results are almost entirely negative.[4] We feel it is possible, therefore, to make a direct comparison of the data from the three cultural groups.

After the junior author had collected her data, she wrote to the senior author informing him of her study. He then arranged to visit her for consultation and for the purpose of doing a reliability check. In January, 1971, the two authors carried out observations together in the homes of four infants in order to obtain data for testing inter-observer reliability and for the standardization of scores on the dependent variables used in describing infant and caretaker behaviors. The terms "caretaker" and "mother" are used as interchangeable in this paper because the caretaker was the mother in over 90 percent of the observations in each of the three cultures. Table 1 gives the names of the dependent variables used in the analyses along with an estimate of their reliability and the weights used for standardization scores.

The names of the dependent variables are fairly self-explanatory, and have been defined in detail in previous publication (Caudill and Weinstein, 1969). The junior author used these detailed definitions in collecting her data (see Frost, 1970). A brief explanation of the variables is, however, useful for the reader. Starting with the infant behaviors, "awake" is reciprocal with "asleep" and therefore only the scores for "awake" are used here. "Breast or bottle" must be in the infant's mouth at the time of observation in order to be scored. "All food" is a composite variable combining the additive variables of "breast or bottle" and "semisolid food" such as commercially prepared baby foods, crackers, biscuits, and so forth which must be in the infant's mouth at time of observation. Since there is very little use of semisolid food at 3 to 4 months of age in Japan, we do not include this variable here, but rather use the composite variable of "all food." "Finger or pacifier" denotes all such actions as sucking on a finger or hand, or sucking on other objects such as a pacifier or the edge of a blanket. "Total vocal" is a composite variable combining the additive variables of "unhappy" and "happy" vocalizations which must be distinctive voiced sounds;

other sounds such as hiccups and coughs are not scored as vocalization. "Active" means gross bodily movements, usually of the arms and legs, and does not include minor twitches or startles. "Baby plays" is a composite variable meaning that the baby was playing with an object at the time of observation which was either a "toy," his "hand" or other part of his body, or an "other object" such as a blanket or the edge of a crib. The three additive detailed variables are combined here into the composite variable of "baby plays."

Turning to the caretaker behaviors, "presence of" means that the caretaker must be able both to see and hear the baby at the time of observation. "Feeds" means that the caretaker is offering the infant the breast, bottle, or food. "Diapers" is restricted to the checking for wetness and the taking off and putting on of the diaper and its cover, plus assisting the baby to urinate or defecate, and the cleaning, powdering, and oiling of the baby's body. All other removal, putting on, or rearranging of clothing is scored as "dresses." "Positions" is the manipulation of the baby's body to make him more comfortable. "Pats or touches" is a combined variable meaning rhythmic stroking or patting as in burping, or that the caretaker's hand is resting on the baby's body with the apparent intent of soothing. "Other care" is a general category including other caretaking acts such as adjusting the covers under which the baby is lying, wiping his face, or taking his temperature. "Plays with" means that the caretaker is attempting to amuse or entertain the baby by such acts as playing peek-a-boo, showing the baby a toy, and so forth. "Looks at" means that the caretaker is specifically directing her visual attention to the baby. "Talks to" is a composite variable combining the additive variable of "chats" and "lulls." "Chats" means that the caretaker is talking or singing to the baby in a lively fashion, "lulls" is a very delimited behavior, and means that the caretaker is softly humming or singing a lullaby, or making repetitive comforting noises, with the apparent intent of soothing and quieting the baby or getting him to go to sleep. "In arms" means that the baby is being held in the caretaker's arms or lap, or is being carried by the caretaker. "Rocks" includes all conscious acts of the caretaker to cause the baby to sway rhythmically back and forth; it is not scored when the infant is being carried and is merely being moved up and down by the normal walking motion of the caretaker.

In assessing the reliabilities shown in Table 1 we used the severe criterion of requiring agreement as to the presence of a particular behavior at the level of the individual observation. Because of the visual difficulty, however, under conditions of actual observation of picking the correct column for time on the form in which to check the presence of a behavior, we counted agreement if the two observers had checked the same column or contiguous columns for the presence of a particular behavior. In some places in the raw data for the reliability check, the observers have obviously recorded the same behavior for the infant and caretaker over a 10-minute sheet of 40 columns but are consistently off one column across the entire sheet.

In general the reliability of the dependent variables is satisfactory in each of the three cultures. Altogether there are only three instances in which reliability is poor: a level of 49 percent in the Japanese data and of 56 percent in the Japanese-American data on "positions," and a level of 59 percent in the Japanese-American data on "pats or touches." In part, satisfactory reliability is related to the frequency of occurrence of a dependent variable, and the relative frequency of occurrence of the behaviors of infant and caretaker can be seen in the tables given later in the discussion of the findings.

As pointed out in earlier publication (Caudill and Weinstein, 1969), a variable can be satisfactorily reliable and still be "biased." That is, compared to the scores of a constant observer (Caudill in all three cultures), separate observers in each culture (Notsuki for the Japanese, Weinstein for the American, and Frost for the Japanese-American) may differ proportionately from the constant observer in the same or in opposite directions. For example, on "total vocal" Caudill had 104 percent as many scores as Notsuki, 86 percent as many as Weinstein, and had the same proportion, 100 percent, as Frost. In order to eliminate these differences where present, the scores of the separate observers are standardized to those of the constant observer. Thus, in the example given for "total vocal" Notsuki's scores are increased by a weight of 1.04, Weinstein's are decreased by a weight of .86, and there is no change in Frost's scores. The weights used to standardize the scores for the dependent variables across the three cultures can be seen in Table 1. Without standardization, it is quite possible to have satisfactory reliability among observers within several cultures, but not to know whether the general perception of the observers is the same or different across cultures.

In this article we are primarily interested in the relative position of the Japanese-Americans in comparison with the other two cultural groups on *each* of the behaviors of infant and caretaker considered singly. Thus, our main technique of analysis was an analysis of variance in which the dependent variables were the behaviors of infant and caretaker, and the independent variables were sex of infant and cultural group. In examining the effects of one independent variable we always controlled for the effects of the other. For each dependent variable we made a series of all possible paired-group comparisons (Japanese and American, Japanese and Japanese-American, and American and Japanese-American).[5] We also did a Pearsonian correlational analysis of the dependent variables for each culture in order to look at patterns of intercorrelation, and we will make a limited use of these patterns in reporting our findings.

FINDINGS

In all three sets of paired comparisons for the dependent variables none of the interactions between the independent variables are significant, and there are no findings by sex of infant. Cultural differences, however, are highly significant as can be seen in Tables 2 and 3. The mean frequencies given for the dependent variables in the tables represent their average occurrence over 800 observations for each case, and all significant differences between cultural groups are reported on the basis of a two-tailed test.

The findings for the dependent variables by cultural group are reported on two separate tables because earlier published comparisons of Japanese and Americans

(Caudill and Weinstein, 1969) showed that the dependent variables divided into two groupings which we called (a) the expression and caretaking of the infant's "basic biological needs," and (b) "styles of behavior" by the infant and caretaker. In general, the Japanese and Americans showed no difference in the first grouping, but were distinctively different in the second grouping. We expected that the Japanese-Americans would also show no difference in the expression and care of the infant's basic needs, and would be closer to the Americans in styles of behaving. On the whole, the results are as expected, but with some surprises, particularly in the case of basic needs.

TABLE 2. PAIRED CULTURAL COMPARISONS OF VARIABLES RELATED TO CARE OF THE INFANT'S BASIC NEEDS

DEPENDENT VARIABLES	MEAN FREQUENCIES			CULTURAL COMPARISONS		
	JAPANESE (30 CASES)	AMERICAN (30 CASES)	JAPANESE-AMERICAN (21 CASES)	JAPANESE AND AMERICAN $p<$	JAPANESE AND JAPANESE-AMERICAN $p<$	AMERICAN AND JAPANESE-AMERICAN $p<$
INFANT BEHAVIOR						
Awake	499	489	511	. . .	. . .	. . .
Breast or bottle	66	55	77	. . .	. . .	. . .
All food	68	74	112	. . .	0.001	0.05
CARETAKER BEHAVIOR						
Presence of	549	414	489	0.01	. . .	. . .
Feeds	74	70	113	. . .	0.01	0.01
Diapers	23	17	38	. . .	0.001	0.001
Dresses	13	13	4	. . .	0.001	0.001
Pats or touches	34	46	53	. . .	0.05	. . .
Other care	17	23	11	. . .	. . .	0.05
Looks at	247	293	288	. . .	. . .	. . .

On Table 2 it can be seen that there are no differences in any of the paired comparisons for the amount of time the baby is "awake," and this argues for the biological similarity of the infants with regard to the needs for sleep and awakeness. There also are no statistical differences for the amount of time spent in the intake of milk from "breast or bottle," although the Japanese-American mean is the highest on this variable. On the intake of "all food," however, the Japanese-American babies are significantly greater than the babies in either of the other groups. The reason for this is obviously due to the greater intake of "semisolid food" (which is the difference between the means for "breast or bottle" and "all food") by the Japanese-American babies when coupled with their higher mean on "breast or bottle."

From the above results it is clear that the Japanese-American mother is making a greater use both of milk and semisolid food in the feeding of her baby, and this shows up in the finding that the Sansei mother is greater than either the Japanese or the American mother on the variable of "feeds." The Sansei mother appears to have taken on the American pattern of a greater use of semisolid food without having given up the Japanese pattern of a somewhat greater use of milk, and thus she appears as a sort of super-caretaker in the matter of feeding. Given this finding, it is not surprising that the Sansei mother is also doing more diapering than the mothers in the other two groups, also has a higher mean on patting and touching as a large part of the behavior included under this latter variable consists of burping the baby.

On the remaining variables in Table 2, there are no differences in the paired comparisons on the variable of "looks at," and the Sansei mother is intermediate between the Japanese and American mothers in the amount of time she is in the "presence of" her baby. The significantly lesser amount of time spent by the Sansei mother in dressing her baby compared with the mothers in the other two groups is probably related to differences in climate; observations were evenly spaced throughout the year in all three cultures, and on the average it is colder in Tokyo and Washington, D.C., than it is in Sacramento. Thus, the Yonsei baby was probably more lightly clothed during the winter months. The same reasoning is applicable for the Sansei mother's lower mean on "other care" as this variable includes such behavior as adjusting bedclothes, wiping runny noses, and so forth.

Turning to Table 3, the main variables of interest in terms of the questions with which we began this paper are the vocalization and activity of the infant, and the verbalization to the infant by the caretaker. As can be seen, the Yonsei baby is more like the American than the Japanese baby in his greater amount of happy vocalization and physical activity, and in his lesser amount of unhappy vocalization. Equally, the Sansei mother is more like the American than the Japanese mother in the greater amount of chatting she does to her baby. Moreover, the infant's happy vocalization and the caretaker's chatting to infant are significantly correlated in the American (.39, $p < 0.05$) and Japanese-American (.57, $p < 0.01$) data, but are not so in the Japanese data (−.09, n.s.). These results indicate that American and Sansei mothers are making a greater, and more discriminating (see Caudill, 1971), use of their voices as a means of communicating with their babies and the babies respond accordingly —the more the mother chats to the baby, the more he is happily vocal. The Sansei mothers are also more like the American mothers in several other regards—they do more positioning and less rocking of their babies than do the Japanese mothers. Thus, the major finding from Table 3 is that the Japanese-American mothers and infants are closer in their style of behavior to their American than to their Japanese counterparts.

In some respects, however, the data in Table 3 also show that the Japanese-American mothers and infants have retained certain patterns of behavior from their Japanese cultural heritage. The Sansei mother is more like the Japanese mother in the greater amount of time she spends in playing with her baby, and this finding is probably related to the finding that the Yonsei baby is more like the Japanese baby in playing less by himself. In addition, the Yonsei and Japanese babies are alike in that they do less nonnutritive sucking on "finger or pacifier" than do the American babies. Finally, the Sansei mother is more like the Japanese mother in doing more carrying of the baby in her arms and lulling.[6]

TABLE 3. PAIRED CULTURAL COMPARISONS OF VARIABLES RELATED TO STYLES OF BEHAVING

DEPENDENT VARIABLES	MEAN FREQUENCIES			CULTURAL COMPARISONS		
	JAPANESE (30 CASES)	AMERICAN (30 CASES)	JAPANESE-AMERICAN (21 CASES)	JAPANESE AND AMERICAN $p<$	JAPANESE AND JAPANESE-AMERICAN $p<$	AMERICAN AND JAPANESE-AMERICAN $p<$
INFANT BEHAVIOR						
Finger or pacifier	70	170	45	0.001	. . .	0.001
Total vocal	95	115	135	. . .	0.05	. . .
Unhappy	67	44	27	0.01	0.001	0.05
Happy	30	59	111	0.001	0.001	0.001
Active	51	95	111	0.001	0.01	. . .
Baby plays	83	170	102	0.001	. . .	0.05
CARETAKER BEHAVIOR						
Positions	9	19	25	0.001	0.001	. . .
Plays with	40	23	71	0.05	0.05	0.001
Talks to	104	121	214	. . .	0.001	0.001
Chats	80	119	205	0.01	0.001	0.001
Lulls	23	2	14	0.001	. . .	0.01
In arms	204	132	193	0.05	. . .	0.05
Rocks	49	17	17	0.01	0.05	. . .

CONCLUSION

In general, the main conclusion to be drawn from these data is that the behavior of the Japanese-American mothers and infants is closer to that of the Americans than to that of the Japanese. This is particularly true for the great amount of lively chatting the Sansei mother does to her baby who, in turn, responds with increased happy vocalization and physical activity.

In answer to the arguments with which we began this paper, it would seem, first of all, that the greater activity and happy vocalization of the American baby in contrast to the Japanese baby do not seem to be genetic in origin because the Yonsei baby is like the American baby in these regards even though he is genetically Japanese. Secondly, it would seem that both cultural change and cultural persistence are operating to influence the behavior of the Sansei mothers and their Yonsei babies. On the whole, Sansei mothers have come to behave like other American mothers, but it is also true that in some respects they act like Japanese mothers. And, as would be expected, the Yonsei babies respond appropriately and learn to behave in ways that reflect the cultural style of their parents.

NOTES

[1] Beyond the possible influence of group genetic factors, the question of the effects of nutritional differences might be asked concerning the feeding of babies among Japanese, Americans, and Japanese-Americans. Roughly speaking, there is greater use of breast feeding for a longer period after birth among Japanese mothers and they also delay the introduction of semisolid food longer (usually until about the beginning of the third month) than do American or Japanese-American mothers (who start semisolid food at about the end of the first month). In terms of the nutritional adequacy of the infant's diet, however, there is probably little difference among the three groups since all of the families in each group are urban, middle class, and without serious economic problems.

[2] For a more general discussion, supported by research data, of this question of ethnic identity across three generations of Japanese-American see Masuda, Matsumoto, and Meredith (1970).

[3] The distinction between working as a salaried employee in a large business and working as an owner or employee in a small business is an important one in Japan and has a meaningful influence on the nature of interpersonal relations in the family. For this reason we designed the study of American and Japanese infants to include this distinction as an independent variable. In the analysis of the American and Japanese data (see Caudill and Weinstein, 1969) this variable proved to be of no importance in the American families, and to be of only minor, but still meaningful, importance in the Japanese families where the caretakers in the Japanese independent business families were more present and doing more talking to, carrying, and rocking of their babies who, probably as a consequence, were more awake.

[4] In the internal analysis of the Japanese-American data no interactions are significant, and there are no findings by sex of infant. There is a hint when the dependent variables are considered singly, that firstborn Yonsei infants may be more active, happily vocalizing, and playing by themselves than are later born infants; but, none of the canonical correlations are significant when the entire group of infant dependent variables are considered collectively.

[5] Before doing our paired comparisons of the three cultural groups, we also ran an analysis using all three cultures (Japanese-American, Japanese, American) and sex of infant (male, female) as independent variables in one analysis in order to assure ourselves that we were not capitalizing on extremes in making our paired comparisons. In this overall analysis no interactions are significant, and there are no findings by sex. The comparisons by culture are highly significant, but the similarities and differences between cultural groups appear more clearly in the paired-group analyses.

[6] The Japanese pattern of soothing the baby and getting him to go to sleep is usually a combination of carrying in arms while also lulling and rocking. The Sansei mother seems to have given up rocking, but she still carries and lulls the baby more than the American mother. Frost's more qualitative notes which were made in addition to her quantitative observations provide a number of illustrations of such behavior. For example: "Mrs. H. does not rock her child to sleep, but she plays soft music, holds him in her arms, and dances with him until he falls asleep. She does this before both his morning and afternoon nap. She says that sometimes she spends as much as an hour dancing with him."

REFERENCES

Bronfenbrenner, Urie. Socialization and social class through time and space. *In* Eleanor E. Maccoby, Theodore M. Newcomb, and Eugene L. Hartley (Eds.), Readings in social psychology. (3rd ed.) New York: Henry Holt, 1958.

Caudill, William. Japanese American personality and acculturation. *Genetic Psychology Monographs* (1952), *45,* 3–102. Tiny dramas: vocal communication between mother and infant in Japanese and American families. In William Lebra (Ed.), Mental health research in Asia and the Pacific. Vol. Two. Honolulu, East-West Center Press, 1971.

Caudill, William, DeVos, George. Achievement, culture and personality: the case of the Japanese Americans. *American Anthropologist,* 1956, *58,* 1102–1126.

Caudill, William, and Weinstein, Helen. Maternal care and infant behavior in Japan and America. *Psychiatry, 32,* 12–43.

Clyde, Dean J., Cramer, Elliot M., Sherin, Richard J. Multivariate statistical programs. Coral Gables, Florida: Biometrics Laboratory, University of Miami, 1966.

Frost, Lois. Child raising techniques as related to acculturation among Japanese Americans. Unpublished Master's thesis in anthropology, Sacramento State College, 1970.

Freedman, D. G., and Freedmen N. C. Behavioral differences between Chinese-American and European-American newborns. *Nature, 224,* No. 5225, 1227 only, December 20, 1969.

Kitano, Harry H. L. Japanese Americans: the evolution of a subculture. Englewood Cliffs, New Jersey: Prentice-Hall, 1969.

Masuda, Minoru, Matsumoto, Gary H. and Meredith, Gerald M. Ethnic identity in three generations of Japanese Americans. *Journal of Social Psychology* 1970, *81,* 199–207.

3.5

Play Behavior in the Year-Old Infant: Early Sex Differences

Susan Goldberg
Michael Lewis

Until recently, the largest proportion of studies in child development gave attention to nursery and early grade school children. The literature on sex differences is no exception. A recent book on development of sex differences which includes an annotated bibliography (Maccoby, 1966) lists fewer than ten studies using infants, in

Reprinted from *Child Development,* 1969, *40,* No. 1, 21–31, by permission of the author and The Society for Research in Child Development, Inc. Copyright © 1969 by The Society for Research in Child Development, Inc.

spite of the fact that theoretical discussions (e.g., Freud, 1938 [originally published in 1905]; Piaget, 1951) emphasize the importance of early experience. Theoretical work predicts and experimental work confirms the existence of sex differences in behavior by age 3. There has been little evidence to demonstrate earlier differentiation of sex-appropriate behavior, although it would not be unreasonable to assume this occurs.

Recently, there has been increased interest in infancy, including some work which has shown early sex differences in attentive behavior (Kagan & Lewis, 1965; Lewis, in press). The bulk of this work has been primarily experimental, studying specific responses to specific stimuli or experimental conditions. Moreover, it has dealt with perceptual-cognitive differences rather than personality variables. There has been little observation of freely emitted behavior. Such observations are of importance in supplying researchers with the classes of naturally occurring behaviors, the conditions under which responses normally occur, and the natural preference ordering of behaviors. Knowledge of this repertoire of behaviors provides a background against which behavior under experimental conditions can be evaluated.

The present study utilized a free play situation to observe sex differences in children's behavior toward mother, toys, and a frustration situation at 13 months of age. Because the Ss were participants in a longitudinal study, information on the mother-child relationship at 6 months was also available. This made it possible to assess possible relations between behavior patterns at 6 months and at 13 months.

METHOD

Subjects

Two samples of 16 girls and 16 boys each, or a total of 64 infants, were seen at 6 and 13 months of age (± 6 days). All Ss were born to families residing in southwestern Ohio at the time of the study. All were Caucasian. The mothers had an average of 13.5 years of schooling (range of 10–18 years) and the fathers had an average of 14.5 years of schooling (range of 8–20 years). The occupations of the fathers ranged from laborer to scientist. Of the 64 infants, 9 girls and 10 boys were firstborn and the remaining infants had from 1 to 6 siblings.

The 6-Month Visit

The procedure of the 6-month visit, presented in detail in Kagan and Lewis (1965), included two visual episodes and an auditory episode where a variety of behavioral responses were recorded. The infant's mother was present during these procedures. At the end of the experimental procedure, the mother was interviewed by one of the experimenters, who had been able to observe both mother and infant for the duration of the session. The interviewer also rated both mother and infant on a rating scale. The items rated for the infant included: amount of activity, irritability, response to mother's behavior, and amount of affect. For the mother, the observer rated such factors as nature of handling, amount of playing with the baby, type of comforting behavior, and amount of vocalization to the baby. Each item was rated on a 7-point scale, with 1 indicating the most activity and 7 the least. For the purpose of this study, it was necessary to obtain a measure of the amount of physical contact the mother initiated with the child. Since scores on the individual scales did not result in sufficient variance in the population, a composite score was obtained by taking the mean score for each mother over all three of the touching-the-infant scales. These included: amount of touching, amount of comforting, and amount of play. The composite touch scores (now called the amount of physical contact) resulted in a sufficiently variable distribution to be used for comparison with the 13-month touch data.

The 13-Month Visit

Kagan and Lewis (1965), who employed the same 64 infants for their study, described the procedures used at 6 months, which were similar to those of the present (13-month) study. The only addition was a free play procedure, which will be discussed in detail below.

The playroom, 9 by 12 feet, contained nine simple toys: a set of blocks, a pail, a "lawnmower," a stuffed dog, an inflated plastic cat, a set of quoits (graduated plastic doughnuts stacked on a wooden rod), a wooden mallet, a pegboard, and a wooden bug (a pull toy). Also included as toys were any permanent objects in the room, such as the doorknob, latch on the wall, tape on the electrical outlets, and so forth. The mother's chair was located in one corner of the room.

Procedure

Each *S,* accompanied by his mother, was placed in the observation room. The mother was instructed to watch his play and respond in any way she desired. Most mothers simply watched and responded only when asked for something. The mother was also told that we would be observing from the next room. She held the child on her lap, the door to the playroom was closed, and observation began. At the beginning of the 15 minutes of play, the mother was instructed to place the child on the floor.

Measurement

Two observers recorded the *S*'s behavior. One dictated a continuous behavioral account into a tape recorder. The second operated an event recorder, which recorded the location of the child in the room and the duration of each contact with the mother.

Dictated recording. During the initial dictation, a buzzer sounded at regular time intervals, automatically placing a marker on the dictated tape. The dictated behavior account was typed and each minute divided into 15-second units, each including about three typewritten lines. The typed material was further divided into three 5-second units, each unit being one typed line. Independent experimenters analyzed this typed material. For each minute, the number of toys played with and amount of time spent with each toy was recorded.

Event recorder.   To facilitate recording the activity and location of the child, the floor of the room was divided into 12 squares. For each square, the observer depressed a key on the event recorder for the duration of time the child occupied that square. From this record it was possible to obtain such measures as the amount of time spent in each square and the number of squares traversed. A thirteenth key was depressed each time the child touched the mother. From this record, measure of (a) initial latency in leaving the mother, (b) total amount of time touching the mother, (c) number of times touching the mother, and (d) longest period touching the mother were obtained.

The data analysis presented in this report provides information only on sex differences (a) in response to the mother and (b) in choice and style of play with toys. Other data from this situation are presented elsewhere (Lewis, 1967).

RESULTS

Response to Mother (13 Months)

Open field.   Boys and girls showed striking differences in their behavior toward their mothers (see Table 1). First, upon being removed from their mothers' laps, girls were reluctant to leave their mothers. When Ss were placed on the floor by their mothers, significantly more girls than boys returned immediately—in less than 5 seconds ($p <$ .05 for both samples by Fisher Exact Probability Test). This reluctance to leave their mothers is further indicated by the time it took the children to first return to their mothers. Girls, in both samples, showed significantly shorter latencies than boys. Out of a possible 900 seconds (15 minutes), girls returned after an average of 273.5 seconds, while boys' average latency was nearly twice as long, 519.5 seconds. This difference was highly significant ($p <$ .002, Mann-Whitney U Test). All significance tests are two-tailed unless otherwise specified.

TABLE 1.   SUMMARY OF INFANT BEHAVIOR TO MOTHER IN FREE PLAY SESSION

BEHAVIOR	GIRLS	BOYS	p
Touching mother:			
x latency in seconds to return to mother	273.5	519.5	< .002
x number of returns	8.4	3.9	< .001
x number of seconds touching mother	84.6	58.8	< .03
Vocalization to mother:			
x number of seconds vocalizing to mother	169.8	106.9	< .04
Looking at mother:			
x number of seconds looking at mother	57.3	47.0	< .09
x number of times looking at mother	10.8	9.2	NS
Proximity to mother:			
x time in squares closest to mother	464.1	351.4	< .05
x time in squares farthest from mother	43.8	44.3	NS

Once the children left their mothers, girls made significantly more returns both physical and visual. Girls touched their mothers for an average of 84.6 seconds, while boys touched their mothers for only 58.8 seconds ($p < .03$, Mann-Whitney U Test). Girls returned to touch their mothers on an average of 8.4 times, and boys 3.9 times ($p < .001$, Mann-Whitney U Test). For the visual returns, the number of times the child looked at the mother and the total amount of time spent looking at the mother were obtained from the dictated material. The mean number of times girls looked at the mother was 10.8 (as compared with 9.2 for boys), a difference which was not significant. The total amount of time looking at the mother was 57.3 seconds for girls and 47.0 seconds for boys ($p < .09$, Mann-Whitney U Test).

Finally, vocalization data were also available from the dictated material. The mean time vocalizing to the mother was 169.8 seconds for girls and 106.9 seconds for boys ($p < .04$, Mann-Whitney U Test).

Another measure of the child's response to his mother was the amount of physical distance the child allowed between himself and his mother. Because the observers recorded which squares the child played in, it was possible to obtain the amount of time Ss spent in the four squares closest to the mother. The mean time in these squares for girls was 464.1 seconds; for boys, it was 351.4 seconds ($p < .05$, Mann-Whitney U Test). Moreover, boys spent more time in the square farthest from the mother, although the differences were not significant.

Barrier frustration. At the end of the 15 minutes of free play, a barrier of mesh on a wood frame was placed in such a way as to divide the room in half. The mother placed the child on one side and remained on the opposite side along with the toys. Thus, the child's response to stress was observed.

TABLE 2. SUMMARY OF INFANT BEHAVIOR DURING BARRIER FRUSTRATION

BEHAVIOR	GIRLS	BOYS	p
x number of seconds crying	123.5	76.7	$< .05$
x number of seconds at ends of barrier	106.1	171.0	$< .001$
x number of seconds at center	157.7	95.1	$< .01$

Sex differences were again prominent, with girls crying and motioning for help consistently more than boys (see Table 2). For both samples, amount of time crying was available from the dictated record. Girls' mean time crying was 123.5 seconds, compared with 76.7 seconds for boys ($p < .05$, Mann-Whitney U Test). Boys, on the other hand, appeared to make a more active attempt to get around the barrier. That is, they spent significantly more time at the ends of the barrier than girls, while girls spent significantly more time in the center of the barrier—near the position where they were placed ($p < .01$, Mann-Whitney U Test).

Toy Preference (13 Months)

A second area of experimental interest was toy preference. When the nine toys were ranked in order of the total amount of time they were played with, girls and boys showed similar patterns of preference.

Table 3 presents each toy and the amount of time it was played with. Play with the dog and cat were combined into one category. The toys which were used most were the lawnmower, blocks, and quoits, and those that were used least were the stuffed dog and cat. On a *post hoc* basis, it seems as if the toys which received the most attention were those that offered the most varied possibilities for manipulation.

TABLE 3.   MEAN TIME PLAYING WITH TOYS, BY SEX

	GIRLS	BOYS	p
Total time with:			
Mallet	51.7	60.8	. . .
Bug	50.2	45.3	. . .
Pail	34.6	22.9	. . .
Blocks	126.5	77.5	$<.03$
Lawnmower	220.3	235.6	. . .
Cat plus dog (combined)	31.0	9.1	$<.01$
Quoits	122.7	130.3	. . .
Pegboard	37.2	28.7	$<.05$
Nontoys	6.9	31.0	$<.005$
Putting toys in pail	28.2	43.0	. . .
Banging toys	19.7	34.8	$<.05$
Lawnmowing on other toys	2.8	9.8	. . .
Other manipulation of two toys	28.2	10.3	$<.05$

Although there were no sex differences in overall toy preference, there were significant sex differences in the amount of time spent with individual toys and in the ways toys were used. Girls played with blocks, pegboard, and with the dog and cat (the only toys with faces) more than boys did ($p < .03$, $p < .03$, $p < .01$, respectively, Mann-Whitney U Test).

In terms of style of play, there were also sex differences. Observation of girls' play indicates that girls chose toys which involved more fine than gross muscle coordination, while for boys, the reverse was true—building blocks and playing with dog and cat vs. playing with mallet and rolling the lawnmower over other toys. Moreover, boys spent more time playing with the nontoys (doorknob, covered outlets, lights, etc.; $p < .005$, Mann-Whitney U Test).

In terms of overall activity level, boys were more active than girls. Girls tended to sit and play with combinations of toys ($p < .05$, Mann-Whitney U Test), while boys tended to be more active and bang the toys significantly more than girls ($p < .05$, Mann-Whitney U Test). In addition, the children were rated by two observers on the vigor of their play behavior; a rating of 1 was given for high vigor, 2 was given for medium vigor, and 3 for low vigor. These ratings were made from the dictated material for each minute, so that the final score for each S represented a mean of 15 vigor ratings. The interobserver reliability was $p = 0.78$. The boys played significantly more vigorously than girls (mean for boys was 2.45, varying from 1.2 to 3.0; for girls, the mean was 2.65, varying from 1.9 to 3.0 [$p < .05$, Mann-Whitney U Test]). This vigor difference was also seen in the style of boys' play; for example, boys banged with the mallet and mowed over other toys. Thus, there were not only significant differences in the choice of toys, but also in the way the toys were manipulated. The data indicate that there are important and significant sex differences in very young children's response to their mothers, to frustration, and in play behavior.

Mother-infant touch (6 months).   One possible determinant of the child's behavior toward the mother in the playroom is the mother's behavior toward the child at an earlier age. The 6-month data indicated that mothers of girls touched their infants more than mothers of boys. On the composite score, where 1 indicated most touching and 7 least, there were twice as many girls as boys whose mothers were rated 1–3 and twice as many boys as girls whose mothers were rated 5–7 ($p < .05$, X^2 test). Moreover, mothers vocalized to girls significantly more than to boys ($p < .001$, Mann-Whitney U Test), and significantly more girls than boys were breast-fed rather than bottle-fed ($p < .02$, Mann-Whitney U Test). Thus, when the children were 6 months old, mothers touched, talked to, and handled their daughters more than their sons, and when they were 13 months old, girls touched and talked to their mothers more than boys did. To explore this relationship further, mothers were divided into high, medium, and low mother-touch-infant groups (at 6 months), with the extreme groups consisting of the upper and lower 25 percent of the sample. For the boys at 13 months, the mean number of seconds of physical contact with the mother indicated a linear relation to amount of mother touching (14, 37, and 47 seconds for the low, medium, and high mother-touch groups, respectively; Kruskal-Wallis, $p < .10$). Thus, the more physical contact the mother made with a boy at 6 months, the more he touched the mother at 13 months. For the girls, the relation appeared to be curvilinear. The mean number of seconds of touching the mother for the low, medium, and high mother-touch groups was 101, 55, and 88 seconds, respectively (Kruskal-Wallis, $p < .10$). The comparable distribution for number of seconds close to the mother was 589, 397, and 475 seconds (Kruskal-Wallis, $p < .03$). A girl whose mother initiated very much or very little contact with her at 6 months was more likely to seek a great deal of physical contact with the mother in the playroom than one whose mother was in the medium-touch infant group.

Observation of the mothers' behavior when their infants were 6 months old revealed that five of the seven mothers of girls who showed little physical contact were considered by the staff to be severely rejecting mothers. The data suggest that the child of a rejecting mother continues to seek contact despite the mother's behavior. This result is consistent with Harlow's work with rejected monkeys (Seay, Alexander, & Harlow, 1964) and Provence's work with institutionalized children (Provence, 1965; Provence & Lipton, 1962) and suggests that the child's need for contact with his mother is a powerful motive.

DISCUSSION

Observation of the children's behavior indicated that girls were more dependent, showed less exploratory behavior, and their play behavior reflected a more quiet style. Boys were independent, showed more exploratory behavior, played with toys requiring gross motor activity, were more vigorous, and tended to run and bang in their play. Obviously, these behavior differences approximate those usually found between the sexes at later ages. The data demonstrate that these behavior patterns are already present in the first year of life and that some of them suggest a relation to the mother's response to the infant in the first 6 months. It is possible that at 6 months, differential behavior on the part of the mother is already a response to differential behavior on the part of the infant. Moss (1967) has found behavioral sex differences as early as 3 weeks. In interpreting mother-infant interaction data, Moss suggests that maternal behavior is initially a response to the infant's behavior. As the infant becomes older, if the mother responds contingently to his signals, her behavior acquires reinforcement value which enables her to influence and regulate the infant's behavior. Thus, parents can be active promulgators of sex-role behavior through reinforcement of sex-role-appropriate responses within the first year of life.

The following is offered as a hypothesis concerning sex-role learning. In the first year or two, the parents reinforce those behaviors they consider sex-role appropriate and the child learns these sex-role behaviors independent of any internal motive, that is, in the same way he learns any appropriate response rewarded by his parents. The young child has little idea as to the rules governing this reinforcement. It is suggested, however, that as the child becomes older (above age 3), the rules for this class of reinforced behavior become clearer and he develops internal guides to follow these earlier reinforced rules. In the past, these internalized rules, motivating without apparent reinforcement, have been called modeling behavior. Thus, modeling behavior might be considered an extension or internalization of the earlier reinforced sex-role behavior. However, it is clear that the young child, before seeking to model his behavior, is already knowledgeable in some appropriate sex-role behavior. In that the hypothesis utilizes both early reinforcement as well as subsequent cognitive elaboration, it would seem to bridge the reinforcement notion of Gewirtz (1967) and Kohlberg's cognitive theory (1966) of identification.

The fact that parents are concerned with early display of sex-role-appropriate behavior is reflected in an interesting clinical observation. On some occasions, staff members have incorrectly identified the sex of an infant. Mothers are often clearly irritated by this error. Since the sex of a fully clothed infant is difficult to determine, the mistake seems understandable and the mother's displeasure uncalled for. If, however, she views the infant and behaves toward him in a sex-appropriated way, our mistake is more serious. That is, the magnitude of her displeasure reveals to us the magnitude of her cognitive commitment to this infant as a child of given sex.

Regardless of the interpretation of the observed sex differences, the free play procedure provides a standardized situation in which young children can be observed without interference from experimental manipulation. While behavior under these conditions may be somewhat different from the young child's typical daily behavior, our data indicate that behavior in the play situation is related to other variables, that behavior can be predicted from earlier events, and that it is indicative of later sex-role behavior. The results of the present investigation as well as the work of Bell and

Costello (1964), Kagan and Lewis (1965), and Lewis (in press) indicate sex differences within the first year over a wide variety of infant behaviors. The fact that sex differences do appear in the first year has important methodological implications for infant research. These findings emphasize the importance of checking sex differences before pooling data and, most important, of considering sex as a variable in any infant study.

REFERENCES

Bell, R. Q., & Costello, N.S. Three tests for sex differences in tactile sensitivity in the newborn. *Biologia Neonatorum,* 1964, *1,* 335–347.

Freud, S. Three contributions to the theory of sex. Reprinted in *The basic writings of Sigmund Freud.* New York: Random House, 1938.

Gewirtz, J. The learning of generalized imitation and its implications for identification. Paper presented at the Society for Research in Child Development Meeting, New York, March, 1967.

Kagan, J., & Lewis, M. Studies of attention in the human infant. *Merrill-Palmer Quarterly,* 1965, *11,* 95–127.

Kohlberg, L. A cognitive-developmental analysis of children's sex role concepts and attitudes. In E. Maccoby (Ed.), *The development of sex differences.* Stanford, Calif.: Stanford University Press, 1966.

Lewis, M. Infant attention: response decrement as a measure of cognitive processes, or what's new, Baby Jane? Paper presented at the Society for Research in Child Development Meeting, symposium on "The Role of Attention in Cognitive Development," New York, March, 1967.

Lewis, M. Infants' responses to facial stimuli during the first year of life. *Developmental Psychology,* in press.

Maccoby, E. (Ed.) *The development of sex differences.* Stanford, Calif.: Stanford University Press, 1966.

Moss, H. Sex, age and state as determinants of mother-infant interaction. *Merrill-Palmer Quarterly,* 1967, *13* (1), 19–36.

Piaget, J. *Play, dreams and imitation in childhood.* New York: Norton, 1951.

Provence, S. Disturbed personality development in infancy: a comparison of two inadequately nurtured infants. *Merrill-Palmer Quarterly,* 1965, *2,* 149–170.

Provence, S., & Lipton, R. C. *Infants in institutions.* New York: International University Press, 1962.

Seay, B., Alexander, B. K., & Harlow, H. F. Maternal behavior of socially deprived rhesus monkeys. *Journal of Abnormal and Social Psychology,* 1964, *69* (4), 345–354.

3.6

Mother-Child Interaction in the First Year of Life

Steven R. Tulkin
Jerome Kagan

Psychologists have begun to take more seriously the idea that experiences during infancy may influence development, although the specific functional relations between early experiences and later cognitive skills or personality traits remain unclear. The failure to understand these functional relations has prompted many social scientists and public officials to use categorical labels like "culturally deprived" to designate types of children. These labels are demeaning to the particular groups so labeled and are misleading because they suggest that one group can judge another by noting how similar others are to themselves. Most discussions of cultural deprivation contribute little to our understanding of human development because they do not examine the effects to *specific experiences* on developmental processes.[1]

The purpose of the present report is to examine the experiences of infants from different social class backgrounds. Hess and Shipman (1965) observed preschool children and reported that middle class mothers engaged in more "meaningful" verbal interchanges with their children than working class mothers. It is less clear, however, whether mothers' behaviors with infants also reflect this difference. Descriptive reports of the experiences of young children in poor families (Pavenstedt, 1965, 1967) suggest that social class differences in mother-infant interaction exist, but there has been little systematic observation.

METHOD

The present study reports data collected from 30 middle class and 26 working class Caucasian mothers. Middle class was defined as (a) one or both parents having graduated from college and (b) the father working in a professional job. Working class was defined as (a) either one or both parents having dropped out of high school (but neither having any college) or (b) the father working in a semiskilled or unskilled job. Each mother was observed at home for 2 hours on two separate days with her firstborn baby girl, who was approximately 10 months of age. Premature infants and infants with abnormal medical histories were excluded from the study.

Observation periods were 20 minutes long, separated by 5 minute rest periods. Thus there were six observation periods scheduled for each visit. Mothers were told that the observer (the first author) was investigating infants' behaviors in natural settings, and that it was important for her to act naturally and to engage in her normal activities so that the day would appear "typical" to the infant. The observer carried a small battery-operated timer which, every 5 seconds, emitted a soft tone which the observer heard through an earphone. Code sheets each contained 30 1 x 2-inch squares, and at the sound of the tone, the observer moved his pencil into the next square. Presence of a particular behavior during a 5-second interval was noted on the code sheet by a number or letter representing that behavior. A particular variable could only be tallied once per 5-second interval.

The variables to be examined in the present report were defined as follows:

1. Location: distance of mother from infant, coded each time it changed.
   a. Face to face.
   b. Within 2 feet (within arm's distance).
   c. More than 2 feet away.
2. Physical contact.
   a. Kiss: mother's lips touch child.
   b. Hold: mother supports child's weight (mother carries child, child sits on mother's lap, etc.).
   c. Active physical contact: mother tickles child, bounces child on lap, throws child in air, etc.
3. Prohibitions: mother interferes with or stops an act that had already begun.
   a. Verbal prohibition: negative command (e.g., "stop that" or "don't do that").
   b. Physical prohibition: mother stops child's motor activity or takes object from child.
   c. Prohibition ratios: To control for possible differences in infants' activity levels which could result in some infants receiving more prohibitions than others, a ratio was computed in which the total number of maternal prohibitions was divided by the number of 5-second intervals in which the infant was either walking or crawling. Another possible bias was that infants moving around on the floor would have more opportunities to engage in behaviors that might be prohibited; thus a second ratio was computed in which the total number of maternal prohibitions was divided by the amount of time that the infant was free to crawl or walk on the floor.

4. Maternal vocalization: mother says words to child. Analyzed separately for each location in category 1.
5. Keeping infant busy: mother provides activity for child.
   a. Entertain: mother holds attention of child by nonverbal sounds, body movements such as peek-a-boo, or holding the attention of the child through a toy— such as shaking a rattle. If words were used in conjunction with an entertainment behavior, category 4 was also coded.
   b. Give object: mother gives child an object and makes no effort to hold child's attention.

Infant behaviors were also recorded, but will not be discussed in the present paper.

In addition to the discrete behaviors described above, several other variables were obtained by examining sequences of mother and infant behaviors. These variables were not directly coded in the homes but were derived at a later time from the discrete behaviors of mothers and infants:

1. Positive responses to nonverbal behaviors: coded when infant touched mother or gave an object to mother if this behavior was followed, within the same or the following 5-second interval, by any maternal behavior in categories 2, 4, or 5 above.
2. Percentage of reciprocal vocalization: defined as the percentage of the child's vocalizations which were followed, within the same or the following 5-second interval by a maternal vocalization.
3. Response of child's frets: positive maternal responses (categories 2, 4,.5 and/or moving to within 2 feet of child) were analyzed following "spontaneous" frets, that is, frets for which there was no apparent cause such as maternal prohibitions putting child in playpen, etc.
4. Interaction: defined by both mother and infant acting in response to each other. Although either could initiate the interaction, infant had to respond to mother's behaviors and mother had to respond to infant's. The interaction went on as long as each responded to the other's behaviors within the same or the following 5-second interval. Examples of interaction sequences are: infant touches mother, mother picks up infant, infant vocalizes; mother tickles infant, infant smiles, mother tickles, etc. Interaction could not be initiated by a fret or prohibition, and if it occurred within 1 minute of a fret or prohibition, it was analyzed separately. Two variables describing the interaction are

(a) the number of times interaction was initiated (labeled "interaction episodes") and (b) the total amount of interaction (labeled "total interaction").

TABLE 1. PERCENTAGES OF AGREEMENT ON HOME-OBSERVATION VARIABLES FOR PRETEST INFANTS (N = 10)

VARIABLE	MEDIAN PERCENTAGE	RANGE OF PERCENTAGES
Location	92.0	90–97
Physical contact	90.0	74–95
Prohibitions	84.5	75–100
Maternal vocalizations	81.5	70–88
Entertain	81.5	71–93
Give object	86.5	75–100

When the observers found that their level of agreement was satisfactory, the computation of reliabilities began. Ten "reliability" infants were each observed for 2 hours and percentages of agreement were computed. Percentages were based on tallies from each page of the coding booklet representing a 2½-minute segment). These were computed by dividing the number of agreements per page by the total number of agreements and disagreements per page, for each infant. Resulting percentages appear in Table 1. The overall range was 70–100 percent agreement, and the median percentages were all above 80. For some variables, the frequencies were too low to permit analysis on a page-by-page basis; therefore Pearson product-moment correlations were also computed between the records of the two observers, on the basis of the total number of tallies for each subject over the 2-hour period. These correlations are presented in Table 2. All correlations were above .90. Reliabilities were not computed for variables derived from the coding sheets, as specific rules were followed (e.g., if maternal vocalization follows child vocalization in either the same or the following 5-second interval, code as reciprocal vocalization).

TABLE 2. BETWEEN-SUBJECT CORRELATIONS OF HOME-OBSERVATION VARIABLES FOR PRETEST INFANTS (N = 10)

VARIABLE	CORRELATION
Location	.99
Kiss	.96
Hold	.99
Active physical contact	.97
Verbal prohibitions	.99
Physical prohibitions	.97
Maternal vocalization	.99
Entertain	.94
Give object	.98

Note.—All correlations are significant beyond the .01 level of confidence.

It should be noted that although there was no class difference in the amount of infant fretting or crying, or in the frequency of maternal prohibition, all maternal behaviors within 1 minute of an infant fret or a maternal prohibition were analyzed separately to reduce the variance which might be attributable to differences among the infants.

If other people interacted with the child, their behavior was recorded in categories identical with those listed for maternal behaviors. An additional variable was the total amount of time another adult interacted with the infant.

Variables describing particular aspects of the infant's environment were also recorded during the home visits. The number of toys available and the number of other environmental objects played with (pots, pans, magazines, etc.) were recorded at the end of each 20-minute observation period. The location of the infant was coded by recording the number of minutes which the child spent in a playpen, in a high chair, in a crib, etc. Infants who were placed in walkers or who were free to walk or crawl on the floor were further described by recording the number of minutes during which they were free to roam around any part of the home, rather than being restricted to a particular area. The free-movement condition was labeled "no barriers." Location variables were summed over the entire 4 hours of observation, yielding a range of 0 —240 minutes. The number of minutes that the television or radio were played during each home visit was similarly recorded. Finally, a "crowdedness ratio" was computed for each home by dividing the number of people living in the dwelling unit by the number of rooms.

After the final observation period, the observer spoke informally with mothers about what they felt was important for mothers to do during their infant's first year of life.

Reliability.   The first author "taught" the above coding system to another observer by their jointly observing 10 pretest infants at home, coding maternal and infant behaviors aloud, and discussing any disagreements.

TABLE 3.   CLASS DIFFERENCES IN HOME ENVIRONMENTS

VARIABLE	WORKING CLASS		MIDDLE CLASS		p[a]
	MEAN	SD	MEAN	SD	
Crowdedness ratio (people per room)	0.761	0.172	0.597	0.143	.001
Number of 5-second intervals with interaction with other adults	114.500	165.676	40.433	68.783	.029
Minutes of TV	109.621	92.025	30.033	60.791	.001
Minutes of radio	39.276	55.776	66.467	68.692	.101
Number of toys within reach in 20-minute period	6.016	2.491	7.011	2.181	.117
Number of environmental objects played with in 20-minute period	3.215	1.557	4.531	1.696	.004
Minutes with no barriers	114.500	77.480	168.600	65.296	.006

[a]Independent *t* tests; two-tailed.

RESULTS

Environmental variables.   Table 3 presents data on the infants' homes. The environments of the infants in the two class groups differed along two particular dimensions. First, there was more "extraneous noise" in the working class children's environments. The infants lived in more crowded homes, had more interaction with adults other than their mothers, and spent more time in front of television sets than their middle class counterparts.

TABLE 4.   MATERNAL BEHAVIORS OBSERVED AT HOME

VARIABLE	WORKING CLASS		MIDDLE CLASS		p^a
	MEAN	SD	MEAN	SD	
Interaction:					
Interaction episodes	36.08	19.69	65.97	36.31	.001
Total interaction	132.50	83.44	251.83	144.46	.001
Location:					
Over 2 feet from child	1,402.73	536.38	1,243.27	488.03	.249
Within 2 feet	1,424.50	515.29	1,525.60	459.54	.441
Face to face	53.19	53.66	110.77	113.69	.022
Physical contact:					
Kiss	4.00	6.13	5.73	5.32	.262
Total holding	210.73	179.71	265.17	154.54	.228
Active physical contact	21.42	23.99	31.37	24.01	.128
Prohibitions:					
Verbal only	15.50	9.85	18.33	14.75	.409
Physical only	12.19	10.89	11.00	9.87	.669
Prohibitions ÷ time on floor	36.19	24.72	33.93	51.85	1.000
Prohibitions ÷ walk and crawl	19.04	13.69	16.50	15.20	.522
Responses to nonverbal behaviors:					
Positive response (%), child touches mother	56.36	22.50	63.89	21.03	.206
Positive response (%), child offers object to mother	90.65	15.44	86.40	16.22	.410
Maternal vocalization:					
Over 2 feet away	17.65	15.36	40.57	33.84	.002
Within 2 feet	148.77	73.92	329.37	183.81	.001
Face to face	19.00	15.97	38.20	28.48	.004
Total maternal vocalization	192.00	88.30	422.40	206.41	.001
Reciprocal vocalization (%)	11.27	6.12	20.70	10.19	.001
Keeping infant busy:					
Entertainment	54.65	40.46	99.13	62.08	.003
Give objects	26.23	19.72	38.53	14.76	.010
Response to spontaneous frets:					
Frets (%) to which mother responded	38.36	15.15	58.41	25.46	.001
Latency to respond (number of 5-second intervals)	1.98	0.70	1.62	0.54	.032

Note.—All numbers (except percentages) refer to the number of 5-second intervals in which the behavior occurred. The possible range is 0–2,880.
[a]Independent t tests; two-tailed.

Second, working class infants had less opportunity to explore and manipulate their environments. They had somewhat fewer toys and fewer environmental objects (pots, pans, magazines, etc.) with which to play, and spent less time with "no barriers."

Maternal behavior.   Table 4 presents the behavioral observations. Total interaction was greater in the middle class group, but analysis of specific behaviors revealed that class differences were larger in some areas than in others. Class differences in maternal *behaviors,* in fact, paralleled the findings noted above for "nonbehavioral" variables. The majority of differences centered around the mother's verbal behavior and her attempts to "keep her infant busy." Other aspects of maternal behavior did not reveal social class differences. There was no class difference in the amount of time mothers spent in close proximity to their infants (within 2 feet), although the middle class mothers more often placed their infants in a face-to-face position. There were also no significant differences for frequencies of kissing, holding, or active physical contact. Contrary to expectations, no class differences were found in the frequency of maternal prohibitions, even when controls were introduced for the amount of time infants were free to crawl around and explore. Finally, when infants touched their mothers or handed objects to their mothers, working class mothers responded positively as often as middle class mothers.

The paucity of social class differences for nonverbal variables was in sharp contrast with the dramatic differences found for the mothers' verbal behaviors. Every verbal behavior coded was more frequent among middle class mothers. There was no social class difference in the infants' tendencies to vocalize spontaneously, a result which suggests that the differences in maternal vocalization were not attributable to initial differences among the infants.[2]

Middle class mothers more often entertained their infants and more often gave their infants things with which to play. They also responded to a higher percentage of the infants' spontaneous frets and responded more quickly.

It was noted above that working class infants were involved in interaction with adults other than their mothers more often than middle class infants; thus the present analysis—by limiting itself to *maternal* behaviors—might not reflect the overall amount of social interaction experienced by the infant. Additional anaylses were made noting every occurrence of specific behaviors directed toward the infants, whether or not the mother was involved. These analyses yielded social class differences similar to those reported in Table 4. Thus, regardless of the degree to which the mothers shared their child rearing responsibilities with others, infants from middle and working class families had different experiences.

It should be noted that the present report deals specifically with differences *between* the two social class groups. Large within-class differences were also observed in the present study, however, and it would be erroneous to conclude that middle class children were "enriched" while working class children were "deprived." The class differences appear to be attributable to a subgroup of middle class mothers who were highly verbal with their infants—rather than to a "deprivation" which is uniquely characteristic of working class families.

DISCUSSION

The results indicate that more middle class than working class mothers were extensively involved in verbal interactions with their infants and were more likely to provide their infants with a greater variety of stimulation. These findings parallel previous reports of (a) minimal social class differences in the affective elements of mother-child interaction (Bayley & Schaefer, 1960; Kagan & Freeman, 1963) and (b) larger differences in verbal interaction and cognitive stimulation (Levine, Fishman, & Kagan, 1967; Shipman & Hess, 1966). In fact, Moss, Robson, and Pedersen (1969) found that "less well-educated mothers" provided more physical stimulation for their infants than better educated mothers. Working class mothers, then, care for their infants as extensively as middle class mothers; differences occur mainly in areas involving maternal stimulation of cognitive development.

It is important to understand why the mothers in the present sample interacted with their infants in this manner, and to examine the implications of the present findings for infant intervention programs. Informal discussions with mothers suggested that one source of variance in maternal behavior was the mother's concept of her infant. Some working class mothers did not believe that their infants possessed the ability to express "adult-like" emotions or to communicate with other people. Hence, these mothers felt that it was futile to attempt to interact with their infants. One working class mother who constantly spoke to her daughter lamented that her friends chastized her for "talking to the kid like she was 3 years old." Some working class mothers felt that it was only important for a mother to speak to her infant after the infant began to speak. Weikart and Lambie (1969) also noted that lower income mothers were hesitant "to involve themselves in anything as silly as talking to a baby." Thus, one objective of infant intervention projects might be to emphasize the importance of early verbal stimulation.

Second, working class mothers seemed to feel that they could not have much influence on the development of their children. Many believed that infants are born with a particular set of characteristics, and that environmental influence is minimal. Minuchin, *et al.* (1967) also observed that lower income mothers "seemed to see themselves as powerless, helpless, and . . . not able to do anything" to effect the development of their children. This philosophy may be indicative of a general sense of fatalism which develops when working class people find that they have little power to effect changes in their environment. Thus, a mother's attitudes toward her children are not independent of social and economic conditions, and interventionists must realize that attempts to change maternal *behaviors* without regard to the source of the behaviors—or the relation between these behaviors and other aspects of the social system—may not succeed.

Various other maternal beliefs also appeared to influence behaviors. Some mothers in both class groups, for example, believed that children should be able to explore and discover things for themselves in an atmosphere of minimal adult-imposed structure; other mothers believed in early teaching of "right and wrong" and worried about their children being spoiled. Infants in the former group spent less time in playpens, were prohibited less, and were allowed to play with more environmental objects. Similarly, some mothers stressed the importance of independence training for their infants. One middle class mother said that she had to teach her daughter "to go out, ... to become more independent when she's not near me." She went on to say that she didn't believe that a child should be picked up "for no reason at all, just because maybe she's fussing to be picked up." This mother had the lowest amount of interaction in the middle class group. Other mothers stressed the importance of extensive mother-infant contact and felt that the child had to learn to be dependent before she could learn to be independent. These mothers had more interaction with their daughters. In each case, mothers had fairly specific ideas about the type of child behaviors they were attempting to develop and acted in accord with this model.

It is important for interventionists to respect the values of the families with whom they are working and not attempt to convert other people to their own value systems. One of the goals of intervention programs should be to encourage parents to recognize the influence they have over their children's development and to understand the consequences of various types of experiences. We must retain a relativisitc posture, however, and not insist that one pattern of intellectual skills and personality traits is optimal for all children.

NOTES

[1]A complete discussion of how the "cultural deprivation" concept has hindered our understanding of developmental processes can be found in Tulkin (in press).

[2]Infants' spontaneous vocalization rates were difficult to assess because mothers often elicited vocalization from their infants by entertainment, tickling, maternal vocalizations, etc. It was decided to construct a "solitary-vocalization ratio," which was defined as follows: frequency of infant vocalizaitons when the mother was over 2 feet away, divided by the number of 5-second intervals during which the mother was over 2 feet away. For middle class infants, the ratio was 24.81 with a standard deviation of 5.46; for working class infants, the ratio was 22.97 with a standard deviation of 7–13. The class difference was not significant.

REFERENCES

Bayley, N., & Schaefer, E. Relationships between socio-economic variables and the behavior of mothers toward young children. *Journal of Genetic Psychology,* 1960, *96,* 61–77.

Hess, R. D., & Shipman, V. C. Early experience and the socialization of cognitive modes in children. *Child Development,* 1965, *36,* 869–886.

Kagan, J., & Freeman, M. The relation of childhood intelligence, maternal behaviors, and social class to behavior during adolescence. *Child Development,* 1963, *34,* 899–911.

Levine, J., Fishman, C., & Kagan, J. Sex of child and social class as determinants of maternal behavior. Paper presented at the meeting of the Society for Research in Child Development, New York, March 1967.

Minuchin, S., Montalvo, B., Guerney, B. G., Rosman, B. L., & Schumer, F. L. *Families of the slums: an exploration of their structure and treatment.* New York: Basic, 1967.

Moss, H.A., Robson, K. S., & Pederson, F. Determinants of maternal stimulation of infants and consequences of treatment for later reactions to strangers. *Developmental Psychology,* 1969, *l,* 239–246.

Pavenstedt, E. A comparison of the child rearing environment of upper-lower and very low-lower class families. *American Journal of Orthopsychiatry,* 1965, *35,* 89–98.

Pavenstedt, E. (Ed.) *The drifters.* Boston: Little, Brown, 1967.

Shipman, V. C., & Hess, R. D. Early experience in the socialization of cognitive modes in children: a study of urban Negro families. Paper presented at the Conference on Family and Society, Merrill-Palmer Institute, April 1966.

Tulkin, S. R. An analysis of the concept of cultural deprivation. *Developmental Psychology,* in press.

Weikart, D. P., & Lambie, D. Z. Early enrichment infants. Paper presented at the meeting of the American Association for the Advancement of Science, Boston, December 1969.

3.7

Hospitalism:[1] An Inquiry into the Genesis of Psychiatric Conditions in Early Childhood

Rene A. Spitz

THE PROBLEM

The term *hospitalism* designates vitiated condition of the body due to long confinement in a hospital, or the morbid condition of the atmosphere of a hospital. The term has been increasingly pre-empted to specify the evil effect of institutional care on infants, placed in institutions from an early age, particularly from the psychiatric point of view.[2] This study is especially concerned with the effect of continuous institutional care of infants under one year of age, for reasons other than sickness. The model of such institutions is the foundling home.

Medical men and administrators have long been aware of the shortcomings of such charitable institutions. At the beginning of our century one of the great foundling homes in Germany had a mortality rate of 71.5 percent in infants in the first year of life (1a).[3] In 1915 Chapin (2a) enumerated ten asylums in the larger cities of the United States, mainly on the eastern seaboard, in which the death rates of infants admitted during their first year of life varied from 31.7 percent to 75 percent by the end of their second year. In a discussion in the same year before the American Pediatric Association (3a), Dr. Knox of Baltimore stated that in the institutions of that city 90 percent of the infants died by the end of their first year. He believed that the remaining 10 percent probably were saved because they had been taken out of the institution in time. Dr. Shaw of the Albany remarked in the same discussion that the mortality rate of Randalls Island Hospital was probably 100 percent.

Conditions have since greatly changed. At present the best American institutions, such as Bellevue Hospital, New York City, register a mortality rate of less than 10 percent (4a), which compares favorably with the mortality rate of the rest of the country. While these and similar results were being achieved both here and in Europe, physicians and administrators were soon faced with a new problem: they discovered that institutionalized children practically without exception developed subsequent psychiatric disturbances and became asocial, delinquent, feeble-minded, psychotic, or problem children. Probably the high mortality rate in the preceding period had obscured this consequence. Now that the children survived, the other drawbacks of institutionalization became apparent. They led in this country to the widespread substitution of institutional care by foster home care. . . .

We believe that further study is needed to isolate clearly the various factors operative in the deterioration subsequent to prolonged care in institutions. . . .

MATERIAL

With this purpose in mind a long-term study of 164 children was undertaken. In view of the findings of previous investigations this study was largely limited to the first year of life, and confined to two institutions, in order to embrace the total population of both (130) infants. Since the two institutions were situated in different countries of the western hemisphere, a basis of comparison was established by investigating noninstitutionalized children of the same age group in their parents' homes in both countries. A total of 34 of these were observed. We thus have four environments:

TABLE 1.

ENVIRONMENT	INSTITUTION NO. 1[4]	CORRESPONDING PRIVATE BACKGROUND	INSTITUTION NO. 2	CORRESPONDING PRIVATE BACKGROUND
Number of children	69	11	61	23

PROCEDURE

In each case an anamnesis was made which whenever possible included data on the child's mother; and in each case the Hetzer-Wolf baby tests were administered.

RESULTS

For the purpose of orientation we established the average of the Developmental Quotients for the first third of the first year of life for each of the environments investigated. We contrasted these averages with those for the last third of the first year. This comparison gives us a first hint of the significance of environmental influences for development.

TABLE 2.

TYPE OF ENVIRONMENT	CULTURAL AND SOCIAL BACKGROUND	DEVELOPMENTAL QUOTIENTS	
		AVERAGE OF FIRST FOUR MONTHS	AVERAGE OF LAST FOUR MONTHS
Parental home	Professional	133	131
	Village population	107	108
Institution	"Nursery"	101.5	105
	"Foundling home"	124	72

Children of the first category come from professional homes in a large city; their Development Quotient, high from the start, remains high in the course of development.

Children in the second category come from an isolated fishing village of 499 inhabitants, where conditions of nutrition, housing, hygienic and medical care are very poor indeed; their Developmental Quotient in the first four months is much lower and remains at a lower level than that of the previous category.

In the third category, "Nursery," the children were handicapped from birth by the circumstances of their origin, which will be discussed below. At the outset their Developmental Quotient is even somewhat lower than that of the village babies; in the course of their development they gain slightly.

In the fourth category, "Foundling Home," the children are of an unselected urban (Latin) background. Their Development Quotient on admission is below that of our best category but much higher than that of the other two. The picture changes completely by the end of the first year, when their Developmental Quotient sinks to the astonishingly low level of 72.

Thus the children in the first three environments were at the end of their first year on the whole well developed and normal, whether they were raised in their progressive middle class family homes (where obviously optimal circumstances prevailed and the children were well in advance of average development), or in an institution or a village home, where the development was not brilliant but still reached a perfectly normal and satisfactory average. The children in the fourth environment, though starting at almost as high a level as the best of the others, had spectacularly deteriorated.

The children in Foundling Home showed all the manifestations of hospitalism, both physical and mental. In spite of the fact that hygiene and precautions against contagion were impeccable, the children showed, from the third month on, extreme susceptibility to infection and illness of any kind. There was hardly a child in whose case history we did not find reference to otitis media, or morbilli, or varicella, or eczema, or intestinal disease of one kind or another. No figures could be elicited on general mortality; but during my stay an epidemic of measles swept the institution, with staggeringly high mortality figures, notwithstanding liberal administration of convalescent serum and globulins, as well as excellent hygienic conditions. Of a total of 88 children up to the age of 2½, 23 died. It is striking to compare the mortality among the 45 children up to 1½ years to that of the 43 children ranging from 1½ to 2½ years: usually, the *incidence* of measles is low in the younger age group, but among those infected the mortality is higher than that in the older age group; since in the case of Foundling Home every child was infected, the question of incidence does not enter; however, contrary to expectation, the mortality was much higher in the older age group. In the younger group, 6 died, i.e., approximately 13 percent. In the older group, 17 died, i.e., close to 40 percent. The significance of these figures becomes apparent when we realize that the mortality from measles during the first year of life in the community in question, outside the institution, was less than ½ percent.

In view of the damage sustained in all personality sectors of the children during their stay in this institution we believe it licit to assume that their vitality (whatever that may be), their resistance to disease, was also progressively sapped. In the ward of the children ranging from 18 months to 2½ years only two of the 26 surviving children speak a couple of words. The same two are able to walk. A third child is beginning to walk. Hardly any of them can eat alone. Cleanliness habits have not been acquired and all are incontinent.

In sharp contrast to this is the picture offered by the oldest inmates in Nursery, ranging from 8 to 12 months. The problem here is not whether the children walk or talk by the end of the first year; the problem with these 10-month-olds is how to tame the healthy toddlers' curiosity and enterprise. They climb up the bars of the cots after the manner of South Sea Islanders climbing palms. Special measures to guard them from harm have had to be taken after one 10-month-old actually succeeded in diving right over the more than two-foot railing of the cot. They vocalize freely and some of them actually speak a word or two. And all of them understand the significance of simple social gestures. When released from their cots, all walk with support and a number walk without it.

What are the differences between the two institutions that result in the one turning out normally acceptable children and the other showing such appalling effects?

Similarities

Background of the children.   Nursery is a penal institution in which delinquent girls are sequestered. When, as is often the case, they are pregnant on admission, they are delivered in a neighboring maternity hospital and after the lying-in period their children are cared for in Nursery from birth to the end of their first year. The background of these children provides for a markedly negative selection since the mothers are mostly delinquent minors as a result of maladjustment or feeble-mindedness, or because they are psychically defective, psychopathic, or criminal. Psychic normalcy and adequate social adjustment is almost excluded.

The other institution is a foundling home pure and simple. A certain number of the children housed have a background not much better than that of the Nursery children; but a sufficiently relevant number come from socially well-adjusted, normal mothers whose only handicap is inability to support themselves and their children (which is no sign of maladjustment in women of Latin background). This is expressed in the average of the Developmental Quotients of the two institutions during the first 4 months, as shown in Table 2.

The background of the children in the two institutions does therefore not favor Nursery; on the contrary, it shows a very marked advantage for Foundling Home.

Housing Conditions.   Both institutions are situated outside the city, in large spacious gardens. In both hygienic conditions are carefully maintained. In both, infants at birth and during the first 6 weeks are segregated from the older babies in a special newborns' ward, to which admittance is only permitted in a freshly sterilized smock after hands are washed. In both institutions infants are transferred from the newborns' ward after 2 or 3 months to the older babies' wards, where they are placed in individual cubicles which in Nursery are completely glass enclosed, in Foundling Home the children remain in their cubicles up to 15 to 18 months; in Nursery they are transferred after the 6th month to rooms containing four to five cots each.

One-half of the children in Foundling Home are located in a dimly lighted part of the ward; the other half, in the full light of large windows facing southeast, with plenty of sun coming in. In Nursery, all the children have well-lighted cubicles. In both institutions the walls are painted in a light neutral color, giving a white impression in Nursery, a gray-green impression in Foundling Home. In both, the children are placed in white painted cots. Nursery is financially the far better provided one: we usually find here a small metal table with the paraphernalia of child care, as well as a chair, in each cubicle; whereas in Foundling Home it is the exception if a low stool is to be found in the cubicles, which usually contain nothing but the child's cot.

Food.   In both institutions adequate food is excellently prepared and varied according to the needs of the individual child at each age; bottles from which children are fed are sterilized. In both institutions a large percentage of the younger children are breast fed. In Nursery this percentage is smaller, so that in most cases a formula is soon added, and in many cases weaning takes place early. In Foundling Home all children are breast-fed as a matter of principle as long as they are under 3 months unless disease makes a deviation from this rule necessary.

Clothing.   Clothing is practically the same in both institutions. The children have adequate pastel-colored dresses and blankets. The temperature in the rooms is appropriate. We have not seen any shivering child in either set-up.

Medical Care.   Foundling Home is visited by the head physician and the medical staff at least once a day, often twice, and during these rounds the chart of each child is inspected as well as the child itself. For special ailments a laryngologist and other specialists are available; they also make daily rounds. In Nursery no daily rounds are made, as they are not necessary. The physician sees the children when called.

Up to this point it appears that there is very little significant difference between the children of the two institutions. Foundling Home shows, if anything, a slight advantage over Nursery in the matter of selection of admitted children, of breast-feeding and of medical care. It is in the items that now follow that fundamental differences become visible.

Differences

Toys.   In Nursery it is the exception when a child is without one or several toys. In Foundling Home my first impression was that not a single child had a toy. This impression was later corrected. In the course of time, possibly in reaction to our presence, more and more toys appeared, some of them quite intelligently fastened by a string above the baby's head so that he could reach it. By the time we left a large percentage of the children in Foundling Home had a toy.

Visual Radius.   In Nursery the corridor running between the cubicles, though rigorously white and without particular adornment, gives a friendly impression of warmth. This is probably because trees, landscape and sky are visible from both sides and because a bustling activity of mothers carrying their children, tending them, feeding them, playing with them, chatting with each other with babies in their arms, is usually present. The cubicles of the children are enclosed but the glass panes of the partitions reach low enough for every child to be able at any time to observe everything going on all around. He can see into the corridor as soon as he lifts himself on his elbows. He can look out of the windows, and can see babies in the other cubicles by just turning his head; witness the fact that whenever the experimenter plays with a baby in one of the cubicles the babies in the two adjoining cubicles look on fascinated, try to participate in the game, knock at the panes of the partition, and often begin to cry if no attention is paid to them. Most of the cots are provided with widely spaced bars that are no obstacle to vision. After the age of 6 months, when the child is transferrred to the wards of the older babies, the visual field is enriched as a number of babies are then together in the same room, and accordingly play with each other.

In Foundling Home the corridor into which the cubicles open, though full of light on one side at least, is bleak and deserted, except at feeding time when five to eight nurses file in and look after the children's needs. Most of the time nothing goes on to attract the babies' attention. A special routine of Foundling Home consists in hanging bed sheets over the foot and the side railing of each cot. The cot itself is approximately 18 inches high. The side railings are about 20 inches high; the foot and head railings are approximately 28 inches high. Thus, when bed sheets are hung over the railings, the child lying in the cot is effectively screened from the world. He is completely separated from the other cubicles, since the glass panes of the wooden partitions begin 6 to 8 inches higher than even the head railing of the cot. The result of this system is that each baby lies in solitary confinement up to the time when he is able to stand up in his bed, and that the only object he can see is the ceiling.

Radius of Locomotion.　In Nursery the radius of locomotion is circumscribed by the space available in the cot, which up to about 10 months provides a fairly satisfactory range.

Theoretically the same would apply to Foundling Home. But in practice this is not the case for, probably owing to the lack of stimulation, the babies lie supine in their cots for many months and a hollow is worn into their mattresses. By the time they reach the age when they might turn back to side (approximately the 7th month) this hollow confines their activity to such a degree that they are effectively prevented from turning in any direction. As a result we find most babies, even at 10 and 12 months, lying on their backs and playing with the only object at their disposal, their own hands and feet.

Personnel.　In Foundling Home there is a head nurse and five assistant nurses for a total of 45 babies. These nurses have the *entire* care of the children on their hands, except for the babies so young that they are breastfed. The latter are cared for to a certain extent by their own mothers or by wetnurses; but after a few months they are removed to the single cubicles of the general ward, where they share with at least seven other children the ministrations of *one* nurse. It is obvious that the amount of care one nurse can give to an individual child when she has eight children to manage is small indeed. These nurses are unusually motherly, baby-loving women; but of course the babies of Foundling Home nevertheless lack all human contact for most of the day.

Nursery is run by a head nurse and her three assistants, whose duties do not include the care of the children, but consist mainly in teaching the children's mothers in child care, and in supervising them. The children are fed, nursed, and cared for by their own mothers or, in those cases where the mother is separated from her child for any reason, by the mother of another child, or by a pregnant girl who in this way acquires the necessary experience for the care of her own future baby. Thus in Nursery each child has the full-time care of his own mother, or at least that of the substitute which the very able head nurse tries to change until she finds someone who really likes the child.

DISCUSSION

To say that every child in Nursery has a full-time mother is an understatement, from a psychological point of view. However modern a penal institution may be, and however constructive and permissive its reeducative policies, the deprivation it imposes upon delinquent girls is extensive. Their opportunities for an outlet for their interests, ambitions, activity are very much impoverished. The former sexual satisfactions, as well as the satisfactions of competitive activity in the sexual field, are suddenly stopped: regulations prohibit flashy dresses, vivid nail polish, or extravagant hairdo's. The kind of social life in which the girls could show off has vanished. This is especially traumatic as these girls become delinquent because they have not been able to sublimate their sexual drives, to find substitute gratifications, and therefore do not possess a pattern for relinquishing pleasure when frustrated. In addition, they do not have compensation in relations with family and friends, as formerly they had. These factors, combined with the loss of personal liberty, the deprivation of private property and the regimentation of the penal institution, all add up to a severe narcissistic trauma from the time of admission; and they continue to affect the narcissistic and libidinal sectors during the whole period of confinement.

Luckily there remain a few safety valves for their emotions: (1) the relationship with wardens, matrons and nurses; (2) with fellow prisoners; (3) with the child. In the relationship with the wardens, matrons and nurses, who obviously represent parent figures, much of the prisoner's aggression and resentment is bound. Much of it finds an outlet in the love and hate relationship to fellow prisoners, where all the phenomena of sibling rivalry are revived.

The child, however, becomes for them the representative of their sexuality, a product created by them, an object of their own, which they can dress up and adorn, on which they can lavish their tenderness and pride, and of whose accomplishments, performance and appearance they can boast. This is manifested in the constant competition among them as to who has the better dressed, more advanced, more intelligent, better looking, the heavier, bigger, more active—in a word, the better baby. For their own persons they have more or less given up the competition for love, but they are intensely jealous of the attention given to their children by the matrons, wardens, and fellow prisoners.

It would take an exacting experimenter to invent an experiment with conditions as diametrically opposed in regard to the mother-child relationship as they are in these two institutions. Nursery provides each child with a mother to the nth degree, a mother who gives the child everything a good mother does and, beyond that, everything else she has. Foundling Home does not give the child a mother, nor even a substitute-mother, but only an eighth of a nurse.

We are now in a position to approach more closely and with better understanding the results obtained by each of the two institutions. We have already cited a few: we mentioned that the Developmental Quotient of Nursery achieves a normal average of about 105 at the end of the first year, whereas that of the Foundling Home sinks to 72; and we mentioned the striking difference of the children in the two institutions at first sight. Let us first consider the point at which the developments in the two institutions deviate.

On admission the children of Foundling Home have a much better average than the children of Nursery; their hereditary equipment is better than that of the children of delinquent minors. But while Foundling Home shows a rapid fall of the developmental index, Nursery shows a steady rise. They cross between the 4th and 5th months, and from that point on the curve of the average Developmental Quotient of the Foundling Home drops downward with increasing rapidity, never again to rise (Curve I).

The point where the two curves cross is significant. The time when the children in Foundling Home are weaned is the beginning of the 4th month. The time lag of one month in the sinking of the index below normal is explained by the fact that the Quotient represents a cross-section including all sectors of development, and that attempts at compensation are made in some of the other sectors.

However, when we consider the sector of Body Mastery (Curve II) which is most indicative for the mother-child relationship, we find that the curves of the children in Nursery cross the Body Mastery curve of the Foundling Home children between the 3rd and 4th month. The inference is obvious. As soon as the babies in Foundling Home are weaned the modest human contacts which they have had during nursing at the breast stop, and their development falls below normal.

One might be inclined to speculate as to whether the further deterioration of the children in Foundling Home is not due to other factors also, such as the perceptual and motor deprivations from which they suffer. It might be argued that the better achievement of the Nursery children is due to the fact that they were better provided for in regard to toys and other perceptual stimuli. We shall therefore analyze somewhat more closely the nature of deprivations in perceptual and locomotor stimulation.

First of all it should be kept in mind that the nature of the inanimate perceptual stimulus, whether it is a toy or any other object, has only a very minor importance for a child under 12 months. At this age the child is not yet capable of distinguishing the real purpose of an object. He is only able to use it in a manner adequate to his own functional needs (23a). Our thesis is that perception is a function of emotion of one kind or another. Emotions are provided for the child through the intervention of a human partner, i.e., by the mother or her substitute. A progressive development of emotional interchange with the mother provides the child with perceptive experiences of its environment. The child learns to grasp by nursing at the mother's breast and by combining the emotional satisfaction of that experience with the tactile perceptions. He learns to distinguish animate objects from inanimate ones by the spectacle provided by his mother's face (28a) in situations fraught with emotional satisfaction. The interchange between mother and child is loaded with emotional factors and it is in this interchange that the child learns to play. He becomes acquainted with his surroundings through the mother's carrying him around; through her help he learns security in locomotion as well as in every other respect. This security is reinforced by her being at his beck and call. In these emotional relations with the mother the child is introduced to learning, and later to imitation. We have previously mentioned that the motherless children in Foundling Home are unable to speak, to feed themselves, or to acquire habits of cleanliness: it is the security provided by the mother in the field of locomotion, the emotional bait offered by the mother calling her child, that "teaches" him to walk. When this is lacking, even children two to three years old cannot walk.

FIGURE 1. COMPARISON OF DEVELOPMENT IN "NURSERY" AND "FOUNDLING HOME"

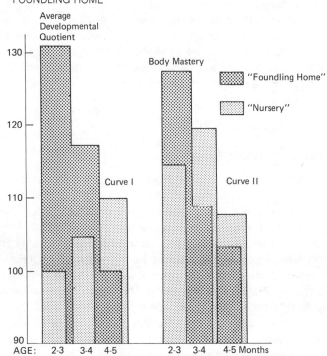

The children in Foundling Home have, theoretically, as much radius of locomotion as the children in Nursery. They did not at first have toys, but they could have exerted their grasping and tactile activity on the blankets, on their clothes, even on the bars of the cots. We have seen children in Nursery without toys; they are the exception—but the lack of material is not enough to hamper them in the acquisition of locomotor and grasping skills. The presence of a mother or her substitute is sufficient to compensate for all the other deprivations.

It is true that the children in Foundling Home are condemned to solitary confinement in their cots. But we do not think that it is the lack of perceptual stimulation *in general* that counts in their deprivation. We believe that they suffer because their perceptual world is emptied of human partners, that their isolation cuts them off from any stimulation by any persons who could signify mother-representatives for the child at this age. The result, as Curve III shows, is a complete restriction of psychic capacity by the end of the first year.

The restriction of psychic capacity is not a temporary phenomenon. It is, as can be seen from the curve, a progressive process. How much this deterioration could have been arrested if the children were taken out of the institution at the end of the first year is an open question. The fact that they remain in Foundling Home probably furthers this progressive process. By the end of the second year the Developmental Quotient sinks to 45, which corresponds to a mental age of approximately 10 months, and would qualify these children as imbeciles.

The curve of the children in Nursery does not deviate significantly from the normal. The curve sinks at two points, between the 6th and 7th, and between the 10th and 12th months. These deviations are within the normal range; their significance will be discussed in a separate article. It has nothing to do with the influence of institutions, for the curve of the village group is nearly identical.

ANACLITIC DEPRESSION

A Circumscribed Psychiatric Syndrome

In the course of this long-term study of infant behavior we encountered a striking syndrome. In the second half of the first year, a few of these infants developed a weepy behavior that was in marked contrast to their previously happy and outgoing behavior. After a time this weepiness gave way to withdrawal. The children in question would lie in their cots with averted faces, refusing to take part in the life of their surroundings. When we approached them we were ignored. Some of these children would watch us with a searching expressions. If we were insistent enough, weeping would ensue and, in some cases, screaming. The sex of the approaching experimenter made no difference in the reaction in the majority of cases. Such behavior would persist for two to three months. During this period some of these children lost weight instead of gaining; the nursing personnel reported that some suffered from insomnia, which in one case led to segregation of the child. All showed a greater susceptibility to intercurrent colds or eczema. A gradual decline in the developmental quotient was observed in these cases.

This behavior syndrome lasted three months. Then the weepiness subsided, and stronger provocation became necessary to provoke it. A sort of frozen rigidity of expression appeared instead. These children would lie or sit with wide-open, expressionless eyes, frozen immobile face, and a faraway expression as if in a daze, appar-

FIGURE 2.   COMPARISON OF DEVELOPMENT IN "NURSERY" AND
"FOUNDLING HOME" DURING THE FIRST FIVE MONTHS

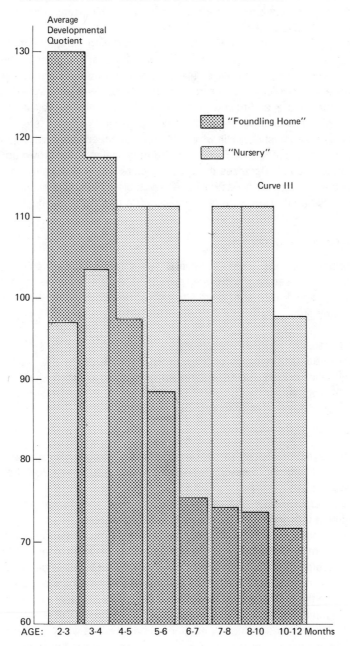

ently not perceiving what went on in their environment. This behavior was in some cases accompanied by autoerotic activities in the oral, anal, and genital zones. Contact with children who arrived at this stage became increasingly difficult and finally impossible. At best, screaming was elicited.

Among the 123 unselected children observed during the whole of the first year of their life we found this clear-cut syndrome in 19 cases. The gross picture of these cases showed many, if not all, of these traits. Individual differences were partly quantitative: i.e., one or the other trait, as for instance weeping, would for a period dominate the picture, and thus would impress the casual observer as the only one present; and partly qualitative: i.e., there was an attitude of complete withdrawal in some cases, as against others in which, when we succeeded in breaking through the rejection of any approach, we found a desperate clinging to the grown-up. But apart from such individual differences the clinical picture was so distinctive that once we had called attention to it, it was easily recognizable by even untrained observers. It led us to assume that we were confronted with a psychiatric syndrome. . . .

Discussion of the Syndrome

The principal symptoms . . . fall into several categories; within each category we have grouped them on a scale of increasing severity. They are not all necessarily present at the same time, but most of them show up at one point or another in the clinical picture. They are:

Apprehension, sadness, weepiness.
Lack of contact, rejection of environment, withdrawal.
Retardation of development, retardation of reaction to stimuli, slowness of movement, dejection, stupor.
Loss of appetite, refusal to eat, loss of weight.
Insomnia.

To this symptomatology should be added the physiognomic expression in these cases, which is difficult to describe. This expression would in an adult be described as depression. . . .

The factors of color and of sex were explored and do not appear to exert demonstrable influence on the incidence of the syndrome.

The youngest age at which the syndrome was manifested in our series was around the turn of the sixth month; the oldest was the eleventh month. The syndrome therefore seems to be independent of chronological age, within certain limits. . . .

There is one factor which all cases that developed the syndrome had in common. In all of them the mother was removed from the child somewhere between the sixth and eighth month for a practically unbroken period of three months, during which the child either did not see its mother at all, or at best once a week. This removal took place for unavoidable external reasons. Before the separation the mother had the full care of the infant, and as a result of special circumstances spent more time with the child than is usual in a private home. In each case a striking change in the child's behavior could be observed in the course of the four to six weeks following the mother's removal. The syndrome described above would then develop. *No* child developed the syndrome in question whose mother was *not* removed. Our proposition is that the syndrome observed developed only in children who were deprived of their love object for an appreciable period of time during their first year of life.

On the other hand, not all children whose mothers were removed developed the same syndrome. Hence, mother separation is a necessary, but not a sufficient cause for the development of the syndrome. ...

Prognosis of the Syndrome

Stages of symptoms.   The static signs and symptoms are those observable phenomena that we are able to ascertain in the course of one or several observations of the infant in question. We have mentioned them in Part II of our study. One of the outstanding signs is the physiognomic expression of such patients. The observer at once notices an apprehensive or sad or depressed expression on the child's face, which often impels him to ask whether the child is sick. It is characteristic, at this stage, that the child makes an active attempt to catch the observer's attention and to involve him in a game. However, this outgoing introduction usually is not followed by particularly active play on the part of the child. In the main it is acted out in the form of clinging to the observer and sorrowful disappointment at the observer's withdrawal.

In the next stage the apprehensiveness deepens. The observer's approach provokes crying or screaming, and the observer's departure does not evoke as universal a disappointment as previously. Many of the cases observed by us fall into the period of what has been described as "eight months anxiety" (4b, 9b, 11b, 18b).

The so-called "eight months anxiety" begins somewhere between the sixth and eighth month and is a product of the infant's increasing capacity for diacritic discrimination (19b) between friend and stranger. As a result of this the approaching stranger is received either by what has been described as "coy" or "bashful" behavior, or by the child's turning away, hanging its head, crying, and even screaming in the presence of a stranger, and refusing to play with him or to accept toys. The difference between this behavior and the behavior in anaclitic depression is a quantitative one. While in anaclitic depression, notwithstanding every effort, it takes upwards of an hour to achieve contact with the child and to get it to play, in the eight months anxiety this contact can be achieved with the help of appropriate behavior in a span of time ranging from one to ten minutes. The appropriate behavior is very simple: it consists in sitting down next to the cot of the child with one's back turned to him and without paying any attention to him. After the above mentioned period of one to ten minutes the child will take the initiative, grab the observer's gown or hand—and with this contact is established, and any experienced child psychologist can lead from this into playing with the child's active and happy participation. In the anaclitic depression nothing of the sort occurs. The child does not touch the observer, the approach has to be moderately active on the observer's part, and consists mostly in patient waiting, untiringly repeated attempts at cuddling or petting the child, and incessant offers of constantly varied toys. The latter must be offered with a capacity to understand the nature of the child's refusal. Some toys create anxiety in some children and have an opposite effect on others; for example, some children are attracted by bright colors but are immediately made panicky if a noise such as drumming is provoked in connection with this brightly colored toy. Others may be attracted by the rhythmic noise. Some are delighted by dolls, others go into a panic and can be reassured by no method at the sight of a doll. Some who are delighted by a spinning top will break into tears when it stops spinning and falls over, and every further attempt to spin it will evoke renewed protest.

When finally contact is made the pathognomonic expression does not brighten; after having accepted the observer the child plays without any expression of happiness. He does not play actively and is severely retarded in all his behavior manifestations. The only signs of his having achieved contact is, on the one hand, his acceptance of toys; and on the other, his expression of grief and his crying when left by the observer. That this qualitative distinction is not an arbitrary one can be seen from the fact that in a certain number of the cases in which the anaclitic depression was manifested late, we could observe the eight months anxiety as well as the anaclitic depression at periods distinct from each other. In one case, for instance, the eight months anxiety actually appeared at 0;7 + 14 and had already completely subsided and disappeared when the anaclitic depression was manifested at 0;11 + 2.

In the next stage the outward appearance of the child is that of complete withdrawal, dejection, and turning away from the environment. In the case of these children even the lay person with good empathy for children has no difficulty in making the diagnosis, and will tell the observer that the the child is grieving for his mother. . . .

Quantitative signs. Quantitative signs can be detected by consecutive developmental tests which, if compared to each other, will at the beginning of the anaclitic depression show a gradual drop of the developmental quotient; this drop progresses with the progression of the disorder (see Fig. 3).

Prognosis: With Intervention

In the beginning of this section we stated that a certain measure could be taken whereupon the syndrome disappeared. The measure taken was in the nature of environmental manipulation. It consisted in returning the mother to the child. The change in the children's observable behavior was dramatic. They suddenly were friendly, gay, approachable. The withdrawal, the disinterest, the rejection of the outside world, the sadness, disappeared as if by magic. But over and beyond these changes most striking was the jump in the developmental quotient, within a period of 12 hours after the mother's return; in some cases, as much as 36.6 percent higher than the previous measurement.

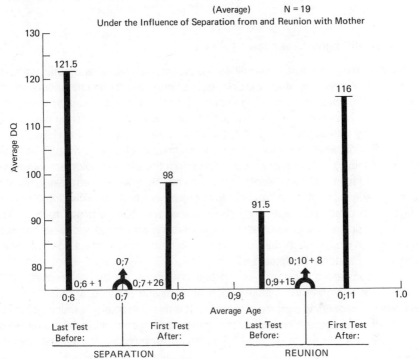

FIGURE 3. VARIATIONS OF DEVELOPMENT QUOTIENT
(Average)   N = 19
Under the Influence of Separation from and Reunion with Mother

Thus one would assume that if adequate therapeutic measures are taken, the process is curable with extreme rapidity and the prognosis is good. The last statement requires some qualification. To our regret we have not been and are not in a position to follow the children in question beyond a maximum of 18 months. It is therefore open to question whether the psychic trauma sustained by them as a consequence of being separated from their mothers will leave traces which will become visible only later in life. We are inclined to suspect something of the sort. For the sudden astonishing jump in the developmental quotient on the return of the love object is not maintained in all cases. We have observed cases in which, after a period of two weeks, the developmental quotient dropped again. It did not drop to the previous low levels reached during the depression. However, compared to these children's pre-depression performance, the level on which they were functioning after their recovery was not adequate. . . .

The spectacular recovery achieved by the children we observed again places before us the question whether we are justified in calling the syndrome a depression, and, if so, whether it should be considered as a phenomenon of more than transitory importance, whether it should not be equated to the transitory depression observable in adults—whether indeed it should not be equated to mourning rather than to depression.

Prognosis Without Intervention

The main reason why, apart from all physiognomic, behavioral and other traits, we feel justified in speaking of an anaclitic depression going far beyond mourning and even beyond pathological mourning is that we have observed a number of cases in which no intervention occurred and where it became only too evident that the process was in no way self-limiting. These cases were the ones observed in Foundling Home. In that institution, where medical, hygienic, and nutritional standards were comparable to those obtaining in Nursery, the separation from the mother took place beginning after the third month, but prevalently in the sixth month. However, whereas in Nursery the separation was temporary and the love object was restored after approximately three months of absence, in Foundling Home the love object was not restored. The picture of depression was as clear-cut as in Nursery, with some additional developments: for the picture of children in advanced extreme cases varied from stuporous deteriorated catatonia to agitated idiocy.

If we compare the pictures of the two institutions we are confronted with a syndrome of a progressive nature which after having reached a critical point of development appears to become irreversible. It is this characteristic which causes us to call the picture depression and not mourning. And beyond this, in Foundling Home we encounter a phenomenon more grave than melancholia. Notwithstanding the satisfactory hygiene and asepsis, the rate of mortality of the infants reared there was inordinately high. In the course of two years 34 of the 91 children observed died of diseases varying from respiratory and intestinal infections to measles and otitis media. In some cases the cause of death was in the nature of cachexia. This phenomenon savors of psychosomatic involvement.

No intervention was effective in the case of the longer lasting separation in Foundling Home. This finding is one of the reasons why we spoke of three months as a critical period. The second reason is that in Nursery we observed towards the end of three months the appearance of that kind of frozen, affect-impoverished expression which had strongly impressed us in Foundling Home. Furthermore, a curious reluctance to touch objects was manifested, combined with certain unusual postures of hands and fingers which seemed to us the precursors of the extremely bizarre hand and finger movements composing the total activity in those infants of Foundling Home whom we described as presenting a picture of stuporous catatonia.

After their recovery in the course of their further development, which to our regret could not be followed beyond 1½ years, the children in Nursery did not show any spectacular changes. As indicated above it, it is therefore impossible at this point to state whether this early depression left any visible traces. One would be inclined to expect some fixation. . . .

Recuperative Trends vs. Institutional Care

An objection might be raised at this point: if anaclitic depression is provoked by inhibiting the locomotion of infants separated from their love object, why is it that a significant number of the infants observed by us in Nursery, the majority in fact, remained unharmed? And what is the reason for the severe nature of one group of infantile depression, for the milder course of the others?

The answer is that in both cases the outcome depends on the measure of success achieved in this institution in providing the infant with a substitute love object. The separation of the infants from their mothers takes place in Nursery between the sixth and ninth month. Another of the inmates is then assigned to the care of the motherless child. The substitute mother thus cares for her own child and for a stranger. Though the enlightened management of Nursery exerts the greatest care, their selection is limited by the available number of inmates. Also it is hardly to be expected that a group of delinquent girls, as these were, will furnish very high grade mother substitutes.

We suggest that when the mother substitute is a good one, depression does not develop. Where the mother substitute turns out to be an aggressive, unloving personality, the parallel to adult melancholia is enacted in real life. Just as in melancholia, the ego is oppressed by a sadistic superego, here the body ego of the infant is oppressed by a sadistic love object substitute.

Inhibited in its motor release, the pent-up aggressive drive is turned against the ego. The child is caught between a hostile love object substitute and its own aggressive drive. Bereft of locomotion, it cannot actively seek replacement for the lost love object among the other grownups in the institution.

An indirect confirmation of this view is contained in the following table, which refers to the original mother-child relationship. In it we tabulate the number of children and the nature of their depression, on the one hand, the nature of the relations between the child and its mother, on the other. The mother-child relation was established by our observation of the way the mother behaved to her child. For the purpose of corroboration these observations then were compared with the information gathered for this purpose from the unusually able headmatron of Nursery. This somewhat complicated procedure made it impossible to procure reliable data on all the 95 children in question; but we did get them on 64, appearing in the table below.

TABLE 3.   MOTHER-CHILD RELATION

	GOOD			BAD		
	INTENSE	MODERATE	WEAK	INTENSE	MODERATE	WEAK
Severe depression	6	11	–	–	–	–
Mild depression	4	–	3	7	–	4
No depression	–	–	2	11	2	14

The figures speak for themselves. Evidently it is more difficult to replace a satisfactory love object than an unsatisfactory one. Accordingly depression is much more frequent and much more severe in the cases of good mother-child relationship. In bad mother-child relationship not a single severe depression occurs. It seems that any substitute is at least as good as the real mother in these cases. . . .

PROVISIONAL CONCLUSIONS

The contrasting pictures of these two institutions (Nursery and Foundling Home), and the depression syndrome described above show the significance of the mother-child relationship for the development of the child during the first year. Deprivations in other fields, such as perceptual and locomotor radius, can all be compensated by adequate mother-child relations. "Adequate" is not here a vague general term. The examples chosen represent the two extremes of the scale. (These findings should not be construed as a recommendation for overprotection of children. In principle the libidinal situation of Nursery is almost as undesirable as the other extreme in Foundling Home. Neither in the nursery of a penal institution nor in a foundling home for parentless children can the normal libidinal situation that obtains in a family home be expected.)

The children in Foundling Home do have a mother—for a time, in the beginning —but they must share her immediately with at least one other child, and from 3 months on, with seven other children. The quantitative factor here is evident. There is a point under which the mother-child relations cannot be restricted during the child's first year without inflicting irreparable damage. On the other hand, the exaggerated mother-child relationship in Nursery introduces a different quantitative factor. To anyone familiar with the field it is surprising that Nursery should achieve such excellent results, for we know that institutional care is destructive for children during their first year; but in Nursery the destructive factors have been compensated by the increased intensity of the mother-child relationship. . . .

POSTSCRIPT

Dr. Spitz wishes to add the following statement, clarifying certain theoretical points omitted in the present condensed version of his articles:

I.   This research supports the proposition that ego formation is an adaptive process, leading to the inception and establishment of a coherent psychic system by the end of the first year.

II.   Consequently so-called "psychiatric disturbances" *before* the establishment of a psychic system cannot be due to genuine *psychic* conflict. Therefore infantile behavior disturbances are not comparable to adult psychiatric disease. They originate actually in disturbances of the survival-ensuring adaptive process of reciprocal affective exchanges between mother and child.

III. These findings disprove also the Kleinian hypothesis on the earliest psychic development and infantile fantasies; the latter cannot be postulated before the establishment of a coherent psychic system. Nor can developmental propositions like the so-called "depressive position" be entertained at an age level at which cognition, volition, representation and even perception is not yet established in a coherent form.

NOTES

[1] This article is a condensed and edited version of two original articles: (1) R. A. Spitz, Hospitalism: An inquiry into the genesis of psychiatric conditions in early childhood, in A. Freud, *et al.* (Eds.), The Psychoanalytic Study of the Child, vol. I. (New York: International Universities Press, 1945), 53–74.; and (2) R. A. Spitz, with the assistance of K. M. Wolf, Anaclitic depression: An inquiry into the genesis of psychiatric conditions in early childhood, II, in A. Freud, *et al.* (Eds), *The Psychoanalytic Study of the Child,* vol. II (New York: International Universities Press, 1946), 313–342.

[2] *Hospitalism* tends to be confused with *hospitalization,* the temporary confinement of a seriously ill person to a hospital.

[3] Numbers in parentheses refer to the bibliography at the end of the paper.

[4] Institution No. 1 will from here on be called "Nursery"; and institution No. 2, "Foundling Home."

REFERENCES (A)

1a. Schlossman, A. Zur Frage der Säuglingssterblichkeit. *Münchner Med. Wochenschrift, 1920, 67.*

2a. Chapin, H. D. Are institutions for infants necessary? *Journal of American Medical Association,* January 1915.

3a. Chapin H. D. A plea for accurate statistics in infants' institutions. *Archives of Pediatrics,* October, 1915.

4a. Bakwin, H. Loneliness in infants. *American Journal of Diseases of Children,* 1942, *63,* 30–40.

5a. Durfee, H., Wolf, K., Anstaltspflege und Entwickling im erstern Lebensjahr. *Zeitschrift fur Kinderforschung,* 1933, *42/3.*

6a. Lowrey, L. G. Personality distortion and early institutional care. *American Journal of Orthopsychiatry,* 1940, *X, 3,* 576–585.

7a. Bender, L., Yarnell, H. An observation nursery: a study of 250 children in the psychiatric division of Bellevue hospital, *American Journal of Psychiatry,* 1941, *97,* 1158–1174.

8a. Goldfarb, W. Infant rearing as a factor in foster home placement. *American Journal of Orthopsychiatry,* 1944, *XIV,* 162–167.

9a. Goldfarb, W. Effects of early institutional care on adolescent personality: Rorschach data. *American Journal of Orthopsychiatry,* 1944, *XIV,* 441–447.

10a. Goldfarb, W. Effects of early institutional care on adolescent personality, *Journal of Experimental Education,* 1943, *12,* 106–129.

11a. Goldfarb, W., & Klopfer, B. Rorschach characteristics of institutional children. *Rorschach Research Exchange,* 1944, *8,* 92–100.

12a. Ripin, R. A study of the infant's feeling reactions during the first six months of life. *Archives of Psychology,* 1930, *116,* p. 38.

13a. Skeels, H. M. Mental development of children in foster homes. *Journal of Consulting Psychology,* 1938, *2,* 33–43.

14a. Skeels H. M. Some Iowa studies on the mental growth of children in relation to differentials of the environment: A summary. *39th Yearbook, National Society for the Study of Education,* 1940, *II,* 281–308.

15a. Skeels, H. M., Updegraff, R., Wellman, B. L., & Williams H. M. A study of environmental stimulation; and orphanage preschool project. *University of Iowa Studies in Child Welfare,* 1938, *15, 4.*

16a. Skodak; M. Children in foster homes. *University of Iowa Studies in Child Welfare,* 1939. *16, 1.*

17a. Stoddard, G. D. Intellectual development of the child: an answer to the critics of the Iowa studies. *School and Society,* 1940, *51,* 529–536.

18a. Updegraff, R. The determination of a reliable intelligence quotient for the young child. *Journal of Genetic Psychology,* 1932, *41,* 152–166.

19a. Woodworth, R. S. Heredity and environment. *Bulletin* 47 Social *Science Research Council,* 1941.

20a. Jones H. E. Personal reactions of the yearbook committee. *39th Yearbook, National Society for the Study of Education* 1940, *I,* 454–456.

21a. Simpson, M. R. The wandering I. Q. *Journal of Psychology,* 1939, *7,* 351–367.

22a. Hetzer, H., Wolf, K. Baby Tests. *Zeitschrift für Psychologie,* 1928, *107.*

23a. Bühler, Ch. *Kindheit und Jugend.* Leipzig, 1931, p. 67.

24a. Compayré, G. *L'evolution intellectuelle et morale de l'enfant.* Paris, 1893.

25a. Stern, Wm. *Psychology of Early Childhood.* London, 1930.

26a. Bühler, K. *Die geistige Entwicklung des Kindes* (4th ed.) Jena, 1942, p. 106 and p. 116.

27a. Tolman, E. C. *Purposive behavior.* New York, 1932, p. 27ff.

28a. Gesell, A., & Ilg, F. *Feeding behavior of infants.* Phila., 1937, p. 21.

29a. Gesell, A., & Thompson, H. *Infant behavior, its genesis and growth.* York, 1934, p. 208.

REFERENCES (B)

1b. Abraham, K. Notes on the psychoanalytical investigation and treatment of manic-depressive insanity and allied conditions. *Selected Papers,* Hogarth, 1927. (Originally 1912.)

2b. Abraham, K. The first pregenital stage of the libido. (Originally, 1916.)

3b. Abraham, K. A short study of the development of the libido, *ibid.*

4b. Bühler, Ch. *Kindheit und Jugend,* Leipzig, 1931.

5b. Fenichel, O. *The Psychoanalytic Theory of Neurosis.* Norton, 1945.

6b. Freud, S. Mourning and melancholia. *Coll. Papers,* IV. (Originally, 1917.)

7b. Glover, E. Examination of the Klein System of child psychology. *this Annual,* 1945, *I.*

8b. Harnik, J. Introjection and projection in the mechanism of depression. *Int. J. Psa.* 1932. *XIII.*

9b. Hetzer, H. and Wolf, K. M. Baby tests. *Zeit. f. Psychol.,* 1928, *107.*

10b. Jacobson, E. Depression; the Oedipus conflict in the development of depressive mechanisms. *Psa. Quarterly,* 1943, *XII.*

11b. Jersild, A. T., & Homles, F. B. Children's fear. *Child Dev. Mon.,* 1935, *20.*

12b. Klein, M. Emotional life and ego development of the infant, with special reference to the depressive position. Controversial Series of the London Psychanalytic Society, *Discussion,* March 1944, *IV.*

13b. Klein, M. *The Psycho-Analysis of Children.* London, 1932.

14b. Klein, M. Mourning and its relation to manic-depression states. *Int. J. Psa., XXI,* 1940.

15b. Klein, M. The Oedipus Complex in the Light of Early Anxieties. *Ibid.,* 1945. *XXVI.*

16b. Rank, O. *Das Trauma der Geburt und seine Bedeutung für die Psychoanalyse,* Int. Psa. Verlag, Wien, 1924.

17b. Riviere, J. Original papers on the genesis of physical conflict in earliest infancy. *Int. J. Psa.,* 1936, *XVII.*

18b. Shirley, M. M. *The first two years. A study of twenty-five babies,* Vol. II. Minneapolis: Minnesota Press, 1933.

19b. Spitz, R. A., & Wolf, K. M. The Smiling Response: A Contribution to the Ontogenesis of Social Relations. *Gen. Psychol. Mon.,* 1946. *XXXIV, I.*

20b. Spitz, R. A. Hospitalism; An inquiry into the genesis of psychiatric conditions in early childhood. *this Annual,* 1945, *I.*

21b. Spitz, R. A., & Wolf, K. M. Diacritic and coenesthetic organizations. *Psa. Rev.,* April, 1945, *32.*

22b. Watson, J. B. *Psychology from the standpoint of a behaviorist.* Philadelphia: Lippincott, 1919. States, Cambridge, Mass.: Harvard University Press (for the Commonwealth Fund), Copyright, 1970, by the President and Fellows of Harvard College.

3.8

Violence Against Children: Physical Child Abuse in the United States

David G. Gil

. . . The impetus for professional and public interest in physical abuse of children was provided in the forties by observations of roentgenologists of cases of unexplained multiple fractures of the long bones of young children found in conjunction with subdural hematomas (swelling or bleeding under the skull between the brain and its protective membrane). Subsequent intensive clinical studies of these strange cases by social workers, pediatricians, and psychiatrists in children's hospitals, clinics and child protective agencies in many communities throughout the country led to the suspicion and eventual confirmation that these unexplained injuries of children were often inflicted by their own parents and caretakers. As a result of these and many other studies, physical abuse of children came to be viewed as a widespread and important medical and social problem, which often resulted in serious, irreversible damage to the physical well-being and emotional development of children and which sometimes even caused their death. The types of injuries inflicted upon children were found to range from minor, superficial bruises and cuts through burns, scaldings, fractures and internal injuries, to intentional starvation, dismemberment and severe injuries to the brain and central nervous system. The circumstances under which the injuries were inflicted were equally varied and ranged from simple disciplinary measures through uncontrollable angry outbursts, often under the influence of alcohol, to premeditated murderous attacks.

Opinions varied widely with respect to the etiology and dynamics of the phenomenon and the characteristics of individuals and families involved. Many investigators concluded that physical abuse of children was an expression of severe personality

Excerpted by permission of the author and publishers from pp. 2–3, 58–60, 122, 133–148 of David G. Gil, *Violence Against Children: Physical Child Abuse in the United States,* Cambridge, Mass.: Harvard University Press (for the Commonwealth Fund). Copyright, 1970, by the President and Fellows of Harvard College.

disorders on the part of the perpetrators who attacked the children in their care. Many students of the phenomenon also noted that severe disturbances of family relationships as well as environmental strains and stresses such as those related to life in poverty were significantly associated with incidents of child abuse. Finally, investigators also noted that some children, because of unusual congenital or acquired characteristics, may occasionally be more prone to provoking abusive attacks against themselves than other, more "normal" children. Definite knowledge as to the nature and scope of physical child abuse was lacking at the time the present series of studies was initiated, however, and widely differing views were held concerning the social, psychological, legal, and administrative treatment and handling of incidents of child abuse. Some professionals expressed optimistic views concerning the potential of therapeutic intervention with abusive parents, while others questioned seriously the value of such intervention, and suggested that emphasis be given to assuring the safety of the abused child by removing him from his family. . . .

One item in the survey was designed to provide an indirect, rough estimate of the upper limit to the annual incidence of child abuse in the United States population. Respondents were asked whether they personally knew families involved in incidents of child abuse resulting in physical injury during the 12 months preceding the interview. Forty-five, or 3 percent of the 1520 respondents, reported such personal knowledge of 48 different incidents in the course of one year. The comprehension of respondents of the definition of child abuse as used in the survey was tested in the interview by means of a supplementary questionnaire that required detailed description and actual identification of each child-abuse incident of which they claimed personal knowledge during the preceding year. In this way the attempt was made to ascertain that all incidents reported in response to this question did indeed occur, and fit the definition used in the survey.

At the time of the survey there were about 110 million adults, 21 years of age and over in the United States, who constituted the universe sampled by the survey. Sample proportions obtained in the survey may be extrapolated to this universe within a known margin of error, which in the case of 3 percent, at the 95 percent level of confidence, is less than 0.7 percent. Accordingly, it is possible to state that 2.3 percent to 3.7 percent of 110 million adults, or 2.53 to 4.07 million adults throughout the United States, knew personally families involved in incidents of child abuse during the year preceding the October 1965 survey.

If each of these adults knew a different family involved in abusing and injuring a child, the number of families abusing children during the year preceding the survey would equal the number of adults having personal knowledge of such families. In that unlikely case the figures 2.53 and 4.07 millions, respectively, would represent, with 95 percent certainty, the lower and upper limits of the annual, nationwide incidence of child abuse resulting in some injury known outside the home of abused children. It must be remembered in this context that some incidents of child abuse are completely unknown beyond the confines of the abused child's home. Information concerning such completely invisible incidents was not expected to be revealed by means of a survey of the type discussed here.

The actual incidence rate of child abuse known outside the abused child's home is, however, likely to be lower than suggested by the foregoing discussion, since some of the 2.53 to 4.07 million adults who according to this estimate personally knew families involved in child-abuse incidents are likely to have known the same family. Data from the survey do not permit an estimate of the proportion of incidents known to more than one person. As far as could be ascertained, there were no multiple known cases at all among those known to the respondents of the survey. Common sense suggests, however, that some of the families involved in abusing children are likely to be known personally to more than one person, and therefore the total number of families known to have abused children is likely to be considerably smaller than the total number of individuals having personal knowledge of such families. Accordingly, the survey provided only an estimate of the *upper limit* in the total United States population of the incidence of child abuse resulting in injury from minimal to fatal, and known beyond the confines of the abused child's home. This upper limit for the year ending October 1965 was between 2.53 and 4.07 million for a population of about 190 million, or about 13.3 to 21.4 incidents per 1000 persons. The actual incidence rate, however, was not determined by the survey and is likely to be considerably lower.

It should be noted once more that this estimate of the upper limit of the annual incidence of child abuse is very rough, having been obtained by means of an indirect method, the reliability and validity of which are unknown. . . .*

While, as already mentioned, nearly all incidents of abuse in the sample cohort took place in the child's own home, they usually occurred in the presence of several persons besides the victim and the perpetrator. Other children from the same household were on the scene in 62.2 percent of the cases, the mother or substitute in 25.9 percent, the father or substitute in 4.6 percent, other adult members of the household in 5.9 percent, children from outside the household in 3.4 percent, and adults from outside the household in 8.2 percent.

The injured child's health and welfare may depend to a considerable extent on actions taken subsequent to an abusive incident. Delay in obtaining help may have serious consequences. A set of items in the comprehensive study focused on this issue. It was learned that the perpetrators themselves initiated help for the victims in 21.2 percent of the incidents. In 35.7 percent of the incidents, members of the victim's household other than the perpetrator initiated help. Thus in 56.9 percent of the cases the child's own family acted to obtain help once they noticed the results of the abusive treatment. School or child-care personnel initiated help in 16.4 percent of the cases, and in 31.7 percent others, such as neighbors or visiting relatives, initiated help for the child. Occasionally help was initiated simultaneously by more than one source. . . .

To gain understanding of physical abuse of children as a phenomenon in American society it seems necessary to overcome the emotional impact of specific incidents, to go beyond the level of clinical diagnosis of individual cases, and to examine trends revealed by data on large cohorts of cases against the background of broader

---

*Ed. Note: Rates of abuse were found to be highest among families of low socioeconomic background, in families headed by females, and in which the birth rate was above average. . . .

social and cultural forces. To conduct such an examination was the objective of the nationwide studies. The following observations suggest a conceptual framework derived from substantive findings of these studies. Based on this framework, several measures to reduce the incidence of physical child abuse in the United States are recommended.

A key element to understanding physical abuse of children in the United States seems to be that the context of child-rearing does not exclude the use of physical force toward children by parents and others responsible for their socialization. Rather, American culture encourages in subtle, and at times not so subtle, ways the use of "a certain measure" of physical force in rearing children in order to modify their inherently nonsocial inclinations. This cultural tendency can be noted in child rearing practices of most segments of American society. It is supported in various ways by communications disseminated by the press, radio, and television, and by popular and professional publications.

Approval of a certain measure of physical force as a legitimate and appropriate educational and socializing agent seems thus endemic to American culture. Yet differences do exist between various segments of American society concerning the quantity and quality of physical force in child rearing of which they approve, and which they actually practice. Thus, for instance, families of low socioeconomic and educational status tend to use corporal punishment to a far greater extent than do middle class families. Also, different ethnic groups, because of differences in their history, experiences, and specific cultural traditions, seem to hold different views and seem to have evolved different practices concerning the use of physical force in child rearing.

Although excessive use of physical force against children is considered abusive and is usually rejected in American tradition, practice, and law, no clear-cut criteria exist, nor would they be feasible, concerning the specific point beyond which the quantity and quality of physical force used against a child is to be considered excessive. The determination of this elusive point is left to the discretion of parents, other caretakers, professional personnel, health, education and welfare agencies, the police, and the courts. Implied in this ambiguous situation is the following question: What kind of forces singly, or in various combinations, result at certain time in culturally unacceptable "excessive" or "extreme" use of physical force against children on the part of caretakers? In other words, why and under what conditions do some persons go beyond a culturally sanctioned level of physical violence against children? Findings from the nationwide surveys suggest the following set of forces:

1. Environmental chance factors;
2. Environmental stress factors;
3. Deviance or pathology in areas of physical, social, intellectual, and emotional functioning on the part of caretakers and/or the abused children themselves;
4. Disturbed intrafamily relationships involving conflicts between spouses and/or rejection of individual children;
5. Combinations between these sets of forces.

Judging by these forces, one concludes that the phenomenon of physical abuse of children should be viewed as multidimensional rather than uniform with one set of causal factors. Its basic dimension upon which all other factors are superimposed is the general, culturally determined permissive attitude toward the use of a measure of physical force in caretaker-child interaction, and the related absence of clear-cut legal prohibitions and sanctions against this particular form of interpersonal violence. A second dimension is determined by specific child rearing traditions and practices of different social classes and ethnic and nationality groups, and the different attitudes of these groups toward physical force as an acceptable measure for the achievement of child rearing objectives. A third dimension is determined by environmental chance circumstances, which may transform an otherwise acceptable disciplinary measure into an unacceptable outcome. A fourth dimension is the broad range of environmental stress factors which may weaken a person's psychological mechanisms of self-control, and may contribute thus to the uninhibited discharge of aggressive and destructive impulses toward physically powerless children, perceived to be the causes of stress for real or imaginary reasons. The final dimension is the various forms of deviance in physical, social, intellectual, and emotional functioning of caretakers and/or children in their care, as well as of entire family units to which they belong.

The following substantive findings from the nationwide studies support the conceptual framework presented here. Culturally determined, permissive attitudes toward the use of physical force against children, and tolerant attitudes toward the perpetrators of such acts, were brought out almost convincingly in the opinions expressed by a majority of respondents to the public opinion survey. Next, a majority of nearly 13.000 abusive incidents reported through legal channels during 1967 and 1968 resulted from more or less acceptable disciplinary measures taken by caretakers in angry response to actual or perceived misconduct of children in their care. Furthermore, a large majority of families involved in these reported incidents of abuse belonged to socioeconomically deprived segments of the population whose income and educational and occupational status were very low. Moreover, families from ethnic minority groups were overrepresented in the sample and study cohorts. Environmental chance factors were often found to have been decisive in transforming acceptable disciplinary measures into incidents of physical abuse resulting in injury, and a vast array of environmental stress situations were precipitating elements in a large proportion of the incidents. Finally, a higher than normal proportion of abused children, their abusers, and their families revealed a wide range of deviance and pathology in areas of physical, social, intellecutal, and emotional functioning.

Before presenting a set of recommendations based on this conceptual framework, several more specific comments concerning selected substantive findings seem indicated.

Physical abuse of children does not seem to be a "major killer and maimer" of children as it was claimed to be in sensational publicity in the mass media of communication. Such exaggerated claims reflect an emotional response to this destructive phenomenon which, understandably, touches sensitive spots with nearly every adult, since many adults may themselves, at times, be subject to aggressive impulses toward children in their care. In spite of its strong emotional impact, and the tragic aspects of every single incident, the phenomenon of child abuse needs to be put into a more balanced perspective. Its true incidence rate has not been uncovered by the nationwide surveys. It seems, nevertheless, that the scope of physical abuse of children resulting in serious injury does not constitute a major social problem, at least in comparison with several more widespread and more serious social problems that undermine the developmental opportunities of many millions of children in American society, such as poverty, racial discrimination, malnutrition, and inadequate provisions for medical care and education.

Reporting levels and rates of physical child abuse did increase in several states from 1967 to 1968, while they decreased in several others. A net increase of about 10 percent occurred during this period throughout the United States. Increases in reporting rates have been interpreted by communications media and other sources as evidence of an increase in real incidence rates. Analysis of reporting patterns, however, does not support such an interpretation. Intrastate changes over time and interstate differences in levels and rates of reporting were found to be associated with differences in legal and administrative provisions and differences in professional concern and actions. They are therefore unlikely to reflect differences and changes in real incidence rates, and claims concerning increases or decreases of real incidence rates are based on insufficient and unreliable evidence.

Although the real incidence rate of all physical child abuse remains unknown in spite of reporting legislation, cohorts of officially reported incidents are likely to be a more adequate representation of the severe-injury segment of the physical child-abuse spectrum than of lesser or no-injury segments, since severity of injury is an important criterion in reporting. If, then, the 6000 to 7000 incidents that are reported annually through official channels are, as a group, an approximate representation of the severe segment of the nationwide abuse spectrum, then the physical consequences of child abuse do not seem to be very serious in the aggregate. This conclusion is based on data concerning the types and severity of injuries sustained by children of the 1967 and 1968 study cohorts. Over half these children suffered only minor injuries, and the classical "battered child syndrome" was found to be a relatively infrequent occurrence. Even if allowance is made for underreporting, especially of fatalities, physical abuse cannot be considered a major cause of mortality and morbidity of children in the United States.

Turning now to an epidemiologic perspective, it should be noted that physical abuse of children, and especially more serious incidents, were found to be overconcentrated among the poor and among nonwhite minorities, and thus seem to be one aspect of the style of life associated with poverty and the ghetto. While it may be valid to argue, on the basis of much evidence, that the poor and nonwhites are more likely to be reported for anything they do or fail to do, and that their overrepresentation in cohorts of reported child abuse may be in part a function of this kind of reporting bias, it must not be overlooked, nevertheless, that life in poverty and in the ghettos generates stressful experiences, which are likely to become precipitating factors of child abuse. The poor and members of ethnic minorities are subject to the same conditions that may cause abusive behavior toward children in all other groups of the population. In addition, however, these people must experience the special environmental stresses and strains associated with socioeconomic deprivation and discrimination. Moreover, they have fewer alternatives and escapes than the nonpoor for dealing with aggressive impulses toward their children. Finally, there is an additional factor, the tendency toward more direct, less inhibited, expression and discharge of aggressive impulses, a tendency learned apparently through lower class and ghetto socialization, which differ in this respect from middle class mores and socialization.

Of considerable interest in terms of the forces contributing to child abuse are findings concerning the troubled past history of many abused children, their parents and perpetrators, and the relatively high rates of deviance in areas of bio-psycho-social functioning of children and adults involved in abuse incidents. In many instances manifestations of such deviance were observed during the year preceding the reported incident. Deviance in functioning of individuals was matched by high rates of deviance in family structure reflected in a high proportion of female-headed households and households from which the biological fathers of abused children were absent. In terms of family structure it is also worth noting that, as a group, families of physically abused children tend to have more children than other American families with children under age 18.

The age distribution of abused children and their parents was found to be less skewed toward younger age groups than had been thought on the basis of earlier, mainly hospital-based, studies. This difference in findings seems due to the fact that younger children tend to be more severely injured when abused and are, therefore overrepresented among hospitalized abused children. More boys than girls seem to be subjected to physical abuse, yet girls seem to outnumber boys among adolescent abused children.

Although more mothers than fathers are reported as perpetrators of abuse, the involvement rate in incidents of child abuse is higher for fathers and stepfathers than for mothers. This important relationship is unraveled when account is taken of the fact that nearly 30 percent of reported abuse incidents occur in female-headed households. Altogether, nearly 87 percent of perpetrators are parents or parent substitutes.

Mention should be made of observation, which support the hypotheses that some children play a contributive role in their own abuse, since their behavior seems to be more provocative and irritating to caretakers than the behavior of other children. Such atypical behavior may derive from constitutional or congenital factors, from environmental experiences, or from both.

Many children in the study had been abused on previous occasions, and siblings of many abused children were abused on the same or on previous occasions. Many perpetrators were involved in incidents of abuse on previous occasions, and many had been victims of abuse during their childhood. The high rate of recidivism reflected in these findings indicates that the use of physical force tends to be patterned into child-rearing practices and is usually not an isolated incident.

Circumstances precipitating incidents of abuse are quite diverse, yet underlying this diversity there seems to be a rather simple structure. A factor analysis of the circumstances of 1380 abusive incidents of the sample cohort resulted in the following refined typology of circumstances of child abuse:

1. Psychological rejection leading to repeated abuse and battering;
2. Disciplinary measures taken in uncontrolled anger;
3. Male babysitter acting out sadistic and sexual impulses in the mother's temporary absence, at times under the influence of alcohol;
4. Mentally or emotionally disturbed caretaker acting under mounting environmental stress;
5. Misconduct and persistent behavioral atypicality of a child leading to his own abuse;
6. Female babysitter abusing child during mother's temporary absence;
7. Quarrel between caretakers, at times under the influence of alcohol.

RECOMMENDATIONS

Measures aimed at the prevention or the gradual reduction of the incidence and prevalence of specified social phenomena cannot be expected to achieve their purpose unless they are designed and executed in a manner that assures intervention on the causal level. Applying a public health model of preventive intervention to the phenomenon of physical abuse of children and proceeding on the conceptualization of its etiology, which has been presented above, I suggest the following measures:

1. Since culturally determined permissive attitudes toward the use of physical force in child rearing seem to constitute the common core of all physical abuse of children in American society, systematic educational efforts aimed at gradually changing this particular aspect of the prevailing child rearing philosophy, and developing clear-cut cultural prohibitions and legal sanctions against the use of physical force as a means for rearing children, are likely to produce over time the strongest possible reduction of the incidence and prevalence of physical abuse of children.

What is suggested here is, perhaps, a revolutionary change not only in the child-rearing philosophy and practices of American society but also in its underlying value system. Such a thorough change cannot be expected to occur overnight on the basis of a formal decision by governmental authority. What would be required is an extended, consistent effort in that direction which must eventually lead to a series of changes in our system of values and in the entire societal fabric.

It is important to keep in mind in this context that educational philosophies tend to reflect a social order and are not its primary shapers. Education tends to recreate a society in its existing image, or to maintain its relative status quo, but it rarely if ever creates new social structures. Violence against children in rearing them may thus be a functional aspect of socialization into a highly competitive and often violent society, one that puts a premium on the uninhibited pursuit of self-interest and that does not put into practice the philosophy of human cooperativeness which it preaches on ceremonial occasions and which is upheld in its ideological expressions and symbols. The elimination of violence from American child rearing philosophy and practice seems therefore to depend on changes in social philosophy and social reality toward less competition and more human cooperativeness, mutual caring, and responsibility.[1]

The foregoing considerations suggest that a close connection may indeed exist between culturally acceptable violence against children and culturally unacceptable violence among adults and among various groups in American society. These considerations also suggest that to the extent that American society may succeed in reducing the amount of violence and abuse which it inflicts collectively on children in the course of their socialization, it may reduce the amount of violence in interpersonal and intergroup relations among adults in this country, and perhaps even in international relations on a global scale.

If physical force could gradually be eliminated as a mode of legitimate interaction between caretakers and children, some other more constructive modes of interaction would have to replace it. Children who were exposed to more constructive relationship patterns would be likely to learn from this experience and to carry it over into their adult relationships. They would no longer be exposed, as they are now, to conflicting signals from their parents and caretakers according to which violence is valued both positively and negatively, but would integrate into their personalities and into their consciousness a value that would reject violence as a mode of human interaction.

Eschewing the use of physical force in rearing children does not mean that inherently nonsocial traits of children would not need to be modified in the course of socialization. It merely means that alternative educational measures would have to replace physical force, since physical force, while perhaps an effective agent of change in human behavior, seems to result in too many undesirable, long-term side effects. Child rearing literature and practice no doubt offer such alternative means of achieving the socially desirable modifications of nonsocial inclinations of children.

It should be recognized that giving up the use of physical force against children may not be easy for adults who were subjected to physical force and violence in their own childhood and who have adopted the existing value system of American society. Moreover, children can sometimes be very irritating and provocative in their behavior and may strain the tolerance of adults to the limit. Yet in spite of these realities, which must be acknowledged and faced openly, society needs to work toward the gradual reduction and, eventually, complete elimination of physical violence toward its young generation if it is serious about its expressed desire to prevent the physical abuse of children.

As a first, concrete step toward developing eventually comprehensive legal sanctions against the use of physical force in rearing children, the Congress of the United States and legislatures of the states could outlaw corporal punishment in schools, juvenile courts, correctional institutions, and other child-care facilities. Such legislation would assure that children would receive the same protection against physical attack outside their homes as the law provides for adult members of society. Moreover, such legislation is also likely to affect child rearing attitudes and practices in American homes, for it would symbolize society's growing rejection of violence against children.[2]

To avoid misinterpretations it should be noted here that rejecting corporal punishment does not imply favoring unlimited permissiveness in rearing children. To grow up successfully, children require a sense of security that is inherent in nonarbitrary structures and limits. Understanding adults can establish such structures and limits through love, patience, firmness, consistency, and rational authority. Corporal punishment seems devoid of constructive educational value, since it cannot provide that sense of security and nonarbitrary authority. Rarely, if ever, is corporal punishment administered for the benefit of the attacked child, for usually it serves the immediate needs of the attacking adult who is seeking relief from his uncontrollable anger and stress. And finally, physical attack by an adult on a weak child is not a sign of strength, for it reflects lack of real authority, and surrender to the attacker's own uncontrollable impulses.

2. Poverty, as has been shown, appears to be related to the phenomenon of physical abuse of children in at least four ways. First, the cultural approval of the use of physical force in child-rearing tends to be stronger among the socioeconomically deprived strata of society than among the middle class. Secondly, there seems to be less inhibition to express and discharge aggressive and violent feelings and impulses toward other persons among members of socioeconomically deprived strata than among the middle class. Thirdly, environmental stress and strain are considerably more serious for persons living in poverty than for those enjoying affluence. Finally, the poor have fewer opportunities than the nonpoor for escaping occasionally from child-rearing responsibilities.

These multiple links between poverty and physical abuse of children suggest that one important route toward reducing the incidence and prevalence of child abuse is the elimination of poverty from America's affluent society. No doubt this is only a partial answer to the complex issue of preventing violence against children, but perhaps a very important part of the total answer, and certainly that part without which other preventive efforts may be utterly futile. Eliminating poverty also happens to be that part of the answer for which this nation possesses the necessary resources, assuming willingness to redistribute national wealth more equitably, and for which it possesses the knowledge of how to effect a change—provided that an unambiguous, high priority, national commitment is made to the unconditional elimination of poverty by assuring to all members of society, without discrimination, equal opportunity to the enjoyment of life through:

> 1. Adequate income derived from employment whenever feasible, or assured by means of a system of nonstigmatizing guaran-

teed-income maintenance based on legal entitlement rather than on charity and bureaucratic discretion;
2. Comprehensive health care and social services;
3. Decent and adequate housing and neighborhoods, free from the stigmatizing milieu and conditions of many existing public-housing programs;
4. Comprehensive education fitting inherent capacities and assuring the realization of each person's potential;
5. Cultural and recreational facilities.

3. Deviance and pathology in areas of physical, social, intellectual, and emotional functioning of individuals and of family units were found to be another set of forces that may contribute to the incidence and prevalence of physical abuse of children. Adequate prevention or ameliorative intervention once an individual or a family is affected by such conditions is known to be very complicated. However, it is also known that these conditions tend to be strongly associated with poverty; the elimination of poverty is therefore likely to reduce, though by no means to eliminate, the incidence and prevalence of these various dysfunctional phenomena. The following measures, aimed at the prevention and amelioration of these conditions and at the strengthening of individual and family functioning should be available in every community as components of a comprehensive program to reduce the incidence of physical abuse of children and also to help individuals and families once abuse has occurred:

a. Comprehensive family-planning programs including the repeal of all legislation concerning medical abortions. The availability of family-planning resources and medical abortions are likely to reduce the number of unwanted and rejected children, who are known to be frequently victims of severe physical abuse and even infanticide. Such provisions would assure that no family would have to increase beyond a size desired by parents and beyond their capacity to care for the children. Women, including single women, would not have to become mothers unless they felt ready for this role. It is important to recall in this context that families with many children, and households headed by females, are overrepresented among families involved in physical abuse of children.

b. Family-life education and counseling programs for adolescents and adults in preparation for marriage and after it. Such programs should be developed in accordance with the assumption that there is much to learn about married life and parenthood which one does not know merely on the basis of sexual and chronological maturity, and the marital and parental relationships can be enriched like all human relationships if one is willing to work toward such enrichment. While such programs should be geared primarily to the strengthening of "normal" families, they could also serve as a screening device for the identification of incipient deviance in any area of individual and family functioning. Such programs should be offered within the public school systems of communities in order to avoid their becoming identified in the mind of the public with deviance-focused agencies.

c. A comprehensive, high quality, neighborhood-based, national health service, financed through general tax revenue and geared not only to the treatment of acute and chronic illness, but also to the promotion and assurance of maximum feasible physical and mental health for everyone.

d. A range of high quality, neighborhood-based social, child-welfare, and child-protective services geared to the reduction of environmental and internal stresses on family life, and especially on mothers who carry major responsibility for the child rearing function. Such stresses are known to precipitate incidents of physical abuse of children, and any measure that would reduce these stresses would also indirectly reduce the incidence of child abuse. Family counseling, homemaker and housekeeping services, mothers' helpers and babysitting services, family and group day-care facilities for preschool and school-age children are all examples of such services. They would all have to be licensed publicly to assure quality. They should be available on a full coverage basis in every community to all groups in in the community and not only to the rich or the very poor. Nor should such services be structured as emergency services; they should be for normal situations, in order tp prevent emergencies. No mother should be expected to care for her children around the clock, 365 days a year. Substitute care mechanisms should be routinely available to offer mothers opportunities for carefree rest and recreation.

Every community needs also a system of social services geared to the assistance of families and children who cannot live together because of severe relationship and/or reality problems. Physically abused children belong frequently to this category, and in such situations the welfare of the child and of the family may require temporary or permanent separation. The first requirement for dealing adequately with such situations is diagnostic service capable of arriving at sound decisions which take into consideration the circumstances, needs, and rights of all concerned. Next, a community requires access to a variety of facilities for the care of children away from their homes.

The administration of services and provisions suggested here should be based on a constructive and therapeutic rather than a punitive philosophy, if they are to serve the ultimate objective—the reduction of the general level of violence and the raising of the general level of human well-being throughout the entire society.

The three sets of measures proposed are aimed at different levels and aspects of physical abuse of children. The first set would attack the culturally determined core of the phenomenon; the second set would attack and eliminate a major condition to which child abuse is linked in many ways; the third set approaches the causes of child abuse indirectly. It would be futile to argue the relative merits of these approaches; all three are important and should be utilized simultaneously. The basic questions seems to be not which measure to select for combating child abuse but whether American society is indeed committed to the well-being of all its children and to the eradication of all violence toward them, be it violence perpetrated by individual caretakers, or violence perpetrated collectively by society. If the answer to this question is an unambiguous yes, then the means and the knowledge are surely at hand to progress toward this objective.

NOTES

[1]See Urie Bronfenbrenner, *Two Worlds of Childhood* (New York: Russell Sage Foundation, 1970).
[2]A unique step in the direction recommended here was taken on June 2, 1970, by the United States District Court in Boston when Chief Judge Charles Wyzanski issued a permanent injunction against corporal punishment in any form under any circumstances in all Boston public schools.

3.9

Adult Status of Children with Contrasting Early Life Experiences: A Follow-Up Study

Harold M. Skeels

I. INTRODUCTION

... The present study is a report on the status as adults of two groups of children originally encountered in Iowa institutions. One group experienced what was then regarded as the normal course of events in a child-caring institution, while the other experienced a specifically designed and implemented intervention program. The findings reported here are concerned with the question of whether and for how long a time mental development is affected by major changes in early environment and, specifically, with the factors significantly associated with deflections in mental development. It is hoped that these findings will contribute to the growing body of evidence on the effects of deprivation and poverty on the young child's ability to learn.

II. THE ORIGINAL STUDY

All the children in this study had become wards of the orphanage through established court procedures after no next of kin was found able to provide either support or suitable guardianship. Of the 25

Excerpted, adapted and reprinted from *Monographs of the Society for Research in Child Development.* Serial No. 105, 1966, *31,* No. 3, by permission. Copyright © 1966 by the Society for Research in Child Development, Inc.

children, 20 were illegitimate and the remainder had been separated from their parents because of evidence of severe neglect and/or abuse. Then as now, the courts were reluctant to sever the ties between child and parents and do so only when clearly presented with no other alternative. All the children were white and of north-European background.

The orphanage in which the children were placed occupied, with a few exceptions, buildings that had first served as a hospital and barracks during the Civil War. The institution was overcrowded and understaffed. By present standards, diet, sanitation, general care, and basic philosophy of operations were censurable. At the time of the study, however, the discrepancies between conditions in the institution and in the general community were not so great and were not always to the disadvantage of the institution. Over the past 30 years, administrative and physical changes have occurred that reflect the economic and social gains of our society. The description of conditions in the institution in the 1930's, therefore, does not apply to the present.

At the time the original study was begun, infants up to the age of 2 years were housed in the hospital, then a relatively new building. Until about 6 months, they were cared for in the infant nursery. The babies were kept in standard hospital cribs that often had protective sheeting on the sides, thus effectively limiting visual stimulation; no toys or other objects were hung in the infants' line of vision. Human interactions were limited to busy nurses who, with the speed born of practice and necessity, changed diapers or bedding, bathed and medicated the infants, and fed them efficiently with propped bottles.

Older infants, from about 6 to 24 months, were moved into small dormitories containing two to five large cribs. This arrangement permitted the infants to move about a little and to interact somewhat with those in neighboring cribs. The children were cared for by two nurses with some assistance from one or two girls, 10 to 15 years old, who regarded the assignment as an unwelcome chore. The children had good physical and medical care, but little can be said beyond this. Interactions with adults were largely limited to feeding, dressing, and toilet details. Few play materials were available, and there was little time for the teaching of play techniques. Most of the children had a brief play period on the floor; a few toys were available at the beginning of such periods, but if any rolled out of reach there was no one to retrieve it. Except for short walks out of doors, the children were seldom out of the nursery room.

At 2 years of age these children were graduated to the cottages, which had been built around 1860. A rather complete description of "cottage" life is reported by Skeels *et al.* (1938) from which the following excerpts are taken:

> Overcrowding of living facilities was characteristic. Too many children had to be accommodated in the available space and there were too few adults to guide them . . . Thirty to thirty-five children of the same sex under six years of age lived in a "cottage" in charge of one matron and three or four entirely untrained and often reluctant girls of thirteen to fifteen years of age. The waking and sleeping

hours of these children were spent (except during meal times and a little time on a grass plot) in an average-sized room (approximately fifteen feet square), a sunporch of similar size, a cloakroom, . . . and a single dormitory. The latter was occupied only during sleeping hours. The meals for all children in the orphanage were served in a central building in a single large dining room. . . .

The duties falling to the lot of the matron were not only those involved in the care of the children but those related to clothing and cottage maintenance, in other words, cleaning, mending, and so forth. . . . With so much responsibility centered in one adult the result was a necessary regimentation. The children sat down, stood up, and did many things in rows and in unison. They spent considerable time sitting on chairs, for, in addition to the number of children and the matron's limited time, there was the misfortune of inadequate equipment. . . .

No child had any property which belonged exclusively to him except, perhaps, his tooth brush. Even his clothing, including shoes, was selected and put on him according to size. [pp. 10–11].

After a child reached the age of 6 years, he began school. His associates were his cottage mates and the children of the same age and opposite sex who lived on the other side of the institution grounds. Although the curriculum was ostensibly the same as that in the local public school, it was generally agreed that the standards were adjusted to the capabilities of the orphanage children. Few of those who had their entire elementary school experience in the institution's school were able to make the transition to the public junior high school.

The orphanage was designed for mentally normal children. It was perpetually overcrowded, although every opportunity to relieve this pressure was exploited. One such relief occurred periodically when new buildings were opened at other institutions, such as at the schools for the mentally retarded. It was not uncommon for a busload of children to be transferred on such occasions. A valued contribution of the psychologists was the maintenance of lists of children who, on the basis of test scores and observable behavior, were regarded as eligible for transfers.

The environmental conditions in the two state institutions for the mentally retarded were not identical but they had many things in common. Patient-inmates were grouped by sex, age, and general ability. Within any one ward, the patients were highly similar. The youngest children tended to be the most severely disabled and were frequently "hospital" patients. The older, more competent inmates had work assignments throughout the institution and constituted a somewhat self-conscious elite with recognized status.

Personnel at that time included no resident social workers or psychologists. Physicians were resident at the schools for the mentally retarded and were on call at the orphanage. Administrative and matron and caretaking staffs were essentially untrained and nonprofessional. Psychological services were introduced in the orphanage in 1932.

Identification of Cases

Early in the service aspects of the program, two baby girls, neglected by their fee-bleminded mothers, ignored by their inadequate relatives, malnourished and frail, were legally committed to the orphanage. The youngsters were pitiful little creatures. They were tearful, had runny noses, and sparse, stringy, and colorless hair; they were emaciated, undersized, and lacked muscle tonus or responsiveness. Sad and inactive, the two spent their days rocking and whining.

The psychological examinations showed developmental levels of 6 and 7 months, respectively, for the two girls, although they were then 13 and 16 months old chronologically. This serious delay in mental growth was confirmed by observations of their behavior in the nursery and by reports of the superintendent of nurses, as well as by the pediatrician's examination. There was no evidence of physiological or organic defect, or of birth injury or glandular dysfunction.

The two children were considered unplaceable, and transfer to a school for the mentally retarded was recommended with a high degree of confidence. Accordingly, they were transferred to an institution for the mentally retarded at the next available vacancy, when they were aged 15 and 18 months, respectively.

In the meantime, the author's professional responsibilities had been increased to include itinerant psychological services to the two state institutions for the mentally retarded. Six months after the transfer of the two children, he was visiting the wards at an institution for the mentally retarded and noticed two outstanding little girls. They were alert, smiling, running about, responding to the playful attention of adults, and generally behaving and looking like any other toddlers. He scarcely recognized them as the two little girls with the hopeless prognosis, and thereupon tested them again. Although the results indicated that the two were approaching normal mental development for age, the author was skeptical of the validity of permanence of the improvement and no change was instituted in the lives of the children. Twelve months later they were reexamined, and then again when they were 40 and 43 months old. Each examination gave unmistakable evidence of mental development well within the normal range for age.

There was no question that the initial evaluations gave a true picture of the children's functioning level at the time they were tested. It appeared equally evident that later appraisals showed normal mental growth accompanied by parallel changes in social growth, emotional maturity, communication skills, and general behavior. In order to find a possible explanation for the changes that had occurred, the nature of the children's life space was reviewed.

The two girls had been placed on one of the wards of older, brighter girls and women, ranging in age from 18 to 50 years and in mental age from 5 to 9 years, where they were the only children of preschool age, except for a few hopeless bed patients with gross physical defects. An older girl on the ward had "adopted" each of the two girls, and other older girls served as adoring aunts. Attendants and nurses also showed affection to the two spending time with them, taking them along on their days off for automobile rides and shopping excursions, and purchasing toys, picture books, and play materials for them in great abundance. The setting seemed to be a homelike one, abundant in affection, rich in wholesome and interesting experiences, and geared to a preschool level of development.

It was recognized that as the children grew older their developmental needs would be less adequately met in the institution for the mentally retarded. Furthermore, they were now normal and the need for care in such an institution no longer existed. Consequently, they were transferred back to the orphanage and shortly thereafter were placed in adoptive homes.

At this point, evidence on the effects of environment on intelligence had been accumulated from a number of studies. The consistent element in normal mental development seemed to be the existence of a one-to-one relationship with an adult who was generous with love and affection, together with an abundance of attention and experiential stimulation from many sources. Children who had little of these did not show progress; those who had a great deal, did.

Since study homes or temporary care homes were not available to the state agency at that time, the choice for children who were not suitable for immediate placement in adoptive homes was between, on the one hand, an unstimulating, large nursery with predictable mental retardation or, on the other hand, a radical, iconoclastic solution, that is, placement in institutions for the mentally retarded in a bold experiment to see whether retardation in infancy was reversible.

By the time these observations were organized into a meaningful whole and their implications were recognized, individual psychological tests were available for all children in the orphanage. As part of a continuing program of observation and evaluation, all infants over 3 months of age were given the then available tests (Kuhlmann-Binet and Iowa Tests for Young Children), and were retested as often as changes seemed to occur. Retests at bi-monthly intervals were not uncommon. Older preschoolers were reexamined at 6- to 12-month intervals; school-aged children, annually or biannually. Children who were showing marked delay in development were kept under special observation.

Children whose development was so delayed that adoptive placement was out of the question remained in the orphanage. The only foreseeable alternative for them was eventual transfer to an institution for the mentally retarded. In the light of the experiences with the two little girls, the possibility was raised that early transfer to such an institution might have therapeutic effects. If not all, then at least some of the children might be able to attain normal mental functioning. In the event they did not, no significant change in life pattern would have occurred, and the child would remain in the situation for which he would have been destined in any case.

This radical proposal was accepted with understandable misgivings by the administrators involved. It was finally agreed that, in order to avoid the stigma of commitment to a state school for the retarded, children would be accepted as "house guests" in such institutions but would remain on the official roster of the orphanage. Periodic reevaluations were built into the plan; if no improvement was observed in the child, commitment would follow. Insofar as possible, the children were to be placed on wards as "only" children.

In the course of time, in addition to the two little girls who have been described and another transferred to the second of the two institutions at about the same time, 10 more children became "house guests." The transfers were spaced over a year's span in groups of 3, 3, and 4. All went to one institution for the mentally handicapped, the Glenwood State School. Unfortunately, the number of "house guests" exceeded the number of "elite" wards of older girls and necessitated the use of some environments that were less desirable. Consequently, in some wards there were more children, or fewer capable older girls, or less opportunity for extra stimulation, with a resulting variation in developmental patterns.

Experimental Group

The experimental group consisted of the 13 children who were transferred from an orphanage for mentally normal children to an institution for the mentally retarded, as "house guests." All were under 3 years of age at the time of transfer. Their development had been reliably established as seriously retarded by tests and observation before transfer was considered. . . .

Those children who happened to be in the infant to 3-year old age range were not ineligible for placement for legal reasons, were not acutely ill, but who were mentally retarded, became members of the experimental group. The entire project covered a span of some three years and was terminated when a change in the administration of the state school reduced the tolerance for such untidy procedures as having "house guests" in an institution. The onset of World War II and the departure of the principal investigator for military service effectively closed the project.

A project such as this could not be replicated in later years because infants were no longer kept exclusively in the orphanage. Temporary boarding homes came to be utilized prior to adoptive placement or for long-term observation and care.

The experimental group consisted of 10 girls and 3 boys, none with gross physical handicaps. Prior to their placement as "house guests" the examinations were routinely administered to them without any indication that they would or would not be involved in the unusual experience.

At the time of transfer, the mean chronological age of the group was 19.4 months (SD 7.4) and the median was 17.1 months, with a range of from 7.1 to 35.9 months. The range of IQ's was from 35 to 89 with a mean of 64.3 (SD 16.4) and a median of 65.0. Additional tests were made of 11 of the 13 children shortly before or in conjunction with the pretransfer tests reported in Table 1, using the Kuhlmann-Binet again or the Iowa Test for Young Children, and the results corroborated the reported scores.

The children were considered unsuitable for adoption because of evident mental retardation. For example, in Case 1, although the IQ was 89, it was felt that actual retardation was much greater, as the child at 7 months could scarcely hold up his head without support and showed little general bodily activity in comparison with other infants of the same age. In Case 3, at 12 months, very little activity was observed, and the child was very unsteady when sitting up without support. She could not pull herself to a standing position and did not creep. Case 11 was not only retarded but showed perseverative patterns of behavior, particularly incessant rocking back and forth. Cases 5, 8 and 13 were classified at the imbecile level. In present-day terms, they would have been labeled "trainable mentally retarded children."

Contrast Group

Since the original purpose of the experiment was to rescue for normalcy, if possible, those children showing delayed or retarded development, no plans had been made for a control or comparison group. It was only after the data had been analyzed that it was found that such a contrast group was available because of the tests that were routinely given to all children in the orphanage. To select such a contrast group, therefore, records were scrutinized for children who met the following criteria:

1. Had been given intelligence tests under 2 years of age.
2. Were still in residence in the orphanage at approximately 4 years of age.
3. Were in the control group of the orphanage preschool study (Skeels et al., 1938).
4. Had not attended preschool.

A total of 12 children were selected on the basis of the criteria and became the contrast group. The mean chronological age of the group at the time of first examination was 16.6 months (SD 2.9), with a median at 16.3 months. The range was from 11.9 to 21.8 months. The mean IQ of the group was 86.7 (SD 14.3) and the median IQ was 90. With the exception of two cases (16 and 24) the children had IQ's ranging from 81 to 103; the IQ's for the two exceptions were 71 and 50 respectively. When the children were examined, it was not known that they were or would become members of any study group. The reexaminations were merely routine retests that were given to all children.

At the ages when adoptive placement usually occurred, nine of the children in the contrast group had been considered normal in mental development. All 12 were not placed, however, because of different circumstances: 5 were withheld from placement simply because of poor family histories, 2 because of improper commitments, 2 because of luetic conditions, 2 because of other health problems, and one because of possible mental retardation.

The subsequent progress of the children in both the experimental and the contrast groups was influenced by individual circumstances. The groups were never identified as such in the resident institution; the members of each group were considered together only in a statistical sense. A child in the experimental group remained in the institution for the mentally retarded until it was felt that he had attained the maximum benefit from residence there. At that point, he was placed directly into an adoptive home or returned to the orphanage in transit to an adoptive home. If he did not attain a level of intelligence that warranted adoptive plans, he remained in the institution for mentally retarded.

The contrast-group members remained in the orphanage until placement. One was returned to relatives, but in most instances the children were eventually transferred to an institution for the mentally retarded as long-term protected residents. A few of the contrast group had been briefly approved for adoptive placement, and two had been placed for short periods. None was successful, however, and the children's decline in mental level removed them from the list of those eligible for adoption.

Description of Experimental and Contrast Groups

Birth Histories

The birth histories of the two groups were not significantly different. Prematurity was of particular interest in relation to the initial tests of intelligence, as a somewhat slower rate of mental and motor development or possible brain damage or retardation may be associated with it.

The contrast group contained only one instance of prematurity.

There were two cases of Caesarean section, one in the experimental group (Case 11) and one in the contrast group (Case 18), but no effect on mental development was indicated in either case. . . .

Medical Histories

In evaluating the medical histories of both the experimental and contrast groups, little of significance was found in the relation between illnesses and rate of mental growth. . . .

Family Backgrounds

Social histories of the children revealed that all in both the experimental and contrast groups came from homes in which the social, economic, occupational, and intellectual levels were low.

Mothers. Information relating to education was available for 11 of the 13 mothers in the experimental group and for 10 of the 12 mothers in the contrast group. The mean grade completed by mothers of children in the experimental group was 7.8, with a median at grade 8. Only two had any high school work; one completed grade 11 and one grade 10 (Cases 3 and 6). In one case, it was doubtful if the second grade had been completed (Case 8). Two (Cases 1 and 5) had dropped out of grade 8 at the age of 16.

In the contrast group, the mean grade completed was 7.3, with a median at 7.5. One mother (Case 19) had completed high school and one had an equivalent of ninth grade education.

Occupational history of mothers, available on seven of the mothers of the experimental group and on nine of the mothers of the contrast group, included mainly housework, either in the homes of their parents or on jobs as domestics. In only one instance was there a higher level (Case 24 of the contrast group); the mother had been a telephone operator and general office worker.

Intelligence tests had been obtained on five of the mothers in the experimental group and on nine of the mothers in the contrast group. The mean IQ for the five mothers of the experimental group was 70.4. with a median at 66. Four mothers had IQ's below 70, and one was classified as normal with an IQ of 100. One additional mother, although not tested, was considered feeble-minded and had gone only as far as the second grade. Of the nine mothers tested in the contrast group, only two had IQ's above 70: one, 79 and the other, 84. The other scores ranged from 36 to 66. The mean IQ was 63, with a median at 62.

Fathers.   Little information was available on the fathers, and in fact, in many cases paternity was doubtful. Ten of the children in each group were illegitimate. In the experimental group, information relating to education was available on only four fathers: two had completed the eighth grade, one had completed high school, and one had gone to high school, but how far was not known. Occupational status was indicated for only three of the fathers: one was a traveling salesman, one a printer, and one a farmhand.

In the contrast group, educational information was available for four fathers. One had completed high school and was considered talented in music (Case 24), two had completed eighth grade (Case 15 and 18), and one, the sixth grade (Case 21). Occupational data were known for eight of the contrast-group fathers: 3 were day laborers, 2 were farmhands, 1 worked on the railroad section, one was a farm renter, and one was in a C.C.C. camp.

A qualitative analysis of social histories seems to justify the conclusion that within these educational and occupational classifications, the parents represented the lower levels in such groups. Most of the fathers and mothers had dropped out of school because they had reached the limits of achievement and were not, in any sense of the word, average for their grade placements. The same may be said about occupational status.

Description of the Environments

Experimental Group

Children in the experimental group were transferred from the orphanage nursery to the Glenwood State School, an institution for mentally retarded, and were placed on wards with older, brighter inmate girls. The wards were in a large cottage that contained eight wards with a matron and an assistant matron in charge and with one attendant for each ward. Approximately 30 patients, girls ranging in age from 18 to 50 years, were on each ward. On two wards (2 and 3), the residents had mental ages of from 9 to 12 years. On two other wards (4 and 5), the mental levels were from 7 to 10 years, and on another (ward 7), the mental ages were from 5 to 8 years. With the exception of ward 7, the wards housed few or no younger children other than the experimental "house guests." It was planned to place one, or at the most two children from the experimental group on a given ward.

As with the first two children, who, by chance, were the first participants in the experiment, the attendants and the older girls became very fond of the children placed on their wards and took great pride in them. In fact, there was considerable competition among wards to see which one would have its "baby walking or talking first." Not only the girls, but the attendants spent a great deal of time with "their children," playing, talking, and training them in every way. The children received constant attention and were the recipients of gifts; they were taken on excursions and were exposed to special opportunities of all kinds. For example, it was the policy of the matron in charge of the girls' school division to single out certain children who she felt were in need of special individualization and to permit them to spend some time each day visiting her office. This furnished new experiences, such as being singled out, receiving special attention and affection, new play materials, additional language stimulation, and meeting other office callers.

The spacious living rooms of the wards furnished ample space for indoor play and activity. Whenever weather permitted, the children spent some time each day on the playground under the supervision of one or more older girls. Here they were able to interact with other children of similar ages. Outdoor play equipment included tricycles, swings, slides, and boxes, etc. The children also began to attend the school kindergarten as soon as they could walk. Toddlers remained for only half the morning and 4- or 5-year-olds, the entire morning. Activities carried on in the kindergarten resembled preschool rather than the more formal type of kindergarten.

As part of the school program, the children attended daily 15-minute exercises in the chapel, which included group singing and music by the orchestra. The children also attended the dances, school programs, moving pictures, and Sunday chapel services.

In considering this enriched environment from a dynamic point of view it must be pointed out that in the case of almost every child, some one adult (older girl or attendant) became particularly attached to him and figuratively "adopted" him. As a consequence, an intense one-to-one adult-child relationship developed, which was supplemented by the less intense but frequent interactions with the other adults in the environment. Each child had some one person with whom he was identified and who was particularly interested in him and his achievements. This highly stimulating emotional impact was observed to be the unique characteristic and one of the main contributions of the experimental setting.

The meager, even desolate environment in the orphanage has been described. The contrast between the richly stimulating, individually oriented experience of the children in the experimental group and the depersonalizing, mass handling, and affectionless existence in the children's home can hardly be emphasized enough.

Table 1. EXPERIMENTAL AND CONTRAST GROUPS: MEAN, MEDIAN, AND STANDARD DEVIATION COMPARISONS OF MENTAL GROWTH FROM FIRST TO LAST TESTS

MEASURE	CHRONO-LOGICAL AGE, MONTHS	MENTAL AGE, MONTHS	IQ	CHRONO-LOGICAL AGE, MONTHS	CHRONO-LOGICAL AGE, MONTHS	MENTAL AGE, MONTHS	IQ	LENGTH OF EXPERIMENTAL PERIOD, MONTHS	CHANGE IN IQ, FIRST TO LAST TEST
	BEFORE TRANSFER			TRANSFER	AFTER TRANSFER				

EXPERIMENTAL GROUP (N = 13)

MEASURE	CA, MONTHS (Before)	MA, MONTHS (Before)	IQ (Before)	CA, MONTHS (Transfer)	CA, MONTHS (After)	MA, MONTHS (After)	IQ (After)	LENGTH OF EXP. PERIOD	CHANGE IN IQ
Mean	18.3	11.4	64.3	19.4	38.4	33.9	91.8	18.9	+27.5
Standard deviation	6.6	4.2	16.4	7.4	17.6	13.0	11.5	11.6	15
Median	16.6	10.8	65.0	17.1	36.8	30.0	93.0	14.5	+28

CONTRAST GROUP (N = 12)

MEASURE	CA, MONTHS (First Test)	MA, MONTHS (First Test)	IQ (First Test)	CA, MONTHS (Transfer)	CA, MONTHS (Last Test)	MA, MONTHS (Last Test)	IQ (Last Test)	LENGTH OF EXP. PERIOD	CHANGE IN IQ
Mean	16.6	14.2	86.7		47.2	28.7	60.5	30.7	−26.2
Standard deviation	2.9	2.9	14.3		5.9	6.4	9.7	5.8	14.1
Median	16.3	13.6	90.0		49.3	29.3	60.0	28.8	−30.0

Source: Adapted from H. M. Skeels & H. B. Dye (1939, Table 3).

Mental Development

The 1922 Kuhlmann Revision of the Binet was used as the standard measure of intelligence, except for two or three tests on children who were 4 years of age or more for whom Stanford-Binet (1916) was used. All examinations were made by trained and experienced psychologists. Test one was the measure of intelligence just prior to transfer. Tests two, three, and the last were given at varying intervals of time following transfer. The last test was given at the end of the experimental period and was the second, third, or fourth, depending on the number of tests available at representative time intervals for a given child.

The comparisons of means, medians, and standard deviations for scores from first to last test for both groups are presented in Table 1. Using the t test, the difference for the experimental group between the means of first and last test was statistically significant at the .001 level. Every child showed a gain of from 7 to 58 points. Three children made gains of 45 points or more, and all but two children gained more than 15 points.

Length of the experimental period was from 5.7 months to 52.1 months. The period was not constant for all children as it depended upon the individual child's rate of development. As soon as a child showed normal mental development, as measured by intelligence tests and substantiated by qualitative observations, the experiment period was considered completed and the child's visit to the school for mentally retarded was terminated. Either he was placed in an adoptive home or returned to the orphanage.

The mental-growth pattern for children in the contrast group was quite opposite that of the experimental group. Using the t test, the difference between the means of first and last tests was statistically significant ($p < .001$) but with the exception of one child who gained 2 points in IQ from first to last test, all children showed losses of from 9 to 45 points. Ten of the 12 children lost 15 or more points in IQ over the period of the study.

In the experimental group, children who were initially at the lower levels tended to make the greater gains. The three children classified at the imbecile level on the first examination made gains of 58, 49, and 45 IQ points. Also, the greatest losses in the contrast group were associated with the highest initial levels. Six children with original IQ's above 90 lost from 29 to 45 points in IQ. While this shift may be partially due to regression, there must have been other factors operating to bring about such a large and consistent change.

Family History and Children's Mental Development

No clear relation between family history information and the mental-growth pattern of the children could be identified.

That the gains in intelligence evidenced by the children of the experimental group were true gains and not the results of vagaries in testing, seems validated. Improvement was noted independently by members of the medical staff, attendants and matrons, and school teachers. Practice effects could not have been a contributing factor to these gains, as the children in the contrast group, who showed continual losses in IQ, actually had more frequent tests than the children in the experimental group.

Parent Surrogates and Children's Mental Development

A close bond of love and affection between a given child and one or two adults who assume a very personal parental role appears to be a dynamic factor of great importance. Nine of 13 children in the experimental group were involved in such relationships. The four other children (Cases 2, 9, 10, and 11) tended to be less individualized on the wards; their relationships with adults were more general, less intense, and did not involve any individual adult. It is significant that the children who experienced the more intense personal relationships made greater gains than those who were limited to more general interactions. The 9 children in the "personal" group made gains in IQ ranging from 17 to 58 points, with an average gain of 33.8 points. The 4 children in the more "general" group made gains of from 7 to 20 points, with an average of 14.

Two children (Cases 10 and 11) showed little progress on ward 7 over a period of 1½ years. This ward differed significantly from the others in that it housed 8 to 12 children of younger ages (3 to 8 years), and the older girls were of a lower mental level. The attendant on the ward was especially fine with young children but was unable to give much individual attention because of the large number of young children. At one time it was feared that the two children would continue to be hopelessly retarded. However, they were subsequently placed as singletons on wards with brighter girls and, after a period of 6 months with the more individualized attention, showed marked gains in intelligence.

First Follow-Up

The experiment ended for each child in the experimental group when the decision was made that he had attained the maximum benefit from his "house-guest" experience. Of the 13, one remained in the institution until adulthood, 5 went directly into adoptive homes from the host institution, 6 had brief periods in the orphanage in transit to adoptive homes, and one was returned to the orphanage for some years and then was committed to the institution for the retarded.

As part of the pre-adoptive procedures and the planned follow-up evaluations, all the children were given individual intelligence tests approximately 2½ years after the close of the experimental period. Thus, the 11 adopted children were tested after approximately 2½ years of living in a family home, and the two children remaining in the institutions, after a similar period of continuing residential care. The mean length of the post-experimental period was 33 months (SD 8.0) and the median 29.8 months, with a range of 21 to 53 months.

The children in the contrast group were still wards of the state institutions and were given routine re-examinations. Those tests that most nearly coincided with the

2½-year-interval testing for the experimental group were used for comparison purposes in this study.

For the contrast group, the mean interval between the follow-up tests and the last experimental-period test was 36.0 months (SD 12.2), with a median of 34.2 months. The 1916 Stanford-Binet was used as the standard measure of intelligence since all the children were past 4 years of age. The means, medians and standard deviations for IQ scores recorded after the follow-up tests for children in the experimental and contrast groups are presented in Table 2.

Mental Development of the Experimental Group

The mean IQ of the 13 children in the experimental group on the follow-up examination was 95.9 (SD 16.3), and the median was 94.0. For the 11 children who had been placed in adoptive homes after the experimental period, the mean IQ at the time of the follow-up study was 101.4; the range of IQ's was from 90 to 118. Changes in IQ for the 11 children ranged from +16 points to –5 points. The greatest gain (16 points) was made by a child (Case 4) who had been placed in a superior adoptive home; the child (Case 5) showing the only loss was in a home considered to be far below the average of the other adoptive homes.

Losses of 17 and 9 points, respectively, were shown by the two children (Cases 9 and 2) who were not placed in adoptive homes. Case 9 had been returned to the orphanage although it was felt that the move was premature.[1] It was true that she became lost in the orphanage group and received very little, if any, individual attention, but whether her development would have been influenced by a different environment is speculative. Case 2, whose IQ was 77 at the close of the experimental period, had remained in the institution for the mentally retarded and, at the time of the follow-up, was expected to require continuing residential care.

Mental Development of the Contrast Group

To facilitate comparisons between the experimental and contrast groups, the time interval between the examinations during the experimental period and the time of examinations for follow-up purposes were kept as nearly the same as possible. For individual children, the test intervals ranged from 20.1 months to 57.6 months. The mean IQ of the 12 children in the contrast group was 66.1 (SD 16.5), a mean gain of 5.6 points over the last test of the experimental period. Despite this small average gain, 8 of the 12 children showed marked mental deterioration between the initial test and the follow-up test. During the three years following the close of the experimental period, a number of changes were made in the group's living situation. Two children (Cases 15 and 16) were transferred to the Glenwood State School, where they experienced essentially the same type of environment as that of the experimental group, but beginning at an older age. The two were 41 months of age at time of transfer. Thirty-four months following this transfer, Case 16 was examined and obtained an IQ of 80, showing a gain of 24 points. She was returned to the orphanage,

Table 2. MENTAL DEVELOPMENT OF INDIVIDUAL CHILDREN AS MEASURED BY REPEATED INTELLIGENCE TESTS EXPERIMENTAL GROUP (N = 13)

	EXPERIMENTAL PERIOD							FOLLOW-UP STUDY				
	BEFORE TRANSFER INITIAL TEST[b]		CHRONOLOGICAL AGE, MONTHS, AT TRANSFER	AFTER TRANSFER LAST TEST[b]		LENGTH OF EXPERIMENTAL PERIOD, MONTHS	CHANGE IN IQ INITIAL TO LAST TEST	FOLLOW-UP TEST[a]		LENGTH OF POST-EXPERIMENTAL PERIOD, MONTHS	CHANGE IN IQ DURING POST-EXPERIMENTAL PERIOD	TOTAL CHANGE IN IQ FROM INITIAL TO FOLLOW-UP TEST
	CHRONOLOGICAL AGE, MONTHS	IQ		CHRONOLOGICAL AGE, MONTHS	IQ			CHRONOLOGICAL AGE, MONTHS	IQ			
Mean	18.3	64.3	19.4	38.4	91.8	18.9	+27.5	71.4	95.9	33.0	+ 4.1	+31.6
Standard deviation	6.6	16.4	7.4	17.6	11.5	11.6	15.0	16.7	16.3	8.0	9.1	17.0
Median	16.6	65.0	17.1	36.8	93.0	14.5	+28.0	67.0	94.0	29.8	+ 1.0	+29.0
CONTRAST GROUP (N = 12)												
Mean	16.6	86.7	...	47.2	60.5	30.7	-26.2	83.3	66.1	36.0	+ 5.6	-20.6
Standard deviation	3.2	13.9	...	5.6	9.7	5.8	14.1	12.3	16.5	12.2	13.8	25.6
Median	16.3	90.0	...	49.3	60.0	28.8	-30.0	81.0	66.0	34.2	+ 6.0	-24.0

[b]Kuhlmann-Binet (1922) IQ.
[c]Stanford-Binet (1916) IQ.

therefore, as continued residence in the institution for mentally retarded seemed unwarranted. Case 15, on the other hand, failed to show any gain after 34 months. An examination six months later resulted in an IQ of 52, a 4-point loss.

Six of the contrast children were transferred to the Woodward State Hospital and School following the close of the experimental period. This transfer was made on a permanent basis, inasmuch as mental retardation and lack of development and adjustment made continued residence in the orphanage seem inadvisable. Four of the children (Cases 14, 17, 18, and 21) were transferred within three months after the close of the experimental period, and the other two (Cases 22 and 24) were transferred 16 months after the close of the experimental period.

The children sent to Woodward experienced a different environment from that of the experimental children who had been "house guests" at Glenwood. The children sent to Woodward were much older at the time of transfer and received, in general, less individual attention and had fewer interactions with adults. They interacted primarily with children of a similar or slightly older chronological age who were mentally more retarded.

Over a period ranging from two to three years, 2 of the 6 transferred children experienced further losses in IQ (Cases 18 and 21), 2 remained relatively constant (Cases 14 and 17), and 2 showed gains (Cases 22 and 24). None attained a level higher than that of borderline intelligence.

The two children who showed marked gains in intelligence had experienced enriched environments. Case 22 was quite the favorite from the time of his transfer. After a year he was placed in the primary group in school. His teacher was especially fond of him and took a great interest in his achievements. The psychologist reported, "Because he was a likable boy with possibilities for improvement under training, he has been given much special attention. His reports show that though he appears quiet and unassuming he has an active imagination and curiosity and often shows initiative." At 6 years of age he surpassed all members of his class in reading skills and in identifying flash cards.

Case 24 was the only one of this transfer group not placed in the nursery ward. He was placed on a ward with older, brighter boys, where his adjustment was consistently satisfactory. Since he was one of the younger boys on the ward, he received additional individual attention from attendants and older boys.

The three contrast children who remained in the orphanage after the close of the original study subsequently also experienced a change of environment. Case 20 did not attend preschool but entered kindergarten at 68 months of age, and he had just completed the year in kindergarten when the follow-up examination was given. Case 23 attended preschool one year, kindergarten one year, first grade one year (with a D average in grades), and, at the time of the follow-up examination, was 9 years of age and in the second grade.

Of the three children who remained in the orphanage, Case 19 had the most enriched and varied experience during the follow-up period and showed by far the greatest gain (22 points) in IQ. Beginning at 5 years of age, he spent one year in preschool and one year in kindergarten. During the year in kindergarten, he was also included in a special mental-growth stimulation study, which was carried on by a research assistant from the State University of Iowa (Dawe, 1942), that included an intensified, individualized program of experimental instruction and frequent trips away from the institution. He was the only child from the contrast group included in this special study.

The last of the contrast children to be accounted for (Case 25) was paroled to his grandparents immediately following the close of the experimental period. The home was a very marginal one, and the family had been on relief for years. At the time of the follow-up examination at 8 years of age, the boy was still in the first grade, doing failing work, and was continually "picked on" by other children. A recommendation was made to transfer the boy to an institution for the mentally retarded.

III. THE FOLLOW-UP STUDY OF ADULT ACHIEVEMENT

Statement of the Problem

The purpose of this follow-up study was to obtain answers to a few very simple questions: What happened to the two groups of children when they became adults? How were the differences in mental growth in childhood reflected in adult achievement and adjustment? Were the two divergent pathways maintained or did they converge over the years? Were there significant changes indicating improvement or regression within and between groups? Was there a relation between adult status and such factors as social history, health history, or environmental experiences?

Reality considerations influenced the kind of information that could be secured. Since the study had not been originally planned as a lifetime follow-up research, certain details of information, predictions that might have been verified, and base-line data were not available. No provision had been made for subsequent visits and, as far as the subjects and the adopting parents were concerned, relationships with the agencies had long since been terminated. In addition, all the issues relating to privacy and confidentiality arose. In view of the small number of cases, it was essential not only to locate every single subject, but to secure maximum and, if possible, uniform information for each. To jeopardize this goal by making excessive demands for time and details and by probing emotionally charged material did not seem justified. The earlier guidelines of a descriptive natural-history approach were accepted as the most appropriate. No attempt was made to convert the adult follow-up into a more penetrating and detailed assessment of dynamics. Hopefully, this needed aspect of research is being pursued by others.

The adult follow-up study began 20 years after the postexperimental follow-up (Skeels & Skodak, 1965). The initial task was to locate and obtain information on every single case in the two groups. In a study based on such small numbers, the failure to locate even two or three cases could materially limit the conclusions or impressions. . . .

Nature of Interviews

Early in the planning, it had been decided not to give intelligence tests to the subjects, now 25 to 35 years of age, because of the many questions that might arise over their relation to the early childhood tests, and because of the possibility of lack of cooperation. It seemed more appropriate to relate the earlier measures of mental development to the adult educational level, occupation, and general social competence attained by the subjects. Personal interviews were used to secure this information. For the experimental group, the adoptive parents (if living) and the subjects were interviewed, usually separately. . . .

General Overall Findings

Survival Data

All 13 subjects in the experimental group reached adulthood. Among the 11 adoptive homes in which subjects were placed as children, both adoptive parents were deceased in two, and the adoptive parents were divorced in one but the adoptive mother had remarried and maintained a relationship with the subject.

In the contrast group, 11 of the 12 subjects were living; one (Case 16) died at the age of 15 while still a resident of the institution for the mentally retarded. None had been placed in adoptive homes.

Mobility

Among the adoptive parents, 2 of the 11 families had moved out of the state, one prior to the first follow-up study and the other later. Of the 13 subjects in the experimental group, 6 including the 2 not placed in adoptive homes, still lived in the state. Of the 7 who had moved out of the state, 2 were residing in Minnesota and 1 each in Arizona, Nebraska, California, Kansas, and Wisconsin.

In the contrast group, 9 of the 11 living subjects still resided within the state of Iowa. One (Case 23) was living in Nebraska, one (Case 22) was located in California (after tracing him from Florida), and he later moved to Montana.

Occupational Levels

The 13 subjects in the experimental group were all self-supporting and none were wards of any institution, public or private. Two, a boy (Case 1) and a girl (Case 6), however, had spent some time in a state correctional school during adolescence. Nevertheless, no member of the group exhibited evidence of antisocial or delinquent behavior, economic dependency, or need for psychiatric or agency support.

Table 3 summarizes the occupational status of the experimental- and contrast-group subjects and their spouses. The women's vocational achievements cannot be

TABLE 3. EXPERIMENTAL AND CONTRAST GROUPS: OCCUPATIONS OF SUBJECTS AND SPOUSES

CASE NO.	SUBJECT'S OCCUPATION	SPOUSE'S OCCUPATION	FEMALE SUBJECT'S OCCUPATION PREVIOUS TO MARRIAGE
Experimental group:			
1[a]	Staff sergeant	Dental technician	. . .
2	Housewife	Laborer	Nurses' aide
3	Housewife	Mechanic	Elementary school teacher
4	Nursing instructor	Unemployed	Registered nurse
5	Housewife	Semi-skilled laborer	No work history
6	Waitress	Mechanic, semi-skilled	Beauty operator
7	Housewife	Flight engineer	Dining room hostess
8	Housewife	Foreman, construction	No work history
9	Domestic service	Unmarried	. . .
10[a]	Real estate sales	Housewife	. . .
11[a]	Vocational counselor	Advertising copy writer[b]	. . .
12	Gift shop sales[c]	Unmarried	. . .
13	Housewife	Pressman-printer	Office-clerical
Contrast group:			
14	Institutional inmate	Unmarried	. . .
15	Dishwasher	Unmarried	. . .
16	Deceased	. . .	. . .
17[a]	Dishwasher	Unmarried	. . .
18[a]	Institutional inmate	Unmarried	. . .
19[a]	Compositor and typesetter	Housewife	. . .
20[a]	Institutional inmate	Unmarried	. . .
21[a]	Dishwasher	Unmarried	. . .
22[a]	Floater	Divorced	. . .
23	Cafeteria (part time)	Unmarried	. . .
24[a]	Institutional gardener's assistant	Unmarried	. . .
25[a]	Institutional inmate	Unmarried	. . .

[a]Male.
[b]B.A. degree.
[c]Previously had worked as a licensed practical nurse.

compared directly with those of the men since women do not have equal opportunities for advancement, and early marriage influences their vocational patterns. In the present study, 8 of the 10 girls were married; 2 married shortly after leaving school and had no employment records (Cases 5 and 8). Case 7 took the examination and was accepted as a stewardess for an air line after graduation from high school, but married instead. She worked as a dining-room hostess for a short time after her marriage. The two cases (2 and 9) who had never been placed in adoptive homes worked as domestics.

The occupational status of the 11 living members of the contrast group was significantly different. The contributions to society of the four residents of state institutions were limited to the unskilled tasks assigned to ward patients. One (Case 25) had intermittent paroles to a grandmother; while with her he occasionally mowed lawns or shoveled walks.

One boy (Case 24) was an employee in the institution for the mentally retarded in which he had been a patient for many years. Upon reaching adulthood, it was felt that his retardation was not sufficient to justify his being kept on as a resident. Placement in a community was attempted but failed completely. He was then placed on the employees' payroll in the institution but continued to live on a patient ward; subsequently, he was made a regular employee and transferred to the employees' home. He had no interests other than his work and had no friends among either inmates or employees.

Of the seven who were employed and living in communities, one (Case 21), a male, was still a ward of an institution for the mentally retarded but out on a vocational-training assignment that eventuated in his discharge from the institution. As a dishwasher in a nursing home he earned $60.00 a month and board and room. Two others, one male (Case 17) and one female (Case 15), previously wards of a state institution for the mentally retarded, were discharged from state supervision and worked as dishwashers in small restaurants. One girl (Case 23) remained in the orphanage from infancy to 17 years and was then returned to her mother. She found employment in a cafeteria where her duties were folding napkins around silverware. On paydays, her mother called for her checks and deposited them in the bank for her.

One man (Case 20) had had brief periods of part-time work on a farm during his teens. He spent his childhood in the orphanage and his adolsecence in a training school for delinquent boys. He escaped from the training school, got to the West Coast, and within a few months was hospitalized following bizarre behavior and a severe depression. He was returned to his home state and has been hospitalized as mentally ill ever since.

Another boy (Case 22) was a "floater" whose travels had taken him from coast to coast. His vocational activities included plucking chickens in a produce house, washing dishes in a hospital kitchen, and doing the heavy packing for shipment in a stationery company. One trip to Iowa and two to the West Coast were made to locate him.

Still another, the last of the employed subjects in the contrast group to be accounted for was the man (Case 19) who stands out from the group in many ways. He became a compositor and typesetter for a newspaper in a city of 300,000, and his income easily equaled that of all the other employed contrast-group members combined.

Comparisons of Occupational Status. . . .

The percentage distribution of family heads by socioeconomic status in the north central region of the United States, 1960, were compared with the distribution of family heads of the experimental and contrast groups. It is apparent that, for the contrast group, again with the consistent exception of Case 19, the subjects are concentrated in the two lowest socio-economic status classifications. The experimental group, however, approximates the distribution of the total population.

Other comparisons of income can be made with census data for employed males in the same general area. Based on principal wage earner, the total experimental group was within the average range of income for employed males in Iowa with earnings of $4224 as compared to $4182–$4782 for men in the labor force; the contrast group, however, had a median annual income of $1200. If the two unmarried women, with annual incomes of $1416 and $1820 are excluded, the median wage for males in the experimental group is $4800.

There were . . . striking differences in incomes between the experimental and contrast groups. The two unmarried women and one unskilled spouse in the experimental group who earned wages of $2200 or less, the lowest in the group, still earned more than the lowest earners in the contrast group. Only one person in the contrast group, Case 19, earned more than the median of the experimental group.

These achievements are particularly significant in view of the fact that the 11 subjects in the experimental group who were placed in adoptive homes at young ages were placed in homes of modest level. As would be expected, there had been some reservations about level of achievement subsequent to adoption, and it was deemed advisable to select homes in which the demands for intellectual and educational achievement would not be too great.

Education

Marked differences were found between the two groups in educational attainment. Mean and median school grades completed by experimental-group subjects and their spouses and by the contrast-group subjects are shown in Table 4.

TABLE 4.   EXPERIMENTAL AND CONTRAST GROUPS: EDUCATION OF SUBJECTS AND SPOUSES

(N = 13)	EXPERIMENTAL GROUP GRADE COMPLETED	SPOUSES GRADE COMPLETED	(N = 12)	CONTRAST GROUP GRADE COMPLETED
Mean	11.68	11.60	. . .	3.95
Median	12.00	12.00	. . .	2.75

Excluding the two cases not placed in adoptive homes (Cases 2 and 9), the mean grade completed for the experimental group was 12.8 and the median, 12. One subject—a male—(Case 11) had a B. A. degree from a state university and had completed some graduate work; another—a male—(Case 10) graduated from a business college; and three of the girls (Cases 3, 4, and 13) had from one semester to 2½ years of college education.

The education of the spouses was comparable to that of subjects in the experimental group. Excluding the spouse of Case 2, who had never been placed in an adoptive home and had had only a sixth grade education, the mean grade completed for spouses was 12.2 and the median, 12.0.

The educational levels attained by subjects in the experimental group, and their spouses, compare favorably with the 1960 Census figures for adults of similar ages for Iowa (U.S. Bureau of the Census, 1936b) and for the United States as a whole (U.S. Bureau of the Census, 1963c). In the 1970 Census, the median grade completed by Iowa adults 25 to 34 years of age was 12.4, and of the white population of similar ages in the United States, 12.2.

The educational levels of the subjects in the contrast group were much lower than those of the experimental group. Using the t test, the difference between the means of the experimental and contrast groups was statistically significant at the .001 level.

A direct comparison between the educational attainments of the two groups is difficult. In most instances, children in the contrast group received their education in state institutions for the mentally retarded. Grade levels there are not directly comparable to those in public school systems. In most instances, grade level reported in this study was based on evidence from standard achievement tests.

Only one subject in the contrast group (Case 19) had an education beyond the eighth grade, and he deserves special mention and explanation. He is not only graduated from high school and had one semester of college but is distinct from the other contrast-group members in that he was the only one with a stable marriage, a family, a home of his own, steady employment in a skilled trade, and earning an income of $6720 in 1963. He was also the one whose experiences least resembled those of the other contrast children. He had had a moderate hearing loss following bilateral mastoidectomy in infancy, and while it was not regarded as a major disability in preschool years and would not have precluded his attending public school, it was felt that he might receive more individual attention and appropriate instruction at a school for the deaf. Following the close of the first follow-up study he was transferred to a residential school for the deaf and completed high school there. He had the added advantage that the matron of his cottage took a special fancy to him because he was one of the youngest children and had no family. He was a frequent guest in her home and in the home of her daughter and son-in-law.

Marital and Family Status

Experimental Group

Eleven of the 13 subjects in the experimental group had married, and one of the 11 had been divorced. The spouses came from the same type of middle class, working class families as the adoptive homes of the experimental subjects, which is indicated by the comparable level of education in each pair and was corroborated during the interviews with parents and subjects.

As far as could be observed in the interviews, the marriages gave every indication of stability and permanence. The one divorce was secured by the husband of an experimental subject who alleged that his wife had been unfaithful and neglected the children. Custody of the five children was awarded to him. His wife had spent some time in a facility for delinquent girls during her adolescence.

Nine of the families had children of their own. Making up this second generation at the time of the study were 28 children ranging in age from 1 to 10½ years; 18 were boys and 10, girls.

Arrangements were made for individual intelligence tests to be given these children (Schenke & Skeels, 1965). The Standard-Binet, form L-M, was given to 22 children, the Stanford-Binet, form L, to one, and the Wechsler Intelligence Scale for Children to two. The Cattell Infant Intelligence Scale was administered to the three children under 2 years of age.

The 28 children had a mean IQ of 103.9 and a median of 104. The range of IQ's was from 86 to 125, and no child tested below the dull-normal level. Only about half of the children had reached school age, but among those who had, grade achievement was commensurate with age.

Examiners were impressed by the fact that none of the children showed any sign of abnormality or organic pathology, and, as a group, were attractive and physically well developed. Personality development and adjustment were considered well within the normal range. In one or two instances, there was some evidence of feelings of insecurity or lack of self-confidence.

Contrast Group

In the contrast group, only two men of the 11 living subjects, had married, Cases 22 and 19. Case 22 had one child, a boy, and subsequently was divorced. He was living in a modest apartment some distance from his family. The boy was examined in the home of his mother at the age of 6 years, 8 months, on the Stanford-Binet, form L-M. An estimated IQ of 66 was obtained. In the examination, the child evidenced signs of possible brain damage of unknown etiology. The mother indicated that she and the boy's father had maintained no permanent address and had traveled about the country a great deal; as a result the child had been cared for by various persons, including the mother's sister and mother, and other persons. The wife stated that her husband had been quite abusive to the boy frequently striking him during fits of rage. She attributed the child's retarded physical and mental development to the mistreatment he had received in the past. The mother had remarried, and she indicated that her current husband was kind to the child and showed him much consideration.

Case 19 is the subject that consistently was the exception within the contrast group. He was married, had four children, and maintained a comfortable home in a very attractive middle-class residential area. His four children were physically well developed, of average size for age, and were very attractive and nicely adjusted. The oldest child, a boy 5 years, 11 months of age, was doing satisfactory work in the first grade and had an IQ of 107 on the Stanford-Binet, form L. The three younger children were girls; when tested the 4½-year-old had an IQ of 117 and the 2½-year-old, 119, on Form L, and the 9-month-old infant had an IQ of 103 on the Cattell Infant Test.

None of the four girls in the contrast group had married. Two had been sterilized in late adolescence prior to work placement in the community.

In neither experimental nor contrast group was there illegitimacy or indication of serious promiscuity.

Institutional Residence: Time and Costs

One measure of the efficacy of different types of intervention programs is derived from a comparison of costs. Length of care in institutions and costs of rehabilitation (retraining, casework services, etc.) must be considered in evaluating the advantages and disadvantages of programs. To determine actual costs of institutional care of experimental- and contrast-group children, monthly per capita costs were secured for the years from 1930 to 1963 from the annual and/or biennial reports of the institutions involved. In reviewing these costs over a 30-year period, it is impressive to note that monthly per capita costs for care in the Iowa institutions increased from approximately $20.00 in 1933 to $250.00 in 1963 (exclusive of capital investments). This increase represents not only actual increases in costs and the decreased purchasing power of the dollar, but, also, increased ratios of staff to resident population, marked expansion of professional staff, much less crowding, and more stimulating educational and nursery-life programs, particularly at the Children's Home.

The actual time spent in residence at one or more of the state institutions was computed for each subject from admission and discharge dates. The contrast between the two groups is impressive. Up to the time of this follow-up study, the 13 children in the experimental group had spent a total of 72 years and 5 months in institutional residence, at a total cost to the state of $30,716.01, whereas the 12 children in the contrast group had spent a total of 273 years in residence, at a total cost of $138,571.68.

For children in the experimental group, the mean length of residence was 5 years, 1 month, with a median at 3 years, 3 months. The mean cost was $2,367.75, the median, $890.22. If one excludes the two cases not placed in adoptive homes, the mean and median periods of residence become 2 years, 5 months, and 3 years, 2 months, respectively, with costs materially reduced to a mean of $1,285.12 and a median of $660.96.

For the contrast group, the mean residence period at the time of the follow-up was 22 years, 9 months, with a median at 21 years, 5 months. Since the members of this group were then in their early thirties, many more years of institutional care can be anticipated. The mean cost (1964) of institutionalization was $11,547.64, and the median $9,108.50. Institutional costs for Case 20 were considerably higher than for other institutionalized subjects for a similar period because he spent over 14 years in state mental hospitals. In these facilities, the per capita costs increased more rapidly in the 1950's than elsewhere because of the improvement in facilities and treatment.

Per capita costs of care for patient residence do not accurately convey the costs for different types of patients. For example, the placement of infants and young children of normal development was accomplished within weeks or, at most, four to five months after admission. During the placement period, the average cost of care was $72.00 for the typical period of 3 months (Skodak, 1939; Skodak & Skeels 1945; 1949). Then, and even more now, a relatively higher drain on professional and casework services was necessary to facilitate adoptions. However, once the child was placed, there was relatively little demand for further agency service.

The costs cited for the experimental group were markedly increased because of the mental retardation that had already occurred to a diagnosable degree and, consequently, that necessitated the active intervention, based on cooperative staff participation, of two independent facilities.

In institutions for the mentally retarded, long-term custodial cases were allocated relatively little professional time. When rehabilitation of patients is attempted, however, professional staff investment and costs become extremely high. Case 17 was considered by the staff of the institution for the mentally retarded to have been an outstanding example of successful rehabilitation. A period of over six years elapsed from the time the search for work placement was begun until the patient was discharged from state supervision. During that time, the case worker from the institution's Social Service Department made 30 or more visits to the young man and to other individuals. These visits were supplemented by services in the community from other agencies: Vocational Rehabilitation, Family Service, and the Community Center. For a period of more than one year, a social worker from one of the local agencies co-signed all checks drawn by the subject on his bank account before it was decided that he could manage his own affairs. It is not surprising that the costs of restoring a patient to the community in a low income, occupationally precarious job, have resulted in the scarcity of such programs.

Still another comparison that reflects the differences in achievement between the two groups and that should be considered in evaluating overall costs is that of federal income tax payments. Tax payments were estimated . . . based on 1963 laws . . .

In the experimental group, these payments were based on family income or on that of the head of the household. Income taxes were paid by all experimental subjects. In the contrast group, on the other hand, four subjects had no income and, therefore, paid no income tax. In the experimental group, the range of tax estimated to have been paid was from $38.00 to $485.00. It should be pointed out that these estimations were based on deductions for a median of three dependents, whereas, in the contrast group, only Case 19 had any dependents.

Income tax payments were estimated for 1963 only. While it is impossible to predict accurately the future employment stability of a wage earner, the fluctuations in income tax assessments, or the effects of changing employment patterns, it is reasonable to assume that those subjects employed at the follow-up will continue to have earnings and make tax payments for an additional 20 to 40 years. The continuity of employment for trained or skilled workers is more likely than for the unskilled, who are more vulnerable to fluctuations in jobs. Since the experimental subjects—and Case 19—had better assurance of continued employment, the difference between contributions to society from the experimental group and costs to society for the contrast group, can be expected to increase with the years.

Analysis of Variable Factors in Relation to Achievement

Medical Histories

An evaluation of the medical histories of the experimental and contrast groups, with few exceptions, revealed no significant relation between illnesses and adult achievement. . . .

Variables Relating to Natural and Adoptive Parents

It would be useful in many kinds of planning if the developmental course of progeny could be predicted. Information about family histories has been seen as providing the basis for such predictions. By inference, educational attainment, vocational success, and general social conformity have been accepted as indications of genetic differences. The unreliability of these indicators can be judged by inspecting, for example, the differences in average educational level between 1930 and 1960, and the differences in educational attainment between contrasting geographic areas of the United States. Delinquency rates, dependence on community agencies, and "general social adequacy" are influenced by many factors other than individual genetic constitution.

Even if the family history data were predictive, the significant items were frequently missing from the case records. History material on the adopting parents, while not quite as meager, also had omissions, since the adoption agency worker's decision that the petitioners did or did not qualify as adoptive parents was frequently based on a global impression. Such details as school grade completed were likely to be interpreted in the light of the worker's own value system.

With the small numbers of cases involved and the frequency of entries such as "no information" or "unknown," any statistical analysis of . . . family histories data is not possible. From long experience in evaluating social histories, an inspection of the available information suggests that even if all the missing data were known the total picture for the experimental and contrast groups would not be materially changed.

The sociocultural levels of the biological parents in both the experimental and contrast groups were similar and represented the lower class in American society. Even within this category they represented a lower selection: many were unemployed, had been known to welfare agencies over the years, or were cited for law infringements.

Adoptive parents of the 11 children in the experimental group could be characterized as coming from the lower middle class. Within this class, in contrast to the biological parents, they represented an upper selection, in that approval for adoptive placement demanded that they be good, solid, substantial citizens in their respective communities and that they be financially capable of supporting a child in the home. The level of these adoptive homes, while representing a marked selection upward in comparison to the natural parents, nevertheless was rated as somewhat below the average level of the adoptive homes in the Skodak-Skeels longitudinal study of 100 adopted children (Skodak, 1939; Skodak & Skeels, 1945; 1949). The selection of relatively modest levels of adoptive homes for the experimental children had been purposeful, and the subsequent development and achievements of the children were similar to or exceeded those that would have been anticipated for natural children in such homes. The question can be raised whether the attainments might have been even higher had the children been placed in homes of higher aspirations and stimulation levels. Conceivably, such placement might have resulted in higher achievement. It is equally possible, on the other hand, that excessive demands and pressures might have resulted in lower achievement.

With such small numbers of subjects and with gaps in information, it is impossible to identify relations between achievement of the subjects and specific characteristics of either the adoptive or natural parents.

IV. IMPLICATIONS

At the beginning of the study, the 11 children in the experimental group evidenced marked mental retardation. The developmental trend was reversed through planned intervention during the experimental period. The program of nurturance and cognitive stimulation was followed by placement in adoptive homes that provided love and affection and normal life experiences. The normal, average intellectual level attained by the subjects in early or middle childhood was maintained into adulthood.

It can be postulated that if the children in the contrast group had been placed in suitable adoptive homes or given some other appropriate equivalent in early infancy, most or all of them would have achieved within the normal range of development, as did the experimental subjects.

It seems obvious that under present-day conditions there are still countless infants born with sound biological constitutions and potentialities for development well within the normal range who will become mentally retarded and noncontributing members of society unless appropriate intervention occurs. It is suggested by the findings of this study and others published in the past 20 years that sufficient knowledge is available to design programs of intervention to counteract the devastating effects of poverty, sociocultural deprivation, and maternal deprivation.

Since the study was a pioneering and descriptive one involving only a small number of cases, it would be presumptuous to attempt to identify the specific influences that produced the changes observed. However, the contrasting outcome between children who experienced enriched environmental opportunities and close emotional relationships with affectionate adults, on the one hand, and those children who were in deprived, indifferent, and unresponsive environments, on the other, leaves little doubt that the area is a fruitful one for further study.

It has become increasingly evident that the prediction of later intelligence cannot be based on the child's first observed developmental status. Account must be taken of his experiences between test and retest. Hunt (1964, p. 212) has succinctly stated that,

> . . . In fact, trying to predict what the IQ of an individual child will be at age 18 from a D.Q. obtained during his first or second year is much like trying to predict how fast a feather might fall in a hurricane. The law of falling bodies holds only under the specified and controlled conditions of a vacuum. Similarly, any laws concerning the rate of intellectual growth must take into account the series of environmental encounters which constitute the conditions of that growth.

The divergence in mental-growth patterns between children in the experimental and contrast groups is a striking illustration of this concept.

The right of every child to be well born, well nurtured, well brought up, and well educated was enunciated in the Children's Charter of the 1930 White House Conference on Child Health and Protection (White House Conference, 1931). Though society strives to insure this right, for many years to come there will be children to whom it has been denied and for whom society must provide both intervention and restriction. There is need for further research to determine the optimum modes of such intervention and the most appropriate ages and techniques for initiating them. The present study suggests, but by no means delimits, either the nature of the intervention or the degree of change that can be induced.

The planning of future studies should recognize that the child interacts with his environment and does not merely passively absorb its impact. More precise and significant information on the constitutional, emotional, and responsive-style characteristics of the child is needed so that those environmental experiences that are most pertinent to his needs can be identified and offered in optimum sequence.

The unanswered questions of this study could form the basis for many lifelong research projects. If the tragic fate of the 12 contrast-group children provokes even a single crucial study that will help prevent such a fate for others, their lives will not have been in vain.

NOTES

[1] The return followed a change in administration rather than psychological readiness.

REFERENCES

Dawe, Helen C. A study of the effect of an educational program upon language development and related mental functions in young children. *Journal of Experimental Education*, 1942, *11*, 200–209.

Hunt, J. McV. The psychological basis for using preschool enrichment as an antidote for cultural deprivation. *Merrill-Palmer Quarterly of Behavior and Development,* 1964, *10,* 209–248.

Kirk, S. A. *Early education of the mentally retarded.* Chicago: Univ. of Ill. Pr., 1958.

Kugel, R. B. Familial mental retardation: some possible neurophysiological and psychosocial interrelationships. In A. J. Solnit & Sally Provence (Eds.), *Modern perspectives in child development.* New York: International Universities Press, 1963, 206–216.

Schenke, L. W., & Skeels, H. M. An adult follow-up of children with inferior social histories placed in adoptive homes in early childhood. Study in Progress, 1965.

Skeels, H. M. The mental development of children in foster homes. *Pedagogical Seminar & Journal of Genetic Psychology.* 1936, *49,* 91–106.

Skeels, H. M. Mental development of children in foster homes. *Journal of Consulting Psychology,* 1938, *2,* 33–43.

Skeels, H. M. Some Iowa studies of the mental growth of children in relation to differentials of the environment: a summary. In *Intelligence: its nature and nurture.* 39th Yearbook, Part II. National Society for the Study of Education, 1940, 281–308.

Skeels, H. M. A study of the effects of differential stimulation on mentally retarded children: a follow-up report. *American Journal of Mental Deficiency,* 1942, *46,* 340–350.

Skeels, H. M., & Dye, H. B. A study of the effects of differential stimulation on mentally retarded children. *Proceedings & Addresses of the American Association on Mental Deficiency,* 1939, *44,* 114–136.

Skeels, H. M., & Fillmore, Eva A. The mental development of children from underprivileged homes. *Journal of Genetic Psychology,* 1937, *50,* 427–439.

Skeels, H. M., & Skodak, Marie. Techniques for a high-yield follow-up study in the field. *Public Health Reports,* 1965, *80,* 249–257.

Skeels, H. M., Updegraff, Ruth, Wellman, Beth L., & Williams, H. M. A study of environmental stimulation: an orphanage preschool project. *University of Iowa Studies in Child Welfare,* 1938, *15,* No. 4.

Skodak, Marie. Children in foster homes: a study of mental development. *University of Iowa Studies in Child Welfare,* 1939, *16,* No. 1.

Skodak, Marie, & Skeels, H. M. A follow-up study of children in adoptive homes. *Journal of Genetic Psychology,* 1945, *66,* 21–58.

Skodak, Marie, & Skeels, H. M. A final follow-up study of one hundred adopted children. *Journal of Genetic Psychology,* 1949, *75,* 85–125.

U.S. Bureau of the Census, 1960, *Methodology and scores of socio-economic status.* Working Paper No. 15. Washington, 1963. P. 13 (a).

U.S. Bureau of the Census. U.S. Census Population, 1960. Vol. I. *Characteristics of the population.* Part 17, Iowa. Washington: U.S. Government Printing Office, 1963. Table 103, pp. 17–333. (b).

U.S. Bureau of the Census. U.S. Census Population, 1960. *Detailed characteristics, United States summary.* Final Report PC (L)-ID Washington: U.S. Government Printing Office, 1963. Table 173, pp. 1–406. (c).

Warner, W. L., Meeker, Marchia, & Eells, H. *Social class in America: the evaluation of status.* New York: Harper's Torchbooks, 1960.

Wellman, Beth L. Our changing concept of intelligence. *Journal of Consulting Psychology,* 1938, *2,* 97–107.

White House Conference on Child Health and Protection. *Addresses and Abstracts of Committee Reports, 1930.* New York: Appleton-Century, 1931.

part four
EARLY CHILDHOOD

It is in this period that the effect of ecological factors on human development becomes most clearly apparent. Social structure shapes patterns of family interaction and, thereby, the course of the child's behavior and growth. In making the case for the small family, Lieberman summarizes research on the effects of family size. Rothbart documents differences in mother-child interaction as a function of the child's ordinal position. Next, the studies by Parke and Baumrind demonstrate the impact of differing patterns of discipline on the development of the child, and Blehar suggests possible disruption of mother-child attachment as a result of the child's early experience with day care.

The next three studies reflect different points of view with respect to social class differences in development and the need for intervention. First Bee and her colleagues argue that social class variations in task performance are the result of differing mother-child interaction. Tulkin provides a more theoretical approach, warning against acceptance of the concept of "cultural deprivation." Finally, Bronfenbrenner, in a review article, evaluates different strategies of early intervention, identifies parent involvement as a crucial component of effective programs, and points to "family support systems" as the keystone for future social policy and action in this sphere.

The role of extrafamilial contexts for development is examined in the next set of studies: Freud and Dann's dramatic follow-up of children rescued from Nazi concentration camps demonstrates the power of the children's group in sustaining emotional security and psychological growth. The way in which "social labeling" of the child can affect others' treatment of him, and thereby his own capacity to function, is demonstrated by Brophy and Good's study of teacher behavior.

The influence of that new and now ubiquitous member of virtually every American family—the television set—is examined in the next three articles. The first, by Liebert and Baron, provides a concrete example of the experimental studies which served as a basis for the Surgeon General's report. In the second, Garbarino calls attention to a major omission in the studies carried out to date on the effects of the television on children. The third focuses attention on the legislative process and social policy as it examines congressional inquiries into televised violence.

4.1

Reserving a Womb: Case for the Small Family

E. James Lieberman

"If people only made prudent marriages, what a stop to population there would be!"—Thackeray.

If conceiving babies were nearly as hard as rearing them well, small families would be more common. Some parents feel that child rearing is not more hazardous with a large family, and many good results are in evidence. But for most of us, child rearing is so complicated and challenging that there is not much to be taken for granted. New knowledge about child development, emphasis on the importance of the early years, and the discovery of subtle but significant differences between new-born infants all lend weight to the idea that "maternal instinct" while essential is not enough. (1) Sound information is needed, too. The profusion of articles and books on child rearing is not an indictment of the American family but public testimony of myriad private concerns that are entirely appropriate for parents of this and any age.

TRENDS IN THE UNITED STATES

In the United States average family size has fluctuated from as many as eight per woman in colonial days to 2.3 during the depression and over three since then. The birth rate has been falling steadily in recent years, but the national growth rate is still ahead of most other industrialized countries. This growth is due not to uncontrolled reproduction among the poor, but to the deliberate attainment of three and four children by the more prosperous majority of our population. In fact, the poor prefer smaller families than the average but attainment of their goals has been more difficult. It takes only two children to replace two parents in the next generation, if the children survive to reproductive maturity. Since there is a slight amount of attrition, the actual size of family required for a stable population is 2.2, given our present standards of health and longevity.

Most Americans determine their family size on personal, not demographic considerations. Of course, population growth cannot go on indefinitely in a finite space, with finite resources. Anyone who has lately tried to get out of a large city on Friday afternoon cr into a national park for a weekend will probably conclude that there are enough people here already! Hopefully, we have sufficient time and individual and community wisdom to bring family size and community size into harmonious relationship on a voluntary basis.

Reprinted from the *American Journal of Public Health*, 1970, *60*, 87–92, by permission of the author and the American Public Health Association.

Surveys indicate that the two-child family was preferred by more people in 1940 than in the last decade. The three- and four-child family seems to be gaining as an ideal. There is an astonishing number of unplanned pregnancies even in recent years and, what is worse, a good many unwanted children. Family building is a process in which the ideals of inexperience are transformed by realities of parenthood with the result that preferred family size may change. Experts in both child development and demography attest to the great significance of the difference between family size of four, three, and two. (2, 3)

There is a good deal of research on family size and birth order, (4) but little that can make precise distinctions between two, three, and four children—the range which is the most common preference today. Furthermore, the studies do not take into account whether the children in these families were wanted or unwanted—often a difficult thing to ascertain. Presumably, wanted children in large families will do as well or better than unwanted children in small families, but as would be expected, there are more unwanted children in large families than in small families.

FAMILY SIZE EFFECTS ON CHILDREN

The 1964 Presidential Task Force on Manpower Conservation found that about 70 percent of Selective Service mental rejectees come from families of four children or more, though only 33 percent of the nation's children come from such families. A further breakdown shows that 47 percent of rejectees come from the 11 percent of children who are members of families with six or more offspring! Interpretation is difficult because large family size and poverty are associated and cannot be separated for analysis. (6)

The Scottish Mental Survey of 1947 gets around this difficulty by separating the effects of social class and family size in its measure of intelligence. All 11-year-olds were subjects of the study, which showed progressive decline in intelligence score with increasing family size regardless of social class. Scores did correlate with social class too: the richer, the better. But family size took its toll within each grouping, so that children of small lower class families excelled those from the large middle class homes, and so on. (7) In the United States several studies have shown that the development of intellect is favored by the small family environment. One interpretation is that parents have less time for verbal interaction with a larger number of children; verbal proficiency is the crux of success in intelligence tests and in education generally.

Concerning personality development, important work on family density—number and spacing of children—has been done at the National Institute of Mental Health. Second and later-born boys were studied for vigor and lethargy at birth, and for dependence or independence at age two and a half. The findings contest the stereotype that children from large (high density) families are more self-reliant and mature. In the nursery school setting they demand more frequent contact with teacher than their peers from small families, which the scientists theorize is due to relative maternal deprivation at home. Even at birth, there are significant differences, the infants from smaller families being more vigorous and responsive. But when the differences at birth are controlled for, those at two and a half remain significant, i.e., there is an environmental as well as a congenital factor. Social class did not influence the results. As might be expected, in the more congested families, observers found significantly less contact with the child initiated by the mother. There was no correlation between family density and friendliness with peers, so the teacher-seeking behavior cannot be written off as extroversion. (9)

Other studies show that (a) successive children do not receive the parental warmth granted their predecessors, (10) and (b) relative maternal unconcern toward younger siblings characterizes some large families. (11) Child development specialists stress the importance of maternal deprivation due to illness, death, or separation. It is likely that another form of maternal and paternal deprivation occurs regularly in crowded families and, furthermore, that this is related to prolonged dependency behavior.

Physical development also seems to be retarded by increased family size. A British study found that average height and weight for age decreased as family size increased, despite the fact that birth weights increase with parity. This may be due to poorer nutrition or factors affecting it; e.g., emotion or infection. Birth spacing may be more important in that the older child receives less attention at mealtime when a new baby is born. (12)

Eighth- and eleventh-grade students from small families in Michigan reported better relations with their parents than those from larger families. (13) In a study of Ohio fifth-graders from families of at least two children, researchers found that offspring in smaller families had more favorable relations with both parents and siblings. (14)

Not all studies favor small families. Some researchers have been unable to show any significant difference between large and small families on criteria of adjustment. (15, 16) Bossard and Boll (17) sum up their survey as follows: Small families have the advantage of more parental attention, but possible disadvantage of too much intensive parenthood, pressure to achieve, and exaggerated feeling of importance in a group; large families tend to be less planned, with less intensive parenting, early acceptance of realities, more crises, more group emphasis with organization, discipline, conformity, and specialization of function among children. The small family theme is planning, rationalism and prudence oriented toward achievement in a complex, changing society. The desire for a large family, significantly, is not prominent among offspring of prolific parents: only 30 percent of children from large families endorsed the idea wholeheartedly.

EFFECTS UPON PARENTS

A recent British study found more ill health—both physical and mental—in parents of larger families, especially mothers, which is attributed to the increased strain imposed upon them by caring for a larger number of children. There was no association between family size and income and none between social class and health in the population sampled. (18)

Other studies have found (a) in discordant marriages, the chance for successful outcome decreases as the number of children increases; (19) (b) happiness was associated with the desire for children, whether couples had any or not at the time, and poorest adjustment was found among those with unwanted children; (20) (c) an inverse relationship existed between marital adjustment and family size, i.e., more children, less adjustment; also, there was a correlation between marital adjustment and success in controlling fertility according to the desires of the couple; (21) (d) having more than one child early in marriage correlated with poorer marital adjustment. (22)

Family planning is clearly related to marital adjustment, and good communication between spouses is known to correlate with effective family planning. (23) Good marriages get better with parenthood and the poor ones get more children. This phenomenon deserves closer attention because it is a very vicious cycle of maladaptation.

DISCUSSION

The two-child family does not seem so oppressively small when we note that, at various times and places, it has become the mode and without grievous consequences; for example, in contemporary Scandinavia, Japan, and Hungary, and in segments of populations, such as women college graduates and Jewish couples in this country.

Most of the accidental pregnancies that occur nowadays turn out to be the first and second children. Many couples whose use of contraceptives, if any, has been casual, will start family planning conscientiously only after reaching their desired family size. This laxity can jeopardize marital stability and compromise the development of infants born too close together. Besides those marriages that occur because the girl is pregnant, there are many more "young marrieds" who become parents before they smooth out their nuptial ruffles. Although divorce rates have remained relatively constant, the number of children affected (1.18 per divorce) has increased significantly, reflecting the rising proportion of couples with children.

Prudence in the matter of starting a family requires some interval for marital adjustment. Young couples need and can well afford an interval of marriage without children. Child spacing is also an important matter, all of which comes down to a strong recommendation that couples learn and adopt effective family planning measures from the start of their sexual relationship. By practicing birth control at the outset, couples are more likely to gain the experience and skill necessary to achieve the desired number and spacing of offspring. This is important for parents who want the best in life for their children.

It is more rational and responsible to have few or none than to have unwanted children. The decision to have a child will rarely be clear-cut; ambivalence, conscious or unconscious, will often be present: a wanted child is sometimes or somehow not wanted, and vice versa. Our society is unequivocal about the desirability of marriage and child rearing, and for most of human history that social imperative expressed the statistical necessity for birth rates to keep ahead of high death rates. The necessity is now gone—in terms of human history not long gone—and while social pressure for large families has lessened, the very small family or childless couple is apparently still in some disfavor.

"You should have as many children as you can afford" is a precept that has a surprising following, even today, despite the fact that "affording" economically may have little to do with competence in child rearing. A community with finite resources cannot "afford" a rich child any better than a poor one. Each child takes up a seat in school, a bed in the hospital, and eventually a parking place. Given the burgeoning knowledge of child development and the demographic picture, it is timely to begin educating school children about family size and structure, (24) so as to remove any stigma associated with small family size and to provide people with the knowledge and the means necessary to realize their parental wishes.

It is high time for more of the attitude: "We want to raise two children well, with time left over for adult pursuits for both husband and wife." Indeed, there is some research evidence to support the idea that the woman who wants to work will be a better mother for half a day with a part-time job and good help than for a full day with no relief and no chance to exercise and replenish her adult capacities. The part-time working mother of one or two children can have time enough for both activities and have wifely charm to spare. (25, 26)

Two children would be sufficient for more of us if (a) we could have the choice of sex; (b) we were not afraid of losing a child, and (c) we did not need to make good our mistakes with the firstborn by having extra chances later. In a few more decades, we will probably be able to choose the sex of our offspring. It is true that the smaller the family, the greater the emotional investment in each child and the more over-whelming is the prospect of losing one, but odds are extremely good that a one-year-old will survive to adulthood and the main hindrance thereto—accidental death—is preventable. As for recouping our errors, this is a dubious practice on several counts; prevention is worth more than a pound of cure. Greater readiness for parenthood should reduce the number of false starts, and where trouble has already occurred, investment of resources—family and professional—for that child is likely to be a better prescription than trying once again.

Actions speak louder than words and sanctions for small families would be enhanced by the behavior of social pacesetters as well. The more affluent members of society cannot merely sanction small families for the poor, as if those with less money should have fewer children. The most important psychological advantages for having few children apply to the rich as well as to the poor. Of course, one cannot completely separate economic from psychological advantages . The Institute of Life Insurance recently estimated that the cost of rearing a child to age 18 for a family with an annual income of $6,600 amounted to $23,800, not including college!

There is a way to have more children without increasing the population. Nowa-days, adoption agencies are more willing to consider requests from fertile couples.

There are still many unadopted children—a tragedy which is overwhelming, if we dare to contemplate it. Some people who have the means and the desire for many children may find an optimum answer in the combination of natural and adopted children. At present, adoption is the one sure way to balance the sexes in a family.

The small family question is more than a matter of quality—good or bad—versus quantity, but quality of diverse kinds. Most parents will recognize some minute differences between their children at birth, perhaps despite what they have been told about environment and heredity. But how many know enough, have time enough, or have sanctions from wherever it counts to exploit the individualities of their different children?

I would hate to see a standardized family emerge as the price of population stability. There will be some who will want one child or none and a few who will want many. Since more individualization of children and parents can occur in small families, we can expect healthy variety not only to endure but thrive under conditions where all children are wanted children, and overpopulation is no longer a threat.

Acknowledgement

The author wishes to acknowledge the valuable assistance of Mrs. Susan Roth in the preparation of this paper.

REFERENCES

1. Bell, Richard Q. A. Reinterpretation of the direction of effects in studies of socialization. *Psychology. Rev.,* 1968, 75, 81–95.

2. Westoff, C. F. "The Fertility of the American Population." In R. Freedman (Ed.), *The Vital Revolution.* New York: Anchor, 1964. Pp. 110–122.

3. Day, L. H., & Day, A. T. *Too many americans.* Boston: Houghton, 1964; New York: Delta, 1965.

4. Clausen, J. A. Family size and birth order as influences upon socialization and personality: bibliography and abstracts. New York: Soc. Science Research Council, 1965. (mimeo.) 182.

5. Westoff, C. F., Potter, R. G., Sagi, P. C. *The third child.* Princeton, N.J.: Princeton University Press, 1963.

6. President's Task Force on Manpower Conservation. *One third of a nation.* Washington, D.C.: Gov. Ptg. Office, 1964.

7. Scottish Council for Research in Education. *Social implications of the 1947 Scottish mental survey.* London, 1953. P. 48.

8. Clausen, J. A. *Family structure, socialization and personality.* Rev. Child Development Res. Hoffman and Hoffman (Eds.). New York: Russell Sage Foundation, 1966. Pp. 1–54.

9. Waldrop, Mary F., & Bell, R. Q. Relation of preschool dependency behavior to family size and density. *Child Development,* 1964, 35, 1187–1195.

10. Lasko, J. Parent behavior toward first and second children. *Genetic Psychol. Monogr.* 49:97–137, 1954.

11. Kent, N., & Davis, R. Discipline in the home and intellectual development. *Brit J. Med Psychol.,* 1957, 27–33.

12. Grant, M. W. Family size. *Brit. J. Social Med.,* 1964, 18, 35–42.

13. Nye, F. I. Sibling number, broken homes, and adjustment. *Marriage & Family Living,* 1952, 14, 327–30.

14. Hawkes, G. R.; Burchinal, L.; Gardner, B. Size of family and adjustment of children. *Ibid.,* 1958, 20, 65–58.

15. Hamilton, G. V. In H. T. Christensen, & R. E. Philbrick. Family size a factor in the marital adjustments of college couples. *Am. soc. Rev.,* 1952, 17, 306–312.

16. Leslie, G. R. *The family in social context.* New York: Oxford, 1967. Pp. 514–516.

17. Bossard, J. H. S., & Boll, E. *The large family system.* Philadelphia: University of Pennsylvania Press, 1956.

18. Hare, E. H., & Shaw, J. K. A study in family health: Health in relation to family size. *Brit. J. Psychiat.* June 1965, 3, 475, 461–466.

19. Mowrer, E. R., *et al. Domestic discord.* Chicago: Chicago University Press, 1928. Cited by Lewis Terman, *et al. Psychological factors in marital happiness.* New York: McGraw, 1938. P. 173.

20. Burgess, E. W., & Cottrell, L. S. *Predicting success or failure in marriage.* New York: Prentice-Hall, 1939. P. 260.

21. Reed, R. B. Social and psychological factors affecting fertility: The interrelationship of marital adjustment, fertility control, and size of family. *Milbank Mem. Fund Quart.,* 1947, 25, 383–425.

22. Hurley, J. R., & Palonen, D. Marital satisfaction and child density among university student parents. *J. Marr. Fam.,* 1967, 29, 483–484.

23. Rainwater, L. *Family design.* Chicago: Aldine, 1965.

24. Wayland, S. R. Family planning and the school curriculum. In Berelson, B. (Ed.), *Family planning and population programs.* Chicago: University of Chicago Press, 1966. Pp. 353–362.

25. Yarrow, M. R.; Scott, P.; & deLeeuw, C. Childrearing in families of working and nonworking mothers. *Sociometry,* 1962, 25, 122–140.

26. Morrow, W. R., & Wilson, R. C. Family relations of bright high-achieving and under-achieving high school boys. In M. Kornich (Ed.), *Underachievement.* Springfield: Thomas, 1965. Pp. 188–199.

27. Etzioni, A. Sex control, science and society. *Science,* Sept. 1968, 161, 1107–1112.

ADDENDA

Christensen, H. T. Children in the family: Relationship of number and spacing to marital success. *J. Marr. Fam.,* (May) 1968, 30, 2, 283–289.

Datta, L.-E. Birth order and potential scientific creativity. *Sociometry,* March 1968, 31, 1, 76–88.

Groat, H. T., & Neal, A. G. Social Psychological correlates of urban fertility. *Am. Sociolog. Rev.,* December 1967, 32, 6, 945–959.

Pohlman, E. *Psychology of birth planning.* Cambridge: Schenkman, 1969.

Population Council. American attitudes on population policy; recent trends. *Studies in Family Planning* No. 30, May 1968.

Tuckman, J., & Regan, R. A. *Size of family and behavioral problems in children. J. Genet. Psychol.,* 1967, 111, 151–160.

4.2

Birth Order and Mother-Child Interaction in an Achievement Situation

Mary K. Rothbart

Most research on the effects of birth order has concentrated on identifying personality characteristics that vary as a function of ordinal position. Although such research often concludes with hypotheses about differing socialization experiences for children of different ordinal positions, only a few studies have attempted to observe the actual behavior of parents toward children of differing birth order. The present study presents a test of hypotheses about differential socialization of first- and later-born children in an achievement situation. It is part of a larger study in which mothers' interactions with firstborn and second-born children were observed in a structured interaction setting.

Reprinted from Rothbart, Mary K. Birth order and mother-child interaction in an achievement situation. *Journal of Personality and Social Psychology,* 1971, *17,* No. 2, 113–120. Copyright © 1971 by the American Psychological Association, and reproduced by permission.

The general finding that the firstborn tends to gain greater eminence in school and later life (Altus, 1966; Sampson, 1965; Schacter, 1963), though recently disputed (Bayer, 1966), has led to questions about the kinds of parental expectations and pressures for success exerted upon the firstborn as compared with the second-born. In addition, numerous studies have considered possible IQ differences between firstborn and later-born children (Sampson, 1965). These studies often have had conflicting results; in infant tests (Bayley, 1965; Cushna, 1966), slight differences in favor of firstborns have been found. Bayley, however, reports that these differences are small, and seem to have no cumulative effect or relation to later intelligence test scores.

What, then, are other variables that might prompt the firstborn to higher academic levels in later life? It has been suggested that greater parental pressures are directed toward the firstborn's achievement and acceptance of responsibility (Davis, 1941; McArthur, 1956; Rosen, 1961), that the firstborn is often given the role of parent surrogate (Sutton-Smith, Roberts, & Rosenberg, 1964), that the parents talk and interact more with the firstborn (Bossard, 1945), and pay more attention to the firstborn (Koch, 1954). Rosen (1961) and Phillips (1956) have proposed that since parents have no frame of reference in their expectations for the firstborn, they tend to overestimate his ability more than the second-born's, setting higher standards for his performance.

Work done on the relation of birth order and eminence thus suggests numerous questions for this study: Do parents exert greater pressure on their firstborn to excel in his work? Do parents have higher or more unrealistic expectations for their first child? Are parents more likely to praise and criticize the performance of the first child than the second? When a parent instructs his child, are his explanations more complex and at a higher level for the firstborn than the second? In the present study these questions were investigated through an observation of mothers supervising their firstborn or second-born children in the performance of a variety of tasks.

METHOD

The experimenter compared mother-child interactions for 5-year-old firstborn and second-born boys and girls from two-child, same-sex families. In a 2 X 2 design, sex of child and birth order were the independent variables. Mothers were asked to supervise their children in the performance of five different tasks, two of which involved explanations by the mother.

Subjects

Subjects were kindergarten children from the Palo Alto Unified School District and their mothers. Subjects were chosen from two-child families only, where both children were of the same sex and there was an approximate age difference of 2 years between the subject and his sibling. Half of the subjects had a 3-year-old younger sibling; half had a 7-year-old older sibling. Of a total of 56 subjects, 30 were girls and

26 were boys. Distributions were matched with respect to age of the subject and age difference with the sibling. Approximately the same proportion of children in each group (67 percent) came from professional homes. One important variable on which groups were not matched was age of mother, with mothers whose second-born children were 5 years old, as would be expected, significantly older than mothers whose firstborn children were 5 years old.

Mothers were introduced to the study by a letter from the school district director of research, who described the purpose of the study as investigating differences between children of different birth orders. After the mothers had received the letter, sessions were scheduled by telephone. Of over 60 mothers asked to take part in the study and pretest, only 2 were unable to participate.

Procedure

All interaction sessions were held in a specially equipped trailer provided by Stanford University's Laboratory of Human Development. Since subjects came from all parts of the city, the trailer was located at four different schools providing the same situation for all subjects. The trailer was divided into three rooms, with two large rooms at either end and a small central observation room containing one-way mirrors and recording equipment. Tasks were performed in one large room; children played with toys in the other large room while the mother was given instructions. In the case of six firstborn boys and seven firstborn girls, the younger sibling was also present in the toy room, since the experimenters offered baby-sitting to participating mothers. Two experimenters, the author and another woman experienced in working with children, were present for all sessions. When the mother and child arrived, introductions were made, and subjects were shown the experimental room. One experimenter then invited the child to come into the playroom for a short time.

The mother was then seated at a card table, and instructions were given to her by the experimenter. The instructions, developed with the help of nine pretest subjects, began:

> What we'd like to try to do as soon as [*name of child*] comes back in is to set up and record several simple situations that you probably go through with him fairly often. Most of the situations will involve you describing or explaining something to him, or supervising his work on a problem. Of course, it's best if you can be as natural as possible, and act toward him as you usually do.

The mother was then introduced to the five tasks she was to engage in with her child. The situations were as follows:

Conversation.   The mother was asked first of all to ask her child what he had seen in the other room, to "get an idea of his usual conversation." The playroom contained a special toy (a set of dump trucks), along with a workbench, coloring book, paper, crayons, and two children's books. The mother did not know what the playroom contained. The conversation was designed to put subjects at ease at the beginning of the session, to provide an indication of the number of questions asked the child by his mother, and the specificity and correctness of the child's recall.

Cartoons. The mother was asked to show her child two four-frame "Peanuts" cartoons by the artist Charles Schulz, and to explain to him what was happening in the cartoons. The cartoons offered a set of somewhat ambiguous stimulus materials that the mother could structure a great deal or not at all. The mother could simply read the cartoon, she could point out emotions displayed by the cartoon characters, and for one cartoon, she could draw a moral lesson. It was thus possible to get a measure of the complexity of the mother's explanation, along with the amount of time she spent explaining the cartoons.

Picture. Mothers were given a picture of 20 zoo animals and were asked, initially, to show the child the picture for a 3-minute period. During this time, the mother, or child could name the animals aloud. The mother was then to turn the picture over for 3 minutes and ask the child to remember as many of the animals as he could. She was allowed to prompt him as much as she wished. The mother was also asked to estimate the number of animals her child would be likely to remember, after being told that the average child of his age would remember 10 animals. This situation proved to be a powerful measure of the mother's pressure on the child to perform well. Most children attempted to stop the task at some point during the recall period, and a measure was made of pressure exerted on the child to continue.

Explanation. Mothers were given a simple diagram of the workings of a water tap, along with an extremely complicated written description of how a water tap works. The language was technical, and included some information about water pressure that was tangential to the explanation. The mother was asked to show the diagram to the child, and explain to him in her own words how the water tap worked. This situation allowed a measure of complexity and length of the mother's explanation, along with her use of praise and criticism.

Puzzle. The last situation was a difficult geometric puzzle, on which the mother was asked to supervise her child. She was given a model of how the puzzle should look when it was completed, and told that she could help the child as much as she wanted without actually showing him the solution to the puzzle. The time allowed for working on the puzzle was 6 minutes, after which the experimenter made sure that the child successfully completed the puzzle if he had not yet done so. The mother was also asked to estimate how quickly her child would be likely to solve the puzzle on a 6-point scale ranging from "very slowly and with difficulty" to "very rapidly."

After the mother was given the initial instructions, she was provided with a shorter written version of the oral instructions, and the child was returned to the room to begin the tasks. The experimenter remained in the room with the mother and child to answer the mother's questions about procedure and to make sure the correct order of tasks was followed. The entire session was tape-recorded.

After the tasks were completed, the child was given paper construction materials, and the mother, a questionnaire to complete during a 15-minute period while the experimenter was out of the room. (These data have not yet been analyzed.) The mother was also asked if she and the child would straighten the room before the experimenter returned. Two brooms, one large and one child-size, were conspicuously located in the corner of the room, and the experimenter noted the extent of the child's involvement in the cleanup. When the 15 minutes had elapsed, the experimenter returned to ask the mothers a few questions about rules she had for her children, and the session was then terminated. (Interview data have also not yet been analyzed.)

Coding Procedures and Reliabilities

Coding for data analysis was based for the most part on tape recordings of the five tasks completed by the mother and child. This coding was blind, with all tape recordings coded by the author and 21 recordings coded independently by a second rater for reliability. In addition, length of interactions was timed, and the child's level of performance on the conversation, picture, and puzzle was rated. The average reliability coefficient was .92; the only achievement scale with a reliability of .80 or below was the mother's structuring of the puzzle task, where $r = .79$.

The basic statistical analysis for all variables was a two-way analysis of variance (Sex X Birth Order). In addition, items on the same general variable, for example, mother's pressure for achievement, were intercorrelated. When correlations were significant at the .01 level, standard scores of these measures were added to form larger scales, and analyses of variance, applied to scale scores. When individual variables failed to correlate or Ns were unequal, separate analyses were carried out.

RESULTS

Results are summarized in Tables 1, 2, and 3. For all measures, the meaning of a score corresponds to the name of the scale. For example, a high score on the pressure for achievement variable indicates strong pressure for achievement. In data analysis, it was first necessary to determine whether performance of firstborns and second borns differed significantly on the tasks assigned them. If there were actual differences in the success or failure of first- and second-borns, these differences might have, in turn, differentially affected their mothers' behavior, greatly complicating an interpretation of differences on maternal variables.

Measures of the child's performance, including the number of playroom objects described in the conversation, number of zoo animals recalled, and time to complete the puzzle, failed to correlate with each other. The direction of recall differences was the same, with higher means for first children, but no significant differences were found (see Table 1). The time required to solve the puzzle showed a significant interaction ($F = 5.34$, $df = 1/51$, $p < .05$), with firstborn girls and second-born boys taking longer to solve the puzzle. The puzzle was fortunately the last task assigned, so differential child performance on the puzzle could not have affected the mother's behavior toward her child on any subsequent tasks.

TABLE 1. MEANS AND STANDARD DEVIATIONS FOR VARIABLES DESCRIBING CHILD'S BEHAVIOR

| | GIRLS | | | | BOYS | | | |
| | FIRSTBORN | | SECONDBORN | | FIRSTBORN | | SECONDBORN | |
AREA AND VARIABLE	M	SD	M	SD	M	SD	M	SD
Performance								
Conversation	4.91	4.08	3.92	3.01	5.80	3.39	4.33	2.87
Picture	9.60	4.63	8.53	3.02	8.38	4.73	7.46	4.14
Puzzle time	3.38	1.33	2.87	1.42	2.42	.90	3.35	1.45
Adoption of responsibility								
Cleanup involvement	3.43	1.28	3.21	1.25	3.30	1.95	2.38	1.43

The first general maternal variable examined was the mother's estimate of her child's performance. It was thought that this variable would be reflected in (a) the mother's response to a direct question about her child's likely performance on a concrete task; (b) a measure of complexity of the mother's explanation, with mothers who have higher estimates of their child's performance using more complex and detailed concepts in their explanations; and (c) the mother's structuring of tasks for her child. If the mother of the second-born is more aware of her child's level of understanding, she might be expected to give him a more structured introduction to a task.

Mothers estimated their child's performance for both the picture and puzzle tasks. For the picture estimate, there was a barely significant birth-order effect ($F = 3.31$, $df = 1/48$, $p < .10$), with mothers tending to have a higher estimate of the first child's performance; however, a stronger interaction ($F = 5.55$, $df = 1/48$, $p < .05$) indicated that the birth-order difference was contributed by the mother's higher estimate for the first girl than for the second girl (see Table 2). The direction of estimates was reversed for the puzzle, with higher estimates for firstborn boys and second-born girls, and no indication of a birth-order effect. The puzzle differences were not significant.

Two measures were made of the mother's complexity of explanation. For the water tap explanation, a count was made of the number of technical terms used by the mother, for example, "water pressure," "valve," and "cylindrical stopper." For the cartoons, a count was made of the number of different features of the picture described, for example, sizes of cars, number of pieces of the snowman, and of interpretations made by the mother (e.g., "The little dog is copying the big dog."). The two measures of complexity failed to correlate significantly with each other, but the direction of differences for both measures was the same: mothers tended to give a more complex description to the first child. This difference was only significant for the water tap explanation ($F = 4.35$, $df = 1/52$, $p < .05$).

Measures were also made of the mother's structuring of tasks, that is, the amount of information she gave the child about what would happen in a task and what he would be expected to do. Structuring for the picture and the puzzle surprisingly failed to correlate. There were no significant differences found in structuring the picture task, or agreement in direction of findings for the picture and puzzle. For structuring the puzzle, a strong interaction was found ($F = 9.61$, $df = 1/51$, $p < .01$). Mothers structured the puzzle task more for firstborn girls and second-born boys, those groups that in fact performed less well on the puzzle than the other two groups.

A second general variable thought to correlate with later achievement of the child was the sheer amount of interaction of the mother with the child. This was measured by the amount of time spent in the conversation and explanation and the number of questions asked by the mother in the conversation, cartoons, and explanation tasks. Since time spent in conversation and explanation correlated .47, these variables were combined, and analysis showed no differences for either the grouped or separate data. Standard scores of number of questions were also combined, yielding only a barely significant sex difference ($F = 3.35$, $df = 1/52$, $p < .10$), with mothers tending to ask more questions of their daughters than of their sons (see Table 2).

TABLE 2.   MEANS AND STANDARD DEVIATIONS FOR VARIABLES DESCRIBING MOTHER'S BEHAVIOR

| | GIRLS | | | | BOYS | | | |
| | FIRSTBORN | | SECONDBORN | | FIRSTBORN | | SECONDBORN | |
AREA AND VARIABLE	M	SD	M	SD	M	SD	M	SD
Expectations								
Picture estimate	12.13	3.93	9.07	1.83	10.25	2.83	11.00	2.31
Puzzle estimate	3.27	.96	3.60	1.05	3.50	.80	3.00	1.22
Explanation complexity	8.47	5.98	5.40	2.77	7.00	4.30	5.85	2.61
Cartoon complexity	5.27	1.75	5.20	2.48	5.92	3.04	5.00	2.61
Picture structuring	1.93	1.10	2.07	1.10	2.00	1.21	1.92	1.11
Puzzle structuring	2.47	.74	1.80	.86	1.92	.79	2.54	.66
Length of interaction								
Conversation and								
explanation time	4.06	2.16	4.23	1.92	3.38	1.47	4.17	1.17
Number of questions	6.98	3.11	5.98	1.67	5.27	2.22	5.49	1.64
Pressure for success								
Pressure for naming	3.07	.70	2.13	1.13	2.75	.87	2.15	1.14
Pressure for remembering	2.90	.32	1.50	.71	2.17	.71	2.20	.79
Anxious intrusiveness	3.33	1.50	2.47	1.13	2.50	1.00	1.85	.90
Praise and criticism								
Praise	1.27	1.66	1.40	1.82	1.82	1.82	.84	1.02
Tells child he is correct	19.87	8.04	19.20	9.10	17.17	10.47	19.31	9.59
Tells child he is incorrect	3.87	4.85	2.07	2.15	1.33	.98	2.77	3.06

The difference probably proposed most often about achievement socialization of firstborn and later-born children involves the prediction of greater pressures for success and greater parental involvement in the firstborn's performance. The first direct measure of pressure for achievement was pressure for naming, a rating of the speed at which zoo animals were named by the mother and child, that is, whether there was leisurely discussion or whether animals were named rapidly and repeated several times before the end of the period. Pressure for remembering rated the mother's reaction to the child's desire to stop trying to recall the names of animals—whether she allowed him to stop or insisted that he continue until the time was up. The two scales were positively correlated with each other ($r = .30$, $p < .05$), and both showed highly significant birth-order effects (pressure for naming, $F = 8.87$, $df = 1/51$, $p < .01$; pressure for remembering, $F = 8.05$, $df = 1/38$, $p < .01$), with mothers exerting more pressure on firstborns than on second borns. Ns for the pressure for remembering variable were smaller, since not all subjects attempted to stop working on the task. The pressure for remembering variable also showed a significant interaction ($F = 9.76$, $df = 1/38$, $p < .01$), with greater differential pressure for girls than for boys (see Table 2).

More indirect measures of achievement variables were amount of time spent in conversation and explanation, and the number of questions asked by the mother. As described above, no differences were found in interaction time, while mothers showed a tendency to ask more questions of their daughters than their sons, with no birth-order effects.

After doing all coding, raters made an overall judgment of the extent to which the mother seemed to intrude herself into the child's performance in a worried or anxious way. Raters achieved good agreement ($r = .88$) on this variable, and it yielded a significant birth-order effect ($F = 5.92$, $df = 1/51$, $p < .05$), with mothers showing higher anxious intrusiveness for firstborns than for second borns. A significant sex difference was also found ($F = 5.45$, $df = 1/51$, $p < .05$), with mothers exerting more anxious intrusiveness on girls than on boys (see Table 2). The intrusiveness variable was included in intercorrelations for both pressure and help-giving variables. It correlated with conversation time ($r = .34$, $p < .01$); the number of questions asked in the conversation, cartoons, and explanation (rs = .38, .26, and .41, ps < .01, .05, and .01, respectively,); the mother's help giving on the picture ($r = .48$, $p < .01$); and on the puzzle ($r = .41$, $p < .01$), even though these last two measures failed to correlate with each other.

A related variable was the extent to which the mother evaluated and reinforced her child's ongoing performance through the use of praise and criticism. If the mothers were more involved in their firstborn's performance, they might be expected to give him more praise and criticism. Since the number of occurences of praise and criticism were relatively small, they were initially combined over all tasks except the conversation. The direction of differences for use of criticism was opposite to that of use of praise. The data, however, were confounded by the fact that the second-born girl and firstborn boy had actually performed better on the puzzle task than the firstborn girl and second-born boy. When praise and criticism data from the puzzle task were discarded, the differences for praise were in the same direction, that is, for more praise to the second-born girl and firstborn boy, but not significant. The frequencies of use of criticism were so low that a chi-square test was performed to see whether the four groups differed according to the mothers' use of criticism (see Table 3). There was a slight tendency for mothers of firstborn girls to use criticism more than the other groups. ($x^2 = 6.67$, $p < .10$, two-tailed).

TABLE 3. CHI-SQUARE FOR MOTHER'S CRITICISM OF CHILD

	GIRLS		BOYS	
REACTION	FIRSTBORN	SECONDBORN	FIRSTBORN	SECONDBORN
Mother criticizes	8	2	2	4
Mother does not criticize	7	13	9	9

Note.—$x^2 = 6.67$, $p < .10$.

A closely related measure, this one taken over all situations except the puzzle, was the number of times the mother told her child that he was correct or incorrect. There were no significant differences in telling the child he was correct, but a significant interaction was found for telling the child he was incorrect ($F = 4.31$, $df = 1/51$, $p < .05$), with the mother more likely to tell the firstborn girl or the second-born boy that he had done something wrong.

Finally, in an attempt to measure the mother's encouragement of her child's responsible behavior, a rating was made of the child's involvement in cleaning up the room. Ratings of cleanup were made from the experimenter's descriptions, with a scale ranging from the mother doing all of the cleanup (low score) to the child doing all of the cleanup (high score). The cleanup scale yielded a significant interaction ($F = 8.39$, $df = 1/47$, $p < .01$), with a larger difference between firstborn and second-born boys in the direction of firstborn boys participating more in the cleanup.

DISCUSSION

The present study showed no tendency for mothers to interact more with firstborns, or to have a general overestimation of the firstborn's ability. Indeed, there was a notable lack of correlation among measures intended to assess the mother's estimate of her child's ability. The mother's behavior appears to be affected more by the nature of the particular task than by some general notion of her child's ability. This finding may not be surprising in view of the fact that subjects were 5 years old at the time of the study; the mothers would have had sufficient time to observe that their children were more successful at some tasks than at others. It seems likely that any generalized overestimate of the firstborn child's ability would be more evident in the mother's behavior toward the infant or every young child than toward the 5 year old.

The strongest birth-order difference among the estimate measures was the mother's tendency to give a more complex technical explanation to the firstborn; on the less technical cartoons, differences were in the same direction, but not significant. Apparently, even if the mother does not show a generalized overestimate of the first child's ability, she nevertheless uses more complex language with the firstborn than the second-born child. Whether she is overrating the firstborn child's ability to understand or simply providing him with better intellectual stimulation than the second-born child is a question for further research.

In considering measures of maternal pressure for success, a comparison of this study's findings with those of Hilton (1967) is of value. She gave mothers differential information about their child's success or failure in order to compare mothers' interactions with firstborn and second-born children on a puzzle task. Hilton reported greater maternal interference with firstborn and only children (grouped together) on several variables: mothers of firstborn and only children were rated as "more involved," were more likely to initiate work in the puzzle task, and gave more task-oriented suggestions and direct help to the firstborn child. While a detailed analysis of maternal help-giving data from the present study is not completed, the measure of overall anxious intrusiveness is highly relevant to the question of maternal interference with the firstborn. Mothers of firstborns were rated as more intrusive than mothers of second-borns, with mothers also more intrusive toward girls than boys. Another finding which may be related to interference is that mothers exerted more pressure for achievement on the firstborn in the picture task, just as mothers of firstborns were more likely to initiate the puzzle task in Hilton's study. Results of both studies suggest that mothers are more intrusive into the performance of firstborn than second-born children, although the present study found this accentuated for the firstborn girl. It is possible that the mother's greater interference with the firstborn provides such a readily accessible source of support that the firstborn may depend more on others for support in achievement situations. The firstborn's later success in school may be mediated to some extent by his dependency on others for setting standards for his performance.

A major difference in the findings of the two studies, however, is that while Hilton failed to find consistent differences in the mother's behavior as a function of the sex of the child, results of the present study favor the view that maternal behavior toward the first- or second-born child is also influenced by his sex. For example, the firstborn girl seems to have evoked the most extreme responses from the mother. The pressure for remembering variable showed greater differential pressure on the firstborn girl as compared to the second-born girl, in addition to a birth-order difference; the mother gave a higher estimate of her firstborn girl's performance on the picture; the mother was more likely to tell the first girl she was incorrect, and showed a tendency to be more likely to criticize her; and the mother showed most anxious intrusiveness toward the firstborn girl. There is a striking similarity between these findings and those of Cushna (1966), reported by Sutton-Smith and Rosenberg (1970). Cushna's subjects were 16–19-month-old children from middle class families. When mothers were asked to determine their children's performance on a number of tasks, mothers were found to be more involved in influencing the performance of firstborn children, but in different ways for boys and girls. Mothers were more supportive and cautious in directing their boys, but more demanding, exacting, and intrusive toward their firstborn girls.

The second-born girl seems to be shown both less criticism and less pressure to achieve than the firstborn girl. Her mother expected less from her on the picture task, and less often told her that she was incorrect. The firstborn boy shared with the firstborn girl greater maternal pressure for achievement, but only on the first part of the picture task; the birth-order difference on the pressure for remembering variable was contributed chiefly by the mother's pressure on the firstborn girl. The mother gave her firstborn boy a more complex explanation and showed greater anxious intrusiveness toward the firstborn boy than toward the second-born boy, but showed no greater intrusiveness toward the firstborn boy than toward the second-born girl. The direction of differences was also for the firstborn boy to be told he was incorrect less often than was the second-born boy. The mother's pressure for the firstborn boy's achievement and intrusiveness into his performance thus seems somewhat tempered in comparison with her pressures on the firstborn girl. Finally, the second-born boy seems to have received less pressure and interference from the mother than the firstborn boy, but was also more likely to be told that he was incorrect than the firstborn boy.

It is interesting to speculate about the more extreme pressure and intrusiveness exhibited toward the firstborn girl in this study. One possibility is that of all ordinal positions, the mother most closely identifies with the firstborn girl, since the firstborn girl most resembles the mother at any given time. This could lead to both greater pressure for achievement and to less satisfaction with the child's performance, since it is difficult to fulfill high expectations. The mother may also feel something of an attraction toward the firstborn boy that would temper her behavior toward him, and a sense of rivalry toward the firstborn girl, in a role reversal of the Oedipal triangle. Her feelings, both positive and negative, may be less extreme toward the second-born girl or boy. It was found in a previous study (Rothbart & Maccoby, 1966) that parents tended to respond more permissively toward a child's voice of the opposite sex; this differential reaction may be stronger for the firstborn in the family, and less accentuated in the parent's reaction to the later born.

An additional finding of interest is that while firstborn boys were involved in the cleanup to as great an extent as either first- or second-born girls, the second-born boy was less likely to be involved in the cleanup. Cleaning up, while a measure of adoption of responsibility, is an activity that is also highly sex typed in the feminine direction. The differences found may reflect a ceiling effect in the behavior of girls which could mask a higher adoption of responsibility for the firstborn to be found in a more neutral (or masculine) activity. In addition, the findings may reflect the greater masculine identification of the second-born boy in an all-male family that has been reported elsewhere (Rosenberg & Sutton-Smith, 1964).

It should be noted that the families of the present study are very limited. Only two-child, same-sex families were involved, with only *mother*-child interaction observed. The value of observing fathers interacting with their children seems apparent from the Sex X Birth Order interactions found in this study. We might expect that in such research, the firstborn boy would occupy the extreme position occupied by the firstborn girl in the present study. It would also be of value to include cross-sex sibling pairs and families of a larger size than two children, although with needed controls for size of family, sex, and spacing of siblings, such research becomes very difficult.

REFERENCES

Altus, W. D. Birth order and its sequelae. *Science,* 1966, 151, 44–49.

Bayer, A. E. Birth order and college attendance. *Journal of Marriage and Family Living,* 1966, *28,* 480–484.

Bayley, N. Comparisons of mental and motor test scores for ages 1–15 months by sex, birth order, race, geographical location, and education of parents. *Child Development,* 1965, *36,* 379–411.

Bossard, J. H. S. Family modes of expression. *American Sociological Review,* 1945, *10,* 226–237.

Cushna, B. Agency and birth order differences in very early childhood. Paper presented at the meeting of the American Psychological Association, New York, September 1966.

Davis, A. American status systems and the socialization of the child. *American Sociological Review,* 1941, *6,* 345–354.

Hilton, I. Differences in the behavior of mothers toward first- and later-born children. *Journal of Personality and Social Psychology,* 1967, *7,* 282–290.

Koch, H. L. The relation of "Primary Mental Abilities" in five- and six-year olds to sex of child and characteristics of his sibling. *Child Development,* 1954, *25,* 209–223.

McArthur, C. Personalities of first and second children. *Psychiatry,* 1956, *19,* 47–54.

Phillips, E. L. Cultural vs. intropsychic factors in childhood behavior problem referrals. *Journal of Clinical Psychology,* 1956, *12,* 400–401.

Rosen, B. C. Family structure and achievement motivation. *American Sociological Review,* 1961, *26,* 574–585.

Rosenberg, B. G., & Sutton-Smith, B. Ordinal position and sex-role identification. *Genetic Psychology Monographs,* 1964, *70,* 297–328.

Rothbart, M. K. *Birth order and mother-child interaction.* (Doctoral dissertation, Stanford University) Ann Arbor, Mich.: University Microfilms, 1967. No. 67–7961.

Rothbart, M. K., & Maccoby, E. E. Parents' differential reactions to sons and daughters. *Journal of Personality and Social Psychology,* 1966, *4,* 237–343.

Sampson, E. E. The study of ordinal position: Antecedents and outcomes. In B. Maher (Ed.), *Progress in experimental personality research.* Vol. 2. New York: Academic Press, 1965.

Schachter, S. Birth order, eminence, and higher education. *American Sociological Review,* 1963, *28,* 757–767.

Sutton-Smith, B., Roberts, J. M., & Rosenberg, B. G. Sibling associations and role involvement. *Merrill-Palmer Quarterly of Behavior and Development,* 1964, *10,* 25–38.

Sutton-Smith, B., & Rosenberg, B. G. *The sibling.* New York: Holt, Rinehart & Winston, 1970.

4.3

Some Effects of Punishment on Children's Behavior

Ross D. Parke

A casual review of magazines, advice to parent columns, or (until recently) the psychological journals quickly reveals that there is considerable controversy concerning the usefulness of punishment as a technique for controlling the behavior of young children. For many years, the study of the impact of punishment on human behavior was restricted to armchair speculation and theorizing. In part, this paucity of information was due to the belief that punishment produced only a temporary suppression of behavior and that many undesirable side effects were associated with its use. Moreover, ethical and practical considerations prohibited the employment of intense punishment in research with human subjects—especially children—thus contributing to this information gap.

Through both studies of child rearing and laboratory investigations, however, some of the effects of punishment on children's social behavior are being determined. It is the main aim of this paper to review these findings and assess the current status of our knowledge concerning the effects of punishment.

TIMING OF PUNISHMENT

A number of years ago at Harvard's Laboratory of Human Development, Black, Solomon and Whiting (1960) undertook a study of the effectiveness of punishment for producing "resistance to temptation" in a group of young puppies. Two training conditions were used. In one case, the dogs were swatted with a rolled-up newspaper just *before* they touched a bowl of forbidden horsemeat. The remaining pups were punished only *after* eating a small amount of the taboo food. On subsequent tests—even though deprived of food—the animals punished as they approached the food showed greater avoidance of the prohibited meat than did animals punished after committing the taboo act. This study is the prototype of a number of studies recently carried out with children, and it illustrates control over children's behavior.

In recent studies of the effects of timing of punishment on children's behavior, the rolled-up newspaper has been replaced by a verbal rebuke or a loud noise, and an attractive toy stands in place of the horsemeat. For example, Walters, Parke and Cane (1965) presented subjects with pairs of toys—one attractive and one unattractive—on a series of nine trials. The 6- to 8-year-old boys were punished by a verbal rebuke. "No, that's for the other boy," when they chose the attractive toy. As in the dog study, one group of children was punished as they approached the attractive toy, but before they actually touched it. For the remaining boys, punishment was delivered only after they had picked up the critical toy and held it for two seconds. Following the punishment training session, the subjects were seated before a display of three rows of toys similar to those used in the training period and were reminded not to touch the toys. The resistance-to-deviation test consisted of a 15-minute period during which the boy was left alone with an unattractive German-English dictionary and, of course, the prohibited toys. The extent to which the subject touched the toys in the absence of the external agent was recorded by an observer located behind a one-way screen. The children's data paralleled the puppy results: the early punished children touched the taboo toys less than did the boys punished late in the response sequence. This timing of punishment effect has been replicated by a number of investigators (Aronfreed & Reber, 1965; Parke & Walters, 1967; Cheyne & Walters, 1969).

Extensions of this experimental model indicate that this finding is merely one aspect of a general relation: *the longer the delay between the initiation of the act and the onset of punishment, the less effective the punishment for producing response inhibition.* This proposition is based on a study in which the effects of four delay of punishment positions were examined (Aronfreed, 1965). Using a design similar to Walters, Parke and Cane (1965), Aronfreed punished one group of children as they reached for the attractive toy. Under a second condition, the subject was permitted to pick up the attractive toy and was punished at the apex of the lifting movement. Under a third condition, six seconds elapsed after the child picked up the toy before punishment was delivered. In the final group, six seconds after the child picked up the toy he was asked to describe the toy and only then was punishment administered. The time elapsing between the experimenter's departure until the child made the first deviation steadily decreased as the time between the initiation of the act and the delivery of punishment increased.

Punishment may be less effective in facilitating learning as well as less effective in facilitating resistance to temptation if the punishment is delayed. Using a learning task in which errors were punished by the presentation of a loud noise combined with the loss of a token, Walters (1964) found that punishment delivered immediately after the error speeded learning more than did punishment which was delayed 10 seconds or 30 seconds.

In addition, the importance of timing of punishment may be contingent on a variety of other features of punishment administration, such as the intensity of the punishment, the nature of the agent-child relationship, and the kind of verbal rationale accompanying the punishment. The effects of these variables will be examined in the following sections.

INTENSITY OF PUNISHMENT

It is generally assumed that as the intensity of punishment increases the amount of inhibition will similarly increase. It is difficult to study severity of punishment in the laboratory due to the obvious ethical limitations upon using potentially harmful stimuli in experimentation with children. Until recently most of the evidence concerning the relative effectiveness of different intensities of punishment derived either from animal studies or from child rearing interview studies.

The animal studies (e.g., Church, 1963), in which electric shock is most often used as the punishing stimulus, have supported the conclusion that more complete suppression of the punished response results as the intensity of the punishment increases. On the other hand, the child rearing data relating to the effects of intensity on children's behavior have not yielded clear-cut conclusions. It is difficult, however, to assess the operation of specific punishment variables using rating scales of parent behavior because most of these scales confound several aspects of punishment, such as frequency, intensity, and consistency (Walters & Parke, 1967). Differences between scale points may, therefore, be due to the impact of any of these variables, either alone or in combination.

Recent laboratory studies have avoided some of these shortcomings and have yielded less equivocal conclusions concerning the effects of punishment intensity on children's behavior. Using the resistance-to-deviation approach already described, Parke and Walters (1967) punished one group of boys with a soft tone (65 decibels) when they chose an attractive but prohibited toy. A second group heard a loud tone (96 decibels) when they chose the attractive toy. In the subsequent temptation test, children who were exposed to the loud punisher were less likely to touch the prohibited toys in the experimenter's absence than were boys exposed to a less intense version of the tone. This finding has been confirmed using a noxious buzzer as the punishing stimulus (Cheyne & Walters, 1969; Parke, 1969).

This research has also yielded some suggestive evidence concerning the impact of intensity variations on other aspects of punishment, the degree of inhibition produced by early and late punishment was similar. Under low intensity conditions, however, the early punished subjects showed significantly greater inhibition than did subjects punished late in the response sequence. Thus, timing of punishment may be less important under conditions of high intensity punishment. However, the generality of this conclusion is limited by the narrow range of delay of punishment intervals that have been investigated. Perhaps when punishment is delayed over a number of hours, for example, this relationship would not hold. Further research is clearly required.

Other research has indicated, however, that high intensity punishment may not always lead to better inhibition or be more effective in controlling children's behavior than low intensity punishment. A study by Aronfreed and Leff (1963), who investigated the effects of intensity of punishment on response inhibition in a temptation situation, illustrates this possibility. Six- and seven-year old boys were given a series of choice trials involving two toys roughly comparable in attractiveness, but which differed along certain stimulus dimensions that the child could use to distinguish between punished and nonpunished choices. For two groups, a simple discrimination between red and yellow toys was required; the other groups of subjects were exposed to a complex discrimination between toys which represented passive containers and toys with active internal mechanisms. The punishment consisted of verbal disapproval (no), deprivation of candy, and a noise. The intensity and quality of the noise were varied in order to control the noxiousness of the punishment. Following training, each child was left alone with a pair of toys of which the more attractive one was similar in some respects to the toys that had been associated with punishment during the training procedure. Provided that the discrimination task was relatively simple, response inhibition was more frequently observed among children who received high intensity punishment. When the discrimination task was difficult, however, "transgression" was more frequent among children under the high intensity punishment than among children who received the milder punishment. Thus, the complex discrimination task combined with high intensity punishment probably created a level of anxiety too high for adaptive learning to occur. When subtle discriminations are involved, or when the child is uncertain as to the appropriate response, high intensity punishment may create emotional levels that clearly interfere with learning and therefore retard inhibition of undesirable behaviors.

NATURE OF THE RELATIONSHIP BETWEEN THE AGENT AND RECIPIENT OF PUNISHMENT

The nature of the relationship between the socializing agent and the child is a significant determinant of the effectiveness of punishment. It is generally assumed that punishment will be a more effective means of controlling behavior when this relationship is close and affectional than when it is relatively impersonal. This argument assumes that any disciplinary act may involve in varying degrees at least two operations—the presentation of a negative reinforcer and the withdrawal or withholding of a positive one (Bandura & Walters, 1963). Physical punishment may, in fact, achieve its effect partly because it symbolizes the withdrawal of approval or affection. Hence, punishment should be a more potent controlling technique when used by a nurturant parent or teacher.

Sears, Maccoby, and Levin (1957) provided some evidence in favor of this proposition. Mothers who were rated as warm and affectionate and who made relatively frequent use of physical punishment were more likely to report that they found spanking to be an effective means of discipline. In contrast, cold, hostile mothers who made frequent use of physical punishment were more likely to report that spanking was ineffective. Moreover, according to the mothers' reports, spanking was more effective when it was administered by the warmer of the two parents.

A study by Parke and Walters (1967) confirmed these child rearing findings in a controlled laboratory situation. In this investigation, the nature of the experimenter-child relationship was varied in two interaction sessions prior to the administration of punishment. One group of boys experienced a 10-minute period of positive interaction with a female experimenter on two successive days. Attractive constructional materials were provided for the children and, as they played with them, the female experimenter provided encouragement and help and warmly expressed approval of their efforts. A second group of boys played with relatively unattractive materials in two 10-minute sessions while the experimenter sat in the room without interacting with the children. Following these interaction sessions, the children underwent punishment training involving verbal rebuke and a noxious noise for choosing incorrect toys. In the subsequent test for response inhibition, children who had experienced positive interaction with the agent of punishment showed significantly greater resistance to deviation than boys who had only impersonal contact.

It is difficult to determine whether this effect is due to an increase in the perceived noxiousness of the noise when delivered by a previously friendly agent or whether the result derives from the withdrawal of affection implied in the punitive operation. Probably it was a combination of these two sources of anxiety which contributes to our findings. A study by Parke (1967), while not directly concerned with the relative importance of these two components, shows that nurturance-withdrawal alone, unaccompanied by noxious stimulation, can effectively increase resistance to deviation in young children. Two experimental treatments were employed. In one condition—the continuous nurturance group—the subjects, six- to eight-year-old boys and girls, experienced 10-minutes of friendly and nurturant interaction with either a male or female experimenter. Subjects in the nurturance-withdrawal group experienced five minutes of nurturant interaction, followed by five minutes of nurturance-withdrawal during which the experimenter turned away from the child, appeared busy, and refused to respond to any bid for attention. Following these manipulations, all subjects were placed in a resistance-to-deviation situation, involving a display of attractive, but forbidden, toys. In the instructions to the subject, it was made clear that if the subject conformed to the prohibition, the experimenter would play with him upon returning. In this way the link between resistance-to-deviation and nurturance was established. As in previous experiments, a hidden observer recorded the child's deviant activity during the 15-minute period that the adult was absent from the room. The results provided support for the hypothesis, with subjects in the nurturance-withdrawal group deviating significantly less often than subjects in the continuous-nurturance condition.

However, it was also found that nurturance-withdrawal influenced girls to a greater degree than boys, and that the effect was most marked with girls experiencing withdrawal of a female agent's nurturance.

These data are consistent with previous studies of nurturance-withdrawal, which have indicated that withdrawal of affection may motivate the previously nurtured child to engage in behavior that is likely to reinstate the affectional relationship (e.g., Hartup, 1958; Rosenblith, 1959, 1961). In the present study, the greater resistance to deviation of the subjects in the inconsistent nurturance condition may thus reflect an attempt to win back the experimenter's approval through conformity to his prohibition.

REASONING AND PUNISHMENT

In all of the studies discussed, punishment was presented in a relatively barren cognitive context. Very often, however, parents and teachers provide the child with a rationale for the punishment they administer. Is punishment more effective when accompanied by a set of reasons for nondeviation? Field studies of child rearing suggest that the answer is positive. For example, Sears, Maccoby, and Levin (1957), in their interview investigation of child rearing practices, found that mothers who combine physical punishment with extensive use of reasoning reported that punishment was more effective than mothers who tended to use punishment alone. Field investigations, however, have yielded little information concerning the relative effectiveness of different aspects of reasoning. In the child-training literature, reasoning may include not only descriptions of untoward consequences that the child's behavior may have for others, but also the provision of examples of incompatible socially acceptable behaviors, explicit instructions on how to behave in specific situations, and explanations of motives for placing restraints on the child's behavior. Moreover, these child-training studies do not indicate the manner in which the provision of reasons in combination with punishment can alter the operation of specific punishment parameters such as those already discussed—timing, intensity, and the nature of the agent-child relationship.

It is necessary to turn again to experimental studies for answers to these questions. First, laboratory investigations have confirmed the field results in that punishment is more effective when accompanied by a rationale. Parke (1969), for example, found that when children, in addition to being punished, were told that a toy was "fragile and may break," greater inhibition occurred than when children were punished without an accompanying rationale. In a later experiment, Parke and Murray (1971) found that a rationale alone is more effective than punishment alone. However, comparison of the results of the two studies indicates that the combination of punishment and a rationale is the most thoroughly effective procedure.

To understand the impact of reasoning on the timing of punishment effect, let us examine a pioneering set of studies by Aronfreed (1965). In the earlier timing experiments, cognitive structure was minimized and no verbal rationale was given for the constraints placed on the child's behavior. In contrast, children in a second group of experiments were provided, in the initial instructions, with a brief explanation for not handling some of the toys. In one variation, for example, the cognitive structuring focused on the child's intentions. When punished, the child was told: "No, you should not have *wanted* to pick up that thing." The important finding here was that the addition of reasoning to a *late*-timed punishment markedly increased its effectiveness. In fact, when a verbal rationale accompanied the punishment the usual timing of punishment effect was absent; early- and late-timed punishments were equally effective inhibitors of the child's behavior. Other investigators have reported a similar relation between reasoning operations and timing of punishment (Cheyne & Walters, 1969; Parke, 1969). In these latter studies, the reasoning procedures presented in conjunction with punishment did not stress intentions, but focused on the consequences of violation of the experimenter's prohibition.

The delay periods used in all of these studies were relatively short. In everyday life, detection of a deviant act is often delayed many hours or the punishment may be postponed, for example, until the father returns home. An experiment reported by Walters and Andres (1967) addressed itself directly to this issue. Their aim was to determine the conditions under which a punishment delivered four hours after the commission of a deviant act could be made an effective inhibitor. By verbally describing the earlier deviation at the time that the punishment was administered, the effectiveness of the punishment was considerably increased in comparison to a punishment that was delivered without an accompanying restatement. An equally effective procedure involved exposing the children to a videotape recording of themselves committing the deviant act just prior to the long-delayed punishment. A partially analogous situation, not studied by these investigators, involves parental demonstration of the deviant behavior just before delivering the punishing blow. In any case, symbolic reinstatement of the deviant act, according to these data, seems to be a potent way of increasing the effectiveness of delayed punishment.

A question remains. Do reasoning manipulations alter the operation of any other parameters besides the timing of the punishment? Parke (1969) examined the modifying impact of reasoning on the intensity and nurturance variables. When no rationale was provided, the expected intensity of punishment effect was present: high intensity punishment produced significantly greater inhibition than low intensity punishment. However, when a rationale accompanied the punishment, the difference between high and low intensity of punishment was not present.

As noted earlier, children who experience nurturant interaction with the punishing agent prior to punishment training deviate less often than subjects in the low nurturance condition. However, this effect was present in the Parke (1969) study only when no rationale accompanied the noxious buzzer. When the children were provided with a rationale for not touching certain toys, the children who had experienced the friendly interaction and the children who had only impersonal contact with the agent were equally inhibited during the resistance-to-deviation test period. Taken together, these experiments constitute impressive evidence of the important role played by cognitive variables in modifying the operation of punishment.

FIGURE 1.   STABILITY OF DURATION OF DEVIATION OVER THREE
FIVE-MINUTE PERIODS FOR HIGH-COGNITIVE AND LOW-
COGNITIVE STRUCTURE CONDITIONS

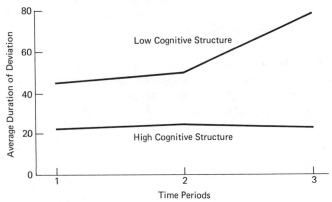

A common yardstick employed to gauge the success of a disciplinary procedure
is the permanence of the inhibition produced. It is somewhat surprising, therefore, that
little attention has been paid to the stability of inhibition over time as a consequence
of various punishment training operations. One approach to this issue involves calcu-
lating changes in deviant activity occurring during the resistance-to-deviation test
session in experimental studies. Does the amount of deviant behavior increase at
different rates, for example, in response to different training procedures? As a first
step in answering this question, Parke (1969) divided the 15-minute resistance-to-
deviation test session into three five-minute periods. As Figure 1 indicates, the low
cognitive structure subjects (no rationale) increased their degree of illicit toy touching
over the three time periods while the degree of deviation over the three intervals did
not significantly change for the high cognitive structure (rationale provided) subjects.
Cheyne and Walters (1969) have reported a similar finding. These data clearly indicate that the stability of inhibition over time was affected by the reasoning or cognitive
structuring procedures. The most interesting implication of this finding is that inhibition
—or internalization—may *require* the use of cognitively oriented training procedures.
Punishment techniques that rely solely on anxiety induction, such as the noxious
noises employed in many of the experiments discussed or the more extreme forms
of physical punishment sometimes used by parents, may be effective mainly in securing only short-term inhibition.

However, children often forget a rationale or may not remember that a prohibition
is still in force after a lengthy time lapse. A brief reminder or reinstatement of the
original punisher or rationale may be necessary to insure continued inhibition. To
investigate the impact of such reinstatement on the stability of inhibition was the aim
of an experiment by Parke and Murray (1971). In this study, following the typical
punishment training procedure, the 7- to 9-year-old boys were tested immediately for
resistance-to-deviation and then retested in the same situation one week later. Half

of the children were "reminded" of the earlier training by the experimenter. For example, in the case of the boys who were punished by a buzzer during the training session, the experimenter sounded the buzzer a single time and reminded the children that it signalled that they should not touch the toys ("You shouldn't touch the toys"). For children who received rationales unaccompanied by any punishment, the experimenter merely restated the rationale ("Remember, those toys belong to another boy" or " "They are fragile and may break") before leaving the children alone with the toys. For the remaining children, no reminder or reinstatement of the earlier training was provided. As Figure 2 indicates, reinstatement of the original training clearly increased the permanence of the response inhibition.

FIGURE 2.   STABILITY OF INHIBITION OVER ONE WEEK WITH AND WITHOUT REINSTATEMENT

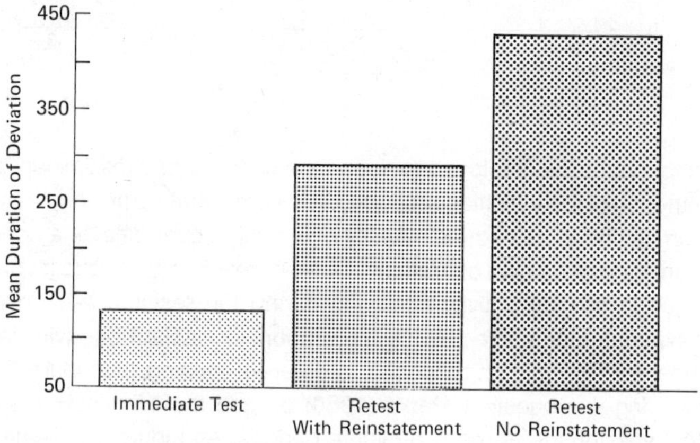

The type of research reviewed here does not provide us with any information concerning the relative effectiveness of reasoning procedures for producing behavioral control at different ages. It is likely that developmental trends will be discovered in light of recent Russian work (e.g., Luria, 1961) which indicates that the child's ability to use verbal behavior to control motor responses increases with age. Possibly with younger children response inhibition will be most successfully achieved by a reliance on physical punishment techniques which stress the production of anxiety. With older children, punishment techniques which diminish the role of anxiety and which stress the role of verbal control of motor behavior through the appeal to general rules will be more effective in producing response inhibition (Parke, 1970).

CONSISTENCY OF PUNISHMENT

In naturalistic contexts, punishment is often intermittently and erratically employed. Consequently, achieving an understanding of the effects of inconsistent punishment is a potentially important task. Data from field studies of delinquency have yielded a few clues concerning the consequences of inconsistency of discipline. Glueck and Glueck (1950) found that parents of delinquent boys were more "erratic" in their disciplinary practices than were parents of nondelinquent boys. Similarly, the McCords (e.g., McCord, McCord, & Howard, 1961) have found that erratic disciplinary procedures were correlated with high degrees of criminality. Inconsistent patterns involving a combination of love, laxity, and punitiveness, or a mixture of punitiveness and laxity alone were particularly likely to be found in the background of their delinquent sample. However, the definition of inconsistency has shifted from study to study in delinquency research, making evaluation and meaningful conclusions difficult (Walters & Parke, 1967).

To clarify the effects of inconsistent punishment on children's aggressive behavior, Parke and Deur (Parke & Deur, 1970; Deur & Parke, 1970) conducted a series of laboratory studies. Aggression was selected as the response measure in order to relate the findings to previous studies of inconsistent discipline and aggressive delinquency. An automated Bobo doll was used to measure aggression. The child punched the large, padded stomach of the clown-shaped doll and the frequency of hitting was automatically recorded. In principle, the apparatus is similar to the inflated punch toys commonly found in children's homes. To familiarize themselves with the doll, the boys participating in the first study (Parke & Deur, 1970) punched freely for two minutes. Then the children were rewarded with marbles each time they punched the Bobo doll for a total of 10 trials. Following this baseline session, the subjects experienced one of three different outcomes for punching: termination of reward (no outcome), receipt of marbles on half the trials and a noxious buzzer following the other half, or consistent punishment by the buzzer. Half the children were also told that the buzzer indicated that they were playing the game "badly," while the remaining boys were informed that the buzzer was a "bad noise." All the boys had been informed that they could terminate the punching game whenever they wished. The main index of persistence was the number of hitting responses that the child delivered before voluntarily ending the game. The results were clear: subjects in the no outcome group made the greatest number of punches, while the continuously punished children delivered the fewest punches; the inconsistently punished children were in the intermediate position. The results were not affected by the labeling of the buzzer; whether the buzzer meant "playing the game badly" or "a bad noise" made no difference. This laboratory demonstration confirms the common child rearing dictum that intermittent punishment is less effective than continuous punishment.

Parents and other disciplinary agents often use consistent punishment only after inconsistent punishment has failed to change the child's behavior. To investigate the effectiveness of consistent punishment *after* the child has been treated in an inconsistent fashion was the aim of the next study (Deur & Parke, 1970). Following the baseline period, subjects underwent one of three different training conditions. One group of boys was rewarded for 18 trials, while a second group of children received marbles on nine trials and no outcome on the remaining trials. A final group of boys was rewarded on half of the trials but heard a noxious buzzer on the other nine trials. The children were informed that the buzzer indicated that they were playing the game "badly."

To determine the effects of these training schedules on resistance to extinction (where both rewards and punishers were discontinued) and on resistance to continuous punishment (where every punch was punished) was the purpose of the next phase of the study. Therefore, half of the children in each of the three groups were neither rewarded nor punished for hitting the Bobo doll and the remaining subjects heard the noxious buzzer each time they punched. The number of hitting responses that the child made before voluntarily quitting was, again, the principal measure.

FIGURE 3. MEAN NUMBER OF PUNCHES IN POST-TRAINING PERIOD AS A FUNCTION OF CONSISTENCY OF REWARD AND PUNISHMENT

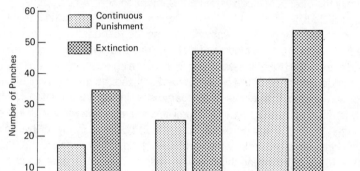

The results are shown in Figure 3. The punished subjects made fewer hitting responses than did subjects in the extinction condition, which suggests that the punishment was effective in inhibiting the aggressive behavior. The training schedules produced particularly interesting results. The inconsistently punished subjects showed the greatest resistance to extinction. Moreover, these previously punished children tended to persist longer in the face of consistent punishment than the boys in the other training groups. The effects were most marked in comparison to the consistently rewarded subjects. The implication is clear: the socializing agent using inconsistent punishment builds up resistance to future attempts to either extinguish deviant behavior or suppress it by consistently administered punishment.

The particular form of inconsistency employed in this study represents only one of the variety of forms of inconsistency which occurs in naturalistic socialization. Consistency, as used in the present research, refers to the extent to which a single agent treats violations in the same manner each time such violations occur. Of equal importance would be studies of inter-agent inconsistency. For example, what effect will one parent rewarding aggressive behavior and the other parent punishing the same class of behaviors have on the persistence of aggressive response patterns? Similar inconsistencies between teacher and parental treatment of deviant behavior and the discrepancies between peer and teacher reactions require examination.

UNDESIRABLE CONSEQUENCES OF PUNISHMENT

The foregoing paragraphs indicate that punishment is effective in producing response suppression. Nevertheless, punishment may have undesirable side effects which limit its usefulness as a socializing technique. In the first place, the teacher or parent who employs physical punishment to inhibit undesirable behaviors may also serve as an aggressive model. Bandura (1967) has summarized this viewpoint as follows: "When a parent punishes his child physically for having aggressed toward peers, for example, the intended outcome of this training is that the child should refrain from hitting others. The child, however, is also learning from parental demonstration how to aggress physically. And the imitative learning may provide the direction for the child's behavior when he is similarly frustrated in subsequent social interactions" (1967, p. 43).

Evidence supporting this position is, at best, indirect. There is a sizeable body of data indicating a relation between the frequent use of physical punishment by parents and aggressive behavior in their children (Becker, 1964). However, the increases in aggression could possibly be due to the *direct* encouragement that punitive parents often provide for behaving aggressively outside the home situation. Alternatively, highly aggressive children may require strong, physically punitive techniques to control them. Thus, even if it is assumed that the punitive parent acts as an aggressive model there is no evidence demonstrating that children imitate the aggressive behaviors the disciplinarian displays while punishing the child. It is recognized that exposure to aggressive models increases aggressive behavior in young children (Bandura, 1967). It is of questionable legitimacy, however, to generalize from Bobo doll studies to children imitating a physically punitive adult who is often carrying out a justified spanking in line with his role as parent or teacher.

The results of a study by Slaby and Parke (1968) are relevant. Children were exposed to a film-mediated model who was disciplined for touching prohibited toys. In one case, the film agent "spanked" the child for touching the toys. In the second case, the adult on the film "reasoned" with the deviant model after detecting the violation of the prohibition. In addition to testing the child's resistance to deviation, the amount of aggression that a child would direct to a peer was assessed. Under the guise of helping the experimenter teach the other child arithmetic problems, the subject was given the opportunity to punish the other child by "punching" him each time he made a mistake. A punch was administered by depressing a button on the subject's panel which activated a punching machine in the adjacent room. Both the number and intensity of punches were recorded for each subject. The subjects who saw the physically punitive disciplinarian were more aggressive than the children exposed to the verbal reasoning sequence.

The effect was most marked, however, in the case of subject-observers who were the same age as the film model (7-year-olds). Older children tended not to show the effect. Clearly, model-subject similarity is an important factor in this type of imitation study and replication of the study with film models of different ages is necessary. The results for the 7-year-olds are shown in Figure 4.

FIGURE 4. AGGRESSION AND TYPE OF DISCIPLINARY MODEL

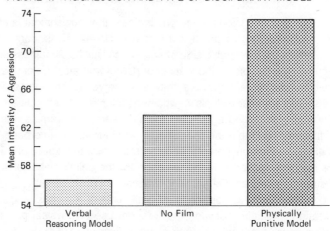

Another undesirable consequence of punishment is the effect on the agent-child relationship. As a result of punishment, the child may be motivated to avoid the punishing parent or teacher. Consequently, the socialization agent may no longer be able to direct or influence the child's behavior. Conditions such as the classroom often prevent the child from physically escaping the presence of the agent. Continued use of punishment in an inescapable context, however, may lead to passivity and withdrawal (Seligman, Maier, & Solomon, 1969) or adaptation to the punishing stimuli themselves. In any case, whether escape is possible or not, the quality of the agent-child relationship may deteriorate if punishment is used with high frequency; punishment administered by such an agent will, therefore, be less effective in inhibiting the child.

The undesirable effects of punishment mentioned here probably occur mainly in situations where the disciplinary agents are indiscriminately punitive. In child-training contexts where the agent rewards and encourages a large proportion of the child's behavior, even though selectively and occasionally punishing certain kinds of behavior, these side effects are less likely to be found (Walters & Parke, 1967).

REINFORCEMENT OF INCOMPATIBLE RESPONSES: AN ALTERNATIVE TO PUNISHMENT

In light of these undesirable consequences, it may be worthwhile to consider other ways in which deviant behavior can be controlled.

Reinforcement of incompatible responses is one such technique. Brown and Elliot (1965) asked several nursery school teachers to ignore aggressive acts and only encourage behaviors that were inconsistent with aggression, such as cooperation and helpfulness. Encouraging these alternative behaviors resulted in a marked decrease in classroom aggression. More recently, Parke, Ewall, and Slaby

(1972) have found that encouraging college subjects for speaking helpful words also led to a decrease in subsequent aggression. In an extension of this work, Slaby (1970) found a similar effect for 8- to 12-year-old children. The lesson is clear: speaking in a manner that is incompatible with aggression may actually inhibit hostile actions. Words, as well as deeds, can alter our physical behaviors. The advantage of the incompatible response technique for controlling behavior is that the unwanted side effects associated with punishment can be avoided.

CONCLUSION

This review leaves little doubt that punishment can be an effective means of controlling children's behavior. The operation of punishment, however, is a complex process and its effects are quite varied and highly dependent on such parameters as timing, intensity, consistency, the affectional and/or status relationship between the agent and recipient of punishment, and the kind of cognitive structuring accompanying the punishing stimulus.

It is unlikely that a socialization program based solely on punishment would be very effective; the child needs to be taught new appropriate responses in addition to learning to suppress unacceptable forms of behavior. "In fact, in real-life situations the suppressive effect of punishment is usually only of value if alternative pro-social responses are elicited and strengthened while the undesirable behavior is held in check. The primary practical value of studies of parameters that influence the efficacy of punishment is ... to determine the conditions under which suppression will most likely occur" (Walters & Parke, 1967, p. 217). From this viewpoint, punishment is only one technique which can be used in concert with other training tools such as positive reinforcement to shape, direct, and control the behavior of the developing child.

REFERENCES

Aronfreed, J. Punishment learning and internalization: Some parameters of reinforcement and cognition. Paper read at biennial meeting of Society for Research in Child Development, Minneapolis, 1965.

Aronfreed, J. *Conduct and Conscience.* New York: Academic Press, 1968.

Aronfreed, J., & Leff, R. The effects of intensity of punishment and complexity of discrimination upon the learning of an internalized inhibition. Unpubl. mss., Univ. of Pennsylvania, 1963.

Aronfreed, J., & Reber, A. Internalized behavioral suppression and the timing of social punishment. *J. pers. soc. Psychol.,* 1965, *1,* 3–16.

Bandura, A. The role of modeling processes in personality development. In W. W. Hartup, & Nancy L. Smothergill (Eds.), *The young child: Reviews of research.* Washington: National Association for the Education of Young Children, 1967, 42–58.

Bandura, A., & Walters, R. H. *Social learning and personality development.* New York: Holt, Rinehart & Winston, 1963.

Becker, W. C. Consequences of different kinds of parental discipline. In M. L. Hoffman, & L. W. Hoffman (Eds.), *Review of child development research.* Vol. 1. New York: Russell Sage Foundation, 1964. Pp. 169–208.

Black, A. H., Solomon, R. L., & Whiting, J. W. M. Resistance to temptation in dogs. Cited by Mowrer, O. H., *Learning theory and the symbolic processes.* New York: John Wiley, 1960.

Brown, P., & Elliot, R. Control of aggression in a nursery school class. *J. exp. child Psychol.,* 1965, *2,* 103–107.

Cheyne, J. A., & Walters, R. H. Intensity of punishment, timing of punishment, and cognitive structure as determinants of response inhibition. *J. exp. child Psychol.,* 1969, *7,* 231–244.

Church, R. M. The varied effects of punishment on behavior, *Psychol. Rev.,* 1963, *70,* 369–402.

Cowan, P. A., & Walters, R. H. Studies of reinforcement of aggression: I. Effects of scheduling. *Child Develpm.,* 1963, *34,* 543–551.

Deur, J. L., & Parke, R. D. The effects of inconsistent punishment on aggression in children. *Develpm. Psychol.,* 1970, *2,* 403–411.

Glueck, S., & Glueck, E. *Unraveling juvenile delinquency.* Cambridge: Harvard Univ. Press, 1950.

Hartup, W. W. Nurturance and nurturance-withdrawal in relation to the dependency behavior of preschool children. *Child Develpm.,* 1958, *29,* 191–201.

Luria, A. R. *The role of speech in the regulation of normal and abnormal behavior.* New York: Liveright, 1961.

McCord, W., McCord, J., & Howard. A. Familial correlates of aggression in non-delinquent male children. *J. abnorm. soc Psychol.,* 1961, *62,* 79–93.

Parke, R. D. Nurturance, nurturance-withdrawal and resistance to deviation. *Child Develpm.,* 1967, *38,* 1101–1110.

Parke, R. D. The role of punishment in the socialization process. In R. A. Hoppe, G. A. Milton, & E. C. Simmel (Eds.), *Early Experiences and the Processes of Socialization.* New York: Academic Press, 1970. Pp. 81–108.

Parke, R. D. Effectiveness of punishment as an interaction of intensity, timing, agent nurturance and cognitive structuring. *Child Develpm.,* 1969, *40,* 213–236.

Parke, R. D., & Deur, J. The inhibitory effects of inconsistent and consistent punishment on children's aggression. Unpubl. mss., Univ. of Wisconsin, 1970.

Parke, R. D., Ewall, W., & Slaby, R. G. Hostile and helpful verbalizations as regulators of nonverbal aggression. *J. pers. soc. Psychol.,* 1972, in press.

Parke, R. D., & Murray, S. Re-instatement: A technique for increasing stability of inhibition in children. Unpubl. mss., Univ. of Wisconsin, 1971.

Parke, R. D., & Walters, R. H. Some factors determining the efficacy of punishment for inducing response inhibition. *Monogr. Soc. Res. Child Develpm.*, 1967, *32* (Serial No. 109).

Rosenblith, J. F. Learning by imitation in kindergarten children. *Child Develpm.*, 1959, *30,* 69–80.

Rosenblith, J. F. Imitative color choices in kindergarten children. *Child Develpm.*, 1961, *32,* 211–223.

Sears, R. R., Maccoby, E. E., & Levin, H. *Patterns of child rearing.* Evanston, Ill.: Row, Peterson, 1957.

Seligman, M. E. P., Maier, S. F., & Solomon, R. L. Unpredictable and uncontrollable aversive events. In F. R. Brush (Ed.), *Aversive conditioning and learning.* New York: Academic Press, 1969.

Slaby, R. G. Aggressive and helpful verbalizations as regulators of behavioral aggression and altruism in children. Unpubl. doctoral dissertation, Univ. of Wisconsin, 1970.

Slaby, R. G., & Parke, R. D. The influence of a punitive or reasoning model on resistance to deviation and aggression in children. Unpubl. mss., Univ. of Wisconsin, 1968.

Walters, R. H. Delay-of-reinforcement effects in children's learning. *Psychonom. Sci.,* 1964, *1,* 307–308.

Walters, R. H., & Andres, D. Punishment procedures and self-control. Paper read at Annual Meeting of the American Psychological Association, Washington, D.C., Sept., 1967.

Walters, R. H., & Parke, R. D. The influence of punishment and related disciplinary techniques on the social behavior of children: Theory and empirical findings. In B. A. Maher (Ed.), *Progress in Experimental Personality Research,* Vol. 4. New York: Academic Press, 1967, Pp. 179–228.

Walters, R. H., Parke, R. D., & Cane, V. A. Timing of punishment and the observation of consequences to others as determinants of response inhibition. *J. exp. child Psychol., 1965, 2,* 10–30.

4.4

Some Thoughts About Childrearing

Diana Baumrind

INTRODUCTION

I want to speak with you today about my research findings relating patterns of parental authority to dimensions of competence in young children, and to share with you the conclusions I draw from those findings.

There are a few points I want to make before I discuss the findings themselves. . . .

1. First, there is no such thing as a *best* way to raise children. Each individual family's total life situation is unique. A generalization which makes sense on a probability basis must be tailored to fit an individual family's situation, if indeed it fits at all. It is each parent's responsibility to become an expert on his own children, using information in books or parent effectiveness encounter groups or, best of all, by careful observation and intimate communication with the child.

2. Secondly, the generalizations which I make have a reasonable probability of being true for a particular sample, but the extent to which that sample is respresentative of a population, say eight years later, remains in question. Moreover, the extent to which any individual family is similar to the families in the sample affects how relevant the findings are for that family. In addition, the relationships found are not strong enough to predict for the individual family.

3. Third, to have any social meaning at all, research findings must be *interpreted* and integrated. Yet the interpretations I make of my findings may well be disputed by other equally expert investigators. I will speak *strongly* for my interpretations because I am that sort of person. But each of you must evaluate the relevance to your own family of what I say, and you must do so in the light of your personal value system and experience.

I should tell you that my *subjective* assurance about what I say rests as much upon my personal experience as a parent, as on my research findings. I have three daughters whose ages are 11, 13 and 15. My theories and my practice coincide rather well (I think), and I am subjectively satisfied with the effectiveness of what I call

This selection was originally presented as a talk to the Children's Community Center in Berkeley, California, May 14, 1969, by Diana Baumrind, Research Psychologist and Principle Investigator for the Parental Authority Research Project. University of California at Berkeley. The program of research discussed in this paper was supported by research grant HD-02228 from the National Institute of Child Health and Human Development, U.S. Public Health Service.

"authoritative parental control" in achieving my *personal* aim. I will generalize to say it is possible, if parents wish to—IF parents wish to—to control the behavior of children, even of adolescents, and to do so without suppressing the individuality and willfulness of the child or adolescent. What gets in the way of most parents who *do* wish to control the behavior of their children more effectively is lack of *expertness* as parents, *indecisiveness* about the application of power, *anxiety* about possible harm resulting from demands and restrictions, and *fear* that if they act in a certain way they will lose their children's love. Nowadays I think more parents are concerned about maintaining the approval of their children than vice versa, and, indeed, many parents become paralyzed with indecision when their authority is disputed, or their children are angered by discipline.

Now I will tell you something about my research.

RESEARCH VARIABLES

For the past eight years my staff and myself have been gathering data on the behavior of preschool children in nursery schools and in structured laboratory situations. Each child studied has been observed for at least three months. These data were related to information obtained about the parent-child interaction, and about the parents' beliefs and values. We made two home visits to each family between the difficult hours of five to eight in the evening, then subsequently interviewed the mother and father separately. So far more than 300 families have participated in the study, most of them middle class, well educated families.

A. Child Variables

I think it is important to tell you what kinds of behavior we were looking for so that you will know what I mean by such general terms as "competence" when speaking of the child, or "authoritative parental control" when speaking of the parent.

In all correlational studies of children's social behavior, at least two dimensions are revealed. One dimension may be called *Responsible vs. Socially Disruptive Behavior.* The other dimension may be called *Active vs. Passive Behavior.* These two dimensions are independent of each other—that is, a socially responsible child can run the gamut from very active and self-assertive to very quiet and socially passive. Or, a socially disruptive child may be an active terrorist or he may be sullen, passive and detached from other children.

When we call a child *socially responsible,* we mean that relative to other children his age the child takes into account the ongoing activities of other children enough not to disrupt them—he will facilitate the routine of the group; he does not actively disobey or undermine the rules of the school; he can share possessions with other children; he is sympathetic when another child needs help; he does not try to get another child into trouble, and so on.

When we speak of a child as *active,* we are referring to the independent, self-motivated, goal-oriented, outgoing behavior of the child. When we call a child highly active, he is relative to other children his age likely to go after what he wants forcefully, to show physical courage, to be a leader, to feel free to question the teacher, to persevere when he encounters frustration, to show originality in his thinking, and so on.

Seventy-two very explicitly defined items were used by the raters to describe each child in relation to these two dimensions.

When I report my findings to you later on and I speak of the most *competent* group of children, I am speaking about children who were rated by the observers as being very active and very responsible. I am comparing these children to other children who are less competent in the sense that raters judged them to be lacking in self-assertiveness and self-control, or to be socially disruptive.

Clearly, any definition of competence makes certain tacit assumptions about the proper relationship of the individual to society. The child is *competent* to fulfill himself and succeed in a given society. The same qualities might not be as effective in a differently organized society. To the extent that an investigator believes that successful accommodation to the ongoing institutions of a society defines competence, he will stress the *social responsibility* dimension of competence. If an investigator believes in revolutionary change, he may reject social responsibility as a criterion of competence. To the extent that an investigator values thrust, potency, dominance, and creative push, he will stress *activity* as a dimension of competence. If, by contrast, he believes in an Eastern ideal—such as Zen Buddhism—an investigator may reject dominance and push as criteria of competence, emphasizing instead receptivity, openness, egolessness, and unwilled activity. My definition of *competence* assumes the importance both of accommodation to social institutions, and of self-assertive and individualistic action in relation to these institutions. In the preschool years, I regard the development of *social responsibility* and of *individuality* as equally important for both sexes, although I suppose that our society, at least in the past, has placed the emphasis in adulthood on activity and individuality for boys, and on responsibility and conformity for girls.

B. Parent Variables

Now I would like to tell you about what we were looking for when we observed parents with their children. Our focus has been upon facets of parental authority which might conceivably predict dimensions related to competence in young children. More specifically, we measured dimensions such as the following:

1. *Directive vs. nondirective behavior*—that is, the extent to which the child's life is governed by clear regulations and the parent in charge sets forth clearly the daily regimen for the child.

2. *Firm vs. lax enforcement policy*—the extent to which the parent enforces directives, resists coercive demands of the child, requires the child to pay attention to her when she speaks, and is willing to use punishment if necessary to enforce her demands.

3. *Expects vs. does not expect participation in household chores*—we measured the extent to which parents require the child to help with household tasks, to dress himself, to put his toys away, and to behave cooperatively with other family members.

4. *Promotes respect for established authority vs. seeks to develop on equalitarian, harmonious relationship with child*—here we sought to measure what is generally thought of as authoritarian control and its opposite, i.e. the extent to which the parent assumes a stance of personal infallibility on the basis of her role as parent rather than on the basis of her specific competencies and responsibilities, and requires of the child that he defer to her without question.

We also measured such variables as:

1. The extent to which the parent encourages self-assertion and independent experimentation.

2. The extent to which the parent uses reason and explanation when directing the child.

3. The extent to which the parent values individuality in behavior and appearance by contrast or in addition to social acceptability.

METHODS USED TO STUDY PARENT ATTITUDES AND BEHAVIOR

In studying parental attitudes and practices we used a variety of methods. As I have already indicated, we visited the home on two occasions between the hours of five and eight, and took complete notes on the interactions which transpired. We then interviewed the mother and the father separately, discussing with each the possible ways in which the presence of the observer might have affected the behavior witnessed during the home visit. We talked with parents about their general position on child rearing, their attitudes towards permissiveness, directiveness, and the use of reason, what their ideals were for the child, and so on.

Some parents have asked how we thought the presence of the observer in the home affected the interactions we witnessed. Our general conclusion is that while most families censored some behavior (such as intense emotional shows of love or anger), the interactions we observed and rated with regard to the variables we were measuring predict pretty well how parents interact with their children. We may think about the information we obtain from home visits somewhat as we do about on-the-job tests for a prospective employee. An employer can predict the typing efficiency of a prospective employee from a five-minute typing test on standardized material. While the typist will not handle all kinds of typing tasks in the same way that she does the typing test copy, her handling of the test copy will predict pretty accurately her general speed, her knowledge of format, and her ability to spell. Under the kind of pressure that preschoolers produce during the hours of five and eight, parents generally become sufficiently involved with their customary tasks so that they fall back upon their most practiced responses, modifying these perhaps in accord with their ideals. Very few parents sought consciously to disguise this customary behavior. Since our focus is upon conscious child rearing practices and values, the observational situation is reasonably successful in providing relevant information about parental practices and values. If we were concerned primarily with incidents of highly charged emotional events, direct observation in the home would probably not have provided us with the needed information. Most studies of the effects of child rearing practices in the past have used less valid data than home visits. They have relied upon psychological tests, or self-report, or experimental observation in the laboratory setting. With all its drawbacks, then, we found that the combination of direct observation in the home setting, with interview and self-report, gave us relatively valid information of the kind we were seeking.

CONCLUSIONS FROM THE STUDY

These are the general conclusions which we drew from our data about the child rearing antecedents of *responsible vs. irresponsible behavior* and *active vs. passive behavior.*

In the middle class group we studied, parental practices which were intellectually stimulating and to some extent tension-producing (e.g., socialization and maturity demands and firmness in disciplinary matters) were associated in the young child both with self-assertion and social responsibility. Techniques which fostered self-reliance whether by placing demands upon the child for self-control and high level performance, or by encouraging independent action and decision-making, were associated in the child with responsible and independent behavior. Firm discipline in the home did not produce conforming or dependent behavior in the nursery school. For boys, especially, the opposite was true. Firm, demanding behavior on the part of the parent was not correlated with punitiveness or lack of warmth. The most demanding parents were, in fact, the warmest.

These conclusions concerning the effects of disciplinary practices are consistent with the findings of a second study we conducted (Baumrind, 1967). In that study, a group of nursery school children who were both responsible and independent were identified. These children were self-controlled and friendly on the one hand, and self-reliant, explorative, and self-assertive on the other hand. They were realistic, competent, and content by comparison with the other two groups of children studied. In the home setting, parents of these children were consistent, loving, and demanding. They respected the child's independent decisions, but were very firm about sustaining a position once they took a stand. They accompanied a directive with a reason. Despite vigorous and at times conflictual interactions, their homes were not marked by discord or dissensions. *These parents balanced much warmth with high control, and high demands with clear communication about what was required of the child.* By comparision with parents of children who were relatively immature, parents of these highly mature children had firmer control over the actions of their children, engaged in more independence training, and did not reward dependency. Their households were better coordinated and the policy of regulations clearer and more effectively enforced. The child was more satisfied by his interactions with his parents. By comparison with parents of children who were relatively unhappy and unfriendly, parents of the mature children were less authoritarian, although quite as firm and even more loving.

A POSITION ON CHILD REARING

I would like now to move from a report of research findings into a presentation of some of my conclusions about child rearing. I want to make clear that experts in the field disagree just as parents do. The meaning I derive from my research findings is affected by my personal values and life experience, and is not necessarily the meaning another investigator would derive.

I have been quoted as opposing permissiveness, and to a certain extent that is true. I would like to describe my position on permissiveness in more detail. I think of the permissive parent as one who attempts to behave in a nonevaluative, acceptant, and affirmative manner toward the child's impulses, desires, and actions. She consults with him about policy decisions and gives explanations for family rules. She makes few demands of household responsibility and orderly behavior. She presents herself to the child as a resource for him to use as he wishes, not as an ideal for him to emulate, nor as an active agent responsible for shaping or altering his ongoing or future behavior. She allows the child to regulate his own activities as much as possible, avoids the exercise of control, and does not insist that he obey externally defined standards. She attempts to use reason and manipulation, but not overt power, to accomplish her ends.

The alternative to adult control, according to Neill, the best known advocate of permissiveness, is to permit the child to be self-regulated, free of restraint, and unconcerned about expression of impulse, or the effects of his carelessness. I am quoting from *Summerhill* now:

> *Self-regulation means the right of a baby to live freely, without outside authority in things psychic and somatic.* It means that the baby feeds when it is hungry; that it becomes clean in habits only

when it wants to; that it is never stormed at nor spanked; that it is always loved and protected (1964, p. 105, italics Neill's).

I believe that to impose anything by authority is wrong. The child should not do anything until he comes to the opinion—his own opinion—that it should be done (1964, p. 114, italics Neill's).

Every child has the right to wear clothes of such a kind that it does not matter a brass farthing if they get messy or not (1964, p. 115).

Furniture to a child is practically nonexistent. So at Summerhill we buy old car seats and old bus seats. And in a month or two they look like wrecks. Every now and again at mealtime, some youngster waiting for his second helping will while away the time by twisting his fork almost into knots (1964, p. 138).

Really, any man or woman who tried to give children freedom should be a millionaire, for it is not fair that the natural carelessness of children should always be in conflict with the economic factor (1964, p. 139).

Permissiveness as a doctrine arose as a reaction against the authoritarian methods of a previous era in which the parent felt that her purpose in training her child was to forward not her own desire, but the Divine Will. The parent felt that since the obstacle to worldly and eternal happiness was self-will, that the subduing of the will of the child led to his salvation. The authoritarian parent of a previous era was preparing his child for a hard life in which success depended upon achievment, and in which strength of purpose and ability to conform were necessary for success. With the advent of Freudian psychology and the loosening of the hold of organized religion, educated middle class parents were taught by psychologists and educators to question the assumptions of their own authoritarian parents. Spock's 1946 edition of *Baby and Child Care* advocated the psychoanalytic view that full gratification of infantile sucking and excretory and sexual impulses were essential for secure and healthful adult personalities. The ideal educated, well-to-do family in the late 1940's and 1950's was organized around unlimited acceptance of the child's impulses, and around maximum freedom of choice and self-expression for the child.

However by 1957 Spock himself changed his emphasis. He said, in the 1957 edition of his famous book, "A great change in attitude has occurred and nowadays there seems to be more chance of conscientious parent's getting into trouble with permissiveness than with strictness."

I would like now to examine certain of the assumptions which have been made in support of permissiveness, most of which, when examined in a research setting, have not been supported.

1. One assumption previously made was that scheduled feeding and firm toilet training procedures have as their inevitable consequences adult neuroses. This apparently is not so. Unless the demands put upon the infant are unrealistic—as might be the demand for bowel training at five months—or the parent punishes the infant cruelly for failure to live up to her demands—scheduled feeding and firm toilet training do not appear to be harmful to the child.

2. A second assumption, that punishment, especially spanking, is harmful to the child, or not effective in controlling behavior, is also not supported by recent research findings. On the contrary, properly administered punishment has been shown by the behavior therapists to be an effective means of controlling the behavior of children. This hardly comes as a surprise to most parents. Brutal punishment *is* harmful to the child. Threats of punishment not carried out are harmful to the child. A parent who threatens to punish must be prepared to deal with escalation from the child by prompt administration of punishment. She cannot appease. Otherwise the threat of punishment will actually *increase* the incidence of undesirable behavior, since it is just that undesirable behavior which will cause the parent to cancel the punishment, in an attempt to appease the child.

While *prompt* punishment is usually most effective, it is important for the parent to be certain that the child knows exactly why he is being punished, and what kind of behavior the parent would prefer and why. While extremely rapid punishment following a transgression works best in training a rat or a dog, a human child is a conscious being and should be approached as one. It should not be enough for a parent, except perhaps in critical matters of safety, to *condition* a child to avoid certain kinds of behavior by prompt punishment. The parent's aim is to help the child control his own behavior, and that end requires the use of reason and the bringing to bear of moral principles to define what is right and what is wrong conduct.

Properly administered punishment, then, provides the child with important information. The child learns what it is his parent wants, and he learns about the consequences of not conforming to an authority's wishes.

3. A third assumption that advocates of permissiveness have made is that unconditional love is beneficial to the child, and that love which is conditional upon the behavior of the child is harmful to the child. I think that the notion of unconditional love has deterred many parents from fulfilling certain important parental functions. They fail to train their children for future life and make them afraid to move towards independence. Indulgent love is passive in respect to the child—not requiring of the child that he become good, or competent, or disciplined. It is content with providing nourishment and understanding. It caters to the child and overlooks petulance and obnoxious behavior—at least it tries to. The effect on the child of such love is often not good. Once the child enters the larger community, the parents are forced to restrict or deprive. Accustomed as the child is to immediate gratification, he suffers greater deprivation at such times than he would if he were accustomed to associating

discipline with love. He does not accept nor can he tolerate unpleasant consequences when he acts against authority figures. Such a child, even when he is older, expects to receive, and is not prepared to give or to compromise. The rule of reciprocity, of payment for value received, is a law of life that applies to us all. The child must be prepared in the home by his parents to give according to his ability so that he can get according to his needs.

The parent who expresses love unconditionally is encouraging the child to be selfish and demanding while she herself is not. Thus she reinforces exactly the behavior which she does not approve of—greedy, demanding, inconsiderate behavior. For his part, the child is likely to feel morally inferior for what he is, and to experience conflict about what he should become. I believe that a parent expresses her love most fully when she demands of the child that he become his best, and in the early years helps him to act in accordance with *her* image of the noble, the beautiful, and the best, as an initial model upon which he can create (in the adolescent years) his own ideal.

On the other hand, I do believe that to the extent that it is possible, a parent's *commitment* to the child should be unconditional. That is, the parent should stay contained *in* the experience with the child, no matter what the child does. Parental love properly expressed comes closest in my mind to the Christian notion of *Agape*. The parent continues to care for the child because it is her child and not because of the child's merits. Since she is human, the quality of her feeling for him depends upon the child's actions, but her interest in his welfare does not depend upon his actions and is abiding. This abiding interests is expressed not in gratifying the child's whims, nor in being gentle and kind with him, nor in approval of his actions, nor even in approving of what he is as a person. Unconditional *commitment* means that the child's interests are perceived as among the parent's most important interests, and that (no matter what the child does) the parent does not desert the child. But the love of a parent for a child must be demanding—not demanding of the unconditional commitment it offers—but rather demanding of the reciprocal of what if offers. The parent has the right—indeed, the duty—to expect obedience and growth towards mature behavior, in order that she can discharge her responsibilities to the child, and continue to feel unconditional commitment to his welfare. (Only parents are required, as an expression of love, to give up the object of that love, to prepare the object of love to become totally free of the lover.)

AUTHORITATIVE VERSUS AUTHORITARIAN PARENTAL CONTROL

Now that I have discussed the concept of permissiveness in child rearing, I would like to explain the distinction which I make between *authoritarian* and *authoritative* parental control.

I think of an *authority* as a person whose expertness befits him to tell another what to do, when the behavioral alternatives are known to both. An authority does not have to *exercise* his control, but it is recognized by both that by virtue of his expertness and his responsibility for the actions of the other, he is fit to exercise authority in a given area.

By *authoritative parental control* I mean that, in relation to her child, the parent should be an authority in the sense just defined.

1. *In order to be an authority, the parent must be expert.* It seems to me that many parents and teachers have come to the conclusion that they are not expert on matters which pertain to the young people placed in their charge. Therefore, since they are not expert, they abandon their role as authorities. I think instead that they should become more expert. Parents often do need more information about children of all ages than they have, in order to be expert. But much of what a parent needs to know she can learn from observing her child and listening to him. A parent must permit her child to be a socialization agent for her, as well as the other way, if the parent is to acquire the information about the child and his peer group that she needs in order to make authoritative decisions about matters which affect the child's life. Unlike the authoritarian parent, the authoritative parent modifies her role in response to the child's coaching. She responds to suggestions and complaints from the child and then transmits her own more flexible norms to her child. In this way, by becoming more expert, the parent legitimates her authority and increases her effectiveness as a socializing agent.

2. *In order to be authoritative, the parent must be willing and able to behave rationally, and to explain the rationale for her values and norms to the child.* The parent does not have to explain her actions all the time to the child, especially if she knows that the child knows the reason but is engaging in harrassment. But a parent does need to be sure that she herself knows the basis for her demands, and that the child also knows, within the limits of his understanding, the reasons behind her demands.

In authoritarian families the parent interacts with the child on the basis of formal role and status. Since the parent has superior power, she tells the child what to do and does not permit herself to be affected by what he says or does. Where parents do not consult with children on decisions affecting the children, authority can only rest on power. As the child gets older and the relative powers of parent and child shift, the basis for parental authority is undermined. Even the young child has the perfect answer to a parent who says, "you must do what I say because I am your mother," and that answer is, "I never asked to be born." The adolescent can add, "Make me," and many say just that when parents are unwise enough to clash directly with an adolescent on an issue on which the adolescent has staked his integrity or autonomy.

3. *In order to be authoritative, the parent must value self-assertion and willfulness in the child.* Her aim should be to prepare the child to become independent of her control and to leave her domain. Her methods of discipline, while firm, must therefore

be respectful of the child's actual abilities and capacities. As these increase, she must share her responsibilities and prerogatives with the child, and increase her expectations for competence, achievement, and independent action.

I believe that the imposition of authority even against the child's will is useful to the child during the first six years. Indeed, power serves to legitimate authority in the mind of the child, to assure the child that his parent has the power to protect him and provide for him.

The major way in which parents exercise power in the early years is by manipulating the reinforcing and punishing stimuli which affect the child. What makes a parent a successful reinforcing agent or an attractive model for a child to imitate is his effective power to give the child what he needs—i.e., the parent's control over resources which the child desires, and his willingness and ability to provide the child with these resources in such a manner and at such a time that the child will be gratified and the family group benefitted. Thus, practically as well as morally, gratification of the child's needs within the realistic economy of the family, is a precondition for the effective imposition of parental authority. An exploited child cannot be controlled effectively over a long period of time. The parent's ability to gratify the child and to withhold gratification legitimates his authority. The child, unlike the adolescent, has not yet reached the level of cognitive development where he can legitimate authority, or object to its imposition, on a principled basis.

By early adolescence, however, power based on physical strength and control of resources cannot and should not be used to legitimate authority. The young person is now capable of formal operational thought. He can formulate principles of choice by which to judge his own actions and the actions of others. He has the conceptual ability to be critical even though he may lack the wisdom to moderate his criticism. He can see clearly many alternatives to parental directives; and the parent must be prepared to defend rationally, as she would to an adult, a directive with which the adolescent disagrees. Moreover, the asymmetry of power which characterizes childhood no longer exists at adolescence. The adolescent cannot be forced physically to obey over any period of time.

When an adolescent refuses to do as his parent wishes, it is more congruent with his construction of reality for the parent simply to ask him, "why not?". Through the dialogue which ensues, the parent may learn that his directive was unjust; or the adolescent may learn that his parent's directive could be legitimated. In any case, a head-on confrontation is avoided. While head-on confrontation won by the parent serves to strengthen parental authority in the first six years, it produces conflict about adult authority during adolescence.

Although a young person need feel no commitment to the social ethic of his parents' generation, he does have, while he is dependent upon his parents, a moral responsibility to obey rational authority, i.e. authority based on explicity, mutually-agreed-upon principles. The just restrictions on his freedom provide the adolescent with the major impetus to become self-supporting and responsible to himself rather than to his parents.

THE RELATIONSHIP OF INDIVIDUAL FREEDOM TO CONTROL

To an articulate exponent of permissiveness in child rearing, such as Neill, freedom for the child means that he has the liberty to do as he pleases without interference from adult guardians and, indeed, with their protection. Hegel, by contrast, defines freedom as the appreciation of necessity. By this he means that the man frees himself of the objective world by understanding its nature and controlling his reactions to its attributes. His definition equates the concept of freedom with power to act, rather than with absence of external control. To Hegel, the infant is enslaved by virtue of his ignorance, his dependence upon others for sustenance, and his lack of self-control. The experience of infantile omnipotence, if such he has, is based on ignorance and illusion. His is the freedom to be irresponsible, a very limited freedom, and one appropriate only for the incompetent.

For a person to behave autonomously, he must accept responsibility for his own behavior, which in turn requires that he believe the world is orderly and susceptible to rational mastery and that he has or can develop the requisite skills to manage his own affairs.

When compliance with parental standards is achieved by use of reason, power, and external reinforcement, it may be possible to obtain obedience and self-correction without stimulating guilt reactions. To some extent the parent's aggressiveness with the child stimulates counteraggressiveness and anger from the child, thus reducing the experience of guilt and of early internalizations of standards whose moral bases cannot yet be grasped. When the child accepts physical punishment or deprivation of privileges as the price paid for acts of disobedience, he may derive from the interaction greater power to withstand suffering and deprivation in the service of another need or an ideal and, thus, increased freedom to choose among expanded alternatives in the future.

Authoritarian control and permissive noncontrol both shield the child from the opportunity to engage in vigorous interaction with people. Demands which cannot be met or no demands, suppression of conflict or sidestepping of conflict, refusal to help or too much help, unrealistically high or low standards, all may curb or understimulate the child so that he fails to achieve the knowledge and experience which could realistically reduce his dependence upon the outside world. The authoritarian and the permissive parent may both create, in different ways, a climate in which the child is not desensitized to the anxiety associated with nonconformity, nor willing to accept punishment for transgressions. Both models minimize dissent, the former by suppression and the latter by diversion or indulgence. To learn how to dissent, the child may need a strongly held position from which to diverge and then be allowed under some circumstances to pay the price for nonconformity by being punished. Spirited give and take within the home, if accompanied by respect and warmth, may teach the child how to express aggression in self-serving and prosocial causes and to accept the partially unpleasant consequences of such actions.

The body of findings on effects of disciplinary practices give provisional support to the position that authoritative control can achieve responsible conformity with group standards without loss of individual autonomy or self-assertiveness.

4.5

Anxious Attachment and Defensive Reactions Associated with Day Care

Mary Curtis Blehar

Full-day group care for infants and toddlers differs from home care in two major ways. A child in group care is reared by multiple caregivers rather than by one or a few figures, and he is separated daily from his primary mother figure. Bowlby (1969, 1973) hypothesized that an infant is biased genetically to maintain a degree of proximity to his mother figure, and predisposed toward becoming attached to her. Does full-time group day care constitute a sufficient departure from the environment to which a child's behavioral systems are preadapted to generate anomalies in the development of attachment? More specifically, can an infant develop an attachment to his mother figure if he spends nine or ten hours a day with substitute caregivers in a group setting? Can a young child who has already become attached to his mother figure sustain a normal relationship with her despite the repeated, long daily separations implicit in day care? There is a dearth of research addressed to these questions.

Caldwell, Wright, Honig, and Tannenbaum (1970) studied the effects of day care on infants who entered care in the first year of life or early in the second year. They focused on a number of variables purporting to reflect the strength of child-mother attachment—affiliation, nuturance, absence of hostility, permissiveness, dependency, happiness, and emotionality. Finding no significant differences between their day-care and home-reared groups, they concluded that full-time day care did not prevent children from developing attachments of normal strength to their mothers.

This study was undertaken as a doctoral dissertation at the Johns Hopkins University. An early version of this paper was presented at the biennial meeting of the Society for Research in Child Development, at Philadelphia, March, 1973, in a symposium entitled "Anxious Attachment and Defensive Reactions." I wish to thank Mary D. Ainsworth and Julian Stanley for their critical comments and Mary B. Main for her assistance in the data analysis. Reprinted by permission of the author and the Society for Research in Child Development, Inc. Copyright © 1974 (forthcoming) by the Society for Research in Child Development.

The present study concerns older children, who were at home with their mothers either two or three years before beginning day care. It addresses itself not to the question of day care's effects on attachment formation processes, but to the effects of repeated daily separations on qualitative aspects of established attachment relationships.

Research into children's responses to major separations, lasting weeks or months, has demonstrated adverse effects, the severity of which depend on a number of factors, such as the child's age, the length of the separation, and the availability of responsive substitute caregivers. In one notable study, Robertson and Bowlby (1952) observed three distinct phases in children's reactions to major institutional separation. Initially, there occurred a protest phase followed by a despair phase. If the separation was very long and conditions were depriving, children would manifest a detachment phase, marked by loss of interest in the mother and superficiality in interpersonal relationships. Detachment was interpreted as a defensive behavioral pattern stemming from repression of anxiety and ambivalence occasioned by separation.

Reunion behaviors of children after major separation typically consist of angry rejection of or apparent indifference to the mother, alternating with heightened attachment behaviors (Heinicke and Westheimer, 1965). However, detached children tend to persist in this mode, sometimes indefinitely, before reestablishing a relationship, usually of a permanently anxious quality (Robertson and Bowlby, 1952). Ainsworth (personal communication), having examined Robertson and Bowlby's data, reported that younger children in their sample (between 1 and 2½) were more likely to develop detachment than older children (between ages 3 and 4), who were more capable of maintaining an attachment to the mother, albeit of an anxious quality.

Although some disturbance is a predictable outcome of separation once a child has become attached, distress can be attenuated if he has the opportunity to form a close relationship with a substitute figure (e.g., Robertson and Robertson, 1971) or if he remains in a familiar environment while separated from his mother (Yarrow, 1961).

In order to assess the possibility that day care could affect attachment, the strange situation, a technique sensitive to qualitative differences in the mother-child relationship, was chosen. This situation first elicits exploration behavior, and then through a series of separations and reunions, heightened attachment behavior. Ainsworth, Bell, and Stayton (1971) classified 1-year-olds into three groups chiefly on the basis of reunion behaviors. The first group was active in seeking and maintaining proximity to and contact with the mother upon reunion. A second group sought little proximity or contact, but actively avoided proximity and interaction. A third group mixed seeking proximity and contact with resistance of contact and interaction. Stable relationships were found, both between infant's strange-situation behavior and his home behavior, and between his behavior and maternal behavior. Infants in the first group had histories of harmonious interaction with the mother, while infants in the other groups had histories of disturbed interaction. Ainsworth and Bell (1970) compared avoidant and resistant behaviors observed in the strange situation with detachment and ambivalence others have noted in young children after major separation.

Although Ainsworth has used her situation to study individual differences in attachment, others (Maccoby and Feldman, 1972; Marvin, 1972) have also used it to observe normative patterns of attachment behavior and changes in patterns over the first four years of life. They found a gradual decline in seeking contact with the mother upon reunion, and then in seeking proximity to her. Maintaining contact upon reunion tended to disappear by age 2 and seeking of proximity tended to disappear by age 4. Separation protest declined more sharply around age 3.

In the present study, the strange situation was used to compare responses to separation from and reunion with the mother in groups of day-care and home-reared children. Depending on one's theoretical point of view, there are three predictions that can be made: (1) day-care children will behave no differently from the controls, on the assumption that day care does not affect attachment; (2) day-care children will be less distressed by separation and will exhibit less strongly heightened attachment behaviors upon reunion because of their more frequent experiences with separation; (3) day-care children will exhibit disturbances in attachment related to daily separation; and the disturbance will be related to the child's developmental level at the time of entering day care.

METHODS

Subjects

The subjects were 40 middle class children, all but one white. Twenty were enrolled in full-time group day care and 20 were reared by their mothers at home. Ten of the day-care group had entered centers at a mean age of 25.66 months (SD = 1.81 months) and ten at a mean age of 34.83 months (SD = 2.45 months). Both groups had been enrolled for approximately the same length of time when observed—4.55 months for the younger group (SD = 2.56 months) and 4.78 months for the older group (SD = 1.69 months). When observed they had mean ages of 30.23 months (SD = 2.20 months) and 39.62 months (SD = 1.98 months) respectively. The mean ages of the home-reared groups at the time of observation were 30.23 months (SD = 1.98) months and 39.46 months (SD = 1.95 months). Equal numbers of males and females were observed at each age level.

One assumption underlying the comparison was that the groups were equivalent on variables affecting the quality of attachment other than the daily separations implicit in day care. This assumption would be unnecessary in an experimental study which randomly assigned children to day care or home rearing, but such a study would be extremely difficult to carry out. However, all children were from middle class homes, both in terms of parental education and income. Both parents were present in the home. Measures of the home environment which support the assumption of equivalence between the groups will be reported below. Eighty percent of day-care children and 60 percent of home-reared children were firstborn. Four day-care children had been cared for by baby-sitters approximately four months before starting group day care. Three home-reared 40-month-olds attended nursery school two or three mornings a week.

Cooperation in collecting a day-care sample was obtained from private centers that followed traditional nursery school regimes with little emphasis on structured academic programs. The degree of structuring in play and the amount of organized group activities were greater for the older children than for the younger. Children were segregated into groups of 2 and 3-year-olds, 4-year-olds, and 5-year-olds. Two caregivers were assigned to each group, and they did not shift over the course of the week. On the average, caregivers tended to remain in their positions for three years. At age 4 and again at age 5, children moved up into a new group with new caregivers. In the 2- and 3-year-old group, the ratio of caregivers to children was 1 to 8, or 1 to 6, depending on the center. A registered nurse was on hand daily at two of the centers. Names of all children attending the centers were provided beforehand by the directors and from this list parents were contacted individually. All but one agreed to cooperate. Pediatricians in private practice supplied names of home-reared children, and all but two parents contacted agreed to participate.

Procedure

The first part of the procedures entailed a home visit of an hour-and-a-half duration to each mother-child pair by the investigator. Its purposes were to establish rapport with the mother, to instruct her about the study, and to assess the general quality of stimulation provided the child by his home environment. Each visit was rated on the Inventory of Home Stimulation, devised by Caldwell (1970). The majority of the items were straightforward, and depended on firsthand observation of the home and of mother-child interaction rather than on maternal report alone. For example, it was noted if the mother spoke spontaneously to the child at least twice, if she caressed or kissed him, if books were present and visible, or if he had a pet. A measure of the mother's empathy or social sensitivity was obtained by use of a Q-sort technique devised by Hogan (1969). The mother was rated by the observer immediately after each visit.

Approximately two weeks later, each mother-child pair participated in a standardized strange situation at Johns Hopkins University. The experimental room had a 9 X 9 foot area of clear floor space. One wall contained one-way vision mirrors. Near the opposite wall stood a child's chair with toys heaped on and around it. Near the window on one side of the room was a chair for the mother and opposite it a chair for the stranger. The situation consisted of eight episodes, each, except for the first, three minutes long (see Table 1).

A continuous description of the child's behavior was dictated into recorders which also picked up the sound of a buzzer every 15 seconds. The transcribed narrative reports were marked off into time intervals. In 65 percent of the cases, there were two independent observers, and in the other cases, the investigator served as sole observer. The second observer, in all but four instances, was an individual who was naive about the hypotheses of the study or unaware of the child's group membership. Two women played the role of stranger in all but three cases when a substitute had to be found. The first woman was stranger for 12 home-reared and 9 day-care children, and the second woman was stranger for 8 home-reared and 8 day-care children. Individual narrative reports were consolidated for analysis and three types of measures were extracted: frequency measures, percentage measures, and scores of social interaction with the mother and the stranger.

TABLE 1.   STRANGE SITUATION EPISODES

EPISODE NUMBER	DURATION	PARTICIPANTS	DESCRIPTION OF EPISODE
1. . .	30 seconds, approximately	Observer, mother, child	Observer ushers mother and child in the room. Child is set down on the floor.
2. . .	3 minutes	Mother, child	Child is free to explore. Mother reads a magazine.
3. . .	3 minutes	Stranger, mother child	Stranger enters, sits quietly for a moment, interacts with mother, then with child.
4. . .	3 minutes*	Stranger, child	Mother leaves. Stranger remains with child; responds to his advances or comforts him if necessary.
5. . .	3 minutes	Mother, child	Stranger leaves as mother enters. Mother comforts child if he is distressed, then reinterests him in toys.
6. . .	3 minutes*	Child	Mother leaves child alone in room.
7. . .	3 minutes*	Stranger, child	Stranger enters; attempts to comfort child if distressed; returns to her chair.
8. . .	3 minutes	Mother, child	Mother enters as stranger leaves. Mother behaves as in episode 5.

*The duration of episode was curtailed if the child became very distressed.

Frequency measures and percentages.   Four measures were obtained by making counts of the frequency of the following behaviors: exploratory manipulation, crying and oral behavior, and distance interaction with the mother. Exploratory manipulation was defined as shaking, banging, turning over, or other active involvement with a toy. Crying was defined as distressed vocalization, ranging from a fuss to a full-blown cry. Oral behavior was defined as chewing or sucking fingers or toys. For these behaviors, a frequency count of the 15-second intervals in which they occurred was obtained. Distance interaction was a composite of the absolute frequency of smiling and showing a toy to the mother and the 15-second interval frequency of vocalizations to the mother. Relative frequency of vocalization was used because it was extremely difficult to determine in a time interval when a particular vocalization stopped and another started in those cases where the child talked almost incessantly. The distance interaction measure (taken from Maccoby and Feldman, 1972) was used only in Episode 2 when the mother was noninterventive in order to obtain an index of the child's spontaneous interest in her. In Episode 3, the presence of the stranger reduced the behavior to a very low level. The following coefficients of interobserver reliability were obtained for the frequency measures: exploratory manipulation, .98; oral behavior, .90; distance interaction, .85; and crying, .98.

Percentages of children who approached and touched the mother in reunion episodes, who exhibited oral behavior, who cried, and who resisted contact and interaction were also used in conjunction with the frequency measures and the social interaction scores.

Social interaction scores. Another part of the analysis involved detailed codings of socially interactive behaviors with the mother and with the stranger on the basis of the narrative reports. Each child was scored on seeking proximity, and contact, avoiding proximity and interaction, and resisting contact and interaction. Intensity of search behavior for the mother during separation episodes was also scored. The scoring system was adopted with only minor modifications from Ainsworth, Bell, and Stayton (1971). The following is a brief description of the contents of the behavioral categories.

Proximity- and contact-seeking behaviors include active approach, clambering up, active gestures such as reaching, partial approaches, and vocal signals.

Proximity- and interaction-avoiding behaviors pertain to episodes which normally elicit approach, or greeting. Behaviors include backing away, ignoring, gaze aversion, and looking away. Avoiding the mother is scored only in reunion episodes.

Contact- and interaction-resisting behaviors include angry attempts to push away, hit or kick the adult, squirming to get away from the adult, pushing away toys, or displays of temper when the adult attempts to intervene in the child's ongoing activities.

Search behavior includes following mother to the door, trying to open it, going to the mother's chair, looking at her chair, and looking at the door. The behaviors imply that the child is seeking to regain proximity to the absent mother.

The behaviors were scored independently by two judges, one of whom was unaware of the child's rearing group classification, and the following coefficients of the interscorer agreement were obtained: seeking proximity to the mother .97; to the stranger, .98; resistance of mother, .93; of stranger, .92; avoiding of mother, .94; of stranger, .88; search behavior, .98.

Methods of analysis. Analyses of variance were conducted for all measures obtained from the home visit and all measures obtained from the strange situation but orality. In this case, a nonparametric test was used because the skewness of the distribution. Separate analyses were performed for behavior to mother and to stranger. There were three independent variables—age, sex, and rearing group—forming a 2 X 2 X 2 factorial design, and one within-subjects repeated measure of episode.

Scores on each behavior to the mother and to the stranger and on frequency measures were obtained for each episode, and a total score for a behavior was obtained by summing scores for the relevant episodes. The interaction of episode with the independent variables was also examined.

RESULTS

Testing the Equivalence of Groups

Table 2 gives the mean scores for the day-care and home-reared groups on the Inventory of Home Stimulation and its subscales. None of the differences was significant. The empathy measure likewise did not discriminate significantly between mothers of the day-care and home-reared children. Although detailed assessments of each mother's sensitivity to her child's signals and communications were not made, the groups' equivalence on the measures obtained suggests that the children observed were receiving normal mothering and stimulation from their home environment adequate for healthy development.

TABLE 2. GROUP MEANS FOR THE INVENTORY OF HOME STIMULATION

	DAY CARE	HOME CARE
1. Total Score	35.30	35.80
2. Emotional-verbal responsiveness of mother	9.40	8.95
3. Avoidance of restriction and punishment	4.79	5.20
4. Organization of physical and temporal environments	5.85	5.85
5. Provision of appropriate play materials	8.25	8.30
6. Maternal involvement with child	3.40	3.95
7. Opportunities for variety in daily stimulation	3.70	3.85

Behavior in the Strange Situation

Table 3 presents a summary of the ANOVA findings. Sex and age differences were relatively few and will not be discussed further. Episode effects are highly significant and in agreement with those reported elsewhere by Ainsworth and Bell (1970). Differences in attachment behavior to the mother between first and later-born children were also examined by ANOVAs and were not significant. However, the data are consistent in showing rearing group differences and interactions of age with rearing group.

Exploratory behavior. Table 3 indicates a significant age X rearing group interaction in the total amount of exploratory manipulation occurring in the strange situation,

TABLE 3. SUMMARY OF ANOVA FINDINGS

SOURCE OF VARIATION	EXPLORATORY MANIPULATION	CRYING	DISTANCE INTERATION TO MOTHER	PROXIMITY TO MOTHER	RESISTING TO MOTHER	AVOIDING OF MOTHER	PROXIMITY TO STRANGER	RESISTING OF STRANGER	AVOIDING OF STRANGER	SEARCH
Sex						.025	.025		.001	
Rearing Group		.05	.025		.05	.0005	.05		.0005	
Age							.025			
Sex × Rearing Group										
Sex × Age										
Rearing Group × Age	.025	.10		.10						
Sex × Rearing Group × Age						.005	.05			.05
Episode	.0005	.001	NA			.10	.10	.025	.0005	.0005
Sex × Episode										
Rearing Group × Episode					.10				.005	
Age × Episode										
Sex × Rearing Group × Episode										
Sex × Age × Episode								.05	.10	
Rearing Group × Age × Episode				.025						
Sex × Rearing Group × Age × Episode										

289

F(1,32) = 6.93, p < .025. Day-care 40-month-olds were lowest in exploration ($\bar{X}$ = 7.48) and home-reared 40-month-olds were highest ($\bar{X}$ = 9.68). Day-care 30-month-olds were intermediate between their home-reared age counter-parts ($\bar{X}$ = 8.9 versus $\bar{X}$ = 8.2) and the older home-reared children. All groups decreased in exploration during separation episodes, but these changes were most marked in the older day-care group and least marked in the older home-reared group.

Separation behaviors. A significant main effect, F(1,32) = 4.60, p < .05, indicates that total crying was higher in day-care children than in home-reared children. However, an age X rearing group interaction, F(1,32) = 3.78, p < .07, suggests that the main effect may be accounted for chiefly by differences in the 40-month-old groups (40-month-old day-care $\bar{X}$ = 3.3 versus 40-month-old home-reared $\bar{X}$ = .22). In the 30-month-old groups, day-care children were only slightly higher in amount of crying than home-reared children ($\bar{X}$ = 1.72 versus $\bar{X}$ = 1.57).

Oral behavior in episode 7 was also more conspicuous in day-care children than in home-reared children (randomization test for two independent samples: p < .0005). Orality occurred most frequently in episode 7, apparently a result of anxiety over the mother's absence compounded by the appearance of the stranger when the mother was expected to return. Forty-five percent of day-care children but only 15% of home-reared children engaged in oral behavior in this episode, X^2 (1) = 4.29, p < .05.

Search behavior in episodes 4, 6, and 7 was another indicator of separation anxiety since it represented attempts to regain proximity to the absent mother by going to the door or at least looking at her chair. An age X rearing group interaction, F(1,32) = 5.14, p < .05, depicted in figure 1, indicates that day-care 40-month-olds searched most for the mother ($\bar{X}$ = 3.72) and home-reared 40-month-olds searched least ($\bar{X}$ = 2.05). The two 30-month-old groups were much closer together in total amount of search, although the home-reared children showed slightly stronger behavior ($\bar{X}$ = 3.15 vs. $\bar{X}$ = 2.75). The older day-care children were conspicuous for engaging in active search (i.e., going to the door and attempting to open it) even in episode 4 when children in the other groups tended to maintain exploratory manipulation, and merely looked at the door, if they displayed any search at all.

Behavior to the Mother

Distance interaction. Home-reared children of both ages interacted more with their mothers across a distance in episode 2 than did day-care children ($\bar{X}$ = 6.08 vs. $\bar{X}$ = 4.06) as is indicated by a main effect, F(1,32) = 6.66, p < .025. This finding could be interpreted as indicating that day-care children are more independent of their mothers, at least in their free-play activities, than home-reared children. However, a negative correlation (r = −.42, p < .01) between distance interaction in episode 2 and resistant and avoidant behaviors directed toward the mother in later reunion episodes suggests that little interaction of this type before separation is a precursor of negative tendencies, which become more apparent in the reunion episodes and which indicate a disturbance in the mother-child relationship.

Proximity-seeking behaviors. Figure 2 shows that group differences in seeking the mother's proximity tended to be small in preseparation episodes 2 and 3, but increased in reunion episodes, age X rearing group X episode interaction, $F(3,96) = 3.85$, $p < .025$. In episode 5, day-care 40-month-olds showed heightened attachment behavior, whereas their home-reared age counterparts showed little. In episode 8, the older day-care group continued to increase somewhat in proximity seeking, and the older home-reared group declined slightly. Home-reared 30-month-olds showed clear heightening of attachment behaviors in this episode, whereas their day-care counterparts tended to decrease somewhat in proximity seeking. The contrast in this episode between the combined day-care 30-month-old and home reared 40-month-old means and the other two means combined is significant (Scheffé test, $p < .025$) and accounts for most of the variance in the interaction. Past strange situation work (e.g., Ainsworth, Bell, and Stayton, 1971) has shown that individual differences in seeking the mother's proximity are most clearly highlighted after separation in the reunion episodes, and especially after two separations in the second reunion, Episode 8.

FIGURE 1.   AGE X REARING GROUP INTERACTION
FOR SEARCH BEHAVIOR

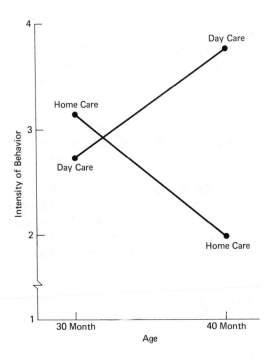

FIGURE 2.   AGE X REARING GROUP X EPISODE INTERACTION FOR
PROXIMITY SEEKING TO MOTHER

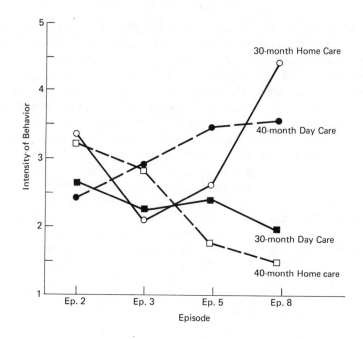

The percentage of children in each group who actually approached and touched the mother upon reunion in Episode 8 was also calculated. Although two of the findings are only trends, day-care 40-month-olds seemed more likely to do so than their home-reared counterparts (60 percent versus 10 percent: Fisher's exact test, two-tailed; $p < .07$ approach; 60 percent versus 0 percent: $p < .025$, touch). Day-care 30-month-olds seemed less likely to do so than their home-reared age counterparts ($\overline{X} = 30$ percent vs. 90 percent, $p < .025$, approach; 10 percent vs. 60 percent, $p < .10$, touch).

Resisting and avoiding behaviors.   Day-care children resisted the mother more than home-reared children, $F(1,32) = 5.22$, $p < .05$. The behavior occurred in only 20 percent of day-care and home-reared 30-month-olds but in 60 percent of the older day-care group. It was completely absent in the older home-reared group. This finding suggests that the older day-care children were somewhat more overtly ambivalent towards the mother than the other groups. Proximity-avoiding behaviors upon reunion are also more conspicuous in day-care children of both ages than in home-reared children ($\overline{X} = 3.2$ versus $\overline{X} = 1.8$), $F(1,32) = 16.36$, $p < .005$, although they occurred more markedly in the younger day-care group than in the older group.

Behavior to the Stranger

Day-care children sought less proximity to the stranger than did home-reared children, $F(1,32) = 4.40$, $p < .05$, but an age $\times$ rearing group interaction, $F(1,32) = 5.24$, $p < .05$, suggests that the younger home-reared children accounted for this difference by seeking a moderate amount of proximity to the stranger. Resistance of the stranger was higher in day-care 40-month-olds than in the other groups, especially during separation Episodes 4 and 7, as a rearing group $\times$ age $\times$ episode interaction, $F(1,32) = 4.30$, $p < .05$, indicates. In general, day-care children of both ages were more avoidant of the stranger than home-reared children, $F(1,32) = 13.26$, $p < .001$. An interaction of rearing group $\times$ exisode, $F(2,64) = 6.26$, $p < .005$, indicates that home-reared children were most wary of the stranger in Episode 3 and became more accepting of her later on during separation episodes. In contrast, day-care children found the stranger increasingly aversive as the situation proceeded (Scheffé test $p < .025$).

Differences in the children's responses to the two women who served chiefly as stranger were also examined. These differences tended to be quite small and none was significant.

DISCUSSION

The above findings demonstrate that day-care children of both ages interacted less with their mothers across a distance before separation in Episode 2 than did home-reared children. During separations, they cried more, and showed more oral behavior, and more avoidance of the stranger. Upon reunion with the mother, they exhibited more avoidant and resistant behaviors. However, the findings also indicate important age differences. Day-care 40-month-olds showed more heightening of attachment behaviors and more distress as a result of separation than did day-care 30-month-olds, whereas in the home-reared groups the opposite age trend was found. The work of Maccoby and Feldman (1972) and Marvin (1972) indicates that the home-reared groups behaved in a manner typical of normal children of these ages. However, in comparison to the older home-reared children, children who began day-care at 35 months of age explored less, were more distressed by separations, and sought more proximity to and contact with the mother upon reunion, although these bids were mixed with resistance and avoidance. In comparison to the younger home-reared children, children who began day-care at 25 months of age sought little proximity to or contact with the mother upon reunion, but showed heightened proximity- and interaction-avoiding tendencies.

The findings of anxious ambivalent attachment behavior in the older day-care children and avoidant behavior in younger day-care children are consistent with age differences reported in children's responses to major separation. During major separation, it is also the younger children (age 1 to 2½) who are more likely to become detached and to respond to the mother with indifference upon reunion, whereas the older children (age 3 to 4) are less likely to consolidate detachment and more likely to respond to reunion with the mother in an anxious ambivalent fashion. Thus, the results of the present study suggest that many repetitions of minor separation may have effects similar in form to major separations.

More recently, Ainsworth (1973) has reported that repetition of the strange-situation procedure after a 2-week interval sensitizes rather than habituates 1-year-olds to separation. This finding also lends credence to the notion that the reunion behaviors of the day-care groups in the present study may be attributable to a sensitizing effect of daily separation.

It is generally acknowledged that detachment is a more serious outcome of major separation than anxious attachment, because as long as a child remains detached, he is limited in his ability to form close interpersonal relationships. Anxious attachment, even if ambivalent, signifies that the child is capable of maintaining a close relationship, and, indeed, under favorable conditions, he may reestablish a normal relationship. In the absence of longitudinal data, it is impossible to ascertain the significance for later development of either the anxious attachment observed in the older day-care group or the avoidant behavior observed in the younger day-care group. However, the possibility exists that the mother-avoiding tendencies of the younger children may signal a more substantial disruption of the child-mother attachment—at least in the short term—than the anxious behavior of the older children, even though at first glance the younger children seem less overtly disturbed.

The finding that younger day-care children are also more avoidant of strangers than their home-reared peers runs counter to a "common sense" expectation that children who are exposed to a variety of adults would affiliate more readily with strangers than those reared within the more sheltered confines of the nuclear family. Nevertheless, this finding is congruent with those of Tizard and Tizard (1971) who found young children reared in residential nurseries more afraid of strangers than home-reared children; and those of Heinicke and Westheimer (1965) who found previously separated children highly fearful of persons they had seen months before during separation. It is possible that day-care children may react to a stranger's presence in an unfamiliar environment as a cue that separation from the mother is about to take place; or there may be a more general relationship between the anxiety vs. security that a child experiences in his primary attachment relationship and the anxiety vs. security he demonstrates in dealing with unfamiliar individuals.

The results of the present study are at variance with those of Caldwell, Wright, Honig, and Tannenbaum (1970) who found no differences between day-care and home-reared infants on several behavioral measures purporting to relate to attachment. There are a number of factors which may account for this discrepancy. First, the staff of Caldwell's center may have provided care so highly individualized that the relationship with the substitute caregiver compensated for adverse reactions to separation from the mother. Second, children accustomed to group care from infancy (as Caldwell *et al.'s* sample was) may not experience the same overt disruption of the relationship with the mother as do children shifted from home care to day care at age

2 or 3. Third, Caldwell and her associates failed to distinguish between those who entered day care relatively early and relatively late. Had interactions between age and rearing group not been examined in the present study, no differences between day-care and home-reared children would have been found on manipulation of toys, search behavior, contact with the mother, or seeking of proximity.

For example, Caldwell *et al.* compared groups on strength of attachment, measured by the intensity of seeking proximity to the mother. Since the younger day-care children in the present study sought relatively little proximity whereas the older children sought much proximity, and since the opposite was true in the home-reared groups, day-care and home-reared children would have appeared equally "intensely" attached, if age differences had not been taken into account. On the other hand, the present study highlights resistant and avoidant behaviors as indicative of qualitative disturbances in attachment relationships. Absence of proximity seeking in reunion coupled with proximity avoiding is interpreted to reflect a reaction against ambivalence and anxiety rather than weak attachment. Hence, a failure on Caldwell *et al.*'s part to attend to the relationship between proximity seeking and negative behaviors and to focus chiefly on strength of proximity seeking may have obscured the effects so conspicuous in the present study.

It may be asked to what extent the results of this study can be attributed to separation rather than to differences which existed between day-care and home-reared groups prior to the day-care experience. The strange-situation procedure has been used previously to highlight differences between home-reared infants who had experienced relatively harmonious relationships with a sensitive mother and those who had experienced disturbed relationships with an insensitive mother. In the case of the present day-care group, there is no evidence that their mothers were any less sensitive or responsive to their children, when at home, than mothers of home-reared children. However, there is some evidence that the quality of the mother's personality (and hence presumably her mothering practices) can influence the intensity and duration of any adverse effects of substitute care (Moore, 1964, 1969). Although the families of the day-care children fell well within the normal range, it is possible that they differed from families of home-reared children on more subtle dimensions, which may have interacted with the experience of day care to create disturbances in attachment.

Hence, further research should attempt to elucidate the relationship between the child's prior experiences and his reaction to day care. It may be that prior disturbed mother-child interaction, more general family instability, or previous experiences of separation, may exacerbate a child's reactions to daily separations. It is also possible that a close relationship with a responsible adult in a center may compensate greatly for separation from the mother but if this substitute relationship is of such importance, then it becomes critical that children experience stability in their caregivers. In view of the present high turnover of day-care staff, this issue deserves immediate attention as does the issue of whether alternative methods of care, such as family day care or part-time group care are more suited to young children's needs than full-time group care. Whether or not research establishes immediate adverse effects, longitudinal studies of day-care children into adolescence are necessary to show that there are no "sleeper" effects. It is essential that research be designed to deal with day care as a separation experience as well as a multiple-mothering experience, and in this, the classical separation literature can serve as a guide to variables on which day-care and home-reared groups may be compared. It is not sufficient to compare groups on "strength" of attachment measures. Such measures may show that a child is attached to his mother, but they do not deal with the issue of whether day care can affect the security vs. anxiety he experiences in this primary relationship.

REFERENCES

Ainsworth, M. D. S. Anxious attachment and defensive reactions in a strange situation and their relationship to behavior at home. Paper presented at the biennial meeting of the Society for Research in Child Development, Philadelphia, March, 1973.

Ainsworth, M. D. S., & Wittig, B. A. Attachment and exploratory behavior of one-year-olds in a strange situation. In B. M. Foss (Ed.), *Determinants of infant behaviour IV.* London: Methuen, 1969, 111–136.

Ainsworth, M. D. S., and Bell, S. M. V. Attachment, exploration, and separation: Illustrated by the behavior of one-year-olds in a strange situation. *Child Development,* 1970, *41,* 49–67.

Ainsworth, M. D. S., Bell, S. M., & Stayton, D. Individual differences in strange-situation behavior of one-year-olds. In H. R. Schaffer (Ed.), *The origins of human social relations.* London: Academic Press, 1971.

Bowlby, J. *Attachment and loss.* Vol. 1. *Attachment.* London: Hogarth, 1969. (New York: Basic Books.)

Bowlby, J. *Attachment and loss.* Vol. 2. *Separation.* London: Hogarth, 1973.

Caldwell, B. M., Wright, D. M., Honig, A. S., & Tannenbaum, J. Infant day care and attachment. *American Journal of Orthopsychiatry,* 1970, *40,* 397–412.

Heinicke, C. M., & Westheimer, I. *Brief separations.* New York: International Universities Press, 1965.

Hogan, R. Development of an empathy scale. *Journal of Consulting and Clinical Psychology,* 1969, *33,* No. 5, 307–316.

Maccoby, D., & Feldman, S. Mother-attachment and stranger reactions. *Monographs of the Society for Research in Child Development,* 1972, *37,* 146.

Marvin, R. Attachment-, exploratory-, and communicative-behavior of two, three, and four-year-old children. Unpublished doctoral dissertation, University of Chicago, 1972.

Moore, T. Children of full-time and part-time mothers. *International Journal of Social Psychiatry,* 1964, *2,* 1–10.

Moore, T. Stress in normal childhood. *Human Relations,* 1969, *22,* 235–250.

Robertson, J., and Robertson, J. *Young children in brief separations*. New York: Quadrangle Books, 1971.

Robertson, J., & Bowlby, J. Responses of young children to separation from their mothers. *Courrier: Centre International d L'Enfrance,* 1952, 131–142.

Stayton, D. J., & Ainsworth, M. D. S. Individual differences in infant responses to brief, everyday separations as related to other infant and maternal behaviors. *Developmental Psychology,* in press.

Tizard, J., & Tizard, B. The social development of two-year-old children in residential nurseries. In H. R. Schaffer (Ed.), *The origins of human social relations*. London: Academic Press, 1971.

Yarrow, L. J. Maternal deprivation: Toward an empirical and conceptual evaluation. *Psychological Bulletin,* 1961, *58,* 459–496.

4.6

Social Class Differences in Maternal Teaching Strategies and Speech Patterns

Helen L. Bee
Lawrence F. Van Egeren
Ann Pytkowicz Streissguth
Barry A. Nyman
Maxine S. Leckie

Many studies of children and parents are based on the assumption that parents, particularly mothers, mediate between the child and the outer world, and in so doing transfer to the child the benefits and limitations of their own personalities, conflicts, and cognitive and emotional resources. While most research within this framework has dealt with personality development, there is recent evidence that the quality of mother-child interactions influences the child's cognitive development as well (cf. Bee, 1967; Bing, 1963; Witkin, Dyk, Faterson, Goodenough, & Karp, 1962). Bing (1963) found differential patterns of children's cognitive ability related to maternal behavior in a structured interaction situation and to mothers' reports of child rearing practices, while Bee (1967) demonstrated a relationship between a child's susceptibility to distraction and certain features of the parent's interactions with him.

Reprinted from *Developmental Psychology,* 1969, *1,* No. 6, 726–734. Copyright © 1969 by the American Psychological Association and reproduced by permission.

Distinctive mother-child relationships have also been used recently to account for social class differences in children's cognitive abilities. Hess (1968), for example, contented that children from disadvantaged homes are not *un*socialized when they reach school, but are socialized in a way that fosters substandard learning. Hess and Shipman (1965, 1967, 1968) proposed that two of the major dimensions of social class differences related to children's learning are the maternal speech and the maternal teaching strategies.

In comparing teaching strategies of middle and lower class black mothers with their 4-year-old children, Hess and Shipman (1965) found that middle class mothers used more direct and efficient teaching strategies than lower class mothers. The quality of the mother's teaching strategy was in turn related to the level of the child's cognitive functioning. In fact, the maternal teaching behavior was as good a predictor of the child's cognitive behavior as IQ measures.

The importance of maternal speech was first emphasized by Bernstein (1961). He postulated the presence of two "linguistic modes" used for communication and organization of experience. Lower class parents, he suggested, typically use a "public" language mode, characterized by a very rigid and restricted grammatical usage. Middle class parents typically use a "formal mode," in which language is used more flexibly, exploiting its structural possibilities for richer and more varied communication. The existence of such social class differences in language modes was later demonstrated by Bernstein (1962a, 1962b), and by Hess and Shipman (1965, 1967, 1968), who found that middle class parents used more complex syntax, longer sentences, more qualifying (discriminating) modifiers, and fewer personal pronouns. Hess and Shipman also found a connection between the linguistic mode used by the mother and the child's level of cognitive functioning.

The present study was designed to provide a general replication of earlier findings on social class differences in maternal language behavior and teaching strategies, and to explore further the dimensions of mother-child interactions that may be associated with the child's cognitive development. To do so, mother-child interactions were observed in both structured and unstructured settings and the mother's behavior language was studied in an interview.

The research reported is part of a larger project in which social class differences in both mother-child interaction and children's cognitive functioning were studied as a starting point for an evaluation of a Head Start program. The present report deals only with the social class differences in mother-child interactions and maternal language. Subsequent publications will report on social class differences in children's cognitive functioning, patterns of mother-child interaction, and the impact of Head Start experience.

METHOD

Subjects

The subjects were 114 children (ages 4–0 to 5–5) and their mothers, 76 lower social class families (37 boys and 39 girls), and 38 middle class families (22 boys and 14 girls).

Half of the lower class sample eventually entered a Head Start program, and were selected from the list of applicants at six Head Start centers. The remaining 38 lower class families were obtained through a variety of sources: (a) families who had applied to Head Start but were ineligible either because they lived outside the areas serviced by the local program, or because their income was somewhat over the Office of Economic Opportunity poverty guidelines, and (b) families living in public housing projects who had 4-year-olds eligible for Head Start but who had not applied.

The middle class group consisted of University of Washington staff and student families. Thirty-eight volunteer families with children of the appropriate age were located by means of a letter sent to all graduate students at the Universtiy.

A comparison of the two social class groups on a number of demographic variables appears in Table 1. The two groups differed in the ways that are typically used to define social class. Middle class families had significantly higher income, the mothers were better educated, and there were fewer children. In addition, fathers were present in all but two of the middle class homes, but in only 34 of 76 lower class homes.

Two features of the middle class sample require some special comment. First, middle class families were intentionally selected whose educational level and academic achievement motivation was higher than for the typical middle class family. This particular comparison group was chosen because we were interested in familial variables related to (and predictive of) school success in children, and wished to maximize the difference in expected school success. Second, the middle class sample was entirely white, while the lower class sample was two-thirds black. This was a direct and unavoidable result of the other selection criteria, since approximately two-thirds of the local Head Start children are black, and almost 100 percent of the University graduate students are white. The reader should bear in mind that when we refer to the "middle class" sample, we refer to "highly educated white middle class" families—the families whose children typically excel in school.

TABLE 1. COMPARISON OF LOWER CLASS AND MIDDLE CLASS GROUPS ON DEMOGRAPHIC VARIABLES

VARIABLE	LOWER CLASS[a] $\bar{X}$	MIDDLE CLASS[b] $\bar{X}$	t
Family income	$4,594	$6,852	4.97**
Mother's education in years	11.46	14.89	8.01**
Number siblings or other children in home	3.44	2.55	2.75*
Number adults in home	1.63	2.00	3.33*
Child's age in months	53.238	53.895	<1.00

[a] $N = 76$.
[b] $N = 38$.
*$p < .01$.
**$p < .001$.

Procedures and Scores Derived

Each mother and child was seen in a four-part session lasting approximately 1 1/2 hours. The pair was first brought into the "waiting room" where their interaction was observed and recorded (by one of two observers) for 10 minutes. The mother was then interviewed while the child was given a series of 13 brief tests of cognitive and motivational behavior. The mother and child were then reunited for a series of problem-solving interactions, administered by one of two experimenters, in which the mother's teaching strategies were observed and recorded. Only the interactional and interview behavior are presented in this article; the details of the individual tests given to the children are described elsewhere (Bee, Nyman, Pytkowitz, Sarason, & Van Egeren, 1968).

Waiting room. The 12 X 13 foot waiting room was furnished with a couch, armchair, and magazine table in one corner, with toys (paper and crayons, mailbox, jack-in-the-box, trucks and cars, toy piano, knock-out bench, and small rubber animals and people) scattered throughout the room on small tables and on the floor. The floor of the room was marked into equal quadrants so that the child's movement could be recorded. An observer watching through a one-way mirror recorded mother and child verbalizations in coded categories. Every 15 seconds, the observer also scored the mother's level of attention to her child in one of four categories and recorded the child's movement about the room and from one toy to another. The observation was terminated after 10 minutes and the observer, using notes and a tape recording of the interaction, made final scorings in each category.

A total of 20 scores were derived from the waiting room situation. Verbal responses by the mother were scored in one of seven categories, as below. The percentage of agreement for each category, based on 12 families scored by two independent observers, is given in parentheses.

1. Control: An attempt by the mother to stop or modify the child's activity in preemptory fashion. (85 percent)
2. Suggestion: A helpful statement soliciting a change or modification of the child's activity. (85 percent)
3. Information: A statement directed at informing or giving facts. (83 percent)
4. Question: A statement directed at asking, interrogating, or inquiring. (88 percent)
5. Approval: A statement giving a favorable opinion of the child's activity or product. (85 percent)
6. Ignoring: Lack of response when the child made a specific bid for help or attention. (91 percent)
7. Disapproval: A statement giving an unfavorable opinion of the child's activity or product. (85 percent)

The child's verbalizations and movements were scored in one of nine categories, as the following.

8. General seeking: A general bid for help, assistance, or attention. (89 percent)
9. Question: A request for specific information. (84 percent)
10. Demand: A statement from the child demanding an action from the mother. (88 percent)
11. Information: A statement giving information gratuitously. (85 percent)
12. Rejection: A rejection of the mother's control, suggestion, or question statement. (100 percent)
13. Acceptance: Acceptance of a control, suggestion, or question statement from the mother. (78 percent)
14. Ignoring: No response to a control, suggestion, or question from the mother. (85 percent)
15. Toy shifts: Movement from one toy to another.
16. Space shifts: Movement from one quadrant of the room to another.

The mother was also scored, every 15 seconds, in one of the following four categories, according to her level of attention to the child.

17. Level 0, no attention: Mother did not look up or speak to the child. (80 percent)
18. Level 1, occasional but brief attention: Mother glanced at, but did not speak to the child. (65 percent)
19. Level 2, moderate attention: Mother looked at the child for a substantial portion of the period, or spoke occasionally. (80 percent)
20. Full attention: Mother looked at the child continuously, and may have spoken in addition. (77 percent)

Raw scores (category frequencies) were converted to rate-per-minute scores for each category.

The interrater agreement for the verbalization and attention categories, as shown above, ranged from 65 to 100 percent with only three categories falling below 80 percent. No reliability estimates were obtained for space or toy shifts.

Problem solving. Mother and child were brought together in a separate room for the problem-solving interaction. Two problems, a "toy-rearrangement" task and a "house-building" task, were administered, but because the toy-rearrangement task proved to be too easy for many of the children, only the house-building task was scored and analyzed. For the house-building task the mother and child were seated on one side of a table with the experimenter on the other side. The experimenter showed the child a toy house constructed out of 17 blocks, with seven different shapes and four colors. The child was given an identical 17-block set and instructed to build a house that was just the same as the model. The mother was then told: "You can give as much or as little help as you like, whatever you think will help—to do his best." Mother and child were then allowed to work on the house until the task was completed. If no progress was being made and the mother was not making any effort to encourage the child to continue, the session was terminated at 10 minutes.

Verbal interactions were recorded on tape and transcribed, with all scoring of verbalizations by mother and child done from the typed transcripts. Nonverbal intrusive behavior by the mother was recorded by the experimenter at the time of the interaction.

Each of the mother's verbalizations was scored in 1 of 11 content categories, but because many categories of verbalization did not occur frequently enough for comparison, or because they were not task relevant, the analysis presented here relates to only 4 verbal categories, and 1 nonverbal category. As before, the percentage of agreement, based on 92 families scored by two independent raters, is given in parentheses.

1. Nonquestion suggestion: A statement indicating what the mother wants the child to do next (e.g., "Find a yellow one like this."). (89 percent)
2. Question suggestion: Suggestion, as above, but stated in interrogative form (e. g., "Where does this yellow one go?"). (91 percent)
3. Positive feedback: An expression of approval about what the child had already done, or general approval of the child (e. g., "Good."). (90 percent)
4. Negative feedback: An expression of disapproval about what the child had already done, or general disapproval of the child. (e.g., "That's not too good."). (81 percent)
5. Nonverbal intrusion: Placement of a block or other physical problem solving such as moving the model, or handing the child a block to use.

All suggestions from the mother, whether they were stated in interrogative form or not, were also scored on a 3-point scale of specificity:

6. Level 1. Orienting suggestions, focusing strategies, suggestions that restrict the attention to some major segment of the task (e.g., "Look at the lady's house." "Let's start on the front."). (85 percent)
7. Level 2: Suggestions about specific pieces, or specific locations on the house, but not both (e.g., "Find a yellow one like this.")' (73 percent)

8. Level 3: Solutions. Suggestions indicating both which piece was to be used and where it was to be placed (e.g., "Put that one over here."). (75 percent)

Of the seven child-verbalization categories, those that occurred with sufficient frequency to be analyzed were:

9. Acceptance: A verbal acceptance of a suggestion from the mother. (71 percent)
10. Rejection: A verbal rejection of a suggestion from the mother. (52 percent)
11. Dependency bids: A verbal bid for help, attention, or approval. (84 percent)

The responses in each category were summed for each mother and child. Since the amount of time spent on the task was variable, raw scores were converted to rate-per-minute scores.

All protocols were scored from the transcripts by both experimenters, disagreements were discussed, and a common score obtained. Percentage of agreement, as reported above, ranged from 73 to 91 percent for the maternal behavior categories, and from 52 to 84 percent for the child-behavior categories. No reliability estimate is available for nonverbal intrusions since they were scored only by the experimenter who administered the tests.

Interview. The 45-minute interview with the mother included a biographical data sheet, 26 standard open-ended questions, and 4 role-playing questions. The analysis of syntactical features of the mothers' speech was based on the first 5 open-ended questions, and only they will be of concern here. These questions asked the mother to describe her child, to indicate the "best" thing about him, the things about him that were of most concern to her; what was the most important thing she thought she could give to or do for her child; and what she tried to teach him.

The analysis of the mother's speech, based on transcriptions of the interview, yielded five scores:

1. Quantity of speech: total number of words spoken.
2. Mean sentence length: total number of words divided by the total number of complete sentences.
3. Adjective/verb quotient: total number of adjectives divided by the total number of verbs.
4. Syntactic complexity: number of subordinate clauses divided by the number of sentences.
5. Percentage of personal pronouns: number of personal pronouns divided by the total number of words.

Since scoring of the speech sample involved simple counting procedures, no reliability estimates were calculated.

RESULTS

Waiting Room

In comparison to lower class mothers, middle class mothers were less controlling, less disapproving, and gave more information to their children in the waiting room. Middle class mothers also gave their children more attention; they were scored more frequently at Attention Level 2, and less frequently at Attention Level 1. Middle class children, in comparison to lower class children, were lower in acceptance of controls and questions, higher in spontaneous information statements, and lower on both toy and space shifts.

Problem Solving

Comparisons of the two groups indicated first that the middle class mothers and children spent significantly more time on the house-building task than did the lower class mothers and children. Second, the middle class mothers' suggestions to their children were less specific than the suggestions given by lower class mothers, and in comparison to lower class mothers, middle class mothers gave more suggestions in the form of questions. Finally, the middle class mothers more often told their children what they were doing correctly rather than what they were doing wrong. Middle class children did not differ from their lower class peers in their reactions to or requests for help.

Interview

Significant social class differences were obtained on all five measures of maternal speech. Middle class mothers used more words, longer sentences, greater syntactic complexity, a high adjective-verb quotient, and a lower percentage of personal pronouns.

Differences in maternal behavior associated with race of mother and sex of child.

Since the lower class group included both blacks and whites, while the middle class group was entirely white, the possibility exists that race rather than social class accounts for the differences in behavior described above. In addition, there were differing numbers of boys and girls in the various racial and social class groups. To assess both effects, two-way analyses of variance were performed on each variable described above, with sex of child and a combination of racial and social class groups as the two between-subjects variables. Lower class blacks were compared with lower class whites and middle class whites.

Main effects on the race-social comparison were obtained for 12 variables, but follow-up analyses showed that the differences were clearly racial in only four instances. That is, in only four cases were the two white groups equivalent, and both significantly different from the lower class black group. Black mothers were significantly lower than both white groups on rate of positive feedback, question suggestions, and total interaction in the problem-solving session. Black children were significantly lower on information statements in the waiting-room situation. In the case of total interaction in the problem-solving session, the differences are somewhat misleading, since there were also differences between the groups in the total time spent on the problem. When the mean *rate* of interaction was determined for each group, the white lower class group showed the highest rate (16.1 statements per minute), with the lower class black group the lowest (12.1 statements per minute).

In addition to those variables on which clear racial differences were obtained, there were four on which all groups differed from each other. On three of these (mother's suggestions at Specificity Level 1, mother's physical intrusiveness, and child's bids for help during problem solving) the differences were such that the lower class black group was lowest, followed in order by the lower class white and the middle class white groups. On one variable (mother's rate of negative feedback), all groups differed, but in this instance it was the lower class white group that showed the highest rate of negative feedback, followed in turn by the lower class black and middle class white groups. On one additional variable (mother's suggestions at Specificity Level 2) lower class white mothers differed from both remaining groups.

In no instance was a main effect of sex of child obtained. However, sex of child interacted with the racial-social class breakdown on 14 variables. The pattern of interaction varied greatly from one variable to another, and there was no systematic effect to be noted. In some instances the social class or racial differences were more marked for boys, in some instances for girls, with neither the mother-child interaction situation nor the type of variable differentiating the two types of pattern.

DISCUSSION

The data presented here provide a clear and consistent portrait of social class differences in maternal behavior. Middle class mothers, regardless of the situation, used more instruction, less physical intrusion, less negative feedback, and were generally more in tune with the child's individual needs and qualities. Their speech patterns were also notably more complex than those of the lower class mothers. Several specific features of the results deserve separate comment.

First, it is clear from the analysis of maternal speech that there were social class differences in linguistic codes of the type described by Bernstein (1961, 1962a, 1962b) for a British sample and by Hess and Shipman (1965, 1967, 1968) for a Midwest black sample. The speech of middle class mothers, in the present study, was similar on all five language measures to what Bernstein has referred to as the "formal" or "elaborated" mode. The fact that these differences were related to social class rather than race, taken together with previous findings by Hess and Shipman and by Bernstein, suggests that social class differences in linguistic style are stable and pervasive.

The second major portion of the results concerns the maternal teaching strategies in the problem-solving setting. The strategy used by many middle class mothers on the house-building task seems to be optimal in a number of respects. The middle class mother tended to allow her child to work at his own pace, offered many general structuring suggestions on how to search for a solution to the problem, and told the child what he was doing that was correct. She allowed the child to take his time and seldom worked on the house herself. Such a procedure seemed to encourage the child to explore the problem on his own and did not focus attention on his failures. The general structure offered by the mother may help the child to acquire learning sets (strategies) that will generalize to future problem-solving situations. In contrast, the lower class mother as a rule did not behave in ways that would encourage the child to attend to the basic features of the problem. Her suggestions were highly specific, did not emphasize basic problem-solving strategies, and seldom required reply from the child. Indeed, she often deprived the child of the opportunity to solve the problem on his own by her nonverbal intrusions into the problem-solving activity. In the use of such a strategy, there is very little demand made on the child's capacities to respond, and it is difficult to imagine that the child learns much from such an interaction that would generalize to other problem-solving settings.

This analysis of the problem-solving interaction also suggests the importance of certain new types of dependent variables. In particular, the division of the form of suggestions into questions and nonquestions appears to be a potentially fruitful approach. Certainly the implications for the child of a predominantly interrogative style, as opposed to an imperative style, are substantial, since questions provoke thought and verbal replies, while imperative statements generally demand only a specific action.

The third major source of data in the present study was the unstructured waiting-room situation. During the 10-minute wait, the interactions of lower class mothers and their children were more negative and restrictive than the interactions of middle class mothers and children. Lower class mothers were less attentive and made more controlling and disapproving statements to the child. This greater control and disapproval of lower class mothers is consistent with findings from previous studies of social class differences in child rearing practices, summarized by Bronfenbrenner (1958). In addition, the negative-restrictive pattern in the waiting room also bears some similarity to behavior in the problem-solving setting, where lower class mothers were more critical and controlling and appeared to be less sensitive to the child's rhythm of activity.

Thus far we have discussed the differences in maternal behavior as though they represent relatively enduring aspects of the different environments surrounding the middle and lower class child. This general interpretation rests on two important assumptions. The first is that the behavior of the mothers in the laboratory is not atypical of their interaction with their children at home. The second is that the children, by their own behavior, did not place radically different response demands on the two groups of mothers.

Concerning the first assumption, it was obvious to the interviewers and observers that to some extent the mothers and children were on their "good" behavior in the laboratory. And yet we were also impressed with the spontaneity, cooperativeness, and relaxed and frank attitude of most mothers in both groups. We could detect no obvious systematic differences between the two groups of mothers in situational anxiety or genuine involvement in the tasks set for them.

Concerning the second assumption, the two groups of children differed little in the problem-solving situation. The lower class child's greater hyperactivity (space shifts and toy shifts) in the waiting room may have made some contribution to the lower class mother's high rate of controlling and disapproving statements there, but the lower class mother's tendency toward control in the problem-solving setting, where the children differed little, suggests that the greater tendency toward control of the lower class mother is not simply a response to a more-difficult-to-manage child.

Finally, although a discussion of the social class differences in the test performance of the children in our sample will be presented in a later paper, a further word should be said about the implications of the social class differences in maternal behavior obtained here. Our findings, as those of Hess and Shipman, provide evidence of an impoverished language environment and ineffectual teaching strategies experienced by the lower class child. Such a child may learn a good deal about what *not* to do, or at least about global rules of conduct, but he may not be well equipped with the language tools or learning sets required for a systematic approach to the analysis of problems. He has not, judging from our results, been encouraged to learn general techniques of problem solving, and he has not been exposed to the highly differentiated language structure that is most suitable for verbally mediated analysis of the environment. If the mother's role as a teacher is as important for the child's cognitive functioning as it would appear to be, then it is not surprising that there are large social class differences in the measured cognitive functioning of children, and in their ultimate school performance.

REFERENCES

Bee, H. L. Parent-child interaction and distractibility in 9-year-old children. *Merrill-Palmer Quarterly,* 1967, *13*, 175–190.

Bee, H. L., Nyman, B. A., Pytkowicz, A. R., Sarason, I. G., & Van Egeren, L. A study of cognitive and motivational variables in lower and middle class preschool children: An approach to the evaluation of the impact of Head Start, Volume 1. University of Washington Social Change Evaluation Project, Contract 1375, Office of Economic Opportunity, 1968.

Bernstein, B. Social class and linguistic development: A theory of social learning. In A. H. Halsey, J. Floud, & C. A. Anderson (Eds.), *Education, economy, and society.* New York: Free Press, 1961.

Bernstein, B. Linguistic codes, hesitation phenomena, and intelligence. *Language and Speech,* 1962, *5,* 31–46. (a)

Bernstein, B. Social class, linguistic codes, and grammatical elements. *Language and Speech,* 1962, *5,* 221–240. (b)

Bing, E. Effect of child rearing practices on development of differential cognitive abilities. *Child Development,* 1963, *34,* 631–648.

Bronfenbrenner, U. Socialization and social class through time and space. In E. E. Maccoby, T. M. Newcomb, & E. L. Hartley (Eds.), *Readings in social psychology.* (3rd ed.) New York: Holt, 1958.

Hess, R. D. Early education as socialization. In. R. D. Hess & R. M. Bear (Eds.), *Early education.* Chicago: Aldine, 1968.

Hess, R. D., & Shipman, V. Early experience and the socialization of cognitive modes in children. *Child Development,* 1965, *34, 869–886.*

Hess, R. D., & Shipman, V. Cognitive elements in maternal behavior. In J. P. Hill (Ed.), *Minnesota symposium on child psychology.* Vol. 1. Minneapolis: University of Minnesota Press, 1967.

Hess, R. D., & Shipman, V. Maternal influences upon early learning: The cognitive environments of urban pre-school children. In R. D. Hess & R. M. Bear (Eds.), *Early education.* Chicago: Aldine, 1968.

Witkin, H. A., Dyk, R. B., Faterson, H. F., Goodenough, D. R., & Karp, S. A. *Psychological differentiation.* New York: Wiley, 1962.

4.7

An Analysis of the Concept
of Cultural Deprivation

Steven R. Tulkin

The term "cultural deprivation" is commonly used to summarize the presumed reasons why lower-class and minority group children show deficits in the development of "intellectual skills." However, there are serious limitations to the validity of the concept of cultural deprivation, and psychologists and educators should reevaluate their roles in programs which attempt to "enrich" the lives of "deprived" populations. The cultural deprivation concept is limited in that (*a*) it does not advance psychology as a science because it does not focus attention on how specific experiences affect developmental processes; (*b*) it ignores cultural relativism; and (*c*) it neglects political realities, which are likely to be primarily responsible for many of the traits observed in deprived populations. The limitations described under (*a*) are discussed only briefly, since they are likely to be most familiar to social scientists.

THE IMPORTANCE OF PSYCHOLOGICAL PROCESSES

The concept of cultural deprivation has often made it easy for social scientists to overlook the importance of the *processes* by which environmental experiences influence development. Jessor and Richardson (1968) stated:

> To speak, for example, of maternal deprivation as an explanation is to attempt to account for certain characteristics of infant develop-ment by the absence of the mother rather than by the presence of some specifiable set of environmental conditions. While mother ab-sence may be a useful and convenient way to summarize or symbol-ize the conditions which will likely be present, the important point is that development is likely to be invariant with or related to the condi-tions which are present, not with those which are absent [p. 3].

Research concluding that social class or racial differences are found on particu-lar developmental or intellectual tasks does not further understanding of develop-ment, unless we examine the actual processes that contributed to the differences. Wolf (1964) urged researchers to distinguish between status variables (class, race, etc.) and process variables (the actual *experiences* of children which contribute to their cognitive growth). He rated parents on 13 process variables descriptive of interactions between parent and child. The items fell under the headings of parental press for academic achievement and language development, as well as provision for general learning. He found a correlation of .76 between these process variables and IQ measures of fifth-grade students. Similarly, Davé (1963) obtained a multiple correlation of .80 between process variables and school achievement. These are substantially higher than the correlations of .40 to .50 which are typically reported between socioeconomic status and measures of intelligence or school achievement.

NEED FOR CULTURAL RELATIVISM

Many authors who discuss deprived populations appear to disregard cultural relativism, despite the attempts—predominantly from anthropologists—to emphasize the importance of cultural relativism in understanding minority subcultures in the United States. Writers have enumerated certain characteristics of black American culture, for example, which can be traced to the cultural patterns of its African origin (Herskovits, 1958). Other authors have argued that particular minority groups possess cultures of their own, which have "developed out of coping with a difficult environment" here in the United States (Riessman, 1962). Despite the recognition of the need for relativism, middle class Americans, including professionals, have difficulty remaining relativistic with regard to minority cultures. Gans (1962) discussed the difficulties encountered by middle class "missionaries" in understanding the Italian-American subculture he studied in Boston's West End. He observed that West End parents made frequent use of verbal and physical punishment, and commented that "to a middle class observer, the parents' treatment often seems extremely strict, and sometimes brutal." Gans, however, felt that

> the torrents of threat and cajolery neither impinge on the feelings of parental affection, nor are meant as signs of rejection. As one mother explained to her child, "We hit you because we love you." People believe that discipline is needed constantly to keep the child in line with and respectful of adult rules, and without it he would run amok [pp. 59–60].

Another example of a subcultural pattern which is foreign to middle class observers was reported by Lehmer (1969). She noted that Navajo children would not compete for good grades in school, and explained that Navajo customs emphasized cooperation, not competition: "In Navajo tradition, a person who stands out at the expense of his brother may be considered a 'witch' [p. D-4]." Does this low need for achievement reflect cultural deprivation or cultural difference?

Why is it so difficult for outsiders to acknowledge subcultural behavior patterns? Gans (1962) believed that the difficulty stemmed from the observers' missionary outlook:

> [They] had to believe that the West Enders' refusal to follow object-oriented middle class ways was pathological, resulting from deprivations imposed on them by living in the West End. They could not admit that the West Enders acted as they did because they lived within a social structure and culture of their own [pp. 151–152].

In fact, Gans had earlier stated that one of the tenets of West End Life was a rejection of "middle-class forms of status and culture." In other words, it was culturally valued to be culturally deprived.

The difficulty of achieving a relativistic approach to the study of subcultures has made research difficult, because minority group children are constantly evaluated by middle class standards. One issue of current interest to psychologists is whether black ghetto residents are less able to communicate verbally, or are simply less proficient in "standard English." It is claimed by many researchers that lower class subjects are verbally deficient, and the deficits are "not entirely attributable to implicit 'middle class' orientations [Krauss & Rotter, 1968]." Other experts have argued that black English is a fully formed linguistic system in its own right, with its own grammatical rules and unique history (Baratz & Shuy, 1969; Labov, 1967; Stewart, 1967, 1969a). These critics have stated that black language is "different from standard American English, but no less complex, communicative, rich, or sophisticated [Sroufe, 1970]"; and argued that research reporting language "deficits" among black children reflects only the middle class orientation of the research instruments and procedures. Supporting this argument Birren and Hess (1968) concluded that

> studies of peer groups in spontaneous interaction in Northern ghetto areas show that there is a rich verbal culture in constant use. Negro children in the vernacular culture cannot be considered "verbally deprived" if one observes them in a favorable environment—on the contrary, their daily life is a pattern of continual verbal stimulation, contest, and imitation [p. 137].

Similarly, Chandler and Erickson (1968) observed *naturally occurring* group interaction and reported data which disputed the findings of Bernstein (1960, 1961) and others that middle class children more commonly used "elaborated" linguistic codes while lower classes typically spoke with "restricted" codes. Chandler and Erickson found that the use of restricted or elaborated linguistic codes was not as closely related to the social class of speakers as had been suggested by other researchers.

> Both inner-city and suburban groups . . . were found to shift back and forth between use of relatively "restricted" linguistic codes and relatively "elaborated" codes. These shifts were closely related to apparent changes in the degree of shared context between group

> members. Examples of extremely abstract and sophisticated inquiry among inner-city Negro young people were found in which a highly "restricted" linguistic code was employed [p. 2].

If black English and standard English are simply different languages, one cannot be seen as more deficient than the other (Sroufe, 1970). Most schools, however, demand that students use standard English, and frequently black children who have been classified by their schools as "slow learners" are able to read passages of black English with amazing speed and accuracy (Stewart, 1969b). Similarly, Foster (1969) found that the introduction of nonstandard English dialect increased the ability of tenth grade disadvantaged students "to comprehend, to recall, and to be fluent and flexible in providing titles for verbal materials." Black students ($N = 90$) also scored higher than white students ($N = 400$) on Foster's (1970) Jive Analogy Test (H. L. Foster, personal communication, 1971).

This argument does not imply that the teaching of standard English is an infringement of the rights of minority cultures. It is necessary that students learn standard English, but there is a difference between emphasizing the development of positive skills which may facilitate a successful adaptation to a particular majority culture versus devaluating a group of people who may not emphasize the development of these particular skills. As Baratz and Baratz (1970) suggested, research should be undertaken to discover the *different* but not pathological forms of minority group behavior. "Then and only then can programs be created that utilize the child's differences as a means of helping him acculturate to the mainstream while maintaining his individual identity and cultural heritage [p. 47]".

An Objective Look at the Middle Class

The cultural bias of middle class America has not only hindered an appreciation of the attributes of minority cultures, but it has also prevented an objective evaluation of middle class culture. Psychologists do not write about the "deficiencies" of the middle class, but the cultural relativist might find a great deal to write about. Coles (1968) suggested that it may be appropriate to label middle class children deprived, because

> they're so nervous and worried about everything they say—what it will mean, or what it will cost them, or how it will be interpreted. That's what they've learned at home, and that's why a lot of them are tense kinds, and, even worse, stale kids with frowns on their faces at ages 6 or 7 [p. 277].

Similarly, Kagan (1968) hypothesized that middle class children were more anxious about failing than lower class children. He noted that lower class children may be less anxious about making a mistake and, therefore, more likely to answer questions and make decisions "impulsively." Most people would agree that an impulsive style could be a hindrance to the development of abstract analytical thinking, but researchers have paid little attention to the possible virtues of an impulsive (or "spontaneous," "nonanalytical") style, and have not considered the consequences of attempting to discourage this style. Maccoby and Modiano (1966) spoke to this point in their discussion of differences among children in Mexico City, Boston, and a rural Mexican village. They noted that, people socialized into the modern industrialized world often lose the ability to experience. "They are," the authors suggested, "like people who see a painting immediately in terms of its style, period, and influences, but with no sense of its uniqueness [p. 268]." Maccoby and Modiano concluded by cautioning that

> as the city child grows older, he may end by exchanging a spontaneous, less alienated relationship to the world for a more sophisticated outlook which concentrates on using, exchanging, or cataloguing. What industrialized man gains in an increased ability to formulate, to reason, and to code the ever more numerous bits of complex information he acquires, he may lose in decreased sensitivity to people and events [p. 269].

But it is quite doubtful if psychologists would call him culturally deprived.

Relativism Toward Other Cultures

Psychologists frequently label American minority groups as culturally deprived, but they are less likely to make value judgments about other cultures. In fact, social scientists are reasonably tolerant of child rearing practices observed in other cultures which would be devaluated if they were found in a minority group in the United States. Rebelsky and Abeles (1969), for example, observed American and Dutch mothers with their 0–3-month-old infants. They found that a Dutch baby typically slept in a low closed bed with a canopy overhead. Dutch mothers kept the infant's room cool—"for health reasons"—necessitating infants being "tightly covered under blankets, often tied into the crib with strings from their sheets." Further, the authors reported comparisons showing that "American mothers looked at, held, fed, talked to, smiled at, patted, and showed more affection to their babies more often than did Dutch mothers." These findings, however, were not used to condemn Dutch mothers. The authors related the differences in parental behavior to cultural variations in the parents' conceptions of infancy. For example, they noted that

> Even if a [Dutch] parent sees a child awake and wanting to play or look around, ... he is not likely to respond to this wish or to the behavior which implies this wish because of fear of "spoiling" the baby (stated by 9 of the 11 mothers in Holland), or because of the belief that a baby in this age range should sleep and not play or stay awake [pp. 16–17].

Observations also revealed that Dutch infants had fewer toys with which to play. By 3 months of age, almost half of the Dutch babies still had no toys within sight or touch. The authors explained that Dutch mothers were concerned that "toys might keep the babies awake or overstimulate them." There were also cultural differences in the mothers' reactions to their infants crying.

> Crying meant a call for help to U.S. mothers; they often reported lactating when they heard the cry. In Holland, crying was considered a part of a baby's behavior, good for the lungs and not always something to stop. In addition, though a mother might hear the cry in Holland and interpret it as a hunger cry, she still would not respond if it was not time for the scheduled feeding [pp. 7–8].

Rebelsky and Abeles did not suggest that Dutch mothers were rejecting or depriving their infants. They did not argue that intervention was necessary to change the patterns of mother-infant interaction. They concluded, instead, that both United States and Dutch cultures "may be training very different kinds of people, yet with each culture wanting the ones they produce." Such data reported for a group of lower income American mothers might be followed by a call for a massive intervention program, or possibly the removal of the infants from their homes.

A similar cultural comparison was reported by Caudill and Weinstein (1966, 1969) who investigated maternal behavior in Japan and in the United States. The authors reported that American mothers talked more to their infants, while Japanese mothers more frequently lulled and rocked their infants. These differences were seen as reflecting different styles of mothering:

> The style of the American mother seems to be in the direction of stimulating her baby to respond . . . whereas the style of the Japanese mother seems to be more in the direction of soothing and quieting her baby [1966, p. 18].

In both cultures, the "style" of mothering was influenced by the prevailing conception of infancy. Caudill and Weinstein (1969) reported that in Japan

> The infant is seen more as a separate biological organism who from the beginning, in order to develop, needs to be drawn into increasingly interdependent relations with others. In America, the infant is seen more as a dependent biological organism who, in order to develop, needs to be made increasingly independent of others [p. 15].

American mothers, following their conception of infancy, pushed their infants to respond and to be active; Japanese mothers, also following their conception of infancy, attempted to foster reduced independent activity and greater reliance on others. As a part of this pattern, the Japanese tended to place less emphasis on clear verbal communication. Caudill and Weinstein reasoned that "such communication implies self-assertion and the separate identity and independence of the person" which would be contrary to the personality which Japanese mothers were attempting to build into their children. Thus, in Japan, as in Holland, mothers related to their infants in a manner consistent with their beliefs and values.

Caudill and Weinstein (1966) also reported data showing that according to American "standards," the Japanese infants might be considered "deficient." They engaged in less positive vocalization and spent less time with toys and other objects: "The Japanese infant," they said, "seems passive—he spends much more time simply lying awake in his crib or on a *zabuton* (a flat cushion) on the floor [p. 16]." The authors further reported that a study by Arai, Ishikawa, and Toshima (1958) found that—compared to American norms—Japanese infants showed a steady decline on tests of language and motor development from 4 to 36 months of age. Caudill and Weinstein, however, remained relativistic. They commented that although Arai, Ishikawa, and Toshima seem somewhat distressed that the "Japanese mothers were so bound up in the lives of their infants that they interfered with the development of their infants in ways which made it difficult to meet the American norms," Caudill and Weinstein (1969) did not share the Japanese authors' concern over the lack of matching the American norms: "We do not believe that the differences we find are necessarily indications of a better or a worse approach to human life, but rather that such differences are a part of an individual's adjustment to his culture [p. 41]." Again, it is doubtful if the same conclusion would have been reached had the data been collected from a minority subculture in the United States.

A final example of the need for cultural relativism involves a study of Ashkenazic and Sephardic Jews in Brooklyn (Gross, 1967). Both groups were solidly middle class, and lived only two blocks apart. Both had been long established in this country and spoke English in their homes. On entering school, however, the Ashkenazic children averaged 17 points higher on a standard IQ test, a disparity similar in magnitude to that often reported between children of white suburbs and black slums.

Gross pointed out that it is generally assumed that inferior performance in school necessarily reflects deprivation and lack of opportunity. He argued, on the contrary, that each culture has its own ideas of what is important—some emphasize one skill, some another. Despite their children's lower IQ scores the Sephardic mothers were not deprived, however one defines the term: "In many cases they had minks, maids, and country homes." The Sephardic mothers were all native born, high school graduates, and none worked. The children "were blessed with privilege, money, and comfort, but their level of academic readiness was similar to that of their underprivileged Israeli counterparts."

Gross explained that the difference was related to cultural tradition: The two communities represented different routes into the middle class—the Ashkenazim through success in school and the Sephardim through success in the marketplace. The author concluded that educational unpreparedness could be found among the "financially well-to-do" as well as among the lower classes, and suggested that this finding should be a "caution signal to social engineers." Gross questioned those who advocate changing lower class blacks to conform to the life styles and values of middle class whites, and suggested that there was an element of "white colonialism" in the attempt to "reshape the economically underprivileged in the image of the education-minded intellectually oriented academicians."

Gross's final point merits expansion, because intervention is becoming a big business in the United States today. The federal government is spending large amounts of money on intervention programs, and some social scientists fear that the interventionists will totally disregard subcultural systems in their attempts to "save" the "deprived" children.

> When we force people of another culture to make an adjustment to ours, by that much we are destroying the integrity of their personalities. When too many adjustments of this sort are required too fast, the personality disintegrates and the result is an alienated, dissociated individual who cannot feel really at home in either culture [Lehmer, 1969, p. D-4].

Why is it so common for researchers to remain relativistic in their discussions of socialization practices in other nations, while being intolerant of subcultural differences among lower income and minority groups in this country? One could propose that each nation socializes its children according to prevailing cultural values so that regardless of the fact that practices in other nations are different, children in each country develop the personalities and intellectual skills needed for success in their own particular social systems. This theory would argue that it is inappropriate to apply cultural relativism to subcultures because a person's success remains defined by the majority culture. Keller (1963), for example, argued that "cultural relativism ignores the fact that schools and industry are middle class in organization and outlook."

Cultural relativism and success in "schools and industry," however, are *not* mutually exclusive. It is possible to teach children the skills needed for articulation with the majority culture, while encouraging them to develop a pride in their own family or cultural heritage, and to utilize the particular skills which their own socialization has strengthened. A majority culture can, however, promote a narrow definition of success in order to ensure that the power of the society remain in the hands of a relatively select group within the society. Thus, by maintaining that any deviation from the white middle class norm represents cultural deprivation, the white middle class is guarding its position as *the* source of culture—and power—in this nation. Cultural deprivation, then, is not just a psychological or educational issue; it is also very much a political issue.

POLITICS AND CULTURAL DEPRIVATION

Subcultural influences may represent a legitimate explanation for some of the behavior observed in particular lower income or minority populations, but these influences should not be regarded as the sole determinant of life styles in these groups. Social scientists must also consider the way in which the majority culture, by its tolerance for social, political, and economic inequality, actually contributes to the development, in some subgroups, of the very characteristics which it considers "depriving." Responsibility, then, lies not with the subpopulations—for being "deprived"—but rather with the "total environmental structure that disenfranchises, alienates [and] disaffects [Hillson, 1970]." Fantini (1969) echoed this argument when he suggested that the "problem" of disadvantaged school children may not be rooted in the learner's "environmental and cultural deficiencies" but rather with the system—"the school and its educational process." He suggested the need for reorientation "from our present 'student-fault' to a stronger 'system-fault' position."

One of the most obvious system faults—and one that is quite relevant to child development—is inadequate medical care for the poor. Social scientists investigating cultural deprivation have paid insufficient attention to the ways in which poor physical health, both of mothers during pregnancy and of infants early in life, can influence the child's developmental progress. The incidences of inadequate prenatal nutrition, premature births, and complications of delivery which can lead to brain injuries are all greater among lower income and nonwhite groups (Abramowicz & Kass, 1966; Knoblock & Pasamanick, 1962). The effects of these medical differences are not unknown. Kagan (1965), for example, noted that one of the possible consequences of minimal brain damage during the perinatal and early postnatal periods is "increased restlessness and distractability, and inability to inhibit inappropriate responses during the pre- and early school years." The effects of malnutrition on developing cognitive skills have also been reported (Brockman & Ricciuti, 1971). We do not know the extent to which developmental "deficits" of lower income- and minority group children can be traced to these differences in their *medical* histories. This is a clear-cut case where responsibility for deprivation falls mainly on the *majority* culture.

Society as a whole is also responsible for other behavior patterns observed in deprived groups. Liebow (1967) argued that many of the behavior patterns he observed among lower class blacks were "a direct response to the conditions of lower class Negro life. . . ." His most cogent example involved the "delay of gratification" variable. The frequent finding that lower class (usually black) children prefer a smaller reward given immediately rather than a larger reward given later is often cited as a serious handicap to their schoolwork. It is often hypothesized that the child rearing practices employed by lower class parents lead children to prefer immediate gratification; and attempts are being made to change these practices and to teach the children to defer gratification. Liebow demonstrated that, although socialization patterns may encourage behaviors which are seen as reflecting a preference for immediate gratification, the socialization patterns do not represent the primary determinant of this pattern. He argued that the so-called preference for immediate gratification derives from the conditions of life encountered in this population. The *realities of life* represent the causal agent; the child rearing patterns are only intermediary variables. The importance of Liebow's argument merits thorough examination.

What appears as a "present-time" orientation to the outside observer is, to the man experiencing it, as much a future orientation as
that of his middle class counterpart. The difference between the two
men lies not so much in their different orientations to time as in their
different orientations to future time or more specifically, to their different futures.

As for the future, the young streetcorner man has a fairly good
picture of it. . . . It is a future in which everything is uncertain except
the ultimate destruction of his hopes and the eventual realization of
his fears. The most he can reasonably look forward to is that these
things do not come too soon. Thus when Richard squanders a
week's pay in two days it is not because, like an animal or a child,
he is "present-time oriented," unaware of or unconcerned with his
future. He does so precisely because he is aware of the future and
the hopelessness of it all.

Thus, apparent present-time concerns with consumption and indul-
gences—material and emotional—reflect a future-time orientation. "I
want mine right now" is ultimately a cry of despair, a direct response
to the future as he sees it [pp. 64–68].[1]

To encourage greater delay of gratification, interventionists should focus on the
conditions causing the "hopelessness" and "despair" in lower income populations,
rather than emphasizing the necessity of changing child rearing patterns. Other researchers have also noted that "conditions of life" represented major causal factors
contributing to parental practices and child development. Minturn and Lambert (1964)
interviewed mothers in six cultural settings (New England, Mexico, Philippines,
Okinawa, India, and Kenya) and found that situational constraints in the mothers'
immediate life space were primary determinants of their responses. Hess and Shipman (1966) analyzed situational constraints among lower income Americans and
noted that

a family in an urban ghetto has few choices to make with respect to
such basic things as residence, occupation, and condition of housing, and on the minor points of choice that come with adequate
discretionary income. A family with few opportunities to make
choices among events that affect it is not likely to encourage the
children to think of life as consisting of a wide range of behavioral
options among which they must learn to discriminate [p. 4].

The same authors (Shipman & Hess, 1966) spoke specifically about language development:

The lower class mother's narrow range of alternatives is being con-
veyed to the child through language styles which convey her attitude
of few options and little individual power, and this is now being
reflected in the child's cognitive development [p. 17].

Gordon (1969) reported specific data. He found that within the "poverty group" the amount of verbal interaction directed toward an infant was related to the "mother's view of her control of her destiny." The extent to which an individual feels he has some control over his destiny is also related to a whole myriad of variables associated with educational achievement. Coleman, Campbell, Hobson, McPartland, Mood, Weinfeld, and York (1966) found that, among minority group students, this factor was the best predictor of academic success. Similarly, Rotter (1966) argued that

> the individual who has a strong belief that he can control his own destiny is likely to (a) be more alert to those aspects of the environment which provide useful information for his future behaviors;(b) take steps to improve his environmental position; (c) place greater value on skill or achievement reinforcements and be generally more concerned with his ability, particularly his failures; and (d) be resistive to subtle attempts to influence him [p. 25].

There is little doubt that the realistic perception of the poor that they have little control over their lives leads not only to the "hopelessness" and "despair" observed by Liebow, but also to less concern with education, and reduced academic success.

Interventionists must concern themselves with these social, economic and political realities of lower class life and see the relations between these realities and indexes of parental behavior and intellectual development. Several interventionists have moved in this direction. Schaefer (1969) reported that "current stresses and the absence of social support influence maternal hostility, abuse, and neglect of the child." He suggested that intervention programs hoping to change a mother's behavior toward her child needed to "alleviate the stress and increase the support of mothers at the time the initial mother-child relationship is developed."

Similarly, Kagan (1969) spoke of the "need for ecological change" to improve the conditions of life among lower class populations. He emphasized that the interventionists needed to be sensitive to "the communities' belief as to what arrangements will help them," and that the changes should be directed toward facilitating the development of a "sense of control over the future."

Other researchers have come to the same conclusion. Pavenstedt (1967) reported that every member of her staff concurred "in the conviction that far-reaching social and economic change must take place in order to alter fundamentally the lives of the families" they observed. Stodolsky and Lesser (1968) suggested that intervention programs "would probably be a lot more successful if we were to modify the conditions which probably lead to many of these [parental] behaviors; namely, lack of money and of access to jobs." Liebow (1967) presented the most convincing argument:

> We do not have to see the problem in terms of breaking into a puncture proof circle, of trying to change values, of disrupting the lines of communication between parent and child so that parents

> cannot make children in their own image, thereby transmitting their culture inexorably, ad infinitum. No doubt, each generation does provide role models for each succeeding one. Of much greater importance for the possibilities of change, however, is the fact that many similarities between the lower class Negro father and son (or mother and daughter) do not result from "cultural transmission" but from the fact that the son goes out and independently experiences the same failures, in the same areas, and for much the same reasons as his father. What appears as a dynamic, self-sustaining cultural process is, in part at least, a relatively simple piece of social machinery which turns out, in rather mechanical fashion, independently produced look-alikes. The problem is how to change the conditions which, by guaranteeing failure, cause the son to be made in the image of the father [p.223].

Intervention programs must effect changes in the conditions of life, and not ignore these issues by merely attempting to change behavior patterns. Intervention programs which do attempt to change the "conditions of life," however, may encounter political opposition, simply because to change the conditions of life necessitates a wider distribution of power and wealth. While it is beyond the scope of the present discussion to examine closely the politics of poverty, it is necessary to understand why poverty may be difficult to eliminate.

All poor peoples do not share the characteristics which Lewis (1965) calls the "culture of poverty" or which researchers have labeled "deprived." Lewis reported that these characteristics are found only among the poor people who occupy a "marginal position in a class-stratified, highly individuated, capitalistic society" in which there is a "lack of effective participation and integration of the poor in the major institutions of the larger society." He reported, for example, that

> many of the primitive or preliterate peoples studied by anthropologists suffer from dire poverty which is the result of poor technology and/or poor natural resources, or of both, but they do not have the traits of the subculture of poverty. Indeed, they do not constitute a subculture because their societies are not highly stratified. In spite of their poverty they have a relatively integrated, satisfying and self-sufficient culture [p. xlviii].

Where a "culture of poverty" exists, however, the poor are less than poor: They are poor while others are rich, and they do not have the power to demand their "fair share." Thus, Lewis aptly characterized the fight for equality in this country as a "political power struggle" and pointed out that, rather than allowing poor people to participate effectively in society, many of those currently holding power "emphasize the need for guidance and control to remain in the hands of the middle class. . . ." The culture of poverty will not be obliterated, however, until power is shared. The elimination of physical poverty per se may not be enough to eliminate the culture of poverty; more basic political changes may be necessary. Some might even argue that a political revolution is the only means of redistributing power and wealth, thus eliminating the culture of poverty. Lewis noted that

> by creating basic structural changes in society, by redistributing wealth, by organizing the poor and giving them a sense of belonging, of power and of leadership, revolutions frequently succeed in abolishing some of the basic characteristics of the culture of poverty even when they do not succeed in abolishing poverty itself [p. liii].

To illustrate, Lewis went on to report:

> On the basis of my limited experience in one socialist country—Cuba —and on the basis of my reading, I am inclined to believe that the culture of poverty does not exist in the socialist countries. After the Castro Revolution I found much less of the despair, apathy, and hopelessness which are so diagnostic of urban slums in the culture of poverty. The people had a new sense of power and importance. They were armed and were given a doctrine which glorified the lower class as the hope of humanity [p. xlix].

The purpose of this discussion is not to encourage political revolution,[2] but rather to point out the complexities of attempting to understand the behavior of people who differ from us—culturally, financially, or any way. It is easier to think of these other people as "groups," and more difficult to think of them as individuals who differ a great deal among themselves—just as members of our own group do. It is easier to think of them as wanting to be like us and needing us to help them; it is more difficult to reject the philosophy of the "white man's burden" and allow people the freedom to retain life styles which differ from the ones we know. It is easy to blame people for what we have defined as their "deficits," but more difficult to consider how we as a society might have contributed to the problems we have defined as "theirs."

IMPLICATIONS FOR RESEARCH[3]

The present author has conducted research on social class differences in maternal behavior and cognitive development (Tulkin, 1968, 1970). He does not advocate that scientists abandon or censor this type of research. However, social scientists need to reevaluate their role in research affecting minority groups (including poor white); and possibly establish a set of guidelines or recommendations to prevent the misuse of research. There are precedents for such guidelines in that psychotherapists ascribe to a set of "ethical standards," and experiments involving human subjects are also regulated. The proposed guidelines could be established by a panel consisting of minority group educators and community leaders, along with those members of the scientific community who have an interest in this type of research. These recommendations might not be binding, but instead would represent an attempt to make research more valid, and hopefully more relevant to the needs of the community. There are several areas in which guidelines might be helpful.

Understanding the Culture

Anthropologists continue to point out the inappropriateness of examining another culture through the experiential framework of one's own (Conklin, 1962; Frake, 1962). The psychologists investigating developmental patterns among minority group children should attempt to understand the "realities of life" in these populations, and how these realities affect life styles. These insights could be developed in several ways: (a) living in the minority group community; (b) holding meetings with community people—not just professionals from the same minority group as the subjects—to discuss any proposed research; and, most important, (c) including minority group (or community) members on the research team at every level of responsibility, from the initial planning of the project through the analysis and interpretation of data. Some effort in this area is sorely needed if research involving human behavior in minority group populations hopes to yield valid conclusions.

Methodological Improvements

Recommendations are also needed in the area of employing more rigorous controls in studies comparing various population groups. Research designs which compare lower income minority children to middle income white children are so confounded that no clear conclusions can be reached. Controlling for social class does not even equate experiential patterns among various populations (Tulkin, 1968). If social scientists hope to understand the processes by which differences develop they must use designs which employ strict controls for economic level (family income, crowded housing conditions, etc.), family milieux (broken homes, family size, birth order, maternal employment, etc.), health of child (prematurity, nutrition, complications of delivery, etc.), and possibly various aspects of the parents' own histories (e.g., birth order and family size). Without these controls, the experiences which contribute to developmental differences cannot be properly investigated.

Finally, we need to reduce the error variance introduced by our testing procedures. Sroufe (1970) criticized researchers who report differences in the performance of white and minority group subjects in laboratory testing situations, because the facilities themselves may "provide different stimuli for the lower class mother than for the faculty wife." Sroufe questioned, for example, whether "a university waiting room [was] a suitable place for observing restrictions placed by lower class mothers on their children." Lore (1969) reported the results of a series of animal experiments that supported Sroufe's argument. Lore noted that many experimenters who compared restricted and nonrestricted animals attributed the differences they found to "deficits" in experientially deprived animals; but, upon further study, the differences appeared to reflect only "an exaggerated fear reaction" elicited by the testing procedure.

> For normally reared subjects, the test setting includes many stimulus
> elements that have been encountered previously. . . . However, for
> restricted animals, the totally unfamiliar test setting apparently elicits
> a severe emotional reaction that is incompatible with any form of
> adaptive behavior [p. 482].

Lore's own data revealed that when tests were conducted in the "home-cage" the behavior of the deprived animals was "entirely comparable to that of subjects exposed to far richer environments." The author's conclusion—which should be heeded by researchers examining the behaviors of minority group populations—is that one cannot infer that "deficits" exist when his test procedures have a different stimulus value to the groups he is attempting to compare.

Community Relevance

The proposed guidelines must also make research more relevant to the needs of minority group communities. The need for change in this area is evidenced by the statement of Whitney Young, National Director of the Urban League, who in 1968 called for a "moratorium" on studies of the Negro family (Young, 1968). Similarly, Robert Williams, Past Chairman of the Association of Black Psychologists, asked his white colleagues to stay out of black neighborhoods (Williams, 1969). These statements reflect the feeling among minority group leaders that their communities are being "exploited" by white professionals. Just as white businessmen came into the ghettos, made their money, and retreated to the suburbs, white professionals are applying for federal funds, going into the ghettos, testing subjects, and returning to their universities to write papers describing the "deprivations" they encountered; in both cases the community has gained nothing. If researchers are going to use minority communities to advance the science of child development (and their own reputations), they should be willing to compensate the communities by structuring their research programs to be relevant to the needs of the people they are using. As was pointed out above, the *real* needs of the community are likely to be the *primary* determinants of many of the behavior patterns which have been labeled as "depriving" anyway.

Community needs vary, but some are universal: The need for jobs, job training, and vocational counseling; and the need for health care and legal services. Perhaps the greatest need is for the community to become self-sufficient. Thus, an intervention program initiated by a noncommunity agency should have as its goal turning the program over to the community itself, with the outside agency acting as a consultant as long as its services were requested. Interventionists would then be social change agents, and not missionairies. The "missionary" approach which is common among interventionists, is illustrated by Pavenstedt's (1967) stated goals:

> It is our tenet that *in order to lead out of misery, as well as out of
> intellectual dearth, intervention must begin very early and must be
> concerned with total personality development.* we set ourselves the

task of bettering their early upbringing, we wanted to prepare them for the competitive struggle with which their parents were incapable of coping [pp. 4–5].

A different type of program was reported by Karnes, Studley, Wright, and Hodgins (1968), who attempted at least minimal social change by relying heavily on the participation of low income mothers in their intervention program. They found that

mothers of low educational and low income levels can learn to prepare inexpensive educational materials and to acquire skills for using such materials to foster the intellectual and linguistic development of their children at home [p. 182].

Karnes *et al.* attributed the success of their program to the participation of the mothers. Similarly, Gilmer (1969) reported that "the effectiveness of programs in stimulating younger children in the home is attributable to the variable of maternal involvement."

Effective involvement of parents, however, is related to the role which parents are asked to play. Chilman (1968) noted that in most intervention programs "lip service" is given to parental involvement, but parents are usually "seen as minor auxiliaries to the major effort." Karnes *et al.,* in contrast, emphasized that mothers were "fully recognized as important members of the educational team," and were actively involved in developing materials to be used with their children.

Because the mothers had made many of the instructional materials and understood their use, they could approach the teaching of their children with confidence. They could readily observe the progress of their children and were immediately rewarded for their mutual efforts [pp. 182–183].

Finally, the mothers were paid for attending meetings and participating in the program.

Karnes's program did not actually effect major structural changes in the *community,* and thus does not illustrate the ideal model for intervention work which has been proposed; but the program did more than most to enable participants to change themselves as a result of the program, rather than assuming that the community would continue to rely on the professionals to "lead (them) out of misery" (Pavenstedt, 1967). The question now is whether the mothers trained by Karnes *et al.* are eligible to apply for federal funds to expand the intervention work to other families; and whether Karnes *et al.* will assist the mothers in this venture and be available to consult with them, and to help them evelute the success of their intervention. If this type of program could be developed then nobody would be exploited: Karnes *et al.* would have their data—and publications; the mothers in the study would have learned something about child development and would have more confidence in themselves; and the community would have federal funds, new jobs, and a sense of pride that community members were helping each other. It may finally be the end of the "white man's burden."

NOTES

[1]Liebow also pointed out that there is no intrinsic connection between "present-time" orientation and lower class persons:

> Whenever people of whatever class have been uncertain, skeptical or downright pessimistic about the future, "I want mine right now" has been one of the characteristic responses. ... In wartime, especially, all classes tend to slough off conventional restraints on sexual and other behavior (i. e., become less able or less willing to defer gratification). And when inflation threatens, darkening the future, persons who formerly husbanded their resources with commendable restraint almost stampede one another rushing to spend their money. ... [Thus] present-time orientation appears to be a situation-specific phenomenon rather than a part of the standard psychic equipment of cognitive lower class man [pp. 68–69].

[2]Nor does the author wish to imply that political and economic changes would provide an automatic panacea for all of our nation's ills. We do need to broaden our perspective, however, and understand that some of the problems which we spend time and money fighting are, in reality, our own creations.

[3]Various colleagues who have read the present article suggested that there is only one implication of the above discussion with regard to research with minority populations: Don't do any. This conclusion may be justified, but it is unlikely to be adopted. Therefore, the following "compromises" are presented.

REFERENCES

Abramowicz, M., & Kass, E. H. Pathogenesis and prognosis of prematurity. *New England Journal of Medicine*, 1966, *275*, 878.

Arai, S., Ishikawa, J., & Toshima, K. Developpement psychomoteur des enfants Japonais. *La Revue de Neuropsychiatrie Infantile et d'Hygiène Mentale de l'Enfance, 1958, 6*, 262–269. Cited by W. Caudill & H. Weinstein, Maternal care and infant behavior in Japan and America. *Psychiatry*, 1969, *32*, p. 41.

Baratz, J. C., & Shuy, R. W. (Eds.) *Teaching black children to read*. Washington, D.C.: Center for Applied Linguistics, 1969.

Baratz, S. S., & Baratz, J. C. Early childhood intervention: The social science base of institutional racism. *Harvard Educational Review*, 1970, *40*, 29–50.

Bernstein, B. Language and social class. *British Journal of Sociology*, 1960, *11*, 271–276.

Bernstein, B. Social class and linguistic development: A theory of social learning. In A. H. Halsey. H. Floud, & C. A. Anderson (Eds.), *Education, economy and society*. Glencoe, Ill.: Free Press, 1961.

Birren, J. E., & Hess, R. Influences of biological, psychological, and social deprivations on learning and performance. In *Perspectives on human deprivation*. Washington, D.C.: Department of Health, Education, and Welfare, United States Government Printing Office, 1968.

Brockman, L. M., & Ricciuti, H. N. Severe protein-calorie malnutrition and cognitive development in infancy and early childhood. *Developmental Psychology,* 1971, *4,* 312–319.

Caudill, W., & Weinstein, H. Maternal care and infant behavior in Japanese and American urban middle class families. Bethesda, Md.: National Institute of Mental Health, 1966. (Mimeo)

Caudill, W., & Weinstein, H. Maternal care and infant behavior in Japan and America. *Psychiatry,* 1969, *32,* 12–43.

Chandler, B. J., & Erickson, F. D. *Sounds of society: A demonstration program in group inquiry.* (Final Rep. No. 6–2044) Washington, D.C.: United States Government Printing Office, 1968.

Chilman, C. S. Poor families and their patterns of child care: Some implications for service programs. In L. L. Dittmann (Ed.), *Early child care.* New York: Atherton Press, 1968.

Coleman, J. S., Campbell, E. Q., Hobson, C. J., McPartland, J., Mood, A. M., Weinfeld, F. D., & York, R. L. *Equality of educational opportunity.* Washington, D.C.: United States Government Printing Office, 1966.

Coles, R. Violence in ghetto children. In S. Chess & A. Thomas (Eds.), *Annual progress in child psychiatry and child development.* New York: Brunner/Mazel, 1968.

Conklin, H. C. The ethnographic study of cognitive systems. In *Anthropology and human behavior.* Washington, D.C.: Anthropological Society of Washington, 1962.

Davé, R. H. The identification and measurement of environmental variables that are related to educational achievement. Unpublished doctoral dissertation, University of Chicago, 1963.

Fantini, M. D. Beyond cultural deprivation and compensatory education. *Psychiatry and Social Science Review,* 1969, *3,* 6–13.

Foster, H. L. Dialect-lexicon and listening comprehension. Unpublished doctoral dissertation, Teachers College, Columbia University, 1969.

Foster, H. L. Foster's Jive Lexicon Analogies Test. Series II. Buffalo: Office of Teacher Education, State University of New York, 1970. (Mimeo)

Frake, C. L. The ethnographic study of cognitive systems. In *Anthropology and human behavior.* Washington, D.C.: Anthropological Society of Washington, 1962.

Gans, H. J. *The urban villagers: Group and class in the life of Italian-Americans.* New York: Free Press of Glencoe, 1962.

Gilmer, B. Intra-family diffusion of selected cognitive skills as a function of educational stimulation. *George Peabody College DARCEE Papers.* Vol 3. Nashville, Tenn.: George Peabody College, 1969.

Gordon, I. J. *Early child stimulation through parent education.* (Final Rep. No. PH5-R-306) Washington, D.C.: Department of Health, Education and Welfare, United States Government Printing Office, 1969.

Gross, M. *Learning readiness in two Jewish groups.* New York: Center for Urban Education, 1967.

Herskovits, M. *The myth of the Negro past.* Boston: Beacon Press, 1958.

Hess, R. D., & Shipman, V. C. Maternal attitude toward the school and the role of pupil: Some social class comparisons. Paper presented at the Conference on Curriculum and Teaching in Depressed Urban Areas, Columbia University, June 1966.

Hillson, M. The disadvantaged child. *Community Mental Health Journal,* 1970, *6,* 81–83.

Jessor, R., & Richardson, S. Psychosocial deprivation and personality development. In *Perspectives on human deprivation.* Washington, D.C.: United States Government Printing Office, 1968.

Kagan, J. Information processing in the child. In P. H. Mussen, J. J. Conger, & J. Kagan (Eds.), *Readings in child development and personality.* New York: Harper & Row, 1965.

Kagan, J. On cultural deprivation. In D.C. Glass (Ed.), *Environmental influences.* New York: Rockefeller University Press, 1968.

Kagan, J. Social class and academic progress: An analysis and suggested solution strategies. Paper presented at the meeting of the American Association for the Advancement of Science, Boston, December 1969.

Karnes, M. B., Studley, W. M., Wright, W. R., & Hodgins, A. S. An approach for working with mothers of disadvantaged preschool children. *Merrill-Palmer Quarterly,* 1968, *14,* 173–184.

Keller, S. The social world of the urban slum child: Some early findings. *American Journal of Orthopsychiatry,* 1963, *33,* 823–834.

Knoblock, H., & Pasamanick, B. Mental subnormality. *New England Journal of Medicine,* 1962, *266,* 1092–1097.

Krauss, R. M., & Rotter, G. S. Communication abilities of children as a function of status and age. *Merrill-Palmer Quarterly,* 1968, *14,* 161–174.

Labov, W. Some sources of reading problems for Negro speakers of nonstandard English. In A. Frazier (Ed.), *New directions in elementary English.* Champaign, Ill.: National Council of Teachers of English, 1967.

Lehmer, M. Navajos want their own schools. *San Francisco Examiner and Chronicle,* December 15, 1969.

Lewis, O. *La Vida: A Puerto Rican family in the culture of poverty.* New York: Random House, 1965.

Liebow, E. *Tally's corner: A study of Negro streetcorner men.* Boston: Little, Brown, 1967.

Lore, R. K. Pain avoidance behavior of rats reared in restricted and enriched environments. *Developmental Psychology,* 1969, *5,* 482–484.

Maccoby, M., & Modiano, N. On culture and equivalence. I. In J. S. Bruner, R. R. Olver, & P. M. Greenfield (Eds.), *Studies in cognitive growth.* New York: Wiley, 1966.

Minturn, L., & Lambert, W. W. *Mothers of six cultures.* New York: Wiley, 1966.

Pavenstedt, E. (Ed.) *The drifters.* Boston: Little, Brown, 1967.

Rebelsky, F., & Abeles, G. Infancy in Holland and in the United States. Paper presented at the meeting of the Society for Research in Child Development, Santa Monica, March 1969.

Riessman, F. *The culturally deprived child.* New York: Harper & Row, 1962.

Rotter, J. B. Generalized expectancies for internal versus external control of reinforcement. *Psychological Monographs,* 1966, 80 (1, Whole No. 609).

Schaefer, E. S. Need for early and continuing education. Paper presented at the meeting of the American Association for the Advancement of Science, Boston, December 1969.

Shipman, V. C., & Hess, R. D. Early experiences in the socialization of cognitive modes in children: A study of urban Negro families. Paper presented at the meeting of the Conference of Family and Society, Merrill-Palmer Institute, April 1966.

Sroufe, L. A. A methodological and philosophical critique of intervention-oriented research. *Developmental Psychology,* 1970, *2,* 140–145.

Stewart, W. A. Sociolinguistic factors in the history of American Negro dialects. *The Florida FL Reporter,* 1967, *5,*(2).

Stewart, W. A. Linguistic and conceptual deprivation—fact or fancy? Paper presented at the meeting of the Society for Research in Child Development, Santa Monica, March 1969. (a)

Stewart, W. A. On the use of Negro dialect in the teaching of reading. In J. C. Baratz & R. W. Shuy (Eds.), *Teaching black children to read.* Washington, D.C.: Center for Applied Linguistics, 1969. (b)

Stodolsky, S., & Lesser, G. Learning patterns in the disadvantaged. In S. Chess & A. Thomas (Eds.) *Annual progress in child psychiatry and child development.* New York: Brunner/Mazel, 1968.

Tulkin, S. R. Race, class, family and school achievement. *Journal of Personality and Social Psychology,* 1968, *9,* 31–37.

Tulkin, S. R. Mother-infant interaction in the first year of life: An inquiry into the influences of social class. Unpublished doctoral dissertation, Harvard University, 1970.

Williams, R. L. The changing image of the black American: A socio-psychological appraisal. Paper presented at the meeting of the American Psychological Association, Washington, D.C., September 1969.

Wolf, R. M. The identification and measurement of environmental process variables related to intelligence. Unpublished doctoral dissertation, University of Chicago, 1964.

Young, W. Invited address presented at the meeting of the American Association on Mental Deficiency, Boston, May 1968.

4.8

Is Early Intervention Effective?

Urie Bronfenbrenner

I. THE PROBLEM

Does early intervention have any enduring effects? The 1960's saw the widespread adoption in this country of preschool programs aimed at counteracting the effects of poverty on human development. Although some of these programs produced dramatic results during the first few months of operation, the question of long-term impact has remained unanswered for lack of extended follow-up data. Recently, however, research results have become available which shed some light on five questions of considerable scientific and social import:

1. Do children in experimental programs continue to gain in intellectual development so long as intervention continues, or at least do they maintain the higher level achieved in the initial phase?
2. Do children continue to improve, or at least to hold their own, after termination of the program, or do they regress to lower levels of function once the program is discontinued?
3. Is development enhanced by beginning intervention at earlier ages, including the first years of life?
4. In terms of long-range impact, what kinds of programs are most effective?
5. Which children from what circumstances are most likely to benefit in the long run from early intervention?

II. THE NATURE AND LIMITATIONS OF THE DATA

Follow-up data are available from two types of early intervention projects: Those conducted in group settings outside the home, and those which involve regularly scheduled home visits by a trained person who works both with the child and his parents, usually the mother. We have attempted to insure comparability in our analysis by reviewing only those studies which (1) include follow-up data for at least two years after termination of intervention; (2) provide information on a matched control group; and (3) provide data which are comparable to results in other studies.

This is a condensed version of a longer report: *Is Early Intervention Effective?* Washington, D.C.: Department of Health, Education and Welfare, Office of Child Development, 1974.

TABLE 1. DESCRIPTION OF MAJOR PROJECTS

IDENTIFYING DATA	SAMPLE	NATURE OF INTERVENTION	EXPERIMENTAL AND CONTROL GROUPS
Howard University Preschool Program Washington, D.C. Elizabeth Herzog (Herzog, Newcomb, & Cisin, 1973, 1972a, 1972b; Kraft, Fuschillo, & Herzog, 1968)	Black children in generally good health from families selected at random from four census tracts in Washington inner-city neighborhoods. All parents had to agree in advance to have their children attend the preschool program if selected. No other requirements. Approximately 68% of families below poverty line; 18% on welfare, median income about $3,500 but extending up to $10,000. About 25% of parents graduated from high school, 90% unskilled labor, remainder skilled and semiprofessional. 28% of the mothers worked, and apparently all of the fathers when present. No father in 40% of the homes. Median number of children in the family 4. The "no-show" rate was over 30% during the recruitment phase, but attrition was very low thereafter.	"A well-run middle class nursery school, with no specific "enrichment" features." Children attended full day for 5 days a week. Each group of 12 had its own teacher and two or three teachers' aides. Weekly parent meetings were held at the university plus individual contacts with families, usually unscheduled." In the hope of consolidating any benefits . . . a series of special school situations was arranged for the 30 experimental children during the three years immediately following nursery school." These included being in the same class in kindergarten, extra teachers and aides, an enriched curriculum, special trips, and assignment of a social worker to the children's families.	30 children from one census tract were designated as the experimental group and 69 from the other three tracts as the control group. The experimental group ended up with a higher percentage of intact families (66% versus 16%), and slightly smaller families.
Perry Preschool Project Ypsilanti, Michigan David P. Weikart (Weikart, D. P., et al., 1970; Weikart, 1967)	Black children from disadvantaged homes residing in a city of 50,000 on the fringe of metropolitan Detroit. To qualify all children had to have IQ's between 50 and 85 with no discernible organic involvement. In addition, families had to fall below a low cutting point on a cultural deprivation scale based primarily on parents' education and occupation, and also number of persons per room in the home. Parents' education averaged below tenth grade; occupations over 70% unskilled; half the families are on welfare; no information on income; 14% of fathers unemployed. Average number of	Half-day classes, five days a week, from mid-October through May for two years. Curriculum derived mainly from Piagetian theory and focused on cognitive objectives. Four teachers for each group of 24 children with emphasis on individual and small group activities. Teachers made weekly 90-minute home visit "to individualize instruction through a tutorial relationship with the student and to make parents knowlegeable about the educative process . . . mothers were encouraged to observe and participate in as many teaching activities as possible during the home visits."	Children from the total sample were divided at random into experimental and control groups with some adjustment to assure matching on social class, IQ, boy/girl ratio, and percent of working mothers. The groups appear to be well matched on other variables as well. Although there were 5 waves of experimental and control groups initiated over a period of years, the waves have been pooled in reporting follow-up data.

Program	Population and Selection	Program Description	Results / Design
	dren have no father in the home; about 28% working mothers. There appears to have been little self-selection of families in the sample and attrition during the course of the project has been low.		
Early Training Project Nashville, Tennessee Susan W. Gray (Gray & Klaus, 1970; Klaus & Gray, 1968)	Black children from families "considerably below" the poverty line. Selected on the basis of parents' occupation (unskilled or semiskilled), education (average below eighth grade), income (average $1,500), and poor housing conditions. No data on welfare status or percent of parents unemployed; one-third of the homes with no father; median number of children per family 5. Both self-selection of families at entry and attrition over the course of the study appear to have been minimal.	In summer, daily morning classes emphasized the development of achievement motivation, perceptual and cognitive activities, and language. Each group of 19 had a black head teacher and three or four teaching assistants divided equally as to race and sex. In dealing with the children, staff emphasized positive reinforcement of desired behavior. The weekly home visit stressed the involvement of the parent in the project and in activities with the child. Home visits lasted through the year.	Sixty-one children from the same large city were divided at random into two experimental groups (E1 and E2) and one control group (C1). The remaining control group, (C2), consisted of 27 children from like backgrounds residing in a similar city 65 miles away. Group E1 attended the ten-week intervention program for three summers plus three years of weekly meetings with a trained home visitor when preschool was not in session. Group E2 began the program a year later with only two years of exposure.
Philadelphia Project Temple University E. Kuno Beller (1972)	Children from urban slum areas of North Philadelphia, 90% black. Families in target mainly employed in unskilled or semi-skilled labor with median income of $3,400. Children admitted to the nursery group were selected from families responding to a written invitation, who also met the following criteria: "dependency of family on public services, mothers working, and broken homes." Kindergarten group consisted of children from the same classroom attended by nursery children, but without prior nursery experience. First grade group was composed of children entering the same classrooms but without prior nursery or kindergarten experience. Attrition was 10% by the time the original groups reached fourth grade.	Nursery groups composed of 15 children with one head and one assistant teacher for four half days a week, with a fifth day devoted to staff meetings, teacher training, and parent conferences. "The program was a traditional one" emphasizing "curiosity for discovery . . . creativity . . . warm, personalized handling of the child. . . balance of self-initiated instructed activities." Kindergarten and first grade classes consisted of 25 to 30 children, meeting five half days a week, with one head teacher and an aide or assistant teacher. Work with parents and home visits were conducted by a home-school coordinator.	A major purpose of the research was to examine the effect of age at entry into school by examining intellectual development of three comparison groups starting in nursery, kindergarten, and first grade respectively. Groups were matched on age, sex, and ethnic background. No data are available on comparability of the three groups in terms of education, socioeconomic status, or family structure. Comparison at time of entry into school, on three different tests of intelligence and on other psychological measures, however, revealed no significant differences. The children from all three groups attended the same classrooms through Grade II, but by Grade III children were dispersed over many schools.

331

TABLE 1. *(cont'd)*

IDENTIFYING DATA	SAMPLE	NATURE OF INTERVENTION	EXPERIMENTAL AND CONTROL GROUPS
Indiana Project Indiana University Bloomington, Indiana Walter L. Hodges (Hodges *et al.*, 1967)	Five-year-old children in good health, predominantly white from Bloomington and from small semirural Indiana communities, selected on the basis of low-rated "psychosocial deprivation, and Binet intelligence score between 50 and 85. Average length of schooling for parents just below tenth grade. No information on welfare status or income. Fathers' occupation approximately 70% unskilled and 8% semiskilled; 12% unemployed; one-third of the mothers work; 20% of the homes have no father present; average number of children in the family 5; no information is available on the degree of self-selection among sample families. There was only one slight attrition over the course of the study.	Group E1 was exposed to a special "diagnostically-based curriculum" designed to remedy specific deficits of individual children through "an intensive, structured, cognitively-oriented" program. The children met daily for morning sessions. To increase the likelihood of adoption of the program by the public schools, "the teacher to child ratio was smaller in the present study than that reported in the other preschool projects. . .For the same reason, no work was done with the families of the subjects."	One experimental group (E1) and control group (C2) were constituted by random assignment. Group E1 attended one year of the specially-designed kindergarten program in Bloomington. C2 was composed of at-home controls from the same city. Children in Group C1 attended regular kindergartens newly established in several semirural Indiana towns. This was a "traditional kindergarten," providing facilities and equipment similar to those for C2, but without the special "diagnostically-evolved" curriculum. Group C3 consisted of at-home controls in these same localities. In general, the families in the experimental group were rated by investigators as more disadvantaged than those in the control group but this difference is not reflected in indices of socioeconomic status, family size, parents' education, or occupation.
Infant Education Research Project Washington, D.C. Earl S. Schaefer (Schaefer, 1972a, 1968; Schaefer & Aaronson, 1972; Infant Education Research Project, undated)	Fifteen month old Black male infants selected from door-to-door surveys of families in two low socioeconomic inner-city neighborhoods in Washington. To be accepted, families had to meet four criteria: (1) income under $5,000; (2) mother's education under 12 years; (3) occupation either unskilled or semiskilled; and (4) willingness to have infant participate in either experimental or control group. In addition, "an attempt was made to choose participants from relatively stable homes, not so noisy or overcrowded as to inter-	Trained tutors worked with each child in the home for one hour a day, five days per weeks, from the time the child was 15 months old until three years of age. The main emphasis was on development of verbal and conceptual abilities through the use of pictures, games, reading, and puzzles. "Participation of the mother and of other family members in the education of the infant was encouraged but not required."	Chosen from different neighborhoods to avoid contamination. "Comparisons between the groups revealed only small differences, many of which favored the control group, on the family variables that might be expected to influence the child's intellectual development."

fere with the home tutoring sessions." No other background information available. Of the 64 subjects in the original sample, 48 (equally divided between experimental and control group) were available for the final follow-up.		Randomized by housing project. The several experimental and control groups differ on age of entry into the program (2 vs. 3, see Table 3), length and intensity of intervention, and prior experience. Groups E1 and E2 had one year of the regular program at two years of age followed by a much abbreviated program in the second year as follows. Group E1 received seven visits in which the focus of attention was on the kit of materials with no involvement of the mother in interaction with the child. Group E2 was given the regular program but with half as many visits as in the first year. Group E3 received the full program for two years beginning at two years of age. Groups E4 and E5 were both given one year of the regular program at age three, but Group E5 had served the previous year as a "placebo" control group which had received the semiweekly visits but without exposure to the special kit of materials or encouragement of mother–child interaction. The visitor simply brought a gift and played records for the child. Seven of the eight groups are generally comparable on major background variables, but one control group (C2) was far out of line—with better educated mothers, smaller families, higher occupational status, no absent fathers, etc.
Verbal Interaction Project Mineola, New York Phyllis Levenstein (1972a, 1970)	Infants 2 to 3 years of age, 90% black, from disadvantaged families in three Long Island suburbs. To qualify, mothers had to be eligible for low income housing with an education not higher than high school graduation. About 25% of the families were on welfare. Average education of parents was eleventh grade; fathers apparently all employed; about 65% unskilled or semiskilled. About 35% of the fathers absent. Average number of children per family 3–4. Self-selection involved in willingness of mothers in experimental group to participate. Attrition especially high in untreated control groups. Average IQ of mothers of children in the experimental groups was 83; in the control group 88.	Semiweekly half-hour visits in the home for seven months each year by trained worker who stimulated interaction between mother and child with the aid of a kit of toys and books referred to as VISM (Visual Interaction Stimulus Materials).

With respect to the third criterion, it is regrettable that the only comparable measures available from most studies are IQ scores (usually the Stanford-Binet) and, for older children, school achievement tests. This circumstance seriously qualifies the conclusions that can be drawn. Thus we have no systematic information about effects of intervention programs outside the cognitive realm, and even within that sphere standarized tests of intelligence and achievement are limited in scope and subject to a marked middle class bias. Not only are they typically administered by middle class professionals in middle class settings, but the kinds of objects, facts, and activities with which the tests are concerned are far more common in middle class than in less favored environments. As a result, the scores obtained inevitably underestimate the potential of children from disadvantaged families.

Nevertheless, few scientists or citizens would dismiss as unimportant the demonstration that a particular strategy of early intervention had enabled children from disadvantaged backgrounds to solve problems of the type presented on tests of intelligence at a level of competence comparable to that of the average child of the same age. Whereas performance below the norm on tests of this kind cannot be taken as firm evidence that the child lacks mental capacity, attainment of the norm year after year does mean that the child both possesses intellectual ability and can use it. It is from this perspective that the present analysis was undertaken.

In this analysis, we review seven studies which meet the criteria mentioned above (summarized in Table 1) and draw from additional studies which, although they do not satisfy all requirements, add important clarifications.

III. METHODOLOGICAL PROBLEMS

Before turning to an interpretation of the results, several methodological complications must be noted.

1. If low IQ is used as a criterion for admission to the program (as in the Weikart and Hodges studies), the initial gains are appreciably inflated by regression to the mean. This phenomenon is responsible for the mistaken but often cited conclusion that the most deprived children are the ones who profit most from intervention programs. In fact, the opposite is the case (see below).
2. A child whose parents are interested in his development and are eager to take advantage of opportunities for him is likely to be more advanced in and to gain more from an intervention program. Thus failure to control for differences in parents' motivation leads to spurious results.
3. Recent evidence (Herzog *et al.,* 1972b) indicates that programs involving children from relatively less deprived homes are likely to achieve more favorable results. In comparing effects from different projects, this source of variation must be taken into account.

4. In evaluating results of intervention, other possible sources of
    confounding include children's age (the effects of deprivation
    increase as the child gets older), and diffusion effects from
    experimental to control group (i.e., the latter begins to adopt the
    practices of the former).

IV. SOME EFFECTS OF PRESCHOOL INTERVENTION IN GROUP SETTINGS

The results of group intervention studies are summarized in Table
2. For each study, the table records the number of subjects, IQ's
achieved in successive years by experimental and control groups,
and the differences between them. The scores given first are those obtained by both
groups before the program began. A double-line indicates the point at which intervention was terminated. At the bottom, major changes over time are summarized in terms
of initial gain (before-after difference in the first year of treatment), gain two years after
all intervention was terminated (shown because it permits a comparison of all seven
studies), and overall gain (difference between initial IQ and last follow-up score three
to four years after the children left the program). Also shown are differences between
these gains for the experimental and control group. Finally, the bottom row records
the average grade equivalent attained on a test of academic achievement administered in the final year of follow-up. Unless otherwise noted, significant differences
between experimental and control groups for each year are designated by asterisks,
one for the 5 percent level and two for 1 percent. The absence of asterisks indicates
that the difference was not reliable. Ordinarily, no significance tests are available for
gain scores, but these are shown in the few instances when they were computed by
the original investigator.

Two striking patterns become apparent. First, preschool intervention produces
substantial gains in IQ so long as the program lasts. But the experimental groups do
not continue to make gains when intervention continues beyond one year, and, what
is more critical, the effects tend to "wash out" after intervention is terminated. The
longer the follow-up, the more obvious the latter trend becomes (Weikart, Gray).
There appear to be some exceptions to the generally regressive trend, but these are
faulted by methodological artifacts—regression to the mean in the Hodges and Weikart programs; inadequate control for parents' motivation in the nonrandom comparison groups of the Beller and Gray projects.

Additional support for our conclusion comes from DiLorenzo's evaluation of
long-term effects of preschool programs in New York State. Although DiLorenzo
(1969) still found significant differences between experimental and control groups on
achievement tests administered in first grade, these differences were no longer
present at the end of second grade.

The DiLorenzo study also adds some new evidence on the comparative effectiveness of different types of preschool programs. The data presented suggest that
most significant differences between experimental and control groups were found in

TABLE 2. EFFECTS ON LATER INTELLECTUAL DEVELOPMENT OF INTERVENTION PROGRAMS IN PRESCHOOL SETTINGS

	HERZOG			WEIKART			GRAY					BELLER				HODGES			
	1	2	3	4	5	6	7	8	9	10	11	12	13	14	15	16	17	18	19
	E	C	E-C	E	C	E-C	E_1	E_2	C_1	C_2	$\bar{E}-C_1$[b]	C_1	C_2	C_3	E	C_1	C_2	C_3	$\bar{E}-C_2$
N	30	66-62		58-13[a]	65-15[a]		19	19	18	23		57-50	53-46	57-53	11	11	13	13	
Age 3 Before	81	85	-4	79.7	79.1	.6	87.6	92.5[c]	85.4	86.7	-1.4[c]								
After	91	85	6	95.8	83.4	12.4**	102.0	92.3[c]	88.2	87.4	11.8*[c]								
Age 4 Before	96	88	8**	94.7	82.7	12.0**	96.4	94.8	89.6	86.7	6.0	92.1							
After							97.1	97.5	87.6	84.7	9.7*								
Kindergarten Before															74.5	75.0	74.5	72.5	0
After	97	90	7	90.5	85.4	5.1*	95.8	96.6	82.9	80.2	13.3*[g]	98.6	91.2		93.8	87.5	80.9	81.3	12.9*
Grade I	95	89	6	91.2	83.3	7.9**	98.1	99.7	91.4	89.0	7.5*	98.4	94.4	89.9	97.4	83.2	91.7	84.8	5.4
Grade II	92	87	5	88.8	86.5	2.3	91.2	96.0	87.9	84.6	5.7*	97.8	92.8	88.6	94.9	85.5	89.2	86.5	5.7
Grade III	87	87	0	89.6	88.1	1.5	–	–	–	–	–	97.6	93.1	89.3					
Grade IV							86.7	90.2	84.9	77.7	3.5*[e]	98.4	91.7	88.6					
Initial gain	10	0	10	16.1	4.3	11.8	14.4	5.0	2.8	.7	6.9	6.5*	3.2	-1.3	19.3	12.5	6.4	8.8	12.9
Gain 2 years after	14	4	10	11.5	4.2	7.3	3.6	3.5	2.5	-2.1	1.1	6.3[d]	1.6[d]	-.6[d]	20.4	10.5	14.7	12.0	5.7
Overall gain	6	2	9	9.9	9.0	.9	-.9	-2.3	-.5	-9.0	1.3	6.3[d]	.5[d]	-1.3[d]					
Achievement level	no difference			2.1	.6	1.5*[f]	3.7	4.0	3.8	3.4	.2	–	–	–	2.1	2.0	1.8	1.5	.4

a. N's decrease because only earlier waves reached grade school (see Table 1).
b. Published significance level includes C_2.
c. Intervention began one year later in E_2; hence C_1 includes E_2 for this age group only.
d. Significance of difference not tested.
e. Difference significant for the distal control group (C_2) only.
f. Difference significant for girls only.
g. A reduced parent intervention program was continued through grade one.
(Double line designates point at which intervention was terminated.)

highly structured, cognitively oriented programs. Furthermore, these programs produced the most pronounced long-term effects. Karnes (1969) reports similar findings. In comparing Montessori programs to structured, cognitively oriented programs, she concludes that structure per se is not crucial. Rather, the greatest and most enduring gains are made in structured programs which include an emphasis on verbal and cognitive training.

The intervention programs reported above were carried out over one or two year's time. Deutsch (1971) reports results of more extended intervention conducted with severely disadvantaged inner city children over a five-year period. After five years of the program, the difference between the experimental and control groups in the third grade was a nonsignificant four points.

These findings raised the important issue of the effect of program length. Of the programs reported in Table 2, four extended longer than one year. Of these, only one (Herzog) showed some rise after the first year. Two indicated no change (Weikart and (Gray E_2) and the third (Gray E_1), like Deutsch's, exhibited a decline. It is significant, in light of Herzog's conclusion "The less they have the less they learn" (Herzog, *et al.*, 1972b), that the Gray and Deutsch samples were the most economically depressed of any included in the analysis.

The hope that group programs begun in the earliest years of life produce greater and more enduring gains is also disappointed. In a project directed by Caldwell (Braun and Caldwell, 1973) children entering intervention programs before the age of three did no better than later entrants, with duration of participation held constant.

One ray of hope emanates from Follow-Through, a nationwide, federally sponsored program, which extends the basic philosophy of Head Start into the primary grades (Stanford Research Institute, 1971a, 1971b). Some early findings indicate that Follow-Through children made significantly larger fall-to-spring gains in achievement than did children in the control group. Furthermore, greatest gains were made by participants who were below the OEO poverty line and by children who had previously participated in Head Start. Finally, highly structured curricula produced the greatest gains. These findings, though encouraging, must be viewed with caution because of inadequate matching between experimental and control families in socioeconomic characteristics and parental motivation. Nevertheless, the possibility exists that the comprehensiveness of the Head Start and Follow-Through programs—including family services and health and nutritional care—accounted for the more enduring gains.

The long-term effectiveness of Follow-Through is yet to be determined. Many of the declines apparent in Table 2 occurred after first grade. Other studies (Deutsch, Gray) report a drop in IQ occurring beyond the first grade level even while the program was still in operation. It has been fashionable to blame the schools for the erosion of competence in disadvantaged children after six years of age. The decline in Deutsch's experimental subjects, who were at the time in an innovative and enriched educational program, suggests that the fault lies in substantial degree beyond the doors of the school. Additional findings lend support to this conclusion. The children who profited least from intervention programs and who showed the earliest and most rapid decline were those who came from the most deprived social and economic backgrounds. Especially relevant in this regard were such variables as the number of children in the family, the employment status of the head of the household, the level of parents' education, and the presence of only one parent in the family.

The impact of such environmental factors is reflected in a study by Hayes and Grether (1969). Rather than assessing academic gains from September to June, as is done conventionally, they looked at changes from June to September—that is, over the summer. They found that, during summer vacation, white children from advantaged families either held their own or continued to gain, whereas youngsters from disadvantaged and black families reversed direction and lost ground. Hayes and Grether conclude that differences over the summer months account for 80 percent of the variation in academic performance between economically advantaged whites and children from nonwhite families. Accordingly, they argue that intervention efforts are best directed at the home. Our analysis of home-based programs, however, did not lead to such a verdict. Rather, as indicated below, it suggested combining elements from both strategies in a sequential manner.

V. SOME EFFECTS OF HOME-BASED INTERVENTION

The form of Table 3 is the same as that of Table 2, but the substance is happily different. The experimental groups in most home-based programs not only made substantial initial gains but these gains increased and continued to hold up rather well three to four years after intervention had been discontinued. The fact that matched controls also exhibited gains in IQ over time is probably due to the special characteristics of the families who participated in home-based intervention: first, the parents were all volunteers who were then randomly assigned to experimental or control groups; thus, all were motivated to provide educational experiences for their children and were willing to accept a stranger into their home. Second, participants in these programs were from relatively less disadvantaged backgrounds, thus providing some corroboration for Herzog's sobering verdict, "The less they have, the less they learn." (Herzog et al., 1972b) But other important factors distinguish these home-based programs: they begin working with children at an earlier age, and they emphasize one-to-one interaction between the child and adult.

However, this one-to-one interaction appears to require special participants. For example, a tutor visiting on a daily basis produces only temporary gains (Schaefer, 1968; Kirk, 1969). From their analyses of the reasons for the failure of this type of program, Schaefer (Schaefer & Aaronson, 1972) concluded that a necessary and crucial component was maternal interest and direct involvement in the teaching process. Schaefer's (1972) insistence on a "family-" rather than "child-centered" approach is exemplified in a project developed by Levenstein. She developed strategies to maximize mother-child interaction around educational materials which she provided. Viewed as a whole, the results from Levenstein's five differentially treated experimental groups suggest that the earlier and more intensely mother and child were stimulated to engage in communication around a common activity, the greater and more enduring the gain in IQ achieved by the child.

TABLE 3. EFFECTS ON LATER INTELLECTUAL DEVELOPMENT OF HOME-BASED INTERVENTION PROGRAMS

	SCHAEFER[a]			LEVENSTEIN I[c]					LEVENSTEIN II				
	1	2	3	4	5	6	7	8	9	10	11	12	13
	E	C	$E-C$	E_1	E_2	E_3	C_1	$\bar{E}-\bar{C}_1$[d]	E_4	E_5	C_2	C_3	$\bar{E}-\bar{C}$
N	24	24		6	7	21	8	8	8	15	7	10	
Age 1 Before	105.9	109.2	-3.3[b]										
After	95.3	89.4	5.9										
Age 2 Before	99.6	90.2	9.4	82.8	82.6	90.1	91.4	-8.7	91.1	87.6	91.3	91.0	-3.5
After				101.8	101.1	101.8	89.8	11.6*	101.3	102.4	95.8	—	6.4
Age 3 Before	105.6	89.4	16.2	102.6	105.0	108.6							
Age 4 Before	99.1	90.1	9.0	98.5	103.6	108.2	85.0	16.0[b]	106.6				
Kindergarten Before	97.8	92.8	5.0										
After				—	—	107.2	—	—	—	103.8	101.1	—	—
Grade I	100.6	96.9	3.7	98.8	100.6	—	88.8	10.9[b]	104.5	94.4	104.3	96.3	0
Initial gain	-10.6	-19.8	9.2	19.0*	18.5*	11.7*	-1.6	20.4*	10.2	14.8*	4.5	—	8.7[b]
Gain 2 years after	-8.1	-16.4	8.3	15.7*	21.0*	17.1*	-6.4	24.8[b]	15.5*	6.8[b]	—	—	5.3
Overall gain	-5.3	-12.3	7.0	16.0*	18.0*		-2.6	19.6	13.4[b]	—	12.9	—	2.2
Achievement level	.7	.7	0	1.2	1.4		1.2	.1	2.1	1.5	1.6		.2

a. Bayley Infant Scale was used for first three testing periods; Binet thereafter.
b. No significant tests available for this value and rest of column.
c. Catell Test used at age 2.
d. $E = \frac{1}{2}(E_1 + E_2)$.
(Double line designates point at which intervention was terminated.)
(Single broken line designates point of entry into school.)

To facilitate this mother-child interaction, Levenstein trained home visitors, whom she called Toy Demonstrators. After first using professionals, she found that non-professional low income mothers were equally competent in this role. Their task was to demonstrate the use of the toys, but far more importantly, to "treat the mother as a colleague in a joint endeavor in behalf of the child" (Levenstein, 1970a, p. 429). Levenstein strongly emphasized that the Demonstrators "keep constantly in mind that the child's primary and continuing educational relationship is with his mother" (1970a, p. 429). The task of the Demonstrator was to enhance this relationship. Thus Levenstein not only created a structured-cognitive program, but directed it at the mother-child system. Furthermore, the mother, rather than a stranger-expert, is the primary agent of intervention.

The resulting reciprocal interaction between mother and child involves both cognitive and emotional components which reinforce each other. When this recipro-cal interaction takes place in an interpersonal relationship that endures over time (as occurs between mother and child), it leads to the development of a strong emotional attachment which, in turn, increases the motivation of the young child to attend to and learn from the mother. It is important, as demonstrated in the Levenstein project, that this process be reinforced when the child's dependency on the mother is greatest— that is, in the second year of life (Bronfenbrenner, 1968). In addition, Levenstein reports that neither a friendly visit with mother and child, nor the mere provision of instructional materials, was sufficient by itself to produce the major effect; the critical element appeared to involve mother-child interaction around a common activity.

This reciprocal process may explain the enduring effectiveness of home interven-tion programs. Since the participants remain together after intervention ceases, the momentum of the system insures some degree of continuity for the future. As a result, the gains achieved through this kind of intervention strategy are more likely to persist than those gained in group preschool programs, which, after they are over, leave no social structure with familiar figures who can continue to reciprocate and reinforce the specific adaptive patterns which the child has learned. In emphasizing the primary role of the parent, and in carrying out the invervention at home, Levenstein maximizes the possibility that gains made by the child will be maintained.

But is it necessary to involve both the mother and child? Perhaps the same result can be obtained by working mainly with the mother? Karnes et al. (1969) developed a program which included home visits, but emphasized weekly group meetings of the mothers and lasted 15 months instead of seven as in the Levenstein study. At the end of the program, the experimental group obtained a mean IQ of 106, 16 points higher than the comparison group. To control for factors associated with home and family, Karnes et al. also compared IQ scores of the experimental subjects with those that had been obtained by older siblings when they were of the same age. A 28 IQ point difference in favor of the experimental group was found.

Encouraged by these findings, Karnes and her colleagues sought to create an optimal intervention strategy by combining the mother-intervention with a preschool program for the children themselves. The results were disappointing, at least by comparison. The children entered the program at age four. After two years there were no differences in IQ between the experimental and control group, and the latter actually scored reliably higher in tests of language development. Why the marked difference in effectiveness? The authors cite one crucial change in the program: the introduction of a group preschool experience. This, combined with a reduction in the number of at-home visits, may have led the mothers to believe that they no longer played the critical role in furthering the development of their children. As Karnes describes it,

> These changes, which seemed relatively minor at the time, coupled with the child's preschool attendance may have significantly altered the mother's perception of her role in this program. In the short-term study, the mother was aware that she was the only active agent for change in her child, and as she became convinced of the merit of the program, she increasingly felt this responsibility. . . . In the longer study, mothers appreciated the value of the activities for their children but may have overemphasized the role of the preschool in achieving the goals of the program. Teachers, through their actions rather than direct statement, may have unwittingly reinforced this devaluation of mother-child interaction by making the purpose of home visits the delivery of materials to absentee mothers. The emphasis of home visits had changed from concern over mother-child interaction to concern over the presence of materials, and it was not unreasonable for some mothers to feel that the materials themselves were the essential ingredient in effecting change. (Karnes, 1969c, pp. 211–212)

The effectiveness of parent intervention also appears to vary as a function of age. Evidence from a number of studies (e.g. Gilmer *et al.,* 1970; Karnes, 1968, 1969b; Levenstein, 1970a) indicates that the greatest gains are obtained with two year olds, and tend to be smaller with older preschoolers, becoming negligible when children are not enrolled until five years of age. Further support for this conclusion comes from Gilmer *et al.* (1970), in an investigation of the effect of home-based intervention on siblings of the target child. Results indicated that younger siblings of those in the parent-intervention groups benefited even more from the program than did the target children.

In the same study, Gilmer and her colleagues also demonstrated a further complexity as a function of age. In addition to looking at effects on siblings, these investigators compared the relative effectiveness of group-, home- and combined programs with four and five-year-old participants. They found that the group program was most effective initially, but scores rapidly declined after discontinuation of the program. The parent intervention groups, while not exhibiting as dramatic gains, nevertheless sustained their advantage longer than the group-centered children. Thus, although parent intervention did not achieve as high gains in the later preschool period, it appeared to retain its power to sustain increases attained by whatever means, including group programs in preschool settings.

VI. A SEQUENTIAL STRATEGY FOR EARLY INTERVENTION

Gilmer's results suggest the possibility of a phased sequence beginning with parent intervention in the first two years of life, followed by the addition of group programs in the late preschool and early school years. A program involving such a phased sequence is currently being carried out by Gordon (1971, 1972, 1973) with indigent families from 12 Florida counties. A weekly home visit is being conducted for the first two years of life, with a small group setting being added in the third year. About 175 children were randomly distributed into eight groups, systematically varied with respect to age at entry and length of exposure to the program, with one group receiving no treatment whatsoever.

Although no measures of intellectual level were obtained at the beginning of the program, Gordon (1973) has recently reported Binet IQ's for each group five years after intervention was started; that is, from two to four years after "graduation." Of the seven experimental groups, the only three that still differed from controls by more than five IQ points (with means from 95 to 97 in the last year of follow-up) were those that had received parent intervention in the first year of life and continued in the program for either one or two consecutive years. Groups which started parent intervention later, whose participation was interrupted for a year, or who were exposed to parent and group intervention only simultaneously, did not do as well. Moreover, the addition of group intervention in the third year for children under four did not result in a higher IQ for those groups that had this experience. Indeed, in both instances in which parent intervention in the second year was followed by the addition of preschool in the third, the mean scores showed a drop over the two-year follow-up period. In contrast, the two groups for whom parent intervention was continued for a second year without the addition of a group program either held their own or gained during the follow-up period, despite the fact that they were tested three rather than only two years after intervention had ended.

Taken as a whole, Gordon's results lend support to the following conclusions:

1. The generalization that parent intervention has more lasting effects the earlier it is begun can now be extended into the first year of life.
2. When parent intervention precedes group intervention, there are enduring effects after completion of the program, at least throughout the preschool years.
3. The addition of a group program after parent intervention has been carried out for a one or two-year period clearly does not result in additional gains, and may even produce a loss, when the group intervention is introduced as early as the third year of life. This type of sequential intervention does seem effective, however, for older children.

But what if the preschool component is not added until the children are four or five years old?

A partial answer comes from the evaluation of a Supplementary Kindergarten Intervention Program developed by Weikart *et al.* (Radin, 1969). The program involved disadvantaged kindergarten children of high ability and consisted of two components in various experimental combinations: (1) a special class supplementing the regular kindergarten session with a Piagetian, cognitively oriented curriculum, and (2) a home visit program to plan similar activities with the mother which she subsequently carried out with her child. The children who experienced the full program—both group and home—exhibited higher IQ gains than those who experienced the supplementary program plus kindergarten, or kindergarten only. But, more importantly, an analysis comparing children who had attended a preschool program involving intensive parent intervention, with those who had not, revealed that children who had had the earlier parent involvement experience gained more in IQ during the SKIP program. Furthermore, children who experienced no parent intervention, either in preschool or school, but who spent a full day first in regular kindergarten and then in the SKIP Piaget course, fell six points in IQ during the kindergarten year. The impact of the classroom program was negative in the absence of any previous or concomitant parent intervention—particularly since it kept the child away from home for a full day.

Radin (1972) has just replicated her findings in a second study designed to provide a direct test of the hypothesis that prior exposure to parent intervention enhances the impact of subsequent group programs. Three matched groups of 21–28 four-year-olds from lower class homes were exposed to a preschool program supplemented with biweekly home visits. In one group, the visitor worked directly with the child, the mother not being present. In a second group, the visitor employed the same activities as a basis for encouraging mother-child interaction. In the third group, mother-child intervention was supplemented by a weekly group meeting led by a social worker and focusing on child rearing practices conducive to the child's development. At the end of the first year, all three groups made significant gains in IQ but did not differ reliably from each other. In addition, the mothers in the two treatments involving parent intervention showed changes in attitude interpreted as more conducive to the child's development, with the greatest shift observed in the group receiving home visits supplemented by weekly meetings.

During the following year, when the children were attending regular kindergarten (with no parent intervention program), the children who had been tutored directly in the preceding year made no additional gains in IQ, whereas the two groups exposed to prior parental intervention achieved further increases of 10 to 15 points. Radin concludes:

> In general the findings of this study suggest that a parent education component is important if the child is to continue to benefit academically from a compensatory preschool program, although there may be no immediate effect on the youngsters. . . . A parent program does appear, however, to enhance the mothers' perception of themselves as educators of their children and of their children as individuals capable of independent thought. Thus, perhaps, new maternal behaviors are fostered wihich are conducive to the child's intellectual functioning. (p. 1363.)

It is to be emphasized that Radin's parent program, like all the other effective parent strategies we have examined, focuses attention on interaction between parent and child around a common activity. This approach is to be distinguished from the widespread traditional forms of parent education involving courses, dissemination of information and counseling addressed only to the parent. There is no evidence for the effectiveness of such approaches (Amidon & Brim, 1972).

Radin's data indicate that the beneficial influence of parent intervention is substantial if it is introduced before the child enters school, but the effect is reduced if home visits are not begun until the kindergarten year. But what of the influence of parent intervention in the later school years? Smith (1968) demonstrated that parent involvement, albeit different in form, continues to be effective through the sixth grade. Her project included 1,000 children from low income housing projects, most of them black. Smith asked parents to support the child's educational activities without being actively involved in teaching, as in the preschool programs. Support consisted of such things as insuring household quiet during homework time, reading books in the presence of the children, and listening to children read. This program produced significant gain in scores on reading achievement in both the second and fifth grades. Once again the family emerges as the system which sustains and facilitates development, spurred by educational experience outside the home. These findings, however, do not displace our earlier conclusion: the optimal time for parent intervention is in the first three years of life.

In summary, intervention programs which place major emphasis on involving the parent *directly* in activities fostering the child's development are likely to have constructive impact at any age, but the earlier such activities are begun, and the longer they are continued, the greater the benefit to the child.

But one major problem still remains. Given that the optimal period for parent intervention is in the first three years of life, or at least before the child enters school, implementation of this strategy still requires the cooperation of the parents at home. But many disadvantaged families live under such oppressive circumstances that they are neither willing nor able to participate in the activities required by a parent intervention program. Inadequate health care, poor housing, lack of education, low income and the necessity for full-time work all continue to rob parents of time and energy to spend with their children. Does this mean that the best opportunity for the child must be foregone? Is there an alternative course?

VII. THE ECOLOGY OF EARLY INTERVENTION

One radical solution to this problem, being tried by Heber, involves removing the child from his home for most of his waking hours, placing him in an environment conducive to his growth and entrusting primary responsibility for his development to persons specifically trained for the job (Heber *et al.*, 1972). The sample for this study consisted of black mothers with newborns who were living in a severely depressed area of Milwaukee and who had IQ's of 75 or less. The experimental group of children attended an intensive, cognitively structured program taught by paraprofessional-teachers selected from the children's own neighborhood. The children entered the program at the age of three months and stayed at the center from 8:45 in the morning until 4:00 in the afternoon. Each child remained with his primary teacher on a one-to-one basis until he reached 12 to 15 months of age. Later, children were placed in small groups of two to four per teacher. A parallel program conducted for the mother involved two phases: job training and training in home economics and child rearing skills.

With respect to the cognitive development of the children, the program has been astoundingly successful and will probably continue to be so long as intervention lasts. At age 5½, the control and experimental groups were separated by 30 IQ points, with a mean of 124 for the latter.

Given our frame of reference, the success is not unexpected, since the program fulfills the major requirements we have stipulated as essential or desirable for fostering the cognitive development of the young child. With one particular person remaining the primary agent of intervention, group experiences were gradually introduced emphasizing language and structured cognitive activities. The entire operation was carried out by a group of people sharing and reinforcing a common commitment to young children and their development.

But what will happen when intervention is discontinued remains an open question. In addition, the costs of the program are prohibitive in terms of large-scale applicability. Nor have the ethical questions of removing a child from his home been dealt with. Is there another approach which does not entail these problems?

An affirmative answer to this question is suggested by Skeels (1969), in a follow-up study of two groups of mentally retarded, institutionalized children, who constituted the experimental and control groups in an experiment he had initiated 30 years earlier. (Skeels, Updegraff, Wellman, & Williams, 1938; Skeels & Dye, 1939). The average IQ of the children and of their mothers was under 70. When the children were about two years of age, 13 of them were placed in the care of female inmates at a state institution for the mentally retarded, with each child being assigned to a different ward. The control group was allowed to remain in the original—also institutional—environment, a children's orphanage. During the formal experimental period, which averaged a year and a half, the experimental group showed a mean rise in IQ of 28 points from 64 to 92, whereas the control group dropped 26 points. Upon completion of the experiment, it became possible to place 11 of the experimental children in legal adoption. After 2½ years with their adoptive parents, this group showed a further nine-point rise to a mean of 101. Thirty years later, all of the original 13 children, now adults, in the experimental group were found to be self-supporting, all but two had completed high school, with four having one or more years of college. In the control group, all were either dead or still institutionalized. Skeels concludes his report with some dollar figures on the amount of taxpayer's money expended to sustain the institutionalized group, in contrast to the productive income brought in by those who had been raised initially by mentally deficient women in a state institution.

The Skeels experiment is instructive on two counts. First, if Heber demonstrated that disadvantaged children of mothers with IQ's under 75 could, with appropriate intervention, attain an IQ well above the norm, Skeels showed that retarded mothers themselves can achieve the same gains for children under their care at substantially less expense. How was this accomplished? First, Skeels points out that almost every experimental child was involved in an intense, one-to-one relationship with an older adult. Not only did the children enjoy this close interpersonal relationship, but the girls and the attendants "spent a great deal of time with 'their children' playing, talking, and training them in every way." (Skeels, pp. 16–17) The grounds and house also afforded a wide range of toys and activities, and all children attended a nonstructured preschool program as soon as they could walk.

Thus three of the essential components of the sequential strategy we previously identified are included in the Skeels research: the initial establishment of an enduring relationship involving intensive interaction with the child; priority, status, and support for the "mother-child" system; the introduction, at a later stage, of a preschool program, but with the child returning "home" for half the day to a highly available mother substitute. The only element that is missing is the systematic involvement of the child in progressively more complex activities, first in the context of the mother-child relationship, and later, in the curriculum of the preschool program. Had these elements of cognitively challenging experience been present, it is conceivable that the children would have shown even more dramatic gains in IQ, approaching the levels achieved by Heber's experimental group.

Both the Skeels and Heber experiments demonstrate the effectiveness of a major transformation in the environment for the child and the behavior of the persons principally responsible for his care and development. We shall refer to this kind of reorganization as *ecological intervention*. The aim is to effect changes in the *context* in which the family lives that enable the family as a whole to exercise the functions necessary for the child's development.

The need for ecological intervention arises when the conditions of life are such that the family cannot perform its childrearing functions even though it may wish to do so. Under such restrictive circumstances, no direct form of intervention aimed at enhancing the child's development is likely to have much impact. For children living in the most deprived environments, the first step in any strategy of intervention must be to provide the family with adequate health care, nutrition, housing, and employment. It is clear that such ecological intervention is not being carried out today precisely because it requires major institutional changes.

But even when the basic needs for survival are met, the conditions of life may be such as to prevent the family from functioning effectively in its child rearing role. As we have seen, an essential prerequisite for the child's development is an environment which provides not only the opportunity but also support for parental activity. Once this is established, the style and degree of parent-child interaction becomes a crucial factor.

Skodak and Skeels (1949) demonstrate this in a study of the effects of adoption on the development of 100 children whose true parents were both socioeconomically disadvantaged and mentally retarded. The children were placed in foster families who were above average in economic security and educational and cultural status. The average IQ of the children's true mothers was 86; by the age of 13 the mean IQ of their children placed in foster homes was 106. A thorough analysis revealed that among the group of adopted children, those who made the greatest sustained gains were those who had experienced "maximal stimulation in infancy with optimum security and affection following placement at an average of three months of age" (Skodak & Skeels, 1949, p. 111).

These three investigations demonstrate the effectiveness of massive ecological intervention. But two of them involved placing institutionalized children in foster homes. When the child remains a member of his family, such a course is problematic. Can anything be done for such disadvantaged families, whose basic needs for survival are being met but whose lives are so burdened as to preclude opportunity for effective fulfillment of the parental role?

No answers are available to this question from our analysis of the research literature, for, as we have indicated, ecological intervention is as yet a largely untried endeavor both in our science and in our society. It seems clear, however, that certain urgent needs of families will have to be met in ways which provide support and status for parents in their childrearing activities. Possibilities exist in four major areas:[1]

1. The world of work—part-time jobs and flexible work schedules;
2. The school—parent apprentice programs in the schools to engage older children in supervised care of the young, involvement of the parents in work at school;
3. The neighborhood—parent-child groups for mutual assistance, family centers for services demonstrations, and cross-age activities;
4. The home—prenatal training in nutrition, medical care, etc., homemaker service, emergency insurance, television teaching.

Programs focused on these themes, addressed to both children and adults, would contribute to making parenthood a more attractive and respected activity in the eyes of children, parents, and the society at large.

VIII. SOME PRINCIPLES OF EARLY INTERVENTION: A SUMMARY

Although further research is needed to replicate results and eliminate alternative interpretations, some principles can be stated specifying the elements that appear essential for the effectiveness of early intervention programs.

First, the family seems to be the most effective and economical system for fostering and sustaining the child's development. Without family involvement, intervention is likely to be unsuccessful, and what few effects are achieved are likely to disappear once the intervention is discontinued.

Secondly, ecological intervention is necessary for millions of disadvantaged families in our country—to provide adequate health care, nutrition, housing, employment, and opportunity and status for parenthood. The evidence demonstrates that even children from severely deprived backgrounds of mothers with IQ's below 70 or 80 are not doomed to inferiority by unalterable constraints either of heredity or environment. But it is certain that ecological intervention will require major changes in the institutions of our society.

Thirdly, a long range intervention program may be viewed in terms of five sequential stages:

1. Preparation for parenthood—child care, nutrition, and health training;
2. Before children come—adequate housing, economic security;
3. The first three years of life—establishment of a child-parent relationship of reciprocal interaction centered around activities which are challenging to the child; home visits, group meetings, to establish the parent as the primary agent of intervention;
4. Ages four through six—exposure to a cognitively oriented preschool program along with continued parent intervention;
5. Ages six through twelve—parental support of the child's educational activities at home and at school, parent remains primary figure responsible for the child's development as a person.

In completing this analysis, we reemphasize the tentative nature of the conclusions and the narrowness of the IQ and related measures as aspects of the total development of the child. We also wish to reaffirm a deep indebtedness to those who conducted the programs and researches on which this work is based, and a profound faith in the capacity of parents, of whatever background, to enable their children to develop into effective and happy human beings, *once our society is willing to make conditions of life viable and humane for all its families.*

NOTES

[1]For a more extensive discussion, see: U. Bronfenbrenner, The origins of alienation. *Scientific American,* August, 1974.

REFERENCES

Amidon, A., & Brim, O. G. What do children have to gain from parent education? Paper prepared for the Advisory Committee on Child Development, National Research Council, National Academy of Science, 1972.

Bee, H. L. Van Egeren, L. F., Streissguth, A. P., Nyman, B. A., & Leckie, M. S. Social class differences in maternal teaching strategies and speech patterns. *Developmental Psychology,* 1969, *1,* 726–734.

Bell, R. Q. A reinterpretation of the direction of effects in studies of socialization. *Psychological Review,* 1968, *75,* 81–95.

Beller, E. K. Impact of early education on disadvantaged children. In S. Ryan (Ed.), *A report on longitudinal evaluations of preschool programs.* Washington, D.C.: Office of Child Development, 1972.

Beller, E. K. Personal communication, 1973.

Bereiter, C., & Engelmann, S. *Teaching disadvantaged children in the preschool.* Englewood Cliffs, N.J.: Prentice-Hall, 1966.

Bissell, J. S. *The cognitive effects of preschool programs for disadvantaged children.* Washington, D.C.: National Institute of Child Health and Human Development, 1971.

Bissell, J. S. *Implementation of planned variation in Head Start: First year report.* Washington, D.C.: National Institute of Child Health and Human Development, 1971.

Bloom, B. S. *Compensatory education for cultural deprivation.* New York: Holt, Rinehart and Winston, 1965.

Bogatz, G. A., & Ball, S. *The second year of Sesame Street: A continuing evaluation.* Vols. 1 and 2. Princeton, N.J.: Educational Testing Service, 1971.

Braun, S. J., & Caldwell, B. Emotional adjustment of children in daycare who enrolled prior to or after the age of three. *Early Child Develop-and Care,* 1973, *2,* 13–21.

Bronfenbrenner, U. The changing American child: A speculative analysis. *Merrill-Palmer Quarterly,* 1961, *7,* 73–84.

Bronfenbrenner, U. Early deprivation: A cross-species analysis. In S. Levine & G. Newton (Eds.), *Early experience in behavior.* Springfield, Ill.: Charles C. Thomas, 1968. (a)

Bronfenbrenner, U. When is infant stimulation effective? In D. C. Glass (Ed.), *Environmental influences.* New York: Rockefeller University Press, 1968. (b)

Bronfenbrenner, U. *Two worlds of childhood: U.S. and U.S.S.R.* New York: Russell Sage Foundation, 1970.

Bronfenbrenner, U. The roots of alienation. In U. Bronfenbrenner (Ed.), *Influences on human development.* Hinsdale, Ill.: Dryden Press, 1972.

Bronfenbrenner, U. Developmental research and public policy. In J. M. Romanshyn (Ed.), *Social science and social welfare.* New York: Council on Social Work Education, 1973.

Bronfenbrenner, U., & Bruner, J. The President and the children. *New York Times,* January 31, 1972.

Caldwell, B. M., & Smith, L. E. Day care for the very young—prime opportunity for primary prevention. *American Journal of Public Health* 1970, *60,* 690–697.

Coleman, J. S. *Equality of educational opportunity.* Washington, D.C.: U.S. Office of Education, 1966.

Deutsch, M. Minority group and class status as related to social and personality factors in scholastic achievement. *Society for Applied Anthropology Monograph No. 2.* Ithaca, N.Y.: New York State School of Industrial and Labor Relations, Cornell University, 1960.

Deutsch, M., *et al. Regional research and resource center in early childhood: Final report.* Washington, D.C.: U.S. Office of Economic Opportunity, 1971.

Deutsch, M., Taleporos, E., & Victor, J. A brief synopsis of an initial enrichment program in early childhood. In S. R. Ryan (Ed.), *A report on longitudinal evaluations of preschool programs.* Washington, D.C.: Office of Child Development, 1972.

DiLorenzo, L. T. *Pre-kindergarten programs for educationally disadvantaged children: Final report.* Washington, D.C.: U.S. Office of Education, 1969.

Gardner, J., & Gardner, H. A note on selective imitation by a six-week-old infant. *Child Development,* 1970, *41,* 1209–1213.

Gilmer, B., Miller, J. O., & Gray, S. W. *Intervention with mothers and young children: Study of intra-family effects.* Nashville, Tenn.: DARCEE Demonstration and Research Center for Early Education, 1970.

Gordon, I. J. *A home learning center approach to early stimulation.* Gainesville, Florida: Institute for Development of Human Resources, 1971.

Gordon, I. J. *A home learning center approach to early stimulation.* Gainesville, Florida: Institute for Development of Human Resources, 1972.

Gordon, I. J. *An early intervention project: A longitudinal look.* Gainesville, Florida: University of Florida, Institute for Development of Human Resources, College of Education, 1973.

Gray, S. W., & Klaus, R. A. Experimental preschool program for culturally-deprived children. *Child Development,* 1965, *36,* 887–898.

Gray, S. W., & Klaus, R. A. The early training project. The seventh-year report. *Child Development,* 1970, *41,* 909–924.

Hayes, D., & Grether, L. The school year and vacation: When do students learn? Paper presented at the Eastern Sociological Convention, New York, 1969.

Hebb, D. O. *The organization of behavior.* New York: John Wiley, 1949.

Heber, R., Garber, H., Harrington, S., & Hoffman, C. *Rehabilitation of families at risk for mental retardation. Madison, Wisc.: Rehabilitation Research and Training Center in Mental Retardation, University of Wisconsin, October, 1972.*

Hertzig, M. E., Birch, H. G., Thomas, A., & Mendez, O. A. Class and ethnic differences in responsiveness of preschool children to cognitive demands. *Monograph of the Society for Research in Child Development,* 1968, *33,* No. 1.

Herzog, E., Newcomb, C. H., & Cisin, I. H. Double deprivation: The less they have the less they learn. In S. Ryan (Ed.), *A report on longitudinal evaluations of preschool programs.* Washington, D.C.: Office of Child Development, 1972. (a)

Herzog, E., Newcomb, C. H., & Cisin, I. R. But some are poorer than others: SES differences in a preschool program. *American Journal of Orthopsychiatry,* 1972, *42,* 4–22. (b)

Herzog, E., Newcomb, C. H., & Cisin, I. H. *Preschool and Postscript: An evaluation of the inner-city program.* Washington, D.C.: Social Research Group, George Washington University, 1973.

Hess, R. D., Shipman, V. C., Brophy, J. E., & Bear, R. M. *The cognitive environments of urban preschool children.* Chicago: University of Chicago Graduate School of Education, 1968.

Hess, R. D., Shipman, V. C., Brophy, J. E., & Bear, R. M. *The cognitive environments of urban preschool children: Follow-up phase.* Chicago: University of Chicago Graduate School of Education, 1969.

Hodges, W. L., McCandless, B. R., & Spicker, H. H. *The development and evaluation of a diagnostically based curriculum for preschool psychosocially deprived children.* Washington, D.C.: U.S. Office of Education, 1967.

Hunt, J. McV. *Intelligence and experience.* New York: Ronald Press, 1961.

Infant Education Research Project. Washington, D.C.: U.S. Office of Education Booklet #OE-37033.

Jones, S. J., & Moss, H. A. Age, state, and maternal behavior associated with infant vocalizations. *Child Development,* 1971, *42,* 1039.

Kagan, J. On cultural deprivation. In D. C. Glass (Ed.), *Environmental influences.* New York: Rockefeller University Press, 1968.

Kagan, J. *Change and continuity in infancy.* New York: John Wiley, 1971.

Karnes, M. B., Studley, W. M., Wright, W. R., & Hodgins, A. S. An approach to working with mothers of disadvantaged preschool children. *Merrill-Palmer Quarterly,* 1968, *14,* 174–184.

Karnes, M. B. *Research and development program on preschool disadvantaged children: Final report.* Washington, D.C.: U.S. Office of Education, 1969.

Karnes, M. B., & Badger, E. E. Training mothers to instruct their infants at home. In M. B. Karnes, *Research and development program on preschool disadvantaged children: Final report.* Washington, D.C.: U.S. Office of Education, 1969. (a)

Karnes, M. B., Hodgins, A. S., & Teska, J. A. The effects of short-term instruction at home by mothers of children not enrolled in a preschool. In M. B. Karnes, *Research and development program on preschool disadvantaged children: Final report.* Washington, D.C.: U.S. Office of Education, 1969. (b)

Karnes, M. B., Hodgins, A. S., & Teska, J. A. The impact of at-home instruction by mothers on performance in the ameliorative preschool. In M. B. Karnes, *Research and development program on preschool disadvantaged children: Final report.* Washington, D.C.: U.S. Office of Education, 1969. (c)

Karnes, M. B., Teska, J. A. , Hodgins, A. S., & Badger, E. D. Educational intervention at home by mothers of disadvantaged infants. *Child Development,* 1970, *41,* 925–935.

Karnes, M. B., Zehrbach, R. R., & Teska, J. A. An ameliorative approach in the development of curriculum. In R. K. Parker (Ed.), *The preschool in action.* Boston: Allyn and Bacon, 1972.

Kirk, S. A. *Early education of the mentally retarded.* Urbana, Ill.: University of Illinois Press, 1958.

Kirk, S. A. The effects of early education with disadvantaged infants. In M. B. Karnes, *Research and development program on preschool disadvantaged children: Final report.* Washington, D.C.: U.S. Office of Education, 1969.

Klaus, R. A., & Gray, S. W. The early training project for disadvantaged children: A report after five years. *Monographs of the Society for Research in Child Development,* 1968, *33,* (4, Serial # 120).

Kraft, I., Fushillo, J., & Herzog, E. Prelude to school: An evaluation of an inner-city school program. *Children's Bureau Research Report Number 3.* Washington, D.C.: Children's Bureau, 1968.

Levenstein, P. Cognitive growth in preschoolers through verbal interaction with mothers. *American Journal of Orthopsychiatry,* 1970, *40,* 426–432.

Levenstein, P. *Verbal Interaction Project.* Mineola, N.Y.: Family Service Association of Nassau County, Inc., 1972. (a)

Levenstein, P. But does it work in homes away from home? *Theory Into Practice,* 1972, *11,* 157–162. (b)

Levenstein, P. Personal communication, 1972. (c)

Levenstein, P., & Levenstein, S. Fostering learning potential in preschoolers. *Social Casework,* 1971, *52,* 74–78.

Levenstein, P., & Sunley, R. Stimulation of verbal interaction between disadvantaged mothers and children. *American Journal of Orthopsychiatry,* 1968, *38,* 116–121.

Moss, H. A. Sex, age, and state as determinants of mother-infant interaction. *Merrill-Palmer Quarterly,* 1967. *13,* 19–36.

Radin, N. The impact of a kindergarten home counseling program. *Exceptional Children,* 1969, *36,* 251–256.

Radin, N. Three degrees of maternal involvement in a preschool program: Impact on mothers and children. *Child Development,* 1972, *43,* 1355–1364.

Radin, N., & Weikart, D. A home teaching program for disadvantaged preschool children. *Journal of Special Education,* Winter 1967, *1,* 183–190.

Resnick, M. B., & Van De Riet, V. *Summary evaluation of the Learning to Learn program*. Gainesville, Florida: University of Florida, Department of Clinical Psychology, 1973.

Rheingold, H. L. The social and socializing infant. In D. A. Goslin, *Handbook of socialization theory and research*. Chicago: Rand McNally, 1969.

Schaefer, E. S. *Progress report: Intellectual stimulation of culturally-deprived parents.* Washington, D.C.: National Institute of Mental Health, 1968.

Schaefer, E. S. Need for early and continuing education. In V. H. Denenberg (Ed.), *Education of the infant and young child*. New York: Academic Press, 1970.

Schaefer, E. S. Personal communication, 1972. (a)

Schaefer, E. S. Parents as educators: Evidence from cross-sectional longitudinal and intervention research. *Young Children,* 1972, *27,* 227–239. (b)

Schaefer, E. S., & Aaronson, M. Infant education research project: Implementation and implications of the home-tutoring program. In R. K. Parker (Ed.), *The preschool in action*. Boston: Allyn and Bacon, 1972.

Schoggen, M., & Schoggen, P. *Environmental forces in home lives of three-year-old children in three population sub-groups.* Nashville, Tenn.: George Peabody College for Teachers, DARCEE Papers and Reports, Vol. 5, No. 2, 1971.

Skeels, H. M. Adult status of children from contrasting early life experiences. *Monographs of the Society for Research in Child Development,* 1966, *31,* Serial # 105.

Skeels, H. M., & Dye, H. B. A study of the effects of differential stimulation on mentally retarded children. *Proceedings and Addresses of the American Association on Mental Deficiency,* 1939, *44,* 114–136.

Skeels, H. M., Updegraff, R., Wellman, B. L. & Williams, H. M. A study of environmental stimulation: An orphanage preschool project. *University of Iowa Studies in Child Welfare,* 1938, *15,* #4.

Skodak, M., & Skeels, H. M. A final follow-up study of 100 adopted children. *Journal of Genetic Psychology,* 1949, *75,* 85–125.

Smith, M. B. School and home: Focus on achievement. In A. H. Passow (Ed.), *Developing programs for the educationally disadvantaged*. New York: Teachers College Press, 1968.

Soar, R. S. An integrative approach to classroom learning. NIMH Project Number 5-R11MH01096 to the University of South Carolina and 7-R11MH02045 to Temple University, 1966.

Soar, R. S. Follow-Through classroom process measurement and pupil growth (1970–71). Gainesville, Florida: College of Education, University of Florida, 1972.

Soar, R. S., & Soar, R. M. Pupil subject matter growth during summer vacation. *Educational Leadership Research Supplement,* 1969, *2,* 577–587.

Sprigle, H. Learning to learn program. In S. Ryan (Ed.), *A report of longitudinal evaluations of preschool programs.* Washington, D.C.: Office of Child Development, 1972.

Stanford Research Institute. Implementation of planned variation in Head Start: Preliminary evaluation of planned variation in Head Start according to Follow-Through approaches (1969–70). Washington, D.C.: Office of Child Development, U.S. Department of Health, Education and Welfare, 1971. (a)

Stanford Research Institute. Longitudinal evaluation of selected features of the national Follow-Through program. Washington, D.C.: Office of Education, U.S. Department of Health, Education and Welfare, 1971. (b)

Tulkin, S. R., & Cohler, B. J. Child rearing attitudes on mother-child interaction among middle and working class families. Paper presented at the 1971 meeting of the Society for Research in Child Development.

Tulkin, S. R., & Kagan, J. Mother-child interaction: Social class differences in the first year of life. *Proceedings of the 78th Annual Convention of the American Psychological Association,* 1970, 261–262.

Van De Riet, V. *A sequential approach to early childhood and elementary education.* Gainesville, Florida: Department of Clinical Psychology, University of Florida, 1972.

Weikart, D. P. *Preschool intervention: A preliminary report of the Perry Preschool Project.* Ann Arbor, Mich.: Campus Publishers, 1967.

Weikart, D. P. A comparative study of three preschool curricula. A paper presented at the Bi-annual meeting of the Society for Research in Child Development, Santa Monica, Calif., March 1969.

Weikart, D. P., *et al. Longitudinal results of the Ypsilanti Perry Preschool Project.* Ypsilanti, Mich.: High/Scope Educational Research Foundation, 1970.

Weikart, D. P., Kamii, C. K., & Radin, M. *Perry Preschool Progress Report.* Ypsilanti, Mich.: Ypsilanti Public Schools, 1964.

Weikart, D. P., Rogers, L., Adcock, C., & McClelland, D. *The cognitively oriented curriculum.* Washington, D.C.: National Association for the Education of Young Children, 1971.

4.9

An Experiment in Group Upbringing

Anna Freud
Sophie Dann

INTRODUCTION

The experiment to which the following notes refer is not the outcome of an artificial and deliberate laboratory setup but of a combination of fateful outside circumstances. The six young children who
are involved in it are German-Jewish orphans, victims of the Hitler regime, whose
parents, soon after their birth, were deported to Poland and killed in the gas cham-
bers. During their first year of life, the children's experiences differed; they were
handed on from one refuge to another, until they arrived individually, at ages varying
from approximately six to twelve months, in the concentration camp of Tereszin.[1]
There they became inmates of the Ward for Motherless Children, were conscientiously cared for and medically supervised, within the limits of the current restrictions
of food and living space. They had no toys and their only facility for outdoor life was
a bare yard. The Ward was staffed by nurses and helpers, themselves inmates of the
concentration camp and, as such, undernourished and overworked. Since Tereszin
was a transit camp, deportations were frequent. Approximately two to three years after
arrival, in the spring of 1945, when liberated by the Russians, the six children, with
others, were taken to a Czech castle where they were given special care and were
lavishly fed. After one month's stay, the 6 were included in a transport of 300 older
children and adolescents, all of them survivors from concentration camps, the first
of 1,000 children for whom the British Home Office had granted permits of entry. They
were flown to England in bombers and arrived in August 1945 in a carefully set-up
reception camp in Windermere, Westmoreland where they remained for two months.
When this reception camp was cleared and the older children distributed to various
hostels and training places, it was thought wise to leave the six youngest together,
to remove them from the commotion which is inseparable from the life of a large
children's community and to provide them with peaceful, quiet surroundings where,
for a year at least, they could adapt themselves gradually to a new country, a new
language, and the altered circumstances of their lives.

This ambitious plan was realized through the combined efforts of a number of
people. A friend of the former Hampstead Nurseries, Mrs. Ralph Clarke, wife of the
Member of Parliament for East Grinstead, Sussex, gave the children a year's tenancy

Reprinted with slight abridgment from *The Psychoanalytic Study of the Child,* Vol. VI, pp. 127–168,
by permission of the author and the International Universities Press, Inc. Copyright 1951 by
International Universities Press, Inc.

of a country house with field and adjoining woodland, "Bulldogs Bank" in West Hoathly, Sussex, containing two bedrooms for the children, with adjoining bathrooms, a large day nursery, the necessary staff rooms, a veranda running the whole length of the house and a sun terrace.

The Foster Parents' Plan for War Children, Inc., New York, who had sponsored the Hampstead Nurseries during the war years 1940–1945, took the six children into their plan and adopted Bulldogs Bank as one of their colonies. They provided the necessary equipment as well as the financial upkeep.

The new Nursery was staffed by Sisters Sophie and Gertrud Dann, formerly the head nurses of the Baby Department and Junior Nursery Department of the Hampstead Nurseries respectively. A young assistant, Miss Maureen Wolfison, who had accompanied the children from Windermere was replaced after several weeks by Miss Judith Gaulton, a relief worker. Cooking and housework was shared between the staff, with occasional outside help.

The children arrived in Bulldogs Bank on October 15, 1945. The personal data of the six, so far as they could be ascertained, were as shown in the following table [page 357].

Meager as these scraps of information are, they establish certain relevant facts concerning the early history of this group of children:

1. That four of them (Ruth, Leah, Miriam, Peter) lost their mothers at birth or immediately afterward; one (Paul) before the age of twelve months, one (John) at an unspecified date;

2. That after the loss of their mothers all the children wandered for some time from one place to another, with several complete changes of adult environment. (Bulldogs Bank was the sixth station in life for Peter, the fifth for Miriam, etc. John's and Leah's and Paul's wanderings before arrival in Tereszin are not recorded.);

3. That none of the children had known any other circumstances of life than those of a group setting. They were ignorant of the meaning of a "family";

4. That none of the children had experience of normal life outside a camp or big institution.

BEHAVIOR TOWARD ADULTS ON ARRIVAL

On leaving the reception camp in Windermere, the children reacted badly to the renewed change in their surroundings. They showed no pleasure in the arrangements which had been made for them and behaved in a wild, restless, and uncontrollably noisy manner. During the first days after arrival they destroyed all the toys and damaged much of the furniture. Toward the staff they behaved either with cold indifference or with active hostility, making no exception for the young assistant Maureen who had accompanied them from Windermere and was their only link with the immediate past. At times they ignored the adults so completely that they would not look up when one of them entered the room. They would turn to an adult when in some immediate need, but treat the same person as nonexistent once more when the need was fulfilled. In anger, they would hit the adults, bite or spit. Above all, they would shout, scream, and use bad language. Their speech, at the time was German with an admixture of Czech words, and a gradual increase of English words. In a good mood, they called the staff members indiscriminately *Tante* (auntie), as they had done in Tereszin; in bad moods this was changed to *blöde Tante* (silly, stupid auntie). Their favorite swearword was *blöder Ochs* (the equivalent of "stupid fool"), a German term which they retained longer than any other.

NAME	DATE AND PLACE OF BIRTH	FAMILY HISTORY	AGE AT ARRIVAL IN TERESZIN	AGE AT ARRIVAL IN BULLDOGS BANK
John	18.12.1941 Vienna	Orthodox Jewish working class parents. Deported to Poland and killed.	Presumably under 12 months	3 years 10 months
Ruth	21.4.1942 Vienna	Parents, a brother of 7 and a sister of 4 years were deported and killed when Ruth was a few months old. She was cared for in a Jewish Nursery in Vienna, sent to Tereszin with the Nursery.	Several months	3 years 6 months
Leah	23.4.1942 Berlin	Leah and a brother were illegitimate, hidden from birth. Fate of mother and brother unknown. Brother presumed killed.	Several months	3 years 5 months Arrived 6 weeks after the others owing to a ring-worm infection.
Paul	21.5.1942 Berlin	Unknown	12 months	3 years 5 months
Miriam	18.8.1942 Berlin	Upper middle-class family. Father died in concentration camp, mother went insane, was cared for first in a mental hospital in Vienna, later in a mental ward in Tereszin where she died.	6 months	3 years 2 months
Peter	22.10.1942	Parents deported and killed when Peter was a few days old. Child was found abandoned in public park, cared for first in a convent, later, when found to be Jewish, was taken to the Jewish hospital in Berlin, then brought to Tereszin.	Under 12 months	3 years

GROUP REACTIONS

Clinging to the Group

The children's positive feelings were centered exclusively in their own group. It was evident that they cared greatly for each other and not at all for anybody or anything else. They had no other wish than to be together and became upset when they were separated from each other, even for short moments. No child would consent to remain upstairs while the others were downstairs, or vice versa, and no child would be taken for a walk or on an errand without the others. If anything of the kind happened, the single child would constantly ask for the other children while the group would fret for the missing child.

This insistence on being inseparable made it impossible in the beginning to treat the children as individuals or to vary their lives according to their special needs. Ruth, for instance, did not like going for walks, while the others greatly preferred walks to indoor play. But it was very difficult to induce the others to go out and let Ruth stay at home. One day, they actually left without her, but kept asking for her until, after approximately twenty minutes, John could bear it no longer and turned back to fetch her. The others joined him, they all returned home, greeted Ruth as if they had been separated for a long time and then took her for a walk, paying a great deal of special attention to her. . . .

Inability to be separated from the group showed up most glaringly in those instances where individual children were singled out for a special treat, a situation for which children crave under normal circumstances. Paul, for example, cried for the other children when he was taken as the only one for a ride in the pony cart, although at other times such rides were a special thrill to him as well as to the others. On another, later, occasion the whole group of children was invited to visit another nursery in the neighborhood. Since the car was not large enough to take everybody, Paul and Miriam were taken earlier by bus. The other four, in the car, inquired constantly about them and could not enjoy the trip nor the pleasures prepared for them, until they were reunited.

Type of Group Formation

When together, the children were a closely knit group of members with equal status, no child assuming leadership for any length of time, but each one exerting a strong influence on the others by virtue of individual qualities, peculiarities, or by the mere fact of belonging. At the beginning, John, as the oldest, seemed to be the undisputed leader at mealtimes. He only needed to push away his plate, for everybody else to cease eating. Peter, though the youngest, was the most imaginative of all and assumed leadership in games, which he would invent and organize. Miriam too played a major role, in a peculiar way. She was a pretty, plump child, with ginger hair, freckles and a ready smile. She behaved toward the other children as if she were a superior being, and let herself be served and spoiled by them as a matter of course. She would sometimes smile at the boys in return for their services, while accepting Leah's helpfulness toward herself without acknowledgement. But she, too, did not guide or govern the group. The position was rather that she needed a special kind of attention to be paid to her and that the other children sensed this need and did their best to fulfill it. The following are some recorded examples of this interplay between Miriam and the group:

> *November 1945.* Miriam, on a walk, has found a tiny pink flower, carries it in her hand but loses it soon. She calls out "flower!" and John and Paul hurry to pick it up for her, a difficult task since they wear thick gloves. Miriam drops the flower again and again, never makes an attempt to pick it up herself, merely calls "flower!" and the boys hurry to find it.

> *March 1946.* From the beginning Miriam liked to sit in comfortable chairs. In the winter she would drag such a chair to the fireplace, put her feet on the fire guard and play in that position. When outdoor life began again, Miriam had a chair in the sandbox. She even helped weed the garden while sitting in a chair. But it did not happen often that she had to fetch a chair herself, usually the other children carried it into the garden for her. One day, Miriam and Paul played in the sandbox after supper. Suddenly Paul appears in the house to fetch Miriam's chair. When told that the evening was too cold already for outdoor play and that they had better both come in, he merely looks bewildered and says: "But Miriam wants chair, open door quickly."

> *May 1946.* Miriam drops her towel, turns around and says: "Pick it up, somebody." Leah picks it up for her.

> *July 1946.* Miriam enters the kitchen, calls out: "Chair for Miriam, quickly." She looks indignant when she sees no child in the kitchen and nobody to obey her orders. She does not fetch the chair herself but goes out again.

> *August 1946.* Ruth is found in Miriam's bed in the morning and is asked to get up. Miriam replies instead of Ruth: "Oh no, she much better stays here. She has to wait to fasten Miriam's buttons."

> *August 1946.* Miriam bangs her hand on the table and says to John: "Can't you be quiet when I want to talk?" John stops talking.

The children's sensitiveness to each other's attitudes and feelings was equally striking where Leah was concerned. Leah was the only backward child among the six, of slow, lower average intelligence, with no outstanding qualities to give her a special status in the group. As mentioned before, Leah's arrival in Bulldogs Bank was delayed for six weeks owing to a ringworm infection. During this period the five other children had made their first adaptation to the new place, had learned some English, had established some contact with the staff and dropped some of their former restlessness. With Leah's coming, the whole group, in identification with her, behaved once more as if they were all newcomers. They used the impersonal *Tante* again instead of first names for the members of the staff. They reverted to talking German only, shouted and screamed and were again out of control. This regression lasted approximately a week, evidently for the length of time which Leah herself needed to feel more comfortable in her new surroundings.

Positive Relations within the Group: Absence of Envy, Jealousy, Rivalry, Competition

The children's unusual emotional dependence on each other was borne out further by the almost complete absence of jealousy, rivalry and competition, such as normally develop between brothers and sisters or in a group of contemporaries who come from normal families. There was no occasion to urge the children to "take turns"; they did it spontaneously since they were eager that everybody should have his share. Since the adults played no part in their emotional lives at the time, they did not compete with each other for favors or for recognition. They did not tell on each other and they stood up for each other automatically whenever they felt that a member of the group was unjustly treated or otherwise threatened by an outsider. They were extremely considerate of each other's feelings. They did not grudge each other their possessions (with one exception to be mentioned later), on the contrary lending them to each other with pleasure. When one of them received a present from a shopkeeper, they demanded the same for each of the other children, even in their absence. On walks they were concerned for each other's safety in traffic, looked after children who lagged behind, helped each other over ditches, turned aside branches for each other to clear the passage in the woods, and carried each other's coats. In the nursery they picked up each other's toys. After they had learned to play, they assisted each other silently in building and admired each other's productions. At mealtimes handing food to the neighbor was of greater importance than eating oneself.

Behavior of this kind was the rule, not the exception. The following examples merely serve the purpose of illustration and are in no way outstanding. They are chosen at random from the first seven months of the children's stay at Bulldogs Bank:

> *October 1945.* John, daydreaming while walking, nearly bumps into a passing child. Paul immediately sides with him and shouts at the passer-by: "Blöder Ochs, meine John, blöder Ochs Du!" ["Stupid fool, my John, you stupid fool!"]

> *November 1945.* John refuses to get up in the morning, lies in his bed, screams and kicks. Ruth brings his clothes and asks: "Willst Du anziehen?" ["Don't you want to put them on?"] Miriam offers him her doll with a very sweet smile. John calms down at once and gets up.

November 1945. John cries when there is no cake left for a second helping for him. Ruth and Miriam offer him what is left of their portions. While John eats their pieces of cake, they pet him and comment contentedly on what they have given him. . . .

December 1945. Paul has a plate full of cake crumbs. When he begins to eat them, the other children want them too. Paul gives the biggest crumbs to Miriam, the three middle-sized ones to the other children, and eats the smallest one himself. . . .

December 1945. Paul loses his gloves during a walk. John gives him his own gloves, and never complains that his hands are cold. . . .

January 1946. A visitor gives sweets to the children in the kitchen. Peter and Leah immediately demand a sweet for Miriam who is alone in the nursery. . . .

March 1946. John has a temper tantrum when a ladybird, which he has caught, flies away. Leah hurries to him, strokes his hair, picks up his basket and all the carrots which he dropped out. She carried both John's and her own full baskets on the way home. . . .

March 1946. Paul receives a parcel with clothes, toys, and sweets from his American foster parents, a new experience in the children's lives. The excitement is great but there is no sign of envy. The children help to unpack, hold whatever Paul gives them to hold, welcome what he gives them as presents but accept the fact that he is, and remains, the owner of most of the contents of the parcel. . . .

April 1946. On the beach in Brighton, Ruth throws pebbles into the water. Peter is afraid of waves and does not dare to approach them. In spite of his fear, he suddenly rushes to Ruth, calls out: "Water coming, water coming," and drags her back to safety. . . .

Discrimination Between Group Members: Antipathies and Friendships

Although the positive reactions of the children extended to all members of the group, individual preferences or their opposite were not lacking. There was a certain discrimination against Leah on the part of the other girls, as the following recordings indicate:

February 1946. When Miriam cries, Leah runs immediately to comfort her, although Miriam each time screams: "Not Leah," and then accepts comfort from the other children.

April 1946. Ruth is very helpful toward Leah, looks after her on walks and helps her to dress and undress. But her behavior

indicates that these actions are duties, imposed by Leah's comparative clumsiness, rather than acts of friendship.

There were, further, close and intimate friendships between individual children, as for example between Paul and Miriam.

October 1945. On his first evening in Bulldogs Bank, Paul
goes to bed, saying with a deep sigh: "My Miriam."

October 1945. Paul is very fond of Miriam. He gives her toys
and serves her at mealtimes. Sometimes he takes her doll, walks
with it round the room and returns it to her.

November 1945. On her third day in Bulldogs Bank, Miriam
had been given a doll from which she became inseparable in day-
and nighttime. No other child was allowed to touch it except Paul
who sometimes took it for a walk round the room.

On November 11, Miriam gives the doll to Paul when saying
good night and goes to sleep without it.

On November 12, she gives him the doll again in the evening
but later cries in her bed. Paul, who has the doll in bed with him, gets
up and calls through the closed door: "Miriam, dolly!" Miriam gets
her doll and Paul goes to sleep without it. . . .

Aggressive Reactions within the Group

With the exception of one child the children did not hurt or attack each other in the
first months. The only aggressiveness to which they gave vent within the group was
verbal. They quarreled endlessly at mealtimes and on walks, mostly without any
visible provocation. . . .

The disputes ended sometimes in a general uproar, sometimes in a concerted
attack on any adult who had tried to interfere and appease the quarrel; mostly the
quarrel merely petered out when some new event distracted the children's attention.

After the children had entered into more normal emotional relationships with the
adults and had become more independent of each other, word battles diminished and
were replaced to some degree by the fights normal for this age. This second phase
lasted approximately from January to July, when the relations between the children
became peaceful again on a new basis.

The only child whose reactions did not fit in with the general behavior of the group
was Ruth. She behaved like the others so far as being inseparable from the group
was concerned, did not want to be left alone and worried about absent children. She
also did her share of comforting others or of helping Leah, the latter especially after
Leah began to call her "my Ruth." But apart from these reactions, she was moved
by feelings of envy, jealousy, and competition, which were lacking in the other children
and which made her actions stand out as isolated instances of maliciousness or
spitefulness. In this connection it is interesting to remember that Ruth is the only child
among the group who has a recorded history of passionate attachment to a mother

substitute. The evidence is not sufficient to establish with certainty that it is this past mother relationship which prevented her from merging completely with the group, and which aroused normal sibling rivalry in her. On the other hand, the difference between her and the other children's behavior together with the difference in their emotional histories seems too striking to be a mere coincidence.

The following are instances of Ruth's negative behavior in the group. Between October and January these instances were daily events. They lessened considerably after she had formed a new attachment to Sister Gertrud and they disappeared almost altogether after June. . . .

October 1945. Ruth takes other children's toys, shows a very pleased, triumphant expression.

October 1945. Peter has to wear a bonnet to protect a bandage where he has cut his head. Ruth takes off his bonnet repeatedly.

November 1945. Peter gets soap in his eyes at bathtime and cries. Ruth watches him. When he has almost ceased crying, her watchful expression changes suddenly to a malicious one. She snatches the piece of soap and tries to put it into Peter's eye.

November 1945. Each child receives a sweet. Ruth keeps hers until the others have finished eating theirs. Then she offers her sweet to one child after the other, withdrawing it as soon as the child touches it. Repeats this for 20 minutes and again later until the children stop paying attention to her. . . .

January 1946. John, Miriam, and Peter are isolated with stomatitis. Ruth cannot stand the extra care given to them and takes out her jealousy on Paul and Leah by hitting and biting them. Her aggressiveness ceases again when the patients recover. . . .

May 1946. The children pick flowers which grow behind high nettles. They are warned to avoid being stung. John continues but moves and picks carefully. After a while he cries out as he gets stung: "Die Ruth, die Ruth push." Ruth stands behind him, pushing him into the nettles with a malicious expression on her face. . . .

AGGRESSIVENESS TOWARD THE ADULTS

As reported above, the children behaved with strong and uncontrolled aggression toward the adults from their arrival. This aggression was impersonal in its character, not directed against any individual and not to be taken as a sign of interest in the adult world. The children merely reacted defensively against an environment which they experienced as strange, hostile, and interfering.

On arrival it was striking that the form of aggressive expression used by the children was far below that normal for their age. They used biting as a weapon, in the manner in which toddlers use it between eighteen and twenty-four months. Biting reached its peak with Peter, who would bite anybody and on all occasions when angry; it was least pronounced with Leah who showed very little aggression altogether. For several weeks John and Ruth would spit at the adults, Ruth also spitting on the table, on plates, on toys, looking at the adults in defiance. Similarly, Peter, when defying the staff, urinated into the brick box, on the slide, into the toy scullery, or wetted his knickers.

After a few weeks, the children hit and smacked the adults when angry. This happened especially on walks where they resented the restrictions imposed on them in traffic.

Shouting and noisy behavior was used deliberately as an outlet for aggression against the adults, even though the children themselves disliked the noise.

Toward spring these very infantile models of aggressiveness gave way to the usual verbal aggressions used by children between three and four years. Instead of hitting out, the child would threaten to do so, or would say: "Naughty boy, I make noise at you," and then shout at the top of their voices. Other threats used by the children were: "Doggy bite you." Paul once used: "Froggy bite you." After a visit to Brighton in April, where Peter had been frightened of the waves, a new threat was used by them: "You go in a water." They sometimes tried to find water so as to carry out the threat.

From the summer 1946 onward, the children used phrases copied from the adults to express disapproval: "I am not pleased with you."

The following samples of aggressive behavior are chosen from a multitude of examples of similar or identical nature during the first three months.

> *October 1945.* Mrs. X from the village returns the clean laundry. Both John and Peter spit at her when she enters the nursery.

> *October 1945.* A painter works in the nursery with a high ladder. Peter, who climbs on the ladder, is lifted down by Sister Gertrud. He spits at her and shouts: "Blöde Tante, blöder Ochs!" ["Stupid auntie, stupid fool."] . . .

> *October 1945.* John hits Mrs. Clarke repeatedly.

> *November 1945.* Sister Gertrud polishes shoes and tells Ruth not to play with the shoe polish. Ruth spits at her, throws the box with polish down the stairs and runs through the house, shouting: "Blöder Ochs, Gertrud."

FIRST POSITIVE RELATIONS WITH THE ADULTS

The children's first positive approaches to the adults were made on the basis of their group feelings and differed in quality from the usual demanding, possessive behavior which young children show toward their mothers or mother substitutes. The children began to insist that the members of the staff should have their turn or share; they became sensitive to their feelings, identified with their needs, and considerate of their comfort. They wanted to help the adults with their occupations and, in return, expected to be helped by them. They disliked it when any member of staff was absent and wanted to know where the adults had been and what they had done during their absence. In short, they ceased to regard the adults as outsiders, included them in their group and, as the examples show, began to treat them in some ways as they treated each other.

Sharing with the Adults

Christmas 1945. The children are invited to a Christmas party in Mrs. Clarke's house. They receive their presents with great excitement. They are equally thrilled when they are handed presents for the staff, they call out: "For Gertrud," "For Sophie" with great pleasure, and run back to Mrs. Clarke to fetch more presents for them.

December 1945. When Mrs. Clarke, who has been visiting, leaves, Ruth demands to be kissed. Then all the children have to be kissed. Then John and Ruth call out: "Kiss for Sophie."

December 1945. The children are given sweets in the shop and demand a "sweet for Sophie." After leaving the shop, they want to make sure that she has received the sweet. Sister Sophie opens her mouth for inspection and, in so doing, loses her sweet. The children are as upset as if they had lost one of their own sweets. John offers his but Sister Sophie suggests that she can wait to get another on returning home. When they reach home after an hour's walk with many distracting events, Peter runs immediately to the box of sweets to fetch one for Sophie.

Considerateness for the Adults

November 1945. When the children are told that one of the staff has a day off and can sleep longer in the morning, they try to be quiet. If one or the other forgets, the others shout: "You quiet. Gertrud fast asleep."

November 1945. Sister Sophie has told the children that the doctor has forbidden her to lift heavy weights. Paul asks: "Not too heavy?," whenever he sees her with a tray or bucket.

May 1946. Leah, though a noisy child, tries hard to keep quiet when her Judith is tired.

Equality with the Adults: Helpfulness

December 1945. The children become keen on fetching from the kitchen what is needed. They carry logs, set chairs and tables. They help to dress and undress themselves and to tidy up.

January 1945. Ruth sees a woman with a shopping bag in the street. She approaches her and takes one handle silently to help carrying it.

April 1946. The children are alone in the nursery after breakfast. Ruth and Peter each take a broom and sweep up the rubbish. When Sister Sophie enters, they call to her: "We tidy up nicely."

May 1946. Miriam begins to help Sister Sophie in the kitchen when the latter is called away. When she returns Miriam has dried four big dishes, twelve bowls, sixteen spoons and has placed them tidily on a tray.

On a similar occasion Miriam is found on a chair in front of the sink, her arms up to the elbows in soapy water, with most of the washing-up done . . .

Sensitiveness to Adults: Identification

March 1946. Ruth and John lag far behind on a walk. When they reach the others eventually, Peter calls to them: "You naughty boys, you dragging behind; Sophie calling and calling and calling. You not coming, Sophie cross and sad!" Then he turns to Sister Sophie and says in a low voice: "You still cross and sad?" When she nods, he repeats his speech.

May 1946. While the children are picking bluebells, Sister Sophie listens intently to the calling of birds. Paul suddenly puts his hand into hers and says: "You cross with everybody?" Though she assures him that she is not cross, merely absent-minded, he leaves his hand in hers to comfort her.

SECOND PHASE OF POSITIVE RELATIONS TO ADULTS: PERSONAL RELATIONSHIPS

Several weeks after arrival in Bulldogs Bank the first signs of individual personal attachments to adults appeared, alongside with and super-imposed on the relationships based on community feelings. These new attachments had many of the qualities which are well known from the relationship of young children to their mothers or mother substitutes. Attitudes such as possessiveness, the wish to be owned, exclusive clinging appeared, but they lacked the intensity and inexorability which is one of the main characteristics of the emotional life at that age. During the year's stay at Bulldogs Bank these ties of the children to the adults in no way reached the strength of their ties to each other. The children went, as it were, through the motions and attitudes of mother relationships, but without the full libidinal cathexis of the objects whom they had chosen for the purpose.

Examples of Owning and Being Owned

Miriam was the first to say "Meine Sophie, my Sophie" at the end of October.

Peter, the youngest, was the next to show a personal attachment. At the end of November he cried on several occasions when Sister Gertrud left the room. He began to say: "Meine Gertrud" and shortly afterward called himself "Gertrud's Peter." He picked flowers for her and liked her to bathe him. But his attachment was in no way exclusive and he did not mind being with somebody else. He was fond of Sister Sophie too and disliked her going away.

Ruth very soon afterward showed a first preference for Mrs. Clarke. She began showing pleasure in seeing her, kissed her once spontaneously and said on another occasion: "Is bin [I am] Mrs. Clarke's Ruth."

Leah was a clinging child who made advances to every visitor and even to people passing in the street. She became attached to the assistant Judith, would hold her hand on walks, picked flowers for her and sang sometimes all day long: "My Judith bathes me all the time!" But the apparent warmth of this relationship was belied by the fact that she continued to attach herself to every stranger.

John called the young assistant "his" Maureen. His attachment showed more warmth than those of the others but was broken again, unluckily, by Maureen's leaving.

Examples of Conflicting Relationships

Several children had considerable difficulties in choosing their mother substitutes, their positive feelings wavering uncertainly between the adult figures. John, after being left by Maureen, attached himself to Sister Gertrud, and shortly afterward became fond of Sister Sophie. Neither relationship was exclusive or very passionate and consequently he seemed to have no difficulties in maintaining both simultaneously. In contrast to this, Miriam, who was attached equally to Sisters Sophie and Gertrud, suffered badly from the consequent conflict of feeling. She lived in a constant state of tension without finding relief and satisfaction in her relationships. During Sister Sophie's absence, she "wrote" and dictated long letters to her and she was full of happiness on Sister Sophie's return. But the preference for Sister Sophie, which seemed established at the time, gave way once more to a preference for Sister Gertrud in the course of a few weeks.

Examples of Resentment of Separations

Even though the children's attachments to their mother substitutes took second place in their emotional lives, they deeply resented the absences or the leaving of the adults.

> *January 1946.*   Sister Sophie has left the house together with Mrs. Clarke. When she returns a few hours later, Peter refuses to say good night to her. He turns to the other side and says: "You go, you go to a Mrs. Clarke."

> *March 1946.*   When Sister Sophie returned to Bulldogs Bank after an absence of two months, Peter refused to let her do anything for him for a week, would not even take bread or sweets from her. Whenever she left the house, he asked: "You go in a London?"
>
> He regained his affection for her through a process of identification with her interests. Five weeks after her return the children played that they took a bus ride to London. When asked what they wanted to do there, Peter said: "Go in a Miss X's house." Peter saying: "Miss X all better?" From then onward, he called the patient "Peter's Miss X," cuddled and kissed Sister Sophie and held her hand on walks although the children usually preferred to walk on their own. . . .

Example of Attachment to a Mother Substitute

The only child to choose a real mother substitute was Ruth, an exception which is easily explainable on the basis of her former attachment to the superintendent of the Children's Ward in Tereszin. She chose as her object Sister Gertrud, and developed toward her the same demandingness, aggressive possessiveness, and wish for exclusive attention which had characterized her earlier relationship, a mixture of emotions which is well known from children in the toddler stage and at later ages from those who have gone through the experience of loss, separation, rejection, and disappointments in their earliest object relationships. Ruth's lack of satisfaction and insecurity expressed itself with regard to Sister Gertrud in the constantly repeated phrase: "And Ruth? And Ruth?"

Example of a Passionate Father Relationship

The only child to form a passionate relationship to a father figure was Miriam. Since Miriam arrived in Tereszin at the age of six months, her father having been killed some time previously, it cannot be presumed that what she went through was a past father relationship transferred to a new object, rather that it was the need for a father which found a first outlet in this manner:

> *January 1946.*   Mr. E., a neighbor, visits the Nursery for a whole afternoon and teaches the children songs. At the time, Miriam

seems more interested in his picture book than in his person. But in the evening she begins to cry for him. She wakes up in the night twice and cries for him and keeps asking for him during the next two days.

March 1946. Miriam has seen Mr. E. more often lately. He has brushed her hair once in the evening and she insists on his doing it again. On evenings when he does not come, her hair is not brushed at all since she will not allow anybody else to touch it.

She flushes whenever she sees him. About twenty times a day she says: "Meine Mr. E.—meine Sophie."

March 1946. Mr. E. says about Miriam: "I have never seen anything like her. That girl is puffing and panting with passion." . . .

ORAL EROTISM: MASTURBATION

There was a further factor which accounted for the children's diminished capability to form new object relationships. As children for whom the object world had proved disappointing, and who had experienced the severest deprivations from the oral phase onward they had had to fall back to a large degree on their own bodies to find comfort and reassurance. Therefore oral-erotic gratifications persisted with each child in one form or another. Ruth, besides, had a habit of scratching herself rhythmically until she bled, and of smearing with the blood. One child, Paul, suffered from compulsive masturbation.

Peter, Ruth, John, and Leah were all inveterate thumb-suckers, Peter and Ruth noisily and incessantly during the whole day, John and Leah more moderately, gradually reducing it to bedtime only. Miriam sucked the tip of her tongue, manipulating it with her teeth until she fell asleep. With Peter, sucking changed in spring to "smoking" carried out with match sticks, twigs, grass blades, then again to sucking his thumb when cross, angry, or at bedtime only. With Ruth sucking persisted even while she was carrying out interesting activities such as threading beads or playing with plasticene.

Since the children's sucking was noisy and obvious they often heard remarks from passers-by or in shops that they should stop or that "their thumbs would be cut off." Contrary to their usual oversensitiveness they remained completely indifferent on such occasions, not even needing reassurance. Sucking was such an integral and indispensable part of their libidinal life that they had not developed any guilt feelings or conflicting attitudes concerning it.

That the excess of sucking was in direct proportion to the instability of their object relationships was confirmed at the end of the year, when the children knew that they were due to leave Bulldogs Banks and when sucking in daytime once more became very prevalent with all of them.

This persistence of oral gratifications, more or less normal under the circumstances, which fluctuated according to the children's relations with the environment, contrasted strongly with Paul's behavior, where compulsive sucking and masturbation manifested themselves as a complicated and, at the time, inaccessible symptom.

Paul, in his good periods was an excellent member of the group, friendly, attentive and helpful toward children and adults, and capable of friendship. Though not aggressive himself, he was always ready to come to another child's rescue and take up arms against an aggressor. But when he went through one of his phases of compulsive sucking or masturbating, the whole environment, including the other children, lost their significance for him. He ceased to care about them, just as he ceased to eat or play himself. He did not bother to take part in his favorite communal activities such as sorting the laundry or lighting fires. He did not defend himself, or anybody else, merely cried passively when something or somebody made him unhappy. These spells attacked him at any time of the day, while playing, when eating at the table, and during work. He was only free of masturbation on walks, when he sometimes sucked his thumb but otherwise showed a completely changed, cheerful, and interested attitude.

In masturbating Paul used his hands, soft toys, picture books, a spoon; or rubbed himself against furniture or against other people. When sucking, his whole passion was concentrated on face flannels or towels which he sucked while they were hanging on their hooks. He also used a corner of his dungarees, of his coat and the arms of a doll, which he sucked while it was hanging from his mouth. For a period of several weeks he treated the children's used bibs or feeders as so many fetishes, rubbing them rhythmically up and down his nose while sucking, treasuring all six feeders in his arms, or pressing one or more between his legs. When on a walk, he sometimes looked forward to these ecstasies with the joyous exclamation "Feeder—feeder!" Since he was indifferent to the same feeders when they were freshly laundered, it may be concluded that his erotic excitation was connected with the smell belonging to a feeding situation.

RELATIONS TO THE OUTSIDE WORLD

In Tereszin, i.e., up to the ages of 3 to 3½, the children had led the existence of inmates of a Ward, within a restricted space, with few or no toys, with no opportunities for moving about freely, for contact with animals, for observing nature. They had not shared or observed the lives of ordinary people and, in the absence of strong emotional ties to the people who looked after them, they had lacked the normal incentives for imitating the adults and for identifying with them. Consequently, their knowledge of the external world, their ability to understand and to deal with it, were far below the level of their ages and of their intelligence.

INDOOR AND OUTDOOR ACTIVITIES

During their first weeks in Bulldogs Bank, the children were unable to use play material. The only toys which attracted their attention from the start were the soft toys, dolls, and teddy bears which were adopted as personal possessions and not so much played with as used for auto-erotic gratification (sucking, masturbation), or in replacement of it. All the children without exception, took their dolls or teddy bears to bed with them. When a child failed to do so in the evening, it would invariably wake up in the middle of the night, crying for the missing object.

The first play activity, which the children carried out with passionate eagerness, was the pushing of furniture, the usual favorite occupation of toddlers who have just learned to walk. They began their day in the morning with pushing chairs in the nursery and returned to this activity at intervals during the day, whenever they were free to do so. After they had learned to play in the sandpit, they used sand for the same purpose, pushing a supply of it along the whole front of the veranda by means of an inverted chair. They would revert to pushing furniture even on coming home from long walks, or when tired.

Gradual progress in their physical ability to handle objects and to manage their own possessions coincided with the growth of the children's emotional interest in the adult world. This led to the wish to "help," to share the work of the adults and, as described above, to fetch and carry, to set chairs and tables, etc., activities which were carried out surprisingly well. For a short while, the wish to be equal to the adults in these matters led to a frenzy of independence, as the following example shows:

> In November, the children are taken for their first bus ride. The situation has been explained to them beforehand, also that the ride will be short and that they will have to get out quickly at the bus stop. They have promised to cooperate, and they leave their seats without protest at the appointed time. But when the conductor and a passenger try very kindly to help them down the steps, they push them away, and shout and scream that they want to do it alone. Finally Miriam lies on the road, her face almost blue with fury, Paul sits next to her, kicking and screaming, the others cry and sob.

While such a phase of independence brought marked increases in the skill and range of the children's activities, in periods of an opposite emotional nature the advances seemed to be lost once more. In January all the children went through a phase of complete passivity, and dependence on the adults, corresponding to the change of their relationships with them from the more impersonal community feelings to warmer personal attachments. During this time they refused to do anything for themselves, wanted to be fed, dressed, etc., and did not cooperate in work. Their ambivalent attitude toward the adults, the outgoing and withdrawal of emotion toward them, was reflected in the sphere of activities by violent demands to be helped and looked after like a helpless infant, coupled with an equally violent refusal to accept the care. In such moods the children would run away from being dressed, push the tables and chairs away when they had been set for a meal, refuse to carry even their own belongings, etc.

After approximately six months stay in Bulldogs Bank, these violent upheavals gave way to more ordinary and stable modes of progress.

In March 1946 the children began to lose interest in their soft toys and took picture books to bed with them for "reading." For some time each child was content to have any book. From April onward the children demanded books in which they were particularly interested.

When Miriam received her postcard from Mr. E. and "wrote" her answer on it before going to sleep in the evening, "reading" came to an end and "writing" took its place. Several children had received letters and parcels from their American foster parents and "wrote" to them in bed. At first they used pencils indiscriminately, after a while they chose their colors. The imaginary letters written at that time dealt with matters such as Sister Sophie's absence, news about animals, flowers, etc., i.e., interests in the external world which had taken the place of the exclusive autoerotic activities of the bedtime hour.

In the second half of their year in Bulldogs Bank, the children became increasingly interested in the usual nursery school occupations. At the end of the year they had become able to concentrate on an occupation for as much as an hour. They had become able to handle scissors, pencils, paint brushes, blunt needles, and enjoyed painting, cutting out, doing puzzles, and threading beads. Even then they preferred "grownup work" to nursery occupations and carried it out very efficiently.

After the beginnings, which had showed the children to be backward in their play by as much as 18 months or two years, it was all the more impressive to watch the speed with which they passed through consecutive stages of play activity making up for development which had been misssed.[2]

Absence of adequate experience with consequent backwardness in understanding and behavior was even more striking outdoors than indooors. The children lacked the city child's knowledge of traffic, shops, busy streets, etc., and the country child's familiarity with animals, trees, flowers, and all types of work. They knew no animals except dogs, which were objects of terror. They did not know the name of a single plant and had never picked or handled flowers. They seemed to know no vehicles and were completely oblivious of the dangers of the road. Consequently their walks on the country road, through the village or the lanes and paths were exciting events during which innumerable new impressions crowded in on them.

Parallel to the speed of their development in the sphere of play, the children passed rapidly through the various stages of experience and behavior with regard to outdoor events, which are usually gone through between the ages of two and four. Their interest in animals, once awakened, was accompanied by the usual animal play, identification with animals and observation of animals. Interest in cars went from an initial terror of being "made too-too by a car" to a pride in being able to manage crossings, to admonish others to do so, and to distinguish between the types of car. Before they left Bulldogs Bank the children had acquired the experience normal for country children of their age. They knew most trees and practically all the common flowers by name and asked for information when meeting new specimens. They distinguished weeds from plants; they picked flowers with long stems instead of tearing their heads off as at first. They were greatly helped in making up for lost time by the interest of the village people who showed them their animals, permitted them to come into their gardens, gave them flowers, explained their tools, allowed them to look inside their vans or behind counters, all of it new experiences of unique importance for the children.

Retardation in Modes of Thinking

In dealing with the mass of experience which crowded in on them, the children revealed, during the first weeks, some characteristic peculiarities which are worth noting in individuals of their ages.

A first perception of an object, or the experiencing of an event, together with the naming of it, left an impression on their minds far overriding all later ones in strength and forcefulness. This was clearly demonstrated on several occasions.

A pony in the field had been introduced to the children as a donkey by mistake, and the first ducks which they met had been misnamed geese. In both cases it took several weeks to undo the wrong connection between object and word. In spite of repeated efforts at correction, the children clung to the names connected with their first image of the animal.

The first leaf shown to the children was an ivy leaf. For a whole month every green leaf was called ivy leaf.

When the children noticed a plane overhead for the first time and asked where it was going, they were told that it was going to France. "Going to France" remained a fixed attribute of every plane from then onward. During the whole year they called out: "Aeroplane going to France," whenever they heard a plane overhead.

The first time that letter writing had come into the children's lives was on the occasion of Sister Sophie's absence. All later letters, imagined or dictated by them retained the opening phrases which they had used then: "Dear Sophie in a London in a Miss X's house. Miss X all better," regardless of the fact that Sister Sophie had returned long ago and that the letters were addressed to other people.

The first English song which the children learned in Bulldogs Bank was "Bah bah black sheep." Though they learned and sang many other nursery rhymes during their stay, "Bah bah black sheep" remained in a class of its own. They would sing it when cheerful or as a treat for somebody on special occasions.

When talking of people the children would name them according to their most interesting attribute or possession, or would name these objects after them. Mrs. Clarke, for example, had two small dogs which were the first friendly dogs known to the children and played an important role in helping them to overcome their terror of dogs. In December all children called Mrs. Clarke: "Miss Clarke's doggies." Objects given by her to the children were called by the same name. A big electric stove which came from her house was called by Peter: "Miss Clarke's doggies." Green porridge bowls given by her as a Christmas present were called Mrs. Clarke by everybody.

> *December 1945.* When washing up, John says: "You wash Mrs. Clarke. I dry Mrs. Clarke. Look at that, Mrs. Clarke all dry."

January 1946. Ruth throws Peter's green bowl on the floor. Three children shout: "Mrs. Clarke kaputt, poor Mrs. Clarke all kaputt."

The examples quoted in this chapter reveal primitive modes of thinking which are shown by children in their second year of life. The overwhelming strength of a first link between an object or event and its name is characteristic for the time when children first learn to speak, or—to express it is metapsychological terms—when word representations are first added to the images (object representations) in the child's mind. The inability to distinguish between essential and nonessential attributes of an object belongs to the same age (see example of aeroplanes). Instances of naming where this is directed not to a single limited object but to a whole idea related to it (see example of "Miss Clarke's doggies") are forms of "condensation," well known from the primary processes which reveal themselves normally in dream activity, and continue in the second year of life as a mode of waking thought.

That these infantilisms in the sphere of thinking were not based on a general mental retardation with the children under observation was borne out by their adequate, adapted reasoning and behavior in situations with which they felt familiar (such as household tasks, community affairs, etc.); that they were not merely a function of the reversal in their emotional development is suggested by the fact that they overcame them before their libidinal attachments had changed decisively. That the rapid growth of life experience brought about an equally rapid advance in the modes of dealing with it mentally, suggests rather that it was the extreme dearth of new perceptions and varied impressions in their most impressionable years which deprived the children of the opportunity to exercise their mental functions to a normal degree and consequently brought about a stunting of thought development. . . .

LANGUAGE PROBLEMS

While passing through the phases of development as described above, the children had the added task of learning a new language, a necessity which made adaptation more difficult since it rendered them inarticulate in the transition period. They talked German on arrival, mixed with Czech which they had picked up after leaving Tereszin. Ruth's mixture of German and Czech was especially difficult to understand. The members of the staff began to talk English in front of the children and with them after a week and ceased talking German altogether after approximately seven weeks.

Surprisingly enough, there was no violent refusal on the part of the children to adopt the new language. The only outbursts of this kind came from Paul. In October, while repeating English words, which he liked to do, he became furious suddenly: "Is nicht motor car, is Auto, blöde Tante!" "Nicht good morning Paul, guten Morgen Paul!" On the other hand, Paul was the first to realize that the new language was essential to make contact with the village people. At the time when the other children still looked unhappy and withdrawn, he attracted everybody's attention by a very pleasant smile. People smiled and waved at him, though he could only say "hallo" in answer. His first English sentence was spoken in a deliberate effort to make contact:

> In December, the children passed one of the cottages whose owner came to the gate and gave flowers to them. Paul said: "Flowers," after some thinking "Lovely flowers," and then "Many lovely flowers, thank you!" The woman was so pleased that she kissed him.

John and Peter followed Paul in using their English words to draw attention to themselves, and soon used more English than German nouns. In a transitional phase they used composite nouns, made up of both languages, such as "auto-car," "doggy-Hund," "dolly-Puppe," "Löffel-spoon," etc. The girls, who were worse speakers altogether, followed much more slowly. The first adjectives and adverbs were used from the fifth week after beginning.

It was of evident concern to the children that the difference in their speed of learning English caused differences between them where there had been unity before. Many of their word battles centered around these points, as the following examples show:

> *December* (at mealtime).
> Leah: "Brot."
> Ruth: "Is bread."
> Leah: "Brot."
> Ruth (half crying): "Nis Brot, is bread."
> Leah (shouting): "Brot."
> Ruth (crying): "Is bread."
> Paul: "Is bread, blöder Ochs Leah."
> John: "Is nis blöder Ochs."
> Paul (shouting): "Is blöder Ochs John."
> John (screaming): "Is nis blöder Ochs."
> Sister Sophie: "Don't cry, nobody is a blöder Ochs."
> Paul (as loud as possible): "Blöder Ochs du, blöder Ochs Sophie."
> John: "Sophie is nis blöder Ochs."
> Peter (all smiles): "Nis blöder Ochs Sophie."
> Paul: Is hau dich" (turns against Peter).
> Peter: "Please bread."
> Paul gets bread for Peter and passes it to him.
>
> *January* (At mealtime).—
> Paul: "Look, ich big Teller, siehst du?"
> John: "Nis Teller, is plate."
> Paul: "Oh nein."
> John: "Is nis Teller, is in endlich [English?] plate."
> Paul (shouts): "Oh nein."
> Sister Sophie: "John is quite right, Teller is plate in English."

Paul: "Look, ich big plate."
John: "Clever boy John."
Peter: "No, clever boy Sophie," etc.

These differences disappeared again after January, when the whole group spoke English, among themselves as well as to the adults. They tried to express everything in English, using a picturesque language where the absence of verbs made expression difficult. . . .

For a long time the children clung to the German negation *nicht* (which must have played an overwhelmingly great part in their restricted lives). For some weeks in spring it was used together with its English counterpart as "not-nicht," before it was finally dropped.

The only German word which the children retained throughout the year was *meine* (my). Although the children knew and used the English equivalent, they would revert to the German *meine* when very affectionate: "Meine Gertrud," "Meine dolly."

By August the last German words, with this single exception, had disappeared, though the understanding of the German language as such had ceased much earlier. When a visitor talked German to the children in April, they laughed as if at a joke. In May, a German prisoner of war talked German to Ruth who looked completely blank. In June another visitor who knew the children from Windermere talked German to them; there was absolutely no reaction.

With the adaptation to the new language the children had made a further decisive step toward the break with their past, which now disappeared completely from their consciousness.

CONCLUSION

"Experiments" of this kind, which are provided by fate, lack the satisfying neatness and circumscription of an artificial setup. It is difficult, or impossible, to distinguish the action of the variables from each other, as is demonstrated in our case by the intermingled effects of three main factors: the absence of a mother or parent relationship; the abundance of community influence; and the reduced amount of gratification of all needs. It is, of course, impossible to vary the experiment. In our case, further, it proved impossible to obtain knowledge of all the factors which have influenced development. There remained dark periods in the life of each child, and guesswork, conclusions, and inferences had to be used to fill the gaps.

Under such circumstances, no claim to exactitude can be made for the material which is presented here and it offers no basis for statistical considerations. This experiment staged by fate accentuates the action of certain factors in the child's life (demonstrated through their absence or their exaggerated presence). . . .

The six Bulldogs Bank children, are, without doubt, "rejected" infants in this sense of the term. They were deprived of mother love, oral satisfactions, stability in their relationships and their surroundings. They were passed from one hand to another during their first year, lived in an age group instead of a family during their second and third year, and were uprooted again three times during their fourth year. A description of the anomalies which this fate produced in their emotional life and of the retardations in certain ego attitudes is contained in the material. The children were hypersensitive, restless, aggressive, difficult to handle. But they were neither deficient, delinquent, nor psychotic. They had found an alternative placement for their libido and, on the strength of this, had mastered some of their anxieties, and developed social attitudes. That they were able to acquire a new language in the midst of their upheavals, bears witness to a basically unharmed contact with their environment. . . .

NOTES

[1]Theresienstadt in Moravia.

[2]See in this respect the paper by Lotte Danzinger and Lieselotte Frankl (2) on the test results with Albanian infants who, according to custom, spend their first year tied down in their cradle. The authors watched some of these infants being taken out of the cradle and allowed to play with toys. While they at first appeared extremely backward in comparison with other children, they nearly caught up with them (though not completely), when they had played with the toys for some hours only. As explanation, the authors suggest that inner processes of maturation had taken place and progressed in spite of the deprivations.

See also Phyllis Greenacre's comprehensive article on "Infant Reactions to Restraint" (4).

REFERENCES

Burlingham, D. T. *Twins.* London: Imago Publ. Co., 1951.

Danziger, L., & Frankl, L. "Zum Problem der Funktionsreifung," *Ztsch. f. Kinderforschung,* XLIII, 1934.

Freud, A., & Burlingham, D. *Infants Without Families,* New York: Int. Univ. Press, 1944.

Greenacre, P. Infant reactions to restraint. In Clyde Kluckhohn and Henry A. Murray (Eds.), *Personality.* New York: A. Knopf, 1948.

Werner, H. *Comparative psychology of mental development.* Chicago: Follet, 1948.

4.10

Teachers' Communication of Differential Expectations for Children's Classroom Performance: Some Behavioral Data

Jere E. Brophy
Thomas L. Good

Rosenthal and Jacobson (1968) assert on the basis of controversial research presented in *Pygmalion in the Classroom* that teachers' expectations for student performance function as self-fulfilling prophecies. The "expectancy effects" in the Oak School experiment described in *Pygmalion* are not as consistent as the authors' interpretations of them would suggest, however, and even the support that they do provide is questionable on methodological grounds (Barber and Silver, 1968; Snow, 1969; Thorndike, 1968). Even if the data and their interpretation are accepted, the Rosenthal and Jacobson work remains only a demonstration of the *existence* of expectancy effects; their study did not address itself to any of the events intervening between the inducement of teacher expectations and the administration of the criterion achievement test. The present study focuses on these intervening processes, applying the method of classroom interaction analysis to identify and document differential teacher behavior communicating different teacher expectations to individual children.

The lack of data concerning the causal mechanisms at work in the Rosenthal and Jacobson study, combined with the tendency in most secondary sources to oversimplify or exaggerate their findings has cast an aura of magic or mystery around expectation effects. Consequently, it is important to conceptualize such phenomena as outcomes of observable sequences of behavior. The explicit model assumed in the present research may be described as follows:

1.   The teacher forms differential expectations for student performance;
2.   He then begins to treat children differently in accordance with his differential expectations;

Excerpted and reprinted from Jere E. Brophy and Thomas L. Good, *Teachers' Communication of Differential Expectations for Children's Performance: Some Behavioral Data,* Report Series No. 25, The Research and Development Center for Teacher Education, The University of Texas at Austin, 1969, by permission.

3. The children respond differentially to the teacher because they are being treated differently by him;

4. In responding to the teacher, each child tends to exhibit behavior which complements and reinforces the teacher's particular expectations for him;

5. As a result, the general academic performance of some children will be enhanced while that of others will be depressed, with changes being in the direction of teacher expectations;

6. These effects will show up in the achievement tests given at the end of the year, providing support for the "self-fulfilling prophecy" notion.

A series of interrelated studies will be required to systematically investigate the full model from beginning (how do teachers form differential expectations in the first place?) to end (how do children change so as to begin to conform more closely to teacher expectations?). The present study deals with the second step: given differential teacher expectations, how are they communicated to the children in ways that would tend to cause the children to produce reciprocal behavior? To begin to answer this question, the present study approached the problem through classroom interaction analysis. In contrast to the usual classroom interaction study, however, the present research focused on dyadic interaction between the teacher and individual children.[1]

METHOD

Subjects

The research was carried out in four first-grade classrooms in a small Texas school district which serves a generally rural and lower-class population. However, a large military base located within the district contributes about 45 percent of the students in the school in which observations were taken. Children from the base tend to be from more urban backgrounds and of a somewhat higher socioeconomic status than the local children. The ethnic composition of the school is about 75 percent Anglo-American, 15 percent Mexican-American and ten percent Afro-American, which is representative of the general population of the area.

Research was carried out in four of the nine first grade classrooms in the school, chosen because there were no assistant teachers present to complicate the picture (the other five classrooms had preservice teacher interns assisting the head teacher). The four teachers involved were asked to rank the children in their class in the order of their achievement. These instructions were deliberately kept vague to encourage the teachers to use complex, subjective criteria in making their judgments. The rankings were then used as the measure of the teachers' expectations for classroom performance for the children in their classes. In each class, three boys and three girls high on the teacher's list (highs) and three boys and three girls low on the teacher's list (lows) were selected for observational study. The highs were simply the first six eligible children on the list. This was generally true also for the lows, although a few children low on the lists were excluded from the study because they could not speak English fluently or because of suspected emotional or biological disturbance. Substitutes for each type of child (high boys, high girls, low boys, low girls) were also identified and these were individually observed on days when children in the designated sample were absent.

The teachers had been told that the study was concerned with the classroom behavior of children of various levels of achievement. They were not informed that their own behavior as well as that of the children was being specifically observed. Furthermore, the teachers thought that observations were being taken on everyone in the class and did not know that specific subgroups had been selected for study. By selecting subjects from the extremes of the distributions of teacher's rankings, the chances of discovering differential teacher treatment of the students were maximized. However, the school practiced tracking, achieving homogeneity within the nine classrooms by grouping the children according to readiness and achievement scores. Thus, at least in terms of test scores, objective differences among the children (and, therefore, objective support for the validity of teacher expectations) was minimized.

Observation System

Since the object of the research was to focus on differential treatment of different children, the observation system developed was addressed only to dyadic contacts between the teacher and an individual child, with lecture-demonstration and other teacher behavior directed to the class as a group being ignored. Although the types of interactions coded were partly dictated by the range of situations seen in pilot studies, certain features of the coding system were built in for their specific relevance to the study of communication of differential teacher expectations. One major and consistent feature was that the source of the interaction was always coded, so that it could be determined later whether the interaction was initiated by the teacher or by the child. . . .

Results

Other than the large class differences, the data are most notable for the consistency of expectancy group differences on variables measuring the tendency to seek out the teacher and initiate contact with her. Children for whom the teacher held high expectations (highs) raised their hands more frequently and initiated more procedural and especially more work-related interactions than did children for whom the teachers held low expectations (lows). The class X expectancy group interactions with regard to child-initiated contacts reflect degree rather than direction of effect. The highs exceeded the lows in each class for hand raising, initiating work-related interactions, and total child-initiated response opportunities (the hand-raising effect excludes

Class 1, where it could not be assessed because the teacher never asked open questions while her class was being observed). The highs also exceeded the lows in three of the four classes in initiating procedural interactions. There was a negligible reversal in Class 2, where this type of interaction was very infrequent (highs averaged 1.50, lows averaged 1.67). The only exception to the pattern of significant differences between highs and lows in child-initiated interactions occurred in the measure of calling out answers in the reading groups. The mean difference is in favor of the highs, but it is not a significant difference and the effect occurred in only one of the four classes. The data for child-initiated contacts may be summarized, then, in the statement that, outside the reading group at least, the highs seek out the teacher and initiate interactions with her more frequently than the lows. The difference is especially notable in work-related interactions: the highs much more frequently show their work to the teacher or ask her questions about it, and they initiate many more response opportunities.

The data for contacts initiated or controlled by the teacher are less clear than for those initiated by the children. The highs were called on more frequently to answer open questions, but the teacher initiated more procedural and work-related interactions with the lows and afforded them slightly more response opportunities. None of these differences reach significance, however. The only significant difference occurred with teacher-afforded behavioral criticisms, which more frequently went to the lows than the highs. This effect showed an important interaction with sex, due to the high frequency of teacher criticisms directed at boys in the low group. Males in the low group averaged 8.25 teacher behavior criticisms, as compared with 2.25 for boys in the high group (the corresponding figures for girls are 1.58 and 1.83). Sex also interacted with expectancy in the measure of hand raising, and again the boys in the low group were notably different from the other three groups. These boys averaged 6.25 on the hand-raising measure as compared to 17.75 for the boys of the high group (corresponding figures for the girls are 11.50 and 15.58).

The data regarding interactions initiated or controlled by the teacher may be summarized as follows: there is a tendency for the teachers to initiate more contacts with the lows than with the highs, but the teachers cannot be said to have been compensating for the superiority of the highs in child-initiated contacts because the trend is not completely consistent and because the only significant differences occur with teacher criticisms rather than with work-related contacts or provision of response opportunities. While the data for child-initiated contacts showed strong expectancy group differences, the measures of teacher-initiated interactions were much more closely related to sex than to expectancy. Boys were higher than girls on all measures of teacher-initiated contacts; significantly so for work-related interactions, behavioral criticisms, and total teacher-afforded response opportunities. When teacher-child dyadic contacts of all types are totaled, a clear difference favoring boys is evident; there is no difference between expectancy groups. Differences between the highs and the lows are in quality rather than quantity of interaction with the teacher. . . .

The highs produced more correct answers and fewer incorrect answers than the lows, had fewer problems in the reading groups, and achieved higher average scores on the Stanford Achievement Test given at the end of the year. They also were given more praise and less criticism than the lows by the teachers. The direction of difference follows this pattern in all four classes for every variable except for the total correct answers, where the group means were equal in one class. Thus the class by expectancy interactions affected the degree but not the direction of expectation effects.

Sex effects also appeared, with boys producing more correct answers and receiving more criticism than girls. The other, nonsignificant, differences in favor of boys are consistent with the finding noted above that boys tend to have more interactions with the teacher than girls. A sex by expectancy group interaction occurs for the measure of total criticism which is similar and related to the one reported for behavioral criticism. For the boys in the low group, teacher criticism was present in 32.50 percent of their dyadic contacts with the teacher. The corresponding figure for the high boys is 13.25 percent, for the low girls 16.17 percent and for the high girls 8.25 percent.

In summary, the data show that teacher expectancy consistently predicts objective measures of classroom performance, objective achievement test scores, and rates of teacher praise and criticism. . . .

Significant group differences on these measures suggest that the teachers were systematically, although not necessarily deliberately or consciously, treating one group more favorably than the other. The first two measures concern provision of response opportunities to the children, and may be considered in combination with the data previously discussed. Since the highs create more response opportunities for themselves than the lows, do the teachers compensate for this by calling on the lows more frequently? The data suggest only a slight tendency in this direction at best. The teachers definitely do not compensate by asking the lows more direct questions, since the mean on this variable for the lows is less than that for the highs, although not significantly. The mean for direct questions in the low group would have been increased if "discipline" questions had been included in their figures. These were very special questions which appeared only in the low group, but not with sufficient frequency to be analyzed as a separate variable. "Discipline" questions were direct questions which ostensibly asked for academic content ("what's the next word, John?"), but which were directed at children not paying attention. In these instances the teacher's questions appeared to function as control techniques rather than as response opportunities, and so they were not included in the totals for the direct questions. If they had been included the results would have been an increase in the mean for direct questions in the low group, but this mean value would still be below that for the highs.

The one teacher measure which does suggest some compensation concerns the teacher's behavior in calling on children to answer open questions. When the number of times the child is called on is weighted by the number of times he raised his hand to seek a response opportunity, the resulting recognition rates showed a significant difference in favor of the lows. However, this difference seemed due more to the large difference in hand raising rate between the two groups of children rather than to any systematic compensation efforts by the teachers. The recognition rates are not adjusted for the fact that more highs than lows were likely to be raising their hands seeking an opportunity to answer a given question, so that a single response opportunity had less effect on the recognition rates of the highs than on those of the lows. The rates may be adjusted by treating the highs and the lows as groups and discounting hand raising by other members of the group when one member of the group is called on. When the hand raising totals are reduced in this manner, the resultant recognition rates still favor the lows, although the difference no longer approaches statistical significance.

In summary, the data on quantity of contacts are neutral with regard to expectation effects. The highs initiate more work-related contacts and create more response opportunities for themselves than do the lows, but there is no unequivocal evidence to suggest that the teachers are systematically either exaggerating or compensating for these differences among the children.

The data for the last five variables comprise the major findings of the study, since they provide direct evidence that the teachers' differential expectations for performance were being communicated in their classroom behavior. The measures involved are all concerned with the teachers' reactions to the children's attempts to answer questions and read in the reading group. All are percentage or ratio measures which take into account absolute differences in the frequencies of the various behaviors involved so as to enable a direct comparison to be made between the teachers' behavior toward the two groups when faced with equivalent situations. The data show that the teachers consistently favored the highs over the lows in demanding and reinforcing quality performance. Despite the fact that the highs gave more correct answers and fewer incorrect answers than did the lows, they were more frequently praised when correct and less frequently criticized when incorrect or unable to respond. Furthermore, the teachers were more persistent in eliciting responses from the highs than they were with the lows. When the highs responded incorrectly or were unable to respond, the teachers were more likely to provide a second response opportunity by repeating or rephrasing the question or giving a clue than they were in similar situations with the lows. Conversely, they were more likely to supply the answer or call on another child when reacting the the lows than the highs. This group difference was observed both for difficulties in answering questions and for problems in reading during reading group. Finally, the teachers failed to give any feedback whatever only 3.33 percent of the time when reacting to highs, while the corresponding figure for lows is 14.75 percent, a highly significant difference.

Group differences in the direction of expectancy effects occur for all four classes on three variables; small reversals occur in the measure of criticism following wrong responses in one class and in the measure regarding teachers' reactions to reading problems in another class. These are the only measures for which the class by expectancy interaction is significant.

Significant sex effects also appear as they have previously. These show that boys receive more direct questions from the teacher than girls and that they are praised more frequently when giving correct answers. The difference on direct questions fits in with the general finding that boys tend to have more interactions of all kinds with the teachers than girls. The data concerning praise are more surprising, in view of the preponderance of criticism toward boys noted earlier. Taken together, the data on teacher praise and criticism suggest that the teachers are generally more evaluative in responding to boys and more objective in responding to girls. Boys are praised more often after correct responses and criticized more often after incorrect responses or failures to respond, although the latter difference is not statistically significant. The general preponderance of critical comments toward boys noted earlier is apparently due to behavioral criticisms rather than to critical comments made during work-related interactions.

DISCUSSION

The data which show objective differences among the children related to their sex and achievement levels, are quite consistent with previous findings. The finding that high-achieving students receive more teacher praise and support (Hoehn, 1954; de Groat and Thompson, 1949; Good, 1970) was confirmed in the present study. Hoehn's suggestion that the differences between high and low achieving students in the interaction with their teachers were in quality rather than quantity of interaction is also compatible with present findings. The finding that teachers have more disapproval contacts with boys than girls has also been frequently reported (Meyer and Thompson, 1956; Lippitt and Gold, 1959; Jackson and Lahaderne 1966). Meyer and Thompson (1956) also reported greater praise toward boys, as was found in the present study in work-related interactions. Taken together, the findings on sex differences in the present study may be summarized as follows: boys have more interactions with the teacher than girls and appear to be generally more salient in the teacher's perceptual field. Teachers direct more evaluative comments toward boys, both absolutely and relatively. The largest and most obvious absolute differences in evaluative comments occur with teacher criticism and disapproval, which are directed far more frequently at boys. However, much of this difference appears to come in the form of behavioral criticisms and disciplinary contacts rather than criticisms of academic performance in work-related contacts. The difference appears attributable to more frequent disruptive behavior among boys which brings criticism upon themselves rather than to a consistent teacher set bias toward being more critical toward boys than girls in equivalent situations. The latter statement agrees closely with the conclusion of Davis and Slobodian (1967), who studied teacher provision of response opportunities and evaluation of children's performance in reading groups.

While sex differences are attributable to objective differences in the classroom behavior of the children, the data show that differences related to teacher expectancy are only partly attributable to the children themselves. When the latter differences are statistically controlled through the use of percentage measures, it is seen that the teachers systematically discriminate in favor of the highs over the lows in demanding and reinforcing quality performance. Teachers do, in fact, communicate differential performance expectations to different children through their classroom behavior, and the nature of this differential treatment is such as to encourage the children to begin to respond in ways which would confirm teacher expectancies. In short, the data confirm the hypothesis that teachers' expectations function as self-fulfilling prophecies, and they indicate some of the intervening behavioral mechanisms involved in the process. Despite large differences in the frequencies of the various behaviors observed in the four classrooms, expectancy effects were consistent across the four teachers (two of the teachers favored the highs on four of the last five measures, while the other two favored the highs on all five measures).

Although the direction of difference in treatment of highs and lows was constant across teachers, there were observable differences in degree. In particular, one teacher stood out as extreme in this regard, while another showed relatively small differences, even though the direction of difference was constant. It is of interest that the latter teacher, who showed the least discrimination between highs and lows, was the teachers who did not group the children by achievement in her classroom seating pattern. It is also worthy of note that although the teachers' expectations were highly related to the children's achievement test scores within classes, the achievement scores are not so closely related to the previous readiness and achievement data which were used as the basis of tracking into classrooms. That is, the class achievement of some classes was higher than expected, while that of others was lower. While not enough classes were included to allow a statistical test, the data suggest that the achievement levels of the classes were related to the teachers' performance demands and expectations. . . .

NOTES

[1]In the study of dyadic interaction the individual child (or teacher-child dyad) becomes the unit of analysis, rather than the class as a group. For a discussion of the advantages of this method for studying traditional teacher effectiveness variables and of applications of the method to problems that cannot be approached through ordinary interaction analysis methods, see Good and Brophy (1969).

REFERENCES

Barber, T. X., & Silver, M. J. Fact, fiction and the experimenter bias effect. *Psychological Bulletin Monographs,* 1968, *70,* 6, Part 2.

Davis, O. L. Jr., & Slobodian, J. J. Teacher behavior toward boys and girls during first grade reading instruction. *American Educational Research Journal,* 1967, *4,* 261–269.

de Groat, A. F., & Thompson, G. G. A study of the distribution of teacher approval and disapproval among sixth grade pupils. *Journal of Experimental Education,* 1949, *18,* 57–75.

Good, T. L. Which pupils do teachers call on? *Elementary School Journal,* 1970, *70,* 190–198.

Good, T. L., & Brophy, J. Analyzing classroom interaction: a more powerful alternative. Report Series No. 26, Research and Development Center for Teacher Education, The University of Texas at Austin, 1969.

Hoehn, A. J. A study of social status differentiation in the classroom behavior of nineteen third-grade teachers. *Journal of Social Psychology,* 1954, *39,* 269–292.

Jackson, P. W., & Lahaderne, H. M. Inequalities of teacher-pupil contacts. Expanded version of a paper delivered at the American Psychological Association Meeting, New York City, September, 1966.

Lippitt, R., & Gold, M. Classroom social structure as a mental health problem. *Journal of Social Issues,* 1959, *15,* 40–49.

Meyer, W. J., & Thompson, G. G. Sex differences in the distribution of teacher approval and disapproval among sixth-grade children. *Journal of Educational Psychology,* 1956, *47,* 385–396.

Rosenthal, R., & Jacobson, L. *Pygmalion in the classroom: Teacher expectation and pupils' intellectual development.* New York: Holt, Rinehart and Winston, Inc., 1968.

Snow, R. E. Unfinished pygmalion. *Contemporary Psychology,* 1969, *14,* 197–199.

Thorndike, R. L. Review of Rosenthal, R. and Jacobson, L. Pygmalion in the Classroom. *American Educational Research Journal,* 1968, *5,* 708–711.

4.11

Some Immediate Effects
of Televised Violence
on Children's Behavior

Robert M. Liebert
Robert A. Baron

In his review of the social and scientific issues surrounding the portrayal of violence in the mass media, Larsen (1968) noted that we may begin with two facts: "(1) Mass media content is heavily saturated with violence, and (2) people are spending more and more time in exposure to such content [p. 115]." This state of affairs has been used by both laymen and professionals as the basis for appeals to modify the entertainment fare to which viewers, particularly children and adolescents, are exposed (Merriam, 1964; Walters, 1966; Walters & Thomas, 1963; Wertham, 1966). Other writers, however, have argued that the kind of violence found on television or in movies does not necessarily influence observers' "real-life" social behavior (Halloran, 1964; Klapper, 1968). A few have even characterized the portrayal of violence as potentially preventing the overt expression of aggression, at least under some circumstances (Feshbach, 1961; Feshbach & Singer, 1971).

In view of the controversy, it is hardly surprising that recent years have seen a substantial increase in the number of experimental studies directed to this issue. An effort has been made to determine whether children will learn and/or be disinhibited in their performance of aggressive acts as a function of exposure to symbolic aggressive models (e.g., in cartoons, movies, stories, and simulated television programs). This research has indicated consistently that children may indeed *acquire,* from even a very brief period of observation, certain motoric and verbal behaviors which are associated with aggression in life situations. More specifically, it has been repeatedly shown that after viewing a film which depicts novel forms of hitting, kicking, and verbal abuse, children can, when asked to do so, demonstrate this learning by reproducing these previously unfamiliar behaviors with a remarkable degree of fidelity (Bandura, 1965; Hicks, 1965). Taken together with the large body of research on the observational learning of other behaviors (Flanders, 1968), the available evidence appears to leave little doubt that the learning of at least some aggressive responses can and does result from television or movie viewing.

Equally important, however, is the question of whether the observation of violence will influence children's performance of aggressive acts when they have *not* been specifically asked to show what they have seen or learned. Several experiments appear to provide evidence relating to this issue (Bandura, Ross, & Ross, 1961, 1963a, 1963b; Rosekrans & Hartup, 1967). In these studies, subjects have typically been exposed to live or filmed aggressive scenes, then placed in a free play situation with a variety of toys or other play materials. Results obtained with these procedures have shown repeatedly that the exposure of young children to aggression produces increments in such play activities as punching inflated plastic clowns, popping balloons, striking stuffed animals, and operating mechanized "hitting dolls."

It has been argued by critics (Klapper, 1968) that findings such as those reviewed above are not directly relevant to the question of whether exposure to televised aggression will increase children's willingness to engage in behavior which might actually harm another person. Since this criticism was advanced, a human victim has replaced the inanimate target in at least four more recent investigations (Hanratty, 1969; Hanratty, Liebert, Morris, & Fernandez, 1969; Hanratty, O'Neal, & Sulzer, 1972; Savitsky, Rogers, Izard, & Liebert, 1971). These later studies have demonstrated clearly that exposure to the behavior of filmed aggressive models may lead young children to directly imitate aggression against a human, as well as a "toy," victim.

Despite the newer evidence, critics may still question whether exposure to the type of violence generally depicted on regularly broadcast television shows will produce similar effects. Likewise, it is important to consider the possible *disinhibitory* effects (cf. Lovaas, 1961; Siegel, 1956) rather than only the direct *imitative* effects of observing aggressive models. Although such effects have previously been observed with adult subjects and violent scenes taken from motion pictures (e.g., Berkowitz, 1965; Berkowitz & Rawlings, 1963; Walters & Thomas, 1963), in no previous investigation known to the authors has the influence of televised violence on interpersonal aggression been examined for young children. It was with these latter questions that the present research was primarily concerned. We sought to determine whether exposure to violent scenes taken directly from nationally telecast programs increases the willingness of young children to engage in aggressive acts directed toward another child.

METHOD

Participants

Population sampled. The sample was drawn both from Yellow Springs, Ohio, a small college town, and from a larger and more conservative neighboring community, Xenia. The participants were brought to Fels Research Institute in Yellow Springs by one of their parents, in response to a newspaper advertisement and/or a letter distributed in local public elementary schools asking for volunteers to participate in a study of the effects of television on children. To assure that no potential participants were turned away because of scheduling inconveniences, parents were invited to select their own appointment times (including evenings or weekends), and transportation was offered to those who could not provide it for themselves.

Subjects. The subjects were 136 children, 68 boys and 68 girls. Sixty-five of the participants were 5 or 6 years of age at the time of the study; the remaining 71 subjects were 8 or 9 years of age. Within each age group and sex the children were assigned randomly to the treatment conditions. Approximately 20 percent of the children in this study were black: virtually all of the remainder were white. The economic backgrounds from which these participants came were widely varied. Although economic characteristics were not used as a basis for assignment to treatments, inspection suggested that the procedure of random assignment had adequately distributed them among the experimental groups.

Experimental personnel. One of the investigators greeted the parent and child at the outset, served as the interviewer, and obtained informed parental consent for the child's participation. A 28-year-old white female served as experimenter for all the children, and two other adult females served as unseen observers throughout the experiment.

Design

A 2 X 2 X 2 factorial design was employed. The three factors were sex, age (5–6 or 8–9 years old), and treatment (observation of aggressive or nonaggressive television sequences).

Procedure

Introduction to the situation. Upon the arrival of parent and child at the institute, the child was escorted to a waiting room containing nonaggressive magazines and other play materials while the parent was interviewed in a separate room. During the interview, the nature of the experiment was disclosed to the parent, questions were invited and answered, and a written consent to the child's participation was obtained.[1]

Experimental and control treatment. After the interview, but without permitting the parent and the child to interact, the experimenter escorted each subject individually to a second waiting room containing children's furniture and a television videotape monitor. The television was then turned on by the experimenter, who suggested that the child watch for a few minutes until she was ready for him. The experimenter left the child to watch television alone for approximately 6½ minutes; the subjects were in fact continuously observed through a concealed camera and video monitor. For all groups, the first 120 seconds of viewing consisted of two 1-minute commercials videotaped during early 1970. The first of these depicted the effectiveness of a certain paper towel, and the second advertised a humorous movie (rated G). The commercials were selected for their humor and attention-getting characteristics.

Thereafter, children in the experimental group observed the first 3½ minutes of a program from a popular television series, "The Untouchables." The sequence, which preserved a simple story line, contained a chase, two fist-fighting scenes, two shootings, and a knifing. In contrast, children in the control group viewed a highly active 3½-minute videotaped sports sequence in which athletes competed in hurdle races, high jumps, and the like. For all subjects, the final 60 seconds of the program contained a commercial for automobile tires. Before the end of this last commercial, the experimenter reentered the room and announced that she was ready to begin.

Assessment of willingness to hurt another child. The subject was next escorted by the experimenter from the television room to a second room and seated at a response box apparatus modeled after the one employed by Mallick and McCandless (1966). The gray metal response box, which measured approximately 17 X 6 inches, displayed a red button on the left, a green button on the right, and a white light centered above these two manipulanda. The word "hurt" appeared beneath the red button, while the word "help" appeared beneath the green button. Several plastic wires led from the response box to a vent in the wall. The experimenter explained to the subject that these wires were connected to a game in an adjacent room and that "one of the other children is in the next room right now and will start to play the game in just a minute." She further explained that the game required the player in the other room to turn a handle and that the white light would come on each time the other child in the next room started to turn the handle, thus activating the red and green buttons.

The experimenter continued:

> When this white light comes on, you have to push one of these two buttons. If you push this green button, that will make the handle next door easier to turn and will help the child to win the game. If you push this red button, that will make the handle next door feel hot. That will hurt the child, and he will have to let go of the handle. Remember, this is the *help* button, and this is the *hurt* button [indicating]. See, it says *help* and *hurt*. . . . You have to push one of these two buttons each time the light goes on, but you can push whichever one you want to. You can always push the same button or you can change from one button to the other whenever you want to, but just remember, each time the light goes on, you can push only one. So if you push this green button then you help the other child and if you push this red button then you hurt the other child. Now if you push this green button for *just a second,* then you *help the other child just a little,* and if you push this red button down for *just a second,* then you *hurt the other child just a little.* But if you push this green button down a little longer, then you help the other child a little more, and if you push this red button down a little longer, then you hurt the other child a little more. *The longer you push the green button, the more you help the other child* and *the longer you push the red button, the more you hurt the other child.*

This explanation, with slightly varied wording, was repeated a second time if the child did not indicate comprehension of the instructions. After being assured that the subject understood the task, the experimenter left the room.[2]

Although all the subjects were led to believe that other children were participating, there was, in fact, no other child; the entire procedure was controlled in the next room so as to produce 20 trials, with an intertrial interval of approximately 15 seconds. Each child's response to each trial (appearance of the white light) and the duration of the response, recorded to the hundredth of a second, was automatically registered. When the subject had completed 20 trials, the experimenter reentered the room and announced that the game was over.

Assessment of aggressive play. The influence of televised violence on the children's subsequent play activities was also explored, although this issue was of secondary interest in the present research (the study being primarily concerned with interpersonal aggression rather than aggression aimed at inanimate objects). After completing the button-pushing task, the child was escorted to a third room (designated the "play room") across the hallway. The room contained two large tables, on each of which appeared three attractive nonaggressive toys (e.g., a slinky, a cookset, a space-station) and one aggressive toy (a gun or a knife). Two inflated plastic dolls, 36 inches and 42 inches in height, also stood in the room. The child was told that he would be left alone for a few minutes and that he could play freely with any of the toys.

All the children were observed through a one-way vision mirror, and their aggressive behavior was recorded using a time-sampling procedure. One point was scored for the occurrence of each of three predetermined categories of aggressive play (playing with the knife, playing with the gun, assaulting either of the dolls) during the first 10 seconds of each of ten ½-minute periods. In order to assess interobserver reliability for this measure, 10 subjects were observed independently by the two observers. Their agreement using the scoring procedures was virtually perfect ($r = .99$).

At the end of the play period, the experimenter reentered the room and asked the child to recall both the television program which he had seen and the nature of the game he had played. (All children included in the analyses were able to recall correctly the operation of the red and green buttons and the essential content of the television programs to which they had been exposed.) The child was then escorted to the lounge where the parent was waiting, thanked for his or her participation, rewarded with a small prize, and asked not to discuss the experiment with his or her friends.

RESULTS

Willingness to Hurt Another Child

The single overall measure which appears to capture the greatest amount of information in this situation is the total duration in seconds of each subject's aggressive responses during the 20 trials. Since marked heterogeneity of variance was apparent among the groups on this measure, the overall 2 X 2 X 2 analysis of variance was performed on square-root transformed scores (i.e., $x' = \sqrt{x} + \sqrt{x+1}$, Winer, 1962). The means for all groups on this measure are presented in Table 1. The analysis itself reveals only one significant effect: that for treatment conditions ($F = 4.16$, $p < .05$).

TABLE 1. MEAN TOTAL DURATION (TRANSFORMED) OF AGGRESSIVE RESPONSES IN ALL GROUPS

PROGRAM SHOWN	5-6-YEAR-OLDS		8-9-YEAR-OLDS	
	BOYS	GIRLS	BOYS	GIRLS
Aggressive	9.65	8.98	12.50	8.53
N	15	18	20	17
Nonaggressive	6.86	6.50	8.50	6.27
N	15	17	18	16

Children who had observed the aggressive program later showed reliably more willingness to engage in interpersonal aggression than those who had observed the neutral program.

Several supplementary analyses, which may serve to clarify the nature of this overall effect, were also computed. For example, a subject's total duration score may be viewed as the product of the number of times he aggresses and the average duration of each of these aggressive responses. Moreover, these two measures are only moderately, although reliably, related in the overall sample ($r = +.30, p < .05$). Analysis of variance for the average duration of the hurt responses reveals only a significant program effect that directly parallels the effects for total duration ($F = 3.95$, $p < .05$). The means for all groups on this measure are presented in Table 2. In contrast, analysis of the frequency measures fails to show any significant effects, although the tendency for the younger children is in the same direction.

TABLE 2. MEAN AVERAGE DURATIONS (TOTAL DURATION/NUMBER OF HURT RESPONSES) OF AGGRESSIVE RESPONSES IN ALL GROUPS

PROGRAM SHOWN	5–6-YEAR-OLDS		8–9-YEAR-OLDS	
	BOYS	GIRLS	BOYS	GIRLS
Aggressive	3.42	2.64	5.18	3.07
Nonaggressive	2.55	2.09	2.07	1.57

Note.—The number of subjects for each cell in this analysis is the same as that shown in Table 1.

Helping Responses

One possible explanation of the higher total aggression scores shown by the aggressive program group is that these children were simply more aroused than their nonaggressive treatment counterparts. To check on this interpretation, an overall analysis of variance was performed on the total duration of the help responses, employing the same square-root transformation described above. Presumably, if general arousal accounted for the effects of the hurt measure, the aggressive program groups should also show larger help scores than the nonaggressive program groups. However, contrary to the general arousal hypothesis, the effect of the treatments on this

TABLE 3. MEAN TOTAL DURATION (TRANSFORMED) OF HELPING RESPONSES IN ALL GROUPS

PROGRAM SHOWN	5–6-YEAR-OLDS		8–9-YEAR-OLDS	
	BOYS	GIRLS	BOYS	GIRLS
Aggressive	10.81	11.66	11.32	19.97
Nonaggressive	10.76	14.12	11.59	10.69

Note.—The number of subjects for each cell in this analysis is the same as that shown in Table 1.

measure was not significant; the overall F comparing the aggressive program subjects' prosocial responses with those of the nonaggressive program observers was only 1.17. The one effect of borderline significance which did appear in this analysis was a Program $\times$ Sex $\times$ Age interaction ($F = 3.91$, $p \cong .05$). As can be seen in Table 3, in which these data are presented, the interaction results from the very large helping responses shown by older girls who saw the aggressive program and the relatively large helping responses shown by younger girls who saw the nonaggressive one.

As a second check on the possibility that the longer durations in the aggressive program groups simply reflected a general arousal, a similar analysis was performed on the average duration scores of the help responses. In contrast to the comparable measure for aggressive responses, no significant differences for any of the main effects or interactions appeared on this measure (main effect for treatments, $F = 1.24$) although paralleling the total duration measure, the older girls who saw the aggressive program showed particularly long average durations. Finally, to show from a correlational approach that the overall help and hurt scores were not merely alternate measures of the same phenomenon, the product-moment correlation between the two sets of scores was computed. The resulting r of $-.24$ reflects a weak but significant ($p < .05$, two-tailed) negative relationship. Thus, overall, it appears clear that a specific disinhibition regarding *aggressive* behavior was produced by observing the televised aggression. This cannot be explained as a general arousal effect.

Aggression in the Play Situation

The mean aggressive play scores for all subjects are presented in Table 4. A 2 $\times$ 2 $\times$ 2 analysis of variance of these data revealed significant main effects for treatment ($F = 8.01$, $df = 1/128$, $p < .01$) and sex ($F = 37.87$, $df = 1/128$, $p < .001$). In addition, the Treatment $\times$ Sex ($F = 4.11$, $df = 1/128$, $p < .05$), Treatment $\times$ Age ($F = 4.28$, $df = 1/128$, $p < .05$), and Treatment $\times$ Sex $\times$ Age ($F = 4.68$, $df = 1/128$, $p < .05$) interactions were all significant. As is apparent from inspection of Table 4, these interactions arose from the fact that, although children exposed to the aggressive program tended to show a higher level of aggressive play than children exposed to the nonaggressive one in all simple comparisons, the effect was much greater for the younger boys than for any of the remaining groups.

TABLE 4. MEAN NUMBER OF TIME-SAMPLED AGGRESSIVE PLAY RESPONSES IN ALL GROUPS

PROGRAM SHOWN	5-6-YEAR-OLDS		8-9-YEAR-OLDS	
	BOYS	GIRLS	BOYS	GIRLS
Aggressive	7.13	2.94	5.65	3.00
Nonaggressive	3.33	2.65	5.39	2.63

Note.—The number of subjects for each cell in this analysis is the same as that shown in Table 1.

DISCUSSION

The overall results of the present experiment provide relatively consistent evidence for the view that certain aspects of a child's willingness to aggress may be at least temporarily increased by merely witnessing aggressive television episodes. These findings confirm and extend many earlier reports regarding the effects of symbolically modeled aggression on the subsequent imitative aggressive behavior of young observers toward inanimate objects (e.g., Bandura, Ross, & Ross, 1963a; Hicks, 1965; Rosekrans & Hartup, 1967). Likewise, the present data are in accord with other studies which have shown disinhibition of both young children's aggressive play and older viewers' willingness to shock another person after observing filmed aggressive modeling. As in many earlier studies, subjects exposed to symbolic aggressive models regularly tended to behave more aggressively than control group subjects tested under identical circumstances. Further, the present results emerged despite the brevity of the aggressive sequences (less than 4 minutes), the absence of a strong prior instigation to aggression, the clear availability of an alternative helping response, and the use of nationally broadcast materials rather than specially prepared laboratory films.

The various measures employed, considered together, provide some clarification of the nature of the effects obtained in the overall analysis. The significant effect for the total duration measure appears to stem predominantly from the average duration of the subjects' aggressive responses. In fact, as seen in Table 2, the group means on this measure did not overlap; the *lowest* individual cell mean among those who observed the aggressive program was higher than the *highest* mean among those groups who observed the nonaggressive program.

It should also be recalled that the instructions given to all children emphasized that a brief depression of the hurt button would cause only minimal distress to the other child, while longer depressions would cause increasingly greater discomfort. This fact, coupled with the finding that the overall average duration of such responses was more than 75 percent longer in the aggressive program group than in the control group, suggests clearly that the primary effect of exposure to the aggressive program was that of reducing subjects' restraints against inflicting severe discomfort on the ostensible peer victim, that is, of increasing the *magnitude* of the hurting response. With the exception of the older girls, this effect was not paralleled by an increment in the corresponding measures of helping; thus it cannot be attributed to simple arousal effects.

It should be noted that the measure of aggressive play responses was obtained after all the subjects had been given an opportunity to help or hurt another child. Thus the observed effects might reflect an interaction between the programs and some aspect of the hurting/helping opportunity rather than the simple influence of the programs themselves. While the present data do not permit us to address the possibility of such interactions directly, it is clear that the obtained results are consistent with earlier studies in which other types of aggressive scenes were used and where there were no such intervening measures.

The present experiment was designed primarily to determine whether children's willingness to engage in interpersonal aggression would be affected by the viewing of violent televised material. Within the context of the experimental situation and dependent measures employed, it appeared that this was indeed the case. However, it is clear that the occurrence and magnitude of such effects will be influenced by a number of situational and personality variables. It is thus important to examine the antecedents and correlates of such reactions to violence in greater detail. In view of the fact that a child born today will, by the age of 18, have spent more of his life watching television than in any other single activity except sleep (Lesser, 1970), few problems seem more deserving of attention.

NOTES

[1]Since no specific information could be provided in public announcements or over the telephone, it appeared necessary to have parents accompany their children to the institute in order to assure that no child participated without the informed consent of his parents. In order to defray the costs of transportation, baby sitters for siblings who remained at home, and the like, and to eliminate economic biases which might otherwise have appeared in the sample, a $10 stipend was given the parent of each participant. No parent who appeared for the interview declined to allow his or her child participate.

[2]Nine children, all in the 5–6 year-old age group, were terminated prior to the collection of data because they refused to remain alone, cried, or left the experimental situation. Twenty-three other children participated in the entire experiment but were not included in the sample. Of these, 14 (5 in the younger age group and 9 in the older group) did not understand or follow instructions for the response box, 7 (3 younger and 4 older children) played or explored the room instead of watching television. The data for the remaining 2 children were not recorded properly due to the technical difficulties. All potential participants brought to the institute by their parents who were not eliminated for the reasons listed above were included in the experimental sample.

REFERENCES

Bandura, A. Influence of models' reinforcement contingencies on the acquisition of imitative responses. *Journal of Personality and Social Psychology,* 1965, *1,* 589–595.

Bandura, A., Ross, D., & Ross, S. A. Transmission of aggression through imitation of aggressive models. *Journal of Abnormal and Social Psychology,* 1961, *63,* 575–582.

Bandura, A., Ross, D., & Ross, S. A. Imitation of film-mediated aggressive models. *Journal of Abnormal and Social Psychology,* 1963, *66,* 3–11. (a)

Bandura, A., Ross, D., & Ross, S. A. Vicarious reinforcement and imitative learning. *Journal of Abnormal and Social Psychology,* 1963, *67,* 601–607. (b)

Berkowitz, L. Some aspects of observed aggression. *Journal of Personality and Social Psychology,* 1965, *2,* 359–369.

Berkowitz, L., & Rawlings, E. Effects of film violence on inhibitions against subsequent aggression. *Journal of Abnormal and Social Psychology,* 1963, *66,* 405–412.

Feshbach, S. The stimulating versus cathartic effects of a vicarious aggressive activity. *Journal of Abnormal and Social Psychology,* 1961, *63,* 381–385.

Feshbach, S., & Singer, R. D. *Television and aggression.* San Francisco: Jossey-Bass, 1971.

Flanders, J. P. A review of research on imitative behavior. *Psychological Bulletin,* 1968, *69,* 316–337.

Halloran, J. D. Television and violence. *The Twentieth Century,* 1964, *174,* 61–72.

Hanratty, M. A. Imitation of film-mediated aggression against live and inanimate victims. Unpublished master's thesis, Vanderbilt University, 1969.

Hanratty, M. A., Liebert, R. M., Morris, L. W., & Fernandez, L. E. Imitation of film-mediated aggression against live and inanimate victims. *Proceedings of the 77th Annual Convention of the American Psychological Association,* 1969, *4,* 457–458. (Summary)

Hanratty, M. A., O'Neal, E., & Sulzer, J. L. The effect of frustration upon imitation of aggression. *Journal of Personality and Social Psychology,* 1972, *21,* 30–34.

Hicks, D. J. Imitation and retention of film-mediated aggressive peer and adult models. *Journal of Personality and Social Psychology,* 1965, *2,* 97–100.

Klapper, J. T. The impact of viewing "aggression": Studies and problems of extrapolation. In O. N. Larsen (Ed.), *Violence and the mass media.* New York: Harper & Row, 1968.

Larsen, O. N. *Violence and the mass media.* New York: Harper & Row, 1968.

Lesser, G. S. Designing a program for broadcast television. In F. F. Korten, S. W. Cook, & J. I. Lacey (Eds.), *Psychology and the problems of society.* Washington, D.C.: American Psychological ASsociation, 1970.

Lovaas, O. I. Effect of exposure to symbolic aggression on aggressive behavior. *Child Development,* 1961, *32,* 37–44.

Mallick, S. K., & McCandless, B. R. A study of catharsis of aggression. *Journal of Personality and Social Psychology, 1966, 4,* 591–596.

Merriam, E. We're teaching our children that violence is fun. *The Ladies' Home Journal,* 1964, *52,* 44, 49, 52.

Rosekrans, M. A., & Hartup, W. W. Imitative influences of consistent and inconsistent responses consequences to a model on aggressive behavior in children. *Journal of Personality and Social Psychology,* 1967, *7,* 429–434.

Savitsky, J. C., Rogers, R. W., Izard, C. E., & Liebert, R. M. The role of frustration and anger in the imitation of filmed aggression against a human victim. *Psychological Reports, 1971, 29,* 807–810.

Siegel, A. E. Film-mediated fantasy aggression and strength of aggressive drive. *Child Development,* 1956, *27,* 365–378.

Walters, R. H. Implications of laboratory studies for the control and regulation of violence. *The Annals of the American Academy of Political and Social Science,* 1966, *364,* 60–72.

Walters, R. H., & Thomas, E. L. Enhancement of punitiveness by visual and audiovisual displays. *Canadian Journal of Psychology,* 1963, *16,* 244–255.

Wertham, F. Is T.V. Hardening us to the war in Vietnam? *New York Times,* December 4, 1966.

Winer, B. J. *Statistical principles in experimental design.* New York: McGraw-Hill, 1962.

4.12

A Note on the Effects of Television Viewing

James Garbarino

Concern with the effects of television viewing began with the earliest introduction of broadcast and reception facilities in the late 1930's and early 1940's. As early as 1936, the question was raised by the British social psychologist T. H. Pear, "What differences will television make to our habits and mental attitudes?" (Pear, 1936). Some 36 years and numerous investigations later, Pear's question remains largely unanswered.

The most recent compendium of research findings, the report to the Surgeon General, entitled *Television and Growing Up: The Impact of Televised Violence,* (1972) is addressed almost exclusively to the problem of assessing the relation of television to aggressive behavior in children and adolescents. In addition, some attention is given to matters such as the number of hours viewed, development of program choice, program content, and "changing patterns of television use." What is disturbing about the report to the Surgeon General is that like much of the research which has gone before, it fails to address the question of the effect of television on the socialization process within the family. More specifically: How does the television viewing both by the child and his parents affect parent-child interaction? How does the use of television as a "babysitter" by parents affect the parent-child relationship? How does the child's free and largely autonomous access to such powerful entertainment affect his other activities?

While little has been done to answer these questions directly there is indirect evidence which is germane and illuminating. Relevant data are cited in the report to the Surgeon General, as well as in two previous large-scale investigations (Schramm,

Lyle, and Parker, 1961; Himmelweit, Oppenheim, and Vince, 1958). But the facts seem to have gone unnoticed because of the inadequacy of the perspective which looks only for direct effects upon the child, rather than viewing the impact on the family interactional system.

Much of the relevant research was done in the transitional period—i.e. the 1950's —when alternatives to the "television culture" were still viable. A major reason reported for initial purchase of a television set was to bring the family together in the home (Riley, Cantwell, and Ruttiger, 1949; Hamilton and Lawless, 1956). Yet television viewing was shown to be a largely noninteractive activity. One study reported that 78 percent of the respondents indicated no conversation occurring during viewing except at specified times such as commercials (and 60 percent indicated that no other activity was engaged while viewing) (Maccoby, 1951). The same investigator described the television viewing setting in the following terms:

> The television atmosphere in most households is one of quiet absorption on the part of the family members who are present. The nature of the family social life during a program could be described as "parallel" rather than interactive, and the set does seem quite clearly to dominate family life when it is on. (Maccoby, 1951, p. 428)

Such is the role of television in family interaction—or lack of it—as described in the early 1950's. Distressingly, 36 percent of respondents in one survey reported that television viewing was the only family activity participated in during the week (Hamilton and Lawless, 1956). This same study concluded that television viewing became a substitute for social activity both within and outside the family circle.

If this evidence suggests anything, it is that—at least during the 1950's—television contributed to "parallel" rather than "interactive" social activity within the family. That this had an effect upon the "habits and mental attitudes" of the viewers—adults and children—seems at the very least plausible. That television had a direct effect upon child rearing patterns seems clearer.

It has been repeatedly found that parents generally do not know how many hours their children view television (e.g., Albert and Melaine, 1958). This result has generally been intepreted as strictly a methodological problem—which to be sure it is. But it is also a substantive finding—or at least can be, given the proper conceptual framework. The fact that children watch television to an extent which is not precisely known to their parents supports the notion that television provides a dimension of experience which is often independent of adult supervision, discussion, guidance, etc.. For example, the choice of viewing time and programs is largely a decision of the child (Hess and Goldman, 1962; Lyle and Hoffman, 1971; McLeod et al., 1971). The rising number of households in which there are two or more sets—over 35 percent in 1969 (Statistical Abstract 1969)—can only contribute to the autonomy of children's viewing. That this independence from parental association and influence may generalize to other areas seems not implausible.

Earlier surveys did probe the relation of television to the process of child rearing. In one study, mothers were asked: "Has TV made it easier or harder to take care of the children at home?" Fifty-four percent replied "easier," 33 percent replied "no difference," and 3 percent replied "harder" (Maccoby, 1951). One investigator reported the following comment from a mother in this regard: "It's much easier—it's just like putting him to sleep" (Maccoby, 1951, p. 439). The same investigator concluded that, "Mothers comment that TV keeps the children much quieter—there is less roughhousing and less bothering the parents with questions." (Maccoby, 1951, p. 440). In response to the statement, "TV keeps the children quiet," in one study 62 percent replied "strongly agree," 26 percent replied "somewhat agree," and 12 percent replied, "disagree." (Hess and Goldman, 1961). What were those children doing while they were so quiet? Was their "silence" enhancing their attachment to people, to activities, or simply to television sets? The question is a rhetorical one. The answer is, of course, a matter of speculation.

To assess the impact of television viewing upon socialization—for present and future generations as the children of the "television culture" become the parents of that culture—is a problem of a magnitude at least as great as that to which the report to the Surgeon General is addressed. The early findings suggest that television had a disruptive effect upon interaction and thus presumably human development, which by the year 1972 may have become not an anomaly but a pervasive element of the culture; by 1972, 96 percent of all American households had one or more television sets and an average viewing time in excess of two hours per day (Report to the Surgeon General, 1972). It is not unreasonable to ask: "Is the fact that the average American family during the 1950's came to include two parents, two children and a television set somehow related to the psychosocial characteristics of the young adults of the 1970's?"

Except for the sketchy data presented above we do not know the answer. And, because television has become an inextricable part of the culture, we may now not be able to find out.

REFERENCES

Albert, R. and Meline, H. The influence of social status on the uses of television. *Public Opinion Quarterly,* 1958, *22,* 145–151.

Belson, W. Measuring the effects of television: A description of method. *Public Opinion Quarterly,* 1958, *22,* 11–18.

Hamilton, R., & Lawless, R. Television within the social matrix. *Public Opinion Quarterly,* 1956, *20,* 393–403.

Hess, R., & Goldman, H. Parents' views of the effect of television on their children. *Child Development,* 1962, *33,* 411–426.

Himmelweit, H. T., Oppenheim, A. N., & Vince, P. *Television and the child: An empirical study of the effects of television on the young.* London: Oxford University Press, 1958.

Maccoby, E. Television: Its impact on school children. *Public Opinion Quarterly,* 1951, *15,* 423–444.

Merrill, I. Broadcast viewing and listening by children. *Public Opinion Quarterly,* 1961, *15,* 263–276.

Pear, T. H. What television might do. *Listener,* November 18, 1936.

Rees, M. Achievement motivation and content preferences. *Journalism Quarterly,* 1967, *44,* 688–692.

Riley, J., Cantwell, F., & Ruttiger, K. Some observations on the social effects of television. *Public Opinion Quarterly,* 1949, *13,* 223–234.

Robinson, J. Television and leisure time: Yesterday, today and (maybe) tomorrow. *Public Opinion Quarterly,* 1969, *33,* 210–222.

Schramm, W., Lyle, J., & Parker, E. B. *Television in the lives of our children.* Stanford: Stanford University Press, 1961.

Surgeon General's Scientific Advisory Committee. *Television and growing up: The impact of televised violence.* Washington, D.C.: U.S. Government Printing Office, 1972.

Sweetser, F. Home television and behavior: Some tentative conclusions. *Public Opinion Quarterly,* 1955, *19,* 79–84.

United States Department of Commerce. *Statistical Abstract of the United States.* Washington D.C.: U.S. Government Printing Office, 1969.

4.13

Congressional Inquiries into TV Violence

Robert M. Liebert
John M. Neale
Emily S. Davidson

As early as 1954, Senator Estes Kefauver, then Chairman of the Senate Subcommittee on Juvenile Delinquency, questioned the need for violent content on television entertainment. Network representatives claimed at that time that research on the effects of violence viewing upon children was inconclusive, although they admitted that some risk existed. In addition, Harold E. Fellows, President and Chairman of the

Excerpted, by permission of the authors and publishers from pp. 146–156 of Robert M. Liebert, John M. Neale and Emily S. Davidson, *The Early Window; Effects of Television on Children and Youth.* New York: Pergamon, Inc., 1973. Copyright ©, 1973.

Board of the National Association of Broadcasters, promised that the NAB would undertake research on the impact of television programming on children.

THE DODD HEARINGS

In 1961, Senator Thomas Dodd, then chairman of the same subcommittee, inquired about violence on children's television. Testimony during hearings revealed that the television industry's use of violence had remained both rampant and opportunistic. (2)

> *An independent producer was asked to "inject an 'adequate' diet of violence into scripts" . . . Another network official wrote 'I like the idea of sadism.' . . . 'Give me sex and action' demanded one executive.* (p. 40)

Also it was clear that the previously promised research had not been carried out. Leroy Collins, the new president of the NAB explained: (2)

> *Soon [after Mr. Fellows' testimony] the television code review board undertook a pilot study of "viewer attitudes" to determine the feasibility of a broader study, but about that time the Columbia Broadcasting System announced that it was engaged in sponsoring a survey which, while broader, would cover essentially the same ground. In view of this overlapping inquiry, NAB deferred to CBS in order that the larger survey could go ahead in preference to the narrower inquiry which the NAB had initiated. It is anticipated that the CBS project will be completed by the end of this summer [1961] and that* the final report will be published before the end of this year. (pp. 593–594)

The report in question was published in 1963 by Gary Steiner. (3) The title, *The People Look at Television,* indicates clearly the subject matter of the volume: the attitudes and beliefs of parents and other viewers about the effects of television on children, not the actual effects as determined by scientific investigation.

But the earlier hearings did have an impact, which one observer described this way: (4)

> *[The subcommittee staff for the 1961 Dodd hearings] noted that many network series mentioned in early testimony as especially violent were being syndicated, and shown on independent stations throughout the country. One committee aide observed: "It's as if they used our 1961 hearings as a shopping list!" Many of the programs were scheduled at earlier hours than before, and were reaching younger audiences.* (p. 203)

In 1961, industry spokesmen again promised more research. (1)

> ... we are moving significantly in this area [of research on effects of television on children] now. At a meeting of our joint radio and television board of directors last week approval was given to proceed with the initial planning of an NAB research and training center in association with one of the leading universities in the nation. (p. 594)

James T. Aubrey and Frank Stanton, executives of CBS, as well as executives of NBC and ABC agreed to participate in industry-wide research.

In 1962, the industry co-sponsored the Joint Committee for Research on Television and Children, along with the United States Department of Health, Education and Welfare. This committee, which consisted almost entirely of network personnel, solicited research proposals from various members of the scientific community. Unfortunately, it became clear in 1964 that few of these proposals were being carried out. In fact, only three papers were even begun as a result of the work of the joint committee. The first, by Dr. Ruth Hartley, constituted a criticism and analysis of the inadequacies of research which was detrimental to the industry, not an investigation of the actual effects. (5) A second was conducted by Dr. Seymour Feshbach, a leading proponent of the catharsis hypothesis. (14) The third study was not even completed.

In 1964, as Senator Dodd's hearings continued, network executives again promised to do more research. By this time the excuses had become rather pathetic. When asked by Dodd what had been done, NBC Executive Vice President Walter D. Scott replied this way: (1)

> I have asked the same question, Senator, because I have wondered why there has not been more in the way of results up to this point. I have been reminded by our people who are working very actively and closely with the Committee that it is appropriate to bear in mind that the work of scholars frequently sets its own pace and that time may be the price we must pay for meaningful results. As I understand it, they have had work done by a very large number of competent scholars in the field of social sciences. I understand that there have been something like one hundred separate projects that have been studied, that these have been narrowed down, that they are now at the stage of being ready to go ahead with, I believe, either five or six specific projects, out of which they hope to get some meaningful answers. (p. 595)

No new research was ever published or reported by the Committee. Scott went on to become NBC's board chairman.

THE VIOLENCE COMMISSION

In 1968, the National Commission on the Causes and Prevention of Violence held hearings on the role of the mass media. Once again, network executives were questioned about the promised research; once again, it was not forthcoming. By this time, the networks were arguing that *they* should not be doing research anyway. One ABC executive stated: (2)

> *Research should be done from an objective standpoint and one that the public would be satisfied with as being done objectively, rather than that which is directly financed by our particular company.* (p. 598)

The networks evidently felt no responsibility to determine the effects of television for their own use in determining program content.

Network executives also suggested that research was impossible due to the lack of adequate research design. Dr. Frank Stanton, then president of CBS and himself a Ph.D. psychologist, remarked: (2)

> *It isn't unwillingness on the part of the industry to underwrite the research. It is that no one in the thirty-odd years I have been in the business has come up with a technique or methodology that would let you get a fix on this impact. . . . These people from the outside [of the industry] have been given every encouragement, every funding they have asked for to come up with methodology, and this is the field that is very illusive [sic] and it doesn't do any good to spend a lot of money and come up with facts somebody can punch his fingers through.* (p. 598)

Less than 2 years later "people from the outside" funded by the Federal government had come up with a number of research plans which did permit "a fix on this impact." It was possible all along.

THE SURGEON GENERAL'S NIMH INQUIRY

In 1969, Senator John O. Pastore, Chairman of the Senate Sub-Committee of the Senate Commerce Committee sent a letter to Health, Education, and Welfare Secretary Robert Finch, which said in part: (7)

> *I am exceedingly troubled by the lack of any definitive information which would help resolve the question of whether there is a causal connection between televised crime and violence and antisocial behavior of individuals, especially children. . . . I am respectfully requesting that you direct the Surgeon General to appoint a commit-*

tee comprised of distinguished men and women from whatever pro-
fessions and disciplines deemed appropriate to devise techniques
and to conduct a study under his supervision using those techniques
which will establish scientifically insofar as possible what harmful
effects, if any, these programs have on children.

Secretary Finch directed Surgeon General William H. Stewart to select a committee to authorize and examine evidence relevant to questions about the effects of
television on children. The Surgeon General, announcing that he would appoint an
advisory panel of scientists respected by the scientific community, the broadcasting
industry, and the general public, requested nominations from various academic and
professional associations (including the American Sociological Association, the
American Anthropological Association, the American Psychiatric Association, and the
American Psychological Association), distinguished social scientists, the NAB and the
three major networks. From the many names suggested, the office of the Surgeon
General drew up a list of 40, and sent it to the presidents of the National Association
of Broadcasters and the three national commercial broadcast networks. The broadcasters were asked to indicate "which individuals, if any, you would believe would
not be appropriate for an impartial scientific investigation of this nature." They responded with a list of seven names:

Leo Bogart, executive vice president and general manager of the
Bureau of Advertising of the American Newspaper Publishers Association. Dr. Bogart had previously published a book on television.

Albert Bandura, professor of psychology at Stanford, and an interna-
tionally acknowledged expert on children's imitative learning. Bandura, now president-elect of the American Psychological
Association, had published numerous research articles which demonstrated that children can learn to be more aggressive from watching TV.

Leonard Berkowitz, Vilas professor of psychology at the University
of Wisconsin, principal investigator of an extensive series of studies
showing that watching aggression can stimulate aggressive behavior. Author of two books on aggression, Berkowitz served as a
consultant to the 1969 Task Force on Mass Media and Violence.

Leon Eisenberg, professor and chairman of the Department of Psychiatry at Harvard University.

Ralph Garry, then professor of educational psychology at Boston
University, author of a book on children's television, and a principal
consultant to the U.S. Senate Subcommittee on Juvenile Delinquency. He is now at the Ontario Institute for Studies in Education.

Otto Larsen, professor of sociology at the University of Washington
and editor of *Violence and the mass media.*

Percy H. Tannenbaum, then professor of psychology and communication at the University of Pennsylvania, and prominent for his theoretical analyses of the arousing effects of media entertainment
depicting violence and sex. He has recently been appointed professor in the Graduate School of Public Policy, University of California
at Berkeley.

While these distinguished men were blackballed, the industry secured 5 of the
12 positions for its own executives and consultants. They were:

Thomas Coffin, vice president of NBC
Ira H. Cisin, CBS consultant
Joseph T. Kapper, director of CBS social research
Harold Mendelsohn, CBS consultant
Gerhart D. Wiebe, former CBS executive

This odd selection procedure, of systematic inclusion and exclusion, was not
intended to be a matter of the public record. Even the non-network members of the
committee, all of whom are well respected by the scientific community, were not told
anything about it. When the procedure was uncovered by Stanford professor Edwin
Parker and Senator Lee Metcalf, HEW Secretary Robert Finch tried to explain away
the travesty as handily as he could, saying that the selection was designed to assure
impartiality. James J. Jenkins, then chairman of the American Psychological Association's board of professional affairs, took a different view. He described the procedure
as deplorable and analogized: (8)

It looks like an exemplar of the old story of the "regulatees" running
the "regulators" or the fox passing on the adequacy of the eyesight
of the man assigned to guard the chicken coop. (pp. 951–952)

It is important, though, that the Committee was not directly involved in the
commissioning of new research. Instead, 1 million dollars was made available for
support of independent projects through the National Institute of Mental Health.
About 40 formal proposals were submitted. They were then reviewed by *ad hoc*
panels of prominent scientists who were not themselves members of the Committee
(by then known as the Surgeon General's Scientific Advisory Committee on Television and Social Behavior). Twenty-three projects were selected and funded in this
way: the investigators were free to proceed with their contracted research without
interference, and to prepare technical research reports of their findings and of any
conclusions they deemed appropriate.

The Advisory Committee Report

Prior to the publication of the individual investigators' reports the committee reviewed
them, as well as previous research, and submitted a report to the Surgeon General.

The post had changed hands since the project began, having passed to Jesse Steinfeld who released both a brief summary, as well as the Committee's full report in January 1972.

Although indicating that a causal relationship between violence viewing and aggression by the young had been found, the Committee report was unfortunately worded so as to lead to misunderstanding, and the summary was flatly misleading. One journalist, Jack Gould of the New York Times, wrote a "scoop" story of the report with the headline, "TV Violence Held Unharmful to Youth." (9)

The Committee's hedging may or may not have been predictible, given its diverse composition and the political pressure to produce a unanimously signed document. At any rate, the private goings on were surely not dull. According to John P. Murray, research coordinator for the project and one of the few non-Committee members who was present during the deliberations: (10)

> There was a big move by Government officials to get a consensus report. There was a lot of anger, the meetings were extremely tense with the warring factions sitting at either end of the table, glaring at each other, particularly toward the end. (p. 28)

The result was undoubtedly a compromise, with the "network five" scoring its share in the battle. According to Newsweek, in a story "correcting" its earlier interpretation: (11)

> At one point during the committee meetings . . . former CBS consultant Wiebe raised his eyes from a particularly damning piece of evidence and grumbled: "This looks like it was written by someone who hates television." But the most ardent defender of the industry was CBS research director Joseph Klapper, who lobbied for the inclusion, among other things, of a plethora of "howevers" in the final report. (p. 55)[1]

Many of the researchers associated with the project felt that their work had been represented inaccurately, at least to the extent of minimizing what seemed a clear relationship between viewing of TV violence and youngsters' aggressive behavior. Dr. Monroe Lefkowitz, Principal Research Scientist at the New York State Department of Mental Hygiene wrote in a letter to Senator Pastore:

> The Surgeon General's Scientific Advisory Committee on Television and Social Behavior in my opinion ignores, dilutes, and distorts the research findings in their report, "Television and Growing Up: the Impact of Televised Violence." As a contributor of one of the technical reports whose study dealt with television violence and aggressive behavior . . . I feel that the Committee's conclusions about the causal nature of television violence in producing aggressive behavior are hedged by erroneous statements, are overqualified, and are potentially damaging to children and society . . .

Lefkowitz' response is strong, but it is by no means unique. Matilda Paisley, in a report of Stanford University's Institute for Communication Research (*Social policy research and the realities of the system: violence done to TV research*), indicates that fully half of the researchers who replied to her questionnaire stated that the results of their own research had not been adequately reported by the Committee. (10) Some typical replies, with letters substituted for respondents' names, appear below:

> *Respondent B commented that, "In fact, they went too deep on some of our extraneous findings, in order to obscure the main conclusion." Respondents G, L, and P spoke of "strange emphases," "misleading focus," and "selective emphases," respectively. Respondents E and F spoke of errors in reporting their research. Respondent T stated that "the conclusions are diluted and overqualified."*

One item on the Paisley questionnaire read: *Whatever the findings of your own research suggest,* * *which of the following relationships of violence viewing to aggressiveness do you feel now is the most plausible?*

(a) viewing television violence increases aggressiveness;
(b) viewing television violence decreases aggressiveness;
(c) viewing television violence has no effect on aggressiveness;
(d) the relationship between the violence viewing and aggressiveness depends on a third variable or set of variables:
(e) other, please specify?

None of the 20 investigators who responded to this question selected answer (b); none selected (c). Clearly, then, these researchers felt that there was a relationship between TV violence and aggressiveness, and that the long touted catharsis hypothesis was untenable. Seventy percent of the respondents simply selected response (a): viewing television violence increases aggressiveness. All of the remainder qualified their replies with some version of alternatives (d) or (e).

The Pastore Hearings

In March 1972, shortly after the publication of the technical reports, Senator Pastore held further hearings to clarify the situation. (12) When questioned by Senator Pastore and members of his subcommittee, Ithiel de Sola Pool, a member of the Surgeon General's Advisory Committee, commented:

> *Twelve scientists of widely different views unanimously agreed that the scientific evidence indicated that the viewing of television violence by young people causes them to behave more aggressively.* (p. 47)

---

*Almost half of the investigators were involved in projects which did not bear directly on this question.

Alberta Siegel, another Committee member, remarked:

> *Commercial television makes its own contribution to the set of factors that underlie aggressiveness in our society. It does so in entertainment through ceaseless repetition of the message that conflict may be resolved by aggression, that violence is a way of solving problems.* (p. 63)

Pool and Siegel were among the academic members of the Committee; they had pressed for a strong report on the basis of the data all along. But even Ira Cisin, Thomas Coffin, and the other "network" Committee members agreed that the situation was sufficiently serious to warrant some action.

The networks' chief executives also testified. Julian Goodman, President of NBC, stated:

> *We agree with you that the time for action has come. And, of course, we are willing to cooperate in any way together with the rest of the industry.* (p. 182)

Elton H. Rule of the American Broadcasting Company promised:

> *Now that we are reasonably certain that televised violence can increase aggressive tendencies in some children, we will have to manage our program planning accordingly.* (p. 217)

Surgeon General Steinfeld made the unequivocal statement that:

> *Certainly my interpretation is that there is a causative relationship between televised violence and subsequent antisocial behavior, and that the evidence is strong enough that it requires sane action on the part of responsible authorities, the TV industry, the Government, the citizens.* (p. 28)

Although few social scientists would put the seal "Absolutely Proven" on this, or any other body of research, the weight of the evidence and the outcry of the news media did become sufficient to produce a belated recognition of the implications of the research. Testimony and documentation at the Hearings of the Subcommittee on Communications, U.S. Senate, were overwhelming. Senator Pastore now had his answer. It is captured entirely in the following interchange, late in the hearings, between Pastore and Dr. Eli Rubinstein. (Rubinstein was Vice-Chairman of the Surgeon General's Committee and, in Dr. Steinfeld's absence, monitored the research and refereed the Committee.)

> *SENATOR PASTORE. And you are convinced, like the Surgeon General, that we have enough data now [about the effects of television on children] to take action?*

> DR. RUBINSTEIN.   I am, sir.
>
> SENATOR PASTORE.   Without a re-review. It will only sub-
> stantiate the facts we already know. Irrespective of how one or
> another individual feels, the fact still remains that you are convinced,
> as the Surgeon General is convinced, that there is a causal relation-
> ship between violence on television and social behavior on the part
> of children?
>
> DR. RUBINSTEIN.   I am, sir.
>
> SENATOR PASTORE.   I think we ought to take it from there.
> . . . (p. 152)

NOTES

[1]Copyright Newsweek, Inc. 1972. Reprinted by permission.

REFERENCES

1. Baker, R. K. The views, standards, and practices of the television industry. In R. K. Baker and S. J. Ball (Eds.). *Violence and the media.* Washington, D.C.: U.S. Government Printing Office, 1969. Pp. 593–614.

2. Johnson, N. *How to talk back to your television set.* Boston: Atlantic-Little, Brown and Company, 1967.

3. Steiner, G. A. *The people look at television.* New York: Alfred A. Knopf, 1963.

4. Barnouw, E. *A History of broadcasting in the United States. Vol. III—from 1953: The image empire.* New York: Oxford University Press, 1972. P. 203. (Copyright © 1972 by Erik Barnouw.)

5. Hartley, R. L. *The impact of viewing "aggression": Studies and problems of extrapolation.* New York: Columbia Broadcasting System Office of Social Research, 1964.

6. Feshbach, S., & Singer, R. *Television and aggression.* San Francisco: Jossey-Bass, 1971.

7. Cisin, I. H., Coffin, T. E., Janis, I. L., Klapper, J. T., Mendelsohn, H., Omwake, E., Pinderhughes, C. A., Pool, I. de Sola, Siegel, A. E., Wallace, A. F. C., Watson, A. S., & Wiebe, G. D. *Television and growing up: The impact of televised violence.* Washington, D.C.: U.S. Government Printing Office, 1972.

8. Boffey, P. M., & Walsh, J. Study of TV violence. Seven top researchers blackballed from panel. *Science,* May 22, 1970, Vol. 168 pp. 949–952. (Copyright © 1970 by The American Association for the Advancement of Science.)

9. Gould, J. TV violence held unharmful to youth. *The New York Times,* January 11, 1972.

10. Paisley, M. B. *Social policy research and the realities of the system: violence done to TV research.* Institute of Communication Research: Stanford University, 1972.

11. Violence revisited. *Newsweek,* March 6, 1972, pp. 55–56. (Copyright Newsweek, Inc. 1972. Reprinted by permission.)

12. U.S. Congress, Senate. Hearings before the subcommittee on Communications of the Committee on Commerce, March 1972.

part five
MIDDLE CHILDHOOD AND ADOLESCENCE

As the child approaches adolescence, social roles and social systems outside the family play an increasing part in shaping his abilities, motives, and behavior. The complexity of the effect of father absence as an influence is demonstrated by Hetherington, in her review article. Kohn takes up the question of social class again, arguing that the father's occupation is a key determinant of parent-child relationships. Rosen and d'Andrade document the impact of these same kinds of social factors on the child's motivation.

Next, Shapira and Madsen's cross-cultural research shows how a new and deliberately contrived life setting, the Israeli kibbutz, creates a distinctive pattern of social interaction among the children who are its products. The power of deliberately constructed social settings to shape behavior is then even more dramatically illustrated in Sherif's "Robber's Cave Experiment," in which the same groups of middle class white Anglo-Saxon boys were transformed in the space of a few weeks first into a gang of unscrupulous and heartless competitors, then into a group of cooperative and compassionate citizens of the children's community.

Nichols' review of the famous Coleman Report then shows how schools, at least as presently constituted, seem unable to alter the developmental trajectories established by class and race in contemporary American society. And the contrast between our own nation and others is illuminated by Kandel and Lesser's comparative study of adolescence in the United States and Denmark.

The section and the book close on a concern for the developing phenomenon of alienation among children and youth in American society. Bronfenbrenner probes the "roots of alienation" as revealed in research studies, and offers a series of recommendations for modification of basic social institutions, such as business, industry, transportation, and urban planning, in order to provide "support systems" to the family and other socializing agencies bearing responsibility for children and youth.

5.1

The Effects of Father Absence on Child Development

E. Mavis Hetherington
Jan L. Deur

In our society, as within most Western cultures, the intact nuclear family is commonly regarded as the optimal unit for rearing children. Deviations from this norm, such as socialization within an institution or within a one-parent family, are believed to be harmful to the children involved and are frequently cited as possible causes of antisocial behavior (e.g., Report of The National Advisory Commission on Civil Disorders, 1968). This paper is a review of research findings concerning one type of disrupted family, the father-absent family. In it, we have attempted to ascertain whether this type of family structure has any unique behavioral and psychological effects upon children reared in these families, as compared to children from father-present homes.

Early research on this problem was stimulated by the widespread paternal absence precipitated by World War II (Stolz *et al.,* 1954). Fathers who had been in the armed forces and away from their families often reported a sense of alienation from children who were born or were in the early preschool years during their absence. This sense of estrangement seemed to be greater toward sons, whom the fathers frequently regarded as being overprotected "sissies."

Many of these first studies ignored the methodological difficulties inherent in investigations of this problem. They tended to compare a sample of children from father-absent families with those from intact families and note the differences. Unfortunately, the problem is too complex for such a simple approach. For one thing, father absence may be due to a variety of factors, such as separation, divorce, occupational demands, military service, or death. It seems likely that the consequences of paternal absence for the children involved will depend at least partially on the reasons for his absence. Morover, the quality of the marriage and family relationships prior to the father's departure will probably also have a bearing on the nature of the family's subsequent interaction. Indeed, if the father were a major source of conflict within the family, his absence could conceivably have some ameliorative effects upon the remaining family members.

Even if it is assumed that the father's absence results in general hardships for the family, other factors will be extremely important in determining the degree to which the rest of the family is affected by the increased stress. For instance, the manner in which the mother copes with the problems caused by the father's departure is obviously important, as is the type of support provided by relatives, friends, and available father substitutes. In addition, the length and time of separation, presence of siblings, socioeconomic status, and sex, age, and race of the child can also modify the consequences of father absence. Thus, it is clear that the effects may be due to a number of interacting factors which have not yet been well-examined empirically. For this reason, as well as for methodological reasons, any conclusions drawn must be regarded as tentative.

The first part of this paper will discuss some important consequences of father absence which have been investigated in the research literature. Following this, some variables which are probably important modifiers of the father absence experience for children will be examined.

BEHAVIORAL CONSEQUENCES OF FATHER ABSENCE

Social and Emotional Development of Father-Absent Boys

The effects on the development of the child attributed to paternal absence have ranged from minor disruptions in social and emotional development to gross forms of psychopathology. One of the most extensively investigated consequences of father absence has been the sex-role development manifested by the father-absent child. Since most theories of socialization emphasize the parents' role in the process of sex-role development, whether the mechanisms involved are assumed to be identification, imitation, use of rewards and punishments, or the acquisition of social roles, one of the most direct consequences of father absence should be disturbed sex-role behavior in children. Also, since most theories assume that the father is more critical in the development of appropriate sex-typed behaviors in boys than in girls, many studies have focused solely on the effects of father absence on male children.

Sex typing is the process by which children acquire the motives, values, and behaviors regarded as characteristically masculine or feminine. Although some changes are occurring in sex-role standards, recent studies show that both children (Hartley, 1964) and adults (Jenkin & Vroegh, 1969) maintain stereotyped, traditional conceptions of masculinity and femininity. These standards are congruent with Parsons' (1955) classification of the male role as basically *instrumental* and the female role as basically *expressive.* Males in our society are expected to be independent, dominant, assertive, and competent in dealing with problems in the environment. In contrast, females are viewed as more submissive, nurturant, and sensitive in social situations.

Studies of intact families have found that boys reared by warm, dominant, masculine fathers are themselves more masculine, both in their overt behavior and in their stated preferences for various sex-typed activities (Biller & Borstelmann, 1967; Hetherington, 1967). If inversions of the parental power relationship occur in such a manner that the mother exerts more control than the father in decision making and disciplinary functions, considerable disruption in sex typing occurs. It might be assumed that in a father-absent home, the lone parent—the mother—must of necessity assume a more dominant, decisive, instrumental role than in the intact family. It can be assumed further that this increased maternal instrumentality in conjunction with the lack of opportunity for interaction with a father may interfere with the development of appropriate gender roles.

The research literature suggests strongly that the sex-typing process can be attenuated by paternal absence and that such disruptions in sex typing are more directly manifested in younger than in older children, being most marked if the separation has occurred before the age of five. Preschool boys who were separated from their fathers during their early years have been described as less aggressive, more dependent, and as having less masculine self-concepts and game preferences than father-present children. In doll play, these show play patterns more characteristic of preschool girls and exhibit more verbal aggression and less physical aggression than do boys from intact families (Bach, 1946; Sears, 1951). The importance of the age at which separation occurs is indicated in a study by Hetherington (1966) which involved observations by male recreation directors of school-aged boys in a community recreation center. Father-absent boys scored as less masculine on a projective test of sex-role preferences and were reported to be more dependent on peers, less assertive, and to engage in fewer physical contact activities than were father-present boys, but only if separation occurred before the age of five. Boys who were six years of age or older at the time of separation did not differ from children reared in a normal home situation.

Further evidence of the effects of early isolation from the father on masculine development is presented in a cross-cultural study by Burton and Whiting (1961). These authors report that in societies where the child's early social contacts are entirely with his mother or other females, and where the father is excluded from interacting with his infant son, a process of discontinuous identification occurs. The male child must eventually shift from an unusually intense primary identification with the mother, with whom he has had exclusive early contact, to a secondary identification with the masculine role. Such cultures frequently place great emphasis on male initiation rites in an effort to expunge dramatically the primary feminine identification and facilitate the establishment of masculine identification. That such procedures are not always successful is suggested by the high incidence of couvade in these societies. Couvade is a custom which Burton and Whiting suggest is a manifestation of an underlying feminine identification and which requires the husband to go to bed as if for child-bearing during delivery of his offspring by his wife.

Studies of the effects of age of separation from father have usually confounded age with length of separation. It is obvious that if father-absent children of a given age are examined these two variables are positively correlated; the earlier the absence, the longer the separation. Although there is suggestive evidence that longer separations are more damaging, no firm conclusions can yet be drawn.

Although findings reported thus far indicate that father absence disrupts the sex-role development of preschool boys, the results for older boys are less consistent. Lynn and Sawrey (1959), in their studies of the families of Norwegian sailors who were away from home for at least nine months of the year, noted that the eight- and nine-year-old boys in these homes, exhibited more compensatory masculinity than boys of father-absent homes, according to maternal reports. Compensatory masculinity involves inconsistent patterns of extremes in sex-typed behavior. Boys exhibiting compensatory masculinity may at times manifest excessively masculine, assertive forms of behavior and at other times show feminine behaviors such as dependency. It has sometimes been argued that such compensaiton is a result of the father-absent boy's desperate attempts to maintain a masculine identification when no masculine role model is present. In such a situation, rather than acquiring a stable masculine identification, the boy acquires a set of loosely integrated responses which appear to be almost a caricature of the stereotyped masculine role. McCord, McCord and Thurber (1962) found that father-absent boys were more likely than father-present boys to show a pattern of aggressive behavior plus either high dependency on adults or homosexual tendencies—a pattern similar to that noted by Lynn and Sawrey (1959). Other investigators have found no differences between adolescent father-absent and father-present boys (Barclay & Cusumano, 1967), especially if the adolescent was not deprived of his father until after the age of five (Biller & Bahm, 1970).

It might be speculated that with increasing age, father-absent boys gradually become aware of the greater privileges and status of males in our society and develop a preference for the masculine role. However, the facility with which they are able to acquire and perform appropriately masculine behaviors will depend to a large extent upon the availability of masculine models in surrogate fathers, teachers, peers, siblings, and the mass media. Although such availability increases with age, early contact with masculine models, such as male nursery school teachers, might well alleviate the detrimental effects of father absence in the critical preschool years.

Miller (1958) proposes that the toughness and hyper-masculine behavior often found among lower-class adolescent male gangs may be due to the increased proportion of fatherless homes in the lower classes. This exaggerated masculinity, which may be expressed in the form of delinquent behavior, reflects an attempt to compensate for the feminine orientation they have derived from their home life. This should be especially true in the matricentric structure of the black lower class family where the rate of father absence increases from the national norm of one-tenth to almost one-half in some regions (Moynihan, 1965; Pettigrew, 1964).

The broken home is frequently cited as a major factor in delinquency (Monahan, 1957; Toby, 1957; Peterson & Becker, 1965). It is known that children from fatherless homes are overrepresented in delinquent groups (Glueck & Glueck, 1950; Gregory, 1965a). In an interesting cross-cultural corroboration of these findings, Bacon, Child and Barry (1963) noted that in 48 societies there seemed to be a relation between the availability of the father and amount of crime among juveniles.

Other forms of social maladjustment have also been associated with father absence. Father-absent boys are more impulsive, less self-controlled, and less able to delay immediate gratification than father-present boys (Mischel, 1961). These characteristics are manifested in a wide range of populations and situations.

In an extensive study of seventh grade white children (Hoffman, 1970), father-absent boys in contrast to father-present boys had less well-internalized standards of moral judgment. They tended to evaluate the seriousness of an act according to the probability of detection or punishment rather than in terms of interpersonal relations and social responsibility. They were rated by teachers as more aggressive and less willing to conform to rules or show consideration for others. Following transgressions, father-absent boys showed little guilt and were unwilling to accept blame for their own behavior. Instead of accepting responsibility or trying to rectify the situation, these children responded in an immature fashion, denying they performed the act, crying, making excuses, or blaming others. In this study no differences were found between father-present and father-absent girls.

Siegman (1966), in a study of first-year law and medical students, found that males who were without a father for at least one year from age one through four scored higher on self-reported antisocial behaviors such as parental disobedience, property damage, and drinking, than did father-present boys. Suedfeld (1967) found Peace Corps volunteers who were without a father for at least five years before their 15th birthday tended to be among those volunteers who returned prematurely because of adjustment or conduct problems. Before evaluating possible mechanisms which might account for this evidence of lack of self-control and responsibility in father-absent boys, it is appropriate to ask whether girls are similarly affected in a fatherless home.

Social and Emotional Development of Father-Absent Girls

By providing experience and security in interacting with males and reinforcement for appropriate sex-role behavior in his daughter, the father can be a powerful force in the shaping of feminine behavior. Biller and Weiss (1970), in their review of the literature, suggest that "It appears that the more a father participates in constructive interplay with his daughter and the more this interaction involves access for her to learn specific activities defining her feminine role, the more adequate will be her identity" (p. 82). This would appear to suggest, then, that absence of the father may have implications for the feminine sex-typing process also.

There is a paucity of studies on the relation of paternal absence to the development of daughters. Early studies on preadolescent girls yielded few consistent results. There was some indication of greater dependency on the mother by girls who had limited access to their fathers (Lynn & Sawrey, 1959); however, this finding has not been reliable. For example, it is reported in a study by Santrock (1970) that there were no differences in preschool black girls on dependency, aggression, and femininity as a function of father absence. It is only recent evidence, largely based on studies of adolescents, that suggests that the father-daughter relationship may have a more salient effect on the social development of girls than has previously been assumed.

Thus, studies of father-absent girls suggest a reverse pattern to that of father-absent boys in terms of time of appearance of deviant behavior. Behavior of father-absent and father-present girls show few differences in the preschool years. However, differences emerge gradually with age and are clearly present at puberty. Also, in contrast to father-absent boys, the deviant behavior of father-absent girls tends to be closely related to inappropriate patterns of behavior in relating to males rather than disruption in feminine sex typing in terms of interests and activities.

A recent study (Hetherington & Deur, 1970) suggests that adolescent father-absent girls tend to show two marked clusters of disruption in heterosexual behavior. Deviation appeared either as severe sexual anxiety, shyness, and discomfort around males, or as promiscuous and inappropriately assertive behavior with male peers and adults. No such differences were found in the interactions of father-absent girls with other females. The former syndrome appeared to be more frequent when separation was a result of death, and the latter when separation was precipitated by divorce or desertion. Overall, the findings suggest that father-absent girls have not had the opportunity to acquire the social skills necessary for appropriate heterosexual interactions and that this deficiency becomes particularly apparent with the advent of puberty.

The critical function of the father in the feminine development of daughters may be in providing a learning situation in which, through the use of contingent reinforcement, he shapes the daughter's skills for interacting with males. Indeed, it appears that this interpersonal facility is developed first in relating to the father and then generalizes to a sense of competence in interacting with opposite-sexed peers. This combination of security and specific skills in heterosexual social relationships is in turn, however, more likely to elicit positive feedback from males.

Findings on delinquent girls also suggest that paternal absence has its greatest impact on disruption in heterosexual behavior. Although girls are less frequently arrested on delinquency charges than are boys (Glaser, 1965), girls who do become delinquent are more likely than delinquent boys to be the product of a broken home (Monahan, 1957; Toby, 1957), and their delinquency is more often due to sexual misconduct (Cohen, 1955; Claser, 1965).

A Problem in Interpretation

One problem in evaluating the findings on social and emotional adjustment in father-absent children is the fact that these data may reflect stress or conflict in the home rather than the effects of missing father, *per se.* Tuckman and Regan (1966) note that there were more clinic problems from separated and divorced homes than from widowed families, and Burt (1929) found no difference between delinquent and non-delinquent groups following death of the father, although separation and divorce were clearly more prevalent in the delinquent group. This would be consistent with an interpretation of stress as the salient factor in father-absence effects since separation and divorce are probably more often preceded by intrafamily conflict than is death of a parent.

Likewise, McCord et al. (1962) concluded that "the relationship between criminality and paternal absence appears to be largely a result of the general instability of broken homes rather than of paternal absence in itself." Even recidivism among delinquents is more frequent in those from father-absent homes due to divorce than among those from father-absent homes caused by death. It has been suggested (Nye, 1957) that the unhappy intact home may have even more severe consequences for children than the home broken by divorce. Adolescent children from the former reported more delinquent behavior and psychosomatic difficulties than did children from the latter. Finally, Parker and Kleiner (1966) note that mothers in father-absent homes have more psychiatric symptoms than mothers from intact homes. Whether this is a cause or effect of father absence is unclear; however, the implication is that the children in these homes will be subject to a greater degree of stress than children from "normal" homes.

Thus, differences in the social behavior of father-absent children cannot necessarily be attributed to father absence—one must also consider the possibility that other concomitants of paternal absence are the causative agents in the observed differences between father-absent and father-present children.

Cognitive and Academic Correlates of Father Absence

Two types of investigations have predominated in the study of the relation between paternal absence and cognitive functioning in children. The first has concerned general intellectual and achievement deficits; the second has focused on variations in patterns of deficits across a variety of specific cognitive areas.

Since paternal absence is more frequent in the families of lower class and black children, and since such children are generally inferior to middle class and white children in academic achievement, it is essential to control for social class and race in evaluating the effects of fatherless homes on cognitive and academic performance. However, even when appropriate controls are instituted, there seems to be a deficit in cognitive skills manifested by father-absent children. In a well-controlled study, Deutsch and Brown (1964) found that, although black children tend to score lower on IQ tests than white children, much of the deficit may be due to inadequate home conditions, since their analysis indicated that fifth grade father-absent children had lower scores than fifth grade father-present children. Although paternal absence was not associated with such a difference in first grade children, Deutsch and Brown suggest that there may be a cumulative effect of father absence which eventually handicaps cognitive performance.

Other research suggests that even less severe forms of father absence may have implications for cognitive achievement. Blanchard and Biller (1970) studied the effects of early (before age five) vs. late father absence, and low father availability (less than six hours a week) vs. high father availability in intact homes with third grade boys. They found that those in high father availability homes surpassed the other three groups on achievement test scores and classroom grades. The early father-absent boys were found to be underachievers. The boys from intact homes with low father availability and the late father-absent boys were also found to be below grade level expectations, although not as severely as early father-absent boys. Finally, results of a study by Sutton-Smith, Rosenberg, and Landy (1968) suggest that these cognitive deficits may extend into adulthood. They found that *American College Entrance Examination* scores of college students whose fathers were missing for two or more years were generally lower than father-present students, although presence of a like-sex sibling attenuated this difference.

There have also been studies showing that absence of a father may affect certain areas related to sex-typed abilities as well as overall academic performance and tests scores. Carlsmith (1964) notes that "accumulated evidence from a large number of studies on Math and Verbal aptitudes clearly demonstrates that females are generally superior to males in Verbal areas, while males are superior to females in quantative pursuits . . ." (p. 4). Carlsmith's (1964) own findings indicate that high school and college students whose fathers were absent for long periods of time when the children were still very young, showed reversals in the usual Mathematics-Verbal patterning on the *College Board Entrance Examination* or the *Scholastic Aptitude Test.* That is, father-absent boys showed relatively higher verbal scores than mathematics scores, while father-present boys manifested the traditional masculine pattern of greater relative mathematical ability. This pattern was most pronounced for boys who had undergone early and long separation experience. Carlsmith interprets her findings as possibly due to a more feminine cognitive style on the part of father-absent boys based on difficulty in same-sex identification.

Nelsen and Macoby (1966) suggest an alternate explanation for this finding: the *tension-interference hypothesis,* which asserts that " . . . stress and tension interfere more with cognitive function basic to mathematical ability and less with function involved in verbal ability" (p. 271). Thus, Nelsen and Maccoby would expect that a variety of stressful conditions within the home, in addition to paternal absence, could result in mathematics-verbal reversals in both boys and girls. Gregory (1965b) found that the mathematics-verbal reversal in college males was associated not with paternal loss specifically, but with loss of either parent due to divorce, with loss of either parent before 10 years of age, and with remarriage of a remaining parent. Gregory concludes that his findings are more in agreement with the tension-interference explanation than with the sex identification hypothesis.

The tension-interference hypothesis would further predict that quantitative skills for girls as well as boys should drop under increased stress. Nelsen and Maccoby (1966) replicated Carlsmith's findings regarding father absence and the math-verbal patterning, using both male and female college students. In addition, it has been found (Landy, Rosenberg, & Sutton-Smith, 1969) that female college students whose fathers worked night shifts and were therefore presumably less available to them showed decreased quantitative scores on the *American College Entrance Examination,* although their linguistic scores were not affected. Night shift work by fathers during the age period between one and nine years seemed especially disruptive on subsequent achievement scores.

It must be noted, however, that other research findings have not supported the tension-interference theory. Some studies indicate (Sutton-Smith, Rosenberg, & Landy, 1968) that father-absent college students score lower on both quantitative and verbal portions of the *American College Entrance Examination.* This suggests that intrafamily stress may affect overall cognitive performance, not merely quantitive ability. Although it is apparent that there is a relation between paternal absence and disrupted cognitive functioning in children, it is also obvious that the contribution of related mediating factors to this association is not well understood. At the present time neither the deficient sex identification nor the tension-interference hypothesis can adequately account for the available findings.

Effects of Father Absence on Mothers

Our discussion thus far has focused on the effects of paternal deprivation on various aspects of children's behavior. However, it would seem probable that lack of a husband would also influence maternal behavior. Lerner (1954) has listed some of the possible effects on the mother: she may become more hostile toward males; she may feel guilty about her behavior as a wife, and she may feel financial pressure. In addition, separation may lead to a lowering in self-esteem, feelings of unattractiveness and inadequacy as a woman, apprehension about the reliability of others, and resentment or ambivalence toward being forced into the role of a single woman burdened by children (Hetherington & Deur, 1970). Such women also report that they regard their lives as less happy and fulfilling (Tiller, 1958).

It has been suggested that the effects of father absence on children may be due, in large measure, to the mediating influence of the mother (Bach, 1946; Pederson, 1966; Tiller, 1958). The mother's attitudes toward males and masculinity, rejection or love of her children, and specific values and control mechanisms used in relating to her children are likely to have more intense effects on children in a one-parent family. There is some evidence that wives without husbands differ from wives in intact families in their relationships to their children. They place more emphasis on obedience, politeness, and conformity (Tiller, 1958), and are slightly less encouraging of masculine behavior in their sons (Biller, 1969). In attempting to control their children they use more extreme disciplinary practices, ranging from overprotectiveness to harsh power assertive techniques, but which are frequently unsuccessful (Hetherington & Deur, 1970). However, it is difficult to know, in these instances, whether the maternal behaviors preceded, or were a result of, the breaking up of the home.

FACTORS MODIFYING THE EFFECTS OF FATHER ABSENCE

Reason for Separation

It seems reasonable to assert that father absence which results from death may have different consequences from father absence caused by divorce, separation, or desertion, since the latter are more likely to be preceded by familial conflict. Tuckman and Regan (1966) urge that the broken home not be treated as a unitary concept, but rather should be differentiated as much as possible in order that varying consequences of the different types of broken homes can be studied. In their own research, it was noted that the widowed home is more like the intact home in terms of significant referral problems than are separated and divorced homes. It has been observed (Rowntree, 1955) that widowed families have more children than separated or divorced families, and the mother tends to be older in the former than in the latter. This suggests the presence of constellational differences between various types of broken homes as well as the previously mentioned possibility that there is greater psychological stress in divorced and separated families.

Relation with Father Before Absence

In his review of the effects of long- and short-term separation of infants from their mothers, Yarrow (1964) speculates on the various possible consequences of separation as a function of the nature of the preseparation mother-child relationship:

> It has been hypothesized that the child who has had a close relationship with his mother may be better equipped to tolerate separation and to establish a meaningful relationship with a substitute figure than the child who has never experienced an intimate relationship. This variable may, however, have different implications for the immediate and for the long-term consequences. The immediate reactions may be more severe for the child who is deeply attached to his mother, but his later adjustment may be more adequate than the child who has never experienced an intimate relationship. . . . On the other hand, it is likely that permanent separation will be more traumatic, the closer the parent-child relationship (p. 124).

Parallel speculations might be made about the preseparation father-child relationship, although few data exist either to confirm or refute them. Given the fact that most father absence studies are entirely *post hoc,* there has been little opportunity to gather preseparation adjustment or intimacy data and relate it to subsequent reactions to paternal loss. Nevertheless, the importance of such data is obvious in helping to clarify the differential effects found in the father absence situation.

Maternal Characteristics

It has been suggested in previous sections that possible aberrations in the mother's own behavior and adjustment may be responsible in some instances for consequences which have previously been attributed to absence of the husband. However, it should also be noted that maternal adaptability, ego strength, and emotional stability can mitigate the effects of a broken home. Less psychopathology, feminine-aggressive behavior, and delinquency is manifested by adolescent boys from father-absent homes if the mother is warm and nondeviant than if the mother is rejecting and emotionally disturbed (McCord *et al.,* 1962; Pederson, 1966).

It might also be expected that if a mother values and rewards masculine behavior in sons, less disruption in sex typing should occur. Research findings support this position. Maternal encouragement of aggression and masculine behavior is associated with a more masculine self-concept and behaviors in early separated father-absent boys. This relation is not apparent in late separated or father-present boys (Biller & Bahm, 1970; Biller, 1969).

Availability of Surrogate Males

Studies of intact families reveal that masculinity in boys is associated both with amount of contact with adult males (Steimel, 1960) and the presence of male siblings (Brim, 1958; Brown, 1956; Koch, 1956; Sutton-Smith, Roberts & Rosenberg, 1964). For example, in intact two-child families, boys with older brothers are more masculine and assertive than those with older sisters.

These findings extend to studies of broken homes. Two recent studies (Santrock, 1970; Wohlford, Santrock, Berger, & Liberman, 1970) show that although father-absent four- and five-year-old black males were more dependent on adults, less aggressive, and less masculine than father-present boys, those with older brothers were more masculine than those with older sisters. A similar result was obtained for father-absent girls; they were more aggressive and less dependent if they had only older male siblings. Although interaction with older brothers may reduce the impact of paternal absence, other evidence suggests that the presence of a father is more salient in the development of masculinity than that of male siblings (Biller, 1968).

Little systematic research has been done on the effects of father surrogates and interaction with peers on the behavior of father-absent children. However, since such relationships have been found to have a powerful effect on the development of sex-typed behavior in children from intact homes (Steimel, 1960; Patterson, Littman, & Bricker, 1967), it might be expected to have an even more intense impact on father-absent children.

CONCLUSIONS

Father absence appears to be associated with a wide range of disruptions in social and cognitive development in children. The effects seem to be most severe if the father leaves the home during the child's preschool years, but can be modified by positive factors such as an emotionally stable, loving mother who reinforces the child for appropriate sex-typed behavior, and the presence of male siblings.

In boys, the effects on social and personality development appear as feminized behavior during the preschool years, but with increasing age and extra-familial interaction these effects often disappear or are transformed into compensatory masculinity. In contrast, in girls, the effects of father-absence are minimal in the early years. At adolescence, however, a dramatic inability to respond appropriately in heterosexual relations is apparent.

Although deviations in cognitive functioning appear, there is considerable uncertainty as to the form and reasons for these cognitive deficiencies. Since the effects of father absence is such an important practical problem in a nation where 10 percent of children are reared in broken homes, further research might focus on factors which can ameliorate the harmful consequences of paternal separation, as well as pinpoint more precisely the interpersonal processes which mediate these effects.

REFERENCES

Bach, G. R. Father-fantasies and father-typing in father-separated children. *Child Develpm.,* 1946, *17,* 63–80.

Bacon, M. K., Child, I. L., & Barry, H., III. A cross-cultural study of correlates of crime. *J. abnorm. soc. Psychol.,* 1963, *66,* 291–300.

Barclay, A. G., & Cusumano, D. Father-absence, cross-sex identity, and field-dependent behavior in male adolescents. *Child Develpm.,* 1967, *38,* 243–250.

Biller, H. B. A multiaspect investigation of masculine development in kindergarten-age boys. *Genet. Psychol. Monogr.* 1968, *78,* 89–139.

Biller, H. B. Father absence, maternal encouragement, and sex role development in kindergarten-age boys, *Child Develpm.* 1969, *40,* 539–546.

Biller, H. B., & Bahm, R. M. Father absence, perceived maternal behavior, and masculinity of self-concept among junior high school boys, *Develpm. Psychol.,* in press.

Biller, H. B., & Borstelmann, L. J. Masculine development: An integrative review. *Merril-Palmer Qtrly.* 1967, *13,* 253–294.

Biller, H. B., & Weiss, S. D. The father-daughter relationship and the personality development of the female. *J. genet, Psychol.,* 1970, *116,* 79–93.

Blanchard, R. W., & Biller, H. B. Father availability and academic performance among third grade boys. *Develpm. Psychol.,* in press.

Brim, O. G. Family structure and sex role learning by children: A further analysis of Helen Koch's data. *Sociometry,* 1958, *21,* 1–16.

Brown, D. G. Sex-role preference in young children, *Psychol. Monogr.,* 1956–57, (14, Whole No. 421).

Burt, C. *The Young Delinquent.* New York: Appleton, 1929.

Burton, R. V., & Whiting, J. W. M. The absent father and cross-sex identity. *Merrill-Palmer Qtrly.,* 1961, *7,* 85–95.

Carlsmith, L. Effect of early father-absence on scholastic aptitude. *Harvard educ. Rev.,* 1964, *34,* 3–21.

Cohen, A. K. *Delinquent Boys: The culture of the Gang.* Glencoe, Ill.: Free Press, 1955.

Deutsch, M., & Brown, B. Social influences in Negro-white intelligence differences. J. soc. Issues, 1964, 20, 24–35.

Glaser, D. Social disorganization and delinquent subcultures. In H. C. Quay (Ed.), Juvenille Delinquency. New York: Van Nostrand, 1965. Pp. 27–62.

Glueck, S., & Glueck. E. Unravelling Juevenile Delinquency. New York: Common-wealth Fund, 1950.

Gregory, I. Anterospective data following childhood loss of a parent: I. Delinquency and high school dropout. Arch. gen. Psychiat., 1965, 13, 110–120. (a).

Gregory, I. Anterospective data following childhood loss of a parent: II: Pathology, performance and potential among the college students. Arch. gen. Psychiat., 1965, 13, 110–120. (b).

Hartley, R. E. Sex-role identification: A symposium. A developmental view of female sex role definition and identification. Merrill-Palmer Qtrly., 1964, 10, 3–16.

Hetherington. E. M. Effects of paternal absence on sex-typed behaviors in Negro and white preadolescent males. J. pers, soc. Psychol., 1966, 4, 87–91.

Hetherington, E. M. The effects of familial variables on sex typing, on parent-child similarity and on imitation in children. In J. P. Hill (Ed.), Minnesota Symposia on Child Psychology, Vol I. Minneapolis: Univ. of Minnesota Press, 1967. Pp. 82–107.

Hetherington, E. M., & Deur, J. L. The effects of father absence on personality develop-ment in daughters. Unpubl. mss., 1970.

Hoffman, M. L. Father absence and conscience development, 1970, Develpm. Psy-chol. in press.

Jenkin, N., & Vroegh, K. Contemporary concepts of masculinity and femininity. Psychol. Rep., 1969, 25, 679–697. Monogr. Suppl. 2-V25.

Koch, H. L. Sissiness and tomboyishness in relation to sibling characteristics. J. genet. Psychol., 1956, 88, 231–244.

Landy, F., Rosenberg, B. G., & Sutton-Smith, B. The effect of limited father absence on cognitive development. Child Develpm., 1969, 40, 941–944.

Lerner, S. H. Effects of desertion on family life. Soc. Casework, 1954, 35, 3–8.

Lynn, D. B., & Sawrey, W. L. The effects of father absence on Norwegian boys and girls. J. abnorm. soc. Psychol., 1959, 59, 258–262.

McCord, J., McCord, W., & Thurber, E. Some effects of paternal absence on male children. J. abnorm. soc. Psychol., 1962, 64, 361–369.

Miller, W. B. Lower-class culture as a generating milieu of gang delinquency. J. soc. Issues, 1958, 14, 5–19.

Mischel. W. Father-absence and delay of gratification. J. abnorm. soc. Psychol., 1961, 63, 116–124.

Monahan, T. P. Family status and the delinquent child: A reappraisal and some new findings. *Soc. Forces,* 1957, *35,* 250–258.

Moynihan, D. P. *The Negro Family: The Case for National Action.* Washington: U.S. Dept. of Labor, 1965.

Nelsen, E. A., & Maccoby, E. E. The relationship between social development and differential abilities on the scholastic aptitude test. *Merrill-Palmer Qtrly.,* 1966, *12,* 269–289.

Nye, F. I. Child adjustment in broken and in unhappy unbroken homes. *Marriage & Family Living,* 1957, *19,* 356–361.

Parker, S., & Kleiner, R. J. Characteristics of Negro mothers in singleheaded households. *J. Marriage & Family,* 1966, *28,* 507–513.

Parsons, T. Family structure and the socialization of the child. In T. Parsons & R. F. Bales (Eds.) *Family, Socialization, and Interaction Process.* Glencoe, Ill.: Free Press, 1955. Pp. 35–131.

Patterson, G. R., Littman, R. A., & Bricker, W. Assertive behavior in children: A step toward a theory of aggression. *Monogr. Soc. Res. Child Develpm.,* 1967, *32,* (Serial No. 113).

Pedersen, F. A. Relationship between father-absence and emotional disturbance in male military dependents. *Merrill-Palmer Qtrly.,* 1966, *12,* 321–331.

Peterson, D. R., & Becker, W. C. Family interaction and delinquency. In H. C. Quay (Ed.), *Juvenile Delinquency.* New York: Van Nostrand, 1965. Pp. 63–99.

Pettigrew, T. F. *A Profile of the Negro American.* Princeton: Van Nostrand, 1964.

Report of the National Advisory Commission on Civil Disorders. New York: Bantam Books, Inc., 1968.

Rowntree, G. Early childhood in broken families. *Population Studies,* 1955, *8,* 247–263.

Santrock, J. W. Paternal absence, sex typing, and identification. *Develpm. Psychol.,* 1970, *2,* 264–272.

Sears, P. S. Doll play aggression in normal young children: Influence of sex, age, sibling status, father's absence. *Psychol. Monogr.,* 1951, *65,* (6, Whole No. 323).

Siegman, A. W. Father-absence during childhood and antisocial behavior. J. *abnorm. soc. Psychol.,* 1966, *71,* 71–74.

Steimal, R. J. Childhood experiences and masculinity-femininity scores. J. *counsel, Psychol.,* 1960, *7,* 212–217.

Stolz, L. M. *et al. Father Relations of War-Born Children.* Stanford: Stanford Univ. Press, 1954.

Suedfeld, P. Paternal absence and overseas success of Peach Corp volunteers. *J. consult. Psychol.,* 1967, *31,* 424–425.

Sutton-Smith, B., Roberts, J. M., & Rosenberg, B. G. Sibling associations and role involvement. *Merrill-Palmer Qtrly.,* 1964, *10,* 25–38.

Sutton-Smith, B., Rosenberg, B. G. & Landy, F. Father-absence effects in families of different sibling composition. *Child Develpm.,* 1968, *39,* 1213–1221.

Tiller, P. O. Father-absence and personality development of children in sailor families. *Nordisk Psychologi's Monogr. Ser.,* 1958, *9,* 1–48.

Toby, J. The differential impact of family disorganization. *Am. Sociol. Rev.,* 1957, *22,* 505–512.

Tuckman, J. & Regan, R. A. Intactness of the home and behavioral problems in children. *J. child Psychol. & Psychiat.,* 1966, *7,* 225–233.

Wohlford, P., Santrock, J. W., Berger, S. E., & Liberman. D. Older brothers' influence on sex-types, aggressive, and dependent behavior in father-absent children. *Develpm. Psychol.,* in press.

Yarrow, L. J. Separation from parents in early childhood. In M. L. Hoffman & L. W. Hoffman (Eds.), *Review of Child Development Research,* Vol. I. New York: Russell Sage Foundation, 1964, Pp. 89–136.

5.2

Social Class and Parent-Child Relationships: An Interpretation

Melvin L. Kohn

This essay is an attempt to interpret, from a sociological perspective, the effects of social class upon parent-child relationships. Many past discussions of the problem seem somehow to lack this perspective, even though the problem is one of profound importance for sociology. Because most investigators have approached the problem from an interest in psychodynamics, rather than social structure, they have largely limited their attention to a few specific techniques used by mothers in the rearing of infants and very young children. They have discovered, *inter alia,* that social class has a decided bearing on which techniques parents use. But, since they have come at the problem from this perspective, their interest in social class has not gone beyond its effects for this very limited aspect of parent-child relationships.

Reprinted from the *American Journal of Sociology,* 1963, Vol. LXVIII, No. 4, 471–480, by permission of the author and the University of Chicago Press. Copyright 1963 by the University of Chicago.

The present analysis conceives the problem of social class and parent-child relationships as an instance of the more general problem of the effects of social structure upon behavior. It starts with the assumption that social class has proved to be so useful a concept because it refers to more than simply educational level, or occupation, or any of the large number of correlated variables. It is so useful because it captures the reality that the intricate interplay of all these variables creates different basic conditions of life at different levels of the social order. Members of different social classes, by virtue of enjoying (or suffering) different conditions of life, come to see the world differently—to develop different conceptions of social reality, different aspirations and hopes and fears, different conceptions of the desirable.

The last is particularly important for present purposes, for from people's conceptions of the desirable—and particularly from their conceptions of what characterics are desirable in children—one can discern their objectives in child-rearing. Thus, conceptions of the desirable—that is, values[1]—become the key concept of this analysis, the bridge between position in the larger social structure and the behavior of the individual. The intent of the analysis is to trace the effects of social class position on parental values and the effects of values on behavior.

Since this approach differs from analyses focused on social class differences in the use of particular child rearing techniques, it will be necessary to reexamine earlier formulations from the present perspective. Then three questions will be discussed, bringing into consideration the limited available data that are relevant: What differences are there in the values held by parents of different social classes? What is there about the conditions of life distinctive of these classes that might explain the differences in their values? What consequences do these differences in values have for parents' relationships with their children?

SOCIAL CLASS

Social classes will be defined as aggregates of individuals who occupy broadly similar positions in the scale of prestige.[2] In dealing with the research literature, we shall treat occupational position (or occupational position as weighted somewhat by education) as a serviceable index of social class for urban American society. And we shall adopt the model of social stratification implicit in most research, that of four relatively discrete classes: a "lower class" of unskilled manual workers, a "working class" of manual workers in semi-skilled and skilled occupations, a "middle class" of white-collar workers and professionals, and an "elite," differentiated from the middle class not so much in terms of occupation as of wealth and lineage.

Almost all the empirical evidence, including that from our own research, stems from broad comparisons of the middle and working class. Thus we shall have little to say about the extremes of the class distribution. Furthermore, we shall have to act as if the middle and working classes were each homogeneous. They are not, even in terms of status considerations alone. There is evidence, for example, that within each broad social class, variations in parents' values quite regularly parallel gradations of social status. Moreover, the classes are heterogeneous with respect to other factors that affect parents' values, such as religion and ethnicity. But even when all such considerations are taken into account, the empirical evidence clearly shows that being on one side or the other of the line that divides manual from non-manual workers has profound consequences for how one rears one's children.[3]

STABILITY AND CHANGE

Any analysis of the effects of social class upon parent-child relationships should start with Urie Bronfenbrenner's analytic review of the studies that had been conducted in this country during the 25 years up to 1958.[4] From the seemingly contradictory findings of a number of studies, Bronfenbrenner discerned not chaos but orderly change: there have been changes in the child-training techniques employed by middle class parents in the past quarter-century; similar changes have been taking place in the working class, but working class parents have consistently lagged behing by a few years; thus, while middle class parents of 25 years ago were more "restrictive" than were working class parents, today the middle class parents are more "permissive"; and the gap between the classes seems to be narrowing.

It must be noted that these conclusions are limited by the questions Bronfenbrenner's predecessors asked in their research. The studies deal largely with a few particular techniques of child rearing, especially those involved in caring for infants and very young children, and say very little about parents' overall relationships with their children, particularly as the children grow older. There is clear evidence that the past quarter-century has seen change, even faddism, with respect to the use of breastfeeding, or bottle-feeding, scheduling or not scheduling, spanking or isolating. But when we generalize from these specifics to talk of a change from "restrictive" to "permissive" practices—or, worse yet, of a change from "restrictive" to "permissive" parent-child relationships—we impute to them a far greater importance than they probably have, either to parents or to children.[5]

There is no evidence that recent faddism in child-training techniques is symptomatic of profound changes in the relations of parents to children in either social class. In fact, as Bronfenbrenner notes, what little evidence we do have points in the opposite direction: the overall quality of parent-child relationships does not seem to have changed substantially in either class.[6] In all probability, parents have changed techniques in service of much the same values, and the changes have been quite specific. These changes must be explained, but the enduring characteristics are probably even more important.

Why the changes? Bronfenbrenner's interpretation is ingenuously simple. He notes that the changes in techniques employed by middle class parents have closely paralleled those advocated by presumed experts, and he concludes that middle class parents have changed their practices *because* they are responsive to changes in what the experts tell them is right and proper. Working class parents, being less educated and thus less directly responsive to the media of communication, followed behind only later.[7]

Bronfenbrenner is almost undoubtedly right in asserting that middle class parents have followed the drift of presumably expert opinion. But why have they done so? It is not sufficient to assume that the explanation lies in their greater degree of education. This might explain why middle class parents are substantially more likely than are working class parents to *read* books and articles on child rearing, as we know they do.[8] But they need not *follow* the experts' advice. We know from various studies of the mass media that people generally search for confirmation of their existing beliefs and practices and tend to ignore what contradicts them.

From all the evidence at our disposal, it looks as if middle class parents not only read what the experts have to say but also search out a wide variety of other sources of information and advice: they are far more likely than are working class parents to discuss child rearing with friends and neighbors, to consult physicians on these matters, to attend Parent-Teacher Association meetings, to discuss the child's behavior with his teacher. Middle class parents seem to regard child rearing as more problematic than do working class parents. This can hardly be a matter of education alone. It must be rooted more deeply in the conditions of life of the two social classes.

Everything about working class parents' lives—their comparative lack of education, the nature of their jobs, their greater attachment to the extended family—conduces to their retaining familiar methods.[9] Furthermore, even should they be receptive to change, they are less likely than are middle class parents to find the experts' writings appropriate to their wants, for the experts predicate their advice on middle class values. Everything about middle class parents' lives, on the other hand, conduces to their looking for new methods to achieve their goals. They look to the experts, to other sources of relevant information, and to each other not for new values but for more serviceable techniques.[10] And within the limits of our present scanty knowledge about means-ends relationships in child rearing, the experts have provided practical and useful advice. It is not that educated parents slavishly follow the experts but that the experts have provided what the parents have sought.

To look at the question this way is to put it in a quite different perspective: the focus becomes not specific techniques nor changes in the use of specific techniques but parental values.

VALUES OF MIDDLE AND WORKING CLASS PARENTS

Of the entire range of values one might examine, it seems particularly strategic to focus on parents' conceptions of what characteristics would be most desirable for boys or girls the age of their own children. From this one can hope to discern the parents' goals in rearing their children. It must be assumed, however, that a parent will choose one characteristic as more desirable than another only if he considers it to be both important, in the sense that failure to develop this characteristic would affect the child adversely, and problematic, in the sense that it is neither to be taken for granted that the child will develop that characteristic nor impossible for him to do so. In interpreting parents' value choices, we must keep in mind that their choices reflect not simply their goals but the goals whose achievement they regard as problematic.

Few studies, even in recent years, have directly investigated the relationship of social class to parental values. Fortunately, however, the results of these few are in essential agreement. The earliest study was Evelyn Millis Duvall's pioneering inquiry of 1946.[11] Duvall characterized working class (and lower middle class) parental values as "traditional"—they want their children to be neat and clean, to obey and respect adults, to please adults. In contrast to this emphasis on how the child comforts himself, middle class parental values are more "developmental"—they want their children to be eager to learn, to love and confide in the parents, to be happy, to share and cooperate, to be healthy and well.

Duvall's traditional-developmental dichotomy does not describe the difference between middle and working class parental values quite exactly, but it does point to the essence of the difference: working class parents want the child to conform to externally imposed standards, while middle class parents are far more attentive to his internal dynamics.

The few relevant findings of subsequent studies are entirely consistent with this basic point, especially in the repeated indications that working class parents put far greater stress on obedience to parental commands than do middle class parents.[12] Our own research, conducted in 1956–1957, provides the evidence most directly comparable to Duvall's.[13] We, too, found that working class parents value obedience, neatness, and cleanliness more highly than do middle class parents, and that middle class parents in turn value curiosity, happiness, consideration, and—most importantly —self-control more highly than do working class parents. We further found that there are characteristic clusters of value choice in the two social classes: working class parental values center on conformity to external proscriptions, middle class parental values on self-direction. To working class parents, it is the overt act that matters: the child should not transgress externally imposed rules; to middle class parents, it is the child's motives and feelings that matter: the child should govern himself.

In fairness, it should be noted that middle and working class parents share many core values. Both, for example, value honesty very highly—although, characteristically, "honesty" has rather different connotations in the two social classes, implying "trustworthiness" for the working class and "truthfulness" for the middle class. The common theme, of course, is that parents of both social classes value a decent respect for the rights of others; middle and working class values are but variations on this common theme. The reason for emphasizing the variations rather than the common theme is that they seem to have far-ranging consequences for parents' relationships with their children and thus ought to be taken seriously.

It would be good if there were more evidence about parental values—data from other studies, in other locales, and especially, data derived from more than one mode of inquiry. But, what evidence we do have is consistent, so that there is at least some basis for believing it is reliable. Furthermore, there is evidence that the value choices made by parents in these inquiries are not simply a reflection of their assessments of their own children's deficiencies or excellences. Thus, we may take the findings of these studies as providing a limited, but probably valid, picture of the parents' generalized conceptions of what behavior would be desirable in their preadolescent children.

EXPLAINING CLASS DIFFERENCES IN PARENTAL VALUES

That middle class parents are more likely to espouse some values, and working class parents other values, must be a function of differences in their conditions of life. In the present state of our knowledge, it is difficult to disentangle the interacting variables with a sufficient degree of exactness to ascertain which conditions of life are crucial to the differences in values. Nevertheless, it is necessary to examine the principal components of class differences in life conditions to see what each may contribute.

The logical place to begin is with occupational differences, for these are certainly preeminently important, not only in defining social classes in urban, industrialized society, but also in determining much else about people's life conditions.[14] There are at least three respects in which middle class occupations typically differ from working class occupations, above and beyond their obvious status-linked differences in security, stability of income, and general social prestige. One is that middle class occupations deal more with the manipulation of interpersonal relations, ideas, and symbols, while working class occupations deal more with the manipulation of things. The second is that middle class occupations are more subject to self-direction, while working class occupations are more subject to standardization and direct supervision. The third is that getting ahead in middle class occupations is more dependent upon one's own actions, while in working class occupations it is more dependent upon collective action, particularly in unionized industries. From these differences, one can sketch differences in the characteristics that make for getting along, and getting ahead, in middle and working class occupations. Middle class occupations require a greater degree of self-direction; working class occupations, in larger measure, require that one follow explicit rules set down by someone in authority.

Obviously, these differences parallel the differences we have found between the two social classes in the characteristics valued by parents for children. At minimum, one can conclude that there is a congruence between occupational requirements and parental values. It is, moreover, a reasonable supposition, although not a necessary conclusion, that middle and working class parents value different characteristics in children *because* of these differences in their occupational circumstances. This supposition does not necessarily assume that parents consciously train their children to meet future occupational requirements; it may simply be that their own occupational experiences have significantly affected parents' conceptions of what is desirable behavior, on or off the job, for adults or for children.[15]

These differences in occupational circumstances are probably basic to the differences we have found between middle and working class parental values, but taken alone they do not sufficiently explain them. Parents need not accord preeminent importance to occupational requirements in their judgments of what is most desirable. For a sufficient explanation of class differences in values, it is necessary to recognize that other differences in middle and working class conditions of life reinforce the differences in occupational circumstances at every turn.

Educational differences, for example, above and beyond their importance as determinants of occupation, probably contribute independently to the differences in middle and working class parental values. At minimum, middle class parents' greater attention to the child's internal dynamics is facilitated by their learned ability to deal with the subjective and the ideational. Furthermore, differences in levels and stability of income undoubtedly contribute to class differences in parental values. That middle class parents still have somewhat higher levels of income, and much greater stability of income, makes them able to take for granted the respectability that is still problematic for working class parents. They can afford to concentrate, instead, on motives and feelings—which, in the circumstances of their lives, are more important.

These considerations suggest that the differences between middle and working class parental values are probably a function of the entire complex of differences in life conditions characteristic of the two social classes. Consider, for example, the working class situation. With the end of mass immigration, there has emerged a stable working class, largely derived from the manpower of rural areas, uninterested in mobility into the middle class, but very much interested in security, respectability, and the enjoyment of a decent standard of living.[16] This working class has come to enjoy a standard of living formerly reserved for the middle class, but has not chosen a middle class style of life. In effect, the working class has striven for, and partially achieved, an American dream distinctly different from the dream of success and achievement. In an affluent society, it is possible for the worker to be the traditionalist —politically, economically, and, most relevant here, in his values for his children.[17] Working class parents want their children to conform to external authority because the parents themselves are willing to accord respect to authority, in return for security and respectability. Their conservatism in child rearing is part of a more general conservatism and traditionalism.

Middle class parental values are a product of a quite different set of conditions. Much of what the working class values, they can take for granted. Instead, they can —and must—instill in their children a degree of self-direction that would be less appropriate to the conditions of life of the working class.[18] Certainly, there is substantial truth in the characterization of the middle class way of life as one of great conformity. What must be noted here, however, is that *relative* to the working class, middle class conditions of life require a more substantial degree of independence of action. Furthermore, the higher levels of education enjoyed by the middle class make possible a degree of internal scrutiny difficult to achieve without the skills in dealing with the abstract that college training sometimes provides. Finally, the economic security of most middle class occupations, the level of income they provide, the status they confer, allow one to focus his attention on the subjective and the ideational. Middle class conditions of life both allow and demand a greater degree of self-direction than do those of the working class.

CONSEQUENCES OF CLASS DIFFERENCES IN PARENTS' VALUES

What consequences do the differences between middle and working class parents' values have for the ways they raise their children?

Much of the research on techniques of infant- and child-training is of little relevance here. For example, with regard to parents' preferred techniques for disciplining children, a question of major interest to many investigators, Bronfenbrenner summarizes past studies as follows: "In matters of discipline, working class parents are consistently more likely to employ physical punishment, while middle class families rely more on reasoning, isolation, appeals to guilt, and other methods involving the threat of loss of love."[19] This, if still true,[20] is consistent with middle class parents' greater attentiveness to the child's internal dynamics, working class parents' greater concern about the overt act. For present purposes, however, the crucial question is not *which* disciplinary method parents prefer, but when and why they use one or another method of discipline.

The most directly relevent available data are on the conditions under which middle and working class parents use physical punishment. Working class parents are apt to resort to physical punishment when the direct and immediate consequences of their children's disobedient acts are most extreme, and to refrain from punishing when this might provoke an even greater disturbance.[21] Thus, they will punish a child for wild play when the furniture is damaged or the noise level becomes intolerable, but ignore the same actions when the direct and immediate consequences are not so extreme. Middle class parents, on the other hand, seem to punish or refrain from punishing on the basis of their interpretation of the child's intent in acting as he does. Thus, they will punish a furious outburst when the context is such that they interpret it to be a loss of self-control, but will ignore an equally extreme outburst when the context is such that they interpret it to be merely an emotional release.

It is understandable that working class parents react to the consequences rather than to the intent of their children's actions: the important thing is that the child not transgress externally imposed rules. Correspondingly, if middle class parents are instead concerned about the child's motives and feelings, they can and must look beyond the overt act to why the child acts as he does. It would seem that middle and working class values direct parents to see their children's misbehavior in quite different ways, so that misbehavior which prompts middle class parents to action does not seem as important to working class parents, and vice versa.[22] Obviously, parents' values are not the only things that enter into their use of physical punishment. But unless one assumes a complete lack of goal-directedness in parental behavior, he would have to grant that parents' values direct their attention to some facets of their own and their children's behavior, and divert it from other facets.

The consequences of class differences in parental values extend far beyond differences in disciplinary practices. From a knowledge of their values for their children, one would expect middle class parents to feel a greater obligation to be *supportive* of the children, if only because of their sensitivity to the children's internal dynamics. Working class values, with their emphasis upon conformity to external rules, should lead to greater emphasis upon the parents' obligation to impose constraints.[23] And this, according to Bronfenbrenner, is precisely what has been shown in those few studies that have concerned themselves with the over-all relationship of parents to child: "Over the entire 25-year period studied, parent-child relationships in the middle class are consistently reported as more acceptant and equalitarian, while those in the working class are oriented toward maintaining order and obedience."[24]

This conclusion is based primarily on studies of *mother*-child relationships in middle and working class families. Class differences in parental values have further ramifications for the father's role.[25] Mothers in each class would have their husbands play a role facilitative of the child's development of the characteristics valued in that class: Middle class mothers want their husbands to be supportive of the children (especially of sons), with their responsibility for imposing constraints being of decidedly secondary importance; working class mothers look to their husbands to be considerably more directive—support is accorded far less importance and constraint far more. Most middle class fathers agree with their wives and play a role close to what their wives would have them play. Many working class fathers, on the other hand, do not. It is not that they see the constraining role as less important than do their wives, but that many of them see no reason why they should have to shoulder the responsibility. From their point of view, the important thing is that the child be taught what limits he must not transgress. It does not much matter who does the teaching, and since mother has primary responsibility for child care, the job should be hers.

The net consequence is a quite different division of parental responsibilities in the two social classes. In middle class families, mother's and father's roles usually are not sharply differentiated. What differentiation exists is largely a matter of each parent taking special responsibility for being supportive of children of the parent's own sex. In working class families, mother's and father's roles are more sharply differentiated, with mother almost always being the more supportive parent. In some working class families, mother specializes in support, father in constraint; in others, perhaps in most, mother raises the children, father provides the wherewithal.[26]

Thus, the differences in middle and working class parents' values have wide ramifications for their relationships with their children and with each other. Of course, many class differences in parent-child relationships are not directly attributable to differences in values; undoubtedly the very differences in their conditions of life that make for differences in parental values reinforce, at every juncture, parents' characteristic ways of relating to their children. But one could not account for these consistent differences in parents' avowed values.

CONCLUSION

This paper serves to show how complex and demanding are the problems of interpreting the effects of social structure of behavior. Our inquiries habitually stop at the point of demonstrating that social position correlates with something, when we should want to pursue the question, "Why?" What are the processes by which position in social structure molds behavior? The present analysis has dealt with this question in one specific form: Why does social class matter for parents' relationships with their children? There is every reason to believe that the problems encountered in trying to deal with that question would recur in any analysis of the effects of social structure on behavior.

In this analysis, the concept of "values" has been used as the principal bridge from social position to behavior. The analysis has endeavored to show that middle class parental values differ from those of working class parents; that these differences are rooted in basic differences between middle and working class conditions of life; and that the differences between middle and working class parental values have important consequences for their relationships with their children. The interpretive model, in essence, is: social class—conditions of life—values—behavior.

The specifics of the present characterization of parental values may prove to be inexact; the discussion of the ways in which social class position affects values is undoubtedly partial; and the tracing of the consequences of differences in values for differences in parent-child relationships is certainly tentative and incomplete. I trust, however, that the perspective will prove to be valid and that this formulation will stimulate other investigators to deal more directly with the processes whereby social structure affects behavior.

NOTES

[1]"A value is a conception, explicit or implicit, distinctive of an individual or characteristic of a group, of the desirable which influences the selection from available modes, means, and ends of action" (Clyde Kluckhohn, Values and value orientations, in Talcott Parsons and Edward A. Shils (Eds.), *Toward a General Theory of Action* [Cambridge, Mass.: Harvard University Press, 1951], p. 395). See also the discussion of values in Robin M. Williams, Jr., *American Society: A Sociological Interpretation* (New York: Alfred A. Knopf, Inc., 1951), chap. xi, and his discussion of social class and culture on p. 101.

[2]Williams, *op. cit.,* p. 89.

[3]These, and other assertions of fact not referred to published sources, are based on research my colleagues and I have conducted. For the design of this research and the principal substantive findings see my Social class and parental values, *American Journal of Sociology,* LXIV (January, 1959), 337–351; my Social class and the exercise of parental authority, *American Sociological Review,* XXIV (June, 1959), 352–366; and with Eleanor E. Carroll, Social class and the allocation of parental responsibilities, *Sociometry,* XXIII (December, 1960), 372–392. I should like to express my appreciation to my principal collaborators in this research, John A. Clausen and Eleanor E. Carroll.

[4]Urie Bronfenbrenner, Socialization and social class through time and space, in Eleanor E. Maccoby, Theodore M. Newcomb, and Eugene L. Hartley (Eds.), *Readings in Social Psychology* (New York: Henry Holt & Co., 1958).

[5]Furthermore, these concepts employ a priori judgments about which the various investigators have disagreed radically. See, e.g., Robert R. Sears, Eleanor Maccoby, and Harry Levin, *Patterns of Child Rearing* (Evanston, Ill.: Row, Peterson & Co., 1957), pp. 444–447, and Richard A. Littman, Robert C. A. Moore, and John Pierce-Jones, Social class differences in child rearing: A third community for comparison with Chicago and Newton, *American Sociological Review,* XXII (December, 1957), 694–704, esp. p. 703.

[6]Bronfenbrenner, *op. cit.,* pp. 420–422 and 425.

[7]Bronfenbrenner gives clearest expression to this interpretation, but it has been adopted by others, too. See, e.g., Martha Sturm White, Social class, child rearing practices, and child behavior, *American Sociological Review,* XXII (December, 1957), 704–712.

[8]This was noted by John E. Anderson in the first major study of social class and family relationships ever conducted, and has repeatedly been confirmed (*The Young Child in the Home: A Survey of Three Thousand American Families* [New York: Appleton-Century, 1936]).

[9]The differences between middle and working class conditions of life will be discussed more fully later in this paper.

[10]Certainly middle class parents do not get their values from the experts. In our research, we compared the values of parents who say they read Spock, Gesell, or other books on child rearing, to those who read only magazine and newspaper articles, and those who say they read nothing at all on the subject. In the middle class, these three groups have substantially the same values. In the working class, the story is different. Few working class parents claim to read books or even articles on child rearing. Those few who do have values much more akin to those of the middle class. But these are atypical working class parents who are very anxious to attain middle class status. One suspects that for them the experts provide a sort of handbook to the middle class; even for them, it is unlikely that the values come out of Spock and Gesell.

[11]Conceptions of parenthood, *American Journal of Sociology,* LII (November, 1946), 193–203.

[12]Alex Inkeles has shown that this is true not only for the United States but for a number of other industrialized societies as well (Industrial man: The relation of status to experience, perception, and value, *American Journal of Sociology,* LXVI [July, 1960], 20–21 and Table 9.)

[13]Social class and parental values, *op. cit.*

[14]For a thoughtful discussion of the influence of occupational role on parental values see David F. Aberle and Kaspar D. Naegele, Middle class Fathers' occupational role and attitudes toward children, *American Journal of Orthopsychiatry,* XXII (April, 1952), 366–378.

[15]Two objections might be raised here. (1) Occupational experiences may not be important for a mother's values, however crucial they are for her husband's, if she has had little or no work experience. But even those mothers who have had little or no occupational experience know something of occupational life from their husbands and others, and live in a culture in which occupation and career permeate all of life. (2) Parental values may be built not so much out of their own experiences as out of their expectations of the child's future experiences. This might seem particularly plausible in explaining working class values, for their high valuation of such stereotypically *middle class* characteristics as obedience, neatness, and cleanliness might imply that they are training their children for a middle class life they expect the children to achieve. Few working class parents, however, do expect (or even want) their children to go on to college and the middle class jobs for which a college education is required. (This is shown in Herbert H. Hyman, The value systems of different classes: A social psychological contribution to the analysis of stratification, in Reinhard Bendix and Seymour Martin Lipset (Eds.), *Class, Status and Powers: A Reader in Social Stratification* [Glencoe, Ill.: Free Press, 1953], and confirmed in unpublished data from our own research.)

[16]See, e.g., S. M. Miller and Frank Riessman, The working class subculture: A new view, *Social Problems,* IX (Summer, 1961), 86–97.

[17]Relevant here is Seymour Martin Lipset's somewhat disillusioned Democracy and working class authoritarianism, *American Sociological Review,* XXIV (August, 1959), 482–501.

[18]It has been argued that as larger and larger proportions of the middle class have become imbedded in a bureaucratic way of life—in distinction to the entrepreneurial way of life of a bygone day—it has become more appropriate to raise children to be accommodative than to be self-reliant. But this point of view is a misreading of the conditions of life faced by the middle class inhabitants of the bureaucratic world. Their jobs require at least as great a degree of self-reliance as do entrepreneurial enterprises. We tend to forget, nowadays, just how little the small or medium-sized entrepreneur controlled the conditions of his own existence and just how much he was subjected to the petty authority of those on whose pleasure depended the survival of his enterprise. And we fail to recognize the degree to which monolithic-seeming bureaucracies allow free play for—in fact, require—individual enterprise of new sorts: in the creation of ideas, the building of empires, the competition for advancement.

At any rate, our data show no substantial differences between the values of parents from bureaucratic and enterpreneurial occupational worlds, in either social class. But see Daniel R.

Miller and Guy E. Swanson, *The Changing American Parent: A Study in the Detroit Area* (New York: John Wiley & Sons, 1958).

[19]Bronfenbrenner, *op. cit.,* p. 424.

[20]Later studies, including our own, do not show this difference.

[21]Social class and the exercise of parental authority, *op. cit.*

[22]This is not to say that the methods used by parents of either social class are necessarily the most efficacious for achievement of their goals.

[23]The justification for treating support and constraint as the two major dimensions of parent-child relationships lies in the theoretical argument of Talcott Parsons and Robert F. Bales, *Family, Socialization and Interaction Process* (Glencoe, Ill.: Free Press, 1955), esp. p. 45, and the empirical argument of Earl S. Schaefer, A circumplex model for maternal behavior, *Journal of Abnormal and Social Psychology,* LIX (September, 1959), 226–234.

[24]Bronfenbrenner, *op. cit.,* p. 425.

[25]From the very limited evidence available at the time of his review, Bronfenbrenner tentatively concluded: "though the middle class father typically has a warmer relationship with the child, he is also likely to have more authority and status in family affairs" (*ibid,* p. 422). The discussion here is based largely on subsequent research, esp. Social class and the allocation of parental responsibilities, *op. cit.*

[26]Fragmentary data suggest sharp class differences in the husband-wife relationship that complement the differences in the division of parental responsibilities discussed above. For example, virtually no working class wife reports that she and her husband ever go out on an evening or weekend without the children. And few working class fathers do much to relieve their wives of the burden of caring for the children all the time. By and large, working class fathers seem to lead a largely separate social life from that of their wives; the wife has full-time responsibility for the children, while the husband is free to go his own way.

5.3

The Psycho-Social Origins of Achievement Motivation

Bernard C. Rosen
Roy D'Andrade

The purpose of this study is to examine the origins of achievement motivation (*n* Achievement) within the context of the individual's membership in two important groups: family and social class. Specifically, this paper explores, through the observation of family interaction, the relationship between achievement motivation and certain child-training practices, and the relationship between these practices and the parent's social class membership.

The importance of group membership for personality development has been demonstrated many times. Perhaps the most important of these groups is the family, whose strategic role in the socialization process has led investigators to study the

Reprinted with abridgment from *Sociometry,* 1959, *22,* 185–195; 215–218, by permission of the senior author and the American Sociological Association.

nexus between child rearing practices and motivation formation. Thus, Winterbottom (15) examined the relationship between independence-mastery training and achievement motivation and found that achievement motivation is strongest among boys whose mothers (all of whom were middle class) expected relatively early indications of self-reliance and mastery from them.

Since many socialization practices are known to be dissimilar between social groups (3, 4), it might be expected that independence training practices would also differ. A study by McClelland *et al.* (8), later replicated by Rosen (10), demonstrated this to be the case: middle class parents place greater stress upon independence training than lower class parents. The deduction from this finding that classes differ in their level of *n* Achievement was shown to be correct by Rosen (9) who found that, on the average, *n* Achievement scores for middle class adolescents were significantly higher than those for their lower class counterparts.

Significantly, although these studies flow logically from one another. In none of them were all three variables—group membership, child training practices, and *n* Achievement—studied simultaneously. Furthermore, there were certain gaps in these studies which called for theoretical and methodological modifications and additions. The nature of these gaps, and the contributions which it was the research objective of this study to make, are as follows:

Theoretical. The keystone around which studies of the origins of achievement motivation have been built is the notion that training in independent mastery is an antecedent condition of *n* Achievement (6, 15). This approach grew out of McClelland's and his associates' theory of the nature and origins of motivation. They argue that all motives are learned, that "they develop out of repeated affective experiences connected with certain types of situations and types of behavior. In the case of achievement motivation, the situation should involve 'standards of excellence,' presumably imposed on the child by the culture, or more particularly by the parents as representatives of the culture, and the behavior should involve either "competition' with those standards of excellence or attempts to meet them which, if successful, produce positive affect or, if unsuccessful, negative affect. It follows that those cultures of families which stress competition with standards of excellence or which insist *that the child be able to perform certain tasks well by himself*... should produce children with high achievement motivation" (7).

Two distinctly different kinds of child-training practices are implicit in this theory. The first is the idea that the child is trained to do things "well"; the second, the notion that he is trained to perform tasks "by himself." The former has been called *achievement training* (2) in that it stresses competition in situations involving standards of excellence; the latter has been called *independence training* in that it involves putting the child on his own. The failure to disentangle these two concepts has resulted in a focus of attention upon independence training largely to the exclusion of achievement training, although the former is primarily concerned with developing self-reliance, often in areas involving self-caretaking (e.g., cleaning, dressing, amusing, or defending oneself). Although both kinds of training practices frequently occur together, they are different in content and consequences and needed to be examined separately. We believe that of the two training practices, achievement training is the more effective in generating *n* Achievement.

There is another component of independence training—one which is explicit in the idea of independence—that needed further exploration: *autonomy.* By autonomy, we mean training and permitting the child to exercise a certain amount of freedom of action in decision making. Although a related aspect of autonomy—*power*—was studied by Strodtbeck (13), who examined the relationship between power distribution in the family, *n* Achievement, and academic achievement among a group of Jewish and Italian adolescents, no study had examined simultaneously the self-reliance and autonomy components of independence training. The operation of both components, we believed, tends to increase the power of independence training to generate *n* Achievement, since in itself high parental expectations for self-reliance may cause rebellion, fellings of rejection, or of apathy on the part of the child, while autonomy without parental expectations for self-reliance and achievement may be perceived as mere permissiveness or indifference.

In association with parental demands that the child be self-reliant, autonomous, and show evidence of high achievement, there must be sanctions to see that these demands are fulfilled. Winterbottom found that mothers of children with high *n* Achievement gave somewhat more intense rewards than mothers of children with low *n* Achievement. Little was known about the role of negative sanctions, or of the relative impact of sanctions from either parent. Further study was required of the degree and kind of sanctions employed by both parents to see that their demands are met.

Methodological. This study departed from two practices common in studies of the origins of *n* Achievement. The first practice is to derive data exclusively from ethnographic materials; the second, to obtain information through questionnaire-type interviews with mothers. Interviews and ethnographies can be valuable sources of information, but they are often contaminated by interviewer and respondent biases, particularly those of perceptual distortion, inadequate recall, and deliberate inaccuracies. There was a need for data derived from systematic observation of parent-child relations. It is not enough to know what parents *say* their child rearing practices are; these statements should be checked against more objective data, preferably acquired under controlled experimental conditions, that would permit us to *see* what they do. In this study, experiments were employed which enabled a team of investigators to observe parent-child interaction in problem-solving situations that were standardized for all groups and required no special competence associated with age or sex.

An equally strong objection can be raised against the tendency to ignore the father's role in the development of the child's need to achieve. Apart from an earlier study of father-son power relations, no efforts had been made to determine the father's contribution to achievement and independence training—a surprising omission even granted the mother's importance in socializing the child in American society. Although we were not prepared to take a position on the nature of the role relationships between father, mother, and son with respect to this motive, we deliberately created experimental conditions which would enable us to observe the way in which the three members of the family interacted in a problem-solving situation. Finally, this study incorporated in one design the variables of group membership, child-training practices, and motivation, variables that heretofore had not been studied simultaneously. In so doing we hoped to establish the nexus among class membership, socialization practices, and achievement motivation.

HYPOTHESES

This study was designed to provide data that would permit testing two basic hypotheses.

1. Achievement motivation is a result of the following socialization practices: (a) *achievement training,* in which the parents set high goals for their son to attain, indicate that they have a high evaluation of his competence to do a task well, and impose standards of excellence upon tasks against which he is to compete, even in situations where such standards are not explicit; (b) *independence training,* in which the parents indicate to the child that they expect him to be *self-reliant,* while at the same time permit him relative *autonomy* in situations involving decision making where he is given both freedom of action and responsibility for success or failure; (c) *sanctions,* rewards and punishments employed by parents to ensure that their expectations are met and proper behavior is reinforced. Although each contributes to the development of achievement motivation, achievement training is more important than independence training. Neither are effective without supporting sanctions.

2. Differences in the mean level of achievement motivation between social classes is in part a function of the differential class emphases upon independence and achievement training: middle class parents are more likely than lower class parents to stress self-relience, autonomy, and achievement in problem-solving situations, particularly those involving standards of excellence. They are more likely to recognize and reward evidences of achievement, as well as to be more sensitive of and punitive toward indications of failure.

EXPERIMENTAL PROCEDURE

The subjects selected to provide data needed for the testing of these hypotheses about the origins of achievement motivation were 120 persons who made up 40 family groups composed of a father, mother, and their son, aged nine, ten, or eleven. The selection of the family groups began with testing the boy. Seven schools in three northeastern Connecticut towns were visited by the same field worker who administered a Thematic Apperception Test individually and privately to 140 boys, aged nine, ten, or eleven. As is customary in the TAT procedure, the subject was presented with a set of four ambiguous pictures and asked to tell a story about each. His imaginative responses were then scored according to a method developed by McClelland and his associates which involved identifying and counting the frequency with which imagery about evaluated performance in competition with a standard of excellence appears in the thoughts of a person when he tells a brief story under time pressure. Experience has shown that this imagery can be identified objectively and reliably. It is the assumption of this test that the more the individual shows indications of evaluated performance connected with affect in his fantasy, the greater the degree to which achievement motivation is part of his personality (7). The stories were scored by two judges; the Pearsonian coefficient of correlation between scorers was .87, a level of reliability similar to those reported in earlier studies with this measure.

Subjects with scores of plus 2 to minus 4 (approximately the bottom quartile) were labeled as having low n Achievement, those with scores of plus 9 to plus 22 (approximately the top quartile) as having high n Achievement. Any boy with an IQ score below 98, with physical defects, whose parents were separated, or who had been raised during part of his life by persons or relatives other than his parents (e.g., grandparents) was eliminated from the sample.

Forty boys, matched by age, race, IQ, and social class were chosen for further study. All were white, native born, and between nine and eleven years of age; the average was ten years. Half of the boys had high n Achievement scores, half had low scores. In each achievement motivation category, half of the boys were middle class, half were lower class. Their social class position was determined according to a modified version of the Hollingshead Index of Social Position (5) which uses the occupation and education of the chief wage earner—usually the father—as the principal criteria of status. The middle class father (class II or III) held either a professional, managerial, white-collar position or was self-employed as an owner of a small- to medium-size business. Often one or both parents in middle class families were college graduates; all were high school graduates. The parents of lower class (IV or V) boys were quasi-skilled or skilled workers in local factories, or owners of very small farms—often the farmers held factory jobs as well. Relatively few of these parents had completed high school, none had gone beyond high school.

It can be seen that the study was designed in such a way that the subjects fell into one of four cells, with the achievement motivation level of the boys and the class position of the parents as the classificatory variables. Within each cell there were ten families. This four-cell factorial design was constructed so as to facilitate the use of the analysis of variance technique in the statistical analysis of the data.

After the boy was selected, a letter was sent to his parents from the principal of the school asking their cooperation with the investigators. Later, appointments were made over the telephone to visit the families. Cooperation was very good; there were only two refusals. A pair of observers visited each family group, usually at night. There were two teams of observers, each composed of a man and woman. Both teams had been trained together to ensure adequate intra- and interteam reliability.

Once in the home, the observers explained that they were interested in studying the factors related to success in school and eventually to a career, and that the son was one of many boys selected from a cross-section of the community. When rapport had been established, the parents and their son were placed at a table—usually in the kitchen—and it was explained that the boy was going to perform certain tasks.

Experimental Tasks

The observers wanted to create an experimental situation from which could be derived objective measures of the parents' response to their son as he engaged in achievement behavior. Tasks were devised which the boy could do and which would involve the parents in their son's task performance. The tasks were constructed so that the subjects were often faced with a choice of giving or refusing help. At times they were permitted to structure the situation according to their own norms; at other times the experimenters set the norms. In some situations they were faced with decision conflicts over various alternatives in the problem-solving process. The observation of the parents' behavior as their son engaged in these experimental tasks provided information about the demands the parents made upon him, the sanctions employed to enforce these demands, and the amount of independence the child had developed in relations with his parents. A category system, similar to the Bales system (1), was devised to permit scoring interaction between parents and son so that the amount and form of each subject's participation could be examined. The investigators were able to learn from these interaction data how self-reliant the parents expected their son to be, how much autonomy they permitted him in decision-making situations, and what kind and amount of affect was generated in a problem-solving situation.

In creating the experimental tasks an effort was made to simulate two conditions normally present when boys are solving problems in the presence of their parents: (1) tasks were constructed to make the boys relatively dependent upon their parents for aid, and (2) the situation was arranged so that the parents either knew the solution to the problem or were in a position to do the task better than their son. In addition, tasks were created which tapped manual skills as well as intellectual capacities, although intelligence is a factor in any problem-solving situation. It was for this reason that the experimenters controlled for IQ.

In one particular respect the experimental situation was deliberately made atypical. The investigators sought to get the parents involved in the experiment by deliberately building stress into the situation. It was hoped that these *stress experiments* would so involve the parents that they would abandon their protective "company behavior" and generate more authentic action in several hours than could be gained through casual observation over several days. This maneuver was generally successful, although it is impossible to evaluate how and in what way the nature of the experiments and the presence of observers affected the subjects. It is a basic assumption of this study that by studying present-time interaction in a controlled situation one can achieve a valid picture of the patterns of interaction between parents and child most likely to have occurred in the child's earlier years. It is recognized, however, that the conflicting evidence about changes in socialization practices as the child grows older leaves the wisdom of this assumption an open question.

Pretesting had shown that no single task would provide sufficient data to test all hypotheses. Hence, five tasks were constructed, each designed to attack the problem from a somewhat different angle and yet provide certain classes of data that could be scored across tasks. The five tasks used in this study are as follows:

1. *Block Stacking.*   The boys were asked to build towers out of very irregularly shaped blocks. They were blindfolded and told to use only one hand in order to create a situation in which the boy was relatively dependent upon his parents for help. His parents were told that this was a test of their son's ability to build things, and that they could *say* anything to their son but could not touch the blocks. A performance norm was set for the experiment by telling the parents that the average boy could build a tower of eight blocks; they were asked to write down privately their estimate of how high they thought their son could build his tower. The purposes of this experiment were (a) to see how high were the parents' aspirations for and evaluations of their son, e.g., if they set their estimates at, above, or below the norm; (b) to see how self-reliant they expected or permitted their son to be, e.g., how much help they would give him.

There were three trials for this task. The first provided measures of parental evaluations and aspirations not affected by the boy's performance; the second and third trial estimates provided measures affected by the boy's performance. The procedure for the third trial differed from the first two in that the boy was told that he would be given a nickel for each block he stacked. Each member of the family was asked to estimate privately how high the boy should build his tower. No money would be given for blocks stacked higher than the estimate nor would the subject receive anything if the stack tumbled before he reached the estimate. Conservative estimates, hence, provided security but little opportunity for gain; high estimates involved more opportunity for gain but greater risk. The private estimates were then revealed to all and the family was asked to reach a group decision. In addition to securing objective measures of parental aspiration-evaluation levels, the observers scored the interaction between subjects, thus obtaining data as to the kind and amount of instructions the parents gave their son, the amount of help the son asked for or rejected, and the amount and kind of affect generated during the experiment.

2. *Anagrams.*   In this task the boys were asked to make words of three letters or more out of six prescribed letters: G, H, K, N, O, R. The letters, which could be reused after each word was made, were printed on wooden blocks so that they could be manipulated. The parents were given three additional letter blocks, T, U, and B, and a list of words that could be built with each new letter. They were informed that they could give the boy a new letter (in the sequence T, U, B) whenever they wished and could say anything to him, short of telling him what word to build. There was a ten-minute time limit for this experiment. Since this is a familiar game, no efforts were made to explain the functions of the task.

The purposes of this experiment were: (a) to see how self-reliant the parents expected their son to be, e.g., how soon they would give him a new letter, how much and what kind of direction they would give him, if they would keep him working until he got all or most of the words on the list or "take him off the hook" when he got stuck. And (b) to obtain, by scoring interaction between the subjects, measures of the affect generated by the problem-solving process, e.g., the amount of tension shown by the subjects, the positive and negative remarks directed toward one another.

3. Patterns. In this experiment the parents were shown eight patterns, graduated in difficulty, that could be made with Kohs blocks. The subjects were informed that pattern 1 was easier to make than pattern 2, pattern 3 was more difficult than 2 but easier than 4, and so forth. The subjects were told that this was a test of the boy's ability to remember and reproduce patterns quickly and accurately. Each parent and boy was asked to select privately three patterns which the boy would be asked to make from memory after having seen the pattern for five seconds. All three patterns were chosen *before* the boy began the problem solving so that his performance in this task would not affect the choice of the patterns. Where there were differences of choice, as inevitably there were, the subjects were asked to discuss their differences and make a group decision. Insofar as possible the observers took a verbatim account of the decision-making process, scoring for three kinds of variables: (a) the number of acts each subject contributed to the decision-making process, (b) the number of times each individual initated a decision, and (c) the number of times each subject was successful in having the group accept his decision or in seeing to it that a decision was made.

The purposes of this experiment were: (a) to obtain another measure of the parents' evaluations of and aspirations for the boy, e.g., whether they would pick easy or difficult tasks for him to do; (b) to get a measure of the autonomy permitted the boy, e.g., whether they would let him choose his own patterns or impose their choices upon him; and (c) to see how much help they would give him and what affect would be generated by the experiment.

4. Ring Toss. In this experiment each member of the group was asked to choose privately ten positions, from each of which the boy was to throw three rings at a peg. The distance from the peg was delineated by a tape with 1-foot graduations laid on the floor. The subjects were told that this was a test of discrimination and judgment and that after each set of three tosses they would be asked to make a judgment as to the best distance from which to make the next set of tosses. Group decisions were made as to where the boy should stand. The purposes of this experiment were: (a) to see whether the parents imposed standards of excellence upon a task for which no explicit standard had been set, e.g., whether the parents would treat this as a childish game or see it as a task which could and should be done well. Would they choose easy or difficult positions? (b) To determine how much autonomy they permitted their son, e.g., would they let him choose his own position?

5. Hatrack. The Maier Hatrack Problem was used in this experiment. The boy was given two sticks and a C-clamp and instructed to build a rack strong enough to hold a coat and hat. His parents were told that this was a test of the boy's ability to build things. In this task no one was given the solution at the beginning of the experiment. For the first time the parents had no advantage over the boy—a most uncomfortable position for many parents, particularly the fathers. This stress situation was created deliberately to maximize the possibility of the problem generating affect, as was often the case, with some hostility being directed at the observers. After seven minutes the parents were given the solution to the problem. The purposes of this experiment were: (a) to see how self-reliant the parents expected their son to be. After receiving the solution what kind of clues would the parents give the boy? How hard would they expect him to work on his own? (b) To obtain measures of the affect created in an unusually frustrating situation. How would the parents handle their frustration? Would they turn it against the boy?

Category System

References have been made to the use of a category system for scoring interaction between subjects. A brief description of this system, shown in Diagram 1, is in order. Most of the subjects' verbal and some of their motor behavior (e.g., laughing, hand-clapping, scowling) was scored in one of twelve categories. In eight of these categories were placed acts involving relatively strong affect. Four additional categories were used to distinguish between various kinds of statements—either giving, requesting, or rejecting directions—which contained very little or no affect. A distinction was made between negative and positive affective acts. Affective acts associated with explicit or implicit evaluations of the boy's performance which aimed at motivating or changing his behavior were scored differently from affective acts which involved reactions to the boy and only indirectly to his performance.

DIAGRAM 1. THE SYSTEM OF CATEGORIES USED IN SCORING PARENT-CHILD INTERACTION

+X	Expresses approval, gives love, comfort, affection
+T	Shows positive tension release, jokes, laughs
+E	Gives explicit positive evaluation of performance, indicates job well done
+P	Attempts to push up performance through expression of enthusiasm, urges, cheers on
N	Gives nonspecific directions, gives hints, clues, general suggestions
S	Gives specific directions, gives detailed information about how to do a task
aa	Asks aid, information, or advice
ra	Rejects aid, information, or advice
–P	Attempts to push up performance through expressions of displeasure; urges on indicating disappointment at speed and level of performance
–E	Gives explicit negative evaluation of performance, indicates job poorly done
–T	Shows negative tension release, shows irritation, coughs
–X	Expresses hostility, denigrates, makes sarcastic remarks

Directional acts by the parents were remarks designed to help the boy perform his task. A distinction was made between *specific* directions (S) which were acts instructing the subject to do particular things which would facilitate task completion, and *nonspecific* (N) which were acts aimed at giving the subject some information but not specific enough to enable him to rely entirely upon it. It was believed that nonspecific statements were more likely than specific statements to create self-reliance in the child.

The affective acts were schematized in two sets—one positive, the other negative. The first set was comprised of acts involving direct expressions of emotion toward another person, not necessarily in the context of task performance, either of a positive character (+X), such as expressions of love or approval, or of a negative character (−X), such as indications of hostility and rejection. Another set was of acts involving release of tension, either associated with positive affect (+T) such as grins, laughter, jokes, or negative affect (−T) such as scowls, coughs, or irritated gestures. Tension-release acts differ from acts of direct emotion (X) in that the former were not focused toward any person but were diffused, undirected reactions to the general situation. The next set of acts involved parental evaluation of the boy's performance. Those acts in which the parents stated that the boy was doing the task well were scored as positive evaluations (+E), while statements that the boy was doing poorly were scored as negative evaluations (−E). The last two categories involved acts aimed at urging or pushing the boy to perform more effectively. These "pushing up the performance level acts" were scored in one of two categories. Those acts in which the parents "cheered" the boy on while at the same time indicating that they expected him to do better were scored as positive pushing acts (+P); negative pushing acts (−P) were statements in which the parents sought to improve the boy's performance by indicating in a threatening way that they thought he could do better.

Only four kinds of acts were scored for the boy: whether he asked for aid (aa), rejected aid (ra), showed positive tension (+T) or negative tension (−T). An act was defined as the smallest segment of verbal or motor behavior which could be recognized as belonging to one of the twelve categories in the system. The actor rather than the target of the acts was used as the observer's frame of reference.

This category system involves a good deal of inference on the part of the observer—a factor which can make for low observer reliability. To ensure adequate reliability, the interaction in each family was scored by two observers who had been trained to work as a team. In the early stages of the field work tape recordings were taken of family interaction. After the experiments the observers rescored the interaction protocols and discussed scoring differences in order to increase interobserver reliability. Tape recordings were discontinued when the scorers felt that their scores were substantially the same. Each team of observers visited 20 families. The reliability of observers for the gross number of acts scored is high. The Pearsonian coefficient of correlation between the first pair of scorers is plus .93, and for the second pair plus .97. No significant differences between pairs of observers has been discovered. . . .

DISCUSSION AND SUMMARY

The question of how achievement training, independence training, and sanctions are related to achievement motivation may be rephrased by asking, How does the behavior of parents of boys with high *n* Achievement differ from the behavior of parents whose sons have low *n* Achievement?

To begin with, the observers' subjective impressions are that the parents of high *n* Achievement boys tend to be more competitive, show more involvement, and seem to take more pleasure in the problem-solving experiments. They appear to be more interested and concerned with their son's performance; they tend to give him more things to manipulate rather than fewer; on the average they put out more affective acts. More objective data show that the parents of a boy with high *n* Achievement tend to have higher aspirations for him to do well at any given task, and they seem to have a higher regard for his competence at problem solving. They set up standards of excellence for the boy even when none is given, or if a standard is given will expect him to do "better than average." As he progresses they tend to react to his performance with warmth and approval, or, in the case of the mothers especially, with disapproval if he performs poorly.

It seems clear that achievement training contributes more to the development of *n* Achievement than does independence training. Indeed, the role of independence training in generating achievement motivation can only be understood in the context of what appears to be a division of labor between the fathers and mothers of high *n* Achievement boys.

Fathers and mothers both provide achievement training and independence training, but the fathers seem to contribute much more to the latter than do the mothers. Fathers tend to let their sons develop some self-reliance by giving hints (N) rather than always telling "how to do it" (S). They are less likely to push (P) and more likely to give the boy a greater degree of autonomy in making his own decisions. Fathers of high *n* Achievement boys often appear to be competent men who are willing to take a back seat while their sons are performing. They tend to beckon from ahead rather than push from behind.

The mothers of boys with high achievement motivation tend to stress achievement training rather than independence training. In fact, they are likely to be more dominant and to expect less self-reliance than the mothers of boys with low *n* Achievement. But their aspirations for their sons are higher and their concern over success greater. Thus, they expect the boys to build higher towers and place them farther away from the peg in the Ring Toss experiment. As a boy works his mother tends to become emotionally involved. Not only is she more likely to reward him with approval (Warmth) but also to punish him with hostility (Rejection). *In a way, it is this factor of involvement that most clearly sets the mothers of high* n *Achievement boys apart from the mothers of low* n *Achievement boys:* the former score higher on every variable, expect specific directions. And although these mothers are likely to give their sons more option as to exactly (fewer Specifics) what to do, they give them less option about doing something and doing it well. Observers report that the mothers of high *n* Achievement boys tend to be striving, competent persons. Apparently they expect their sons to be the same.

The different emphasis which the fathers and mothers of high *n* Achievement boys place upon achievement and independence training suggest that the training practices of father and mother affect the boy in different ways. Apparently, the boy can take and perhaps needs achievement training from both parents, but the effects of independence training and sanctions, in particular Autonomy and Rejection, are different depending upon whether they come from the father or mother. In order for high *n* Achievement to develop, the boy appears to need more autonomy from his father than from his mother. The father who gives the boy a relatively high degree of autonomy provides him with an opportunity to compete on his own ground, to test his skill, and to gain a sense of confidence in his own competence. The dominating father may crush his son (and in so doing destroys the boy's achievement motive), perhaps because he views the boy as a competitor and is viewed as such by his son. On the other hand, the mother who dominates the decision-making process does not seem to have the same effect on the boy, possibly because she is perceived as *imposing her standards* on the boy, while a dominating father is perceived as *imposing himself* on the son. It may be that the mother-son relations are typically more secure than those between father and son, so that the boy is better able to accept higher levels of dominance and rejection from his mother than his father without adverse affect on his needs to achieve. Relatively rejecting, dominating fathers, particularly those with less than average warmth—as tended to be the case with the fathers of low *n* Achievement boys—seem to be a threat to the boy and a deterrent to the development of *n* Achievement. On the other hand, above-average dominance and rejection, coupled with above-average warmth, as tends to be the case with mothers of high *n* Achievement boys, appear to be a spur to achievement motivation. It will be remembered that the fathers of high *n* Achievement boys are on the average less Rejecting, less Pushing, and less Dominant—all of which points to their general hands-off policy.

It is unlikely that these variables operate separately, but the way in which they interact in the development of achievement motivation is not clear. Possibly the variables interact in a manner which produces cyclical effects roughly approximating the interaction that characterized the experimental task situations of this study. The cycle begins with the parents imposing standards of excellence upon a task and setting a high goal for the boy to achieve (e.g., Ring Toss, estimates and choices in Block Stacking and Patterns). As the boy engages in the task, they reinforce acceptable behavior by expressions of warmth (both parents) or by evidences of disapproval (primarily mother). The boy's performance improves, in part because of previous experience and in part because of the greater concern shown by his parents and expressed through affective reaction to his performance and greater attention to his training. With improved performance, the parents grant the boy greater autonomy and interfere less with his performance (primarily father). Goals are then reset at a higher level and the cycle continues.

REFERENCES

1. Bales, R. F. *Interaction process analysis.* Cambridge, Mass.: Addison-Wesley, 1951.

2. Child, I. L., Storm, T., & Veroff, J. Achievement themes in folk tales related to socialization practice. In J. W. Atkinson, *Motives in fantasy, action and society.* Princeton, N.J.: Van Nostrand, 1958.

3. Erickson, M. C. Social status and child-rearing practices." In T. Newcomb and E. Hartley, *Readings in social psychology.* New York: Holt, 1947.

4. Havighurst, R. J., & Davis, A. Social class differences in child-rearing. *American Sociological Review,* 1955, *20,* 438–442.

5. Hollingshead, A., & Redlick, F. C. Social stratification and psychiatric disorders. *American Sociological Review,* 1953, *18,* 163–169.

6. McClelland, D. C., & Friedman, G. A. A cross-cultural study of the relationship between child-training practices and achievement motivation, appearing in folk tales. In G. E. Swanson, T. M. Newcomb, & E. L. Harley (Eds.), *Readings in social psychology.* New York: Holt, 1952.

7. McClelland, D. C., Atkinson, J. W., Clark, R., & Lowell, E. *The achievement motive.* New York: Appleton-Century-Crofts, 1953.

8. McClelland, D. C., Rindlisbacher, A., & deCharms, R. Religious and other sources of parental attitudes toward independence training. In D. C. McClelland, (Ed.), *Studies in motivation.* New York: Appleton-Century-Crofts, 1955.

9. Rosen, B. C. The achievement syndrome: a psychocultural dimension of social stratification. *American Sociological Review,* 1956, *21,* 203–211.

10. Rosen, B. C. Race, ethnicity, and the achievement syndrome. *American Sociological Review,* 1959, *24,* 47–60.

11. Sakoda, J. M. Directions for a multiple group method of factor analysis. Mimeographed paper, University of Connecticut, June, 1955.

12. Sears, R. R., Maccoby, E. E., & Levin, H. in collaboration with E. L. Lowell, P. S. Sears, & J. W. M. Whiting, *Patterns of child rearing.* Evanston, Ill.: Row, Peterson, 1957.

13. Strodtbeck, F. L. Family interaction, values, and achievement. In D. C. McClelland, A. L. Baldwin, U. Bronfenbrenner, & F. L. Strodtbeck, *Talent and society.* Princeton, N.J.: Van Nostrand, 1958.

14. Tryon, R. C. *Cluster analysis.* Ann Arbor, Mich.: Edwards Brothers, 1939.

15. Winterbottom, M. R. The relation of need for achievement to learning experiences in independence and mastery. In J. W. Atkinson, *Motives in Fantasy, Action, and Society.* Princeton, N.J.: Van Nostrand, 1958.

5.4

Cooperative and Competitive Behavior of Kibbutz and Urban Children in Israel

Ariella Shapira
Millard C. Madsen
Several researchers have attempted to determine the extent of subcultural differences in the cooperative and competitive behavior of children in the United States. McKee and Leader (1955) found preschool children of low socioeconomic level to be more competitive than children of middle class families. Goodman (1952) found Negro children (age 4) to be more competitive than white children, while Sampson and Kardush (1965) found the opposite to be true with older children (age 7–11). Nelson and Madsen (in press) found no differences in cooperation and competition between Negro and white lower class and white middle class 4-year-olds. There are many methodological differences between the above studies, as well as differences of time and place. It is also probably true that subcultural groups in the United States cannot be as rigidly differentiated, with respect to social values and child rearing practices that give rise to differential interdependent behavior, than is possible in other settings.

In an experimental study of subcultural differences in competitive and cooperative behavior, Madsen (1967) found that both rural and urban poor children in Mexico were dramatically more cooperative than Mexican urban middle class children. An attempt was made to account for these differences in performance on experimental tasks by reference to the environmental milieu in which the different subcultural groups had developed. The study reported here was carried out in Israel and used the same techniques to compare two other subcultural groups: children from agricultural social communes (kibbutzim) and those from an urban environment.

Children in an Israeli urban middle class community are encouraged by parents and teachers to achieve and succeed. Competition is an acceptable means of arriving at this goal. In the kibbutz, on the other hand, children are prepared from an early age to cooperate and work as a group, in keeping with the objectives of communal living. Spiro (1965) found, through questionnaires given to parents in the kibbutz, that generosity and cooperation were the most frequently rewarded behaviors, while selfishness and failure to cooperate were among the behaviors most frequently punished.

Reprinted from *Child Development,* June 1969, *40,* No. 2, 609–617, by permission of the author and The Society for Research in Child Development, Inc. Copyright © 1969 by The Society for Research in Child Development, Inc.

The formal teaching methods in the kibbutz are also noted for their minimal emphasis on competitive goals and techniques. Grades and examinations are viewed as unnecessary or even undesirable. Competition, with all its punitive aspects, is far less intense in the classroom of the kibbutz than in that of the city. Not only do the agents of socialization avoid inducing a favorable set toward competition, but also the children themselves develop an attitude against competition. Spiro found that only one out of 28 students saw himself or his peers as being competitively motivated. By far the majority of the students said that their desire was primarily to become equal to their peers or, as Rabin (1965) observed, to raise the achievement level of their group as a whole. Generally, kibbutz children do not accept competition as a socially desirable norm and dislike those who try to excel over members of their own group. This anti-competition attitude is so strong that, according to some teachers, students are ashamed of being consistently at the top of the class. Spiro also found that these cooperative attitudes and behaviors increase with age concomitant with a decrease in competitive motivation.

In line with these basic differences in child rearing practices and values, it was hypothesized that kibbutz children would be more cooperative than urban middle class children when playing a social interaction game with their peers.

METHOD

Subjects

The kibbutz sample included 40 children, 20 boys and 20 girls, ages ranging from 6 to 10 years, with a mean age of 8 years. Children from three different kibbutzim were included: Beit Zerah (in the Jordan valley), Beit Hashita (in the Yisrael valley), and Ein Hahoresh (in the Sharon). Both Ein Hahoresh and Beit Zerah belong to the Hashomer Hatzair, a radical socialist movement which is idealogically the most puritanical of all kibbutz movements in Israel. Beit Hashita belongs to Hakibbutz Hameuhad, a relatively more moderate ideological movement. All of the kibbutz children who played the experimental game knew the children with whom they participated. They were usually from the same *kvutza,* a group within a kibbutz comprised of children who spend almost all their time together.

The city sample consisted of 40 children, 20 boys and 20 girls, ages ranging 6 to 10 years, with a mean age of 8 years. These children were from Mount Carmel, an upper middle class community in which most people have a relatively high income. The children, who were spending their vacation at a summer day camp, had already been together for several weeks and therefore knew each other quite well. This particular group of urban children was chosen because they were quite similar to kibbutz children in intelligence and opportunities for development.

In both samples, by far the majority of the children had been born in Israel.

Apparatus

The Madsen Cooperation Board was used. This board is 18 inches square with an eyelet fastened to each of the four corners. Strings strung through each eyelet are connected to a metal weight which serves as a holder for a ball-point pen filler. A sheet of paper is placed on the board for each trial, thus recording the movement of the pen as Ss pull their strings. Because the string passes through the eyelets, any individual child can pull the pen only toward himself. In order to draw a line through the circles, the children must work together. The essential features of the apparatus and position of circles to be crossed can be seen in Figure 1.

FIGURE 1. MADSEN COOPERATION BOARD

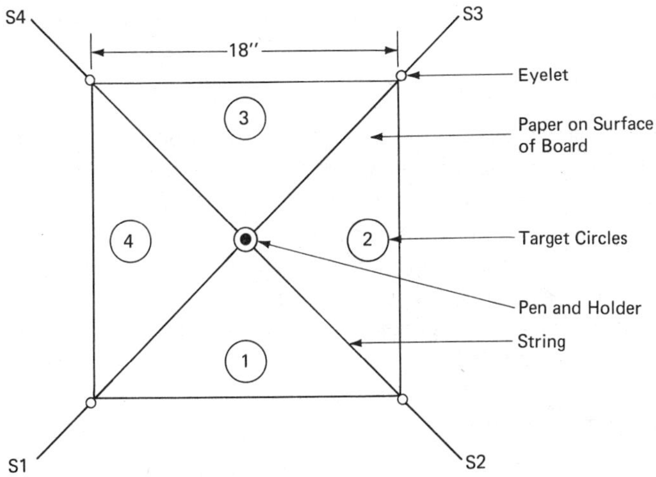

EXPERIMENT I

The purpose of this experiment was to train the Ss in playing the game in a cooperative manner so the children would know how to play cooperatively under the individual reward condition, if motivated to do so. It would also reveal whether there was any preexisting tendency to behave competitively or cooperatively.

Procedure

Two treatment conditions, Group Reward (GR) and Individual Reward (IR), were compared over three trials. In trials 1–3 (GR), all four children received a prize as soon as the group was able to draw a line through the four circles within the time allowed. In trials 4–6 (IR), each of the four players had his own circle and would receive a prize only when his circle was crossed.

Four children of the same sex and approximately the same age were taken from the group (either kibbutz or city) into a separate room. The experimental board was set on a low table. The four children were seated at the four corners of the board and told that they were going to play a game. The children were instructed to hold on to the handles, one in each hand, and to listen to the instructions of the game.

Instructions for Trials 1–3

As you can see, when we pull the strings, the pen draws lines. In this game we are going to pull the strings and draw lines, but in a special way. The aim of the game is for you to draw a line over the four circles within 1 minute. If you succeed in doing this, each one of you will get a prize. If you cover the four circles twice, everyone will get two prizes, and so on. But if you cover less than four circles no one will get a prize. You may talk to each other but are not allowed to touch another child's string or handle. Are there any questions?

While the children were playing the game, E announced the number of circles crossed and also announced when a round of four circles was completed. When 1 minute was up, the children were stopped and E announced and recorded the number of rounds and extra circles the children had crossed.

At this point each child was given a paper bag with his name on it, and the prizes were given out in accordance with the number of rounds completed. Trial 1 was completed and a new sheet of paper was attached to the board. The procedure was repeated for the second and third trials.

Instructions for Trials 4–6

Now the game is going to be somewhat different. Now every one of you gets his own circle. This is David's circle [E writes name on a circle to the right of David]. This is Ron's circle [etc.]. Now, when the pen draws a line across one of the circles, the child whose name is in the circle gets a prize. When it crosses David's circle, David gets a prize; when it crosses Ron's circle, Ron gets a prize, and so on. You will have 1 minute to play before I stop you. Are there any questions?

During this trial, E announced every time a circle was crossed. When the trial was over, E announced and recorded, for each child, the number of times his circle had been crossed. Prizes were given out accordingly. Trials 5 and 6 followed the same procedure as trial 4.

Results

Figure 2 shows the mean number of circles crossed by the two subcultural samples under the group and individual reward conditions. It was indicated by t tests that there were no significant differences between city and kibbutz groups for any of the three GR trials or for the three trials combined. Similar tests indicated significant differences between these groups after the introduction of individual reward (trial 4, $p < .01$; trials 5 and 6, $p < .05$). Both groups crossed fewer circles on trial 4 than on trial 3. While the average drop from trial 3 to trial 4 for city groups was 10.1 circles, the average drop in the kibbutz was 5.6 circles. This difference in the amount of decrease was significant at the .05 level (t test).

Observation indicated that this lowered performance occurred for different reasons. On trial 4, most city groups began competing, thus reducing drastically the number of circles crossed. The kibbutz groups, on the other hand, simply slowed down. The reason for this could have been either because they made an effort to avoid competition or because they were adjusting to the new rules as if it were a different game. It can also be seen from Figure 2 that the kibbutz groups recovered on trials 5 and 6, whereas the city groups never regained the level of performance attained under the GR condition.

FIGURE 2. MEAN NUMBER OF CIRCLES CROSSED PER TRIAL BY KIBBUTZ AND URBAN CHILDREN

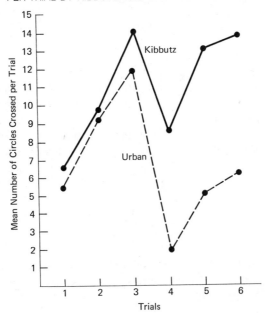

The same pattern of results occurred for both sexes. The mean circles crossed by boys and girls under GR within both groups was nearly identical. However, the difference between kibbutz and city groups under the IR condition was greater for the boys. The mean circles crossed by urban boys was 30.6 fewer than by kibbutz boys, whereas the urban girls crossed a mean of 12.8 fewer circles than the kibbutz girls (trials and Ss collapsed).

EXPERIMENT II

The purpose of this experiment was to compare the behavior of kibbutz and city children in a situation where competition is an adaptive behavior. Since in this situation the circles were at the corners of the page, it was possible for a competitive child to win more prizes than the others by pulling the string sharply toward himself and drawing a line through his own circle.

Procedure

The circles were drawn at the corners of the page so that each child had a circle directly in front of him. The following instructions were given:

> As you see, the circles are now at the corners of the page. This time the game is somewhat different so listen carefully. Again everyone has his own circle. [*E* writes each child's name in the circle closest to him.] Now, when the pen draws a line across the circle of one of the children, that child will get a prize. At this point, we shall stop the game and return the pen to the center of the page and begin again. We will do this four times without changing the page. Are there any questions?

When a line was drawn across one of the circles, *E* stopped the game and recorded the time of the trial and the order. The child whose circle was crossed received a prize. The same procedure was carried out for trials 2, 3, and 4. If no circle was crossed within a minute, *E* stopped the game and began a new trial.

When the experiment was over, *E* gave prizes to those children who had not won many during the game, so that all children received about the same number of prizes. Although the prizes were of little value (candy, gum, and small plastic charms) they were effective reinforcers, as demonstrated by the children's eagerness to work for them.

Results

Any line which passed through an individual circle without deviating more than 1 inch from the direct path from the center starting point to the circle, and which did not reverse directions within those limits, was considered a noncompetitive response.

TABLE 1. MEAN NONCOMPETITIVE RESPONSES FOR KIBBUTZ AND URBAN CHILDREN BY SEX

GROUP	FEMALE	MALE
Kibbutz	2.8	2.4
Urban	2.2	0.6

Lines which violated these criteria were considered competition in that they indicated that children were pulling against each other.

Table 1 gives the mean number of noncompetitive responses for four trials for the two groups, by sex.

Kibbutz groups had more noncompetitive responses than urban groups (mean 2.6 vs. 1.4, respectively), but this difference only approaches significance ($t = 1.70$ $p < .05 < .10$).

Most of the differences between kibbutz and city groups can be attributed to the fact that the city boys were more competitive than city girls as well as both boys and girls from the kibbutzim.

DISCUSSION

The hypothesis that kibbutz children would show more cooperative behavior than city children in Israel was confirmed. Under the individual reward condition in Experiment I, the kibbutz children showed performance superior to that of the city children. Since both groups had learned the task equally well, as evidenced by their similar performances under the group reward condition, differences in performance under the individual reward condition can be attributed to different types of motivational stress in urban and kibbutz environments. Thus, changes in instructions produced different behaviors in city children but not in kibbutz children. The slight improvement in performance for kibbutz groups under the individual reward condition probably reflects the effect of practice as the children continue to follow the cooperative techniques adopted under the group reward condition. Once reward was given out on an individual basis, city children changed the tactics they had used to obtain group rewards and began pulling toward themselves. Even though they obviously realized, after trials 4 and 5, that these competitive procedures were not paying off for any of them, they were unable to stop their irrational competition.

Perhaps of greater interest is the fact that the children themselves did not enjoy the competition and wanted to change the rules. A number of children kept asking E not to write names on the circles, evidently realizing that as long as there were names on the circles they would continue to compete.

At times a child would suggest that they take turns, or help each other, but usually the other children refused. In some isolated cases, the children agreed to cooperate, but the instant one child pulled a little harder, cooperation broke down completely and they all started pulling toward themselves.

Among the kibbutz groups the picture was entirely different. When individual reward instructions were introduced, the first response of most of the groups was to set up rules for cooperation. Some examples of these responses were: "OK gang, let's go in turns," or "Let's help each other," or "We'll start here, then here," etc. Some groups asked E if they were allowed to help each other or whether they could go in rounds like before. When E said they could do as they wished, they always decided upon cooperation. These children were very organized in their performance.

They usually had decided the order before the trial began. During the game they were also very active in directing one another.

The kibbutz children were very eager to do well as a group and tried their best to improve their performance on every subsequent trial. Some of the groups asked to compare their results with other groups and wanted to know what the best score had ever been. Such responses indicate that a desire to achieve and to do well characterizes these children, who do compete with other groups on the kibbutz but not within their group. At the group level, they cooperate and work together as a team.

In most of the kibbutz groups there was a great concern about equality in prizes ("Every one should get the same"). They were so concerned about this that, in many cases, they rotated the starting point so that if they were stopped before a round was completed a different child would get the extra prize on each trial. When, in some isolated cases, one of the children tried to compete against the others, the group usually restrained him.

In general, the results and observations indicate that, when cooperative behavior was adaptive, children of the kibbutz were generally able to cooperate successfully for maximum performance, whereas urban children were usually not able to do so.

Many aspects of kibbutz life and collective education are potentially competitive. The children of the kibbutz, more than those of the city, must compete for the nurses' attention and affection, must compete for the toys they play with, etc. It is possible that because of this, the development of cooperative tendencies is so instrumental to proper functioning of the group and that, without such a development, conflict would be exceptionally severe.

REFERENCES

Goodman, M. E. *Race awareness in young children.* Cambridge, Mass.: Addison-Wesley, 1952.

McKee, J. P., & Leader, F. The relationship of socioeconomic status and aggression to the competitive behavior of preschool children. *Child Development,* 1955, *26,* 175–182.

Madsen, M. C. Cooperative and competitive motivation of children in three Mexican subcultures. *Psychological Reports,* 1967, 20, 1307–1320.

Nelson, L., & Madsen, M. C. Cooperation and competition in four-year-olds as a function of availability of reward and subculture. *Developmental Psychology,* in press.

Rabin, A. I. *Growing up in the kibbutz.* New York: Springer, 1965.

Sampson, E. E., & Kardush, M. Age, sex, class, and race differences in response to a two-person non-zero-sum game. *Journal of Conflict Resolution,* 1965, *9,* 212–220.

Spiro, M. E. *Children of the kibbutz.* Cambridge, Mass.: Harvard University Press, 1965.

5.5

Superordinate Goals in the Reduction of Intergroup Conflict

Muzafer Sherif

In the past, measures to combat the problems of intergroup conflicts, proposed by social scientists as well as by such people as administrators, policy-makers, municipal officials, and educators, have included the following: introduction of legal sanctions, creation of opportunities for social and other contacts among members of conflicting groups; dissemination of correct information to break down false prejudices and unfavorable stereotypes; appeals to the moral ideals of fair play and brotherhood; and even the introduction of rigorous physical activity to produce catharsis by releasing pent-up frustrations and aggressive complexes in the unconscious. Other measures proposed include the encouragement of cooperative habits in one's own community, and bringing together in the cozy atmosphere of a meeting room the leaders of anatagonistic groups.

Many of the measures may have some value in the reduction of intergroup conflicts, but, to date, very few generalizations have been established concerning the circumstances and kinds of intergroup conflict in which these measures are effective. Today measures are applied in a somewhat trial-and-error fashion. Finding measures that have wide validity in practice can come only through clarification of the nature of intergroup conflict and analysis of the factors conducive to harmony and conflict between groups under given conditions.

The task of defining and analyzing the nature of the problem was undertaken in a previous publication.[1] One of our major statements was the effectiveness of superordinate goals for the reduction of intergroup conflict. "Superordinate goals" we defined as goals which are compelling and highly appealing to members of two or more groups in conflict but which cannot be attained by the resources and energies of the groups separately. In effect, they are goals attained only when groups pull together.

INTERGROUP RELATIONS AND THE BEHAVIOR OF GROUP MEMBERS

Not every friendly or unfriendly act toward another person is related to the group membership of the individuals involved. Accordingly, we must select those actions relevant to relations between groups.

Reprinted from the *American Journal of Sociology,* 1958, LXIII, no. 4, 349–356, by permission of the author and the University of Chicago Press. Copyright 1958 by the University of Chicago.

Let us start by defining the main concepts involved. Obviously, we must begin with an adequate conception of the key term—"group." A group is a social unit (1) which consists of a number of individuals who, at a given time, stand in more or less definite interdependent status and role relationships with one another and (2) which explicitly or implicitly possesses a set of values or norms regulating the behavior of individual members, at least in matters of consequence to the group. Thus, shared attitudes, sentiments, aspirations, and goals are related to and implicit in the common values or norms of the group.

The term "intergroup relations" refers to the relations between two or more groups and their respective members. In the present context we are interested in the acts that occur when individuals belonging to one group interact, collectively or individually, with members of another in terms of their group identification. The appropriate frame of reference for studying such behavior includes the functional relations between the groups. Intergroup situations are not voids. Though not independent of relationships within the groups in question, *the characteristics of relations between groups cannot be deduced or extrapolated from the properties of in-group relations.*

Prevalent models of behavior within a group, in the way of cooperativeness and solidarity or competitiveness and rivalry among members, need not be typical of actions involving members of an out-group. At times, hostility toward out-groups may be proportional to the degree of solidarity within the group. In this connection, results presented by the British statistician L. F. Richardson are instructive. His analysis of the number of wars conducted by the major nations of the world from 1850 to 1941 reveals that Great Britain heads the list with 20 wars—more than the Japanese (nine wars), the Germans (eight wars), or the United States (seven wars). We think that this significantly larger number of wars engaged in by a leading European democracy has more to do with the intergroup relations involved in perpetuating a far-flung empire than with dominant practices at home or with personal frustrations of individual Britishers who participated in these wars.[2]

In recent years relationships between groups have sometimes been explained through analysis of individuals who have endured unusual degrees of frustration or extensive authoritarian treatment in their life histories. There is good reason to believe that some people growing up in unfortunate life-circumstances may become more intense in their prejudices and hostilities. But at best these cases explain the intensity of behavior in a given dimension.[3] In a conflict between two groups—a strike or a war —opinion within the groups is crystallized, slogans are formulated, and effective measures are organized by members recognized as the most responsible in their respective groups. The prejudice scale and the slogans are not usually imposed on the others by the deviate or neurotic members. Such individuals ordinarily exhibit their intense reactions within the reference scales of prejudice, hostility, or sacrifice established in their respective settings.

The behavior by members of any group toward another group is not primarily a problem of deviate behavior. If it were, intergroup behavior would not be the issue of vital consequence that it is today. The crux of the problem is the participation by group members in established practices and social-distance norms of their group and their response to new trends developing in relationships between their own group and other groups.

On the basis of his UNESCO studies in India, Gardner Murphy concludes that to be a good Hindu or a good Moslem implies belief in all the nasty qualities and practices attributed by one's own group—Hindu or Moslem—to the other. Good members remain deaf and dumb to favorable information concerning the adversary. Social contacts and avenues of communication serve, on the whole, as vehicles for further conflicts not merely for neurotic individuals but for the bulk of the membership.[4]

In the process of interaction among members, an in-group is endowed with positive qualities which tend to be praiseworthy, self-justifying, and even self-glorifying. Individual members tend to develop these qualities through internalizing group norms and through example by high-status members, verbal dicta, and a set of correctives standardized to deal with cases of deviation. Hence, possession of these qualities, which reflect their particular brand of ethnocentrism, is not essentially a problem of deviation or personal frustration. It is a question of participation in in-group values and trends by good members, who constitute the majority of membership as long as group solidarity and morale are maintained.

To out-groups and their respective members are attributed positive or negative qualities, depending on the nature of functional relations between the groups in question. The character of functional relations between groups may result from actual harmony and interdependence or from actual incompatibility between the aspirations and directions of the groups. A number of field studies and experiments indicate that, if the functional relations between groups are positive, favorable attitudes are formed toward the out-group. If the functional relations between groups are negative, they give rise to hostile attitudes and unfavorable stereotypes in relation to the out-group. Of course, in large group units the picture of the out-group and relations with it depend very heavily on communication, particularly from the mass media.

Examples of these processes are recurrent in studies of small groups. For example, when a gang "appropriates" certain blocks in a city, it is considered "indecent" and a violation of its "rights" for another group to carry on its feats in that area. Intrusion by another group is conducive to conflict, at times with grim consequences, as Thrasher showed over three decades ago.[5]

When a workers' group declares a strike, existing group lines are drawn more sharply. Those who are not actually for the strike are regarded as against it. There is no creature more lowly than the man who works while the strike is on.[6] The same type of behavior is found in management groups under similar circumstances.

In time, the adjectives attributed to out-groups take their places in the repertory of group norms. The lasting, derogatory stereotypes attributed to groups low on the social-distance scale are particular cases of group norms pertaining to out-groups.

As studies by Bogardus show, the social-distance scale of a group, once established, continues over generations, despite changes of constituent individuals, who can hardly be said to have prejudices because of the same severe personal frustrations or authoritarian treatment.[7]

Literature on the formation of prejudice by growing children shows that it is not even necessary for the individual to have actual unfavorable experiences with out-groups to form attitudes of prejudice toward them. In the very process of becoming an in-group member, the intergroup delineations and corresponding norms prevailing in the group are internalized by the individual.[8]

A RESEARCH PROGRAM

A program of research has been under way since 1948 to test experimentally some hypotheses derived from the literature of intergroup relations. The first large-scale intergroup experiment was carried out in 1949, the second in 1953, and the third in 1954.[9] The conclusions reported here briefly are based on the 1949 and 1954 experiments and on a series of laboratory studies carried out as coordinate parts of the program.[10]

The methodology, techniques, and criteria for subject selection in the experiments must be summarized here very briefly. The experiments were carried out in successive stages: (1) groups were formed experimentally; (2) tension and conflict were produced between these groups by introducing conditions conducive to competitive and reciprocally frustrating relations between them; and (3) the attempt was made toward reduction of the intergroup conflict. This stage of reducing tension through introduction of superordinate goals was attempted in the 1954 study on the basis of lessons learned in the two previous studies.

At every stage the subjects interacted in activities which appeared natural to them at a specially arranged camp site completely under our experimental control. They were not aware of the fact that their behavior was under observation. No observation or recording was made in the subjects' presence in a way likely to arouse the suspicion that they were being observed. There is empirical and experimental evidence contrary to the contention that individuals cease to be mindful when they know they are being observed and that their words are being recorded.[11]

In order to insure validity of conclusions, results obtained through observational methods were cross-checked with results obtained through sociometric technique, stereotype ratings of in-groups and out-groups, and through data obtained by techniques adapted from the laboratory. Unfortunately, these procedures cannot be elaborated here. The conclusions summarized briefly are based on results cross-checked by two or more techniques.

The production of groups, the production of conflict between them, and the reduction of conflict in successive stages were brought about through the introduction of problem situations that were real and could not be ignored by individuals in the situation. Special "lecture methods" or "discussion methods" were not used. For example, the problem of getting a meal through their own initiative and planning was introduced when participating individuals were hungry.

Facing a problem situation which is immediate and compelling and which embodies a goal that cannot be ignored, group members *do* initiate discussion and *do* plan and carry through these plans until the objective is achieved. In this process the discussion becomes *their* discussion, the plan *their* plan, the action *their* action. In this process discussion, planning, and action have their place, and, when occasion arises, lecture or information has its place, too. The sequence of these related activities need not be the same in all cases.

The subjects were selected by rigorous criteria. They were healthy, normal boys around the age of 11 and 12, socially well adjusted in school and neighborhood, and academically successful. They came from a homogeneous sociocultural background and from settled, well-adjusted families of middle or lower middle class and Protestant affiliations. No subject came from a broken home. The mean IQ was above average. The subjects were not personally acquainted with one another prior to the experiment. Thus, explanation of results on the basis of background differences, social maladjustment, undue childhood frustrations, or previous interpersonal relations was ruled out at the beginning by the criteria for selecting subjects.

The first stage of the experiments was designed to produce groups with distinct structure (organization) and a set of norms which could be confronted with intergroup problems. The method for producing groups from unacquainted individuals with similar background was to introduce problem situations in which the attainment of the goal depended on the coordinated activity of all individuals. After a series of such activities, definite group structures or organizations developed.

The results warrant the following conclusions for the stage of group formation: When individuals interact in a series of situations toward goals which appeal to all and which require that they coordinate their activities, group structures arise having hierarchical status arrangements and a set of norms regulating behavior in matters of consequence to the activities of the group.

Once we had groups that satisfied our definition of "group," relations between groups could be studied. Specified conditions conducive to friction or conflict between groups was introduced. This negative aspect was deliberately undertaken because the major problem in intergroup relations today is the reduction of existing intergroup frictions. (Increasingly, friendly relations between groups is not nearly so great an issue.) The factors conducive to intergroup conflict give us realistic leads for reducing conflict.

A series of situations was introduced in which one group could achieve its goal only at the expense of the other group—through a tournament of competitive events with desirable prizes for the winning group. The results of the stage of intergroup conflict supported our main hypotheses. During interaction between groups in experimentally introduced activities which were competitive and mutually frustrating, members of each group developed hostile attitudes and highly unfavorable stereotypes toward the other group and its members. In fact, attitudes of social distance between the groups became so definite that they wanted to have nothing further to do with each other. This we take as a case of experimentally produced "social distance" in miniature. Conflict was manifested in derogatory name-calling and invectives, flare-ups of physical conflict, and raids on each other's cabins and territory. Over a period of time, negative stereotypes and unfavorable attitudes developed.

At the same time there was an increase in in-group solidarity and cooperativeness. This finding indicates that cooperation and democracy within groups do not necessarily lead to democracy and cooperation with out-groups, if the directions and interests of the groups are conflicting.

Increased solidarity forged in hostile encounters, in rallies from defeat, and in victories over the out-group is one instance of a more general finding: Intergroup relations, both conflicting and harmonious, *affected the nature of relations within the groups involved.* Altered relations between groups produced significant changes in the status arrangements *within* groups, in some instances resulting in shifts at the upper status levels or even a change in leadership. Always, consequential intergroup relations were reflected in new group values or norms which signified changes in practice, word, and deed within the group. Counterparts of this finding are not difficult to see in actual and consequential human relations. Probably many of our major preoccupations, anxieties, and activities in the past decade are incomprehensible without reference to the problems created by the prevailing "cold war" on an international scale.

REDUCTION OF INTERGROUP FRICTION

A number of the measures proposed for reducing intergroup friction could have been tried in this third stage. A few will be mentioned here, with a brief explanation of why they were discarded or were included in our experimental design.

1. Disseminating favorable information in regard to the out-group was not included. Information that is not related to the goals currently in focus in the activities of groups is relatively ineffective, as many studies on attitude change have shown.[12]

2. In small groups it is possible to devise sufficiently attractive rewards to make individual achievement supreme. This may reduce tension between groups by splitting the membership on any "every-man-for-himself" basis. However, this measure has little relevance for actual intergroup tensions, which are in terms of group membership and group alignments.

3. The resolution of conflict through leaders alone was not utilized. Even when group leaders meet apart from their groups around a conference table, they cannot be considered independent of the dominant trend and prevailing attitudes of their membership. If a leader is too much out of step in his negotiations and agreements with out-groups, he will cease to be followed. It seemed more realistic, therefore, to study the influence of leadership within the framework of prevailing trends in the groups involved. Such results will give us leads concerning the conditions under which leadership can be effective in reducing intergroup tensions.

4. The "common-enemy" approach is effective in pulling two or more groups together against another group. This approach was utilized in the 1949 experiment as

an expedient measure and yielded effective results. But bringing some groups together against others means larger and more devastating conflicts in the long run. For this reason, the measure was not used in the 1954 experiment.

5. Another measure, advanced both in theoretical and in practical work, centers around social contacts among members of antagonistic groups in activities which are pleasant in themselves. This measure was tried out in 1954 in the first phase of the integration stage.

6. As the second phase of the integration stage, we introduced a series of superordinate goals which necessitated cooperative interaction between groups.

The social contact situations consisted of activities which were satisfying in themselves—eating together in the same dining room, watching a movie in the same hall, or engaging in an entertainment in close physical proximity. These activities, which were satisfying to each group, but which did not involve a state of interdependence and cooperation for the attainment of goals, were not effective in reducing intergroup tension. On the contrary, such occasions of contact were utilized as opportunities to engage in name-calling and in abuse of each other to the point of physical manifestations of hostility.

The ineffective, even deleterious, results of intergroup contact without superordinate goals have implications for certain contemporary learning theories and for practice in intergroup relations. Contiguity in pleasant activities with members of an out-group does not necessarily lead to a pleasurable image of the out-group if relations between the groups are unfriendly. Intergroup contact without superordinate goals is not likely to produce lasting reduction of intergroup hostility. John Gunther, for instance, in his survey of contemporary Africa, concluded that, when the intergroup relationship is exploitation of one group by a "superior" group, intergroup contact inevitably breeds hostility and conflict.[13]

INTRODUCTION OF SUPERORDINATE GOALS

After establishing the ineffectiveness, even the harm, in intergroup contacts which did not involve superordinate goals, we introduced a series of superordinate goals. Since the characteristics of the problem situations used as superordinate goals are implicit in the two main hypotheses for this stage, we shall present these hypotheses:

1. When groups in a state of conflict are brought into contact under conditions embodying superordinate goals, which are compelling but cannot be achieved by the efforts of one group alone, they will tend to cooperate toward the common goals.

2. Co-operation between groups, necessitated by a series of situations embodying superordinate goals, will have a cumulative effect in the direction of reducing existing conflict between groups.

The problem situations were varied in nature, but all had an essential feature in common—they involved goals that could not be attained by the efforts and energies of one group alone and thus created a state of interdependence between groups: combating a water shortage that affected all and could not help being "compelling"; securing a much desired film, which could not be obtained by either group alone but required putting their resources together; putting into working shape, when everyone was hungry and the food was some distance away, the only means of transportation available to carry food.

The introduction of a series of such superordinate goals was indeed effective in reducing intergroup conflict: (1) when the groups in a state of friction interacted in conditions involving superordinate goals, they did cooperate in activities leading toward the common goal and (2) a series of joint activities leading toward superordinate goals had the cumulative effect of reducing the prevailing friction between groups and unfavorable stereotypes toward the out-group.

These major conclusions were reached on the basis of observational data and were confirmed by sociometric choices and stereotype ratings administered first during intergroup conflict and again after the introduction of a series of superordinate goals. Comparison of the sociometric choices during intergroup conflict and following the series of superordinate goals shows clearly the changed attitudes toward members of the out-group. Friendship preferences shifted from almost exclusive preference for in-group members toward increased inclusion of members from the "antagonists." Since the groups were still intact following cooperative efforts to gain superordinate goals, friends were found largely within one's group. However, choices of out-group members grew, in one group, from practically none during intergroup conflict to 23 percent. Using chi square, this difference is significant ($P < .05$). In the other group, choices of the out-group increased to 36 percent, and the difference is significant ($P < .001$). The findings confirm observations that the series of superordinate goals produced increasingly friendly associations and attitudes pertaining to out-group members.

Observations made after several superordinate goals were introduced showed a sharp decrease in the name-calling and derogation of the out-group common during intergroup friction and in the contact situations without superordinate goals. At the same time the blatant glorification and bragging about the in-group, observed during the period of conflict, diminished. These observations were confirmed by comparison of ratings of stereotypes (adjectives) the subjects had actually used in referring to their own group and the out-group during conflict with ratings made after the series of superordinate goals. Ratings of the out-group changed significantly from largely unfavorable ratings to largely favorable ratings. The proportions of the most unfavorable ratings found appropriate for the out-group—that is, the categorical verdicts that "all of them are stinkers" or ". . . smart alecks" or ". . . sneaky"—fell, in one group, from 21 percent at the end of the friction stage to 1.5 percent after interaction oriented toward superordinate goals. The corresponding reduction in these highly unfavorable verdicts by the other group was from 36.5 to 6 percent. The overall differences between the frequencies of stereotype ratings made in relation to the out-group during intergroup conflict and following the series of superordinate goals are significant for both groups at the .001 level (using chi-square test).

Ratings of the in-group were not so exclusively favorable, in line with observed decreases in self-glorification. But the differences in ratings of the in-group were not statistically significant, as were the differences in ratings of the out-group.

Our findings demonstrate the effectiveness of a series of superordinate goals in the reduction of intergroup conflict, hostility, and their by-products. They also have implications for other measures proposed for reducing intergroup tensions.

It is true that lines of communication between groups must be opened before prevailing hostility can be reduced. But, if contact between hostile groups takes place without superordinate goals, the communication channels serve as media for further accusations and recriminations. When contact situations involve superordinate goals, communication is utilized in the direction of reducing conflict in order to attain the common goals.

Favorable information about a disliked out-group tends to be ignored, rejected, or reinterpreted to fit prevailing stereotypes. But, when groups are pulling together toward superordinate goals, true and even favorable information about the out-group is seen in a new light. The probability of information being effective in eliminating unfavorable stereotypes is enormously enhanced.

When groups cooperate in the attainment of superordinate goals, leaders are in a position to take bolder steps toward bringing about understanding and harmonious relations. When groups are directed toward incompatible goals, genuine moves by a leader to reduce intergroup tension may be seen by the membership as out of step and ill advised. The leader may be subjected to severe criticism and even loss of faith and status in his own group. When compelling superordinate goals are introduced, the leader can make moves to further cooperative efforts, and his decisions receive support from other group members.

In short, various measures suggested for the reduction of intergroup conflict—disseminating information, increasing social contact, conferences of leaders—acquire new significance and effectiveness when they become part and parcel of interaction processes between groups oriented toward superordinate goals which have real and compelling value for all groups concerned.

NOTES

[1]Muzafer Sherif and Carolyn W. Sherif, *Groups in Harmony and Tension* (New York: Harper & Bros. 1953).
[2]T. H. Pear, *Psychological Factors of Peace and War* (New York: Philosophical Library, 1950), p. 126.
[3]William R. Hood and Muzafer Sherif, Personality oriented approaches to prejudice, *Sociology and Social Research,* XL (1955), 79–85.
[4]Gardner Murphy, *In the Minds of Men* (New York: Basic Books, 1953).
[5]F. M. Thrasher, *The Gang* (Chicago: University of Chicago Press, 1927).
[6]E. T. Hiller, *The Strike* (Chicago: University of Chicago Press, 1928).

[7]E. S. Bogardus, Changes in racial distances, *International Journal of Opinion and Attitude Research,* I (1947), 55–62.

[8]E. L. Horowitz, 'Race Attitudes,' in Otto Klineberg (Ed.), *Characteristics of the American Negro,* Part IV (New York: Harper & Bros., 1944).

[9]The experimental work in 1949 was jointly supported by the Yale Attitude Change Project and the American Jewish Committee. It is summarized in Sherif and Sherif, *op. cit.,* chaps. ix and x. Both the writing of that book and the experiments in 1953–54 were made possible by a grant from the Rockefeller Foundation. The 1953 research is summarized in Muzafer Sherif, B. Jack White, and O. J. Harvey, Status in experimentally produced groups, *American Journal of Sociology,* LX (1955), 370–379. The 1954 experiment was summarized in Muzafer Sherif, O. J. Harvey, B. Jack White, William R. Hood, and Carolyn W. Sherif, Experimental study of positive and negative intergroup attitudes between experimentally produced groups: Robbers cave study (Norman, Okla.: University of Oklahoma, 1954). (Multilithed.) For a summary of the three experiments see chaps. vi and ix in Muzafer Sherif and Carolyn W. Sherif, *An Outline of Social Psychology,* rev. ed. (New York: Harper & Bros., 1956).

[10]For an overview of this program see Muzafer Sherif, Integrating field work and laboratory in small group research, *American Sociological Review,* XIX (1954), 759–771.

[11]E.g., see F. B. Miller, 'Resistentialism' in applied social research, *Human Organization,* XII (1954), 5–8; S. Wapner and T. G. Alper, The effect of an audience on behavior in a choice situation, *Journal of Abnormal and Social Psychology,* XLVII (1952), 222–229.

[12]E.g., see R. M. Williams, *The Reduction of Intergroup Tensions* (Social Science Research Council Bull. 57 [New York, 1947]).

[13]John Gunther, *Inside Africa* (New York: Harper & Bros., 1955).

5.6

Schools and the Disadvantaged (A Summary of the Coleman Report)

Robert C. Nichols

The recent spate of federally financed education programs intended to improve the performance of racial minorities and other disadvantaged groups rests on a foundation of plausible assumptions and commendable intentions but with essentially no data to indicate their probable effectiveness. Will Head Start improve the school performance of deprived children? Will excellent teachers for the poor help break the "cycle of poverty"? Will Negro students learn more in integrated schools? Will the performance of middle class children suffer if they attend school with predominantly lower class children? Will increased expenditures for education result in greater student achievement? There are currently no firm answers to these questions.

Reprinted from *Science,* 9 Dec. 1966, *154,* No. 3754, 1312–1314, by permission of the author and the American Association for the Advancement of Science. Copyright 1966 by the American Association for the Advancement of Science.

Apparently as a reaction to the dearth of information, Section 402 of the Civil Rights Act of 1964 directed the Commissioner of Education to conduct a survey of inequalities in educational opportunities for all groups in the United States. What seemed to be called for was a tabulation of the physical facilities, teachers, and expenditures in schools attended by various minority groups; but at a more fundamental level answers to such questions as those posed above are necessary, since equality of educational opportunity is ultimately defined not by dollars, teachers, and buildings, but by the effects of these facilities on student achievement. Fortunately, the congressional directive was interpreted as including the more basic questions.

Several studies were initiated by the U. S. Office of Education's National Center for Educational Statistics, directed by Assistant Commissioner Alexander M. Mood, a statistician of some note and author of *Introduction to the Theory of Statistics.* The studies were directed by two consultants: James S. Coleman, professor of social relations at Johns Hopkins and author of *The Adolescent Society* and *Introduction to Mathematical Sociology,* among other books; and Ernest Q. Campbell, chairman of the Department of Sociology and Anthropology at Vanderbilt and author of *Christians in Racial Crisis.*

The results of these studies are reported by Colemen, Campbell, Mood, and four USOE staff members—Carol J. Hobson, James McPartland, Frederic D. Weinfeld, and Robert L. York—in Equality of Educational Opportunity (Government Printing Office, Washington, D. C. 1966. 743 pp. $4.25), a thick, paperbound volume filled with tables and charts and accompanied by a separately bound Supplemental Appendix ($3) containing 548 pages of computer-printed correlations. The report shows signs of being hastily put together to meet the two-year congressional deadline. The major findings are imbedded in a mass of trivial detail, and the summary (available as a separate 33-page booklet, $0.30), which appears to have been guided by a desire to avoid disturbing public opinion, is actually misleading. The survey itself, however, was carefully planned and skillfully analyzed. Conducted at a cost of $1.25 million—about half the cost of an F-4 Phantom Jet—it is one of the largest studies yet completed in the field of education, and its startling findings assure it the status of a landmark in educational research.

The principal study was a survey of over 600,000 children enrolled in grades 1, 3, 6, 9, and 12 of about 4,000 schools generally representative of all U.S. public schools, but with some intentional overrepresentation of schools enrolling minority children. The children answered questionnaires about their attitudes and home backgrounds and took tests of educational achievement and verbal and nonverbal ability. Teachers, principals, and superintendents also answered questionnaires, and the teachers took a brief verbal-ability test. A survey of such scope would have been nearly impossible just 15 years ago; but, through the magic of optical scanners, computers, and probably Benzedrine, the current report was released an unbelievable ten months after data collection was started. The survey was met with suspicion and slander in many communities, and school systems in several major cities refused to participate. Complete data were available for only 59 percent of the sampled schools, which shortcoming detracts from the survey's value as a census.

Analyses of the data were concerned with three major questions:

(1) *Are minority groups segregated in public schools?*   To no one's surprise, it was found that segregation prevails. Nationwide, 65 percent of Negroes attended schools in which over 90 percent of the students were Negro, and 80 percent of whites attended schools in which over 90 percent of the students were white. There was greater segregation in the South than in the North. Mexican Americans, American Indians, Puerto Ricans, and Oriental Americans were also segregated, but to a lesser extent than Negroes and whites.

(2) *Are the school facilities for minority children inferior to those for the majority?* On the basis of such indicators of school quality as class size, educational programs, physical facilities, and teacher qualifications, no consistent advantage was found for any one group, and the differences in the quality of education available to the various racial and ethnic groups were small when compared with differences between regions of the country and between metropolitan and nonmetropolitan areas. In terms of these indicators, the educationally deprived groups in the U. S. are not racial or ethnic minorities, but children—regardless of race—living in the South and in the nonmetropolitan North.

(3) *Do the various racial and ethnic groups perform differently from each other on tests of school achievement and of verbal and nonverbal ability?*   The substantial differences between the average test scores of the different racial and ethnic groups were quite similar on the various tests and at the various grade levels. Whites obtained the highest average scores, followed, in order, by Oriental Americans, American Indians, Mexican Americans, Puerto Ricans, and Negroes. "The Negroes' averages tend to be about one standard deviation below those of the whites, which means that about 85 percent of the Negro scores are below the white average" (p. 219). The differences between regions for Negroes followed the pattern for whites, but the regional variation tended to be greater for Negroes. The highest scores were obtained in the metropolitan North and the lowest in the nonmetropolitan South. The highest regional average score for Negroes was below the lowest for whites. . . ."

This survey suffers from problems common to all nonexperimental studies in attempting to assess the effects of natural experiments, which are so messy that one can never be certain that all relevant variables have been taken into account or that the correlations observed in the natural setting would continue to hold if the variables were artificially manipulated. Two uncontrolled variables that come to mind as possible distorting influences in this study are student dropout and migration. If there are differential dropout rates for the various groups, loss of the less able minority students at higher grades may obscure an increasing decrement in group performance. Because of student migration, the student's present school may not be a good indicator of the quality of education to which he has been exposed, and this clouding of the independent variable may make the regression analysis less sensitive to whatever school effects may exist.

It is unfortunate that the sensitivity of the racial issue made it necessary to collect the data from the students anonymously. If each student's name could have been associated with his test scores, a retesting of the same grades in the same schools three years later would have yielded data for a longitudinal study in four segments stretching from the first through the 12th grade.

The study would also have been improved if Jews and possibly Catholics had been identified as additional minority groups, since both are probably subject to some *de facto* segregation in public schools. The higher average performance usually found among Jews would have provided a useful contrast in the attempt to understand the lower average performance of the other minorities.

In view of these shortcomings it is obvious that this is not a good study of the effects of education on minority-group performance; it is just the best that has ever been done. Moreover, it provides the best evidence available concerning the differential effects—or rather the lack of such effects—of schools. AAAS members may find it hard to believe that the $28-billion-a-year public education industry has not produced abundant evidence to show the differential effects of different kinds of schools, but it has not. That students learn more in "good" schools than in "poor" schools has long been accepted as a self-evident fact not requiring verification. Thus, the finding that schools with widely varying characteristics differ very little in their effects is literally of revolutionary significance.

It is not customary for educational practice in the U.S. to be based on research, and these results will likely have little influence on educational policy. The conservatism may be adaptive in this instance, because the findings are too astonishing to be accepted on the basis of one imperfect study. What seems to be required is additional study of differential school effects with better controls for input. However, until these findings are clarified by further research they stand like a spear pointed at the heart of the cherished American belief that equality of educational opportunity will increase the equality of intellectual achievement.

5.7

Youth in Two Worlds: A Summary of Research Results

Denise B. Kandel
Gerald S. Lesser

In this [article] we compare the operation of adolescent societies under different cultural conditions [in the United States and Denmark], and we examine the relative impact on the adolescent of his peer groups as compared to his family. Our interest is in the competing influences of peer groups and adults in different areas of adolescent behavior and under differing cultural conditions. In the two countries, we examine the characteristics of adolescent groups in secondary schools, their academic orientations, patterns of interaction between adolescents and their parents, the consequences of different family patterns for adolescent involvement with peers, the concordance on values, and educational goals within and between generations.

THE DATA

To study the simultaneous influence of several socializing agents upon adolescents under differing cultural conditions, certain methodological conditions were required. We used direct indicators of adolescent behavior and interpersonal influences gathered independently from the different sources of influence. A limited number of schools were selected in each society, with the complete census of adolescents, friends, and parents in these schools studied intensively. Data were collected in spring 1965 from three groups: (1) A total of 2,327 high school students in three American schools and 1,552 in 12 Danish secondary schools were given structured questionnaires administered in a classroom situation; all the students present on the day of questionnaire administration were included in the sample; (2) Students' mothers responded to a mailed, self-administered, structured questionnaire which contained many questions identical to those included in the students' instrument; 68 percent (1,407) of the mothers in the United States and 75 percent (1,098) in Denmark returned their questionnaires; (3) School principals at each school were interviewed and were also asked to fill out a form about the general characteristics and facilities of the school. (Self-adminis-

Excerpted by permission of the publisher from Kandel, Denise B. and Lesser, Gerald S. *Youth in Two Worlds*. San Francisco: Jossey-Bass Inc., 1972. Copyright, 1972, by Jossey-Bass, Inc.

tered questionnaires also were distributed to the teachers in each school. However, since only 30 percent of the Danish teachers returned questionnaires, no data from teachers are presented in this study.)

Our analyses are based alternately upon the total student or total mother samples or upon subsamples of dyads and triads. The adolescent-mother dyads include all matched adolescent-mother pairs (1,141 in the United States, 977 in Denmark) from intact families. The adolescent-best-school-friend dyads include all identified adolescent-best-school-friend pairs (2,157 pairs in the United States, 1,423 in Denmark), regardless of whether there was a mother match. The adolescent-mother-best-school-friend triads number 1,065 in the United States and 905 in Denmark. . . .

RESULTS

The adolescent subculture has been described by some investigators as opposed to the values of adult society and aimed at subverting adult values. Other investigators have described the adolescent subculture as more limited in scope, developing only in areas that are irrelevant to the larger society. Our results support the second of these alternatives. Far from developing a "contra-culture" in opposition to that of adult society, the adolescents we have studied express the values of the adult society.

Moreover, our data also argue against the "exclusive" view—the assumption that the stronger the rejection of adult standards, the stronger the acceptance of peer standards and, conversely, the stronger the commitment to adult standards, the less the need for accepting peer influence. Our data lead to a contrary view: In critical areas, interactions with peers support, express, and specify for the peer context the values of parents and other adults; and the adolescent subculture is coordinated with, and in fact is a particular expression of, the culture of the larger society. Our data indicate that in areas of importance adolescents display high concordance with both parents *and* peers, or low concordance with both. It thus appears that adolescents can display differing levels of generalized social interaction—some adolescents depending heavily upon several external agents, whether parents or peers; others depending little upon either parents or peers. Some adolescents follow conscientiously both parent and peer standards; others may ignore both sources with equal conscientiousness.

Finally, our data also suggest that differences in structure and functioning of schools and families may be coordinated to differences in values of each country. American and Danish values express themselves in the family in the form of parental practices and directives and in the high school in terms of the organization and values of the peer culture. We would therefore argue that the adolescent subculture is best understood as a youthful expression of adult society, dealing with problems unique to adolescence. To understand the adolescent subculture, it is therefore essential to understand the adult culture and its value system.

VALUES IN THE UNITED STATES AND DENMARK

With some exceptions we found considerable difference between the values of Americans and Danes, and rather little difference between adolescents and their parents within either society. This finding in itself suggests that each society develops in its members, both adolescent and adult, a common perspective, so that national differences are larger than generational ones.

Differences between American and Danish values seem associated with two thematic differences. The first is related to achievement; the other, to the family. Americans emphasize achievement more than Danes; Americans emphasize getting somewhere, establishing oneself, and, in this way, gaining the respect or recognition of the community. Central here is a concern for the respect of others, and the belief that it is won by achievement. For example, a much larger percentage of American than Danish parents and adolescents emphasize being a leader in activities, earning money, having a good reputation. Furthermore, the majority of American parents and adolescents believe that the best way to get ahead in life is to work hard, a belief maintained only by a very small minority of Danes, who, in contrast, emphasize getting along with others as the best way to get ahead in life. Comparing the two, we might say that Americans believe that achievement gains the testimony of others to one's worth, which then permits self-acceptance. Danes, in contrast, want to get along with others, to be accepted as someone dependable, in personal rather than achievement terms. The distinction is between winning the regard of others through achievement (characteristic of the American outlook) and simply gaining acceptance as a person (characteristic of the Danish outlook).

The second difference between the American and the Danish outlooks is perhaps more surprising, for it indicates that greater emphasis is placed by Americans on the responsiblity of youth to their families. The specific value items expressing this theme are loyalty to the family, respect for parents, and doing things with the family. As we shall suggest in our interpretation of materials dealing with family structure, the themes of achievement and family responsibility are mutually supportive. The family uses its authority to direct the adolescent toward the end of establishing himself and the adolescent, in turn, must achieve well, in part because his performance will reflect on his family. As Riesman (1950) points out, success is defined variously by various groups in modern American life; but in the last analysis it is measured by the extent to which one has managed to win the regard of others:

> *Approval itself, irrespective of content, becomes almost the only unequivocal good in this situation; one makes good when one is approved of. Thus all power, not merely some power, is in the hands of the actual or imaginary approving group, and the child learns from his parents' reactions to him that nothing in his character, no possession he owns, no inheritance of name or talent, no work he has done is valued for itself but only for its effect on others. . . . To him that hath approval shall be given more approval [p.66].*

ADOLESCENT SOCIAL SYSTEM IN SCHOOLS

For most adolescents, the high school and the family are the two social structures within which life takes place. In the United States, much more than in Denmark, attending classes is only one of a wide variety of activities engaged in by students in schools. There are official and semiofficial assemblies and a host of activities, clubs, and social events. Thus, in addition to academic concerns, the school supports students in both athletic and social activities. Most American schools provide formal recognition for outstanding achievements. Those whose grades are outstanding are listed on honor rolls; those who do well in athletics or in the band are awarded school letters; social prominence is likely to be recognized through elections for various class offices. The attention paid by the American high school to identifying those students who are outstanding seems to correspond to a need of its students for social recognition. There are few equivalent practices in Danish secondary schools; nor are there the alternative routes to establishing oneself as a leader which abound in American schools.

Interactions with Peers. Since all but a small minority of friendships among both American and Danish adolescents are with schoolmates, a description of friendships and peer influences within the school serves adequately as a description of all adolescent friendship groups. Although friendship has somewhat different meanings in the two societies, American adolescents are not different from Danish adolescents in their numbers of friends and in the tendency to choose as friends other adolescents of about the same age and in the same school. For the majority of adolescents, school friendships are their most meaningful friendships and friendships tend to develop on the basis of proximity within the school, such as year in school or school program. Social class background and similarity of interest are much less important criteria.

Our data suggest a difference between American and Danish friendship patterns in the extent of close, mutually recognized bonds. In a number of ways—including relative frequency of visiting of friends ranked as "best," "second best," and "third best"; the smaller number of reciprocated friendship choices; and the greater similarity of attitudes among reciprocated and nonreciprocated friendship choices—American adolescents form several friendships of about the same intensity, while Danish adolescents form one very close tie and then maintain several other, more distant, relationships. These characteristics of friendships among American and Danish adolescents support Lewin's (1948) interpretations of American and European adult social life. Lewin suggested that Americans participate in many friendships, each of which engages a rather superficial level of personality, while Europeans engage in fewer friendships, each of which penetrates more deeply into their personal sphere. These descriptions of contrasting adult styles of social interaction find their counterparts in the characteristics of adolescent friendship patterns.

Status and Recognition. Marked differences exist in the functioning of the school social systems in the United States and Denmark. The American concern with winning the regard of others results in greater sensitivity, among American adolescents, to the way other adolescents are rated on a host of characteristics. Asked to name the best athlete among boys, the best dressed among girls, the best student among both boys and girls, the most popular with the other sex, American adolescents display very high consensus. Danish adolescents display some agreement, but nowhere near the consensus displayed by American adolescents. In the United States adolescents are acutely observant of the performances of their peers and develop agreement among themselves regarding who is outstanding and in what ways. Even more striking cross-cultural differences appear in the identification of members of the leading crowd. In both the United States and Denmark, certain youngsters may be identified as leaders, or as members of the leading crowd. In the United States, however, this characterization comes more easily than in Denmark; many more American than Danish adolescents can name members of the leading crowd, and they display higher consensus than do Danes regarding who is in the leading crowd. However, consensus on leading-crowd members in these Danish schools, while lower than in our sample of [American] schools, is as high among boys as the levels reported by Coleman (1961) for his sample of ten American schools. Leading crowds among adolescents are not a uniquely American phenomenon.

Furthermore, if one accepts that a crucial criterion for the existence of a leading crowd is the grouping together of adolescents named as leaders, then this criterion is met in Denmark as well as in the United States. On the basis of their reciprocated sociometric friendship choices, adolescents were grouped as isolates, members of pairs, or members of cliques. In both countries, students nominated as members of the leading crowd associate with each other in well-defined cliques within the school. Similarly, the frequency of nominations on every one of the other status criteria increases as a function of the adolescent's involvement in social networks. Nominations on status criteria received by clique members are higher than those received by pair members, which are higher than those received by isolates. To the extent that our data allow us to test for this, such recognition appears at times to be a function of high achievement and at times a function of the higher visibility of the achievements of clique members. Indeed, at the same levels of academic performance, students receive the same number of nominations as best students whether they are isolates or members of pairs or of cliques. On the other hand, students who participate in the same number of sports are more likely to be nominated as best athlete if they are socially involved than if they are isolates.

That leading crowds have less prominence in Denmark than in the United States and are less significant components of the adolescent's experience is substantiated by additional findings besides those pertaining to response rates and consensus levels. More Americans than Danes subjectively perceive themselves to be leading-crowd members; and adolescents' self-esteem is related to actual membership in the United States, but not in Denmark.

Although American schools develop more prominent and visible leading crowds than do Danish schools, members of the leading crowd in both countries share similar characteristics: involvement in sociometric networks, achievement in the peer culture, social class background, self-evaluations, and future life goals. Students nominated as members of the leading crowd possess some general leadership quality, so that they are also judged outstanding in other ways as well. Positive and statistically significant correlations obtain between membership in the leading crowd and every single specific criterion in terms of which an adolescent could be rated by his peers in our study: being a good athlete, being well dressed, being a good student, being popular, and even being someone one would choose for a friend. Even though one might conclude that any basis for being outstanding is valued, certain kinds of prominence are more regularly associated with membership in the leading crowd than others: being an athlete for the boys; being well dressed for the girls; being thought popular with the opposite sex for each; and being someone one would choose for a friend, especially for the boys. Being a best student shows the lowest association to leading-crowd membership in both countries. Prominence along the fun, companionship, and sports dimension is more important then prominence along the dimension of scholarship. Nonetheless, whether measured by ability, actual or self-reported grades, or future educational plans, leadership in the peer subculture is associated with superior academic performance. Leaders have higher IQ's, higher objective and self-reported grades, high educational aspirations than nonleaders. At comparably high levels of ability, leaders get better grades than nonleaders. However, this level of academic performance is not matched by a comparable level of interest in an academic role. Leaders in both countries—even in Denmark, where intellectual values are more prominent than in the United States—show less preference for the scholar image than the student body as a whole.

The similarity of leaders in both countries extends to other aspects of their life as well. Leaders are more likely to be from middle class than from working class backgrounds. They are more involved than their peers in activities that bring them in close contact with their peers, such as school clubs, sports, or dating. At each level of social activity, nominations as leading-crowd member are highest for adolescents who belong to cliques. It is out of the convergence of a high level of activity and performance embedded in close interpersonal peer networks that leading crowds arise.

Attitudes Toward Studies and Grades.   By a number of indicators, Danish schools have a stronger intellectual orientation than American schools. When asked how they would like to be remembered in school, a minority of American adolescents wanted to be remembered as a brilliant student; in Danish schools, it is the majority. Americans nominated as best students are less likely to want to be remembered as best students than those nominated as athletes want to be remembered as athletes. The reverse is true in Denmark. Furthermore, more Danish students than American enjoy their studies. The same proportion in both countries stress good grades.

Earlier, we noted that in the United States both parents and adolescents are less often concerned with the intrinsic gratifications of doing satisfying work than they are with the extrinsic rewards of achievement for work done. The same seems true of American adolescents in relation to academic concerns, if we consider that minority for whom good grades are extremely important. It is perhaps not surprising that most American students report that study is not satisfying in itself. What is surprising is that even most top-rank students find studying not satisfying. In the United States, in all categories of adolescents who are in some way identified with scholastic achievement—those who feel themselves to be in the top rank of students, those who are believed by their fellows to be among the best students, those who would like to be remembered as brilliant students, those who plan to continue their education—getting good grades is much more frequently valued than is satisfaction in studying. In Denmark, the percentage of students who very much want good grades is only slightly larger than the percentage of students who say studying is satisfying.

In the United States, high school students want good grades to obtain the rewards available to the successful student (admission to a good college and eventual entrance into a desirable career). The American emphasis on establishing oneself serves to polarize attitudes toward grades. Americans who are not top-rank students are more likely to say that grades are not important than their Danish counterparts, and Americans who are top-rank students are more likely to say that grades are important than their Danish counterparts. The result of this polarization of attitudes is that those American students who have chosen the route of scholastic achievement not only feel different from others in the school but actually exaggerate the extent to which they are different. In the American high school, taking the route of academic achievement means accepting that one's motivations (and not just one's talents) are different. No aspect of this phenomenon appears in the Danish schools: nearly all Danish students who value scholastic achievement perceive congruence in this value between themselves and their environment.

More generally, we find that perceptions of attitudes in the environment are totally a function of the adolescent's personal values and are independent of the distribution of values in the environment, except for a slight effect in dyads. We assessed the distribution of attitudes at different levels of the student's social environment: the school as a whole, the clique, the friendship dyad. Most students attribute their own attitudes to others irrespective of whether no one or everyone in their immediate environment actually holds that value. Given a specific personal attitude, the same proportion of students will perceive that attitude around them, irrespective of the actual distribution of attitudes in the environment. However, American students who value grades project their attributes to others to a much smaller degree than any other group of students.

We may speculate on the process that underlies the uniform belief, among American students, that other students do not value grades. Certainly, students who hold this view are correct: only a minority of students value grades. Yet the near unanimity with which American students make this appraisal seems unjustified by the reality; since a third of the students do not value grades, why should almost no one believe that grades are valued by others? Only a minority among American students think that good grades are important, and even they must dissimulate this fact so as to suggest to their fellows that they are as unconcerned as everyone else. Perhaps admitting a concern for grades is unfashionable, and even unwise, in high school society, especially since achievement itself is not important to the adolescent, although achievement as a way of winning the regard of others is. Such dissimulation, repeated throughout the student body, would result in pluralistic ignorance, in which students systematically underestimate the proportion of their fellows who are interested in grades. In both countries, the school itself seems to have little to do with the development of intellectual interests.

FAMILY STRUCTURE

If we accept that American life is in part motivated by a striving to win the respect of others and that American parents require the respect of their children so as to guide their children's endeavors toward gaining the respect of others, then we may understand the structure developed in the United States by families of adolescents. Despite the presumed permissiveness often attributed to American parents of very young children, American families are much more often authoritarian than are families of Danish adolescents. It is the American parent rather than the adolescent (or the two together) who is likely to make most decisions; parental decisions are less frequently explained; parents establish more rules. Families where the parent alone makes decisions have been characterized as "authoritarian"; where both parent and child decide jointly, as "democratic"; and where the child alone decides as "permissive." The authoritarian pattern is the one most frequently observed in the United States (whether the practices of mothers alone are considered, of fathers alone, or of the two jointly). This pattern is much less frequently observed in Denmark, where the modal family pattern is the democratic. American families have many more rules than do Danish families, especially about behavior which might produce social difficulties for the adolescent or the parents, such as: being in on time at night, observing some limit on dating, and not going out with certain boys or certain girls. American families appear to be more permissive than the Danish only when no social danger is likely to be encountered; an example is "eating dinner with the family," a practice required by more Danish than American families.

The three themes identified so far—the greater emphasis in America than in Denmark on achievement, family responsibility, and authoritarianism—may be interrelated. The greater authoritarianism of the American family stems, at least in part, from the responsibility felt by American parents to supervise the activities of their adolescents so as to ensure that they behave in ways most likely to maintain the respect of others. It is also possible, however, that Danish parents exercise relatively greater control over very young children, which then permits them to allow these children more self-direction in adolescence.

A most striking cross-cultural difference appears on the issue of adolescent independence. Danish adolescents have a strong subjective sense of their independence from family influence; they feel more frequently than do the Americans that they would disregard their parents' wishes about not seeing friends, that their opinions are different from those of their parents, that they are being treated like adults by their parents, and that they get sufficient freedom from their parents. In contrast to the Danes, American adolescents appear unable to behave according to their parents' wishes unless their parents have clear and specific rules for them. These findings, thus, do not support the widespread belief that American adolescents act independently and are encouraged by their parents to be independent at an earlier age than are Europeans.

In both countries, feelings of independence are enhanced when parents have few rules, when they provide explanations for their rules, and when they are democratic and engage the child actively in the decision-making process. Furthermore, feelings of independence from parents in both countries, far from being associated with rebelliousness, are associated with closeness to parents and positive attitudes toward them. By contrast, parental restrictiveness brings with it conflict between the adolescent and the parent. In families where the adolescent feels too little freedom from his parents, he is much more likely to report that it is hard for him to get along with his parents and that there has been conflict with them in the past year. This is only to be expected; in the restrictive family, parents take positions on many more issues. Furthermore, in both the United States and Denmark, the authoritarian pattern of decision-making seems to produce, particularly in adolescent girls, a feeling of distance from the parent. Compared with adolescents from democratic families, adolescents from authoritarian families are more likely to feel that their parents do not explain their decisions; these children also are less likely to bring their problems to their parents and to enjoy doing things with their parents. Thus, while socialization practices of families in the United States and Denmark differ somewhat, the consequences of particular practices for the adolescent are similar within each culture.

American and Danish families also differ in the relative importance of mother and father as parents. In the United States, it is the mother who is most likely to voice the family directives, and to back them with discipline. The American mother almost invariably is responsible for disciplining girls; she is also responsible for disciplining boys somewhat more often than the father is. In Danish families, in contrast, both parents frequently share responsibilities. Not only is shared responsibility less frequent in America, but disagreement between parents about the discipline of adolescents is more frequent; in the case of disagreement, the American mother more often wins. The relative dominance of the American mother may be explained to some extent by a withdrawal of the American father from family interaction. Perhaps the same need for achievement, which is expressed in other ways in the American family, keeps American men committed to the world of work to the point where they are relatively unavailable at home.

The types of issues that American youngsters bring to their parents reflect the dependence of American adolescents upon their parents. American adolescents are likely to discuss problems involving fundamental orientations: morals and values, and the expressions of these values in dating and choice of friends. Half or more of American adolescents would bring these problems to their parents—generally to their mothers—whereas Danish adolescents would more often bring them to friends. Despite the greater prevalence of conflict in American families, American adolescents seem to accept that their parents, and particularly their mothers, are proper advisers in relation to fundamental orientations. In regard to issues that deal with specific plans or programs, however, the American adolescent is apt to consult specialists, such as a teacher or guidance counselor. Such specialists are not available to Danish students, who would consult their parents in these cases. In both countries, parents have a great deal of influence on adolescent decisions regarding continuation of an academic education. American parents continue to concern themselves with the fundamental values and outlook of their children, and with their children's social behavior, long after most Danish parents treat their children as already formed. Despite this, the American parent seems willing to have his adolescent youngster consult specialists for help in just how and where to pursue his fundamental aims.

ROLE OF PEERS

Despite striking differences between the United States and Denmark in the authoritarian or democratic structure of the family, adolescents in both countries turn to their parents for help in solving problems and to their peers for companionship. Americans are more likely to enjoy their friends' over their parents' company, but less likely to rely on their friends for assistance, support, or counsel. Very few American adolescents bring problems of morals and values, or other personal problems, to their friends. A much larger proportion of Danish adolescents than American adolescents bring problems of morals and values to their friends. But Danish parents, as well as American parents, remain the primary source of advice on such matters. However, American adolescents, more than Danish, report that they would respect the opinion of their mothers over that of their best friends.

Subjective peer orientation of adolescents is related to the directiveness of the family. In families that follow the democratic pattern, adolescents respond by more often preferring the company of their parents to that of their friends. Thus, the way parents pattern their relationship with their adolescent children to some extent determines the way the adolescents subjectively experience their relationships with each other. By contrast, family patterns bear no relationship to adolescents' actual patterns of interaction with their peers: either their informal contacts, the frequency with which adolescents see their friends out of school, or the extent to which they are nominated by their classmates on various status criteria. None of these sociometric criteria are related to the quality of the adolescent's relations with his parents. Thus, parental relationships are related to the attitude that is brought to bear on contacts with peers rather than to the extensiveness of the contacts themselves.

RELATIVE INFLUENCE OF PEERS AND PARENTS

American parents often set rules regarding what peers are acceptable as friends or dates, and American adolescents suggest that they abide by such rules when they are set. American adolescents may learn to choose their friends partly in terms of the influence the friends exert. Two processes—parental supervision of friendships and adolescent selection of friendships in terms of values shared with parents—should result in friendships that support parental values. This seems to be true in both countries.

In the critical area of educational goals, adolescents in the United States and Denmark show very high concordance with both their mothers and their best friends. However, parental influence seems the more important factor, when contrasted with the influence of the best friend. Furthermore, the greater influence of parents than peers operates across the entire adolescent age period, in our samples 14–18 years of age. The decreasing influence of parents throughout adolescence has been accepted as fact by many psychologists and sociologists. Our data, however, show a persistence of greater parental than peer influence across all adolescent age groups.

Perhaps the most remarkable negative finding in this study is our failure to demonstrate that the kinds of interactions between parent and adolescent (such as closeness, amount of communication, type of parental authority) affect the degree to which parents are able to transmit their values and goals to their children. These variables are related to the adolescent's subjective report of agreement with parents, but not to actual agreement. These negative results may be a function of the methodology used. However, the possibility remains that parental influence is an all-or-none phenomenon which appears at a very low threshold level, and in all the families in the sample.

More specific parent-child variables do affect degree of concordance between mother and adolescent on college plans. Concordance between mothers' college (or university) aspirations and adolescents' plans for a higher education is moderated by the amount of actual encouragement provided by the mother. Higher academic education is available to a larger proportion of American than Danish adolescents, and its value may be greater in the United States than in Denmark. This, combined with the greater directiveness of American parents, results in many more American than Danish parents' giving strong encouragement to their adolescent children to continue their academic education. In both countries strong encouragement from the mother seems nearly always enough in itself to determine the adolescent's actual plans. Among adolescents whose mothers have college aspirations for them and who receive strong encouragement from their mothers, about nine out of ten in middle class circumstances and eight out of ten in lower class circumstances in the United States (eight and seven, respectively, in Denmark) decide to continue their education. Other family variables which might be expected to moderate mother-child concordance do not play a visible role in our data.

In contrast to mother-adolescent concordance, in both countries concordance between adolescent and best school friend varies according to the intensity of the friendship. The indicators of intensity of friendship are several: (1) whether or not the friendship choice is reciprocated; (2) how frequently the adolescent sees his friend after school; and (3) whether the best school friend is also the best friend overall. The closer the friend, the more his outlook is likely to match that of the adolescent's own. This might come about both through influence of one friend upon another and through selection as friends of individuals with compatible attitudes and values. In the absence of longitudinal data, neither interpretation can be selected over the other.

Furthermore, in both countries, adolescents who disagree with their parents are not especially likely to have peers who support them in their rebellion. Adolescents whose plans do not correspond to those of their parents are less likely to have plans that correspond to those of their best friends. This is only to be expected: peer influences are compatible with, and supportive of, parental influences; for attitudes of peers and parents are mutually supportive. We might generalize to suppose that such mutual support will be found in all other areas considered critical by the parents.

Apart from the issue of educational goals, there is little concordance between adolescent attitudes and those of friends and parents on a variety of other issues. While these negative results are similar to those of other studies, their interpretation is problematical. These results may be a function of the methodology and of the questions we used, as well as of the issues we have focused upon. More extensive batteries of questions—touching on such adolescents' concerns of political values or attitudes toward drugs—are needed.

In summary, peers offer opportunities for fun and companionship; reinterpret parental directives in terms more meaningful to adolescents and specify behaviors and outlooks in areas left to them by parents; and offer a sphere in which the adolescents, particularly the Americans, can begin their careers of winning the respect of others. Parental influence varies according to the issue involved. There is no doubt that with respect to future life goals, in both countries, parental influence is much stronger than peer influence. It is misleading to speak of separate adolescent cultures or of general peer versus parental influences. The particular content area under discussion must be specified. For certain values or areas peers may be more influential than parents; for other issues, the reverse may be true. Indeed, preliminary data from an ongoing panel survey of adolescent drug use indicate that peer influences are more important than parental influences in adolescent marijuana use (Kandel, 1971).

CONCLUSIONS

American and Danish adolescents are surprisingly close to their parents; they tend not to rebel against their authority; they often share with parents goals and aspirations for their future role in society. Whether in quality of family life or personal aspirations for adolescents' future role in society, the findings of this study fail to support the notion of an extensive gap between parents and their adolescent children. Obviously, the present data do not speak to many of the issues that now concern young people, even those in their early teens—issues such as the Vietnam War, the escalation of armed conflicts, relations between blacks and whites in American society, the use of drugs, the contamination of the environment. Awareness of these issues has developed mainly in the last two or three years, after the data for this study were collected.

How can we reconcile our findings with the commonly held belief—both among the general public and a large segment of professional social scientists—that there is a widespread and extensive generation gap, not only in the United States but throughout the world. According to Margaret Mead, this gap exists mainly because technological changes have arisen with such speed that the young are growing up in a world totally different from their parents.

It is obvious that in terms of sheer technology, the present generation has had experience with and takes for granted many innovations that were unknown to most of us in our youth: television, the atomic bomb, computers, moon landings. Yet, growing up involves more than simply the mastery and understanding of ever changing technologies. Growing up also involves the mastery of feelings and of interpersonal relations. The basic processes of developing one's identity remain the same whatever the specific contents involves. The control of aggression, the expression of love, the handling and resolution of interpersonal conflicts, the development of a sense of self—these are perennial issues that must be handled anew by each successive generation of youths. In these areas, irrespective of technological change, an older person will always have something to teach a younger one.

Adelson (1970) attributes the persistent belief in a generation gap to three factors: a tendency to generalize from a narrow and verbal segment of the young to the entire youth population; a tendency to exaggerate the differences between younger and older groups; a tendency to see the mood of the young as a forecast of long-term national tendencies. Some other factors, particularly in the United States, may also explain the contradictions among some of the empirical studies that indicate agreement on values between adolescents and their parents and the perceptions in society at large of strong differences between the generations. These factors may include, on the one hand, a sharp polarization of society and on the other, an ability on the part of youth to act according to their beliefs. American society as a whole is deeply divided. Blacks are polarized against whites, blue-collar workers against white-collar workers, hawks against doves. The young thus express more openly and often more effectively the internal divisions that exist within society at large. It may be less threatening to adults to attribute differences to generations when they actually emanate from differences between race, class, or interest lines within adult society itself. In addition, youth often have the courage and/or naïveté to act out convictions less actively shared by their parents. Adolescents are less subtle, less hypocritical than adults. They may provide an explicit and visible acceptance of values that are implicit, albeit often denied by adult society. Thus, adolescent society often seems to serve as the active conscience of adult society.

REFERENCES

Adelson, J. What generation gap? *The New York Times Magazine,* January 18, 1970, pp. 10–11, 34–36, 45–46.

Coleman, J. S. *The Adolescent Society.* New York: Free Press, 1961.

Kandel, D. Family processes in adolescent drug use. Progress Report. Grant No. MH 19079, October 1971.

Lewin, K. Some social-psychological differences between the United States and Germany. *Character and Personality,* 1936, *4,* 265–293. Reprinted in K. Lewin, *Resolving social conflicts.* New York: Harper & Row, 1948.

Riesman, D. *The lonely crowd.* New Haven: Yale University Press, 1950.

5.8

The Origins of Alienation

Urie Bronfenbrenner

Profound changes are taking place in the lives of America's children and young people. The institution that is at the center of these changes and that itself shows the most rapid and radical transformation is the American family, the major context in which a person grows up. The primary causes and consequences of change, however, lie outside the home. The causes are to be found in such unlikely quarters as business, urban planning, and transportation systems; the ultimate effects of change are seen most frequently in American schools and—not as often but more disturbingly —in the courts, clinics and mental and penal institutions. The direction of change is one of disorganization rather than constructive development.

The disorganization is experienced at two levels. In the first instance it affects the structure and function of society and its primary institutions; then it is rapidly reflected in the structure and function of individual human beings, particularly of those who are still in the process of development: children and young people. The crux of the problem lies in the failure of the young person to be integrated into his society. He feels uninterested, disconnected and perhaps even hostile to the people and activities in his surroundings. He wants "to do his own thing" but often is not sure what it is or with whom to do it. Even when he thinks he has found it—and them—the experience often proves unsuccessful, and interest wanes.

This feeling, and fact, of disconnectedness from people and activities has a name that has become familiar: alienation. My purpose here is to explore the origins of alienation, to identify the circumstances that give rise to it and to consider how these circumstances might be altered in order to reverse the process. As I have suggested, whereas alienation ultimately affects the individual, it has its roots in the institutions of the society, and among these institutions the family plays a particularly critical role. I can therefore begin my inquiry by examining the changes that have taken place in the American family over recent decades.

FAMILY STRUCTURE

The family of 1974 is significantly different from the family of only 25 years ago (Bronfenbrenner & Bruner, 1972). Today almost 45 percent of the nation's mothers work outside the home. The greatest increase has occurred for mothers of preschool children: one in every three mothers with children under six is working today. As more mothers go to work, the number of other adults in the family who could care for the child has shown a marked decrease. For example, 50 years ago half of the households in Massachusetts included at least one other adult besides the parents; today the figure is only 4 percent.

The divorce rate among families with children has risen substantially during the past 20 years. The percent of children from divorced families is almost twice what it was a decade ago. If present trends continue, one child in six will lose a parent through divorce by the time he is 18.

In 1970, 10 percent of all children under six—2.2 million of them—were living in single-parent families with no father in the home, almost double the rate for a decade ago. The average income for a single-parent family with children under six was $3100 in 1970—well below the "poverty" line ($4000 per year for a family of four). Even when the mother worked, her average income of $4200 barely exceeded the poverty level. Among families in poverty, 45 percent of all children under six were living in single-parent households; in nonpoverty families the corresponding figure was only 3.5 percent.

Of the 5.6 million preschool children whose mothers are in the labor force, one million live in families below the poverty line. Another million children of working mothers live in near-poverty (income between $4000 and $7000 for a family of four). All these children would have to be on welfare if the mother did not work. Finally, there are about 2.5 million children under six whose mothers do not work but whose family income is below the poverty level. Without counting the many thousands of children in families above the poverty line who are in need of child-care services, this makes a total of about 4.5 million children under six whose families need some help if normal family life is to be sustained.

The situation is particularly critical for the families of black Americans. Of all black children, 53 percent live in families below the poverty line; the corresponding figure for whites is 11 percent. Of all black children, 44 percent have mothers who are in the labor force; the corresponding figure for whites is 26 percent. Of all black children, more than 30 percent live in single-parent families; the corresponding figure for whites is 7 percent. The census does not provide comparable information for other groups living under duress, such as American Indians, Mexican Americans, whites living in Appalachia. If and when such data become available, they are likely to show similar trends.

During the past decade many of us have become familiar with the plight of poor families in general terms, but we may not yet have recognized the impact of poverty at the concrete level and our own direct responsibility for its destructive effects. A case in point is the scandal of infant mortality. At the latest count in 1971, the U.S.

ranked fourteenth in the world in combating mortality during the first year of life—behind East Germany—and our ranking has been dropping steadily. The overall figures for the U.S., dismaying as they are, mask even greater inequities. Infant mortality is almost twice as high for nonwhites as for whites; within New York City it is three times as high in central Harlem as it is in Forest Hills. Several different studies have related infant mortality to inadequate prenatal care (Kessner *et al.,* 1973). What happens if that care is delivered to poor people? The answer to that question is available in data from the maternal- and infant-care projects that the Department of Health, Education, and Welfare financed in the mid-1960's in slum sections of 14 cities. In the target areas of such programs there was a dramatic drop in infant mortality: from 34.2 per 1000 live births in 1964 to 21.5 in 1969 in Denver, from 33.4

FIGURE 1. INFANT MORTALITY (DEATHS BEFORE ONE YEAR OF AGE) IS ONE OF THE INDEXES OF MATERNAL AND CHILD CARE BY WHICH THE U.S. NO LONGER RANKS WELL AMONG ADVANCED INDUSTRIAL NATIONS. RECENT STUDIES HAVE CORRELATED INFANT MORTALITY SPECIFICALLY WITH POOR PRENATAL HEALTH CARE.

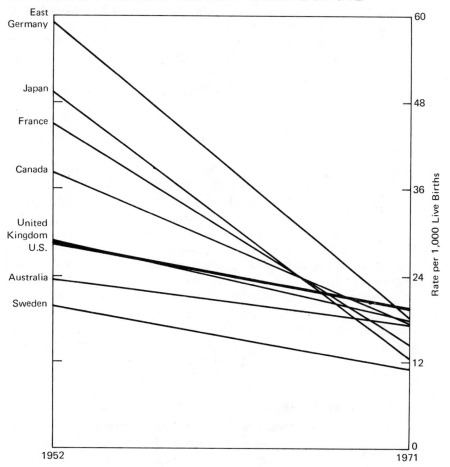

to 13.4 in Omaha, from 25.4 in 1965 to 14.3 in 1969 in Birmingham. Among the populations served by these programs there were also significant reductions in premature births, in repeated teen-age pregnancy, in conceptions by women over 35 and in the number of families with more than four children. It is a reflection of our distorted priorities that these programs are currently in jeopardy—even though their proposed replacement through revenue-sharing is not even on the horizon. The phasing out of these programs will result in a return of mortality to the earlier levels: more infants will die.

The record in infant and maternal care is only one example of this country's failure to support its children and families living in poverty. It is not only disadvantaged families, however, that experience frustration and failure; for families that can get along, the rats may be gone but the rat race remains. The demands of a job that claims mealtimes, evenings, and weekends, as well as days; the trips and moves necessary to get ahead or simply to hold one's own; the increasing time spent commuting, entertaining, going out, meeting social and community obligations—all of these produce a situation in which a child often spends more time with a passive babysitter than with a participating parent.

The forces undermining the parental role are particularly strong in the case of fathers. Compare, for example, the results of a study of middle-class fathers, who told interviewers they were spending an average of 15 to 20 minutes a day playing with their one-year-old infants, with another study in which the father's voice was actually recorded by means of a microphone attached to the infant's shirt. "The data indicated that fathers spend relatively little time interacting with their infants. The mean number of interactions per day was 2.7, and the average number of seconds per day was 37.7" (Rebelsky & Hanks, 1971, p. 65).

Another factor reducing interaction between parents and children is the changing physical environment in the home, in which proliferating television-viewing areas and playrooms and "family rooms" and master bedrooms increasingly separate the generations. Perhaps the ultimate in isolation is reached in a "cognition crib" described in a brochure I recently received in the mail. It is equipped with a tape recorder that can be actuated by the sound of the infant's voice. Frames built into the sides of the crib make possible the insertion of "programmed play modules for sensory and physical practice." The modules come in sets of six, which the parent is "encouraged to change" every three months in order to keep pace with the child's development. Since "faces are what an infant sees first, six soft plastic faces ... adhere to the window." Other modules include mobiles, a crib aquarium, a piggy bank and "ego-building mirrors." Parents are hardly mentioned except as potential purchasers.

¡SOLATION

It is not only parents of whom children are deprived, but also people in general. Developments of recent decades—many in themselves beneficent—conspire to isolate children from the rest of society.

The fragmentation of the extended family, the separation of residential and business areas, the breakdown of neighborhoods, zoning ordinances, occupational mobility, child-labor laws, the abolition of the apprentice system, consolidated schools, super-markets, television, separate patterns of social life for different age groups, the working mother, the delegation of child-care to specialists—all these manifestations of progress operate to decrease opportunity and incentive for meaningful contact between children and people older or younger than themselves.

This erosion of the social fabric isolates not only the child but also his family. In particular, with the breakdown of the community, the neighborhood and the extended family and the rise in the number of homes from which the father is absent, increasingly great responsibility has fallen on young mothers. For some of them the resulting pressures appear to be mounting beyond the point of endurance. The growing number of divorces is now accompanied by a new phenomenon: the unwillingness of either parent to take custody of the child. In more and more families the woman is fleeing without waiting for a formal separation. Increasing numbers of married women are being reported to police departments as missing, and news reports indicate a quantum leap in the number of runaway wives whom private detectives, hired by fathers who are left with the children, are trying to retrieve.

There is a more gruesome trend: the killing of infants under one year of age has been increasing sporadically since 1957 (*Homicide in the United States,* 1967). The infanticide rate rose from 3.1 per 100,000 of the infant population in that year to 4.7 in 1970. A similar pattern appears for less violent forms of child abuse that involve bodily injury. A 1970 survey of more than 1300 families (Gil, 1970) estimated a nationwide total of from two to four million battered-child cases a year, with the highest rates occurring among adolescents. Significantly, more than 90 percent of the incidents took place in the child's home. The most severe injuries occurred in single-parent homes and were inflicted by the mother herself, a fact that reflects the desperation of the situation faced by some young mothers today.

The centrifugal forces generated within the family by its increasing isolation propel its members in different directions. As parents spend more time in work and community activities, children are placed in or gravitate toward organized or informal group settings. Between 1965 and 1970 the number of children enrolled in day-care centers doubled, and the demand today far exceeds the supply. More and more children come home from school to an empty house or apartment. When he is not in preschool or school, the child spends increasing amounts of time in the company of only his age-mates; the vacuum created by the withdrawal of parents and other adults has been filled by the informal peer group. A recent study has found that at every age and grade level children today show greater dependence on their peers than they did a decade ago (Condry & Siman, 1968a). A parallel investigation indicates that such susceptibility to group influence is higher among children from homes in which at least one parent is frequently absent (Condry & Siman, 1968b). Moreover, peer-oriented youngsters describe their parents as being less affectionate and less firm in discipline. Attachment to age-mates appears to be influenced more by a lack of attention and concern at home than by any positive attraction of the peer group

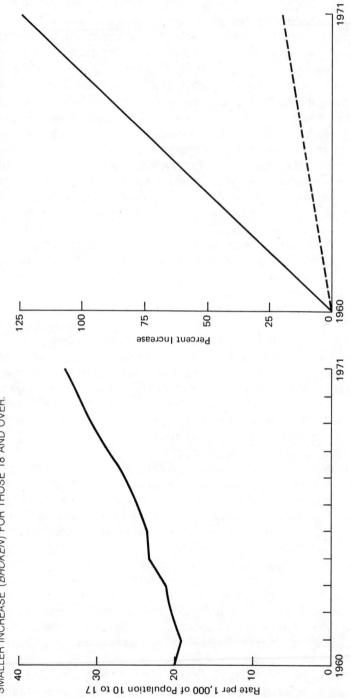

FIGURE 2. INCREASE IN JUVENILE CRIME IS REFLECTED BY THE RATE OF U.S. JUVENILE DELINQUENCY CASES OTHER THAN TRAFFIC OFFENSES (*LEFT*) AND BY THE DISPARITY BETWEEN THE LARGE INCREASE IN ARRESTS OF PEOPLE UNDER 18 (*SOLID*) AND THE SMALLER INCREASE (*BROKEN*) FOR THOSE 18 AND OVER.

itself; in fact, these children have a rather negative view of their friends and of themselves as well. They are pessimistic about the future, rate lower in responsibility and leadership and are more likely to engage in such antisocial behavior as lying, teasing other children, playing hooky or "doing something illegal" (Siman, 1973).

FIGURE 3. INCREASE IN VIOLENT CRIME IS REFLECTED IN FEDERAL BUREAU OF INVESTIGATION STATISTICS COVERING MURDERS AND NONNEGLIGENT MANSLAUGHTERS (*SOLID CURVE AND SCALE AT LEFT*) AND ROBBERIES (*BROKEN CURVE AND SCALE AT RIGHT*) KNOWN TO AND REPORTED BY POLICE DEPARTMENTS.

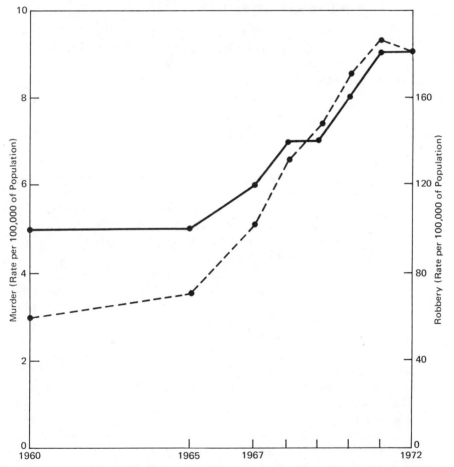

These, of course, are among the milder consequences of alienation. The more serious manifestations are reflected in the rising rates of youthful runaways, school dropouts, drug abuse, suicide, delinquency, vandalism and violence documented for the White House Conference on Children in 1970 (*Profiles of Children,* pp. 78, 79, 108, 179, 180) and in more recent government publications (Report of the New York State Commission, 1973). The proportion of youngsters between the ages of 10 and

18 arrested for drug abuse doubled between 1964 and 1968. Since 1963 juvenile delinquency has been increasing at a faster rate than the juvenile population; more than half the crimes involve vandalism, theft, or breaking and entry; if the present trends continue, one in every nine youngsters will appear in juvenile court before the age of 18. These figures index only offenses that are detected and prosecuted. One wonders how high the numbers must climb before we acknowledge that they reflect deep and pervasive problems in the treatment of children and youth in our society.

THE NEGLECTED FAMILY

What is the ultimate source of these problems? Where do the roots of alienation lie? Scientific studies of human behavior have yielded few generalizations that are firmly grounded in research and broadly accepted by specialists in the field, but there are two answers to the foregoing questions that do meet these exacting criteria.

1. Over the past three decades, literally thousands of investigations have been conducted to identify the developmental antecedents of behavior disorders and social pathology. The results point to an almost omnipresent overriding factor: family disorganization.
2. Much of the same research also shows that the forces of disorganization arise primarily not from within the family but from the circumstances in which the family finds itself and from the way of life that is imposed on it by those circumstances.

Specifically, when those circumstances and the way of life they generate undermine relationships of trust and emotional security between family members, when they make it difficult for parents to care for, educate and enjoy their children, when there is no support or recognition from the outside world for one's role as a parent and when time spent with one's family means frustration of career, personal fulfillment and peace of mind, then the development of the child is adversely affected. The first symptoms are emotional and motivational: disaffection, indifference, irresponsibility and inability to follow through in activities requiring application and persistence. In less favorable family circumstances the reaction takes the form of antisocial acts injurious to the child and to society. Finally, for children who come from environments in which the capacity of the family to function has been most severely traumatized by such destructive forces as poverty, ill health, and discrimination, the consequences for the child are seen not only in the spheres of emotional and social maladjustment but also in the impairment of the most distinctive of human capacities: the ability to think, to deal with concepts and numbers at even the most elementary level.

The extent of this impairment in contemporary American society, and its roots in social disorganization, are reflected in recent studies. A New York State commission on education studied more than 300 schools and reported that 58 percent of the variation in student achievement could be predicted by three socioeconomic factors: broken homes, overcrowded housing, and the educational level of the head of the household; when racial and ethnic variables were introduced into the analysis, they accounted for less than an additional 2 percent of the variation. And there is a secular trend: each year "more and more children throughout the state are falling below minimum competence" (*Report of the New York State Commission on the Quality of Education,* Vol. 1, p. 33).

How are we to reverse this trend? The evidence indicates that the most promising solutions do not lie within the child's immediate setting, the classroom and the school. An impressive series of investigations, notably the studies published by James Coleman in 1966 and by Christopher Jencks in 1972, demonstrates that the characteristics of schools, of classrooms and even of teachers predict very little of the variation in school achievement. What does predict it is family background, particularly the characteristics that define the family in relation to its social context: the world of work, neighborhood and community.

The critical question thus becomes: Can our social institutions be changed—old ones modified and new ones introduced—so as to rebuild and revitalize the social context that families and children require for their effective function and growth? Let me consider some institutions on the contemporary American scene that are likely to have the greatest impact, for better or for worse, on the welfare of America's children and young people.

DAY CARE

Day care is coming to America. The question is what kind. Shall we, in response to external pressures to "put people to work" or for considerations of personal convenience, allow a pattern to develop in which the care of young children is delegated to specialists, further separating the child from his family and reducing the family's and the community's feeling of responsibility for their children? Or will day care be designed, as it can be, to reinvolve and strengthen the family as the primary and proper agent for making human beings human?

As Project Head Start demonstrated, preschool programs can have no lasting constructive impact on the child's development unless they affect not only the child himself but also the people who constitute his enduring day-to-day environment. This means that parents and other people from the child's immediate environment must play a prominent part in the planning and administration of day-care programs and also participate actively as volunteers and aides. It means that the program cannot be confined to the center but must reach out into the home and the community so that the entire neighborhood is caught up in activities in behalf of its children. We need to experiment with putting day-care centers within reach of the significant people in the child's life. For some families this will mean neighborhood centers, for others centers at the place of work. A great deal of variation and innovation will be required to find the appropriate solutions for different groups in different settings.

Such solutions confront a critical obstacle in contemporary American society. The keystone of an effective day-care program is parent participation, but how can parents participate if they work full time—which is one of the main reasons the family needs day care in the first place? I see only one possible solution: increased opportunities and rewards for part-time employment. It was in the light of this consideration that the report of the White House Conference urged business and industry, and governments as employers, to increase the number and the status of part-time positions. In addition the report recommended that state legislatures enact a "Fair Part-Time Employment Practices Act" to prohibit discrimination in job opportunity, rate of pay, fringe benefits and status for parents who sought or engaged in part-time employment.

I should like to report the instructive experience of one state legislator who attempted to put through such a bill, Assemblywoman Constance Cook of New York. Mrs. Cook sent me a copy of her bill as it had been introduced in committee. It began, "No employer shall set as a condition of employment, salary, promotion, fringe benefits, seniority" and so on that an employee who is the parent or guardian of a child under 18 years of age shall be required to work more than 40 hours a week. Forty hours a week, of course, is full time; Mrs. Cook informed me that there was no hope of getting a bill through with a lower limit.

It turned out that even 40 hours was too much. The bill was not passed even in committee. The pressure from business and industry was too great. They insisted on the right to require their employees to work overtime.

There is a ray of hope, however. In the settlement of the United Automobile Workers' 1973 strike against the Chrysler Corporation a limit was placed for the first time on the company policy of mandatory overtime.

These concerns bring us to what I regard as the most important single factor affecting the welfare of the nation's children. I refer to the place and status of women in American society. Whatever the future trend may be, the fact remains that in our society today the care of children depends overwhelmingly on women, and specifically on mothers. Moreover, with the withdrawal of the social supports for the family to which I alluded earlier, the position of women and mothers has become increasingly isolated. With the breakdown of the community, the neighborhood, and the extended family an increasing responsibility for the care and upbringing of children has fallen on the young mother. Under these circumstances it is not surprising that many young women in America are in revolt. I understand and share their sense of rage, but I fear the consequences of some of the solutions they advocate, which will have the effect of isolating children still further from the kind of care and attention they need. There is, of course, a constructive implication to this line of thought, in that a major route to the rehabilitation of children and youth in American society lies in the enhancement of the status and power of women in all walks of life—in the home as well as on the job.

WORK AND RESPONSIBILITY

One of the most significant effects of age segregation in our society has been the isolation of children from the world of work. Once children not only saw what their parents did for a living but also shared substantially in the task; now many children have only a vague notion of the parent's job and have had little or no opportunity to observe the parent (or for that matter any other adult) fully engaged in his or her work. Although there is no systematic research evidence on this subject, it appears likely that the absence of such exposure contributes significantly to the growing alienation among children and young people. Experience in other modern urban societies indicates that the isolation of children from adults in the world of work is not inevitable; it can be countered by creative social innovations. Perhaps the most imaginative and pervasive of these is the common practice in the U.S.S.R., in which a department in a factory, an office, an institute, or a business enterprise adopts a group of children as its "wards." The

FIGURE 4. JUVENILE SUICIDE RATE (FOR ADOLESCENTS FROM 10 TO 19 YEARS OLD) HAS RISEN RECENTLY. THE RATE FOR THE POPULATION AS A WHOLE, IN CONTRAST, HAS STAYED AROUND 11 SINCE WORLD WAR II.

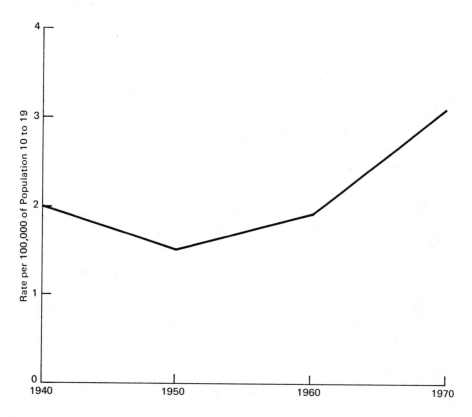

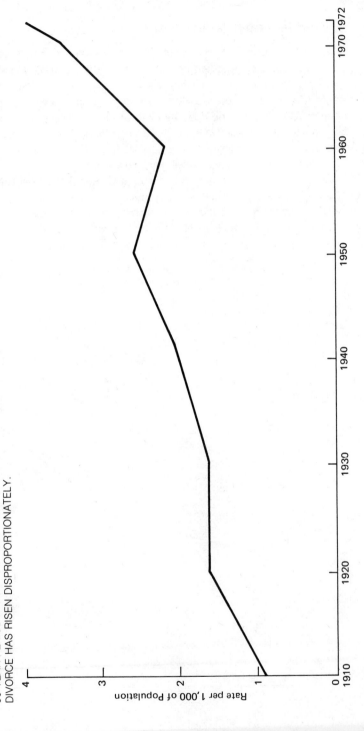

FIGURE 5. DIVORCE RATE, A MIRROR OF SOME OF THE PRESSURES ON THE U.S. FAMILY, HAS DOUBLED IN EACH OF THE PAST TWO 30-YEAR PERIODS. DIVORCE NOW COMES SOMEWHAT LATER IN MARRIAGE, SO THAT THE NUMBER OF CHILDREN INVOLVED IN EACH DIVORCE HAS RISEN DISPROPORTIONATELY.

children's group is typically a school classroom, but it may also include a nursery, a hospital ward, or any other setting in which children are dealt with collectively. The workers not only visit the children's group wherever it may be but also invite the youngsters to their place of work in order to familiarize the children with the nature of their activities and with themselves as people. The aim is not vocational education but rather acquaintance with adults as participants in the world of work.

There seems to be nothing in such an approach that would be incompatible with the values and aims of our own society, and this writer has urged its adaptation to the American scene. Acting on this suggestion, David Goslin of the Russell Sage Foundation persuaded *The Detroit Free Press* to participate in an unusual experiment as a prelude to the White House Conference on Children. By the time it was over two groups of 12-year-old children, one from a slum area and the other predominantly middle class, had spent six to seven hours a day for three days in virtually every department of the newspaper, not just observing but participating actively in the department's work. There were boys and girls in the pressroom, the city room, the composing room, the advertising department and the delivery department. The employees of the *Free Press* entered into the experiment with serious misgivings, but, as a documentary film that was made of the project makes clear, the children were not bored, nor were the adults—and the paper did get out every day.

If a child is to become a responsible person, he not only must be exposed to adults engaged in demanding tasks but also must himself participate in such tasks. In the perspective of cross-cultural research one of the most salient characteristics of the U.S. is what Nicholas Hobbs, a former president of the American Psychological Association, has called "the inutility of childhood." Our children are not entrusted with any real responsibilities. Little that they do really matters. They are given duties rather than responsibilities; the ends and means have been determined by someone else and their job is to fulfill an assignment involving little judgment, decision making or risk. This practice is intended to protect children from burdens beyond their years, but there is reason to believe it has been carried too far in contemporary American society and has contributed to the alienation and alleged incapacity of young people to deal constructively with personal and social problems. The evidence indicates that children acquire the capacity to cope with difficult situations when they have an opportunity to take on consequential responsibilities in relation to others and are held accountable for them.

SCHOOL

Although training for responsibility by giving responsibility clearly begins in the family, the institution that has probably done the most to keep children insulated from challenging social tasks is the American school system. For historical reasons rooted in the separation of church and state this system has been isolated from responsible social concern in both content and actual location. In terms of content, education in America, when viewed from a cross-cultural perspective, seems peculiarly one-sided, emphasizing subject

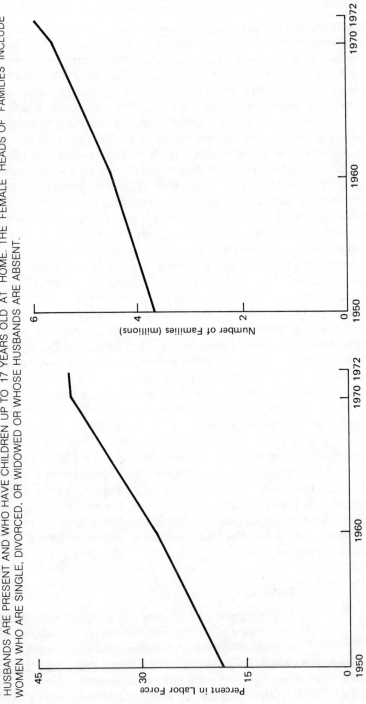

FIGURE 6. STRESS ON MOTHERS IS SUGGESTED BY DATA FOR WORKING MOTHERS (*LEFT*) AND FOR FAMILIES HEADED BY WOMEN (*RIGHT*). THE CURVE AT LEFT SHOWS, SPECIFICALLY, THE LABOR-FORCE PARTICIPATION RATE FOR MARRIED WOMEN WHOSE HUSBANDS ARE PRESENT AND WHO HAVE CHILDREN UP TO 17 YEARS OLD AT HOME. THE FEMALE HEADS OF FAMILIES INCLUDE WOMEN WHO ARE SINGLE, DIVORCED, OR WIDOWED OR WHOSE HUSBANDS ARE ABSENT.

matter to the exclusion of another fundamental aspect of the child's development for which there is no generally accepted term in our educational vocabulary: what the Germans call *Erziehung,* the Russians *vospitanie* and the French *éducation.* Perhaps the best equivalents are "upbringing" or "character education," expressions that sound outmoded and irrelevant to us. In many countries of Western and Eastern Europe, however, the corresponding terms are the names of what constitutes the core of the educational process: the development of the child's qualities as a person —his values, motives, and patterns of social response.

Our schools, and consequently our children, are also physically insulated from the life of the community, neighborhood and families the schools purport to serve, and from the life for which they are supposedly preparing the children. And the insularity is repeated within the school system itself, where children are segregated into class-rooms that have little social connection with one another or with the school as a common community for which members can take active responsibility.

During the past decade the trend toward segregation of the school from the rest of the society has been accelerated by the forces of social disorganization to which I have referred. As a result the schools have become one of the most potent breeding grounds of alienation in American society. For this reason it is of crucial importance for the welfare and development of school-age children that schools be reintegrated into the life of the community.

It is commonplace among educators to affirm that the task of the school is to prepare the child "for life." There is one role in life the overwhelming majority of all children will ultimately play but for which they are given virtually no concrete preparation. It is parenthood. In cross-cultural observations I have been struck by the American child's relative lack of ease in relating to infants and young chil-dren, engaging their interest and enjoying their company. With the important ex-ception of certain minority groups, including blacks, many young people never have experience in extended care of a baby or a young child until they have their own.

A solution to this problem, which speaks as well to the need to give young people in our society genuine and consequential responsibility, is to introduce truly functional courses in human development into the regular school curriculum. These would be distinguished in a number of important ways from units on "family life" as they are now usually taught in the junior high school (chiefly to girls who do not plan to go on to college). Now the material is typically presented in vicarious form, that is, through reading or discussion or possibly through role playing rather than actual role taking. In contrast, the approach being proposed here would have as its core a responsible and active concern for the lives of young children and their families. Such an experi-ence could be facilitated by locating day-care centers and preschool programs in or near schools so that they could be made an integral part of the curriculum. The older children would work with the younger ones on a regular basis, both at school and in the young children's homes, where they would have an opportunity to become ac-quainted with the youngsters' families and their circumstances.

NEIGHBORHOOD

Much of what happens to children and families is determined by the ecology of the neighborhood in which the family lives. The implication of this principle for our own times is illustrated in a research report on the effect of some "new towns" on the lives of children. The study compared the reactions of children living in 18 new model communities in West Germany with those of youngsters living in older German cities. The research was conducted by the Urban and Planning Institute in Nuremberg. According to a report in *The New York Times* (May 9, 1971), in the new towns, "amid soaring rectangular shapes of apartment houses with shaded walks, big lawns and fenced-in play areas, the children for whom much of this has been designed apparently feel isolated, regimented and bored." The study found that the children gauged their freedom not by the extent of open areas around them but by the liberty they had to be among people and things that excited them and fired their imagination.

The implications of such research are self-evident. In the planning and design of new communities, housing projects and urban renewal, both public and private planners need to give explicit consideration to the kind of world being created for the children who will grow up in these settings. Particular attention should be given to the opportunities the environment presents (or precludes) for the involvement of children with people both older and younger than themselves. Among the specific factors to be considered are the location of shops and businesses where children can have contact with adults at work, recreational and day-care facilities readily accessible to parents as well as children, provision for a family neighborhood center and family-oriented facilities and services, the availability of public transportation and—perhaps most important of all—places to walk, sit and talk in common company.

It may be fitting to end this discussion with a proposal for nothing more radical than providing a setting in which young and old can simply sit and talk. The fact that such settings are disappearing and have to be re-created deliberately points both to the roots of the problem and to its remedy. The evil and the cure lie not in the victims of alienation but in the social institutions that produce alienation, and in their failure to be responsive to the most human needs and values of a democratic society.

REFERENCES

Bronfenbrenner, U. Socialization and social class through time and space. In E. E. Maccoby, T. M. Newcomb, and E. Hartley (Eds.), *Readings in social psychology.* (3rd ed.) New York: Holt, 1958, 400–425.

Bronfenbrenner, U. *Two Worlds of Childhood: U.S. and U.S.S.R.* New York: Russell Sage Foundation, 1970.

Bronfenbrenner, U., & Bruner, J. The President and the children. *The New York Times,* January 31, 1972, p. 41.

Cloward, R. D. Studies in tutoring. *Journal of Experimental Education,* Fall 1967, *36,* 14–25.

Coleman, J. S. *Equality of educational opportunity.* Washington, D.C.: U.S. Office of Education, 1966.

Condry, J. C., & Siman, M. A. Characteristics of peer- and adult-oriented children. Unpublished manuscript, Cornell University, 1968. (a)

Condry, J. C., & Siman, M. A. An experimental study of adult versus peer orientation. Unpublished manuscript, Cornell University, 1968. (b)

Devereux, E. C., Jr., Bronfenbrenner, U., & Rodgers, R. R. Child rearing in England and the United States: A cross-national comparison. *Journal of Marriage and the Family,* May 1969, *31,* 257–270.

Garbarino, J. A note on the effects of television. In U. Bronfenbrenner (Ed.), *Influences on Human Development.* Hinsdale, Illinois: The Dryden Press, 1972.

Gil, D. G. *Violence Against Children: Physical child abuse in the United States.* Cambridge, Mass.: Harvard University Press, 1970.

Homicide in the United States 1950–1964. National Center for Health Statistics, Series 20, Number 6. U.S. Department of Health, Education, and Welfare, 1967.

Jarus, A., Marcus, J., Oren, J., & Rapaport, Ch. *Children and families in Israel.* New York: Gordon and Breach, 1970.

Jencks, C. *Inequality.* New York: Basic Books, 1972.

Kessner, D. M., *et al. Infant death: An analysis by maternal risk and health care.* Washington, D.C.: Institute of Medicine, National Academy of Sciences, 1973.

National Commission on Resources for Youth, Inc. *Youth tutoring youth—it worked.* A final report, January 31, 1969. 36 West 44th St., New York, New York 10036.

Parke, B. K. Towards a new rationale for cross-age tutoring. Unpublished manuscript, Cornell University, November 1969.

Profiles of Children: White House Conference on Children. Washington, D.C.: U.S. Government Printing Office, 1970.

Rebelsky, F., & Hanks, C. Father's verbal interactions with infants in the first three months of life. *Child Development,* 1971, *42,* 63–68.

Report of Forum 15. White House Conference on Children, 1970.

Report of the New York State Commission on the Quality, Cost, and Financing of Elementary and Secondary Education. Vol. 1, p. 33.

Report to the President: White House Conference on Children. Washington, D.C.: U.S. Government Printing Office, 1970, pp. 240–255.

Rodgers, R. R. Changes in parental behavior reported by children in West Germany and the United States. *Human Development,* 1971, *14,* 208–224.

Siman, M. A. Peer group influence during adolescence: A study of 41 naturally-existing friendship groups. A thesis presented to the Faculty of the Graduate School of Cornell University for the degree of Doctor of Philosophy, January 1973.

NAME INDEX

SUBJECT INDEX